Accounting Information Systems

Basic Concepts and Current Issues *Second Edition*

Accounting Information Systems

Basic Concepts and Current Issues *Second Edition*

Robert L. Hurt

California State Polytechnic University, Pomona

The McGraw·Hill Companies

ACCOUNTING INFORMATION SYSTEMS: BASIC CONCEPTS & CURRENT ISSUES
Published by McGraw-Hill/Irwin, a business unit of The McGraw-Hill Companies, Inc., 1221 Avenue of the Americas, New York, NY, 10020.

This book is printed on acid-free paper.

1 2 3 4 5 6 7 8 9 0 QPD/QPD 0 9

ISBN 978-0-07-122052-1
MHID 0-07-122052-6

www.mhhe.com

Preface

MESSAGE FROM THE AUTHOR

To the Instructor

Wow—a second edition. Some days I have to pinch myself to realize that colleagues across the United States and around the world appreciated the first edition enough to warrant a second edition. At the same time, I recognize that this book definitely isn't for everyone—in many fundamental ways, it's nontraditional and significantly different from other AIS texts. I really appreciate the feedback I received from many of you; I've tried to incorporate much of it into the new edition, while retaining the features that worked well the first time around.

As in the first edition, I've introduced more fundamental topics early in the book (transaction processing, ethics, internal control, systems documentation). Later chapters apply those topics in various organizational settings. In addition, some chapters include material students have learned/will learn in other accounting courses; indeed, some colleagues questioned the need for journal entry problems and such in an AIS text. Here's my thinking: I've noticed my own students too often do a "memory dump" as they finish each accounting course. I've included topics like journal entries, the FASB conceptual framework, and the time value of money to show students that all areas of accounting are fundamentally linked to one another—and that it's probably not a good idea to erase their personal database of accounting knowledge as they finish each course.

I believe that accounting education in general, and AIS in particular, is about developing a student's ability to think like an accountant—it's not about preparing them to pass a professional exam. So, as in the first edition, I've shied away from a lot of prescriptive rules and "one right way" thinking in addressing AIS issues. Sure—there are some things in accounting that do have "one right answer": The debits and credits better equal each other, databases better follow the rules of normalization, and such. But many things are a matter of judgment: Do you use letters or numbers to label on- and off-page connectors in a flowchart? What's the best way to document an information system? When is it time for an organization to reorganize its business processes, and how should that be done? I hope you'll help your students develop those critical thinking and judgment skills via your own classroom activities—even if your point of view differs from my own on a particular AIS topic.

For better or worse, "assessment" is one of the watchwords of accounting education in the 21st century—especially for AACSB-accredited schools. I've included a lot of features that I hope will assist you in your assessment efforts: clearly stated learning objectives at the start of each chapter, a test bank that's directly connected to those learning objectives, and various levels of thinking and reasoning and ideas you can use for classroom assessment. (You'll find the latter in the new "teaching suggestions" material on the instructor's Web site for the second edition.)

I'm deeply honored that you're using (or considering using) my text for your AIS course. Please contact me if there's something I can do to improve the text and/or make your life in teaching AIS easier and better.

Best regards,

Bob Hurt
RLHurt@csupomona.edu

About the Author

Dr. Robert L. Hurt *California State Polytechnic University, Pomona*

Robert L. Hurt is Professor of Accounting in the College of Business Administration at California State Polytechnic University Pomona, where he teaches Accounting Information Systems, Forensic Accounting, Controllership, and Cost Accounting. Dr. Hurt received his Ph.D. in Management with a concentration in information science from Claremont Graduate University. He also holds an M.S. in Business Administration (concentration in business education) from Cal Poly Pomona and a B.S. in Business Administration (concentration in accounting) from Southeast Missouri State University.

Hallmarks of Dr. Hurt's classroom approach include utilizing active learning, developing students' critical thinking skills, and incorporating information technology to enhance the teaching/learning environment. Dr. Hurt's courses are also competency based to help students focus their efforts on important skills.

Dr. Hurt is published in the *Journal of Accounting Case Research, Strategic Finance, NACADA Journal,* and *Journal of Education for Business.* Bob is active with the Institute of Management Accountants, the Association of Certified Fraud Examiners, and the National Academic Advising Association.

Acknowledgments

We could not produce a textbook of the quality and scope of *Accounting Information Systems: Basic Concepts and Current Issues* without the help of a great number of people.

I talked to many colleagues while preparing the second edition, but one stands out among all of them: Dr. Kevin Dow. Kevin was enormously helpful in more ways than I can count. The "Why Do We Care" stories at the start of each section of the text were Kevin's idea, and he wrote them based on his own experiences in the field. Kevin is genuinely concerned about his students' learning; that attitude came through time and again during our conversations about the second edition. I'm proud to have significant, constructive input from such a thoughtful, engaged educator and scholar on this edition of the text.

The efforts of many people are needed to develop and improve a text. Among these people are the reviewers who point out areas of concern and areas of strength and make recommendations for change. The following professors provided feedback that was enormously helpful in preparing the second edition of *Accounting Information Systems: Basic Concepts and Current Issues.*

Linda Bressler
University of Houston
Terri Brunsdon
University of Akron
Susan Cain
Southern Oregon University
Sandra Cereola
James Madison University
Debra Cosgrove
University of Nebraska–Lincoln
Sandra Devona
Northern Illinois University
Kevin Dow
Kent State University
Jan Gillespie
University of Texas–Austin
Mary Beth Goodrich
University of Texas–Dallas
Rong Huang
Baruch College–CUNY
Yujong Hwang
DePaul University
Ann Lusher
Slippery Rock University
Leisa Marshall
Valdosta State University
Maureen Mascha
Marquette University
Bonnie Morris
West Virginia University
Perseus Munshi
Arizona State University
Vincent Owhoso
Bentley College
Linda Parsons
George Mason University
Timothy Pearson
West Virginia University
Cheryl Prachyl
University of Texas–Arlington
Laura Rickett
Kent State University
Marsha Scheidt
University of Tennessee
Vincent Shea
Kent State University
Patricia Smith
DePaul University
Rodney Smith
University of Arkansas
Patricia Tilley
Central Connecticut State University

I am grateful for the outstanding support from McGraw-Hill. In particular I would like to thank Stewart Mattson, Editorial Director; Dick Hercher, Executive Editor; Janice Hansen, Editorial Assistant; Dean Karampelas, Marketing Manager; Dana Pauley, Project Manager; Debra Sylvester, Production Supervisor; Joanne Mennemeier, Designer; and Balaji Sundararaman, Media Project Manager; all contributed significantly to the project and I appreciate their efforts.

Walkthrough

What's New in This Edition!

Reorganization

- The book is now organized in **five** major parts: Introduction and Basic Concepts, Documentation Techniques, Systems Analysis and Information Technology, Business Processes, and Other Topics in AIS.
- The chapter on **REAL modeling** and event-driven accounting systems has been moved up from Chapter 13 to Chapter 7, giving instructors the flexibility to use any combination of flowcharts/DFDs/REAL models in teaching the course.
- The chapter on **XBRL** has been moved up from Chapter 15 to Chapter 9; material and exercises on XBRL are incorporated as appropriate in other chapters after the topic is introduced.
- Material on **application service providers,** including SAS 70 audits, has been condensed and incorporated in the chapter on e-business and enterprise resource planning.
- Two topics from Chapter 7 in the first edition (factors to consider in selecting information technology and the weighted rating model) have been incorporated in Chapter 8 of the second edition, along with several new topics.

New Topic Coverage

- Chapter 8 (Information Systems Concepts) discusses the systems development life cycle (**SDLC**) and the capability maturity model (**CMM**).
- Part Four (Business Processes) now includes a chapter on **business process management.**

Student Materials

- Every chapter has a **new "AIS in the Business World."**
- Most chapters have **a "reading review problem"** based on the first edition's "AIS in the Business World."
- Every chapter concludes with a **"critical thinking"** section that focuses on developing judgment skills and/or showing students how to apply topics in new settings.
- Figures and illustrations have been updated; many end-of-chapter activities have been updated.
- Every part opens with a new feature: **"Why Do We Care."** Suggested and written by Dr. Kevin Dow, those features show students how the topics in each section are relevant in professional practice.

Instructor Materials

- The **solutions manual** has been updated to reflect new material.
- The Instructor's Online Learning Center incorporates **"teaching suggestions"** for each chapter. They outline activities instructors can use in the classroom to engage students more completely; they also can be used for classroom assessment.

Overall Features

Readability

The writing style has been highly praised. Students easily comprehend chapter concepts because of the conversational tone. The author has made every effort to ensure that the writing style remains engaging, lively, and consistent.

Structure

The text puts the most important, fundamental topics first, followed by applications in transaction cycles. Nice-to-know topics are included and can be covered or not at the instructor's discretion.

Philosophy

The text emphasizes the art of AIS over its "science." It helps students begin to develop their professional judgment as accountants, rather than encouraging them to memorize examples and solutions.

Content

The text incorporates modeling techniques and information technology, but at a level appropriate for accountants rather than CIS majors/professionals. The second edition discusses and applies the systems development life cycle, tying it clearly and directly to accounting. While remaining true to its accounting roots, the text moves beyond a strict accounting orientation; it integrates information technology, behavioral issues, management concerns, quantitative reasoning, and ideas from business law and ethics. Thus, students will have a clear grasp of how AIS concepts impact business practice, regardless of the organizational contexts where they pursue their careers.

Chapter Features

Real-World Examples

Each chapter opens with an illustrative vignette about an AIS issue/concept—in most chapters, those vignettes are based on actual organizations. Thus, students develop a clearer understanding of how AIS works in the "real world."

Chapter **Thirteen**

Other Business Processes

AIS in the Business World

Dr. Mohamed Ali

Dr. Mohamed Ali is an internal medicine physician in Upland, California; his office employs two nurses and a physician's assistant. Dr. Ali offers a variety of services, including smoking cessation and weight loss programs, in addition to his regular medical practice. In response to a trend that started as early as 2004, Dr. Ali maintains his patients' medical records electronically using software from Cerner Corporation (www.cerner.com).

Consider the following comments about electronic medical records (EMR) technology:

> [A study discussed in the *Journal of the American College of Surgeons*] reported that in just 16 months the University of Rochester (N.Y.) Medical Center recouped its initial $485,000 cost for an EMR system serving five outpatient offices and 28 doctors. The study compared actual before- and after-EMR costs of activities such as pulling and filing charts, creating new charts and transcription. The savings with electronic medical records added up to $394,000 a year, meaning annual savings of $280,000 after operating costs, the study said.

Advantages of EMR include labor cost savings, improved records accessibility, and the ability to query databases of patient information. Although security and privacy issues create some concern, information security techniques like encryption can help address them.

Discussion Questions

1. What steps would a doctor take to investigate EMR software?
2. How might an accounting professional be involved with EMR software?

Source: R. Roberts, "Electronic Records Provide Good Return on Investment," *Kansas City Business Journal*, June 8–14, 2007, www.cerner.com/public/Cerner_2.asp?id=26328 (January 22, 2009).

248

Reflection and Critical Thinking

Reflection and Self-Assessment **4.4**

Classify each of the following internal controls as preventive, detective, or corrective. Justify your responses, particularly when a single control can fulfill more than one category.

1. Reconciling a bank statement.
2. Requiring that all purchase requisitions are coordinated through a central purchasing department.
3. Separating the inventory ordering function from the inventory receiving function.
4. Encouraging employees to attend annual seminars on ethical behavior in the workplace and related topics.
5. Conducting surprise counts of cash on hand in a bank teller's cash drawer.
6. Tearing ticket stubs in half at a movie theater when a patron enters.
7. Collecting cash at one window and delivering the order in a different window at a fast food establishment.
8. Enforcing a policy of changing passwords every six months.
9. Locking doors and filing cabinets containing sensitive and valuable equipment and information.
10. Installing an alarm and fire suppression system.

Each chapter presents basic ideas and then encourages students to reflect on those ideas. "Reflection and Self-Assessment" activities throughout each chapter will help students think critically about the material. In addition, each chapter now includes a "critical thinking" application that gets students started down that path.

End-of-Chapter Activities

The homework material remains a strength of the text. The shear number of questions, problems, and Internet assignments will test and therefore expand the students' knowledge of chapter concepts. Further, many chapters include questions and problems that refer back to earlier material in the text and earlier courses in the accounting curriculum to discourage students from doing a "memory wipe" once they've studied a particular topic.

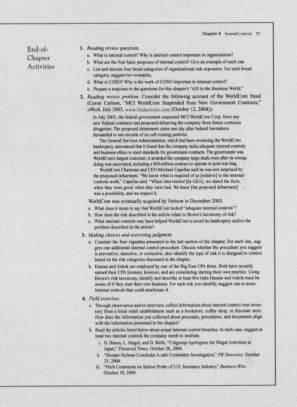

Chapter 4 *Internal Controls* 77

End-of-Chapter Activities

1. *Reading review questions.*
   a. What is internal control? Why is internal control important in organizations?
   b. What are the four basic purposes of internal control? Give an example of each one.
   c. List and discuss four broad categories of organizational risk exposures. For each broad category, suggest two examples.
   d. What is COSO? Why is the work of COSO important in internal control?
   e. Prepare a response to the questions for this chapter's "AIS in the Business World."
2. *Reading review problem.* Consider the following account of the WorldCom fraud (Caron Carlson, "MCI WorldCom Suspended from New Government Contracts," *eWeek,* July 2003, www.findarticles.com (October 12, 2004)):

   > In July 2003, the federal government suspected MCI WorldCom Corp. from any new federal contracts and proposed debarring the company from future contracts altogether. The proposed debarment came one day after federal lawmakers demanded to see records of its call-routing patterns.
   >
   > The General Services Administration, which had been reviewing the WorldCom bankruptcy, announced that it found that the company lacks adequate internal controls and business ethics to meet standards for government contracts. The government was WorldCom's largest customer; it awarded the company large deals even after its wrongdoing was uncovered, including a $45 million contract to operate in post-war Iraq.
   >
   > WorldCom Chairman and CEO Michael Capellas said he was not surprised by the proposed debarment. "We know what is required of us [relative] to the internal controls work," Capellas said. "When interviewed [by GSA], we stated the facts, when they were good, when they were bad. We knew [the proposed debarment] was a possibility, and we respect it.

   WorldCom was eventually acquired by Verizon in December 2005.
   a. What does it mean to say that WorldCom lacked "adequate internal controls"?
   b. How does the risk described in the article relate to Brown's taxonomy of risk?
   c. What internal controls may have helped WorldCom to avoid its bankruptcy and/or the problem described in the article?
3. *Making choices and exercising judgment.*
   a. Consider the four vignettes presented in the last section of the chapter. For each one, suggest one additional internal control procedure. Discuss whether the procedure you suggest is preventive, detective, or corrective; also identify the type of risk it is designed to control based on the risk categories discussed in the chapter.
   b. Hassan and Ashok are employed by one of the Big Four CPA firms. Both have recently earned their CPA licenses, however, and are considering starting their own practice. Using Brown's risk taxonomy, identify and describe at least five risks Hassan and Ashok must be aware of if they start their own business. For each risk you identify, suggest one or more internal controls that could ameliorate it.
4. *Field exercises.*
   a. Through observation and/or interview, collect information about internal control over inventory from a local retail establishment such as a bookstore, coffee shop, or discount store. How does the information you collected about processes, procedures, and documents align with the information presented in the chapter?
   b. Read the articles listed below about actual internal control breaches. In each case, suggest at least two internal controls the company needs to institute.
      i. D. Ibison, L. Saigol, and D. Wells, "Citigroup Apologizes for Illegal Activities in Japan," *Financial Times,* October 26, 2004.
      ii. "Hooper Holmes Concludes A.udit Committee Investigation," *PR Newswire,* October 25, 2004.
      iii. "Fitch Comments on Spitzer Probe of U.S. Insurance Industry," *Business Wire,* October 18, 2004.

Reviewer Comments

I have never read a textbook written in a conversational tone. Students may appreciate this style as it appears that the author is talking directly to them. If anything it may hold their attention a bit longer than a traditionally written text. I appreciate the author's attempt to be innovative!!

Sandra Cereola, James Madison

I believe the organization of the content represents an improvement over existing AIS texts. As I mentioned earlier, I prefer the business processes section prior to information technologies and internal controls.

In terms of approach, there appears to be an attempt to develop an AIS foundation as opposed to co-mingling the AIS foundations with particular software or modeling techniques (e.g., REA). This approach allows the students to focus on developing the basics or foundations prior to topics that depend on the foundations. This is a great improvement over many of the existing texts.

Leisa Marshall, Valdosta State University

One of the best AIS texts out there for an undergraduate course. Great readability and relevant topical coverage! I think students will actually read this!

Mary Beth Goodrich, University of Texas

Excellent approach to introductory/survey course. Instructor can augment with additional material. Gives the necessary background for more advanced courses.

Rob Smith, University of Arkansas

Very comprehensive, but many, many links to aid understanding as well as a good amount of exercises. In addition, the faculty member can add personal experiences and what he/she learned in faculty development activities and easily slip that learning into this course with this text. Nice job!

Linda Bressler, University of Houston

I use this textbook because it is concise and to the point in the coverage of necessary topics.

Anna Lusher, Slippery Rock University

I like the new contents in this textbook, XBRL- and SOX-related discussions. These are very timely and important topics that are hard to find in other textbooks.

Rong Huang, University of New York–Baruch College

Supplements

For the Instructor

Instructor's Online Learning Center (www.mhhe.com/hurt2e) incorporates **"teaching suggestions"** for each chapter. They outline activities instructors can use in the classroom to engage students more completely; they can also be used for classroom assessment.

Instructor's Resource and Solutions Manual includes the solutions to all the discussion questions, end-of-chapter questions and problems, and reflection and self-assessment questions.

Test Bank includes a substantial number of questions in each chapter offering a large pool of material to choose from when creating a test.

EZ Test Computerized Test Bank can be used to create different versions of the same test, change the answer order, edit and add questions, and conduct online testing. Technical support for this software is available at (800) 331-5094 or visit www.mhhe.com/eztest.

PowerPoint Presentations deliver a complete set of slides covering many of the key concepts presented in each chapter.

For the Student

PowerPoint Presentations (www.mhhe.com/hurt2e) are available on the Student Center of the text's Online Learning Center. These presentations accompany each chapter of the text and contain the same slides that are available to the instructor.

Technology

Online Learning Center

www.mhhe.com/hurt2e

For instructors, the book's Web site contains the Instructor's Resource and Solutions Manual, PowerPoint slides, Interactive Activities, Text and Supplement Updates, and links to professional resources.

The student section of the site features online chapter quizzing activities, including a multiple-choice quiz and a key term flashcard quiz to accompany each chapter of text. PowerPoint presentations are also available to download. The author has listed several important links relating to text and professional material.

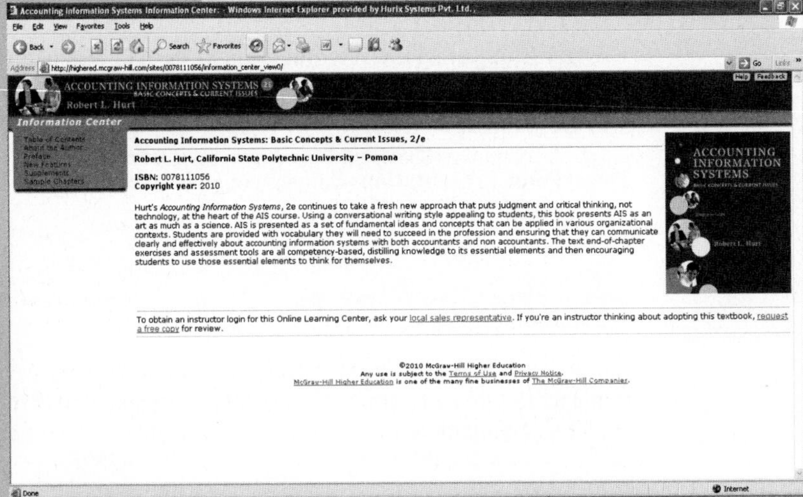

Message from the Author

To the Student

Welcome to the study of accounting information systems (AIS) and the second edition of this book! You've embarked on the first stage of a lifelong education about accounting; AIS touches every area of professional practice, so what you learn in this class will be relevant to you whether your career takes you into public accounting, the corporate world, governmental and not-for-profit accounting, or some other area of practice.

I heard from several students who used the first edition of the book, and I've incorporated many of their suggestions and ideas in this second edition. I've also retained the features from the first edition they found most useful. Here's a list of some of the guiding principles I had in mind as I prepared this new edition for you:

- At its core, AIS is about critical thinking and judgment—it's not fundamentally about journal entries and information technology, although both those and other traditional accounting topics are important in AIS. I've included several activities to help you develop your professional judgment and critical thinking skills because I think the best way to develop those skills is to practice them; I encourage you to "think out loud" with both your fellow scholars and your professors.
- In AIS, many problems have more than one acceptable solution. But don't take that to mean that every solution is acceptable! In other words, a problem might have several "right" answers—but some answers are clearly "wrong."
- For many accounting students, reading an accounting textbook ranks at about the same place as having a root canal at the dentist's office. As in the first edition, I've tried to use a lively, conversational tone that will make reading this text easier for you.
- You want to know that what you learn in school has clear, direct relevance to your career. So, I've used plenty of examples from the literature, my own professional experience, and the professional experience of friends and colleagues with that goal in mind.

AIS will likely be very different than your other accounting courses, in both its content and approach. I think I've written a text that will facilitate your learning and professional development; I hope you'll take the time to provide me feedback about this new edition. Please drop me an e-mail (RLHurt@csupomona.edu) to let me know how I can improve the book in the future. While I cannot promise a response to every single e-mail, I'll do my best to acknowledge your questions/comments and incorporate them in subsequent editions of the text.

Dr. Bob Hurt, C.M.A., C.F.E.

Brief Contents

Contents

Chapter 6
Data Flow Diagramming 105

Chapter 7
REAL Modeling 126

PART THREE
Systems Analysis and Information Technology 145

Look at ways various forms of information technology are used.

Chapter 8
Information Systems Concepts 147

Chapter 9
XBRL 165

Chapter 10
E-business and Enterprise Resource Planning Systems 182

PART FOUR
Business Processes 201

Look at various business processes that cut across organizations.

Chapter 11
Sales/Collection Process 203

Part One

Introduction and Basic Concepts

1. Role and Purpose of Accounting Information Systems
2. Transaction Processing in the AIS
3. Professionalism and Ethics
4. Internal Controls

The ideas in these chapters are fundamental to the study of accounting information systems, regardless of approach or philosophy. They define the nature of accounting information systems, review the accounting cycle, analyze various schools of ethical thought, and provide a firm foundation in internal controls. While these chapters present the four topics at a basic level, the material is reinforced and applied in various contexts throughout the rest of the text.

Scholars, each part of the text will open with a section like this one. Dr. Kevin Dow of Kent State University suggested including this feature in the second edition, and he prepared the text for each of them. These "why do we care" sections will help you understand why AIS topics are important in accounting practice, regardless of the direction your career takes. I'm very grateful to Kevin for suggesting this idea, and for the hard work he put into developing this content.

WHY DO WE CARE ABOUT THE BASIC CONCEPTS OF ACCOUNTING INFORMATION SYSTEMS

These chapters provide the foundation for developing an understanding of how accounting information systems (AIS) impact organizations. Coming into your AIS class, you might assume AIS only pertains to computers and general ledger (GL) software packages and is not relevant to those that enter traditional areas of accounting (such as auditing, financial accounting, management accounting, or tax). But nothing could be further from the truth!

All areas of accounting ultimately use the information generated from the AIS. For example: The auditor relies on the accounting system for integrating quality internal controls. The financial accountant relies on the soundness of the numbers as validated by the accounting system, and the tax accountant relies on the financial transactions as recorded by the accounting system. Management accountants use the information from the AIS for tasks like performance evaluation and cost analysis. Therefore, it is imperative for you to develop a fundamental understanding of this area.

In a broader sense, weaknesses in the AIS affect organizations in other ways. The accounting scandals of 2001 and 2002 (such as Enron, WorldCom, and Global Crossing) demonstrate the dramatic impact such weaknesses can have on both individuals and organizations. Internal controls can be designed to discourage errors or irregularities before they occur. For example, expense reports of a department are reviewed by the authorized account signers prior to payment, to ensure propriety and validity of the expenditure.

Accounting information systems also involve ethical decision making. Those same scandals demonstrate the importance and relevance of making sound ethical decisions in organizations. As such, there is an increased interest in understanding the role that corporate ethics plays in organizations. Ultimately, we do the right thing because it is the right thing to do.

Chapter One

Role and Purpose of Accounting Information Systems

AIS in the Business World

Dairy Queen

When I grew up in St. Louis, Missouri, my mom would often take me and my brothers to Dairy Queen if we'd been especially well behaved. (I'll leave it to you to wonder how often that happened!) But, when I moved to southern California in 1983, I found that Dairy Queen stores were few and far between. So, you can probably imagine how happy I was to find one only a few miles from my home. As a boy, my only interest in visiting was the ice cream; I still enjoy the ice cream today, but I also think about how their accounting information system works whenever I visit.

Dairy Queen is a franchised operation; their web site (www.dairyqueen.com) outlines five steps to owning a franchise. They are

1. Complete a form to request information from the corporate office.
2. Start the application process.
3. Have the application reviewed; if approved, select a site for the store.
4. Begin construction and participate in a management training program.
5. Open the new store.

The whole process, according to the Web site, takes less than a year in most cases.

As you'll learn in this chapter, most accounting information systems have five parts: inputs, processes, outputs, storage, and internal controls. Check out the table below for some examples of each one within the context of a Dairy Queen franchise:

AIS element	Example
Input	Franchise application
Process	Collect franchise fee and deposit it in the bank
Output	Form approving a suggested location
Storage	Database files
Internal control	Multiple reviews of application and related materials

The next time you visit your favorite restaurant (or any similar business), think about its accounting needs and see if you can come up with one or more examples of each element.

Discussion Questions

1. Why do organizations need an accounting information system?
2. In what ways are the systems similar regardless of organizational characteristics (type, size, location)? In what ways are the systems different based on those factors?
3. What are some examples of the five generic AIS elements that would be involved in selling ice cream?

Welcome to the study of accounting information systems (AIS)! AIS is a critically important area of study for future accountants. It ties together what accounting students often see as separate, unrelated areas of accounting: financial, managerial, tax, and governmental. Additionally, AIS brings in considerations from management, finance, and information systems. Finally, a deep, fundamental comprehension of accounting information systems is a great help in the study of auditing.

You'll often hear the phrase "single, correct, deterministic responses" throughout this text—that's another way of saying there is "one right answer."

Many accounting students are drawn to the discipline because of its perceived objectivity; they like solving problems that have "right answers." And your prior study of accounting may have focused on such problems. But, in practice, such problems are few and far between. And even when they exist, you won't be able to look up the right answer in a textbook or solutions manual. Problems and issues in accounting information systems seldom have single, correct, deterministic responses. So, to get you ready to confront and respond to those kinds of problems in practice, I'm including many of them in this textbook. One of this book's main purposes is to help you develop professional judgment and confidence in your ability to analyze **unstructured problems**.

You'll find a paragraph like this one at the beginning of every chapter in the book. The enumerated items are often referred to as "learning objectives" or "expected student outcomes." You can use them to test your own mastery of the topics discussed in each chapter. Be sure to ask your instructor about the relationship between the textbook learning objectives and exams in class.

When you've finished studying this chapter, and completing the activities at its conclusion, you should be able to:

1. Define "accounting information systems."
2. Discuss why AIS is an important area of study for future accountants.
3. Compare and contrast AIS with other areas of study in accounting.
4. Explain the structure of most accounting information systems.
5. Locate and evaluate information sources on accounting information systems.
6. Describe the structure and content of the remainder of this text.

Different university accounting curricula place the AIS course differently. In some schools, AIS is the first course accounting majors take after the introductory sequence. In other programs, AIS is near the end of the required sequence. And you'll find some schools allow students discretion in the timing of AIS study. In my university, students study AIS early in their accounting education—within one or two terms of completing their introductory sequence. But this book can be used in any of the three frameworks mentioned above.

As you can probably tell already, I tend to write in a conversational tone—as if I'm talking to you. I've found students appreciate such an approach, and that it motivates them to read the text more systematically and regularly. If something in the text seems unclear, or could be stated differently to enhance your understanding, I encourage you to contact me with your thoughts. My e-mail is RLHurt@csupomona.edu. While I can't promise a response to every e-mail I receive, I can promise every one will receive serious consideration in future editions of the text.

DEFINITION AND IMPORTANCE OF AIS

An **accounting information system** is a set of interrelated activities, documents, and technologies designed to collect data, process it, and report information to a diverse group of internal and external decision makers in organizations. A well-designed AIS can significantly enhance decision making in organizations by responding to many elements of the Financial Accounting Standards Board Conceptual Framework.

FASB developed the **conceptual framework** in the late 1970s as a guide for the development of future accounting principles. While the jury is still out on whether the conceptual framework has fulfilled that purpose, it is a fundamental part of accounting practice. You also can be fairly confident that you'll see questions on the conceptual framework on most accounting professional exams (CPA, CMA, and the like).

Detailed study of the conceptual framework often comprises the first part of intermediate accounting, so we won't go into great detail on it here. Basically, the conceptual framework looks like the one shown in Figure 1.1. The framework has three levels. The first, at the top of the triangle, explains what accounting is trying to do: provide information for decisions. The second level presents two sets of ideas: What information does accounting provide (elements of financial statements), and what characteristics should the information have to make it useful for decisions (qualitative characteristics)? The third level of the

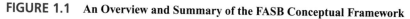

FIGURE 1.1 **An Overview and Summary of the FASB Conceptual Framework**

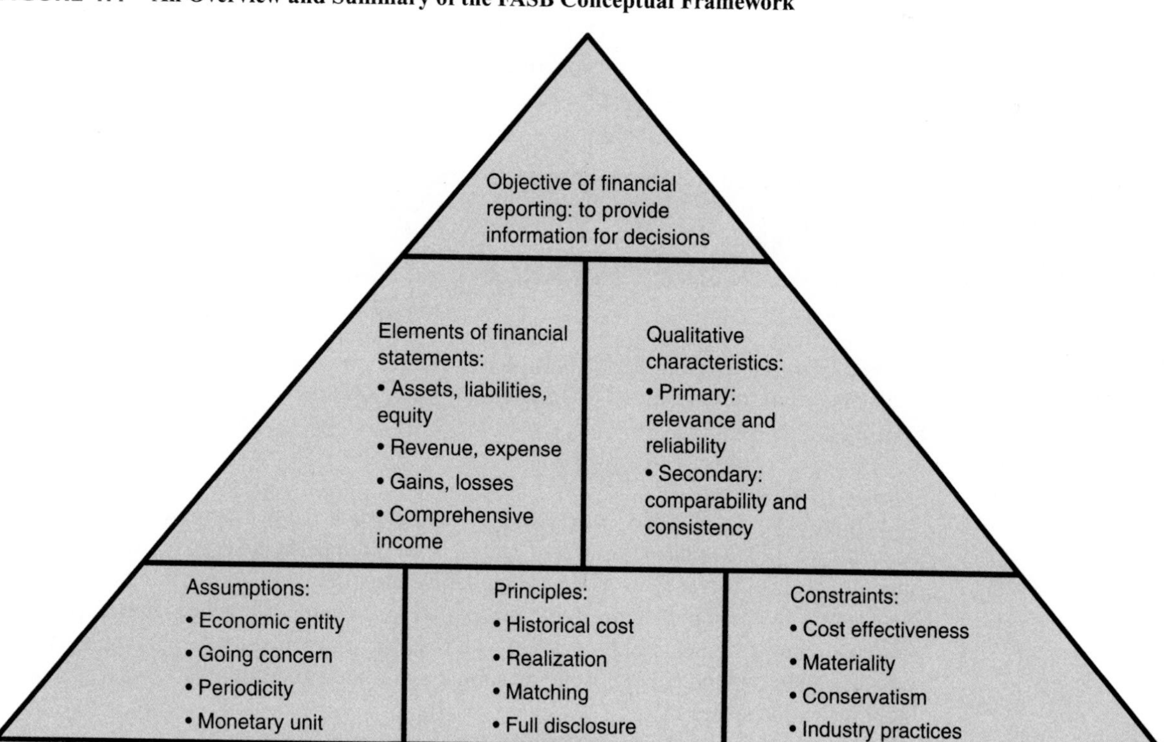

framework highlights some ideas that pervade accounting and the design of accounting information systems (assumptions, principles, and constraints).

A well-designed accounting information system relates to the conceptual framework by

- *Capturing data on the elements of financial statements.* No matter what form they take or information technologies they use, accounting information systems document changes in assets, liabilities, equity, revenues, expenses, gains, and losses. Many continue to use a traditional debit/credit format for doing so, although some scholars in the area have suggested that debits and credits may have less relevance in the future.
- *Transforming those data into relevant and reliable information.* Well-designed accounting information systems also can gather data beyond the elements of financial statements. Items like sales by geographic area, customer characteristics and transaction histories, demand for inventory items, and vendor quality ratings can improve decision making by enhancing the elements of relevance: predictive value, feedback value, and timeliness. Additionally, internal controls in the accounting information system promote reliability (verifiability, neutrality, and representational faithfulness), as you'll see in later chapters.
- *Recognizing and adapting to the cost–benefit constraint.* Accounting information systems are all about choices and trade-offs: What data should I capture? What information technologies should I use to process them? What information should I report? Looking at the conceptual framework diagram in Figure 1.1, you'll see "cost-effectiveness" as one of the constraints on accounting information. Cost-effectiveness reminds us that we can't design the world's perfect accounting information system. Even in the best organizations with the most effective systems, you'll find managers who want more data or different data, who question the system's integrity, and/or who want business processes to be structured differently. As a designer, implementer, and interpreter of accounting information systems, always keep in mind that the benefit of having data, processes, and information must outweigh the costs of obtaining or implementing them. Those costs and benefits might be economic, behavioral, psychological, or financial, but they should always be considered.

Reflection and Self-Assessment 1.1

Based on your prior study of accounting, give two examples of each element of financial statements. Also, find a Web site that discusses the elements of the conceptual framework in greater detail. In your own words, write a definition for each of the qualitative characteristics of accounting information.

You probably noticed the "why should I care" story at the beginning of this section of the book; you'll find one at the start of each section throughout the text. Those stories were suggested by Dr. Kevin Dow at Kent State University; they will show you, in a very concrete way, how the topics in the book are applied in accounting practice. Hopefully, those stories and my comments will convince you that AIS is an area of accounting worthy of your full attention and energy. Next, let's think about the structure of a "typical" accounting information system.

AIS STRUCTURE

I often refer to "organizations" rather than "companies" or "businesses." That's because every organization needs an AIS, but not all organizations are "businesses."

An accounting information system is a set of interrelated activities, documents, and technologies designed to collect data, process them, and report information to a diverse group of internal and external decision makers in organizations. Most accounting information systems comprise five parts, as shown in Figure 1.2.

Each part of the **AIS structure** plays a vital role in its overall efficiency and effectiveness. And each part is filled with the kinds of design choices and cost–benefit trade-offs mentioned earlier. Consider the questions below to illustrate them:

1. *Inputs.* Inputs to an AIS might include documents such as sales invoices and purchase orders. Accountants would also need to ask questions like these to design and/or audit the system:
   a. What kinds of source documents will system users need?
   b. Should the source documents be paper-based, electronic, or both?
   c. How many copies of each source document will be required?
   d. What information should the documents contain?
2. *Processes.* Processing tools can include computers and satellites. Here are some other questions you might ask about processing tools:
   a. Which processing tools should the AIS use?
   b. Should the tools be manual, computer-based, or both?
   c. If computer-based tools are used in the AIS, which software and hardware packages should be implemented?
3. *Outputs.* System outputs for most organizations would include the general-purpose financial statements as well as internal reports such as variance analyses. Other considerations include
   a. Beyond the general-purpose financial statements, what other reports will managers and system users need?
   b. How should the AIS be designed to facilitate their production?
4. *Storage.* Data in an accounting information system could be stored locally (as in a cash register or a transactions file) or remotely (as on an external network). Organizations also might maintain paper-based records of transactions. Relevant questions about storage include
   a. How should data be stored? On paper? Electronically? Both?
   b. Where should data be stored? Locally? Remotely? Both?
   c. How long should data be stored?
   d. Under what conditions can/should data be destroyed?
5. *Internal controls.* We'll explore internal controls in much greater depth later in the text. Most organizations employ internal controls such as daily backup of data and separation

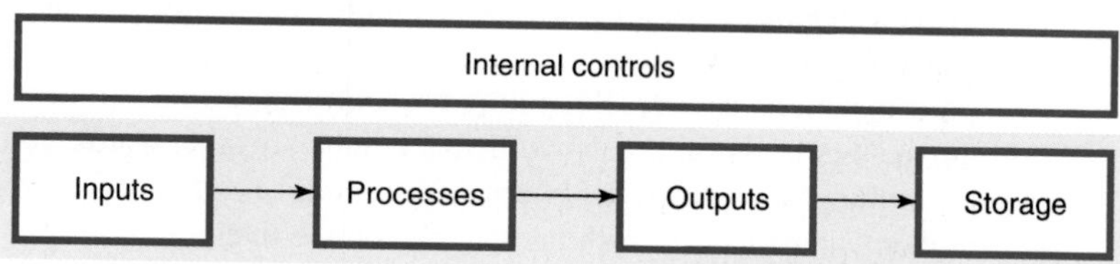

FIGURE 1.2 **Generic AIS Structure**

of duties (custody, authority, and record keeping) to maintain control over specific assets. Other questions might be

a. What controls are necessary to promote information integrity in the AIS?

b. What behavioral effects are the controls likely to have?

c. Are the controls cost-effective?

The preceding questions don't have clear-cut, easy, simplistic answers. They do have "common" or "usual" answers, and that's part of what you'll learn throughout this course. But the rest of what you'll learn may be even more important. You'll learn how to make choices and judgments within the context of accounting information systems—choices and judgments that may not be perfect but that you'll be able to explain, along with their costs and benefits. Additionally, you'll be able to critique and evaluate the choices made by others. At first blush, that kind of thinking may seem daunting. Try to set aside your anxiety so you can think critically. Recognize that even seasoned professionals have to discuss and debate ideas to solve problems.

Reflection and Self-Assessment 1.2

How do you feel about starting a course that doesn't have clear-cut, easy, simplistic answers? What study tools and techniques could you use to develop your ability to respond to open-ended questions?

So, to move you forward toward that goal, let's examine places (other than this book) where you can find information about AIS, as well as some guidelines for evaluating that information.

AIS INFORMATION SOURCES AND INFORMATION LITERACY CONCEPTS

The first time you read this section, you may not understand how it fits into your study of accounting information systems. Here's the connection: Accounting information systems is an emerging field; with the possible exception of forensic accounting and fraud examination, it may be the newest field of study for accounting students. And, unlike other areas of accounting, practitioners and professors alike take different approaches to it. So, throughout the course, you'll often be called upon to do research as part of answering questions/responding to problems/preparing projects.

When your professor assigns a research or current article project, where is the first place you look? If you're like most accounting students, you answered, "the Internet." And, since AIS is such a "hot topic" in today's business world, you're bound to find tons of information on it there. But you're probably not surprised to learn that not all information on the Internet is valid, trustworthy, or reliable. In other words, you can't necessarily believe everything you read on the Internet. You should evaluate information critically for yourself, rather than believe everything you read on the Internet.

Reflection and Self-Assessment 1.3

Society is full of urban legends that may or may not be true. For example, some people believe the Earth is flat. Others believe that the first U.S. landing on the moon was nothing more than a hoax. Choose one of those urban legends or some other you prefer. Find an information source that attempts to assess its validity, and comment on the believability of the source.

According to Dictionary.com, "validity" refers to something that is well grounded or something that is binding. Although validity doesn't appear formally in the conceptual framework, it is definitely implied—particularly by the qualitative characteristics of accounting information.

Depending on the kinds of assignments your instructor gives you this term, you may find yourself doing a lot of research for this class. The point of this section of the chapter is to give you tools to evaluate the information you find during your research—to think about it critically, rather than assuming it's all "true" on its face.

If you'd like to learn more about information competence in general and assess the degree to which you have it, I encourage you to visit the American Association of School Librarians' Web site on the topic: www.ala.org/ala/aasl/aaslproftools/informationpower/informationliteracy.htm.

Basically, information about accounting information systems on the Internet falls into three main groups: sponsored information, popular/practitioner information, and scholarly information. Let's consider the identifiers of each group as objectively as possible, then talk about how to evaluate information you find on the Internet (and, indeed, in other places).

Sponsored/commercial information means that someone has paid a fee or given other consideration to have their information put on the Internet. The main purpose of sponsored/commercial information is to sell products and services. Often, Internet users can access this information free of charge, which may give it the appearance of being objective. Sponsored information sites aren't necessarily 100 percent biased, but they may limit the information they disseminate or the choices available to Internet users. Again, the point isn't to reject all sponsored information sites "out of hand" for research and information purposes; the point is to evaluate them critically using guidelines we'll look at in a few paragraphs. www.investopedia.com is an example of sponsored/commercial information. So, for example, if you were looking for information on a particular piece of software, you might be looking at sponsored/commercial information. Suppose you were investigating various general ledger software packages, such as QuickBooks and Peachtree. You'd expect to get a lot of information from the companies that publish the software, although that information might paint a more optimistic, positive picture than a third-party review.

Popular/practitioner information has gone through a review process prior to publication. It may recount the experiences of a specific company or group of companies, offer suggestions to managers, or present new ideas or ways of thinking. Because popular/practitioner information has passed through a review process prior to publication, it's usually more trustworthy and objective than sponsored information on the Internet. But you should always ask yourself about the author's motivation and the context of the information. For example, if an article talks about the successful implementation of an enterprise resource planning system, consider (among other things) whether the author works for the ERP vendor, the size and industry of the organization, and the resources (human, technological, and monetary) devoted to the project. Consider the Web site for the *Journal of Accountancy* (www.aicpa.org/pubs/jofa/joahome.htm) in this category. If you were responding to a problem about how things happen in practice, such as how companies deal with internal control issues in an e-business environment, you'd probably consult popular/practitioner information.

Scholarly information also has gone through a review process prior to publication. As a future accountant, you may only rarely access scholarly information on AIS. Generally, scholarly information contains a clear research question, a review of related literature, a thorough description of the methods used to answer the question, and the results and conclusions of the research project. This additional detail is necessary so that readers can more easily evaluate the results and conclusions in light of the methodology; the review of related literature helps carve out the "value added" by an individual article in light of what other authors have discovered/written about a topic. *Business Ethics Quarterly* (www.pdcnet.org/beq.html) is a scholarly publication focused on various aspects of business ethics.

A lot of scholarly information may be difficult for you to understand; it's often written by people with advanced degrees, for people with advanced degrees. However, if written clearly and simply, you may benefit from reading the results and/or conclusions of a scholarly research study—particularly if you're looking for "hard evidence" on a topic (such as how people from different cultures respond to ethics issues).

Evaluating information reliability on the Internet comes under the broad heading of "information literacy" or "information competence." For ease of discussion, I'll use the term **information competence** (IC) here, but you're likely to hear both terms in conversation about this topic. IC is much, much broader than the evaluation of information reliability, but we'll limit our discussion here to that aspect of it. According to the California State University's Work Group on Information Competence (Curzon, 1995), it is "the ability to find, evaluate, use, and communicate information in all of its various formats."

Your university library probably has numerous materials on information literacy as well; most librarians are well versed in the topic and eager to share their knowledge with students.

Why is information competence important in the study of accounting information systems? As a relatively new area of study for accountants, AIS is full of emerging concepts, ideas, and issues. Answers to the problems you'll confront in this class are not always found in textbooks but may require significant research. Evaluating the validity of sources you encounter in that research is a critical skill for reaching reliable conclusions and finding genuinely valuable information.

You'll also find a lot of resources about this important topic at www.calstate.edu/LS/Tutorials.shtml.

Many sources can assist you in evaluating information, but I've found the checklist developed by the University of Maryland's University College (UMUC) to be especially helpful. You can find the checklist at http://umuc.edu/library/guides/evaluate.html. The UMUC site presents five evaluation criteria, each with several specific questions you can use in your research. The five criteria are

1. *Authority.* Can you tell who created the information? The purpose of its creation? Can you contact the author or creating organization, or otherwise establish their credentials? For example, authors published in *Strategic Finance* (the monthly publication of the Institute of Management Accountants) are required to provide background and contact information as part of their articles. Reading that information carefully can help you make decisions about authority as you evaluate information for AIS course projects.
2. *Accuracy.* Does the site/article/source tell you where the information came from? Does it contain any obvious errors of fact or misleading graphs, charts, or statistics? Consider, for instance, information presented in a graph. Differences can be exaggerated simply by changing the graph's scaling. Consider Figure 1.3 as an illustration of this point. Notice how the differences appear more pronounced in graph (a) than in graph (b), although the only difference between the two graphs is the scaling on the vertical axis.
3. *Objectivity.* Does the information contain advertising? Is it available freely? By this time in your accounting education, you have probably heard of the Sarbanes-Oxley Act of 2002. We'll explore the details of SOX later in the text, but consider www.soxlaw.com in terms of this information criterion. Figure 1.4 gives you a partial screen shot of the Web site. Although I've found the information there objective and valuable in learning about SOX, notice the "Contact Us" link on the left side. Clicking that link reveals the name of the consulting firm that compiled the information, offering its services to help companies comply with SOX.
4. *Currency.* Can you tell when the source was created/written? When was the last time it was updated? Does the page contain any "dead links"? Later in the text, we'll explore how to create databases of accounting information; one of the important concepts in that area is data normalization. Data normalization refers to the set of rules designers use to ensure that databases are as effective and as efficient as possible.

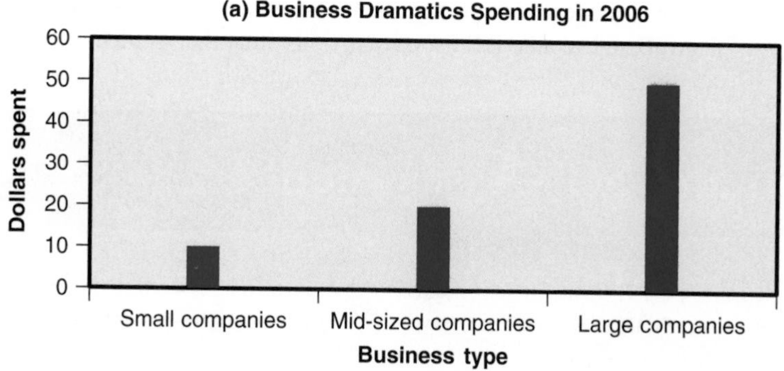

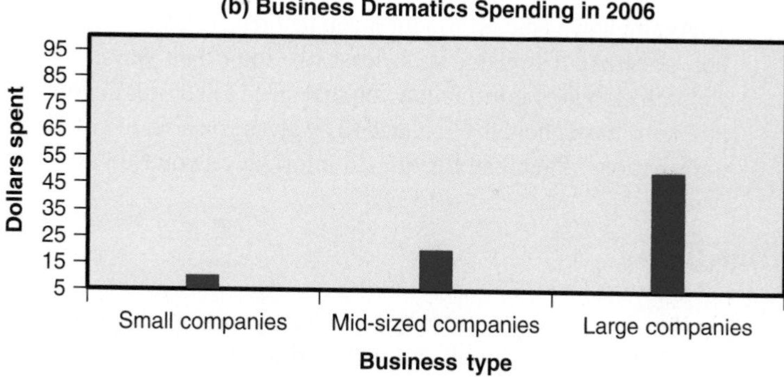

FIGURE 1.3
Data Displays

You'll find the rules of data normalization nicely summarized at www.datamodel.org/NormalizationRules.html. As I prepared this chapter for the first edition, the Web site showed its last update as June 13, 2005. Is that current enough? In this case, it probably is—the rules of data normalization have been well established for quite some time.

5. *Coverage.* Is the source still under construction? Does it cover the subject with sufficient depth? In some sense, all Web sites are always "under construction." In most cases, they have to be updated periodically to stay current and relevant. But if a page is perpetually "under construction," you should consider whether it would be a valuable, trusted source for research and problem solving. Here are a couple links to Web sites "under construction" at the time of this writing: www.conveyor.com/ucz/ and http://access.nku.edu/oca/UnderConstruction.htm.

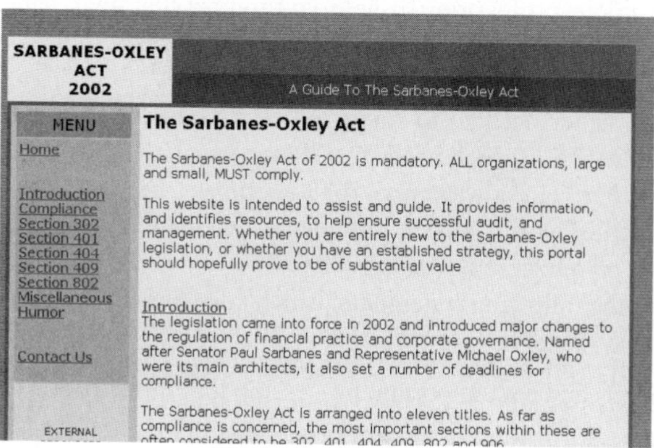

FIGURE 1.4
Sarbanes-Oxley Information Web Site, www.soxlaw.com

I encourage you to point your Web browser to the University of Maryland site listed on page 10 and see the full list of questions and other guidelines there.

Reflection and Self-Assessment 1.4

Use your university's library to find an article reasonably related to accounting. Evaluate the article based on the five criteria listed previously, or some other set your instructor prefers.

Again: how is the information you just read related to your study of accounting information systems? It's related in at least two important ways: (1) it gives you some guidance about the kinds of information you may need to consult in doing research and responding to problems throughout the text, and (2) it gives you a set of criteria you can use to evaluate that information, rather than treating all information you find as the full and absolute "truth."

CRITICAL THINKING

By this time in your university education, you've probably heard at least one professor talk about the need to "think critically." But what exactly does that mean? Dictionary.com defines critical thinking as "the mental process of actively and skillfully conceptualizing, applying, analyzing, synthesizing, and evaluating information to reach an answer or conclusion." And the Critical Thinking Community (www.criticalthinking.org) says that someone who thinks critically does five things:

- Raises vital questions and problems, formulating them clearly and precisely
- Gathers and assesses relevant information, using abstract ideas to interpret it effectively
- Comes to well-reasoned conclusions and solutions, testing them against relevant criteria and standards
- Thinks openmindedly [*sic*] within alternative systems of thought, recognizing and assessing, as needs be, their assumptions, implications, and practical consequences
- Communicates effectively with others in figuring out solutions to complex problems

Every area of accounting requires critical thinking; every day, accountants make judgments and respond to questions that may have more than one acceptable answer. Throughout this book, I'll often ask you to think critically so you can develop the skills you'll need to succeed in our profession. To help you toward that goal, each chapter in the text will contain a section like this one. I hope that studying them will help you develop your critical-thinking skills.

For this chapter, I'd like to focus on the "statement evaluation" exercises you'll find throughout the text. In each of them, I'll give you 10 statements; your job will be to determine if each one is (a) always true, (b) sometimes true, or (c) never true. For those that are "sometimes true," you'll need to provide an explanation; your instructor may include similar exercises on quizzes and exams.

Consider the following statements, which talk about the role of computers in accounting information systems:

1. Computers can be an important processing tool in the AIS.
2. Computers are always an important processing tool in the AIS.
3. Computers are important processing tools in the AIS.

At first blush, without thinking critically, all three statements may seem alike to you—but they're not. Each statement has a unique phrase that differentiates it from the others: "can be," "are always," and "are."

The first statement (Computers can be an important processing tool in the AIS) is always true. When you see the phrase "can be," think of it as meaning "have the potential to be." It's always true that computers have the potential to be an important processing tool—even though they are not used in every AIS.

The second statement (Computers are always an important processing tool in the AIS) is never true. The phrase "are always" means that there are no exceptions. Here's a parallel example: People with blonde hair always have blue eyes. While it's true that people with blonde hair often have blue eyes, the two don't always go together; some people with blonde hair, for example, have green eyes. Similarly, some accounting information systems employ computers as processing tools—but some don't. So it is never true that computers are always an important processing tool in the AIS.

The third statement (Computers are important processing tools in the AIS) is sometimes true. In other words, in some accounting information systems, computers are important processing tools; but in other systems, they are not.

Take a look at the statement evaluation exercise at the end of this chapter. Statement (a) (Data in an accounting information system are stored electronically, such as on a disk) is sometimes true. Statement (b) ("Truth" is one of the qualitative characteristics identified by the FASB conceptual framework) is never true. Statement (c) (The FASB conceptual framework identifies eight elements of financial statements) is always true.

I often tell my students that accounting really isn't about numbers at all; it's really about the use of language. And becoming a critical thinker means, in part, that you're able to use language accurately and precisely. The statement evaluation exercise at the end of each chapter will be challenging for you at first, I'm sure. But, as you practice thinking critically, the exercise will make more sense. If you ever find yourself "stumped" by one of those statements, don't hesitate to drop me an e-mail (RLHurt@csupomona.edu) and let me know; I'll do my best to clarify and point you in the right direction.

TEXT STRUCTURE AND CONTENT

This book is structured in five parts:

Introduction and basic concepts. In the first four chapters, we'll look at topics that form the foundation of most AIS courses. Here in Chapter 1, we examined the basic nature of accounting information systems; we also looked at information literacy and critical thinking. Chapter 2 reviews the accounting cycle and talks about how human judgment and information technology are involved in its activities. Chapter 3 presents material on professionalism and ethics: What does it mean to be a professional, particularly a professional in accounting? And what ethical issues do practicing accountants face? The last chapter in the first part of the book, Chapter 4, explores topics related to internal control, including the following: What purposes do internal controls serve in the AIS? What frameworks can accountants use to design and evaluate internal controls? What risks do organizations face that require strong internal controls? The topics from all four chapters reappear later in the text, where they are applied in various contexts.

Documentation techniques. Whether you're designing a completely new accounting information system, making changes to an existing system, or auditing a system, documentation techniques are important. In these three chapters, we'll look at three common ways accountants create models of accounting information systems: flowcharts

(Chapter 5), data flow diagrams (Chapter 6), and REAL models (Chapter 7). In Chapters 6 and 7, we'll also explore database design. Later chapters on business processes will give you the chance to apply the skills you acquire in systems documentation in more specific contexts.

Systems analysis and information technology. The three chapters in the third part of the book look at ways various forms of information technology are used in the AIS—everything from the relatively traditional (like spreadsheets and others in Chapter 8) to newer topics (like XBRL in Chapter 9 and ERP systems in Chapter 10). In addition, this section contains a brand new chapter on information systems models. In Chapter 8, we'll talk about two ideas that relate to virtually any information system, including the AIS: the systems development life cycle (SDLC) and the capability maturity model (CMM). The SDLC is one good way to build an information system "from the ground up," while the CMM gives systems professionals a tool for determining how sophisticated (mature) an organization's business processes and systems are.

Business processes. The first three chapters in this part of the book take a look at various business processes that cut across organizations: sales/collection (Chapter 11), acquisition/payment (Chapter 12), and other business processes (Chapter 13). We'll take many of the ideas from previous sections and apply them within the context of those business processes: internal control, systems documentation, the SDLC, and information technology. The last chapter in this part of the text (Chapter 14) is brand new to this edition. It talks about ways organizations can manage their business processes with an eye toward making them more effective and efficient.

Other topics in AIS. I've included four chapters in the last part of the text: computer crime and information technology security (Chapter 15), decision-making models and knowledge management (Chapter 16), professional certifications and career planning (Chapter 17), and auditing and evaluating the AIS (Chapter 18). I've included these four topics, which are not often part of other AIS texts, for several reasons: (a) they are areas my own students have been interested in, (b) they provide an opportunity to apply some fundamental topics (internal control, database design, information technology) in new areas, (c) they connect accounting with other areas of business (such as management), and (d) they connect AIS with other areas of accounting (such as auditing).

As always, I encourage you to communicate with me, either on your own or through your professor, about aspects of the book that are working well for you and those that could use some improvement.

Summary

Each chapter in the text ends with a brief summary of its major points, structured in terms of the learning objectives at the beginning of the chapter.

1. *Define "accounting information systems."* An accounting information system (AIS) is a collection of interrelated parts, some of which may incorporate information technology. Its purpose is to collect data, process it into information, and report the information so it can be used by internal and external decision makers.
2. *Discuss why AIS is an important area of study for future accountants.* AIS is important because it cuts across traditional functional lines in accounting. It provides the "big picture" and allows students to develop their critical-thinking and problem-solving skills.
3. *Compare and contrast AIS with other areas of study in accounting.* AIS is like other areas of accounting in that it includes consideration of financial statements and internal reports.

It is different, though, from other parts of accounting. AIS typically includes more open-ended problems that do not have deterministic responses. It also cuts across traditional accounting subdivisions (financial, managerial, and the like) and incorporates material from disciplines outside accounting (such as management and information systems).

4. *Explain the structure of most accounting information systems.* Most AIS incorporate five main parts. Inputs are used to collect data and get them into the system; they include source documents such as checks and invoices. Processing tools transform the data into information; processing tools can be manual or automated. Outputs provide some of the information decision makers need in organizations. Typical outputs of an AIS include the general-purpose financial statements. Internal controls are the policies and procedures established in an AIS to promote information integrity and safeguard assets. And storage refers to the methods for keeping data secure and available.
5. *Locate and evaluate information sources on accounting information systems.* Information on AIS can be found in both traditional and online sources. The chapter grouped information sources into three parts: sponsored/commercial, popular/practitioner, and scholarly. All information, regardless of source, should be evaluated for validity. One useful checklist for information evaluation is provided by the University of Maryland: authority, accuracy, objectivity, currency, and coverage. The ability to find, evaluate, and use information appropriately is often referred to as information competence.
6. *Describe the structure and content of the remainder of this text.* The text is structured in five main parts: (1) introduction and basic concepts, (2) documentation techniques, (3) systems analysis and information technology, (4) business processes and (5) other topics in AIS.

So, as you can see, you're in for a fascinating, highly relevant, diverse study this term in your AIS course. I hope you'll approach your study with enthusiasm and commitment, knowing that what you learn this term will serve you very well in your career as a professional accountant.

Key Terms

These terms are defined in the glossary at the end of the text, as well as in the chapter.

accounting information system, *5*
AIS structure, *7*
conceptual framework, *5*
information competence, *10*
popular/practitioner information, *9*
scholarly information, *9*
sponsored/commercial information, *9*
unstructured problems, *4*

Chapter Reference

Curzon, S. 1995. *Information Competence in the CSU.* www.calstate.edu/LS/Archive/info_comp_report.shtml (May 25, 2005).

End-of-Chapter Activities

1. *Reading review questions.* These questions will help you assess your understanding of the text readings. If you've studied the chapter thoroughly, you should be able to answer them without reference to the text itself. Although these questions appear first, you may find them easier to answer after completing the rest of the end-of-chapter assignments. I urge you to answer them in your own words, rather than with quotations from the text itself.
   a. What is an accounting information system?
   b. Describe the purpose of the FASB conceptual framework. Discuss how it relates to your study of accounting information systems.

c. List and discuss the five parts of a generic accounting information system.

d. Compare and contrast sponsored information, practitioner/public information, and scholarly information.

e. Identify five broad criteria you can use to evaluate information on the Internet and in other sources.

f. In a manner specified by your instructor (e.g., individually or with a group, as a written paper or as an oral presentation), prepare an original response to one or more of the questions for this chapter's "AIS in the Business World."

2. *Reading review problem.* Except for the two chapters that are brand new to this edition (Chapters 8 and 14), every chapter will have a reading review problem in addition to the reading review questions. I'm using the "AIS in the Business World" stories from the first edition as the basis for these reading review problems in the second edition. So, in this chapter, the reading review problem focuses on Dollar General (www.dollargeneral.com). Nash ("Dollar General: 8 Days to Grow," *Baseline* 1, no. 32 (July 2004)) offered the following comments about Dollar General:

You may not have heard of Dollar General, but it's a heavy competitor with Wal-Mart in some areas of the United States. Dollar General (DG) has over six thousand stores in 29 states, generating $6.9 billion in annual sales. The chain successfully opens two stores a day on average, maintaining a profit margin of over 4 percent. A central computer in Tennessee interfaces with each store's cash registers via satellite every night; otherwise, DG employs no computer networks, e-mail, or local inventory tracking servers. While DG can maintain high profit margins through cutting back on systems costs, it does experience significant inventory shrinkage (theft and loss)—about 3 percent of sales annually.

a. Which generic element of most accounting information systems best describes cash registers and satellites as they are used at DG?

b. What kind of information does Nash's article in *Baseline* present? Evaluate Nash's article using the five UMUC criteria presented in the chapter. You can find Nash's article by pointing your Web browser to www.baselinemag.com, then searching for the article title.

c. Use DG's Web site *or* the SEC's EDGAR database (www.sec.gov/edgar.shtml) to find recent outputs of DG's accounting information system. What is the purpose of each of the following forms: 8-K, 424B3, 10-Q, S-8, 10-K. When did DG last file each one of them with the SEC?

d. What policies would you recommend DG institute to reduce its inventory shrinkage?

3. *Making choices and exercising judgment.* As you read in the chapter, AIS is all about making choices and evaluating their costs and benefits. These questions and exercises are designed to help you develop those skills. When I give exercises like these to my own students, they frequently say, "So does this mean there's no right or wrong answer?" You may be thinking the same thing, so I'll tell you what I tell them: The point isn't whether your answer is "right" or "wrong," or even if such answers exist. The point here is for you to make choices and create answers you can defend in the face of other alternatives.

a. RKH Company is a small consulting service based just outside Los Angeles. It has two partners, Sebastian and Viola, and average monthly sales revenue of $25,000. At any one time, Sebastian and Viola have up to three consulting engagements running simultaneously. Monthly expenses include office rent, supplies, utilities, professional magazine subscriptions, and automobile expenses. What form(s) of information technology, if any, should Sebastian and Viola use in their accounting information system? Explain the costs and benefits of your recommendation.

b. Most accounting information systems in use today employ principles of debit and credit for recording transactions. What are the costs and benefits of using the debit/credit system for transaction recording? If the system is destined to fade into disuse, what do you think will replace it?

4. *Field exercises.* These exercises will require you to go out "into the field" to interview an accountant, observe a business process, do library research, or collect other kinds of data. Your instructor may ask you to complete one or more field exercises with a group of students; they also could be used as the basis for a major course writing assignment or presentation.
   a. Interview an accountant or other financial professional in an organization of your choice. Ask what information technologies (if any) are used in the accounting information system and about the costs and benefits of their use. If time permits, also ask for examples of internal controls in the organization. Don't forget to write a thank-you note or e-mail after your interview.
   b. Visit a movie theater, retail store, fast-food outlet, or other business organization near your home or campus. Carefully observe the process of making sales and collecting payments. What processes and tools does the organization use to keep its cash safe?
   c. Visit a local office supply store and ask to see the business documents section. Find examples of at least two documents from the following list: purchase requisition, purchase order, sales invoice, check, remittance advice, and customer statement. Either through a conversation with a store employee, individual research, and/or your own deductive powers and experience, discuss the purpose and use of the documents. List the information on the documents and explain how each information item helps achieve the document's purpose.
5. *Information types.* Using the three classifications discussed in the chapter, determine whether each of the following is sponsored, practitioner, or scholarly in nature.
   a. *Accounting, Behavior and Organizations*
   b. *Harvard Business Review*
   c. *Journal of Accountancy*
   d. *Management Accounting Quarterly*
   e. *MIS Quarterly*
   f. *Strategic Finance*
   g. **www.amazon.com**
   h. **www.findaccountingsoftware.com**
   i. **www.findarticles.com**
   j. **www.quickbooks.com**
6. Other than those listed in Question 5, find one or two examples (each) of sponsored, practitioner, and scholarly Web sites, journals, or other periodicals. Be prepared to explain your choices and their classifications.
7. Look up the following references online or in your school's library. Using the criteria and specific questions from the UMUC Web site referenced in the chapter, evaluate and discuss the quality of each reference. (*Note:* To do a thorough evaluation of these references, you *must* get the list of questions from the UMUC Web site. You won't be able to rely on my summary in the chapter to do your best work.)

   Zipperer, J. "Using Technology to Verify the Books." *Internet World,* October 2002.

   "Sage Launches Accounting Solution for Small Businesses." *Online Product News,* September 2000.

   Bradley, S. "Less Paper, More Security: Electronic Storage Doesn't Mean More Secure Files." *California CPA,* May 2003.

   "Mind Your E-Mail Manners." *Journal of Accountancy,* April 2003.

   Gooderham, P. N., et al. "Accountants as Sources of Business Advice for Small Firms." *International Small Business Journal,* February 2004.

8. *Crossword puzzle.* Each chapter includes an exercise like this one. These puzzles were created with a free tool called Eclipse, available at www.eclipse.com. As you complete each puzzle, don't limit yourself to the list of "important terms" in each chapter.

Across

3. The glue that ties an AIS together.
5. One element in UMUC's information evaluation checklist.
8. General-purpose financial statements, for example.
9. The "S" in AIS.
10. The "A" in AIS.

Down

1. The "I" in AIS.
2. The type of information presented in *Business Ethics Quarterly.*
4. QuickBooks, for example.
6. May include paper-based source documents.
7. Information ______________________: the ability to find and evaluate information.

9. *Terminology.* Each chapter also includes an exercise like this one. Not only will completing them help you master each chapter's vocabulary; you also may find questions like this one on your class exams and accounting professional exams. Please match each item on the left with the most appropriate item on the right.

1. *Business Ethics Quarterly*
2. Comparability and consistency
3. Currency
4. Deterministic
5. Going concern
6. *Journal of Accountancy*
7. Matching
8. Materiality
9. Objective of financial reporting
10. Relevance and reliability

a. A constraint of the conceptual framework
b. A principle of the conceptual framework
c. Accounting information's secondary qualitative characteristics
d. An assumption of the conceptual framework
e. An example of scholarly information
f. Another name for problems with single correct answers
g. Concerns whether information is up-to-date
h. Example of practitioner information
i. Primary qualitative characteristics of accounting information
j. To provide information for decision making

10. *Multiple choice questions.* Each chapter in the text will have 10 multiple choice questions based on its learning objectives. Some of the questions will be "low context." You can typically answer those just by reading the chapter. Other questions will be "high context." High-context questions call for you to exercise judgment in applying the material from the chapter.

1. Which of the following describes an accounting information system?

   I. Paper-based journals and ledgers with manually generated financial statements
   II. A general ledger package, such as Peachtree, that also includes modules for manufacturing and purchasing
   III. Your checkbook

   a. I and II
   b. II and III
   c. I and III
   d. I, II, and III

2. Accounting information systems is similar to other areas of accounting in that

   a. Its problems always have single, correct responses.
   b. It requires aptitude for mathematics.
   c. It helps students understand the conceptual framework of accounting.
   d. It always involves computers.

3. Most accounting systems have five parts. Which of the following is not one of them?

   a. Management judgment
   b. Processes
   c. Internal controls
   d. Outputs

4. Costs and benefits associated with accounting information systems can be

   a. Financial.
   b. Behavioral.
   c. Psychological.
   d. All of the above.

5. Which of the following is the best type of information for accounting research?

   a. Sponsored
   b. Popular
   c. Scholarly
   d. Cannot be determined from the information given

6. Which element of an AIS best describes "making journal entries"?
   a. Input
   b. Process
   c. Output
   d. Storage
7. Which element of an AIS best describes a monthly budget?
   a. Input
   b. Process
   c. Internal control
   d. Output
8. Which element of an AIS best describes "adequate business process documentation"?
   a. Input
   b. Internal control
   c. Output
   d. Storage
9. Which element of an AIS best describes a purchase requisition?
   a. Input
   b. Process
   c. Output
   d. Storage
10. Which of the following is not a quality of information identified by the UMUC taxonomy?
    a. Truthfulness
    b. Authority
    c. Objectivity
    d. Currency

11. *Statement evaluation.* As you learned in the chapter, designing and implementing accounting information systems requires judgment and critical thinking. Each chapter will include an exercise like this one to help you develop those skills. Several statements related to the material in the chapter are listed below; your job is to explain whether each statement is (i) always true, (ii) sometimes true, or (iii) never true. If you answer (ii), explain when the statement is true.

a. Data in an accounting information system are stored electronically, such as on a disk.
b. "Truth" is one of the qualitative characteristics identified by the FASB conceptual framework.
c. The FASB conceptual framework identifies eight elements of financial statements.
d. Information you find on the Internet is reliable.
e. Cost-effectiveness is an important criterion in the design of accounting information systems.
f. A Web site that is "under construction" may have a problem with adequate coverage according to the UMUC information criteria.
g. Both internal and external parties can use information provided by the accounting information system.
h. Most companies have two different accounting information systems: one for internal use and one for external use.
i. In an AIS, source documents are paper-based.
j. Problems and questions in accounting information systems are open-ended; they do not have "right" or "wrong" answers.

Chapter Two

Transaction Processing in the AIS

AIS in the Business World

Transaction Processing at the Restaurant at Kellogg Ranch

According to its Web site (www.rkr.csupomona.edu), "The Restaurant at Kellogg Ranch (RKR) is a student-operated restaurant, serving both lunch and dinner. The restaurant is part of the Hospitality Management curriculum at The Collins College of Hospitality Management at Cal Poly Pomona." As background for writing this vignette, I interviewed Dr. Ben Dewald, a professor in the Collins College.

RKR's chart of accounts is block coded. For example, assets related to food and beverage operations all have four-digit account numbers that begin with "1." Expenses for nonsalable items (such as cleaning supplies for the kitchen) have four-digit account numbers that begin with "7."

RKR's transaction processing software, developed and created by Lawrence Browning, is called DataTrap; it runs as an add-on to Excel. DataTrap organizes RKR's accounting and operating data into several worksheets within a single Excel file. Some of those worksheets include net sales, counts of lunch and dinner items, credits for lunch and dinner items, waste, crew meals for both lunch and dinner, and inventory. RKR uses those data to complete a weekly income statement summary sheet that reports both financial data (such as revenue from lunch, revenue from dinner, breakage expenses, supplies expense) and nonfinancial data (such as the number of guests for lunch and dinner, food cost as a percentage of food revenue).

RKR's transaction processing is complicated a bit by its relationship to the University. It must periodically transmit its financial data to the Cal Poly Pomona Foundation (http://foundation.csupomona.edu/), but the Foundation uses the principles of not-for-profit accounting, not the traditional accrual accounting businesses use. In effect, that reporting arrangement requires RKR to maintain two sets of accounting records: one for internal purposes, which is used for student assignments and management decision making, and one for use by the Foundation as part of its financial relationship with the University.

Discussion Questions

1. What does it mean to say that a chart of accounts is "block coded"? What other coding systems can organizations use for their chart of accounts?
2. What are the advantages and disadvantages of using an Excel add-on for transaction processing?

As I mentioned in Chapter 1, you may be studying accounting information systems near the start or near the finish of your formal accounting education. If you're taking this course before intermediate accounting, you'll likely want to devote significant attention to this chapter, which talks about the steps in the accounting cycle. If you're studying AIS after completing one or more courses in intermediate accounting, your instructor may use this chapter as a review, or skip it altogether.

When you've finished studying this chapter, and completing the activities at its conclusion, you should be able to:

1. Differentiate *accounting* and *bookkeeping.*
2. List, discuss, and complete, in order, the steps in the accounting cycle.
3. Identify common internal controls associated with the accounting cycle.
4. Describe common chart of accounts coding systems.
5. Explain how human judgment and information technology impact the accounting cycle.

Understanding the steps in the accounting cycle is important in the study of AIS. Without grasping the "big picture" of transaction processing, you'll be at a significant disadvantage when we begin talking in later chapters about documentation, internal controls, business processes, and current trends in AIS.

ACCOUNTING AND BOOKKEEPING

Many students and business professionals confuse bookkeeping with **accounting.** Before the advent of information technology, most accountants spent considerable time on bookkeeping tasks. Thankfully, we have tools available to us today that allow us to focus on more interesting and important areas, such as using accounting information for competitive advantage and management decision making.

You can find more information about AAA on its Web site: http://aaahq.org/index.cfm.

The American Accounting Association (AAA) is a group of accounting educators with members all over the world. A committee of the AAA developed the following definition of accounting:

> Accounting is the process of identifying, measuring, and communicating economic information to permit informed judgments and decisions by users of the information.

Note that the definition has three principal elements: identifying, measuring, and communicating.

Implied within the AAA's definition is the **bookkeeping** process: that part of accounting devoted to identifying and measuring the economic information. So you may be able to see why bookkeeping often is confused with accounting. A solid understanding of bookkeeping is essential for any practicing accountant, but knowing the rules and procedures of bookkeeping is by no means sufficient to guarantee success in the accounting profession!

As an undergraduate accounting student at Southeast Missouri State University, I had a friend named Gary. Gary, like me, started his higher education as an accounting major. But, after only one semester (and before taking his first accounting course), Gary changed his major to computer science. When I asked him why, his reply was simple: by the time we graduate, all accountants are going to be replaced by computers. That was in 1977 and the accounting profession is still alive and well. Gary was clearly confusing accounting with bookkeeping. Most bookkeeping today is handled via information technology; accountants can then take the summarized information and complete the remaining tasks in the AAA definition: communicating, facilitating informed judgments, and making decisions.

Reflection and Self-Assessment 2.1

Write your own definition of accounting based on your prior study of the field. What attracted you to the accounting profession? How have your impressions of accounting changed since you were first exposed to it?

Next, we'll look at the steps in the accounting cycle—the process of identifying and measuring economic events that leads to communication and decision making.

ACCOUNTING CYCLE

The **accounting cycle** comprises 10 steps (Spiceland, Sepe, and Tomassini, 2001, p. 60):

1. Obtain information about external transactions from source documents.
2. Analyze transactions.
3. Record the transactions in a journal.
4. Post from the journal to the general ledger accounts.
5. Prepare an unadjusted trial balance.
6. Record adjusting entries and post to the general ledger accounts.
7. Prepare an adjusted trial balance.
8. Prepare financial statements.
9. Close the temporary accounts to retained earnings (at year-end only).
10. Prepare a post-closing trial balance (at year-end only).

Some descriptions of the accounting cycle include an 11th step: prepare reversing entries. But, since the cycle isn't our primary focus here, we'll omit it. You'll learn about reversing entries in intermediate accounting.

Transactions come in two basic types in most accounting information systems: external and internal. **External transactions,** appropriately enough, are those that involve exchanges of goods and services with other individuals and business entities—suppliers, shareholders, government agencies, employees, and the like. **Internal transactions** include adjusting entries, closing entries, and reversing entries. Accountants become aware of external transactions, in most cases, through the use of **source documents.** Source documents can be paper or electronic; their use helps retain some level of objectivity in the accounting information system. They can include purchase orders, remittance advices, and invoices, for example. Common internal controls associated with source documents include

- *Sequential numbering.* For example, the checks in your checkbook are numbered sequentially. Thus, you would know if a check had been used out of sequence, which may indicate an internal control breach.
- *Physical security.* Keeping important source documents physically secure is also important. For example, a company should not keep its blank checks in an easily accessible location; rather, they should be secured (such as in a locked filing cabinet) to prevent unauthorized use.
- *Transaction limits.* A new purchasing agent, for example, might not be authorized to issue purchase orders over a certain amount. Requiring a second signature or supervisory approval can cut down on errors and potential misuse of assets.

Reflection and Self-Assessment 2.2

Identify two additional examples of source documents commonly used in organizations. What essential information would each document need to capture for input into the accounting information system?

Source documents themselves would be a cumbersome way to capture transaction information, so accountants distill the essential information from them and use the principles of transaction analysis to enter them into the accounting information system. Transaction analysis involves five steps:

- Identify the accounts affected by the transaction.
- Identify the effect of the transaction on each account (i.e., increase or decrease).
- Determine the element of financial statements represented by each account. The FASB conceptual framework identifies eight elements of financial statements. We'll confine our discussion here to the five most common: assets, liabilities, equity, revenues, and expenses. The five elements are related through the expanded accounting equation:

$$\text{Assets} = \text{Liabilites} + \text{Equity} + \text{Revenue} - \text{Expense}$$

- Based on the **principles of debit and credit,** determine which kind of entry is required for each account. *Debit* is accounting shorthand for the left side of an account; *credit* is accounting shorthand for the right side. Because the terms *debit* and *credit* have other meanings in general usage, many students have difficulty remembering the principles of debit and credit in an accounting context. But the rules are actually quite straightforward if you relate them back to the equation. On the left side of the equation, the "plus" is on the left, so assets increase with debits and decrease with credits. On the right side of the equation, the "plus" is on the right. Liabilities, equity, and revenue, then, increase with credits and decrease with debits. Because expenses have a minus sign in front of them, the rules are reversed again: expenses increase with debits and decrease with credits.
- Verify that, for each transaction, the total debits equal the total credits. The equality of debits and credits is at the heart of a double-entry accounting system. Without it, we revert to a single-entry system similar to your checkbook. Single-entry systems have no internal checks and balances; they also fail to provide all the meaningful information of double-entry systems. Ensuring that debits and credits are equal is a form of internal control; even if a bookkeeper makes errors in account names and/or amounts, the errors can be corrected if the entries balance.

Reflection and Self-Assessment 2.3

Besides *debit* and *credit,* what other terminology do you know that refers to "left" and "right"? Based on your prior study of accounting, identify two specific examples of each element of financial statements discussed above.

FIGURE 2.1 **General Journal Illustration**

GENERAL JOURNAL — PAGE

	DATE	ACCOUNT TITLE	DOC. NO.	POST. REF.	DEBIT	CREDIT	
1							1
2							2
3							3
4							4
5							5
6							6
7							7
8							8
9							9

You may have heard of "special journals" in your previous study of accounting. Sales journals, for example, have a special structure that facilitates the recording of sales on account only. Very few organizations still use special journals, however, so they are not a major topic of discussion here.

After they've been analyzed, transactions are recorded in a journal. The journal may be paper-based or computerized; it is often referred to as the "book of original entry," since it is the first place a transaction is formally recorded in the accounting information system. The most common form of journal is the general journal, illustrated in Figure 2.1.

In a general journal, debits are recorded first. Credits are indented slightly, as shown below:

9/27/04	Equipment	$80,000	
	Cash		$ 8,000
	Notes payable		72,000

In the preceding transaction, the company purchased equipment with a 10 percent down payment and notes payable for the rest. If a transaction is particularly complex, accountants often will write a short description of it in the journal for clarification.

Reflection and Self-Assessment 2.4

Think of two events that would be important to a business organization that would *not* be recorded in the accounting information system. Explain why they would not be recorded; refer to the FASB conceptual framework as needed to justify your responses.

Then, record each of the following transactions in general journal format:

1. DMN Corporation issued 10,000 shares of $1 par capital stock for $15 per share.
2. Purchased inventory on account, $30,000.
3. Sold inventory with a cost of $6,000 on account for $9,000.
4. Paid current period's salaries, $12,000.
5. Paid creditors on account, $4,000.
6. Received cash from clients on account, $6,000.

In most computerized AIS, a transaction that has been posted to the general ledger cannot be changed or deleted. To promote good internal control, posted transactions can only be corrected with an additional journal entry.

The journal, then, is a chronological listing of all the organization's recordable transactions. But, to produce financial statements and other reports, data in the AIS need to be organized according to the account(s) they affect. The process of posting from the journal to the ledger reorganizes the transactions in that way. Posting by hand takes a lot of time and opens up the AIS to all sorts of errors: transposing numbers, recording in the wrong account, recording on the wrong side, and/or omitting part of a transaction are only a few. In most modern accounting information systems, posting is handled via information technology. While IT doesn't eliminate the possibility of incorrect transaction recording, it does cut down on the time and types of errors noted above.

Preparing a trial balance is the next step in the accounting cycle. A trial balance is a listing of all the accounts in an organization's general ledger, with their balances, that demonstrates the equality of debits and credits in the ledger. Note that the trial balance does not warrant that the AIS is error-free. If, for example, a transaction is posted to the wrong account, but on the correct side, the trial balance will still be in balance. Table 2.1 shows a trial balance.

Once again, information technology is used in most accounting information systems to prepare a trial balance. And a trial balance can serve as an additional form of internal control, ensuring that the ledger accounts balance before preparing the financial statements.

Reflection and Self-Assessment 2.5

Use the trial balance in Table 2.1 and the journal entries you prepared in Reflection and Self-Assessment 2.4 to prepare a new trial balance for DMN Corporation.

TABLE 2.1
Trial Balance

DMN CORPORATION
Trial Balance
September 30, 2004

	Debit	Credit
Cash	$15,800	
Accounts receivable	5,200	
Inventory	4,800	
Equipment	5,000	
Accumulated depreciation		$ 1,400
Accounts payable		2,000
Notes payable		800
Bonds payable		6,000
Capital stock		12,000
Additional paid-in capital		7,400
Retained earnings		2,500
Sales		13,800
Cost of goods sold	6,300	
Advertising expense	5,000	
Depreciation expense	2,800	
Supplies expense	1,000	
Totals	$45,900	$45,900

TABLE 2.2 Adjusting Entries

Type	Description	Example	General Format of Adjustment
Accrued revenues	An organization provides service to its customers before collecting cash	Unbilled client fees	Debit an asset Credit a revenue
Accrued expenses	An organization receives service before paying cash	Unpaid employee wages	Debit an expense Credit a liability
Deferred revenues	An organization receives cash before providing services to clients	Insurance premiums	Debit a liability Credit a revenue
Prepaid expenses	An organization uses up assets that have previously been paid for	Supplies	Debit an expense Credit an asset
Uncollectible accounts	Estimates of amounts clients will be unable or unwilling to pay	Bad debts	Debit an expense Credit a contra-asset
Depreciation	Periodic allocation of an asset's cost to the periods that benefit from its use	Equipment	Debit an expense Credit a contra-asset

The basic idea behind the matching concept is simple: it costs money to make money. But, although simple, the matching concept is profoundly important in accounting. It gives us the theoretical basis for things like depreciation and pension accounting.

The sixth step in the accounting cycle requires accountants to record adjusting entries and post them to the general ledger accounts. In this context, adjusting entries refer to internal journal entries made to account for timing differences in the flow of cash and the recognition of accrual-basis revenues and expenses. Adjusting entries are required by the matching concept in the FASB conceptual framework. Six types of **adjusting entries** are common in most accounting information systems as shown in Table 2.2.

Notice that each adjusting entry requires one account for the income statement and one account for the balance sheet. "Cash" is not involved in any of the preceding types of adjustments. The specific account titles will change depending upon the exact item being adjusted.

Reflection and Self-Assessment 2.6

Describe a specific transaction for each adjustment type noted above. For example, an accrued revenue description might say: "DMN Corporation had unbilled client fees of $2,000." Then, explain how the adjustment would be recorded in the accounting information system. For example, debit Accounts Receivable and credit Sales.

After adjusting entries are journalized and posted, it's a good idea to prepare an adjusted trial balance. The purpose and nature of an adjusted trial balance are the same as for an ordinary trial balance; the only difference is the timing of its preparation. An adjusted trial balance reflects the status of the ledger accounts after the adjusting entries have been posted.

The accounting cycle continues with the preparation of the **general-purpose financial statements.** They are four in number and include

- The *income statement,* which summarizes the results of business operations on the accrual basis for a specified period of time. The income statement reports revenues, expenses, gains, and losses from the accounting information system.
- The *statement of changes in shareholders' equity* reports changes in capital stock and retained earnings accounts for the same period of time as the income statement. Net income increases retained earnings; net losses and declaration of dividends decrease retained earnings. Capital stock can increase or decrease for a variety of reasons, the most common of which is issuance of new shares.
- The *balance sheet* shows the financial position of an organization at a specific point in time. It contains assets (listed in order of their liquidity), liabilities (listed with the most current due dates first), and equity (which comes from the statement of changes in shareholders' equity). Naturally, the assets must equal the liabilities plus equity on the balance sheet.
- The *statement of cash flows* is the relative newcomer to the general-purpose financial statements. Developed in the late 1980s by the Financial Accounting Standards Board, the statement of cash flows reports inflows and outflows of cash for a specified period of time. Cash flows on the statement fall into three categories: operating, investing, and financing. Accountants can choose between the direct and indirect methods of calculating operating cash flows.

You can access the financial statements of publicly traded companies online via EDGAR. EDGAR is administered by the Securities and Exchange Commission; its URL is www.sec.gov/edgar.shtml.

You'll probably have an entire course in auditing as part of your accounting program; we'll also discuss auditing in the last chapter of this text. Audits are important forms of internal control. Internal audits can help promote organizational efficiency and encourage compliance with management directives; external audits ensure that financial statements are prepared in accordance with generally accepted accounting principles.

Reflection and Self-Assessment 2.7

Use EDGAR or some other source to access the financial statements of Martha Stewart Living Omnimedia Inc. What is your assessment of the corporation's financial position and performance based on the statements?

After preparing financial statements, the accounting information system must be readied for the next fiscal period's entries. That objective is accomplished via closing entries. Balances from temporary (nominal) accounts on the income statement are transferred into retained earnings (a real, permanent account in the equity section of the balance sheet). Finally, then, the accounting information system produces a post-closing trial balance. Similar in form to the other trial balances discussed above, the post-closing trial balance differs in content. Since all the nominal accounts have been closed, the post-closing trial balance contains only balance sheet accounts. See the illustration in Table 2.3 for an example.

Most accounting information systems fall into one of two types: view-driven systems or event-driven systems. View-driven systems are the more traditional; they are focused on providing a particular "view" of the data and information—the view provided by the

TABLE 2.3
Post-closing Trial Balance

DMN CORPORATION Post-closing Trial Balance September 30, 2004		
	Debit	**Credit**
Cash	$15,800	
Accounts receivable	5,200	
Inventory	4,800	
Equipment	5,000	
Accumulated depreciation		$ 1,400
Accounts payable		2,000
Notes payable		800
Bonds payable		6,000
Capital stock		12,000
Additional paid-in capital		7,400
Retained earnings		1,200
Totals	$30,800	$30,800

general purpose financial statements. The steps in the accounting cycle are primarily focused on collecting data and reporting information in view-driven systems.

We'll talk about event-driven systems later in the text. Event-driven systems are a fairly recent development in the business world; they focus on capturing more comprehensive information about business events. A view-driven system would be concerned about which accounts and amounts to debit and credit; an event-driven system would capture those data and other details, such as sizes and colors of merchandise ordered. Event-driven systems use relational database technology to provide various ways of viewing the data—it's possible to get the general purpose financial statements from an event-driven system, but it's also possible to get a much greater variety of reports as well.

You may be able to imagine how much time accountants spent simply completing the steps in the cycle before the advent of information technology. Later in the chapter, we'll take a look at how IT has facilitated the accounting cycle, as well as ways in which human judgment is still paramount in its 10 steps.

CODING SYSTEMS

In both manual and automated accounting information systems, each account typically has both a name and a number; account numbers facilitate transaction recording and posting, particularly when the AIS relies heavily on automation. In most cases, you'll walk into an organization with an established chart of accounts; however, at some point in your career, you may need to create a chart from scratch. At a minimum, you'll need to be able to understand your company's and/or clients' charts of accounts. In this section, we'll look at some of the systems used in practice to establish and modify charts of accounts.

Williamson (2006) lists five important reasons for maintaining a clear, logical chart of accounts:

- efficiency of data capture, entry and analysis . . .
- frequency of use and familiarity . . .
- consistency and understanding of use within the organization . . .

- saving on computer processing time and storage . . .
- similar items can be related by means of a coding system, whereas a verbal description could be very inefficient . . .

In addition, Williamson identified several common coding systems often used in organizations; while they are not exhaustive, they do provide a comprehensive overview. So, let's look at four of them briefly.

- *Sequential coding,* as the name implies, simply numbers items in sequence. Think of the checks in your checkbook when you think of sequential coding. In automated accounting information systems, transactions might be assigned sequential numbers by a computer as a method of internal control.
- *Block coding* is quite common in a chart of accounts. Numbers are assigned in blocks; each block is reserved for a particular kind of account. For example, all current asset accounts might start with "1," while equity accounts might start with "5." Thus, you can tell what kind of account you're dealing with simply by looking at its first digit.
- *Hierarchical codes* are a more sophisticated form of block coding. In hierarchical coding, each digit/block of digits conveys important information to people who know the code. The Harvard Law School uses hierarchical coding in its chart of accounts (www.law.harvard.edu/administration/financial/coa). Its codes are organized in seven parts, with each part communicating specific information. Many enterprise resource planning systems, such as PeopleSoft, use hierarchical coding.
- *Mnemonic codes,* by their nature, help people remember the meaning of the code. At my university, as at most universities, course prefixes are mnemonic. ACC is the code for courses in the accounting department, while CIS stands for computer information systems. In an accounting information system, product and customer codes might be mnemonic in nature.

See Table 2.4 for examples of account coding.

While many organizations develop their own unique chart of accounts, some use a standardized chart of accounts. Thorp (1991) talked about the "European Uniform Chart of Accounts" as a way of facilitating information exchange between and within organizations. For example, a company with five geographic locations might use a uniform chart of accounts to make preparing financial statements easier.

TABLE 2.4 Chart of Accounts Coding

Coding System	Example	Format
Sequential	Purchase order numbers	101, 102, 103
Block	Uniform system of accounts for restaurants	Current assets: 101, 105, 109 Plant assets: 202, 206, 208 Current liabilities: 301, 303, 305
Hierarchical	State university	101-11-08-81 101: Big City campus 11: academic affairs division 08: college of business 81: accounting department
Mnemonic	Inventory items	DVR: digital video recorder FSTV: flat-screen television

HUMAN JUDGMENT AND INFORMATION TECHNOLOGY

Susan Wolcott, of Wolcott Lynch Associates, has developed a methodology for enhancing critical thinking and judgment skills. Called the "Steps for Better Thinking," you can find more information about it at www.wolcottlynch.com. We'll be exploring SBT in more depth in the chapter on decision-making models and knowledge management.

Accounting has been a "system" since the 14th century; using information technology tools to assist in the collection, processing, and dissemination of accounting information is a relatively recent phenomenon in the profession. And, while IT has had a profound impact, it has only increased the need for and opportunity to exercise human judgment.

Human judgment comes into play in the AIS in at least the following ways:

- *Designing source documents.* We'll consider issues of forms design in greater detail in future chapters. But, for now, be aware that source documents should be clear and easy to read, omit unnecessary information, and provide plenty of space for filling in required data. Sequential numbering, such as in your checkbook, is also important for strong internal control.
- *Recognizing recordable transactions.* Not every document in an AIS indicates a recordable transaction; further, not every recordable transaction is represented by a source document. Therefore, accountants must exercise professional judgment in recognizing recordable transactions.
- *Estimating amounts and interpreting accounting rules.* Many journal entries, particularly adjusting entries, require the use of estimates. For example, accountants must estimate the useful economic life and salvage value of fixed assets to calculate depreciation. Further, FASB pronouncements and other authoritative accounting documents require significant interpretation. As principles-based accounting standards, such as International Financial Reporting Standards (IFRS), become the norm, interpretation will become even more important.

Principles-based accounting is an alternative to the current rules-based approach. For more information, do a library search on principles-based accounting. You also may consult Howard Stock, "SEC Urges Principles-Based Accounting," *Investor Relations Business,* August 4, 2003, p. 1.

At the same time, **information technology** has cut down on the tedium associated with many steps in the accounting cycle. Transactions can be posted automatically or with the touch of a button; the same applies to closing the accounts at the end of the period. Reports, including the general-purpose financial statements, can easily be generated with the "touch of a button" as well. We'll explore information technology issues in greater depth in Part Three of the book.

CRITICAL THINKING

I'd like to explore two topics with you in this chapter's critical thinking section: recognizing transactions that should be recorded in the AIS and creating a coding system for a chart of accounts.

As you read earlier in the chapter, human judgment is important in several areas of the accounting cycle—one of which is recognizing transactions that should (and should not) be recorded. Consider the three items that follow, along with their explanations:

1. *FNF Corporation sold merchandise with a cost of $800 to customers on account for $1,000.* This transaction should be recorded in the AIS; goods were exchanged between two willing parties, and the evidence of it is clear and objective. Assuming the use of a perpetual inventory system, this transaction would be recorded as follows: debit Accounts Receivable, $1,000; debit Cost of Goods Sold, $800, credit Sales, $1,000; credit Inventory, $800.
2. *During 20x3, FNF Corporation purchased temporary Investments with a cost of $10,000. The market value of those investments at the end of 20x3 was $12,000; FNF classified them as trading securities.* Of course, the initial purchase of the investments should be recorded in the AIS. But the increase in market value also should be recorded.

According to FASB No. 115, trading securities should be reported at their fair value. At first, this idea may seem to violate the objectivity principle of the FASB conceptual framework. The key here, though, is that the market value of the investments is readily determinable by looking at the financial press. An accountant couldn't simply decide to increase the market value based on his/her own judgment; but, if the market value of the investments can be looked up, then the investments must be increased. The $2,000 difference would be referred to as an *unrealized gain,* which means that it hasn't been "economically experienced" by FNF. To experience (realize) the gain, FNF would have to sell the investments.

3. *FNF purchased the land for its headquarters 10 years ago at a cost of $65,000. In 20x3, a real estate investor offered to purchase the land for $165,000.* In this case, the $100,000 would not be recorded in the AIS unless FNF actually sold the land. The fact that they've had an offer to buy it isn't objective enough; in addition, the land is not held as an investment—it's used for their headquarters. So, unlike item 2, the increase in market value would not result in an "unrealized gain" for FNF.

So, as you can tell, recognizing which transactions to record in an AIS requires critical thinking and a solid understanding of accounting principles.

When it comes to designing a chart of accounts, critical thinking is important. Whatever coding system an organization uses (sequential, block, hierarchical, mnemonic), it must be easily understood and rational. Consider the example below, which used a random number generator to assign account numbers in an AIS:

Poorly Designed Chart of Accounts

252	Cash
256	Accounts receivable
311	Accounts payable
698	Wages payable
461	Capital stock
507	Retained earnings
824	Sales
617	Interest earned
633	Cost of goods sold
924	Depreciation expense

There's no "rhyme or reason" to that chart of accounts; you would practically have to memorize each number and account name individually. On the other hand, the chart of accounts could be made much more understandable with a block-coding system:

Block Coded Chart of Accounts

101	Cash
103	Accounts receivable
301	Accounts payable
305	Wages payable
402	Capital stock
406	Retained earnings
501	Sales
701	Interest earned
633	Cost of goods sold
635	Depreciation expense

In the block-coded chart, current assets begin with "1," while current liabilities begin with "3." Equity accounts start with "4." Operating revenue (such as sales) is differentiated from nonoperating revenue (such as interest earned) easily with block coding.

Consider these additional account titles and suggested numbers that would conform to the block-coding system:

105	Inventory
201	Land
203	Equipment
213	Accumulated depreciation—equipment
405	Treasury stock
801	Interest expense

Inventory, as a current asset, has a number starting with "1." Since current assets start with "1" and current liabilities with "3," what kinds of accounts should start with "2"? Long-term assets, such as land and equipment. Notice the numbering similarity between equipment (203) and its related accumulated depreciation account (213). As an equity account, treasury stock has a number that starts with "4." Interest expense starts with an "8" because it would normally be considered a nonoperating expense.

Is block coding the only way to organize a chart of accounts? Definitely not. Is it the best way? In some cases, sure—but not every time. And you could come up with completely different numbers even using a block-coding system. The important idea is being able to explain the coding system to others so that they can use it effectively.

Summary

This chapter, then, has presented a review of the steps in the accounting cycle. Here is the usual summary based on the chapter's learning objectives:

1. *Differentiate accounting and bookkeeping.* Bookkeeping is the part of accounting concerned with recording transactions in the AIS. Accounting goes far beyond that, concerning itself with identifying those transactions and communicating information for decision making.
2. *List, discuss, and complete, in order, the steps in the accounting cycle.* The chapter examined 10 steps in the accounting cycle:
   a. Obtain information about external transactions from source documents.
   b. Analyze transactions.
   c. Record the transactions in a journal.
   d. Post from the journal to the general ledger accounts.
   e. Prepare an unadjusted trial balance.
   f. Record adjusting entries and post to the general ledger accounts.
   g. Prepare an adjusted trial balance.
   h. Prepare financial statements.
   i. Close the temporary accounts to retained earnings (at year-end only).
   j. Prepare a post-closing trial balance (at year-end only).
3. *Identify common internal controls associated with the accounting cycle.* Internal controls include sequentially numbered documents, physical security, transaction limits, equality of debits and credits, trial balances, and audits.

4. *Describe common chart of accounts coding systems.* The chapter discusses four common systems: sequential, block, hierarchical, and mnemonic.
5. *Explain how human judgment and information technology impact the accounting cycle.* Accountants exercise their judgment in deciding which transactions are recordable in the accounting information system. Information technology can be used for a variety of tasks in the cycle: recording transactions, posting them to the ledger, preparing trial balances and financial statements, and closing the accounts.

Accounting education has typically emphasized transaction processing throughout the undergraduate curriculum; understanding this topic is important in your education as an accountant. We'll use it as a foundational topic, exploring more advanced issues throughout the rest of the text.

Key Terms

accounting, *22*
accounting cycle, *23*
adjusting entries, *27*
bookkeeping, *22*
external transactions, *23*
general-purpose financial statements, *28*
human judgment, *31*
information technology, *31*
internal transactions, *23*
principles of debit and credit, *24*
source documents, *23*

Chapter References

Spiceland, J. D., J. F. Sepe, and L. A. Tomassini. 2001. *Intermediate Accounting.* Updated 2nd ed. New York: Irwin/McGraw-Hill.

Thorp, J. A. 1991. "European Uniform Chart of Accounts." *Management Accounting,* July/August, pp. 20–23.

Williamson, D. 2006. "Coding Systems for Accountants: An Introduction." www.duncanwil.co.uk (June 20, 2006).

End-of-Chapter Activities

1. *Reading review questions.*
   a. In your own words, explain the similarities and differences between accounting and bookkeeping.
   b. What systems do accountants use to create and modify a chart of accounts?
   c. What internal controls are common in the accounting cycle?
   d. How is human judgment involved in the accounting cycle?
   e. How has information technology been employed in the accounting cycle?
   f. List and discuss the six common types of adjusting entries found in most accounting information systems.
   g. Explain the purpose and structure of each general-purpose financial statement.
   h. Respond to the questions for the chapter's "AIS in the Business World."
2. *Reading review problem.* In discussing transaction processing at VISA, Steve Marlin ("VISA Tests Transaction Processing System," *Information Week,* no. 999 (July 26, 2004), p. 34) wrote:

   In today's information-based, on-demand economy, credit card companies are being called upon to handle ever greater transaction volumes. In July 2004, VISA USA conducted a system stress test as part of its capacity planning process. The company's transaction processing system managed 6,200 transaction messages per second, representing about 3,100 card purchases. Debit card transactions used more processing capacity than credit card transactions; debit transactions require tracking the movement of funds in real time, whereas credit transactions require a simple yes-or-no decision.

A "debit card transaction" refers to purchasing goods or services with an ATM card. Many such cards also can be used for "credit card" transactions.

a. Does the activity described above more closely resemble accounting or bookkeeping? Explain your answer.
b. Use EDGAR to find the Form 10-K that VISA Inc. filed with the SEC on November 21, 2008. What AIS outputs are included in that filing?
c. Develop a coding system for the operating revenue and operating expense accounts listed in VISA Inc.'s income statement.
d. Explain why the line items in VISA's statement of cash flows (such as Net income and Cash acquired through reorganization) would not require account numbers.

3. *Making choices and exercising judgment.*

a. Which of the following would be recordable transactions in an accounting information system? For each item that would not be a recordable transaction, explain why not.
   i. Purchasing land with a down payment and a note payable.
   ii. Verifying an increase in the market value of land.
   iii. Establishing an exclusive relationship with a raw material supplier.
   iv. Estimating the amount of warranty expense for the next accounting period.
   v. Negotiating with an employees union for wage increases.
b. How will principles-based accounting influence the design of accounting information systems? The steps in the accounting cycle?
c. Use EDGAR to obtain the 2008 financial statements for Home Depot Inc. and Lowes Companies Inc., two large firms in the home improvement industry. Compare their financial statements and comment on which company is stronger.

4. *Field exercises.*

a. Point your Web browser to **www.download.com**. Investigate One-Step Accounting Standard Edition and Free Accounting—two general ledger packages that can help companies with the steps in the accounting cycle. Identify and describe at least two modules in each system; explain the types of accounting transactions the modules are designed to record.
b. Point your Web browser to **www.law.harvard.edu/administration/financial/coa**. Describe Harvard Law School's chart of accounts coding system.
c. Contact an accounting professional at a local organization such as your university, a bank, or a retail store. Find out how he/she employs human judgment and information technology in completing the steps of the accounting cycle.

5. *Journal entries.* Record each of the following transactions in general journal format.

a. Issued 50,000 shares of $1 par capital stock for $35 each.
b. Billed customers for services provided, $10,000.
c. Purchased supplies on account, $3,000.
d. Paid monthly utility bill, $1,500.
e. Verified 20 percent increase in market price of stock.
f. Paid wages for the current month, $6,000.
g. Purchased equipment with a list price of $50,000 by making a 20 percent down payment and financing the remainder with a six-month, 12 percent note payable.
h. Collected cash from customers, $5,000.
i. Paid vendors, $1,400.
j. Recorded one month's accrued interest on note payable.

6. *Adjusting entries.* The unadjusted trial balance for GLP Corporation appears below:

GLP CORPORATION
Trial Balance
September 30, 20x4

	Debit	Credit
Cash	$ 6,000	
Accounts receivable	2,500	
Allowance for bad debts		$ 200
Inventory	4,500	
Supplies	800	
Equipment	15,000	
Accumulated depreciation—equipment		10,000
Accounts payable		1,200
Notes payable		6,000
Deferred fees		900
Capital stock		7,000
Additional paid-in capital		8,000
Retained earnings		11,000
Sales		16,000
Cost of goods sold	13,500	
Advertising expense	5,000	
Wages expense	12,000	
Miscellaneous expense	1,000	
Totals	$60,300	$60,300

End-of-period analysis revealed the following:

a. The market value of equipment had decreased by 30 percent of its original cost. Depreciation for the quarter totaled $1,000.

b. The note payable was signed on August 1, 20x4. Its interest rate was 10 percent, and no interest had been recorded since the signing.

c. Unpaid employee wages at September 30 totaled $1,000.

d. Deferred fees represented a consulting contract signed at the beginning of September. The contract's duration is three months, and the work is spread evenly throughout the contract period.

e. Supplies on hand totaled $150.

f. The market value of capital stock had increased by 15 percent.

g. Actual bad debt write-offs during September were $300; 1 percent of sales will likely become uncollectible in the coming period.

Prepare the required adjusting entries based on the preceding information. Then, prepare an adjusted trial balance.

7. *Financial statements.* Use the adjusted trial balance from Problem 6 to prepare an income statement for the quarter ended September 30, 20x4, and a balance sheet as of September 30, 20x4, for GLP Corporation.

8. *Coding systems.* Which type of coding system is indicated in each of the following independent situations? Be prepared to explain your reasoning.

a. Airport codes (LAX, OGG)

b. Automatically assigned transaction numbers in a cash register

c. Consecutively numbered purchase orders (101, 102, 103, and so on)
d. Dewey Decimal System (used to classify library books)
e. Invoice numbers
f. National Association of Home Builders chart of accounts (look this one up on the Internet)
g. Standard chart of accounts included with QuickBooks
h. Telephone numbers
i. Universal Product Codes (UPCs)
j. ZIP codes (91768, 63135)

9. *Crossword puzzle*

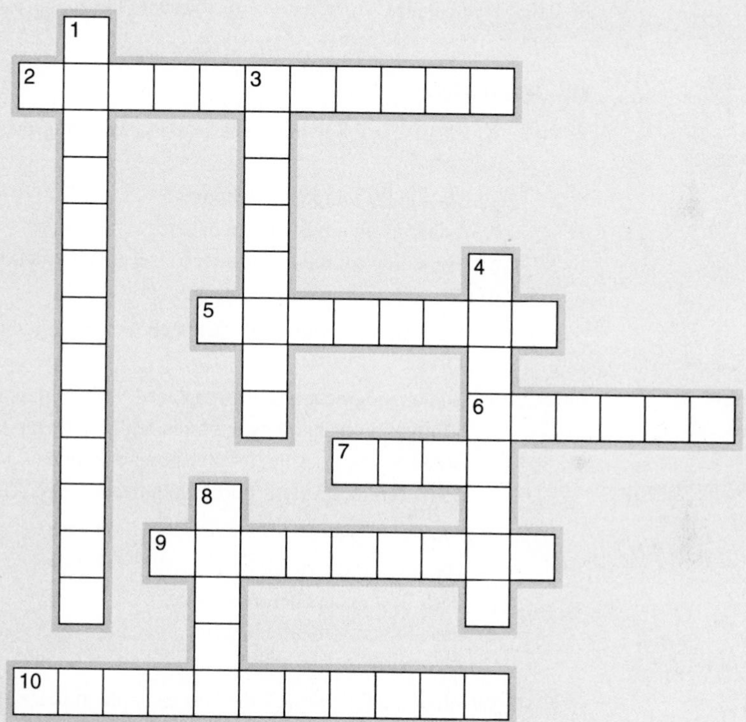

Across

2. Often confused with accounting.
5. Transaction type that describes adjusting entries.
6. Increases to equity accounts.
7. Specific account that is never involved in an adjusting entry.
9. One of the three elements of AAA's definition of accounting.
10. One of the three main elements of AAA's definition of accounting.

Down

1. One of the three elements of AAA's definition of accounting.
3. Transaction type that involves exchanges with suppliers.
4. Conceptual basis for depreciation.
8. Increases to an asset.

10. *Terminology.* Please match each item on the right with the most appropriate item on the left.

1. Accrued revenue	a. Book of original entry
2. Credit	b. Cash is received before service is provided
3. Debit	c. Decreases to revenue
4. Deferred revenue	d. Increases to liabilities
5. Human judgment	e. Purchase orders, invoices, and receipts
6. Information technology	f. Service is provided before cash is received
7. Journal	g. Simplifies the bookkeeping process
8. Posting	h. Transferring information from the journal to the ledger
9. Source document	i. Used to recognize recordable transactions
10. Trial balance	j. Verifies the equality of debits and credits in the ledger

11. *Multiple choice questions.*

1. Which of the following steps in the accounting cycle is most likely to involve human judgment?
   a. Closing the temporary accounts.
   b. Preparing an adjusted trial balance.
   c. Evaluating source documents for recordable transactions.
   d. Preparing financial statements.
2. Which of the following statements about human judgment and information technology is most true?
   a. Human judgment has been replaced by information technology.
   b. Information technology has been replaced by human judgment.
   c. Bookkeeping does not involve human judgment.
   d. Bookkeeping involves information technology.
3. In general, an "accrual" refers to a situation where
   a. The matching concept is violated.
   b. Cash flow occurs before service.
   c. Cash flow occurs after service.
   d. A corporation has unbilled client fees.
4. Which of the following is the best example of deferred revenue?
   a. A newspaper company collects subscription fees before delivering papers.
   b. A student pays her college tuition after the term has begun.
   c. A company signs a note payable due in six months.
   d. A corporation purchases supplies on account.
5. A trial balance:
   a. Demonstrates the lack of fraud in the AIS if its debits equal its credits.
   b. Can be prepared only at the end of the accounting period.
   c. Is another name for the balance sheet.
   d. Proves the equality of debits and credits in the ledger, but does not guarantee an error-free AIS.
6. Which of the following is not a type of coding common in organizations?
   a. Random
   b. Sequential
   c. Hierarchical
   d. Block

7. Internal control can be strengthened in the accounting cycle by
   a. Eliminating human judgment.
   b. Making information easily accessible.
   c. Enforcing transaction limits.
   d. All of the above.
8. A journal entry increases an asset. Which of the following could also be part of the entry?
   a. Decrease in revenue
   b. Increase in expense
   c. Increase in liability
   d. Any of the above
9. A project manager codes a transaction as 12-06-48, where 12 stands for a particular project, 06 denotes the department where the transaction occurred, and 48 indicates the transaction number. Considered as a whole, this coding system is best described as
   a. Block.
   b. Hierarchical.
   c. Mnemonic.
   d. Sequential.
10. Which of the following steps in the accounting cycle is least likely to involve human judgment?
    I. Posting
    II. Coding transactions according to the chart of accounts
    III. Approving transactions before they are recorded
    a. I only
    b. I and II
    c. I and III
    d. I, II, and III

12. *Statement evaluation.* Determine whether each of the following statements is (i) always true, (ii) sometimes true, or (iii) never true. For those that are (ii) sometimes true, explain when the statement is true.

a. Bookkeeping and accounting are two ways of referring to the same thing.
b. If a transaction increases a liability, it will also increase an expense.
c. The accounting cycle involves human judgment.
d. A company's chart of accounts should use block coding.
e. Information technology has eliminated the need for human judgment in the accounting cycle.
f. An "accrual" refers to a situation where a company provides service before receiving cash.
g. An adjusting entry for depreciation recognizes an asset's loss in market value over time.
h. Adjusting entries involve one balance sheet account and one income statement account, but never cash.
i. In automated accounting information systems, block coding facilitates closing entries.
j. The complete accounting cycle incorporates three different forms of a trial balance.

13. *International Financial Reporting Standards (IFRS).* Do an Internet search for information on IFRS. Visit at least two Web sites, including the International Accounting Standards Board, and respond to the following questions about IFRS:

a. Compare and contrast the IFRS framework with the FASB conceptual framework discussed in Chapter 1. List three similarities and three differences between the two.
b. Choose two countries that have adopted IFRS. If an organization had operations in both countries, how would you communicate that fact in their chart of accounts?

Chapter Three

Professionalism and Ethics

AIS in the Business World

Top Flight Travel's Tax Return

John, Ruben, and Mark were partners in Top Flight Travel, a travel agency that focused mainly on the corporate and executive travel markets. John and Ruben were general partners, while Mark was a limited partner. As you may be aware from studying business law, a limited partner's liability is limited to the amount of his/her investment; for general partners, that limitation doesn't apply. As a result, if a partnership is sued, general partners could lose their personal assets in addition to the assets of the partnership itself.

Mark left the day-to-day management of Top Flight to John and Ruben, who had hired Lee to prepare the partnership tax return for 2007. Lee prepared the 2007 return according to IRS rules for partnerships and, early in 2008, sent it to John and Ruben for the partners' signatures prior to filing it with the IRS. The return showed a net loss of around $12,000. A few days later, Lee's phone rang; it was Mark. Their conversation went something like this:

Mark: This tax return you prepared is unacceptable, Lee.

Lee: Really? I hadn't realized you knew much about preparing taxes. What's the problem with the return?

Mark: I invested $50,000 in Top Flight last year, so I want a $50,000 tax write-off.

Lee: Unfortunately, Mark, that's not how things work. Part of your $50,000 investment remains in the company—your tax write-off is based on the company's net loss, not on the amount you invested.

Mark: How did you calculate the net loss?

Lee: The net loss is the difference between the agency's revenues and its expenses. If you check the supporting documentation for the tax return, you'll see the income statement.

Mark: I'm looking at it now. Why doesn't it show any wages expense?

Lee: Wages expense applies only to employees. Since Top Flight is operated by John and Ruben, it doesn't have any wages expense. Anything John and Ruben withdraw from the partnership is deducted from their capital accounts, not treated as an expense.

Mark: I see. What if I buy out John's interest in the partnership and make him an employee?

Lee: You can definitely do that. But buying out John's interest now won't affect last year's tax return.

Mark: It will if you say it happened last year. It's only a few weeks; what's the problem with that?

This story is true, but the name of the travel agency and the names of some of the people have been disguised.

Discussion Questions

1. Is Mark acting unethically? Why, or why not?
2. Should Lee comply with Mark's request? Why, or why not?
3. What ethical codes should accountants follow in their professional careers?

Until recently, accounting professionals were considered among the most ethical people in business. Unfortunately, the unethical acts of a few members of our profession have called that perception into question. Without our sense of professionalism and ethics, accountants in all areas of the economy cannot provide effective, reliable, trustworthy services to our constituents.

Professionalism and ethics are not skills that magically descend upon you once you earn your accounting degree. Indeed, developing them is at least as important as learning software applications, FASB pronouncements, and other technical areas of accounting. In this chapter, we'll consider what it means to be a professional, specifically within the context of accounting. We'll also examine frameworks for ethical decision making and the ethical codes of several accounting professional organizations.

When you complete your study of this chapter, you should be able to:

1. List and discuss characteristics of a professional.
2. Explain how those characteristics apply to the accounting profession.
3. Define *ethics.*
4. Discuss various models/schools of ethical decision making.
5. Explain and apply the professional ethics codes of various accounting professional organizations.
6. Explain how to resolve ethical dilemmas.
7. Give examples of recent ethical cases in accounting.

Although this chapter may mark your first exposure to these issues, it almost certainly will not constitute your last.

PROFESSIONALISM

You probably have heard many people talk about the "accounting profession." And you've probably noticed that people consistently refer to some careers as "professional," but not others. Have you considered what constitutes a "profession"? What is it about accounting that qualifies it as a profession, whereas other valuable and important careers are not labeled as such?

Dr. Nancy Bell (2004) suggests seven **characteristics of a professional.** Although her list is given in the context of insurance and risk management, its elements can be applied equally to accounting. In Dr. Bell's view, a professional

- Communicates effectively.
- Thinks rationally, logically, and coherently.
- Appropriately uses technical knowledge.
- Integrates knowledge from many disciplines.
- Exhibits ethical professional behavior.
- Recognizes the influence of political, social, economic, legal, and regulatory forces.
- Actively seeks additional knowledge.

Consider the idea that a professional communicates effectively. Good communication skills are fundamental in accounting. Our profession uses specialized, technical vocabulary that is not shared by the general population. For example, to the average person on the street, *depreciation* refers to an asset's loss in value over time. In accounting, however, *depreciation* is the periodic allocation of an asset's cost to the periods that benefit from its use—accounting depreciation is unrelated to changes in market value. So, as professionals, part of our job is to explain the differences between accounting depreciation and economic depreciation to those who are outside our profession. The same could be said for a variety of other terms: stock, capital, revenue, expense, and others.

As another example, think about the second characteristic in Dr. Bell's list: a professional thinks rationally, logically, and coherently. I often tell my students that the purpose of earning an accounting degree isn't to prepare to take the CPA exam—or any other accounting professional exam. Rather, the purpose of earning an accounting degree is to teach you how to think like an accountant: rationally, logically, and coherently. One of the most important skills you'll bring to your career is that ability. Being able to think that way develops over time and with practice, through a process of questioning and dialogue. I know some of my students are sometimes reticent to share their thoughts and opinions, out of concern that they'll say something "wrong." But I always try to challenge and encourage them so they can develop their thinking skills. I'm sure your AIS and other accounting professors feel the same way.

Reflection and Self-Assessment 3.1

Choose three of the remaining characteristics in Dr. Bell's list. For each one, give a specific example of how an accounting professional might display it.

McDonald (2001) identified four criteria to be considered a professional:

- *Specialized knowledge base.* Accounting certainly has a specialized knowledge base. Whether we're talking about financial reporting rules, standards for conducting audits, tax research and planning skills, or activity-based accounting processes, the knowledge we share is not part of society's general body of knowledge.
- *Complex skills.* Accounting also involves complex skills. It requires the use of judgment, and also relies on fairly complex computations in some areas (such as pension accounting). Although some accounting software is straightforward and easy to use, some of our IT tools are reasonably sophisticated as well.

FIGURE 3.1 Houle's Ideas about Becoming a Professional

Conceptual	**Performance**
✓ Members are concerned with defining the profession's function in society.	✓ Members learn at least the basics of the fields that underlie specialized knowledge. ✓ Members improve their ability to solve problems. ✓ Members know how to use their profession's practical knowledge. ✓ Members engage in ongoing education in related fields.

Collective identity

- ✓ Current members establish formalized processes for teaching prospective members.
- ✓ Current members create knowledge-based credentials and licenses to test basic skills and performance.
- ✓ Professionals create a "subculture" with (among other things) traditions and specialized language.
- ✓ Members of the profession are supported by a legal framework that protects their rights as professionals.
- ✓ Through the efforts of the profession, the public becomes aware of what they do and what they value.
- ✓ Members are guided by a code of professional ethics.
- ✓ The profession establishes sanctions or punishments for members who do not meet its standards.
- ✓ Members of the profession understand how their work is related to that of other professions.
- ✓ The profession clearly establishes criteria for appropriate relationships with clients.

You can find more information about the PCAOB at www.pcaobus.org/.

- *Autonomy of practice.* Autonomy refers to independence or self-sufficiency. As you'll learn in your later study of auditing, "independence of mind" is an important characteristic for accounting professionals. Historically, the accounting profession was almost completely independent and self-regulating. But ethical scandals, such as Enron, led to the creation of the Public Companies Accounting Oversight Board. The PCAOB "is a private-sector, non-profit corporation, created by the Sarbanes-Oxley Act of 2002, to oversee the auditors of public companies in order to protect the interests of investors and further the public interest in the preparation of informative, fair, and independent audit reports." Although the PCAOB has given less autonomy to auditors, the profession as a whole remains relatively self-sufficient.
- *Adherence to a code of ethical behavior.* Accountants also adhere to codes of ethical behavior. Later in this chapter, we'll examine the ethical codes of three important organizations: the American Institute of Certified Public Accountants, the Institute of Management Accountants, and the Association of Certified Fraud Examiners.

Notice how McDonald's four characteristics connect to the list of seven provided by Dr. Bell. For example, both lists include a component regarding ethical behavior.

Houle (1980) focused on the process of "professionalization," rather than characteristics of a professional. For him, the process by which you become a professional is much more important than a list of characteristics; so, whereas McDonald and Bell are talking about what a professional *is,* Houle discusses the *how* of achieving those characteristics. Consider Figure 3.1 for a brief overview of Houle's thinking on becoming a professional.

Overall, then, Houle's concept of "professionalization" represents a "process or strategy by which a profession gains more respect, privilege, and sometimes, prestige" (Huggett, 2000).

One common element in almost all definitions of professionalism is the emphasis on professional ethics. Next, we'll turn our attention to that important topic.

Reflection and Self-Assessment 3.2

You have just read about the ideas of Bell, McDonald, and Houle regarding professions, professionals, and professionalism. How are the ideas of those three authors connected to one another? Develop your own list of the top five characteristics you want to exhibit as a professional accountant based on those ideas and your own original thinking.

ETHICS

In this section, we'll consider five main topics: definitions of ethics, models of ethical decision making, codes of professional ethics in accounting, processes for resolving ethical dilemmas, and ethics cases in accounting. Although our main focus will be on ethical behavior in the accounting profession, I'm sure you've realized that behaving ethically begins long before you enter that portion of your career. As a student, you make choices about your behavior regularly; consider the following questions as examples:

1. Have you ever presented others' ideas as your own?
2. Have you ever collaborated on an assignment when told specifically to complete it individually?
3. Have you inappropriately accessed homework solutions for your accounting or other courses?
4. Have you, implicitly or explicitly, ignored unethical behavior from your fellow students?

Within the context of accounting information systems, ethical issues include

1. Making realistic, unbiased estimates.
2. Using AIS data appropriately.
3. Maintaining strong internal control over cash and other liquid assets.
4. Paying for software and other forms of information technology.

Consider those questions and issues, and others you may think of for yourself, in the broad context of our further discussion of ethics in the following paragraphs.

What is ethics? The Internet Encyclopedia of Philosophy (2004) says:

> The field of ethics, also called moral philosophy, involves systematizing, defending, and recommending concepts of right and wrong behavior. Philosophers today usually divide ethical theories into three general subject areas: metaethics, normative ethics, and applied ethics. *Metaethics* investigates where our ethical principles come from, and what they mean. *Normative ethics* takes on a more practical task, which is to arrive at moral standards that regulate right and wrong conduct. This may involve articulating the good habits that we should acquire, the duties that we should follow, or the consequences of our behavior on others. Finally, *applied ethics* involves examining specific controversial issues.

Ethics information abounds on the Internet. Consult www.ethics.org, www.business-ethics.com/, and www.usoge.gov/ for more information.

Dictionary.com (2004) offers several other **definitions of ethics,** including "rules or standards governing the conduct of a person or the members of a profession."

In accounting, we are perhaps most concerned with **normative ethics.** What are the rules and standards, whether personal or professional, that guide our professional decision making?

Reflection and Self-Assessment 3.3

One rule/standard that guides ethical decision making in accounting is objectivity. As professional accountants, we have the responsibility to present information as fairly and objectively as possible. Suggest two other rules or standards accountants should observe as part of making ethical decisions.

Merchant and Van der Stede (2003) articulated four basic paradigms for ethical decision making. *Utilitarianism* says that "the end justifies the means." In other words, someone following the **utilitarian model of ethics** would say that as long as you have a successful/favorable outcome, any method of achieving it is justified. Consider, for example, the goal of increasing a company's stock price. No one really knows what causes changes in stock prices, but accounting numbers do have a significant impact. So, a utilitarian ethical model would say it's okay to increase a company's stock price, even if you have to engage in profit manipulation via accounting policy changes.

The **rights and duties** school of ethical thinking feels that all individuals have certain rights; others have the duty not to interfere with those rights. You might think of this model as an "every person for himself/herself" way of thinking. If, for example, a manager has the right to earn a bonus every year, others have the duty not to interfere with that process. The manager may act in ethical or unethical ways to earn the bonus, but, according to this school of ethical thought, others should not impede the managers' actions. At the same time, the manager has a duty not to interfere with the rights of colleagues to earn a bonus.

Decision makers who follow the **justice model** of ethics feel that all people should be given what they deserve. Of course, the tougher question becomes "What do people deserve?" The justice model weighs a person's actions against the results of those actions. For example, an accountant who has worked hard for several years in a CPA firm would likely deserve to be made a partner. On the other hand, a manager who has slacked off, been difficult to work with, and exhibited unprofessional behavior would probably not be deserving of a promotion under the justice school of ethics.

Finally, Merchant and Van der Stede discussed the **virtues model** of ethical behavior. According to this way of thinking, people should do what is right, moral, and virtuous. The virtues model asks managers to look inwardly to determine the rightness of their actions. Although some managers might make distinctions between moral behavior and ethical behavior, those who subscribe to this way of thinking often do not separate the two. So, a manager who adheres to this definition of ethical behavior might have no difficulty in misappropriating assets to help someone in need, since helping someone in need is a moral act.

Of course, those four models of ethical decision making are not the only ones in existence. And few accountants would be likely to know the names of them if asked. They would only know their personal beliefs regarding ethics and ethical decision making. As professional accountants, we also are subject to the ethical codes of the profession.

Reflection and Self-Assessment 3.4

Consider this chapter's "AIS in the Business World." How would Lee respond to his ethical dilemma under each of the preceding models?

The ethics code presented here represents a significant revision; the revised code was discussed in the November 2005 issue of *Strategic Finance.* For more information about the IMA and its ethics code, point your Web browser to www.imanet.org. Click the Ethics Center link.

Most, if not all, professional accounting organizations have codes of ethical behavior for their members. The **ethics code of the Institute of Management Accountants** explains members' responsibilities in four main areas, as shown in Figure 3.2 (Verschoor, 2005).

Note that the IMA code of ethics applies to all members of the Institute, not just those with the C.M.A. certification. The Certified Management Accountant exam tests candidates on the content and application of the IMA code of ethics, typically with cases like the one shown below:

> Rose Swanson is a profit center manager at VLG Corporation. Rose earns an annual salary, plus a bonus based on the difference between forecasted and actual profits. In years when Rose really needs her bonus, she tends to forecast her revenues a bit lower and her expenses a bit higher than in other years. In that way, her forecasted profits are low, and her actual profits are generally higher.

Rose's actions violate several elements of the IMA ethics code, including

- *Competence.* Rose has not prepared complete and clear reports and recommendations after appropriate analyses of relevant and reliable information. Her forecast of earnings is not complete since it misstates the revenue and expense items in an effort to earn a bonus.
- *Integrity.* Rose has engaged in an activity (creating budgetary slack) that prejudices her ability to carry out her duties ethically. By understating expected profits, she also has actively subverted the attainment of VLG's legitimate goals and objectives. The company's intent, clearly, is to reward managers for accurate forecasts. By forecasting inaccurately, she is thwarting the attainment of that goal. She also has violated the standard regarding refraining from engaging in or supporting any activity that would discredit the profession.
- *Credibility.* Rose has violated two standards under credibility. She has not communicated information fairly or objectively; neither has she disclosed all relevant information regarding forecasted profits.

Notice that Rose's case does not violate the confidentiality standards of the IMA ethics code. While many ethics cases touch on elements of all four, not all will. In doing a case analysis, don't try to "force a fit" that doesn't seem to occur naturally.

According to the Association of Certified Fraud Examiners (2004), "All Certified Fraud Examiners must meet the rigorous criteria for admission to the Association of Certified Fraud Examiners. Thereafter, they must exemplify the highest moral and ethical standards and must agree to abide by the bylaws of the ACFE and the **Certified Fraud Examiner Code of Professional Ethics.**" The ACFE code comprises eight segments:

- A Certified Fraud Examiner shall, at all times, demonstrate a commitment to professionalism and diligence in the performance of his or her duties.
- A Certified Fraud Examiner shall not engage in any illegal or unethical conduct, or any activity which would constitute a conflict of interest.
- A Certified Fraud Examiner shall, at all times, exhibit the highest level of integrity in the performance of all professional assignments and will accept only assignments for which there is reasonable expectation that the assignment will be completed with professional competence.
- A Certified Fraud Examiner will comply with lawful orders of the courts and will testify to matters truthfully and without bias or prejudice.

FIGURE 3.2
Institute of Management Accountants Code of Ethics, 2005 Revision

IMA Statement of Ethical Professional Practice

Members of IMA shall behave ethically. A commitment to ethical professional practice includes: overarching principles that express our values, and standards that guide our conduct.

PRINCIPLES

IMA's overarching ethical principles include: Honesty, Fairness, Objectivity, and Responsibility. Members shall act in accordance with these principles and shall encourage others within their organizations to adhere to them.

STANDARDS

A member's failure to comply with the following standards may result in disciplinary action.

COMPETENCE

Each member has a responsibility to

1. Maintain an appropriate level of professional expertise by continually developing knowledge and skills.
2. Perform professional duties in accordance with relevant laws, regulations, and technical standards.
3. Provide decision support information and recommendations that are accurate, clear, concise, and timely.
4. Recognize and communicate professional limitations or other constraints that would preclude responsible judgment or successful performance of an activity.

CONFIDENTIALITY

Each member has a responsibility to

1. Keep information confidential except when disclosure is authorized or legally required.
2. Inform all relevant parties regarding appropriate use of confidential information. Monitor subordinates' activities to ensure compliance.
3. Refrain from using confidential information for unethical or illegal advantage.

INTEGRITY

Each member has a responsibility to

1. Mitigate actual conflicts of interest. Regularly communicate with business associates to avoid apparent conflicts of interest. Advise all parties of any potential conflicts.
2. Refrain from engaging in any conduct that would prejudice carrying out duties ethically.
3. Abstain from engaging in or supporting any activity that might discredit the profession.

CREDIBILITY

Each member has a responsibility to

1. Communicate information fairly and objectively.
2. Disclose all relevant information that could reasonably be expected to influence an intended user's understanding of the reports, analyses, or recommendations.
3. Disclose delays or deficiencies in information, timeliness, processing, or internal controls in conformance with organization policy and/or applicable law.

- A Certified Fraud Examiner, in conducting examinations, will obtain evidence or other documentation to establish a reasonable basis for any opinion rendered. No opinion shall be expressed regarding the guilt or innocence of any person or party.
- A Certified Fraud Examiner shall not reveal any confidential information obtained during a professional engagement without proper authorization.
- A Certified Fraud Examiner will reveal all material matters discovered during the course of an examination which, if omitted, could cause a distortion of the facts.
- A Certified Fraud Examiner shall continually strive to increase the competence and effectiveness of professional services performed under his or her direction.

Unlike the IMA code of ethics, the ACFE code applies only to certified fraud examiners. Becoming a CFE requires both work experience related to fraud detection and prevention and passing a four-part exam in criminology and ethics, financial transactions, fraud investigation, and legal elements of fraud. You can find more information at www.cfenet.com/home.asp.

Although the two codes cover different areas of professional responsibility, notice their similarities. Both codes mention conflicts of interest and the importance of integrity. Impartiality and objectivity are also elements of both the IMA and ACFE codes, as is confidentiality.

The American Institute of Certified Public Accountants has an extensive code of professional conduct for CPAs. It is organized into seven areas:

- Principles of Professional Conduct
- Rules: Applicability and Definitions
- Independence, Integrity, and Objectivity
- General Standards Accounting Principles
- Responsibilities to Clients
- Responsibilities to Colleagues
- Other Responsibilities and Practices

While the details of the **AICPA code of professional conduct** are too extensive to include here in their entirety, you can access the various parts at www.aicpa.org/about/code/index.htm. Since CPAs are charged with serving the public interest, maintaining the highest level of ethical behavior is a paramount consideration.

You'll face countless ethical dilemmas in your professional career, from major choices such as how aggressive accounting practices should be to minor ones such as using office supplies for personal purposes. How do accountants resolve ethical dilemmas? The standards of conduct and ethics codes presented above are more about the "content" of ethical behavior and less about the "process." Next, let's consider the steps you might take to resolve an ethical dilemma in your professional life.

Langenderfer and Rockness (1989) proposed an **eight-step model** for dealing with ethical dilemmas:

1. Identify the facts.
2. Identify the ethics issues and the stakeholders involved.
3. Define the norms, principles, and values related to the situation.
4. Identify the alternative courses of action.
5. Evaluate the consequences of each possible course of action.
6. Decide the best course of action consistent with the norms, principles, and values.
7. If appropriate, discuss the alternative with a trusted person to help gain greater perspective regarding the alternatives.
8. Reach a decision as to the appropriate course of action.

Many companies will have an established practice for resolving ethical issues. They might include discussions with a neutral party (such as an ombuds or ethics officer) or reporting ethical violations anonymously. If a company you work for has an established policy for resolving ethical dilemmas, you should generally follow that policy first. As with many issues in accounting practice, there is no "one right way" to resolve an ethical problem.

If, though, your company has no established policy for dealing with ethics issues, try talking to your supervisor. If your supervisor is involved in unethical conduct, talk to his/her supervisor. After talking with your supervisor, the issue may be resolved. If not, though, take the problem to the next highest level of authority in the organization—with your supervisor's full knowledge. Don't do an "end run" around your boss, unless you suspect his/her involvement in the problem. Continue up the organizational hierarchy until the problem is resolved. In extreme cases, you may need to consider resigning your position with the organization if the issue is egregious and cannot be resolved internally.

These steps are based on the Institute of Management Accountants' recommendations for resolving ethical issues.

Unfortunately, the unethical and unprofessional actions of a small group of accountants have tarnished the profession's reputation in the eyes of the public. To conclude this chapter, let's take a look at a few "infamous" cases of unethical behavior in the profession.

The cases discussed here, along with many others, are available to members of the Association of Certified Fraud Examiners on their Web site (www.cfenet.com).

In the early 20th century, **Charles Ponzi** committed a multimillion-dollar fraud with international postal reply coupons. Ponzi collected money from investors but never purchased the international postal reply coupons. Basically, he was using new investors' money to pay off old investors. This practice has continued to the present day; you may have heard frauds like this one referred to as "pyramid" or "multilevel marketing" schemes. When such a fraud involves the use of securities or financial instruments, we often refer to it as a Ponzi scheme. Ponzi eventually was sentenced to five years in federal prison for mail fraud, followed by an additional seven-to-nine-year sentence in Massachusetts.

In 1952, John Rigas purchased a Pennsylvania cable company for $300. Twenty years later, he and his brother, Gus, created the **Adelphia Communications Corporation.** Adelphia was a family-run business; indeed, *Adelphia* is Greek for "brothers." In the late 1990s, Adelphia purchased Century Communications for $5.2 billion, making it the sixth largest cable company in the United States. John loved the limelight and was quite the philanthropist. But he also had a huge ego. For example, he bought homes for people and also was known to fly people on private planes for medical treatment; at the same time, he personally had to approve every business transaction for Adelphia. Adelphia's fraud was multifaceted. The company funded over $2 billion in personal loans to the Rigas family. Adelphia management engaged in deceptive accounting practices to meet analysts' expectations for profitability; the company also commingled its assets with the Rigas family's personal assets. Ultimately, Adelphia filed for bankruptcy in June 2002 and was delisted from NASDAQ.

The **Enron/Arthur Andersen** debacle may be the best-known accounting fraud in recent history. Enron filed for bankruptcy in December 2001; at that time, it was the largest bankruptcy filing ever. Enron was created in 1985 from the merger of two other companies in the natural gas and pipeline industries. After a few years, though, Enron found itself with mounting liabilities and loss of exclusive control over its pipelines. Based on the recommendation of consultant Jeffrey Skilling, Enron embarked on a new business strategy by creating a "bank" to buy and sell gas. In 1990, Enron created a financial subsidiary and hired Skilling to run it. The financial subsidiary hired the "best and brightest" but subjected them to a brutal performance evaluation system. Eventually, most of Enron's business came from its financial division, rather than from its original gas pipeline activities. Earnings, but not cash flows, continued increasing, and its stock price went up as well for 20 quarters in a row. Meanwhile, Enron's employees continued making deals of increasing risk, unbeknownst to Enron's investors. The company's accounting information system became rife with earnings management, off balance-sheet debt, and related-party transactions. The company also failed to disclose key facts in the notes to its financial statements. Ultimately, Enron's ethical breaches led to its bankruptcy filing; the downfall of Arthur Andersen, one of the then "Big Five" CPA firms, also was closely related to its activities in auditing Enron.

The preceding cases are just three among many in the accounting profession. By applying the principles of professionalism and ethics discussed in this chapter, you will hopefully be able to avoid such situations and help our profession become more respected in the business world.

CRITICAL THINKING

For this chapter's critical thinking application, let's talk about two things: the four schools of ethical decision making and the eight-step process for addressing ethical dilemmas. To provide some context for the discussion, here's the case presented right after Reflection and Self-Assessment 3.4:

> Rose Swanson is a profit center manager at VLG Corporation. Rose earns an annual salary, plus a bonus based on the difference between forecasted and actual profits. In years when Rose really needs her bonus, she tends to forecast her revenues a bit lower and her expenses a bit higher than in other years. In that way, her forecasted profits are low, and her actual profits are generally higher.

As stated earlier in this chapter, Rose's actions are clearly in violation of the IMA code of ethics—nothing will change that. But how would someone subscribing to each of the four schools of ethical thought view Rose's actions? Someone following the *utilitarianism* school would probably view Rose's action as ethical. In strict utilitarianism, actions are less important than results; if Rose's action has a positive result (i.e., she gets her bonus), her action would likely be considered ethical. Likewise, the *rights and duties* school would probably consider her action ethical. Someone using rights and duties as an ethical framework would say that Rose has a right to earn a bonus and/or to set her budget any way she wants; others have the duty not to interfere with her.

Looking through the lens of the *justice* school makes things a bit less clear. From that perspective, the question is: Does Rose deserve her bonus? If Rose is a hard worker, she probably does; if not, maybe she doesn't. I'm sure you can begin to appreciate how complex this question is at this point—what's the definition of a "hard worker"? Could someone judging Rose really evaluate her objectively enough to determine if her actions are ethical? The *virtues* school may be the most straightforward of the four; someone subscribing to it would probably say Rose's action definitely is not ethical. Many people in business would say it's just "not right" to misstate her budget deliberately.

Suppose you were Rose's supervisor and you discovered what she'd been doing. Let's look at Rockness and Langenderfer's eight-step model to determine what course of action you should take.

1. *Identify the facts.* Rose is overstating expenses and understating revenues in her budget so that she can earn a higher bonus.
2. *Identify the ethics issues and the stakeholders involved.* The ethics issue concerns whether or not Rose should be budgeting in that way. The stakeholders (people involved in and affected by the decision) are: Rose, Rose's family, other managers in the organization, stockholders of VLG Corporation, and VLG employees.
3. *Define the norms, principles, and values related to the situation.* We're using the IMA code of ethics as the basis for determining whether Rose is acting ethically. Of course, the AICPA Code of Professional Conduct also could apply, as could VLG's own corporate code of ethics (if they have one).

4. *Identify alternative courses of action.* Rose's supervisor could (a) change the performance evaluation system, (b) talk with Rose and tell her to change her budgeting process, or (c) fire Rose. Of course, those aren't the only three alternatives—Rose's supervisor could come up with many, many others.
5. *Evaluate the consequences of each possible course of action.* Changing the performance evaluation system would take a long time and a lot of effort; in addition, there's no guarantee that Rose (or some other manager) wouldn't find a way to abuse a new system. Talking with Rose will alert her to the fact that her supervisor knows there's a problem; it also gives her a chance to change before taking more drastic action. Firing Rose seems a bit extreme in this case; in addition, VLG would have to be very careful not to single Rose out for firing. If other managers were behaving similarly, but did not lose their jobs, VLG could open itself up to legal action.
6. *Decide the best course of action consistent with the norms, principles, and values.* Deciding the best course of action is definitely a matter of personal choice. From the three alternatives suggested above, I'd probably try the second one. It's the least extreme, and has a pretty good chance of fixing the issue.
7. *If appropriate, discuss the alternative with a trusted person to help gain greater perspective regarding the alternatives.* Rose's boss may want to talk over the decision with a peer.
8. *Reach a decision as to the appropriate course of action.* Rose's supervisor would call Rose in for a conversation about budgeting, letting her know what she needed to change and what would happen if she didn't.

As you can tell, ethical decision making is a complex area—in a fundamental way, such decisions are all about the decision maker's point of view. That helps explain why the professional codes of ethics presented earlier in the chapter are so specific. As you enter the accounting profession, you may sometimes find your personal ethical values conflict with professional ethics. I'm not saying you need to compromise or change your personal ethics—but you need to keep in mind what The Rolling Stones said in one of their well-known songs: "You can't always get what you want." In other words, you may need to do something (or not do something) professionally that would be unacceptable to you personally.

Summary

Ethics and professionalism are important elements of any career in accounting. Accounting educators have two main schools of thought regarding their incorporation in the curriculum: weaving their study into existing accounting courses and/or establishing a separate course devoted to this important topic. This chapter is included here as part of the first approach; here is a summary of its main points:

1. *List and discuss characteristics of a professional.* A professional communicates effectively; thinks rationally, logically, and coherently; appropriately uses technical knowledge; integrates knowledge from many disciplines; exhibits ethical professional behavior; recognizes the influence of political, social, economic, legal, and regulatory forces; and actively seeks additional knowledge.
2. *Explain how those characteristics apply to the accounting profession.* As professionals, accountants have a responsibility to exhibit all seven of the preceding characteristics. Failing to do so violates the public trust.
3. *Define ethics.* The field of ethics has been subdivided into three parts: metaethics, normative ethics, and applied ethics. Each part concerns the ways people make choices between "right" and "wrong."

4. *Discuss various models/schools of ethical decision making.* The chapter outlined Merchant's thoughts in this area. He identified four broad systems for making ethical decisions: utiliarianism, rights and duties, justice, and virtue.
5. *Explain and apply the professional ethics codes of various accounting professional organizations.* Virtually all accounting professional organizations have their own codes of ethics, although the individual codes demonstrate striking similiarities. The IMA code of ethics comprises four parts: confidentiality, competence, integrity, and credibility. The ethics code of the Association of Certified Fraud Examiners contains eight elements, while the AICPA code focuses on seven: Principles of Professional Conduct; Rules: Applicability and Definitions; Independence, Integrity, and Objectivity; General Standards Accounting Principles; Responsibilities to Clients; Responsibilities to Colleagues; and Other Responsibilities and Practices.
6. *Explain how to resolve ethical dilemmas.* If a company policy on resolving ethical dilemmas exists, accountants should follow it. However, if no such guidelines are in place, one good model for making ethical decisions involves eight steps: identify the facts; identify the ethics issues and the stakeholders involved; define the norms, principles, and values related to the situation; identify the alternative courses of action; evaluate the consequences of each possible course of action; decide the best course of action consistent with the norms, principles, and values; if appropriate, discuss the alternative with a trusted person to help gain greater perspective regarding the alternatives; and reach a decision as to the appropriate course of action.
7. *Give examples of recent ethical cases in accounting.* The chapter discussed the classic ethical cases associated with Charles Ponzi, Adelphia Communications, and Enron/Arthur Andersen.

The ability to make ethical decisions does not appear magically when you earn your accounting degree. You must develop the habit of making strong ethical decisions throughout your career, starting with those you confront in your education as an accountant. In the next chapter, we'll look at internal control issues; a strong sense of ethics can be a valuable internal control for virtually any organization.

Key Terms

Adelphia Communications Corporation, *49*
AICPA code of professional conduct, *48*
Certified Fraud Examiner Code of Professional Ethics, *46*
characteristics of a professional, *41*
Charles Ponzi, *49*
definitions of ethics, *44*
eight-step model, *48*
Enron/Arthur Andersen, *49*
Institute of Management Accountants ethics code, *46*
justice model, *45*
normative ethics, *44*
rights and duties, *45*
utilitarian model of ethics, *45*
virtues model, *45*

Chapter References

Association of Certified Fraud Examiners. 2004. *Code of Professional Ethics.* www.cfenet.com/about/codeethics.asp (October 11).

Bell, N. 2004. "Characteristics of a Risk Management and Insurance Professional." www.wsu.edu/belln/ (October 4, 2004).

Dictionary.com. 2004. "Ethics." http://dictionary.reference.com/search?q=ethics (October 4).

Houle, C. 1980. *Continuing Learning in the Professions.* San Francisco: Jossey-Bass.

Huggett, K. 2000. "Professional Development in an Uncertain Profession: Finding a Place for Academic and Career Advisors." *NACADA Journal,* Fall, pp. 46–51.

Internet Encyclopedia of Philosophy. 2004. "Ethics." www.utm.edu/research/iep/e/ethics.htm (October 4).

Langenderfer, H., and J. Rockness. 1989. "Integrating Ethics into the Accounting Curriculum: Issues, Problems, and Solutions." *Journal of Accounting Education,* Spring, pp. 58–69.

McDonald, C. 2001. "A Review of Continuing Professional Education." *Journal of Continuing Higher Education,* Winter, pp. 29–40.

Merchant, K., and W. Van der Stede. 2003. *Management Control Systems.* Upper Saddle River, NJ: Prentice Hall.

Verschoor, C. 2005. "Do the Right Thing: IMA Issues New Ethics Guidance." *Strategic Finance,* November, pp. 42–46.

End-of-Chapter Activities

1. *Reading review questions.*
   a. List and discuss 10 characteristics of a professional and/or professional behavior. Where possible, include a specific example of each characteristic from your own experience as a student.
   b. Define *ethics*. Explain why ethics is so important in the accounting profession.
   c. Compare and contrast the ethics codes of the AICPA, IMA, and ACFE.
   d. What basic schools of thought exist regarding ethical behavior? What are the strengths and weaknesses of each one?
   e. Explain the basic facts of fraud schemes associated with Ponzi, Adelphia, and Enron.
   f. In a manner specified by your instructor, respond to the questions for this chapter's "AIS in the Business World."

2. *Reading review problem.* Consider the following story:

   It was a Saturday afternoon, and the two men at the window table in the club lounge were relaxing over drinks, talking football and a little politics, and cooling down after an hour of tennis. "You're getting the hand of it," Fred Smith joked to Jim Cunningham, who, as he often did, had edged out his longtime friend. "Practice, practice, practice," Jim replied with a laugh. Fred and Jim had been playing tennis together for almost as many years as they had worked at Summitt Manufacturing. Fred is vice president for human resources; Jim is one of the company's accountants. They try to keep Summitt out of the conversation when they get together, but this particular day they broke their own rule by getting into some shop talk. That's when Jim dropped a surprise on Fred. "I don't know if I should tell you this," he said, "but there's something going on at work and you should know about it." Jim then told Fred—in strict confidence—that the company's chief financial officer was planning to have Summitt take an aggressive stance on sales revenue reporting that, in Jim's view, would stretch the boundaries of acceptable accounting practices. Jim's accounting expertise and core responsibilities at Summitt center on the company's real estate holdings; he doesn't deal with sales revenue. But he has a pretty good understanding of what's happening in other areas of the company's financial activities, and he was clearly concerned with what he had picked up about what the CFO wanted to do. If the CFO were to prevail, his accounting method would burnish Summitt's earnings outlook and probably help its stock price. "But it could be risky," Jim told Fred. "It could raise questions" about the firm's methods and even its integrity. What's more, Jim said he wasn't sure the company's top executives understood the nuances of the CFO's approach. "They might get talked into going along with something they're not up to speed on," Jim said. (Source: Brenda Franklin, "Spinning the Numbers," *HR Magazine,* no. 47 (November 2002), pp. 64–69.)

   a. Is Jim acting professionally? Explain your response.
   b. Which of the four schools of ethical thought does Jim follow? Explain your response.
   c. Is the CFO's proposed action ethical? Use one of the professional ethical codes discussed in the chapter to develop your response.

3. *Making choices and exercising judgment.* Econo-lube (taken from the ACFE educator documents at www.cfenet.com).

While living in St. George, Jeff received a coupon in the mail for an oil change for $9.95 at a local Econo-lube. He thought $9.95 was a good deal so he decided to give Econo-lube a try. When Jeff arrived at Econo-lube, the waiting room had approximately five people obviously waiting for their cars to be serviced. He went to the service counter and was greeted by the owner.

Jeff explained to the owner that he would like to use his coupon for the $9.95 oil change. The owner acted very friendly and told him that the price of $9.95 did not actually include a $3.00 oil disposal fee. Also, the coupon was only good for cars that required four quarts of oil so Jeff would have to purchase one more quart to meet the requirements of his car. So the price would be $14.90. Next, Jeff asked for Valvoline 30wt oil because that was what his uncle, who repairs his own work vehicles, recommended he use in this car. The owner immediately told Jeff that 30wt was not right and proceeded to tell Jeff all about his high performance Porsche that he never runs 30wt oil in. Jeff's 1989 Honda was definitely not a Porsche so he persisted. The owner finally agreed to use 30wt oil on the condition that Jeff signs a liability waiver. Jeff also had to pay an extra dollar for each quart of Valvoline brand oil because Econo-lube used a different brand. The $9.95 oil change was now up to $18.90.

Jeff sat down next to a young looking man named Rick who told him he was also in for the great deal on an oil change. As they talked, Jeff learned that this man was recently married and was planning to start college in the fall.

The owner called Rick's name and invited him into the shop to review the "free diagnostic check" details Econo-lube had performed on his car. Rick was with the owner about 5 minutes and came back ghostly white. Jeff asked him what was wrong. He explained that his car was in bad shape. In fact, he felt lucky it had not broken down yet. He was sick that the amount of his estimate was now over $300. When Jeff asked if he was going to let the owner do the work he replied: "Do I really have a choice? My car is in bad shape." He had already given the OK.

After a while the owner called Jeff's name. He greeted Jeff gravely, asked him to come with him into his shop, and told him that his Honda needed some help. He then proceeded through a detailed checklist and showed Jeff everything that was wrong. Apparently, Jeff was lucky not to be dead because his brakes were on the brink of failing. Also, Jeff was told his transmission fluid needed to be drained and the filter replaced—for added effect the mechanic showed how he had opened the plug and saw that the fluid was black. There were also a lot of small "preventative maintenance items." The final item the owner discussed with Jeff was that the O2 sensor needed to be replaced. Of course, Jeff did not know what an O2 sensor was so the owner explained it to him in great detail. In the end Jeff's bill for the oil change was going to be over $400! The good news was that he could have it all done in a couple of hours.

Jeff was tempted to have the charges done, but politely declined and asked for the basic $9.95 oil change (which cost $18.90). Later, Jeff drove the car to an uncle's house and went through a copy of the same checklist with him. About half of the small preventive maintenance items were legitimate things that the uncle recommended. The total of these items cost Jeff no more than $50. The expensive items listed (brakes, transmission filter replacement, O2 sensor) were in good shape and did not need to be replaced at all. In fact, because Jeff's car was a standard transmission, it did not even have a transmission filter. Jeff and his uncle checked the transmission fluid themselves and found it to be clean and clear. Jeff was upset that the owner of the shop would try to take advantage of him so badly but did not pursue the issue any farther.

Did the owner of the Econo-lube in St. George commit fraud? What precautions or controls can consumers use to prevent them from being taken advantage of in a situation like this? Were there any symptoms or indications of fraud present in this case?

4. *Field exercises.*

   a. Research one or more of the following accounting frauds. Report the results of your research in a two- to three-page paper and/or an oral presentation to the class.

      - Lucent Technologies
      - Tyco International
      - Worldcom
      - American Tissue Inc.

   b. Through interviews or other research, find a company's code of ethics. Summarize it and discuss how it is similar to and different from one of the codes of ethics discussed in the chapter.

   c. Point your Web browser to www.cfenet.com. Click the "local chapters" link and find a CFE chapter near you. Attend a meeting, interview a member, or, in cooperation with your instructor, ask a CFE to come and speak to your class.

5. Describe your personal philosophy for making ethical decisions. Your philosophy may be based on one or more of the schools of thought discussed in the chapter; it also may be completely original. Meet with a group of your classmates to discuss your ethical philosophies. Describe a time when you had to make a personal ethical choice; explain the choice you made and its consequences. If confronted with the same decision again, would you make the same choice? Why, or why not?

6. Which school of ethical thought is described in each of the following independent scenarios? Justify your choices.

   a. Julie and Bart were talking over their progress in the accounting program at Big State University. Julie was annoyed at the number of students who cheated on exams and class projects in the program. She told Bart: "If prospective employers find out that cheating is so prevalent here, it will hurt my chances of getting a good job when I graduate—even if I don't cheat!"

   b. Maria is a certified fraud examiner. She is interviewing Rehan about missing inventory. When Maria asked what should be done to the person who stole the inventory, Rehan replied: "They should be locked up and pay a hefty fine."

   c. Anita recently discovered that her co-worker Vicki was engaging in fraudulent activities that harmed their company. She went to her priest for guidance about what to do.

   d. Gil is a financial analyst on Wall Street with an accounting and finance degree from Big State University. In an interview for a popular magazine, he said "Everyone 'cheats' a little when they forecast their financial statements. In the end, it's probably okay because everybody's financial results are a little distorted that way."

7. *Ethics cases* (K. D. Stocks and S. Albrecht, "Ethical Dilemmas," *The Internal Auditor,* June 1993, pp. 24–25).

   a. Upon graduating from Ethics University five years ago, you accepted a job with Peat & Price CPAs. After three years with that firm, you joined MiniCare Health Company as an audit senior and are now an audit manager with that company. Not long after being promoted to audit manager, you noticed that the executives of the company were doing things that you didn't think were appropriate. The company overbilled Medicare on several occasions, and several members of senior management were abusing their positions by taking company perks that were against the company's code of conduct. You have talked to your superior, the financial vice president. He has, in essence, told you to mind your own business. He told you that auditors are to report on controls and assist management, not question it. You are currently making $100,000 a year, far more than you could earn in another company at this stage in your career. Which elements of the IMA ethics code are the company's executives violating? Use the Langenderfer and Rockness eight-step framework to decide how you would respond to this situation.

   b. You are an auditor for International Pharmaceutical Company (IPC), a company that has invested over $200 million in developing a new drug. For tax purposes, the related research and development expenses were written off as deductible expenses on IPC's U.S. corporate tax returns. When the drug was patented, your company set up a Puerto Rican subsidiary to manufacture the drug. The company then transferred the patent to the subsidiary and arranged to purchase the drug from the subsidiary at a high price. IPC justified the transfer price as reasonable because of the high value of the patent, which is now owned by the subsidiary company. You are concerned because you think the price being charged by the subsidiary is excessive and is being used to inflate costs and minimize taxes paid to the U.S. government. You know that tax rates are considerably less in Puerto Rico than in the United States. Is the company violating any elements of the AICPA Code of Professional Conduct? If so, which? Use the Langenderfer and Rockness eight-step framework to decide how you would respond to this situation.

8. Point your Web browser to the AICPA's Code of Professional Conduct at www.aicpa.org/about/code/index.htm. Working on your own or with a group, summarize the code in a paper of not more than three pages. What elements of the code did CPAs violate in the Enron case? Worldcom? Tyco?
9. *Crossword puzzle.* Please use terms from the chapter to complete this puzzle.

Across

2. Company associated with John Rigas.
3. School of ethics that says everyone should get what they deserve.
8. Private sector nonprofit created by Sarbanes-Oxley.
9. One of the four components of the IMA code of ethics.
10. ______ ethics is concerned with standards that regulate right and wrong conduct.

Down

1. Ethical school that says the end justifies the means.
4. Responsibilities to ______: one area of the AICPA code of ethics.
5. A professional thinks this way.
6. ______ of practice: one of McDonald's characteristics of a professional.
7. According to the ACFE ethics code, no CFE can express an opinion regarding this.

10. *Terminology.* Please match each item on the left with the most appropriate item on the right.

1. Associated with pyramid schemes	a. Comply with lawful orders of the courts and will testify to matters truthfully and without bias or prejudice.
2. Autonomy of practice	b. Houle discussed this as part of professionalization.
3. Collective identity	c. McDonald identified this as part of being a professional.
4. Company ethics code	d. One of Bell's characteristics of a professional.
5. Element of integrity	e. People should do what is right and moral.
6. Enron fraudster	f. Ponzi.
7. Integrates knowledge from many disciplines	g. Refuse any gift, favor, or hospitality that would influence or would appear to influence their actions.
8. Part of a CFE's ethical responsibilities	h. Skilling.
9. Specialized knowledge base	i. The first source to consult for workplace ethical dilemmas.
10. Virtues school of ethics	j. The PCAOB reduced, but did not eliminate, this.

11. *Multiple choice questions.*

1. Which of the following is not a characteristic of a professional according to Bell?
   a. Communicating effectively
   b. Actively seeking additional knowledge
   c. Thinking focused on your area of expertise
   d. Demonstrating ethical behavior
2. Which of the following is the best example of accounting's specialized knowledge base?
   a. The AICPA Code of Professional Conduct
   b. The process of reconciling a bank statement
   c. Financial ratio calculations
   d. The rules associated with business combinations
3. The IMA code of ethics and the ACFE code of ethics both mention
   a. Off balance-sheet financing.
   b. Conflicts of interest.
   c. Legal rights of accountants and their clients.
   d. Rules for conducting examinations ethically.
4. Which of the following best describes a Ponzi scheme?
   a. A fraud whereby old investors are paid with money from new investors.
   b. Any fraud that involves a conflict of interest.
   c. A fraud committed with international cooperation.
   d. A fraud involving related-party transactions.
5. Which of the following names is most closely associated with the Enron debacle?
   a. Ponzi
   b. Albrecht
   c. Rigas
   d. Skilling

6. Bell asserted that a professional integrates knowledge from many disciplines. Your study of accounting information systems integrates accounting knowledge with
   a. Information technology.
   b. Business law.
   c. Both of the above.
   d. None of the above.
7. According to the AICPA Code of Professional Conduct, accountants have an ethical responsibility to
   a. Clients only.
   b. Colleagues only.
   c. Both clients and colleagues.
   d. Neither clients nor colleagues.
8. Which branch of ethics is concerned with the source and meaning of ethics?
   a. Metaethics
   b. Normative ethics
   c. Applied ethics
   d. Professional ethics
9. Different accounting organizations (such as the IMA and AICPA) have their own codes of ethics because
   a. They are required by law to do so.
   b. They do not respect one another.
   c. They want to punish their members differently for ethical violations.
   d. The nature of members' work is different.
10. The first resource to consult when confronting a professional ethical dilemma in accounting is
    a. The company's own code of ethics.
    b. A lawyer.
    c. A professional code of ethics.
    d. Dependent upon the decision maker's personal ethical philosophy.

12. *Statement evaluation.* Please indicate whether each of the following statements is (i) always true, (ii) sometimes true, or (iii) never true. For those that are (ii) sometimes true, explain when the statement is true.

a. Legal behavior is the same as ethical behavior.
b. Metaethics and applied ethics are important in the accounting profession.
c. The habit of ethical decision making begins once you have your first professional job.
d. Any response to an ethical dilemma is acceptable, provided the decision maker can justify it.
e. "Pyramid schemes" are, by definition, both illegal and unethical.
f. Effective communication is an important part of professional behavior.
g. To be considered professional, an accountant must have a CPA license.
h. A subordinate can bypass his/her supervisor in reporting an ethical dilemma.
i. Violations of professional codes of ethics can lead to fines, prison, and/or losing your professional license/certification.
j. The best ethical decision makers in accounting follow the utilitarianism school of ethical thought.

Chapter Four

Internal Controls

AIS in the Business World

Identity Theft in Las Vegas

Consider the following story from the December 10, 2008, edition of the *Las Vegas Review-Journal*:

> Authorities unsealed the indictments of 15 people involved in a Eurasian gang on Tuesday, revealing an organized crime ring that raked in about $1.5 million through stolen credit cards and identity theft in the Las Vegas Valley. The suspects are facing federal charges including trafficking and possession of counterfeit devices, identity theft, production and use of counterfeit devices and fraud. [A U.S. attorney] said some of the suspects were involved in "skimming," an act by which a person can obtain credit card information by running the card through a handheld counterfeiting device. The gang members would have people working in restaurants, bars and smoke shops who would scan a customer's credit card on a legitimate machine and then swipe it again with a counterfeiting device.

If you've ever been the victim of that kind of crime, or known someone who was, you know that it can take quite a while to repair the damages.

Discussion Questions

1. What risks do organizations and individuals take when they use credit cards for transactions?
2. What policies and procedures can they put in place to detect, prevent, and or correct situations like the one described?

Source: Lawrence Mower, "ID Theft Operation Outlined," *Las Vegas Review Journal,* December 10, 2008, p. 2B.

Internal controls have been at the heart of accounting information systems practically since AIS emerged as a separate field of study for accounting students. A lack of sound internal controls can have serious consequences for a company—particularly with the advent of Sarbanes-Oxley and the Public Companies Accounting Oversight Board. In this chapter, we'll lay a foundation in the study of internal control; later chapters will apply the basic ideas you learn here to specific contexts within your study of accounting information systems.

When you complete your study of this chapter, you should be able to:

1. Define *internal control* and explain its importance in the accounting information system.
2. Explain the basic purposes of internal control.
3. Describe and give examples of various kinds of risk exposures.
4. Conduct a comprehensive risk assessment.
5. Summarize and explain the importance of the COSO documents on internal control and enterprise risk management.
6. Critique existing internal control systems and design effective internal controls.

A solid understanding of internal controls is important in any area of accounting. If you're considering a career in auditing, you need to be able to assess internal controls as part of an audit. If you're thinking about a career in corporate or not-for-profit accounting, you may have to design internal controls to comply with Sarbanes-Oxley. Internal controls also tie into our discussion of ethics and professionalism in the previous chapter; fundamentally, internal controls exist because, in most organizations, you cannot be assured that everyone will behave ethically and professionally 100 percent of the time.

INTERNAL CONTROL DEFINITION AND IMPORTANCE

You can find COSO's Web site at www.coso.org. Click the "publications" link for executive summaries of the reports discussed here.

So what is internal control? Let's look at three definitions. In *Internal Control: Integrated Framework* (1985), the Committee of Sponsoring Organizations of the Treadway Commission (COSO) defined **internal control** as "a process, effected by an entity's board of directors, management and other personnel, designed to provide reasonable assurance regarding the achievement of objectives in the following categories: effectiveness and efficiency of operations, reliability of financial reporting and compliance with applicable laws and regulations." The New York State Office of the State Comptroller (2004) defined *internal control* as "the integration of the activities, plans, attitudes, policies, and efforts of the people of an organization working together to provide reasonable assurance that the organization will achieve its objectives and mission." Lander (2004, p. 15) defined *internal control* as

> A process designed by, or under the supervision of, the company's principal executive and principal financial officers and implemented by the company's board of directors, management, and other personnel to provide reasonable assurance for the reliability of financial reporting and the preparation of financial statements for external purposes in accordance with generally accepted accounting principles.

Notice that all three definitions of internal control have several common elements:

- *Internal control is a process.* Popular wisdom states that 20 percent of employees in most organizations will not defraud the company under any circumstances; 60 percent of employees will defraud the company if it's easy; and the remaining 20 percent will go out of their way to defraud the company. Internal controls are principally designed, then, for that 60 percent group. Because internal control is a process, it is subject to process improvement; and single correct answers to control problems seldom exist. Accountants must use judgment and experience in designing and implementing internal controls; the controls must be periodically reviewed to ensure their continued effectiveness.

We'll look at business process management later in the text.

- *Internal control necessarily involves people in the organization.* The COSO and Lander definitions lay the responsibility for internal control squarely at the feet of management and the board of directors; the New York State Office definition speaks in broader terms of "the people of an organization working together." Internal controls, therefore, require discussion during design, implementation, and evaluation. They impact human behavior, and control systems designers, as far as possible, must anticipate their behavioral effects.
- *Internal controls are designed to provide reasonable assurance.* Dictionary.com defines reasonable as "governed by or being in accordance with reason or sound thinking; being within the bounds of common sense; not excessive or extreme." So, internal controls should not, and probably cannot, be designed to provide absolute assurance of anything. Going back to our prior discussion of the conceptual framework of accounting, internal controls are subject to a cost–benefit constraint. Their cost must be outweighed by their benefit if they are to be meaningful.
- *Internal controls provide reasonable assurance in a few common areas, such as operations, financial reporting, and human behavior.* When I talk to students and business professionals about internal control, I identify four purposes: safeguarding assets, ensuring financial statement reliability, promoting operational efficiency, and encouraging compliance with management's directives. In short, internal controls are there to help ensure that no one steals from the company and everyone follows the rules.

Why are internal controls important? One answer certainly lies with the purposes of internal control. Most managers, stockholders, employees, and other organizational stakeholders want a company to operate as effectively and efficiently as possible, to have financial statements that are reliable, and to make sure their assets are safe. Apart from those issues, though, internal control is also legally mandated by several important pieces of legislation.

You can find out more about the FCPA on its Web site: www.usdoj.gov/criminal/fraud/fcpa.html.

The **Foreign Corrupt Practices Act** was passed by the U.S. Congress in 1977. U.S. businesses had begun expanding internationally in the mid-1970s. And, in some foreign countries, bribery is an acceptable way of doing business. In fact, an SEC investigation in the 1970s showed that over 400 U.S. companies had paid bribes to foreign officials for a variety of reasons. Although bribery is an acceptable business practice in some countries, it is not in the United States. So, the FCPA was enacted to stop those practices by U.S. businesses and to restore some confidence in U.S. business practices around the world. The FCPA requires corporations covered by its provisions to maintain an adequate system of internal accounting controls. The act also states, "no person shall knowingly circumvent or knowingly fail to implement a system of internal accounting controls or knowingly falsify any book, record, or account." The legislation also mentions the concept of reasonable assurance, defining it as "such level of detail and degree of assurance as would satisfy prudent officials in the conduct of their own affairs." Companies failing to comply with the Foreign Corrupt Practices Act can be subject to both fines and imprisonment.

Details of SOX are available all over the Internet. One site I've found useful is www.soxlaw.com. It is a proprietary site, but the information is accurate and easy to read.

In response to the corporate scandals of the late 20th century, Congress passed the **Sarbanes-Oxley Act of 2002**. Sarbanes-Oxley (SOX for short) is the most sweeping accounting-related legislation business professionals have seen since the FCPA.

It is a broad-reaching act that significantly changed the way U.S. companies do business, as well as impacting the roles of top management, the board of directors, independent auditors, and audit committees. Provisions of SOX related to internal controls include

- Management and the external auditors must assess the company's internal controls on an annual basis.
- Management has certain required disclosures when reporting to the SEC. They include acknowledgment that management is personally and organizationally responsible for the design and implementation of internal controls, particularly as they relate to reasonable assurance of reliable financial statements. Management also must disclose any internal control changes since the last reporting cycle, if those changes are likely to have a noticeable effect on internal controls over financial reporting. Finally, management must certify that they have informed the auditors and the board of director's audit committee of any significant problems or weaknesses in internal control.
- Management must personally sign the required certifications and reports related to the preceding items. The signature cannot be delegated, even via power of attorney.

Many of the SOX requirements related to internal control are found in section 404 of the Act. In practice, people often refer to conducting/having a "404 audit."

So, internal controls are very important for organizations of all types. As an accounting professional, you may be involved in the design, implementation, or evaluation of internal controls as an external (independent) auditor, internal auditor, controller, or consultant.

Reflection and Self-Assessment 4.1

Compare the content and purpose of the FCPA and SOX. What similarities and differences do you notice? If a nonaccountant asked you how you know that financial statements are fair and reliable, what would you say?

To design effective internal controls, accountants and managers should consider the risks associated with doing business. By identifying risks, we can develop controls to mitigate them successfully.

RISKS

Risk is a part of everyday life—both personally and professionally. The question is, are businesses taking risks unnecessarily, to the point that they cannot operate effectively or rely on their accounting systems to produce reliable information?

Most business professionals, including accountants, find it easier to think about risk if they have some organizational structure for doing so. An organizational structure for knowledge, like types of risk, is sometimes referred to as a *taxonomy*.

Reflection and Self-Assessment 4.2

Think about risks you have taken today. For example, you risked that your car wouldn't start when you came to school. You may have taken a risk in leaving your house, residence hall, or apartment later than usual. List six additional risks you've taken today and organize them in some way that makes sense to you.

FIGURE 4.1 Brown's Risk Taxonomy

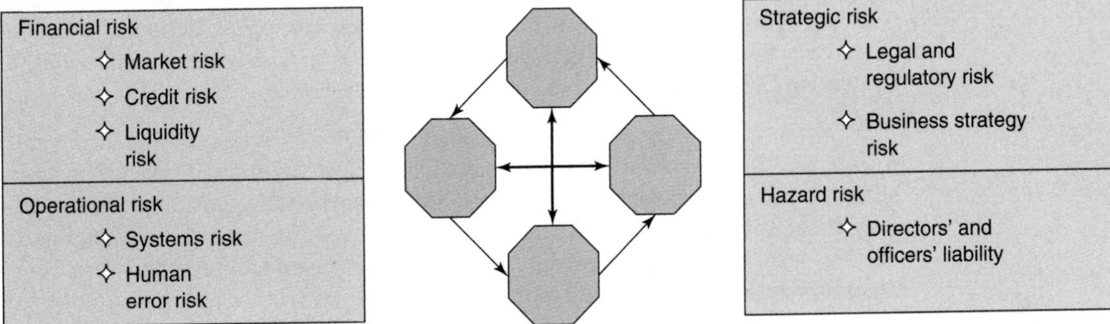

Financial risk
✧ Market risk
✧ Credit risk
✧ Liquidity risk
Operational risk
✧ Systems risk
✧ Human error risk
Strategic risk
✧ Legal and regulatory risk
✧ Business strategy risk
Hazard risk
✧ Directors' and officers' liability

Brown (2001) takes a very practical view toward the management of risk. He identified four categories of risk and suggested eight specific risks within the four categories, as shown in Figure 4.1. Here are some definitions and examples of the elements of **Brown's taxonomy of risk**:

1. *Financial risks* are related to monetary activities. The worldwide financial crisis that started in 2007 had elements of all three forms of financial risk.
   a. *Market risk* refers to changes in a company's stock prices, investment values, and interest rates. For example, if an organization fails to diversify its financial investments adequately, it runs the risk of a significant decrease in value that will impact financial statements.
   b. *Credit risk* is associated with customers' unwillingness or inability to pay amounts owed to the organization. For example, you may have seen department store employees outside of stores during the holiday season. They want you to fill out an application for a credit card, which is virtually guaranteed to get you at least a small amount of credit. While granting credit without a solid investigation will probably boost sales in the short run, the company runs the risk of nonpayment.
   c. *Liquidity risk* involves the possibility that a company will not have sufficient cash and near-cash assets available to meet its short-term obligations. If an organization has no budget or spending plan for its cash and near-cash assets, it is exposed to this risk.
2. *Operational risks* concern the people, assets, and technologies used to create value for the organization's customers.
   a. *Systems risk* relates directly to information technology. As organizations become increasingly dependent on computers and related IT to deliver goods and services to customers, they risk the possibility that IT resources will fail at a critical moment.
   b. *Human error risk* recognizes the possibility that people in the organization may make mistakes. Those mistakes might result in asset misappropriation or theft, divulgence of trade secrets, legal action from breaking laws, or other consequences. For example, a manager might create a hostile work environment for an employee, leading to a sexual harassment lawsuit.

3. *Strategic risks,* according to Brown (2001, p. 44), "relate to the entity's decision-making process at the senior management and board of directors level."
   a. *Legal and regulatory risk* is concerned with the chance that those parties might break laws that result in financial, legal, or operational sanctions. For example, if the CEO and/or the CFO knowingly falsify the reports required by SOX, they may be subject to governmental penalties.
   b. *Business strategy risk* comprises poor decision making related to a company's basis for competing in its markets. You may remember the era of Web-based grocery stores in the United States. Firms such as WebGrocer are now out of business, at least in part because they did not adequately consider the risk associated with trying to develop a new market for a previously nonexistent service.
4. *Hazard risk,* in Brown's taxonomy, has a single category: *directors' and officers' liability.* Organizations in which directors and officers are accused of mismanagement by shareholders, government agencies, employees, or other stakeholders bear this risk in a very direct way. The WorldCom case in this chapter's reading review problem definitely involves legal and regulatory risk, but also could encompass hazard risk if WorldCom's managers were held personally accountable.

Brown's taxonomy of risk is not the only one available for risk assessment. For example, Hollander, Denna, and Cherrington (2000) suggest five categories of risk, some of which overlap with Brown's four categories. The Hollander categories include strategic risk, decision risk, operating risk, financial risk, and information risk. If you completed Reflection and Self-Assessment 4.2 above, you created your own taxonomy of risk. The point here is not which taxonomy is better or the best; your goal should be to work with a comprehensive taxonomy that makes sense to you in identifying risks associated with the design and implementation of accounting information systems.

Reflection and Self-Assessment 4.3

The California State University (CSU) system is the largest four-year higher education system in the United States. In 2004, all 23 CSU campuses adopted PeopleSoft, an enterprise resource planning system, for managing finances, personnel records, and other important functions. The project was referred to as the Common Management System (CMS). Considering Brown's taxonomy of risk, identify five risks the CSU and its management took by making the PeopleSoft decision. You may want to consult the following Web site for more information on the project itself: cms.calstate.edu/T6CMSNewsArchives.asp.

By using a taxonomy to identify risks, accountants, managers, and other organizational stakeholders are in a much better position to establish internal controls that will ameliorate (lessen the impact of) those risks.

COSO FRAMEWORKS

The Committee of Sponsoring Organizations of the Treadway Commission (**COSO** for short) comprises the Institute of Management Accountants, the American Institute of Certified Public Accountants, the American Accounting Association, the Institute of Internal

FIGURE 4.2
Components of the COSO Internal Control Framework

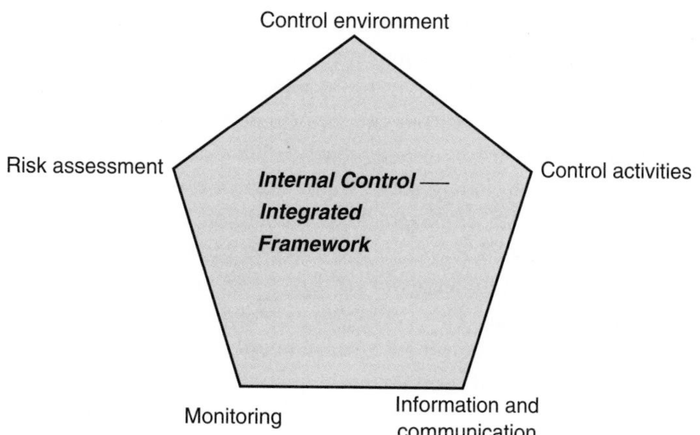

Auditors, and the Financial Executives Institute. COSO's first publication, **Internal Control: Integrated Framework,** suggested five interrelated components for achieving effective internal control: control environment, risk assessment, control activities, information and communication, and monitoring. (See Figure 4.2.) Although each component has its own definition and explanation, the five truly form an *integrated framework* in the best sense of the term. Managers and accountants cannot afford to pay attention to a subset of the five components; they must be considered simultaneously to achieve the internal control objectives discussed earlier in this chapter.

ISACA (Information Systems Audit and Control Association, www.isaca.org) developed another control framework, often referred to as COBIT (Control Objectives for Information and Related Technology). We'll explore COBIT in more depth in our discussion of computer crime later on the text.

The *control environment* refers to the tone at the top of the organization. It reminds accountants and managers that, without the clear, demonstrated commitment of upper management and opinion leaders in the organization, internal control will not be taken seriously elsewhere in the hierarchy. To develop and sustain a strong control environment, managers and other influential people in the organization should

1. Be committed to integrity and ethical behavior.
2. Demonstrate a commitment to competence in carrying out their duties and responsibilities.
3. Actively seek the participation of the board of directors and its audit committee in decisions related to internal control.
4. Maintain a consistent, appropriate management philosophy and operating style.
5. Structure the organization for efficiency, effectiveness, and reasonable internal control.
6. Assign authority and responsibility with integrity and the best interests of the organization in mind.
7. Develop and enforce human resource policies and practices that encourage all employees to maintain a sound internal control system.

Risk assessment is the second component of the integrated framework. It involves using a taxonomy, business experience, research, and dialogue to identify the risks associated with operations. By identifying risks, we can design appropriate, cost-effective internal controls to provide reasonable assurance of safeguarding assets, ensuring financial statement reliability, promoting operational efficiency, and encouraging compliance with management's directives.

The *control activities* refer to the actual internal controls implemented on the basis of the risk assessment. Control activities also can be organized into a number of taxonomies, one of which is based on their purpose and function. *Preventive controls* such as requiring two signatures on checks over $1,000 help prevent errors and irregularities from happening. *Detective controls* such as airport metal detectors help stakeholders determine when an error or irregularity has occurred. Finally, *corrective controls,* which include things like anger management courses or punishments for subverting internal controls, focus on fixing a problem, error, or irregularity after it has occurred.

A single control may serve more than one purpose in the preceding taxonomy. For example, seeing an employee lose his/her job because of consistent cash shortages that cannot be explained serves as a corrective control for one employee, but may serve as a preventive control for a co-worker. Likewise, airport metal detectors could be classified in all three categories. They help prevent dangerous items from being brought on board airplanes; they also detect such substances before they are actually brought on board. Subsequent searches and legal action help correct the problem.

The presence of information technology in an accounting information system requires a different level or set of controls, referred to as information processing controls. *General controls* apply to an entire information system or significant "chunks" of the system. They include items such as backing up data files regularly and installing virus detection and removal software. *Application controls* are associated with a specific IT application such as the accounting information system. For example, most general ledger software packages such as QuickBooks and Peachtree do not allow users to make journal entries where the debits and credits are unequal.

Reflection and Self-Assessment 4.4

Classify each of the following internal controls as preventive, detective, or corrective. Justify your responses, particularly when a single control can fulfill more than one category.

1. Reconciling a bank statement.
2. Requiring that all purchase requisitions are coordinated through a central purchasing department.
3. Separating the inventory ordering function from the inventory receiving function.
4. Encouraging employees to attend annual seminars on ethical behavior in the workplace and related topics.
5. Conducting surprise counts of cash on hand in a bank teller's cash drawer.
6. Tearing ticket stubs in half at a movie theater when a patron enters.
7. Collecting cash at one window and delivering the order in a different window at a fast food establishment.
8. Enforcing a policy of changing passwords every six months.
9. Locking doors and filing cabinets containing sensitive and valuable equipment and information.
10. Installing an alarm and fire suppression system.

Information and communication is the fourth component of COSO's integrated framework. For an internal control system to function effectively, its purpose, methods, and results must be communicated throughout the organization. Employees at all levels should understand the risk exposures they face and the controls employed to mitigate those exposures. They should be able to articulate how their position "fits into" the overall organizational structure and how the work they do every day contributes to fulfilling the objectives of sound internal control: safeguarding assets, ensuring financial statement reliability, promoting operational efficiency, and encouraging compliance with management's directives. Communicating information throughout the organization is a daunting task, particularly in large, decentralized, geographically dispersed organizations. Newsletters, seminars, individual or small group conferences, and focus groups can be used effectively to fulfill this important element of the integrated framework.

Finally, managers must determine the quality of internal control performance, a process known as *monitoring*. As noted previously, SOX mandates internal control monitoring and personal certification by the CEO and CFO of the organization. Companies' objectives and business processes change over time, so the monitoring function is an important part of maintaining good internal control. Monitoring systems can be automated, but many involve human interaction. For example, a company could monitor the number of customer compliments and complaints it receives. Managers, accountants, and/or internal auditors could keep records of the number and estimated dollar cost of internal control breaches. The accounting information system, if properly designed, also can produce reports of internal control costs by category or by type of risk. In a perfect world, internal control monitoring is seen as a formative process, not a summative one. In other words, the results of monitoring should be used to guide employee behavior, as opposed to being used to "whack employees over the head" for small violations of internal control policies.

In 2004, COSO produced a second major document related to internal control: **Enterprise Risk Management: Integrated Framework**. According to the COSO Web site, "the framework defines essential ERM components, discusses key ERM principles and concepts, suggests a common ERM language, and provides clear direction and guidance for enterprise risk management."

According to COSO:

The framework's executive summary is available at www.coso.org/Publications/ERM/COSO_ERM_ExectiveSummary.pdf.

> Enterprise risk management is a process, effected by an entity's board of directors, management and other personnel, applied in strategy setting and across the enterprise, designed to identify potential events that may affect the entity, and manage risk to be within its risk appetite, to provide reasonable assurance regarding the achievement of entity objectives.

Notice that the definition of ERM mentions entity objectives. COSO discusses five categories of objectives for most organizations: strategic, operations, reporting, compliance, and safeguarding of resources. The objectives and categories overlap, of course; also, not all categories are always under the direct control of management. Strategic and operations objectives, for example, can be profoundly influenced by political and economic events around the world.

Whereas the integrated framework for internal control had five components, the ERM framework has eight, as shown in Figure 4.3. Like the five elements of the internal control framework, the eight ERM elements are intimately linked to one another. Here's the way COSO describes them in the executive summary of the ERM documents:

> **Internal Environment**—The internal environment encompasses the tone of an organization, and sets the basis for how risk is viewed and addressed by an entity's people, including risk management philosophy and risk appetite, integrity and ethical values, and the environment in which they operate.
>
> **Objective Setting**—Objectives must exist before management can identify potential events affecting their achievement. Enterprise risk management ensures that management has in place a process to set objectives and that the chosen objectives support and align with the entity's mission and are consistent with its risk appetite.
>
> **Event Identification**—Internal and external events affecting achievement of an entity's objectives must be identified, distinguishing between risks and opportunities. Opportunities are channeled back to management's strategy or objective-setting processes.

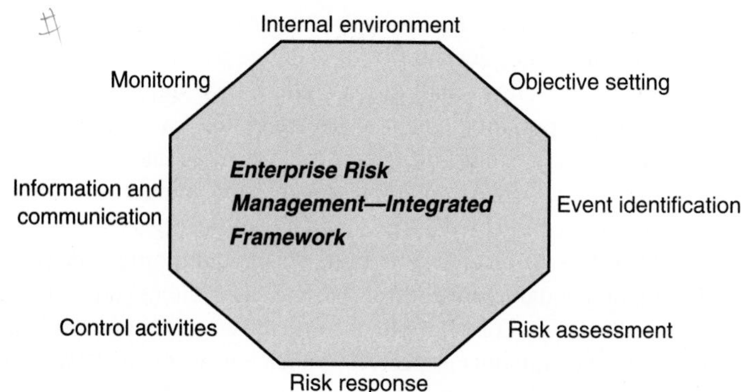

FIGURE 4.3 Enterprise Risk Management Framework

Risk Assessment—Risks are analyzed, considering likelihood and impact, as a basis for determining how they should be managed. Risks are assessed on an inherent and a residual basis.

Risk Response—Management selects risk responses—avoiding, accepting, reducing, or sharing risk—developing a set of actions to align risks with the entity's risk tolerances and risk appetite.

Control Activities—Policies and procedures are established and implemented to help ensure the risk responses are effectively carried out.

Information and Communication—Relevant information is identified, captured, and communicated in a form and timeframe that enable people to carry out their responsibilities. Effective communication also occurs in a broader sense, flowing down, across, and up the entity.

Monitoring—The entirety of enterprise risk management is monitored and modifications made as necessary. Monitoring is accomplished through ongoing management activities, separate evaluations, or both.

The objectives (strategic, operations, reporting, compliance, and safeguarding assets) represent what the organization is trying to accomplish. The eight components of the enterprise risk management framework help managers formulate plans for accomplishment.

In 2006, COSO published *Internal Control over Financial Reporting—Guidance for Smaller Public Companies.* When SOX was passed in 2002, many companies complained about its implementation cost—particularly smaller companies. That late COSO document recognizes that smaller organizations face some unique challenges with respect to internal control, including (COSO, 2006)

- *Resources.* Obtaining sufficient resources to achieve adequate segregation of duties.
- *Management Domination.* Management's ability to dominate activities and significant opportunities for improper management override of processes. This could result in the appearance that business performance goals have been met, when in fact, they have not.
- *Board Expertise.* Recruiting individuals with requisite financial reporting and other expertise to serve effectively on the board of directors and audit committee.
- *Financial Competence.* Recruiting and retaining personnel with sufficient experience and skill in accounting and financial reporting.
- *Running the Business.* Taking critical management attention away from running the business in order to provide sufficient focus on accounting and financial reporting.
- *Information Technology.* Controlling information technology and maintaining appropriate general and application controls over computer information systems with limited technical resources.

The 2006 document lists and discusses 20 basic principles to help smaller organizations achieve strong, effective internal control. In 2009, COSO released "Guidance on Monitoring Internal Control Systems," which focuses on the final element of the ERM framework. You can obtain executive summaries of both the 2006 and 2009 documents on the COSO Web site.

Reflection and Self-Assessment 4.5

Compare (explain similarities) and contrast (explain differences) the integrated frameworks for internal control and enterprise risk management. Do managers need both frameworks? Why, or why not? Explain why the frameworks are important to you as an accounting professional.

Next, we'll turn our attention to a discussion of some common internal control procedures.

INTERNAL CONTROL EXAMPLES

Internal control systems are as unique and different as the organizations and managers that utilize them. But some internal controls are so common that they merit a closer look. While the list below does not represent the "universe" of internal controls, it does give you an introduction to some you're likely to encounter in practice. (The items are listed in alphabetical order so you can refer to them easily later.)

1. *Adequate documentation.* Understanding how things are supposed to happen in an accounting information system is an important first step in designing and assessing internal controls. Process documentation, often in the form of flowcharts (Chapter 5) and/or data flow diagrams (Chapter 6), can help you critique internal controls and determine if they are functioning effectively.
2. *Background checks.* People are the heart of most organizations today. Particularly for employees in sensitive positions, such as those that deal with large amounts of money, background checks are essential. For example, they may reveal financial difficulties or criminal convictions that may create pressure to breach internal controls.
3. *Backup of computer files.* If done regularly, backing up computer files takes only a few minutes—a small inconvenience compared to the alternative of recreating files from scratch. Daily backups ensure that no more than one day's work is lost in the event of a systems failure.
4. *Backup of power supplies.* A few years ago, California was subject to power blackouts when the state's electrical grid was overloaded. During that time, backup power supplies were commonly employed as an internal control. While a computer cannot run indefinitely on a backup power supply, the backup supply can give the user time to save any open files, ensuring they are not lost.
5. *Bank reconciliation.* You probably learned how to reconcile a bank statement in your introductory accounting course. The basic purpose of a bank reconciliation is to account for timing differences between the account holder's records and the bank's records of a cash account. Reconciling the bank statement at least monthly can be helpful in spotting out-of-sequence checks, fraudulent signatures, and errors in the information system.

6. *Batch control totals.* When an accounting information system is processing a group (batch) of documents, users can calculate various control totals to promote data integrity. For example, you could add up the invoice numbers for a group of sales invoices. Would the total have any meaning in the AIS? Probably not. But, as the invoices move through the AIS, the total should remain the same.
7. *Data encryption.* In today's world of wireless networks, data encryption is critically important. Without it, hackers and other computer criminals can easily access, change, and/or steal data, compromising data integrity and privacy throughout the accounting information system.
8. *Document matching.* Whether electronic or paper-based, document matching helps ensure that vendor invoices are only paid when merchandise has been properly ordered and invoiced. The purchasing department would send a copy of all purchase orders to the accounting department; the receiving department would likewise send a copy of the receiving report. Then, when the vendor mails the invoice, an accountant will match the three documents before initiating payment. In practice, we often use the term "three-way match" to describe such an arrangement.
9. *Edit checks.* You've seen edit checks in operation if you've ever purchased books or airline tickets online. The information system "echoes" the data you've entered back to you before it completes final processing. That process allows you to edit the data for any errors or other changes.
10. *Firewalls.* Along with data encryption, a firewall is an important element of AIS security—particularly in a wireless environment. Firewalls are also useful in wired environments. They can prevent unauthorized intrusions into an accounting information system and warn users when such intrusions are detected.
11. *Insurance and bonding.* While insurance and bonding cannot prevent internal control breaches, they can help organizations correct any financial losses they experience as a result. If you've ever hired contractors to work in your home, they were probably bonded. Companies often bond key employees as a safeguard against error and/or fraud.
12. *Internal audits.* We'll look more closely at audits, including internal audits, in the last chapter of the text; your university may even offer a course in internal auditing. Internal audits can reveal indications of fraud, waste, and inefficiency, thus strengthening internal control.
13. *Limit checks.* An accounting information system can incorporate various kinds of limit checks; for example, if a manager is authorized for purchases less than $1,000, a limit check can ensure that the manager doesn't violate the limit for a specific transaction. Most general ledger packages limit transaction dates to the current year; they don't allow users to pre- or post-date transactions.
14. *Lockbox systems.* Lockbox systems help promote strong internal control over cash. Rather than remitting payment directly to an organization, customers send their payment to a lockbox. An independent company, for a fee, monitors the lockbox and deposits cash receipts daily in the bank.
15. *Physical security.* Internal control doesn't have to be extraordinarily sophisticated. Simple actions such as locking doors and securing computers and related equipment can go a long way in safeguarding assets.
16. *Preformatted data entry screens.* Remember that one of the purposes of internal control is promoting operating efficiency. Using preformatted data entry screens for things like customer orders and cash disbursement processing greatly improves data entry efficiency.

17. *Prenumbered documents.* Checks, purchase orders, sales invoices, and other documents should be prenumbered to promote strong internal control. If an accounting information system is automated, the numbers may be assigned using an "auto numbering" function. A seriously out-of-sequence document (such as a check numbered in the 400s when others are in the 100s) can be a warning sign for internal control breaches and/or fraud.
18. *Restrictive endorsement and daily deposits of checks received.* You endorse checks when you deposit them in your bank account; you may use a "blank endorsement," which means your signature alone. Here's the problem: blank endorsements weaken internal control. An unethical person with a fake ID can easily cash such a check at the bank. Restrictive endorsements give the bank more specific instructions that limit the uses of the endorsed check; the most common is "for deposit only," often with an account number included. In addition, all cash receipts (coin, currency, and checks) should be deposited daily in the bank to keep them secure.
19. *Segregation of duties.* Although all of the controls in this list are important, segregation of duties may be the most important of all. Basically, segregation of duties means that, to the extent possible, three different people should each take on one responsibility with respect to a specific asset: authorization for use, physical custody, and recordkeeping. Consider cash, for example: physical custody rests with the bank, while authorization for use is vested with signatories on the account. Recordkeeping refers to both journal entries and bank reconciliations. So, for example, someone authorized to sign checks should not reconcile the bank statement. The same duties (authorization, custody, and recordkeeping) should be separated for other assets, such as inventory, plant assets, and supplies.
20. *User training.* Finally, let's consider user training. All the internal control processes in the world are virtually worthless if people don't know how to apply them. Thus, employees should receive periodic training/reminders about appropriate internal control procedures, their rationales, and the reasons they exist.

Remember: the controls we've just considered are not the sum total of available choices. They are a good beginning, but you should think creatively when designing and critiquing internal control systems—both in class and in practice. Let's conclude this chapter by looking at some ways to apply the ideas of risk management and internal control in various organizational settings.

INTERNAL CONTROL APPLICATIONS

This section of the chapter presents four vignettes illustrating various internal control strengths and weaknesses. Although the names of the individuals and companies involved have been disguised, they represent actual internal control issues in actual organizations.

Vignette #1: Internal Control over Cash

Alphabet Soup Consulting employs a staff of 50 consultants and is managed by a three-person board of directors: Robbie (president), Vicki (vice president), and Richard (treasurer). The company's bylaws specify that checks over $500 require the signatures of two directors to be valid. However, if an invoice over $500 is due and Robbie or Vicki cannot be reached, Richard frequently writes two (or more) smaller checks to cover the total amount. For example, if an invoice totals $900, Richard might write three checks for $300 each or two checks for $450 each. Richard feels justified in his actions because of increased efficiency.

Clearly, Richard's actions constitute a breach of internal controls. Recall the four basic purposes of internal control, and you'll realize that Richard is not fulfilling two of them: safeguarding assets and ensuring compliance with management directives. By implication, he also is interfering with financial statement reliability. To keep Richard from circumventing controls, Alphabet Soup Consulting could take a number of actions, including (1) restricting Richard's access to checks; (2) asking an independent third party, such as the firm's CPA, to handle check writing and bill paying; or (3) removing Richard as a signatory on the account. Each of those controls has a cost, as shown in the table below:

Control	Type	Cost
Restricting Richard's access to checks	Preventive	Decreased efficiency
Asking an independent third party to handle check writing and bill paying	Corrective	Increased monetary cost; time delays in paying bills
Removing Richard as a signatory on the account	Preventive	Extra burden on Robbie and Vicki

So what really happened in this situation? Vicki and Robbie continued to allow Richard to circumvent the company's controls. Richard had no external controls over his spending of the company's money, and Alphabet Soup Consulting eventually went out of business due to poor liquidity.

Vignette #2: Embezzling

Gary and Dan were psychologists in private practice. They employed Christina as a receptionist, and a local CPA firm to handle many (but not all) financial matters. Christina opened the mail, collected cash payments from clients, and wrote checks for Gary's or Dan's signature each month. Each month, the practice would get a bank statement in the mail; Christina was supposed to pass on the bank statement to the CPA firm for reconciliation. Unfortunately, Christina got into a personal financial dilemma. Having access to the company's checks and knowing what Gary's and Dan's signatures looked like, she began forging checks written to her husband. The checks were stored in boxes in an unlocked filing cabinet; Christina would take checks to forge from the bottom of the box so they would not be missed until much later. Additionally, although she had regularly been forwarding the bank statements to the CPA firm, the CPAs had not reconciled them for at least six months. One Saturday, Gary came into the office and noticed the bank statement sitting on Christina's desk. Thinking to save himself and his partner some money, he decided to reconcile the bank statement on his own rather than sending it to the CPA firm. He noticed the out-of-sequence checks with signatures that resembled his and Dan's but were not exactly "right." Christina had embezzled a total of $250,000 before Gary and Dan caught onto her scheme.

The preceding vignette illustrates several important internal controls for cash: sequential numbering of checks (preventive), separation of duties (check writing, check signing, and reconciliation—both preventive and detective), and sequentially numbered documents (preventive). But the system broke down when the CPAs did not do their job by balancing the checkbook monthly (a detective control). In addition, the checks were kept in an unlocked filing cabinet; the company would have achieved stronger internal control by locking up the blank checks more securely (a preventive control).

So what happened? Gary and Dan confronted Christina about her embezzlement. At first, she denied it, but later she confessed when confronted with the evidence. Gary and Dan fired her and she was prosecuted for embezzlement; the bank restored the embezzled funds into Gary and Dan's account, and they hired a new CPA firm.

Vignette #3: Information Technology

The College of Business at Southern State University has over 200 faculty and four information technology staff members. The college's e-mail is maintained on a central server; each administrator, staff member, and professor can check his/her e-mail from any computer in the world that has Internet access. When a new hire comes to work for the college, his/her e-mail password is the same as the e-mail user name. For example, if Dr. J. M. Ortiz is hired as a professor, both his user name and initial e-mail password are *jmortiz.* A small group of students figured out that connection and started hacking into faculty members' e-mail accounts for illicit purposes. David, the lead information technology staff member, therefore introduced several new policies related to e-mail security:

- *Random creation of initial passwords.* Rather than establishing the initial password as the user name, David's staff now uses a password generator to create new passwords for new hires.
- *Mandatory password changes every six months.* New passwords must contain at least six characters. The six characters must contain at least two of the following: capital letters, lowercase letters, or numbers. The passwords cannot be recycled for a period of two years. So, for example, if someone establishes a password of PhdCma1977 for six months, that password cannot be used again for two years after the six-month period ends.
- *Daily file backup.* David and his staff back up the files from the e-mail server every day.
- *Virus, spyware, and spam protection.* The e-mail server, as well as other information technology assets, is equipped with extensive software to prevent, detect, and correct those problems.

The college has experienced no significant internal control problems with information technology since those policies were instituted.

Vignette #4: Inventory

John is the purchasing manager for The Village Bookstore in Claremont, California. He monitors inventory, prepares purchase orders to send to book publishers, and receives the books when they arrive at the store. The bookstore uses a perpetual inventory system, in which inventory records in the accounting information system are updated with every purchase and sale. For example, when books are purchased, the accountant debits inventory and credits accounts payable; when books are sold, the accountant debits cost of goods sold and credits inventory. John also handles merchandise returns when books arrive in unacceptable condition. Since Village uses a perpetual inventory system, John sees no need for periodic counts of inventory—he views them as a waste of time, since the accounting information system is always up-to-date.

Possibly the biggest internal control problem for The Village Bookstore is separation of duties. To safeguard assets and ensure financial statement reliability, three important duties should be borne by different people in most organizations: (1) physical custody of an asset, (2) recordkeeping for the asset, and (3) authorization to use the asset. In this example, John has both physical custody of inventory and authorization for its use. By vesting both those important responsibilities in a single person, it becomes far too easy for John to steal books and tell the accountant they were returned to, or never received from, the publisher. In addition, although the company uses a perpetual inventory system, they still need an annual inventory to promote financial statement reliability.

Thankfully, John was a trustworthy employee. Although he had multiple opportunities to defraud The Village Bookstore, he never did so. An external consultant from a local accounting firm pointed out the bookstore's internal control weaknesses and the company corrected them before they experienced significant financial losses.

TABLE 4.1 Risk/Control Matrix for MP3 Downloads

Risk	Risk Category (Brown)	Internal Control	Internal Control Purpose	Comments
Downloading material you don't like	Human error	Listen to a song excerpt.	Preventive	Most music libraries allow you to listen to a short clip before buying a song.
	Human error	Review a song's details, such as the artist and year.	Preventive	Most songs have related data available: it's just a matter of referring to it.
Song doesn't download correctly	Systems	Get it from another source.	Corrective	You could buy a CD with the song and download it from there. Or you could look at some other online service.
Computer firewall blocks the download.	Systems	Set up firewall to allow downloads from that site.	Preventive/ corrective	If you set up the firewall in advance, this control is preventive. If it happens "after the fact," it's corrective.
No room for new music on the MP3 player.	Systems	Monitor amount of space available on MP3 player.	Detective	Most MP3 players give you a graphic display of the amount of space used and the amount of space available.
	Systems	Buy an MP3 player with more capacity.	Corrective	Of course, you'd have to consider the cost of a new player.
Credit card used for payment isn't accepted.	Credit/liquidity	Only use "gift cards" to pay for music.	Preventive	Your ability to download music, then, would depend on having a gift card available.
	Credit/liquidity	Dedicate one credit card to nothing but this kind of transaction.	Preventive/detective	Unless you download a *lot* of music, it's unlikely the card will reach its credit limit too quickly. Also, using one card for nothing but music downloads would help you detect fraudulent activity.

CRITICAL THINKING

Almost any business transaction has certain associated risks; those risks can be addressed, in many cases, by developing and implementing a few internal controls.

I was walking around my campus a few days ago and noticed the number of students carrying MP3 players of various sorts; I got my first MP3 player in 2007, and I really don't know how I lived without one for so long! As you may be aware, there are two basic ways to add content (music, movies, TV shows, and such) to an MP3 player: uploading from your personal library and downloading from the Internet. Let's think about the risks involved in downloading music from the Internet and identify some associated internal controls; once you've studied this section, you might want to complete a similar analysis for "uploading from your personal library."

To make the discussion a bit more concise and easy to read, I'm going to organize it in a simple "risk/control matrix" (see Table 4.1). Like so many AIS topics, there's no "one right way" to design a risk/control matrix; we'll look at a more detailed one later in the text, and your AIS professor probably has a preferred format as well. So I encourage you not to memorize the format of the matrix; try to stay focused on its content.

This analysis doesn't present all the risks associated with downloading music from the Internet for your MP3 player; I'm giving you a few as examples to show you a good way of thinking about the design of internal controls. I've usually found it most productive to think first about "what could go wrong" with a transaction; that is, what are its associated risks. Then, I think about how I want to handle that risk—what the COSO ERM framework would call a "risk response." And, when I've decided how I want to respond to a risk, I think about ways to enact the response. For example, I don't want to try to download a song to my MP3 player only to discover that I don't have room for it. So, that's a risk I want to try to detect before it happens. I normally do that, as the risk/control matrix points out, by keeping tabs on how much space I have available.

Notice that a specific risk can have more than one associated internal control; it's not a "one-to-one correspondence." Keep in mind, though, that internal controls aren't free—they take time, money, and energy to develop and implement. As we've discussed before, you must always strive to balance the cost of a control with the benefit you receive from it.

Summary

Here is the usual chapter summary, structured according to the learning objectives:

1. *Define* internal control *and explain its importance in the accounting information system.* Internal control refers to the ways an organization keeps its assets safe and ensures that everyone follows estabished organizational procedures. Without solid internal control in the AIS, an organization can open itself up to fraud. Weak internal controls also necessitate more extensive auditing procedures.
2. *Explain the basic purposes of internal control.* Internal control has four basic purposes: (*a*) to safeguard assets, (*b*) to ensure financial statement reliability, (*c*) to promote operational efficiency, and (*d*) to encourage compliance with management's general and specific directives.
3. *Describe and give examples of various kinds of risk exposures.* Taxonomies for classifying and describing organizational risks are numerous in the literature and in practice. Brown advanced a four-part structure: financial risk, operational risk, strategic risk, and hazard risk. Financial risks include not having sufficient cash on hand to meet short-term obligations. Operational risks concern (among other things) the possibility that people will make mistakes. Strategic risks include entering a market not aligned with organizational strategy. Hazard risks relate to fraud and errors committed by the board of directors and/or company management.

4. *Conduct a comprehensive risk assessment.* A risk assessment uses some taxonomy of risk, such as Brown's, to assess the ways a company is exposed to risk. Human judgment and dialogue are integral parts of a risk assessment; business experience is also vital.
5. *Summarize and explain the importance of the COSO documents on internal control.* The Committee of Sponsoring Organizations of the Treadway Commission (COSO) published two documents related to internal control. The first, *Internal Control: Integrated Framework,* has five parts: control environment, risk assessment, control activities, monitoring, and information and communication. The second, *Enterprise Risk Management: Integrated Framework,* comprises eight sections: internal environment, objective setting, event identification, risk assessment, risk response, control activities, information and communication, and monitoring. Both documents give managers comprehensive guidance on risk management and internal control.
6. *Critique existing internal control systems and design effective internal controls.* This process starts with a comprehensive risk assessment. Managers must then consider various responses to risk, as well as the cost–benefit relationship of various internal controls. As with most issues we study in accounting information systems, the design, implementation, and evaluation of internal controls is at least as much "art" as "science." The question most managers face in most organizations is not Which internal controls are the "right" ones? but Which internal controls can I implement in a cost-effective way to provide reasonable assurance of information integrity, asset safety, and procedural compliance?

As you consider the end-of-chapter materials that follow, try not to "second guess" me or your AIS instructor; try, instead, to put yourself in each situation and come up with the most original solutions you can.

Key Terms

Brown's taxonomy of risk, *63*
COSO, *64*
Enterprise Risk Management: Integrated Framework, 67
Foreign Corrupt Practices Act, *61*
internal control, *60*
Internal Control: Integrated Framework, 65
Sarbanes-Oxley Act of 2002, *61*

Chapter References

Brown, B. 2001. "Step-by-Step Enterprise Risk Management." *Risk Management,* September, pp. 43–49.
Committee of Sponsoring Organizations of the Treadway Commission. 1985. *Internal Control: Integrated Framework.* New York: Committee of Sponsoring Organizations of the Treadway Commission.
Committee of Sponsoring Organizations of the Treadway Commission. 2004. *Enterprise Risk Management: Integrated Framework.* New York: Committee of Sponsoring Organizations of the Treadway Commission.
Committee of Sponsoring Organizations of the Treadway Commission. 2006. *Internal Control over Financial Reporting—Guidance for Smaller Public Companies.* New York: Committee of Sponsoring Organizations of the Treadway Commission.
Hollander, A. S., E. L. Denna, and J. O. Cherrington. 2000. *Accounting, Information Technology, and Business Solutions.* 2nd ed. New York: Irwin/McGraw-Hill.
Lander, G. 2004. *What Is Sarbanes-Oxley?* New York: McGraw-Hill.
New York State Office of the State Comptroller. 2004. *Standards for Internal Control in New York State Government.* *www.osc.state.ny.us/audits/audits/controls/standards.htm* (October 18, 2004).

End-of-Chapter Activities

1. *Reading review questions.*
   a. What is internal control? Why is internal control important in organizations?
   b. What are the four basic purposes of internal control? Give an example of each one.
   c. List and discuss four broad categories of organizational risk exposures. For each broad category, suggest two examples.
   d. What is COSO? Why is the work of COSO important in internal control?
   e. Prepare a response to the questions for this chapter's "AIS in the Business World."
2. *Reading review problem.* Consider the following account of the WorldCom fraud (Caron Carlson, "MCI WorldCom Suspended from New Government Contracts," *eWeek,* July 2003, www.findarticles.com (October 12, 2004)):

   > In July 2003, the federal government suspected MCI WorldCom Corp. from any new federal contracts and proposed debarring the company from future contracts altogether. The proposed debarment came one day after federal lawmakers demanded to see records of its call-routing patterns.
   >
   > The General Services Administration, which had been reviewing the WorldCom bankruptcy, announced that it found that the company lacks adequate internal controls and business ethics to meet standards for government contracts. The government was WorldCom's largest customer; it awarded the company large deals even after its wrong-doing was uncovered, including a $45 million contract to operate in post-war Iraq.
   >
   > WorldCom Chairman and CEO Michael Capellas said he was not surprised by the proposed debarment. "We know what is required of us [relative] to the internal controls work," Capellas said. "When interviewed [by GSA], we stated the facts, when they were good, when they were bad. We knew [the proposed debarment] was a possibility, and we respect it.

   WorldCom was eventually acquired by Verizon in December 2005.
   a. What does it mean to say that WorldCom lacked "adequate internal controls"?
   b. How does the risk described in the article relate to Brown's taxonomy of risk?
   c. What internal controls may have helped WorldCom to avoid its bankruptcy and/or the problem described in the article?
3. *Making choices and exercising judgment.*
   a. Consider the four vignettes presented in the last section of the chapter. For each one, suggest one additional internal control procedure. Discuss whether the procedure you suggest is preventive, detective, or corrective; also identify the type of risk it is designed to control based on the risk categories discussed in the chapter.
   b. Hassan and Ashok are employed by one of the Big Four CPA firms. Both have recently earned their CPA licenses, however, and are considering starting their own practice. Using Brown's risk taxonomy, identify and describe at least five risks Hassan and Ashok must be aware of if they start their own business. For each risk you identify, suggest one or more internal controls that could ameliorate it.
4. *Field exercises.*
   a. Through observation and/or interview, collect information about internal control over inventory from a local retail establishment such as a bookstore, coffee shop, or discount store. How does the information you collected about processes, procedures, and documents align with the information presented in the chapter?
   b. Read the articles listed below about actual internal control breaches. In each case, suggest at least two internal controls the company needs to institute.
      i. D. Ibison, L. Saigol, and D. Wells, "Citigroup Apologizes for Illegal Activities in Japan," *Financial Times,* October 26, 2004.
      ii. "Hooper Holmes Concludes A.udit Committee Investigation," *PR Newswire,* October 25, 2004.
      iii. "Fitch Comments on Spitzer Probe of U.S. Insurance Industry," *Business Wire,* October 18, 2004.

c. Point your Web browser to the COSO Web site (www.coso.org). Find the executive summary for *Internal Control over Financial Reporting—Guidance for Smaller Public Companies.* List the 20 principles the document offers as guidance.

5. Internal control has four basic purposes: safeguarding assets, ensuring financial statement reliability, promoting operational efficiency, and encouraging compliance with management's directives. Consider each of the internal control procedures described below. For each procedure, indicate which purpose(s) of internal control it is designed to address.

a. Conducting surprise cash counts.
b. Creating a policy manual.
c. Creating separate departments for purchasing inventory and receiving inventory.
d. Deleting an employee's computer account when the employee retires or is fired.
e. Employing internal auditors.
f. Installing virus cleaning software on all computers.
g. Locking filing cabinets with sensitive documents.
h. Performing background checks on employees.
i. Reconciling the bank statement monthly.
j. Requiring all management employees to take annual vacations.

6. Extreme Canines is "America's favorite celebrity stunt dog show." Their Web site is www.extremecanines.com. Examine the company's Web site and then consider the operational risks listed below. How would each risk be classified using Brown's taxonomy? Justify your responses.

a. The sole supplier of dog food to the company goes out of business.
b. The dogs' kennels are not kept clean.
c. The dogs do not receive the proper vaccinations and immunizations.
d. The company's Web site is temporarily unavailable due to a natural disaster.
e. One of the dogs is injured en route to a performance.
f. Interest rates rise on a company line of credit.
g. Extreme Canines' accountants calculate the company's tax liability incorrectly.
h. Dogs fail to perform tricks correctly in a show.
i. Customers are unable or unwilling to pay for an Extreme Canines show.
j. A new dog bites an audience member.

7. For each risk listed in the preceding problem, suggest one or more internal controls Extreme Canines could institute. Classify each control as preventive, detective, or corrective in nature.

8. The Vermont Teddy Bear Company (www.vtbear.com) works with customers to design custom teddy bears. The bears are individually built and assembled in Vermont, and then are sent out to gift recipients all over the world. The company's mission is "to make the world a better place—one Bear at a time." Consult the company's Web site for information about its operations, philosophy, and history. Then respond to each of the following requirements as directed by your instructor:

a. Conduct a comprehensive risk assessment using the COSO *Internal Control: Integrated Framework.* Your output could be a PowerPoint presentation, a written report, a Web page, or some other form. Consider the following questions as a guide:

   i. How would you describe the control environment at VTB?
   ii. What risks does the company face?
   iii. What control activities would you advise to mitigate the risks?
   iv. How does VTB management communicate with its employees, stockholders, and the public? What additional communication tools would you recommend?

v. How has VTB responded to the Sarbanes-Oxley requirements for internal control monitoring?

vi. Overall, does VTB have a sound, comprehensive internal control structure?

b. Conduct a similar analysis for NetFlix, an online DVD rental service. You can find information about NetFlix at www.netflix.com.

9. (CMA adapted, December 1992) In each of the following independent situations, identify internal control deficiencies and make suggestions regarding their correction/improvement.

a. Many employees of a firm that manufactures small tools pocket some of these tools for their personal use. Since the quantities taken by any one employee were immaterial, the individual employees did not consider the act as fraudulent or detrimental to the company. As the company grew larger, an internal auditor was hired. The auditor charted the gross profit percentages for particular tools and discovered higher gross profit rates for tools related to industrial use than for personal use. Subsequent investigation uncovered the fraudulent acts.

b. A company controller set up a fictitious subsidiary office to which he shipped inventories and then approved the invoice for payment. The inventories were sold and the proceeds deposited to the controller's personal bank account. Internal auditors suspected fraud when auditing the plant's real estate assets. They traced plant real estate descriptions to the assets owned and leased and could not find a title or lease for the location of this particular subsidiary.

c. The manager of a large department was able to embezzle funds from his employer by carrying employees on the payroll beyond actual termination dates. The manager carried each terminated employee for only one pay period beyond the termination date so the employee would not easily detect the additional amount included on the W-2 reporting of wages to the Internal Revenue Service. The paymaster regularly delivered all checks to the department manager, who then deposited the fraudulent checks to a personal checking account. An internal auditor discovered the fraud from a routine tracing of sample entries in the payroll register to the employees' files in the personnel office. The sample included one employee's pay record whose personnel file showed the termination date prior to the pay period audited. The auditor investigated further and discovered other such fraudulent checks.

10. (CMA adapted, June 1994) MailMed Inc. (MMI), a pharmaceutical firm, provides discounted prescription drugs through direct mail. MMI has a small systems staff that designs and writes MMI's customized software. Until recently, MMI's transaction data were transmitted to a third party for processing on their hardware.

MMI has experienced significant sales growth as the cost of prescription drugs has increased and medical insurance companies have been tightening reimbursements in order to restrain premium cost increases. As a result of these increased sales, MMI has purchased its own computer hardware. The computer center is installed on the ground floor of its two-story headquarters building. It is behind large plate-glass windows so that the state-of-the-art computer center can be displayed as a measure of the company's success, attracting customer and investor attention. The computer area is equipped with high-tech fire suppression equipment and backup power supplies.

MMI has hired a small computer operations staff to operate the computer center. To handle the current level of business, the operations staff is on a two-shift schedule, five days per week. MMI's systems and programming staff, now located in the same building, have access to the computer center and can test new programs and program changes when the operations staff are not available. As the systems and programming staff are small and the work demands have increased, systems and programming documentation are developed only when time is available. Periodically, MMI backs up its programs and data files, storing them at an off-site location.

Unfortunately, due to several days of heavy rains, MMI's building recently experienced serious flooding, which reached several feet into the first floor level and affected the on-site hardware, data, and programs.

Based on the preceding narrative, describe at least two specific computer weaknesses for MMI. For each weakness you identify, suggest a way to compensate for it.

11. (CMA adapted, June 1994) Richards Furniture Company is a 15-store chain, concentrated in the southwest, that sells living room and bedroom furniture. Each store has a full-time manager and an assistant manager, who are paid on a salary basis. The cashiers and sales personnel typically work part-time and are paid an hourly wage plus a commission based on sales volume. The company uses cash registers with four-part sales invoices to record each transaction; the invoices are used regardless of the payment type (cash, check, credit card).

    On the sales floor, the salesperson manually records his/her employee number and the transaction, totals the sales invoice, calculates any appropriate discount and the sales tax, and calculates the grand total. The salesperson then gives the sales invoice to the cashier, retaining one copy in the sales book.

    The cashier reviews the invoice and inputs the sale into the cash register. The cash register automatically assigns a consecutive number to each transaction. The cashier is also responsible for obtaining credit authorization approval on credit card sales and approving sales paid by check. The cashier gives one copy of the invoice to the customer and retains the second copy as the store copy. Returns are handled in exactly the reverse manner with the cashier issuing a return slip when necessary.

    At the end of each day, the cashier sequentially orders the sales invoices and provides cash register totals for cash, credit card, and check sales, as well as cash and credit card returns. These totals are reconciled by the assistant manager to the cash register tapes, the total of the consecutively numbered sales invoices, and the return slips. The assistant manager prepares a daily reconciled report for the store manager's review.

    Cash sales, check sales, and credit card sales are reviewed by the manager, who then prepares the daily bank deposit. The manager physically deposits these at the bank and files the validated deposit slip. At the end of the month, the manager performs the bank reconciliation. The cash register tapes, sales invoices, return slips, and reconciled report are then forwarded daily to the central Data Entry Department at corporate headquarters for processing. The Data Entry Department returns a weekly Sales and Commission Activity Report to the manager for review.

    Please respond to the following questions about Richards Furniture Company's operations based on the preceding narrative:

    a. What risks does Richards face?
    b. If you were an unethical customer and/or employee of Richards, how could you defraud the company given their current procedures?
    c. What internal control strengths does the company possess? What risks are those strengths designed to address?
    d. How could internal control be improved at Richards?

12. (CMA adapted, June 1993) PriceRight Electronics Inc. (PEI) is a wholesale discount supplier of a wide variety of electronic instruments and parts to regional retailers. PEI commenced operations a year ago, and its records processing has been on a manual basis except for stand-alone automated inventory and accounts receivable systems. The driving force of PEI's business is its deep-discount, short-term delivery reputation that allows retailers to order materials several times during the month to minimize in-store inventories. PEI's management has decided to continue automating its operations, but, because of cash flow considerations, this needs to be accomplished on a step-by-step basis.

It was decided that the next function to be automated should be sales order processing to enhance quick response to customer needs. PEI's systems consultants suggested and implemented an off-the-shelf software package that was modified to fit PEI's current mode of operations. At the same time, the consultants recommended and installed a computerized database of customer credit standings to permit automatic credit limit checks as the lingering recessionary climate has resulted in an increase in slow paying or delinquent accounts. The new systems modules are described below:

Marketing. Sales orders are received by telephone, fax, mail, or e-mail and entered into the sales order system by marketing personnel. The orders are automatically compared to the customer database for determination of credit limits. If credit limits are met, the system generates multiple copies of the sales order.

Credit. On a daily basis, the credit manager reviews new customer applications for creditworthiness, establishes credit limits, and enters them into the customer database. The credit manager also reviews the calendar month-end accounts receivable aging report to identify slow-paying or delinquent accounts for potential revisions to or discontinuance of credit. In addition, the credit manager issues credit memos for merchandise returns based on requests from customers and forwards copies of credit memos to Accounting for appropriate accounts receivable handling.

Warehousing. Warehouse personnel update the inventory master file for purchases and disbursements, confirm availability of materials to fill sales orders, and establish back-orders for sales orders that cannot be completed from stock on hand. Warehouse personnel assemble and forward materials with corresponding sales orders to Shipping and Receiving. They also update the inventory master file for merchandise returns that are received by Shipping and Receiving.

Shipping and Receiving: Shipping and Receiving accepts materials and sales orders from Warehousing, packs and ships the order with a copy of the sales order as a packing slip, and forwards a copy of the sales order to Billing. Merchandise returns received from customers are unpacked, sorted, inspected, and sent to Warehousing.

Accounting. The Accounting Department comprises three functions relevant to this narrative: Billing, Accounts Receivable, and General Accounting. Billing prices all sales orders received, which takes approximately five days after order shipment. To spread the work effort throughout the month, customers are segregated and placed in 30-day billing cycles. There are six billing cycles for which invoices are rendered during the month. Monthly statements, prepared by Billing, are sent to customers during the cycle billing period. Outstanding carry-forward balances reported by Accounts Receivable and credit memos prepared based on credit requests received from the credit manager are included on the monthly statement. Billing also prepares sales and credit memo journals for each cycle.

Copies of invoices and credit memos are forwarded to Accounts Receivable for entry into the accounts receivable system by customer account. An aging report is prepared at the end of each billing cycle and forwarded to the credit manager.

The accounts receivable journal reflecting total charges and credits processed through the accounts receivable system for each cycle is forwarded to General Accounting. General Accounting compares this information to the sales and credit memo journals and posts the changes to the general ledger.

Based on the preceding narrative:

a. Identify at least two internal control strengths of PEI's system. Indicate why each is a strength.

b. Identify at least three internal control weaknesses in PEI's system. Explain the nature of each weakness and recommend a way to address it.

13. *Crossword puzzle.* Please complete the puzzle below using terminology from the chapter.

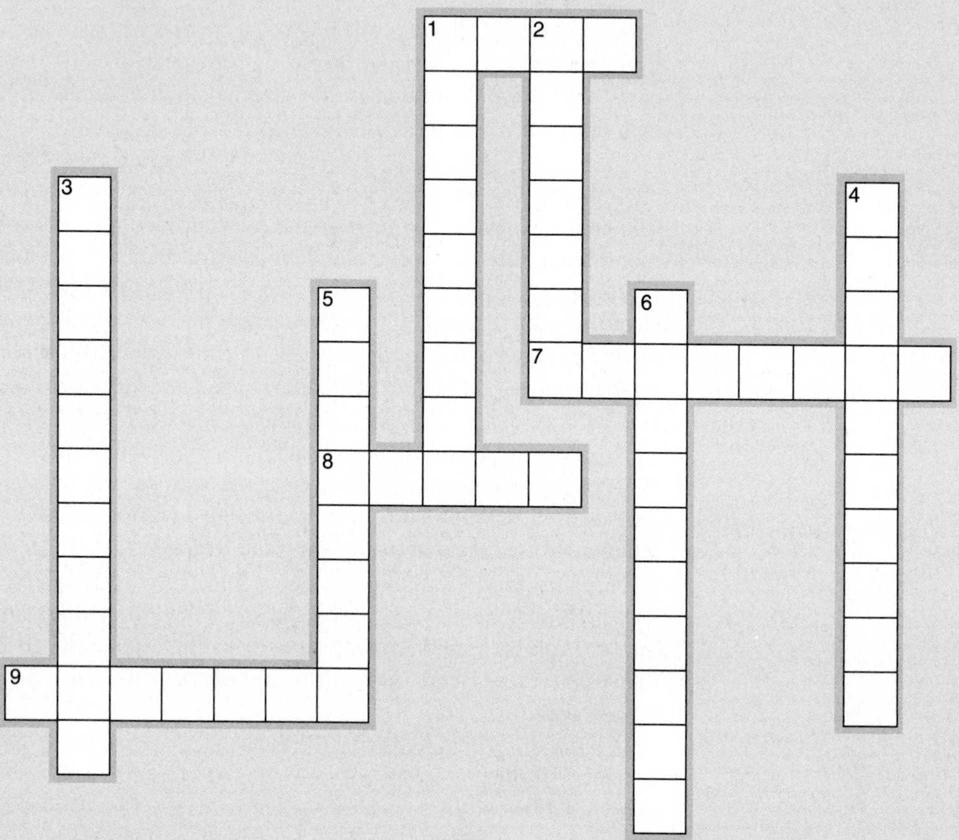

Across

1. 1977 legislation that dealt with internal control.
7. One author of SOX.
8. One author of SOX.
9. Personal _______: a commitment to values and principles.

Down

1. Risk category that includes market risk.
2. Internal control is a _______.
3. Risk category that includes systems risk.
4. Adjective that describes both COSO frameworks.
5. A way of organizing knowledge.
6. Separation of duties is this type of control.

14. *Terminology.* Please match each item on the right with the best item on the left.

1. Avoiding, accepting, reducing, sharing	a. 1977 legislation
2. Foreign Corrupt Practices Act	b. 2002 legislation
3. General controls	c. Apply to a broad range of IT applications
4. Legal and regulatory	d. Internal control example
5. Liquidity	e. A group that offers advice about internal control and enterprise risk management
6. Reasonable assurance	f. Organizational risk example
7. Sarbanes-Oxley Act	g. Risk responses
8. Separation of duties	h. Strategic risk category
9. Systems	i. Type of financial risk
10. COSO	j. What internal controls provide

15. *Multiple choice questions.*

1. Who bears the primary responsibility for establishing and maintaining a sound internal control system in an organization?
   a. Accountants
   b. External auditors
   c. Management
   d. Board of directors
2. Internal controls are designed to
   a. Eliminate risk.
   b. Ensure accurate financial reporting.
   c. Detect fraud.
   d. Provide reasonable assurance.
3. Which of the following is not an element of *Internal Control: Integrated Framework?*
   a. Committee of sponsoring organizations
   b. Control environment
   c. Risk assessment
   d. Monitoring
4. Which of the following statements is not true?
   a. The Sarbanes-Oxley Act requires CEOs to personally attest to the adequacy of internal controls.
   b. The Foreign Corrupt Practices Act predates the Sarbanes-Oxley Act.
   c. A CFO can delegate attestation responsibility for internal controls to a lower-level manager under the provisions of Sarbanes-Oxley.
   d. Managers who violate the Foreign Corrupt Practices Act are subject to both fines and imprisonment.
5. "Risk appetite" is most closely associated with
   a. *Enterprise Risk Management: Integrated Framework.*
   b. Brown's taxonomy of risk.
   c. Sarbanes-Oxley.
   d. Detective internal controls.
6. How are internal controls related to the FASB conceptual framework?
   a. Internal controls ensure that financial statements are true.
   b. Internal controls help fulfill the qualitative characteristics of accounting information.
   c. If internal controls are strong, independent audits to ensure compliance with the conceptual framework are unnecessary.
   d. All of the above are true.

7. The simplest way to secure computer hardware is
   a. Conduct employee background checks.
   b. Complete an annual physical inventory.
   c. Lock and alarm the doors where computer equipment is stored.
   d. Purchase replacement insurance.
8. Which of the following organizations is not a part of COSO?
   a. American Institute of CPAs
   b. Securities & Exchange Commission
   c. American Accounting Association
   d. Institute of Management Accountants
9. Risk responses in COSO's ERM framework include all of the following except
   a. Avoid.
   b. Reduce.
   c. Share.
   d. Eliminate.
10. Enron, WorldCom, and other corporate scandals of the late 20th century were the primary impetus for
    a. Internal auditing.
    b. Foreign Corrupt Practices Act.
    c. *Enterprise Risk Management: Integrated Framework.*
    d. Sarbanes-Oxley Act.

16. *Statement evaluation.* Indicate whether each of the following statements is (i) always true, (ii) sometimes true, or (iii) never true. For those that are (ii) sometimes true, explain when the statement is true.

a. Audits are less time consuming and less expensive in organizations with strong internal control systems.
b. Document matching concepts can be applied to purchases of and payments for office supplies.
c. In companies with strong internal control, only one person has the authority to sign checks.
d. In the ERM framework, risk can be residual or inherent.
e. Information technology eliminates the need for internal control systems.
f. Internal controls prevent fraud.
g. Liquidity risk is more important than other types of risk.
h. Preventive controls are more expensive than detective or corrective controls.
i. Properly implemented lockbox systems eliminate the need for bank reconciliations.
j. Reported weaknesses in internal control will lead to reductions in stock prices.

Documentation Techniques

Part One presented some fundamental ideas about accounting information systems: their nature, the accounting cycle, professionalism and ethics, and internal controls. In Part Two, we'll look at ways to document the AIS. Systems documentation is an important part of auditing; in addition, you'll need to be able to prepare and interpret graphic representations of the AIS. This section discusses three techniques: flowcharting, data flow diagramming, and REAL modeling. Depending on your work environment and the task at hand, you may be called upon to use any one (or more) of the three.

WHY DO WE CARE ABOUT DOCUMENTATION TECHNIQUES

Documentation provides accountants a visual method to help understand processes and procedures, identify internal control weaknesses, and improve the efficiency of the company's accounting systems and business operations. Without documentation, confusion would exist in the firm because of uncertainty and inconsistency in how individual jobs should be done. This confusion would increase the number of mistakes and decrease the timeliness of the accounting transactions, thereby increasing the difficulties of all accountants' jobs and making their lives miserable.

Documentation also provides institutional memory—the collection of documentation because if the only person who knows how to do the task leaves, the company has to recreate the process from scratch. Institutional memory is a collective of facts and experiences held by a group of people.

Take the example of the JM Smucker Company (www.smuckers.com) as they prepared to launch a new product: Smuckers Uncrustables. (You can read about Uncrustables under the "Products/Sandwiches" heading on the Web site.) Smuckers built a new facility that only produces the Uncrustables sandwiches. The controller for this new, built-from-scratch site implemented policies and procedures for the employees of the site to follow, ranging from the handling of raw materials to the recording of product costs. But what would have happened if he left the firm prior to the documentation of the newly implemented policies and procedures? Most likely it would have a significant impact on the new controller as he/she inefficiently gains an understanding of the operations and cause confusion in operating policies and procedures.

Flowcharting

AIS in the Business World

Using Flowcharts for SOX Compliance

As you read in Chapter 4, the Sarbanes-Oxley Act of 2002 (SOX) was a reaction to the corporate accounting scandals of the late 20th century. In discussing some of the positive results of SOX, Harrington stated:

> Companies can find additional uses for Sarbanes-Oxley documentation as a tool for audit committees, a way to enhance employee decisions based on cross-function process information and a means of increasing efficiencies by eliminating duplicate controls. Alltel Corporation (www.alltel.com) documented 100 company processes within the scope of [SOX]. Alltel's internal audit team reports to the company's audit committee. Its process documentation includes six flowcharts per process, supported by memos and narratives. The audit committee can use this information to support its decisions.

She concluded her article with these summary comments:

> CPAs can use the documentation to provide audit committees with more detailed information, to empower all employees to consider cross-functional processes and to lead the entire company in using section-404-type documentation. Since there is no way to avoid the cost, might just as well find ways to spread the expenditures over this greater array of benefits.

So, flowcharts aren't just something you study in AIS class. In fact, in a survey conducted by Bradford, Richtermeyer, and Roberts, nearly half of the respondents reported using flowcharts to document accounting information systems.

Discussion Questions

1. What is "cross-function process information"? Why is it important in business?
2. What is the role of an "audit committee"? How might an audit committee use a flowchart?
3. How can a well-prepared flowchart promote good decision making?

Sources: Cynthia Harrington, "The Value Proposition," *Journal of Accountancy* (September 2005), pp. 77—81; Marianne Bradford, Sandra B. Richtermeyer, and Douglas F. Roberts, "System Diagramming Techniques: An Analysis of Methods Used in Accounting Education and Practice," *Journal of Information Systems* (Spring 2007), pp. 173–212.

In practice, you may often be called upon to evaluate a system's risk exposures; recommend ways to achieve stronger internal control; and/or suggest one or more ways to make a system more efficient and effective. In those situations, you'll want a way to encapsulate the essential features of an accounting information system: its documents, personnel involved, information flows, and related technologies.

When you complete your study of this chapter, you should be able to:

1. List and discuss the purpose and use of systems flowcharts, document flowcharts, program flowcharts, and hardware flowcharts.
2. Explain the basic parts of and design considerations common to all types of flowcharts.
3. Identify and describe common symbols and information technology tools used in flowcharting.
4. Discuss ways flowcharts impact the design, implementation, and evaluation of accounting information systems.
5. Create a risk/control matrix.
6. Create and interpret systems and document flowcharts.

A good flowchart is like a snapshot of an information system. It can tell you, at a glance, where information originates, who handles the information, and how it is summarized for decision making. Like most of the rest of AIS, flowcharting is at least as much art as science. The keys are to make your flowcharts as easy to read and as understandable as possible and to develop them in sufficient detail to provide an accurate picture of what's going on in an accounting information system.

FLOWCHART TYPES AND CONVENTIONS

Basically, a flowchart is a graphical representation of some part of an information system. The information system might be focused on accounting, production, human resources, or marketing; it might be related to a particular project such as launching the space shuttle or evaluating employee performance. Flowcharts have been used by information technology professionals for years to document computer programs; they also can be used to depict the hardware associated with a computer information system.

Flowcharts often are classified by their overall purpose and function:

- **Systems flowcharts** give the user a "big picture" look at an information system. Consider, for example, the process you use to register for classes each term. You use certain documents and types of information technology to select and register for classes; a systems flowchart would combine all of those resources with their related business processes.
- **Program flowcharts** show the logic associated with a computer program. As an accountant, you probably won't have much to do with program flowcharts.
- **Document flowcharts,** as you might expect, show the various documents involved in a system; they also portray the procedures performed on those documents. So, for example, a document flowchart might show your federal income tax return from the time you receive a blank form through its eventual disposition with the Internal Revenue Service.
- **Hardware flowcharts** will probably be a minor concern in your accounting career as well. They show the computers, printers, monitors, input devices, and other hardware elements associated with an information system.

Reflection and Self-Assessment 5.1

What type of flowchart would be most appropriate in each of the following situations?

1. Steps in a Visual Basic program for producing financial statements.
2. Steps associated with purchasing inventory.
3. Relationships between a central server and desktop computers.
4. Path of a sales invoice through an information system.
5. Origination, processing, and termination of a payroll check.
6. Local area network configuration.
7. Employee evaluation process.

Although two different people can look at the same business process and draw flowcharts that are significantly different, they should generally observe some very common conventions (habits) associated with good flowcharting:

1. Flowcharts should be read from top to bottom and left to right—the same way you read a page in a book. Flowcharting, though, is a highly iterative process, meaning that most folks don't "get it right" the very first time. So, the design may not proceed in such a neat and orderly fashion. But, when the final flowchart is produced, users should be able to follow it easily.
2. Flowcharts should have plenty of "white space." In other words, they shouldn't be too crowded on the page. If you're like most accounting students, you're thinking, "How do I know if it's too crowded? Is there a rule?" Well, no. Generally, if you think a flowchart looks too crowded, it probably is. In that case, it needs to be broken up into more than one page for easier reading.
3. Flowcharts should have a title. A bunch of symbols on a page can be confusing to read and evaluate if you don't know what they're trying to present. So, it's a good idea to title your flowchart based on what it represents; for example, "Systems flowchart of the employee evaluation process."
4. Flowcharts should be organized in columns that depict areas of responsibility. For example, purchasing inventory in most organizations involves departmental managers, purchasing agents, and vendors. So, a systems flowchart that shows the purchasing process would typically have three columns—one for each area of responsibility.
5. Documents involved in a business process should have a clear origin and a clear termination. They shouldn't appear "by magic" in the middle of a flowchart, nor should they disappear from the system. Also, the progress of a document should be very clear in a flowchart. For example, the blank tax form you get from the IRS should be clearly distinguished from the completed tax return you send back to them.
6. Rough drafts of flowcharts should be discussed by people involved in the process. Such discussions serve as a "reality check." They also help ensure that the flowchart is easily understood by someone other than the designer.

Adhering to those six conventions will make your flowcharts a lot easier to read and understand; they'll also be considerably more useful in the design, evaluation, and implementation of accounting information systems.

FLOWCHARTING TOOLS AND SYMBOLS

Flowcharts can be designed using a variety of tools, both high-tech and low-tech. On the low-tech end, you can draw a flowchart with paper and pencil. You also can use a flowcharting template, which includes many common flowcharting symbols. While manual methods are useful for "quick and dirty" starts at a flowchart, they can become tedious and messy over time.

You can find more information about Visio at http://support.microsoft.com/ph/2529. Check out SmartDraw on its Web page: www.smartdraw.com. It comes with a free trial that you might find useful for your AIS course.

Fortunately, numerous software programs facilitate the preparation of good flowcharts. Two programs I've found useful are **Microsoft Visio** and **SmartDraw.** Visio is part of the Microsoft Office Suite, so it interfaces fairly well with other programs such as Word, PowerPoint, and Excel. SmartDraw is an independent software program, but it also does a good job with designing all kinds of flowcharts; generally, they also can be read by Office software. Of course, you can use just about any software package that has some graphics capability to design a flowchart—even something as simple as PowerPoint! The advantage of using a program specifically designed for flowcharting, like SmartDraw or Visio, is its adherence to the flowcharting conventions discussed earlier. Additionally, flowcharting programs typically have a wider variety of flowcharting symbols in their libraries than other programs designed for different purposes.

Reflection and Self-Assessment 5.2

Point your Web browser to www.download.com. Search for flowcharting programs. Identify and describe two other programs you could use to create flowcharts.

Because flowcharts represent a kind of "universal language" in information systems design, implementation, and evaluation, they have some common symbols with specific meanings. Consider the **symbols** shown in Figure 5.1, which are just a small subset of the many symbols associated with flowcharting.

Now, let's take a look at how the symbols are put together to construct an actual flowchart.

FIGURE 5.1
Selected Flowcharting Symbols

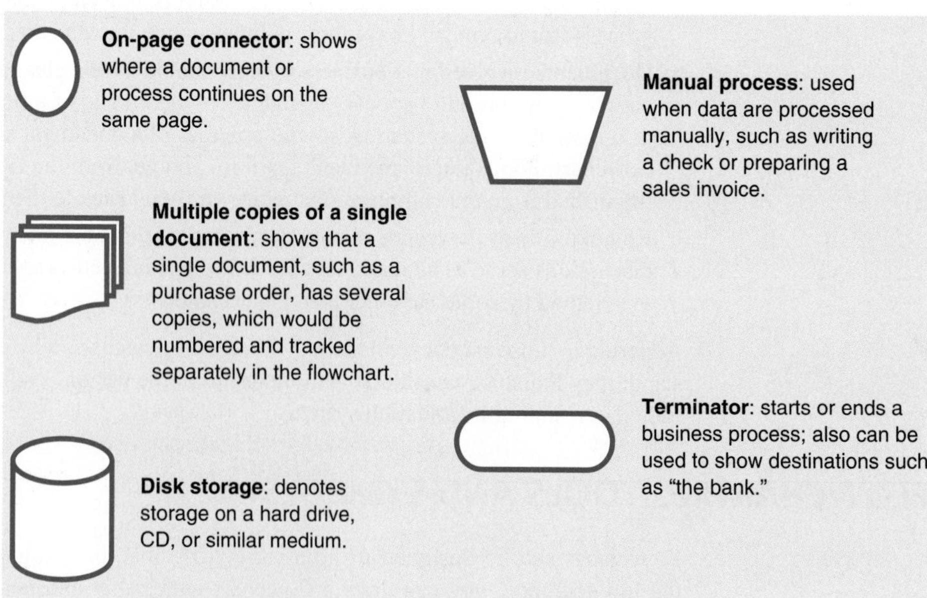

On-page connector: shows where a document or process continues on the same page.
Manual process: used when data are processed manually, such as writing a check or preparing a sales invoice.
Multiple copies of a single document: shows that a single document, such as a purchase order, has several copies, which would be numbered and tracked separately in the flowchart.
Terminator: starts or ends a business process; also can be used to show destinations such as "the bank."
Disk storage: denotes storage on a hard drive, CD, or similar medium.

Reflection and Self-Assessment 5.3

Which flowcharting symbol is used to depict each item below? Give an example as well as a description. (You'll need to do some outside research for this exercise. You could start by examining the "auto shapes" in Word or PowerPoint.)

- Annotation
- Decision
- Nonprocessed document
- Offline process
- Off-page connector
- Online computer process
- Terminal display

SAMPLE FLOWCHARTS

In this section, we'll look at two example flowcharts for common parts of an accounting information system. Carefully read and study each example. As an AIS professional, you'll need to be comfortable in "both directions" with flowcharts; that is, looking at a flowchart and describing it in narrative form *and* reading a narrative description and preparing a flowchart.

Case 1. Cori's Catering Services

Cori is the owner and manager of a catering company. CCS provides complete meals (breakfast, lunch, and dinner), as well as an assortment of hot and cold appetizers and drinks, for groups of 12 to 500. CCS receives orders in three main ways: e-mail, telephone, and personal office consultation. In some cases, the customer has an idea of what he/she wants; in others, the customer relies on Cori's expertise to select appropriate items. For each catering job, Cori prepares an estimate for the client; she files one copy of the estimate and sends the other to the client for approval. The client may make changes to the estimate over the phone, via e-mail, or through a personal consultation. Once the estimate has been finalized, Cori prepares a catering contract for the client's signature. She requires a 50 percent deposit with the signed contract; the remaining catering fees can be paid within 30 days of the catering event. Cori accepts cash and checks; she does not accept credit cards. The client signs the contract and sends it back to Cori. Cori also signs it, files a copy for her own records, and sends a copy with both signatures back to the client. Cori and her staff deliver the catering order as scheduled, and she bills the client for any remaining fees. The client pays the invoice within 30 days and Cori deposits the funds in her bank account.

The flowchart in Figure 5.2 depicts the preceding process from the client's first contact with Cori through the signing of the final contract.

Case 2. University Bookstore

Ordering textbooks in a university bookstore is a massive undertaking that requires good organizational, communication, and coordination skills. The process begins with faculty deciding which textbooks they want to use. Professors communicate relevant information about the textbook (title, author, ISBN, edition, publisher, copyright date) to a department chair or secretary, who consolidates all the orders. That communication may take place with a paper form or an e-mail. In either case, the departmental representative prepares a standard university book requisition form in triplicate: one copy for the requesting faculty member, one for the department, and one for the bookstore. The bookstore receives and consolidates requisition forms from all across the university and prepares purchase orders for textbook publishers. Each purchase order has three copies: one for the publisher, one for the purchasing department, and one for the accounting department. When the publisher sends the books, the bookstore's receiving department prepares two copies of a receiving report; one is filed to indicate that the goods were received, while the second is forwarded to the accounting department. The publisher sends a billing statement (invoice) directly to the accounting department. Once all three documents have been matched and verified, the accounting department writes a check or sends an electronic funds transfer to the publisher. The bookstore staff then sort the books based on class and stock the shelves, where the books await purchase by students.

Figure 5.3 shows a flowchart demonstrating part of the ordering process. Keep in mind that the flowcharts presented here are representative, not definitive. Two different systems analysts

FIGURE 5.2 Partial Flowchart for Cori's Catering Services

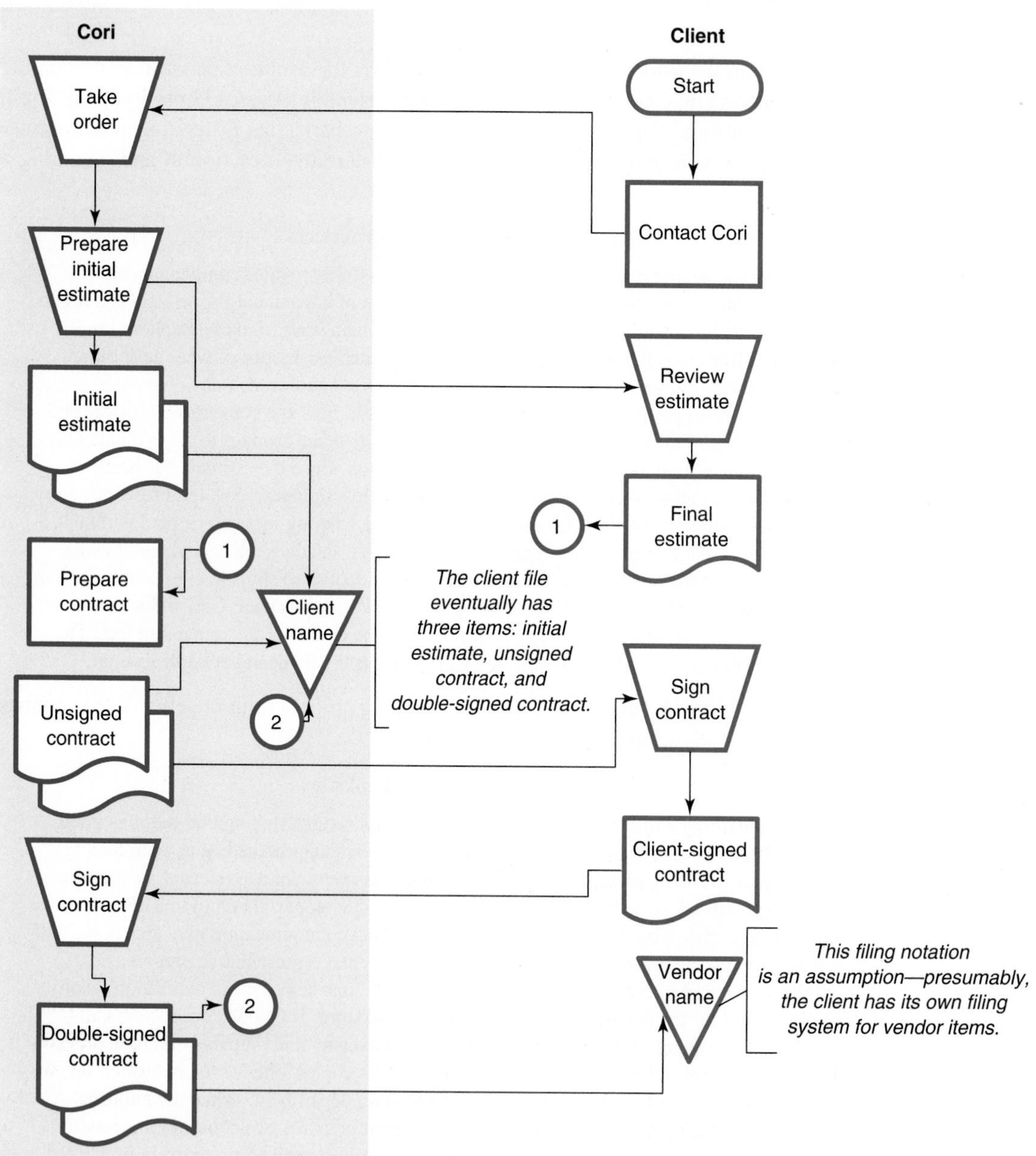

FIGURE 5.3 **Partial Flowchart for University Bookstore**

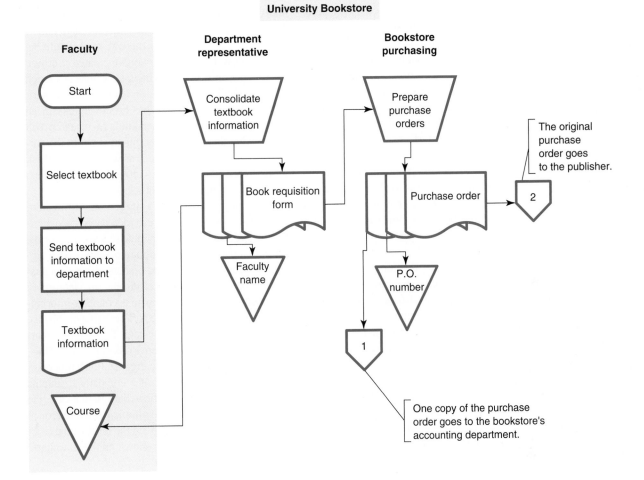

could read the narratives provided and construct flowcharts that look significantly different while still observing the flowcharting rules and conventions presented earlier in the chapter.

FLOWCHARTING AND ACCOUNTING INFORMATION SYSTEMS

So how does all this material relate to your study of accounting information systems? AIS professionals use flowcharts in many different ways, including confirming how a system is currently operating, suggesting improvements to an accounting information system, evaluating internal control deficiencies, and designing procedures manuals.

In your very first accounting job after you graduate, you'll likely be coming into an unfamiliar environment. You may wonder "how things work" in the accounting information system, especially if you're in charge of a particular function such as accounts payable or accounts receivable. Additionally, if you're working for a CPA firm or as a consultant, you may need to confirm how a system is operating currently before you start an audit or make recommendations regarding operational efficiency. In all those cases, a flowchart can be a useful way to conceptualize the big picture of a system. You'd probably want to look over any existing procedures manuals and talk with employees familiar with the system already.

Then, you can try designing a flowchart to model a business process. Once you've completed a first draft, discuss it further with others in the organization. Explain to them what it says and ask if that's the way things "really work" in the company, or if you're misunderstanding something. Remember: The overall goal of a flowchart in this situation is to understand the current state of things—the way they are, not necessarily the way they should be.

If you're looking at a previously constructed flowchart, whether you've created it or not, you can try to spot opportunities for improvement. Critically analyzing a flowchart is a tough job—there are no hard-and-fast rules for doing it. You'll need to draw on your training, experience, and ordinary business sense to identify and describe possible improvements in an accounting information system. Once again, interviewing and other kinds of research will help in this task. Ask employees, for example, what their biggest complaint is about the current process. If they've thought about ways to improve it, listen to those as well. You could ask employees in one-on-one or small group interviews; written surveys, e-mail exchanges, and employee suggestion boxes also can help in gathering ideas about process improvements. In many cases, the employees closest to a process can provide the best suggestions for making things better; in some cases, a system outsider can provide a new, fresh idea based on experience in other organizations. Opportunities for improvements might include redesigning forms, increasing or decreasing the number of copies of a particular form, obtaining authorizing signatures for transactions, filing in a different way (for example, based on date rather than customer name or vice versa), or changing a form from paper-based to electronic (or vice versa).

As noted in Chapter 4, systems risk relates directly to information technology. As organizations become increaingly dependent on computers and related IT to deliver goods and services to customers, they risk the possibility that IT resources will fail at a critical moment.

Flowcharts also can be used to spot internal control deficiencies in an accounting information system. Remember the risk analyses you completed in Chapter 4? A flowchart can enhance them by providing a concrete picture of an accounting information system. To use a flowchart to spot internal control deficiencies, start by making a list of the system's risk exposures. Then, look at the flowchart with those risk exposures in mind. Do any of the organization's processes or documents increase its exposure to specific risks? For example, if a company maintains only an electronic record of inventory purchases, you'll see that in a flowchart. In that case, the company is exposed to a systems risk. What controls has the company implemented to reduce its exposure to systems risk? Are the controls strong and adequate given the level of the risk? For example, does the company also maintain a paper file that is not shown on the flowchart? Or is a paper file missing from the flowchart because it doesn't exist?

A risk/control matrix is a good tool for internal control analysis, especially when combined with a flowchart. Egerdahl (1995) had these comments about risk/control matrices:

> [A risk/control matrix] helps to identify, document and evaluate the system of internal controls. The matrix identifies the threats facing the environment, the components within the facility and the necessary controls. It also provides a risk assessment, evaluation of the controls and any recommendations. In its final format, these elements are presented graphically on one page for ease of understanding and approval by management.

Although risk/control matrices can take on different forms, depending on the designer and purpose, Figure 5.4 gives an example of a very comprehensive format (Roth and Espersen, 2004). Chapter 4 presented a simpler version of a risk/control matrix. Unless your AIS professor specifically tells you otherwise, feel free to use either one to respond to questions and problems in the text.

Here's a bit of explanation about the elements of the risk/control matrix:

- The control objective is a goal or outcome, such as "safeguard cash."
- WCGW stands for "what could go wrong." So, in safeguarding cash, it could be lost or stolen.
- The risk level is management's subjective assessment; in this case, how likely is it that cash will be lost or stolen? Other things being equal, items marked "high" would receive priority over those marked "medium" or "low."

FIGURE 5.4 Risk/Control Matrix

Source: Roth and Espersen, 2004.

Risk/Control Matrix

Process/Subprocess:____________________ Owner(s):____________________

Control Objective	WCGW	Risk Level	Controls	Assertion					Type				Key?		Design?		COSO					Tests	Freq.	By	Oper.	
				E	C	V	R	P	P	D	M	A	Y	N	Y	N	E	R	A	I	M				Y	N

LEGEND

WCGW	Risk Level	Assertion	Type	Key?	Design?	COSO	Oper.
What Could Go Wrong?	H = High M = Medium L = Low	E = Existence C = Completeness V = Valuation R = Rights and Obligations P = Presentation and Disclosure	P = Preventive D = Detective M = Manual A = Automated	Is this a key control? Y = Yes N = No	Will the controls, if they are operating as designed, ensure the objective? Y = Yes N = No	E = Control Environment R = Risk Assessment A = Control Activity I = Information & Communication M = Monitoring	Are the controls operating as designed? Y = Yes N = No

- The *controls* column would comprise the various internal controls in place to lessen the risk. Thinking back to the previous chapter, controls for cash include depositing it in the bank daily; restrictively endorsing checks; and separating custody, authorization, and recordkeeping.
- You'll learn more about *assertions* when you take auditing. Basically, assertions are the "claims" that organizations make about elements of their financial statements.
- The *type* grouping identifies the purpose of each control listed in the controls column. For example, restrictive check endorsements are primarily preventive in nature. Notice that controls also can be classified as manual or automated; for example, if the cash receipts clerk uses a rubber stamp for restrictive endorsements, the process is manual.
- Think of a *key control* as one that is critically important; for example, depositing cash daily in the bank might be a more important/valuable control than separation of duties in a small organization. (I'm not saying that's always true—clearly, judgment and situational factors would be part of determining which controls are key.)
- The *design* columns are fairly self-explanatory. Keep in mind, however, that a single internal control, no matter how strong, is unlikely to prevent problems all on its own. Designers, managers, and auditors must consider the totality of the internal control system.
- We discussed the COSO enterprise risk management framework in the last chapter. The next set of columns in the risk/control matrix connects specific controls to specific parts of the COSO framework: environment, risk assessment, activities, information, and monitoring. Roth and Espersen (2004) state: "There will be few entries on the matrix for the control environment, because that is best tested on the entity-wide level, and for risk assessment, because the matrix itself might be the best risk assessment the organization has done for financial reporting." For example, a bank reconciliation would be a control activity in the COSO framework.
- The remaining columns in the matrix (tests, frequency, by, and operating) would be used by an auditor testing the internal controls.

FIGURE 5.5 Risk/Control Matrix for Cori's Catering Service

Control Objective	WCGW	Risk Level	Controls	Type	Key	Design	COSO
Process orders timely	Order is late	Low	Set up schedule when taking order	P & A	Yes	Yes	Control activity
	Order is incorrect	Low	Repeat information on phone	P & M	No	Yes	Information and communication
			Supply copy of order to client	D & A	Yes	Yes	Monitoring
Estimate accurately	Prices change	Medium	Long-term supply contracts	P & M	Yes	Yes	Risk assessment
	Mathematical errors	Low	Automate calculations	P & A	No	Yes	Control activity
Deliver services accurately	Incorrect time/place	Medium	Verify in writing	P & M	Yes	Yes	Information and communication
	Incorrect items	Low	Verify in writing	P & M	Yes	Yes	Information and communication
Receive payment timely	Lost in mail	Low	Collect remaining payment on delivery	P & M	No	Yes	Control activity
	Client fails to pay	Medium	Credit checks	P & A	Yes	Yes	Risk assessment
	Bad checks	Medium	Collection agency	D & M	No	Yes	Control activity

Figure 5.5 shows a completed matrix based on the Cori's Catering Service vignette presented earlier in this chapter. I've omitted the "assertions" column, as you'll learn more about those in auditing; I've also omitted the columns related to checking the internal controls.

For an example of a procedures manual, see Stoica's *Development of a Procedural Manual for Newly Hired Treasury Analysts at Company X* (2000).

Finally, flowcharts can be a starting point for the development of procedures manuals. A procedures manual is simply an "instruction book" that explains how everyday tasks in an organization are accomplished. Halbert (2003) recommends that "every staff member . . . document his or her duties and write a procedures manual—a time-consuming effort but worth doing." A well-constructed flowchart can easily be "translated" into regular, step-by-step text for use by future employees.

CRITICAL THINKING

As you read earlier in this chapter, developing flowcharts is as much "art" as "science." Therefore, learning to create good, descriptive flowcharts is often a challenge for accounting students—knowing the rules and conventions only takes you part of the way, in just the same way that you can't really learn to drive a car simply by reading a book. So, for this section, I'm going to show you how I usually go about creating a flowchart; please keep in mind that the way I do it is a result of my own experience and training. It's not the "one right way" to develop flowcharts.

If you've had some intermediate accounting already, you probably know the process the Financial Accounting Standards Board uses to develop new accounting pronouncements. In case you haven't studied that yet, here's a summary (Spiceland et al., 2009, p. 14):

1. *Identification of problem.* A measurement or reporting issue is identified by the Emerging Issues Task Force and placed on the FASB's agenda.
2. *The task force.* A task force of approximately 15 knowledgeable persons is appointed to advise the Board on various matters.
3. *Research and analysis.* The FASB's technical staff investigates the issue.
4. *Discussion memorandum (DM).* The DM, a detailed analysis of the problem along with alternative solutions, is prepared and disseminated to interested parties.
5. *Public response.* Public hearings are held to discuss the issue and letters of response are sent to the FASB, which then analyzes this feedback.
6. *Exposure draft (ED).* A preliminary draft of a proposed statement, called an exposure draft, is issued. The ED details the proposed treatment for the problem.
7. *Public response.* Written responses to the ED are accepted and analyzed. The ED is revised, if necessary, depending on the Board's analysis.
8. *Statement issued.* An SFAS [Statement of Financial Accounting Standards] is issued if four of the seven FASB members support the revised ED.

So how would you encapsulate those eight steps in a systems flowchart? First, I usually decide how many columns the flowchart will have, keeping in mind that you need one column for each area of responsibility. In the eight-step process, the groups involved are the Emerging Issues Task Force, the advisory task force, technical staff, the public, and the FASB. So, the flowchart will need five columns. Next, I normally consider what each group does and how to translate those actions into flowcharting symbols. The Emerging Issues Task Force identifies issues; a generic process symbol could be used to represent that. The Board does several things: appoints the advisory task force (generic process or predetermined process symbol), prepares documents (document symbol), analyzes feedback (generic process), and votes (decision symbol). The advisory task force advises the Board, while the technical staff conduct research. The process also involves several documents, each of which should be depicted with a document symbol.

Once I know how many columns and what kinds of symbols to use, it's time to start drawing the flowchart. I usually use graphics software like Visio or SmartDraw; you could also start with a paper-and-pencil sketch. Keep in mind that the flowchart should have a single "start" symbol and a single "end" symbol; it should also follow the rules and conventions discussed at the beginning of this chapter. Once the first draft is done, I discuss it with other people, make any needed changes, and then discuss it again; the flowchart is "done" when it fairly represents the process involved.

Reflection and Self-Assessment 5.4

Try drawing a flowchart of the standard-setting process based on the preceding description. Share your work with at least one other person—perhaps someone in your AIS course. Then, revise the flowchart as needed.

Summary

Here is a summary of the chapter:

1. *List and discuss the purpose and use of systems flowcharts, document flowcharts, program flowcharts, and hardware flowcharts.* A systems flowchart provides a top-level view of an information system; it shows the "big picture" of what is happening. A document flowchart, as the name implies, shows how documents (paper and electronic) flow through an information system, while a program flowchart details the steps in a specific computer program. A hardware flowchart lays out the computers, printers, monitors, and other hardware devices used in an information system.
2. *Explain the basic parts of and design considerations common to all types of flowcharts.* In general, a flowchart should be read from top to bottom and left to right. Since flowcharts are communication tools, they should be easy to read, incorporating plenty of white space. Every flowchart should have a title to make it easier to reference after its creation; flowcharts also should be organized into columns based on areas of responsibility in the information system. Documents should have clear beginning and ending points as well. Finally, flowcharts are usually the product of discussion among colleagues, rather than the product of a single individual.
3. *Identify and describe common symbols and information technology tools used in flowcharting.* Figure 5.1 shows various flowcharting symbols; your individual research (Reflection and Self-Assessment 5.3) revealed more. Two popular IT tools for flowchart creation are SmartDraw and Visio.
4. *Discuss ways flowcharts impact the design, implementation, and evaluation of accounting information systems.* A well-constructed flowchart can give a new accountant or consultant a quick overview of how a system works. Flowcharts also can be used as part of the auditing process and/or to suggest process improvements in the accounting information system, particularly when combined with a risk/control matrix. They also can inform recommendations regarding internal controls.
5. *Create a risk/control matrix.* A risk/control matrix is useful in analyzing internal controls based on a flowchart. Although different formats for the matrix exist, virtually every format has two key features: a list of risks and the controls designed to address them.
6. *Create and interpret systems and document flowcharts.* In working with systems and document flowcharts, you should be able to construct a flowchart from a narrative and create a narrative from a well-prepared flowchart. Three key ideas are important in creating flowcharts: (*a*) strive to achieve a clear representation of the system, not a deterministic response to a particular problem or case situation; (*b*) practice will increase your skill in flowcharting; and (*c*) seldom will your first creation be your final one—flowcharts can almost always be improved via dialogue and consultation with other professionals.

Flowcharting is one of two commonly used documentation techniques for accounting information systems. For accounting students, who typically like dealing with numbers better than words and symbols, they can be challenging. But, with time, practice, and patience, you can learn the art of developing clear, meaningful flowcharts and using them as analytical tools in the accounting information system.

Key Terms

Chapter References

Egerdahl, R. 1995. "A Risk Matrix Approach to Data Processing Facility Audits." *Internal Auditor,* June, pp. 34–40.

Halbert, J. 2003. "Mining Back-Office Operations May Bolster the Bottom Line." *Los Angeles Business Journal,* April 14, www.findarticles.com (last visited November 4, 2004).

Roth, J., and D. Espersen. 2004. "The Matrix Revisited." *Internal Auditor,* August, pp. 87–88.

Spiceland, J. D., J. Sepe, M. W. Nelson, and L. A. Tomassini. 2000. *Intermediate Accounting* 5th ed. New York: Irwin/McGraw-Hill.

Stoica, R. 2000. *Development of a Procedural Manual for Newly Hired Treasury Analysts at Company X.* California State Polytechnic University, Pomona; CA.

End-of-Chapter Activities

1. *Reading review questions.*

a. What is a flowchart? Describe four different kinds of flowcharts and explain which are most often used in an accounting information system.
b. Summarize the rules and conventions commonly observed in the preparation of flowcharts.
c. List and explain the meaning and use of 10 common flowcharting symbols. What sources would you consult for learning about additional symbols not on your list?
d. How are flowcharts used in working with accounting information systems?
e. Respond to the questions for this chapter's "AIS in the Business World."

2. *Reading review problem.* Zions Bancorporation (www.zionsbancorporation.com) established three goals with respect to risk management and internal control: (1) enable the company to better manage risk and reduce loss, (2) strengthen customer service and shareholder value, and (3) meet a variety of regulatory requirements. According to Stone (2003), Zions "decided to deploy a Web-based risk assessment system as part of its enterprise risk management efforts." The company assembled a cross-functional team to define system requirements and establish an overall approach for managing risk. The bank's risk management system is Web-based, allowing the company to share data easily and develop a 'robust risk culture within the organization in which business liens would work proactively to identify, assess and manage risk within the system."

The company embarked on a four-step process for identifying, assessing, and managing risk: (a) identify business objectives and related risks, (b) list and assess the strength of controls, (c) determine actions needed to close control gaps, and (d) ensure accountability and sustainability. Flowcharting is particularly important in the first step of the process, where "users identify the business processes that [a particular] risk impacts and attach a flowchart depicting the process." In addition, accountants can use a well-constructed flowchart to identify and correct internal control gaps. Finally, in Zion's system, a user can search for risks and related internal controls based on business processes depicted in flowcharts.

Source: David L. Stone, "Leveraging Risk Technology," *Internal Auditor,* December 2003, p. 27.

a. What kind(s) of flowchart(s) would be useful to Zions? Explain your response.
b. Consider the four-step risk management process. Identify three to five symbols you would use to create a flowchart of that process; explain your choices.
c. Visit Zions' Web site. Create a risk/control matrix for three risks they might experience.

3. *Making choices and exercising judgment.* Compare and contrast SmartDraw, Microsoft Visio, and one other flowcharting program (if you completed Reflection and

Self-Assessment 5.2, you could use one of the programs you identified there). Prepare a paper and/or PowerPoint presentation that include a recommendation regarding your preferred flowcharting software; justify your recommendation.

4. *Field exercises.* Visit a local restaurant for lunch or dinner. Pay close attention to the steps involved in ordering, receiving, and paying for a meal. Create a flowchart that depicts the process. List and discuss one or two internal controls you observe in the process; also suggest one or two ways the system could be improved.

5. *Flowchart creation.* Create a flowchart based on each of the following independent situations (one flowchart per situation).

   a. Using Figure 5.2 (Partial Flowchart for Cori's Catering Services) and the narrative provided in the chapter, complete the flowchart.

   b. Using Figure 5.3 (Partial Flowchart for University Bookstore) and the narrative provided in the chapter, complete the flowchart.

   c. Horacio is a college student at Feng Shui University. He rents an apartment from the university for $600 a month. On the 15th of every month, Horacio writes a check for the rent. He mails the check to the Housing Services office on campus; in turn, Housing Services sends an e-mail receipt back to Horacio. The mailroom staff in Housing Services makes a copy of the check for Horacio's file and sends the original, with all the other rent checks for the month, to the bank. Once a month, the treasurer of Housing Services reconciles the bank statement. Prepare a flowchart of the preceding scenario.

   d. Consider the process you use to register for classes every term. At Cal Poly Pomona (my university), students see an advisor to determine which classes they need and check their e-mail for their registration appointment time. They then compare the list of needed classes with the offerings for the upcoming term and their personal scheduling constraints and preferences. The students register online or over the phone. The university generates a "fee bill," which may include parking, and e-mails it to the student. Students can pay their fee bills electronically with a credit card or in person with cash or a check. Prepare a flowchart of the Cal Poly Pomona registration process and of your university's registration process (two separate flowcharts).

   e. Visit the Web site of the International Accounting Standards Board. Summarize the process the Board uses to develop International Financial Reporting Standards (IFRS), then create a systems flowchart of the process.

6. (CMA adapted) *Narrative preparation from a flowchart.*

   a. Consider the flowchart in Figure 5.6. Write a narrative description of the business process it depicts.

   b. Consider the flowchart in Figure 5.7. Write a narrative description of the business process it depicts.

7. *Flowchart and system critiques.*

   a. Consider the flowchart in Figure 5.6. Describe at least two strengths and at least two weaknesses of the flowchart itself. Then, identify and describe at least two strengths and at least two weaknesses of the process it depicts. For each process weakness, suggest a way to correct it.

   b. Consider the flowchart in Figure 5.7. Describe at least two strengths and at least two weaknesses of the flowchart itself. Then, identify and describe at least two strengths and at least two weaknesses of the process it depicts. For each process weakness, suggest a way to correct it.

   c. Compare the flowcharts you created for the registration process at your university and Cal Poly Pomona. What risk exposures does each flowchart indicate? What internal controls would you recommend to address each risk exposure?

FIGURE 5.6 Flowchart for Richards Furniture Company

Salesperson
Cashier
Assistant Manager
Manager
Prepare sales invoice
Sales invoice (4 copies)
Three copies go to the cashier; one is retained in the sales book.
Sales invoice (3 copies)
1
Approve sale and process
Assign consecutive number
1
One copy of the validated invoice goes to the customer; one stays in the store, and the third goes to the assistant manager.
Cash register
Tape
Validated invoice, check or cash, return slip
Reconcile and prepare report
Reconciled report
Prepare bank deposit
Deposit documents
To bank
Review bank deposit
Date

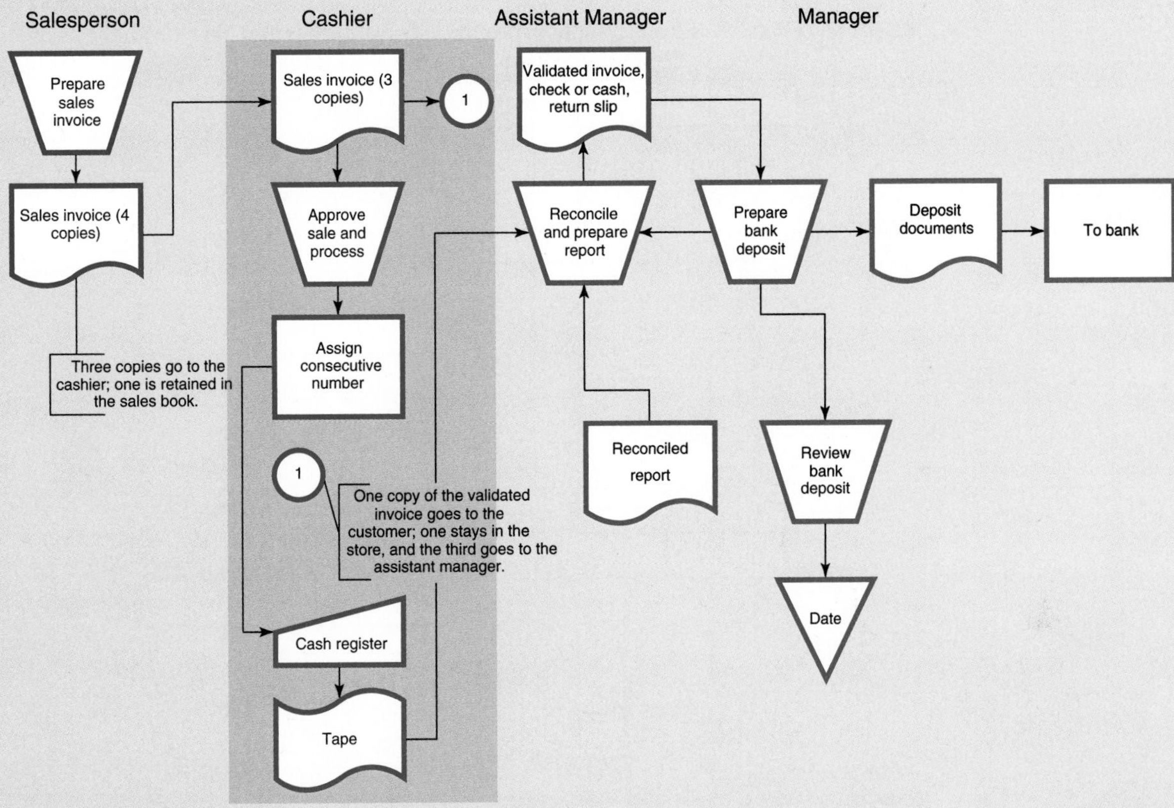

FIGURE 5.7 Flowchart for PriceRight Electronics Inc.

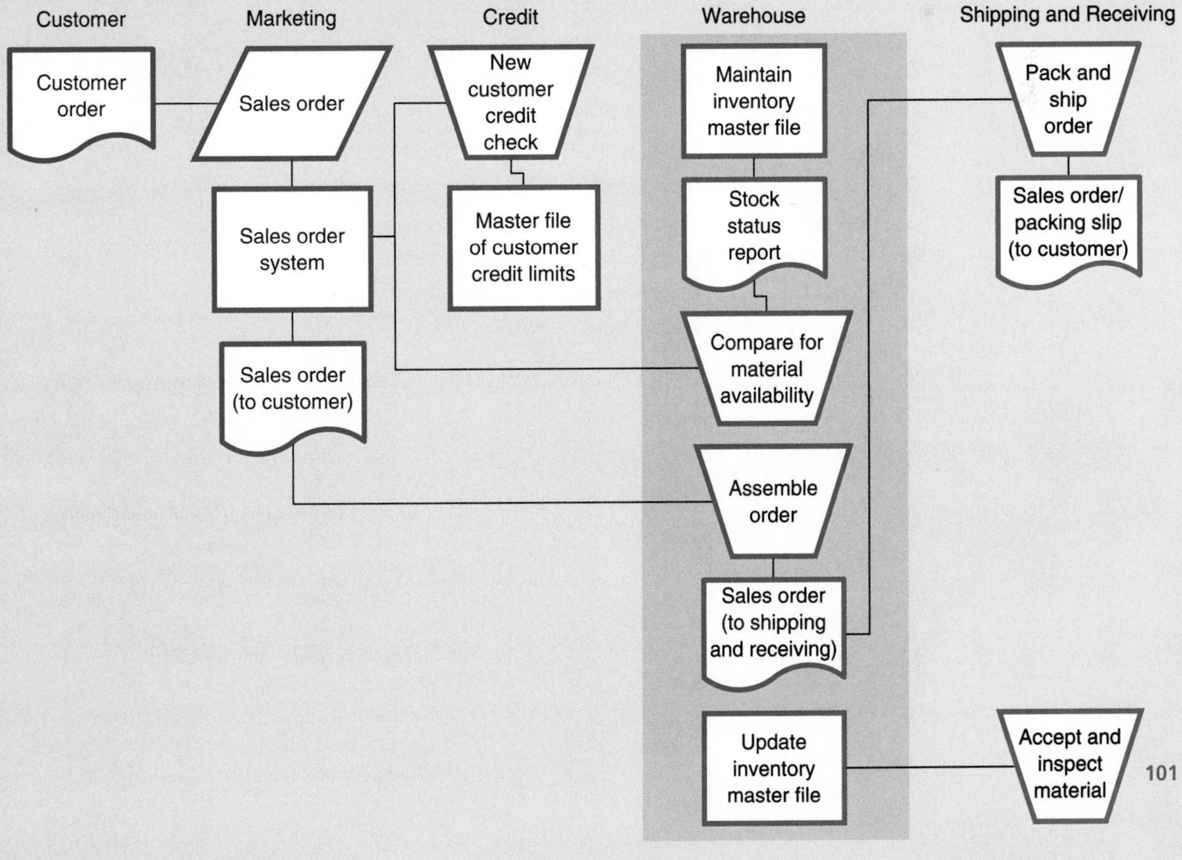

Customer
Marketing
Credit
Warehouse
Shipping and Receiving
Customer order
Sales order
Sales order system
Sales order (to customer)
New customer credit check
Master file of customer credit limits
Maintain inventory master file
Stock status report
Compare for material availability
Assemble order
Sales order (to shipping and receiving)
Update inventory master file
Pack and ship order
Sales order/ packing slip (to customer)
Accept and inspect material

8. *Crossword puzzle.* Please complete the puzzle below with terminology from the chapter.

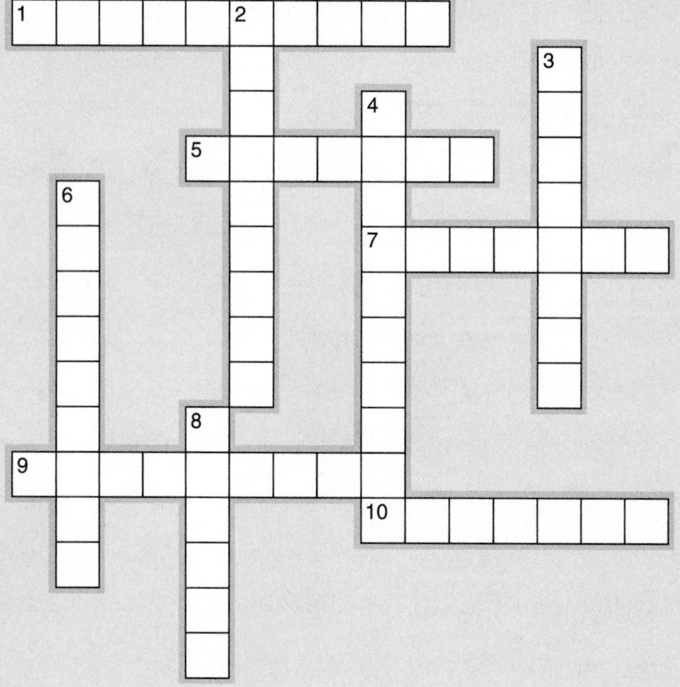

Across

1. Use this to avoid clutter in flowcharts.
5. Flowchart type based on computer code.
7. How flowcharts are organized.
9. Flowcharting is an ______ process—it's seldom "right" the first time.
10. Flowchart that gives the big picture.

Down

2. Flowcharting software example.
3. Flowchart type based on items such as purchase orders.
4. A flowchart can help in preparing a ______ manual.
6. An on-page ______ is represented as a number in a circle.
8. ______ processes are depicted as trapezoids.

9. *Terminology.* Please match each item on the left with the best item on the right.

1. Areas of responsibility
2. Document flowchart
3. Hardware flowchart
4. Inverted triangle
5. Origin and termination
6. Overlapping shapes
7. Program flowchart
8. Spotting internal control deficiencies
9. Systems flowchart
10. Title

a. A flowchart depicting the process of buying a car.
b. Based on lines of computer code.
c. Can trace remittance advices and invoices through a system.
d. Documents in a flowchart should have these.
e. Every flowchart should have one of these.
f. One application of flowcharting in AIS.
g. Represents a file in a flowchart.
h. Shows monitors, input devices, and computers.
i. Used to show multiple copies of a document.
j. What columns represent in a flowchart.

10. *Multiple choice questions.*

1. Vicki prepared a flowchart showing the computer's instructions for calculating payroll. Her flowchart would best be described as a ________ flowchart.
   a. systems
   b. document
   c. program
   d. hardware
2. Which of the following is not a design consideration common to all types of flowcharts?
   a. They should have a title of no fewer than five words.
   b. They should be free of clutter and easy to read.
   c. They should be organized in columns.
   d. They should be read the same way you read a page in a book.
3. SmartDraw and Visio are examples of
   a. Accounting information systems software.
   b. General ledger software.
   c. Presentation graphics software.
   d. Flowcharting software.
4. Which of the following flowcharting packages is the best?
   a. SmartDraw
   b. Visio
   c. WizFlow Flowcharter
   d. Cannot be determined from the information given
5. Which of the following statements is most true?
   a. Different people will probably create identical flowcharts for the same business process.
   b. Flowcharts are a requirement of COSO's enterprise risk management framework.
   c. Flowcharting is a highly iterative process.
   d Flowcharting is the best tool for analyzing risks and establishing internal controls in an accounting information system.
6. Flowcharts are organized in columns that represent
   a. Areas of responsibility.
   b. Business processes.
   c. Documents.
   d. Risk exposures.
7. A database would be represented in a flowchart as a
   a. Square.
   b. Cylinder.
   c. Triangle.
   d. Circle.
8. In a risk/control matrix, internal controls can be classified as
   a. Preventive or detective.
   b. Automated or manual.
   c. Both of the above.
   d. None of the above.
9. Consider the relationship between the COSO enterprise risk management framework and the risk/control matrix presented in the chapter. Which of the following COSO elements would seldom be present in the matrix?
   a. Control environment
   b. Risk assessment
   c. Control activity
   d. Information and communication

10. Flowcharts should be organized and read
    a. From top to bottom, from right to left.
    b. From bottom to top, from left to right.
    c. From top to bottom, from left to right.
    d. In any way that makes sense to the designer.

11. *Risk/control matrices* (builds on Activity 5). Prepare a risk/control matrix for one or more of the companies mentioned in Activity 5 above (other than Cori's Catering Services, which is illustrated in the chapter). Omit the assertions column and the checking columns from your matrix.

12. *Statement evaluation.* Indicate whether each statement below is (i) always true, (ii) sometimes true, or (iii) never true. For those that are (ii) sometimes true, explain when the statement is true.

a. Columns in a systems flowchart denote areas of responsibility.
b. Flowcharts are focused on business documents.
c. Flowcharts should include off-page connectors for easier reading.
d. Monthly bank reconciliations ensure that no one embezzles cash.
e. Once designed, flowcharts do not need to be revised.
f. On-page connectors help keep flowcharts uncluttered and easy to read.
g. Process symbols should be sandwiched between an input and an output.
h. The first step in drawing a flowchart is to decide which software package to use.
i. Two designers would independently create identical flowcharts for the same business process.
j. Visio is the best tool for drawing flowcharts.

Chapter Six

Data Flow Diagramming

AIS in the Business World

Risk Analysis Using Data Flow Diagrams

Consider the following summary of a risk analysis conducted from May to July 2003 (den Braber et al., 2005):

> NetCom is one of the main mobile phone network providers in Norway. Their "MinSide" application offers their customers access to their personal account information via the Internet, enabling them to view and change the properties of their mobile phone subscription. "MinSide" deals with a lot of sensitive customer information that needs to be secure, while at the same time being easily available to the customer in order for the service to remain usable and competitive. The goal of the analysis was to identify risks in relation to the use of the "MinSide" application and, where possible, suggest treatments for these risks. This was achieved through two model-driven brainstorming sessions based on system documentation [including] data flow diagrams.

You can find NetCom's Web page (written in Norwegian) at http://www.netcom.no.

Discussion Questions

1. What is a "model-driven brainstorming session?"
2. How could a data flow diagram be used for risk identification?
3. In what other ways could a data flow diagram be used in accounting information systems?

Source: F. den Braber, A. Mildal, J. Nes, K. Stolen, and F. Vraalsen, "Experiences from Using the CORAS Methodology to Analyze a Web Application," *Journal of Cases on Information Technology* (July–September 2005), pp. 110–30.

In the previous chapter, you learned about the first of three documentation techniques often used in accounting information systems: flowcharting. In this chapter, we consider the second of the three: data flow diagramming. The third technique, REAL modeling, is discussed in the next chapter.

The concepts and ideas of data flow diagramming originated in the broader field of systems analysis and design. Since the accounting information system is a subset of an organization's complete management information system, we can borrow the ideas and techniques for our purposes here. Data flow diagrams (DFDs) incorporate fewer symbols and different "rules" than flowcharts, but they do share many similarities. When you finish studying this chapter, you should be able to:

1. Explain the symbols and design considerations associated with DFDs.
2. Compare and contrast flowcharts and DFDs with regard to purpose, content, structure, and use in accounting information systems.
3. Discuss ways DFDs are used in AIS work.
4. Construct a leveled set of DFDs.
5. Design normalized database tables from a DFD.

Some AIS professionals prefer one documentation method over another, but many use both flowcharts and data flow diagrams depending upon the situation and tasks at hand. In research conducted by Bradford, Richtermeyer, and Roberts (2007), just over 20 percent of respondents reported using data flow diagrams to document information systems. Managers use them to describe business processes, evaluate the current system, design or change a system, and assess the internal control environment.

DFD SYMBOLS AND DESIGN CONSIDERATIONS

Data flow diagrams can be prepared with the same software tools as flowcharts.

Unlike flowcharts, which incorporate a plethora of symbols, data flow diagrams incorporate only four (DeMarco, 1979), which are shown in Figure 6.1.

A **process** is any set of procedures an organization uses to gather data, change the data into information, or report the information to system users. Every process in a data flow diagram has two identifying characteristics: a number and a name. Numbers follow specific conventions, which we'll examine later in this chapter. Process names should always be verb phrases; that is, they should start with an "action word," like approve, record, calculate or check.

FIGURE 6.1
Data Flow Diagram Symbols

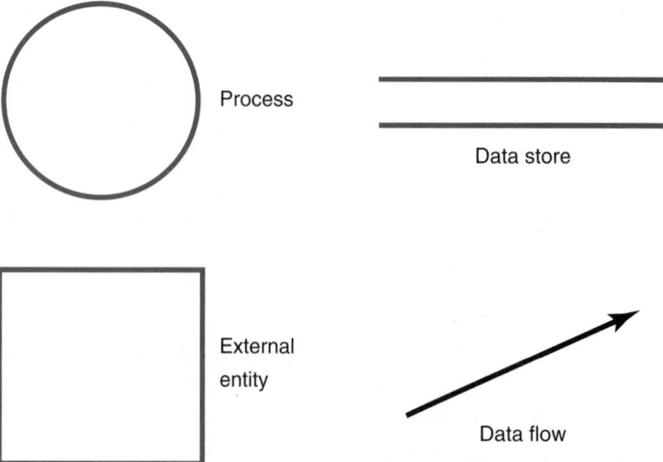

An **external entity** is any person or organization outside the boundary of an information system. Establishing a clear, appropriate system boundary is essential to the construction of a good data flow diagram. Without such a boundary, you'll end up analyzing "the world" every time you want to solve a problem in an accounting information system. Boundaries are a matter of management judgment, and external entities lie outside boundaries. So, for example, if you were constructing a data flow diagram for Home Depot's cash management system as referenced in this chapter's reading review problem, external entities might include customers, suppliers, or the bank. But whether or not a person or an organization is an external entity depends upon your definition of the system, not your definition of the organization. So, for example, if you are processing travel expenses for a marketing staff member, the marketing staff member might be an external entity—even though she is employed in the same organization.

A **data store** is a place for collecting data; you might think of it as a "file," whether paper-based or electronic. Data stores are labeled with noun phrases such as customer data, vendor data, or inventory data. Data stores can be linked to processes or external entities in a data flow diagram; they cannot be linked to one another. Later in this chapter, we'll consider some of the issues involved in creating database files based on the data stores in a DFD.

Finally, a **data flow** is represented by a directional line in a data flow diagram. Data flows should have only one arrow on one end to conform to DFD design conventions. Data flows, like data stores, are labeled with noun phrases: desired information, accounts payable data, customer order data, and the like. When a data flow is labeled in that way, we're referring to the content, not the format. So, for example, a data flow labeled "approved order" could indicate a piece of paper, an e-mail, or an electronic purchase order. Students often try to label data flows with verb phrases—that's a bad idea. Remember, processes are verbs—they tell what happens to data in an information system. A data flow refers to the data itself, not what happens to it.

Hoffner, George, and Valacich (1996) suggested the following **rules/conventions** associated with good data flow diagrams:

1. All processes should have unique names. If two data flow lines (or data stores) have the same label, they should both refer to the exact same data flow (or data store).
2. The inputs to a process should differ from the outputs to a process.
3. Any single DFD should not have more than about seven processes.
4. No process can have only outputs. (This would imply that the process is making information from nothing.) If an object has only outputs, then it must be an external entity.
5. No process can have only inputs. If an object has only inputs, it must be a data store.
6. A process has a verb phrase label. Examples include *prepare check* or *register for classes.*
7. Data cannot be moved directly from one data store to another data store. Data must be moved by a process.
8. Data cannot move directly from an external entity to a data store. Data must be moved by a process that receives data from the entity and places the data into the data store.
9. Data cannot move directly to an external entity from a data store. Data must be moved by a process.
10. A data store has a noun phrase label.
11. Data of any concern to the system cannot move directly from one external entity to another external entity. They must be moved by a process. If data flow directly between external entities without processing, then they are outside the system boundary and omitted from the DFD.
12. An external entity has a noun phrase label.

FIGURE 6.2 Registration Process Level Zero DFD

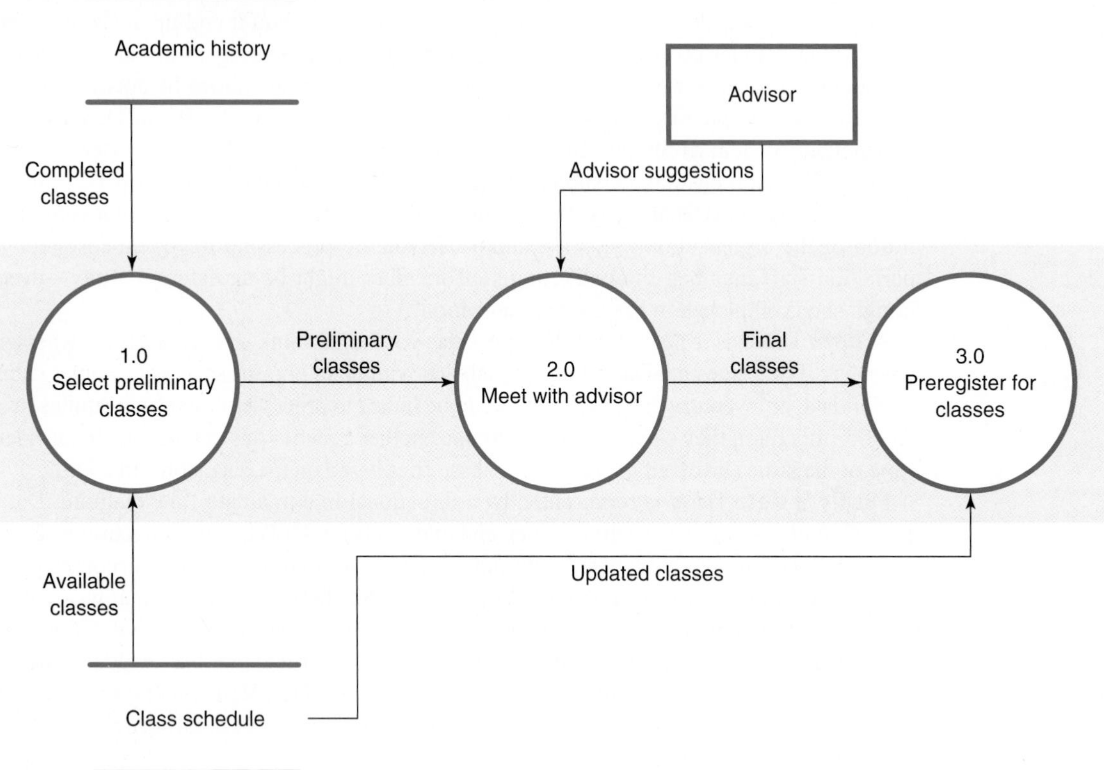

13. A data flow has only one direction between symbols.
14. A data flow cannot go directly back to the same process it leaves. There must be at least one other process that handles the data flow, produces some new data, and returns the original data to the original process.
15. A data flow can go directly into a data store. When it does, it signifies an update (delete, add, or change). Likewise, a data flow can come directly from a data store; in that context, it refers to a retrieval or use of the data in the store.
16. A data flow has a noun phrase label.

Consider the data flow diagram in Figure 6.2, which shows a basic process for registering for classes. The DFD contains three processes associated with registration: selecting preliminary classes, meeting with an advisor, and preregistering for the classes. It has two data stores: academic history (which is the record of all the classes a student has taken and the grades earned in them) and class schedule. Keep in mind that the data stores don't necessarily refer to physical documents—we're focused here on the *data,* not the *format.* The one external entity is the advisor; including the advisor as an external entity is a design judgment.

Data flow diagrams represent a very new way of thinking for most accounting students, so expect a bit of frustration as you become comfortable with this important method of documenting an accounting information system. When my own students experience that frustration, I often remind them of how they may have struggled initially to remember the rules of debit and credit in the AIS. By the time they take an AIS course, however, debiting and crediting accounts seem as routine as driving a car. In time and with practice, you'll develop that same level of comfort regarding designing and interpreting data flow diagrams.

Write a narrative description of the process depicted in Figure 6.2. Also, clearly describe and differentiate the four data flows associated with classes: available, preliminary, final, and preregistered. In other words, how do the four data flows differ from one another? How are they similar?

DATA FLOW DIAGRAMS AND FLOWCHARTS

So now that you know a bit about both, what are the differences between data flow diagrams and flowcharts? Many of the important differences are summarized in the table below:

Characteristic	Data Flow Diagram	Flowchart
Symbols	Four: circle (process), line (data flow), rectangle (external entity), and parallel lines (data store).	Many: rectangle (process), diamond (decision), triangle (file), and others.
Organization	Leveled sets, each depicting more detail than the last.	Columns representing areas of responsibility.
Numbers	Processes are numbered in the following formats: Level Zero, 1.0; Level One, 1.1; Level Two, 1.1.1; and so on.	Numbers are used for on- and off-page connectors, not for processes.
Focus	DFDs focus on data and how they move between business processes, external entities, and data stores.	Flowcharts are concerned with data, but also with documents and processing tools.
Use of "lines"	Lines represent data; they are labeled with noun phrases (e.g., account balance, customer data).	Lines represent movement between processes, areas of responsibility, and the like; they are not labeled.

Both data flow diagrams and flowcharts are useful in the design and implementation of accounting information systems; but systems flowcharts typically provide more detail than a data flow diagram. In a data flow diagram, for example, a business process, such as "receive payment," would be represented with a single numbered circle, a single data flow, and a single external entity:

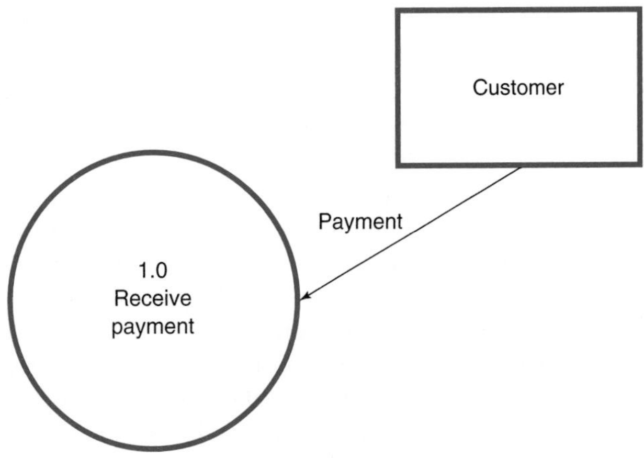

Someone looking at that portion of a Level Zero data flow diagram would not know

- How is the payment transmitted?
- What documents are used in the transaction?
- Who receives the payment?

A flowchart of that same process, on the other hand, might look like this:

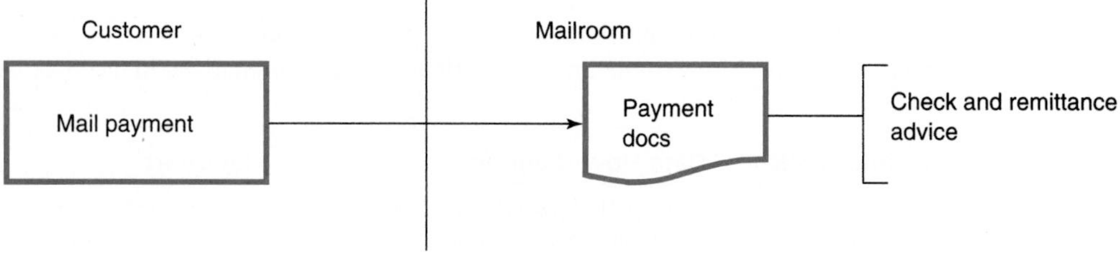

From that flowchart excerpt, we know

- Payments are made through the mail.
- They are received in the company's mailroom.
- Documents include both the customer's check and the remittance advice.

In the DFD, notice that the rectangle denotes the customer (an external entity); in the flowchart, the rectangle denotes a process (mail payment). In the data flow diagram, the process is depicted with a numbered circle. And, in the DFD, the data flow (arrow) has a name; in the flowchart, the data are represented with the document symbol, while the arrow shows the movement of the documents between areas of responsibility.

At this point, you might be wondering why it's necessary to learn more than one systems documentation technique; many students feel that knowing one should be enough. In practice, you might be called upon to create a flowchart as part of a financial statement audit to assess internal controls; you also might need to use a data flow diagram if you want to focus on the data you're auditing, regardless of their format (paper, electronic). Additionally, you will probably need to interpret both kinds of documents at some point in your career. For example, if you were hired by an entrepreneur to design an accounting information system "from scratch," you might first use a data flow diagram to focus on the data and how they are manipulated; the DFD might later be supplemented with a systems flowchart to iron out the details of who is responsible for different tasks, how documents will be named, how many copies of documents will be required, and other detailed issues.

LEVELED SETS OF DFDS

You probably recall from our discussion of flowcharting that flowcharts often span more than one page; the pages are connected with off-page connectors. The point of creating multipage flowcharts is to make them easy to read and interpret.

In the same way, data flow diagrams should be uncluttered and easy to read; but systems analysts use a slightly different method to achieve that goal: **leveled sets** of DFDs. A leveled set of DFDs refers to a collection that models related business processes. The various levels provide increasing detail about the processes in the system.

Table 6.1 shows an overview of the components of a leveled set of DFDs.

TABLE 6.1
Components of a Leveled Set of DFDs

Level Name	Number of DFDs in a Leveled Set	Numbering Format
Context	One	0
Zero	One	1.0, 2.0
One	As many as necessary	Process 1.0 is subdivided into 1.1, 1.2, 1.3 Process 2.0 is subdivided into 2.1, 2.2, 2.3
Two	As many as necessary	Process 1.1 is subdivided into 1.1.1, 1.1.2 Process 2.3 is subdivided into 2.3.1, 2.3.2, 2.3.3
Three	As many as necessary	Process 1.1.2 is subdivided into 1.1.2.1, 1.1.2.2 Process 2.3.1 is subdivided into 2.3.1.1, 2.3.1.2

Just before I sat down to write this evening, I was doing some baking: fudge, pound cake, and ginger cookies. If I wanted to create a set of DFDs for that process (which wouldn't be nearly as much fun as doing the baking itself), the set might have labels and numbers that look like Table 6.2.

Table 6.2 is only talking about the processes—not the external entities, data stores, and data flows. Also notice how the system boundary is defined; it does not include driving to the grocery store or buying all the ingredients. As I mentioned earlier, defining the system boundary is a critically important judgment when preparing DFDs.

Figure 6.3 shows a **context diagram** for a registration system. (I showed you the **Level Zero diagram** first because it's more detailed; in practice, you'd prepare the context diagram first, then the Level Zero diagram.) Figure 6.2 showed a Level Zero diagram

TABLE 6.2
DFD for Baking

Level	Processes
Context	0: Bake tasty treats.
Zero	1.0: Make fudge. 2.0: Make pound cake. 3.0: Make ginger cookies.
One	Process 1.0 is broken down into 1.1: Combine chocolate chips, vanilla, butter, and nuts in a large bowl. 1.2: Cook marshmallows, sugar, and milk in a saucepan. 1.3: Pour mixture from saucepan over mixture in large bowl. 1.4: Stir vigorously until combined. 1.5: Lightly grease pan. 1.6: Pour combined mixture into greased pan. 1.7: Cool and cut. Process 2.0 is broken down into 2.1: Prepare oven and pan. 2.2: Whisk together dry ingredients. 2.3: Mix wet ingredients. 2.4: Combine wet and dry ingredients. 2.5: Pour batter into pan. 2.6: Bake.
Two	Process 2.1 is broken down into 2.1.1: Preheat oven to 375 degrees. 2.1.2: Lightly grease and flour cake pan. Process 2.3 is broken down into 2.3.1: Beat together butter, sugar, and vanilla. 2.3.2: Mix in eggs.

FIGURE 6.3
Registration Process Context Diagram

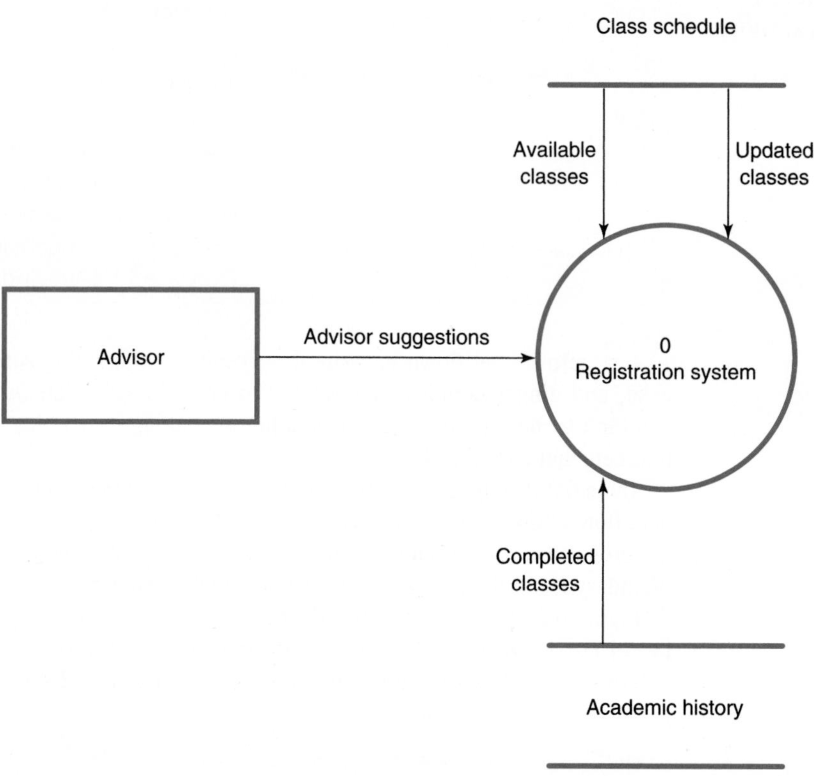

with three processes that are part of the registration system: select preliminary classes, meet with advisor, and preregister for classes.

Figure 6.4 shows a Level One diagram; it breaks down the "select preliminary classes" process from Level Zero into three parts: determine needed classes, determine time constraints, and prepare list for advisor meeting.

Reflection and Self-Assessment 6.2

Try your hand at creating a DFD that decomposes Process 3.0 (Preregister for classes) from Figure 6.2. The processes should have numbers like 3.1 and 3.2.

Here are some questions students often have when they first learn about DFDs:

1. *How many processes should a single DFD have?* There's really no "one right answer" for this question. But most analysts would try to limit the number of processes to seven in a single DFD.
2. *How many levels should be in a leveled set?* Again, it's a matter of judgment and the complexity of the process. For your work in class, you shouldn't need to go past Level Three—most of the time, Level Two will be plenty.

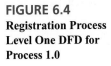

FIGURE 6.4
Registration Process Level One DFD for Process 1.0

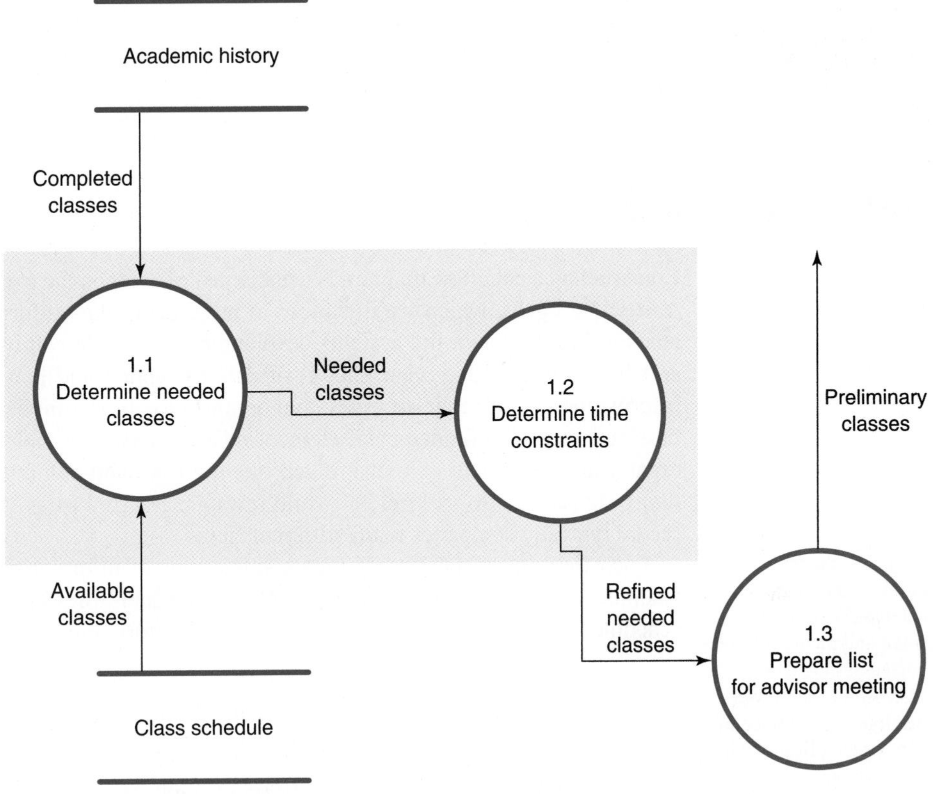

3. *When do you stop breaking down a process?* You stop breaking down a process when it's "self explanatory." At that point, the process is said to be **primitive,** meaning it cannot be broken down any further. If you were preparing a leveled set of DFDs of the accounting cycle for a group of experienced accounting students, a process called "make journal entries" might be considered primitive; but, if the audience for that same set was a group of students in introductory accounting, you might decompose "make journal entries" into its component parts in a new DFD.
4. *Does each process have to be decomposed to the same level?* No. In the cooking example above, notice that Processes 2.1 and 2.3 are broken down further; Process 2.2 is not.
5. *What other documents support the leveled set of DFDs?* In most information systems, you'll find some specialized terminology that needs to be defined. In the cooking example, those terms might include *dry ingredients* from Process 2.2 and *wet ingredients* from Process 2.3. In Figure 6.2, *academic history* might need to be defined. You'd normally prepare a systems dictionary for that purpose; a systems dictionary is very similar to a regular dictionary—it includes terms and their definitions as a reference.
6. *What's the relationship between the levels?* The DFDs at various levels must be **balanced.** In other words, things cannot magically appear and disappear between the levels. For example, look at the context diagram in Figure 6.3; notice that it includes a data flow called "advisor suggestions." Now, look at the Level Zero diagram in Figure 6.2; you see that same data flow. In Figure 6.2, two data flows go into Process 1.0: completed classes and available classes. Look now at Figure 6.4, which breaks down Process 1.0. Both data flows are inputs to Process 1.1.

Reflection and Self-Assessment 6.3

What other data flows are balanced between Figures 6.2, 6.3, and 6.4? Look back at the DFD you created in Reflection and Self-Assessment 6.2; is it balanced?

DATABASE DESIGN

Constructing a data flow diagram is usually just one step in the overall **systems development life cycle,** which we'll explore in more detail the "information systems models" chapter. Later steps in the systems development life cycle call on designers and users to collaborate in deciding what kind(s) of data to capture and how to organize them in an information system; in most cases, that organization is accomplished with relational database software. The fundamental element of a database is a table. **Database tables** are organized in rows and columns, much like the rows and columns of a spreadsheet. Columns are referred to as "fields," while rows are referred to as "records." So, a database record typically comprises many different fields.

Arguably, the most commonly used relational database software for small and medium-sized businesses today is Microsoft Access. We'll just touch the surface of database applications in this text, but you'll know enough to interact successfully with other information systems professionals about their design, use, and maintenance.

Each field in a database captures a single type of information. Consider our ongoing example of a class registration process. One of the data stores in Figure 6.2 is called "Class schedule." In a typical class schedule, you'd find information like

Course prefix	Meeting days
Course number	Meeting times
Course title	Class location
Section number	Instructor last name
Number of units	Instructor first name

So, each of the 10 elements above constitutes a field in the class schedule database. Each record in the database would have a particular value associated with it. For example, at my university, all accounting courses have an "ACC" prefix. Our basic accounting information systems course is ACC 304; its title is "Introduction to Accounting Information Systems."

Each record in a database must have a unique identifier, referred to as a **primary key.** In a database of student information, for example, the primary key might be your student identification number. The Internal Revenue Service uses your Social Security number as a primary key; it identifies you and only you, uniquely and clearly. In a class schedule database, an individual course would probably have a unique reference number, although you could also use a *compound primary key* made up of the course prefix, course number, and section number as well.

Reflection and Self-Assessment 6.4

Consider the data store labeled "Academic history" in Figure 6.2. What fields would you establish in a table to capture that information? What primary key would you use to identify each record in a unique way?

In practice, a single database is likely to contain multiple tables. For example, a credit card company might have one table with customer information, a second table with information about current period charges, and a third table with information about customer payments. Each table captures different information, yet all three are related to one another. For that reason, database tables often include one or more **foreign keys.** A foreign key in one table is nothing more than another table's primary key. For example, the primary key in the customer information table might be the customer's credit card number. When a payment comes in, the credit card company needs to record not only the amount and date of the payment, but also who the payment is from. So, the customer's credit card number (the primary key in the customer information table) would become a foreign key in the payment table.

For the sake of convenience and clarity in talking about database tables, we'll use an underline to denote a primary key and [brackets] to denote a foreign key. Here's an example:

Check number	Payee number
Date written	Payee name
[Payee number]	Payee address
Amount	Payee city
Date paid by bank	Payee state
	Payee ZIP code
	Payee phone number
	Contact person

The column on the left might be called the "check table," while the column on the right could be labeled the "payee table." Organizing the data in a relational database would allow users to ask questions (referred to as **queries**) and create output reports that reflect information. For example, in our two-table database above, we could generate a query as the basis for a report that contains the check number and amount for each payee in the database. Relational databases also can do simple arithmetic operations, such as calculating the average check amount or the number of checks written but not yet paid by the bank as of a certain date. Database queries store instructions, not data. Each time the query is "run," it looks at the current data to get the answer to its question. Storing just the instructions, and not the results, helps keep the database compact and manageable (we'll come back to that idea at the end of this section).

Databases also can contain forms that facilitate data entry. If, for example, you've ever purchased anything on the Internet, you probably filled out a form with information such as your name, address, items ordered, and credit card number. That form would store the data in a table.

Databases of accounting information can grow very large, very quickly. And database users want to be able to access the data quickly and easily. The process of making a database efficient and easy to use is referred to as *data normalization.* In short, data normalization allows database creators and users to minimize database size, optimize table design, and access data more quickly and efficiently. When a database follows the rules of data normalization, it is said to be in "normal form." Altogether, database specialists have conceptualized six normal forms, although the first three typically satisfy most business requirements. And normal forms are "additive"; that is, if a database is in second normal

You can get more information about data normalization at www.datamodel.org or by doing a Web search on "data normalization."

form, it is by definition in first normal form as well. Let's look at the rules for the first three normal forms in more detail.

First Normal Form (1NF): Eliminate Repeating Groups

A database table is in first normal form if it *eliminates repeating groups.* Suppose, for example, you wanted to show which customers had purchased which inventory items. If you attempted to create an "inventory items purchased" field in the customer table, at least two problems would result. First, the field would have to be updated every time a customer purchased a new type of inventory. Second, searching the database for that information would be time-consuming and cumbersome. Succinctly stated, the table would contain repeating groups—inventory item names would be repeated in several customer records.

Customer Name	Inventory Items
Brown	Paper, pens
McLaughlin	Pens, notebooks
Silva	Paper, pens, notebooks
Truong	Paper, notebooks
Zarineh	Notebooks

So how could you eliminate the repeating groups and put the database in first normal form? You could create two tables—one for inventory items and one for customers. The inventory table would have one field for the inventory item name and another field for the customer name. The inventory table would have a compound primary key; each record would be uniquely identified with the combination of the inventory item name AND the customer name.

Inventory Item	Customer
Notebooks	McLaughlin
Notebooks	Silva
Notebooks	Truong
Notebooks	Zarineh
Paper	Brown
Paper	Silva
Paper	Truong
Pens	Brown
Pens	McLaughlin
Pens	Silva

Second Normal Form (2NF): Eliminate Redundant Data

A table is in second normal form if it *eliminates redundant data.* In the table above, both customer names and inventory item names are repeated, although not in groups. (Eliminating repeating groups is the point of 1NF.) Because data items are repeated individually, the 1NF table contains redundant data. If the number of products and/or the number of customers expanded significantly, the database table would take up a lot of "space" on a computer network.

How could we fix that problem and put the database in 2NF? By splitting the 1NF table into separate tables again: one for inventory items, one for customer names, and a third that "marries" the two. The inventory item table would have three records (notebooks, paper, and pens); the customer table would have five records (Brown, McLaughlin, Silva, Truong, Zarineh). The third table, often referred to as a "junction table" would combine the data, thus making searches more efficient. A junction table is required in this case because each inventory item can be associated with many customers, and each customer can be associated with many inventory items. The three tables would look like this (notice the addition of "identification numbers" for each inventory item and each customer):

Inventory Table		Customer Table		Inventory/Customer Table	
Item	**ID**	**Name**	**ID**	**Inventory ID**	**Customer ID**
Notebooks	1	Brown	1	1	2
Paper	2	McLaughlin	2	1	3
Pens	3	Silva	3	1	4
		Truong	4	1	5
		Zarineh	5	2	1
				2	3
				2	4
				3	1
				3	2
				3	3

The tables above are in 2NF; they eliminate data redundancy in that they do not repeat inventory item names and customer names. The data redundancy is eliminated by introducing a third table that stores the ID numbers rather than the full names; the junction table would have a compound primary key, comprised of both fields displayed in the table above.

Third Normal Form (3NF): Eliminate Columns Not Dependent on the Primary Key

A table is in third normal form if it *eliminates columns not dependent on the primary key.* In other words, each field in a table should provide additional information about its primary key. So, if you wanted to include more information about each customer (address and phone number, for example), where would you put it? In the customer table, *not* in the junction table. Although the junction table contains one piece of data about a customer (the customer ID), additional data about the customer does not help us understand more about the relationship between customers and inventory; additional data about the customer help us understand more about the customer and therefore should be included in the customer table. Likewise, additional data about inventory transactions (such as the date and number of items purchased) help us understand more about the data in the junction table and therefore should be included there.

One other note about database design: Never store derivable data in a database table. Derivable data refer to anything that can be calculated, such as a customer's account balance, an employee's age, or the number of inventory items on hand. Use a query to get derivable data. Recall that a query stores instructions, not output. Storing the instructions takes up a lot less room than storing the data itself; also, using a query to derive data allows database users to get current results each time the query is run. So, for example, the junction table above would not contain a field for "total sales." It would contain a field for number of items sold and price per item; you would use a query to calculate the total of each sale.

As noted above, we've barely scratched the surface of using databases in accounting information systems. While data flow diagrams can be used in AIS work regardless of the technology that underlies the system, they are arguably used most often as the basis for designing a relational database. Depending upon the emphasis your instructor places on software in your AIS course, you may develop a basic to intermediate skill level with databases; either way, such knowledge will give you a competitive edge in your accounting career.

CRITICAL THINKING

In the last chapter, we talked about drawing a flowchart of the FASB's new standards approval process; if you completed Reflection and Self-Assessment 5.4, you actually drew the flowchart. To help you understand the similarities and differences between flowcharts and DFDs, let's look at a Level Zero data flow diagram of the same process.

I usually start drawing a DFD by thinking about the system boundary. In this case, I'm going to define the system boundary as the FASB itself; that is, the actual Board members. As a result, the following will be external entities: Emerging Issues Task Force, advisory task force, technical staff, and the public. An alternative definition of the system boundary would be the entire FASB organization, which would include the Board, the EITF, and the technical staff. In that case, external entities would be the advisory task force and the public.

The processes involved in standard setting are described fairly clearly by the steps listed in Chapter 5. They would include (a) develop the agenda, (b) appoint advisory task force, (c) assign technical staff, (d) develop discussion memorandum, (e) get feedback on the DM, (f) develop the exposure draft, (g) get feedback on the ED, and (h) vote. Notice that the list involves seven processes, so we'd really be pushing the limit to include all of them in a single DFD. The good news is not all seven processes need to be shown in the Level Zero diagram. Some of them could potentially be combined, with the detail provided in subsequent levels.

Based on that, a Level Zero DFD might look like Figure 6.5. From the Level Zero DFD, you could decompose Process 3.0 into three processes: 3.1, prepare discussion memorandum; 3.2, obtain DM feedback; and 3.3, prepare exposure draft. Notice how, in the Level Zero diagram, the data flow leaving Process 3.0 is labeled "exposure draft." In the Level One decomposition of Process 3.0, that same data flow should leave Process 3.3 as one way of balancing the diagrams. You also could decompose Process 5.0 into two processes: 5.1, revise exposure draft; and 5.2, vote on revised draft.

At this point, you may be thinking: But what if the FASB votes and the potential new standard doesn't pass? The Board probably wouldn't conduct a vote until they were fairly certain the standard would pass; revision would continue until that point.

Developing data flow diagrams, just like constructing flowcharts, requires practice; in fact, I made three different drafts of Figure 6.5 before it was ready. And another systems professional might suggest additional changes, too. So, try not to be discouraged as you're learning—use constructive feedback to make your diagrams clearer and more readable, keeping in mind the "art versus science" comments from Chapter 5.

FIGURE 6.5 Level Zero DFD of FASB's Standard Development Process

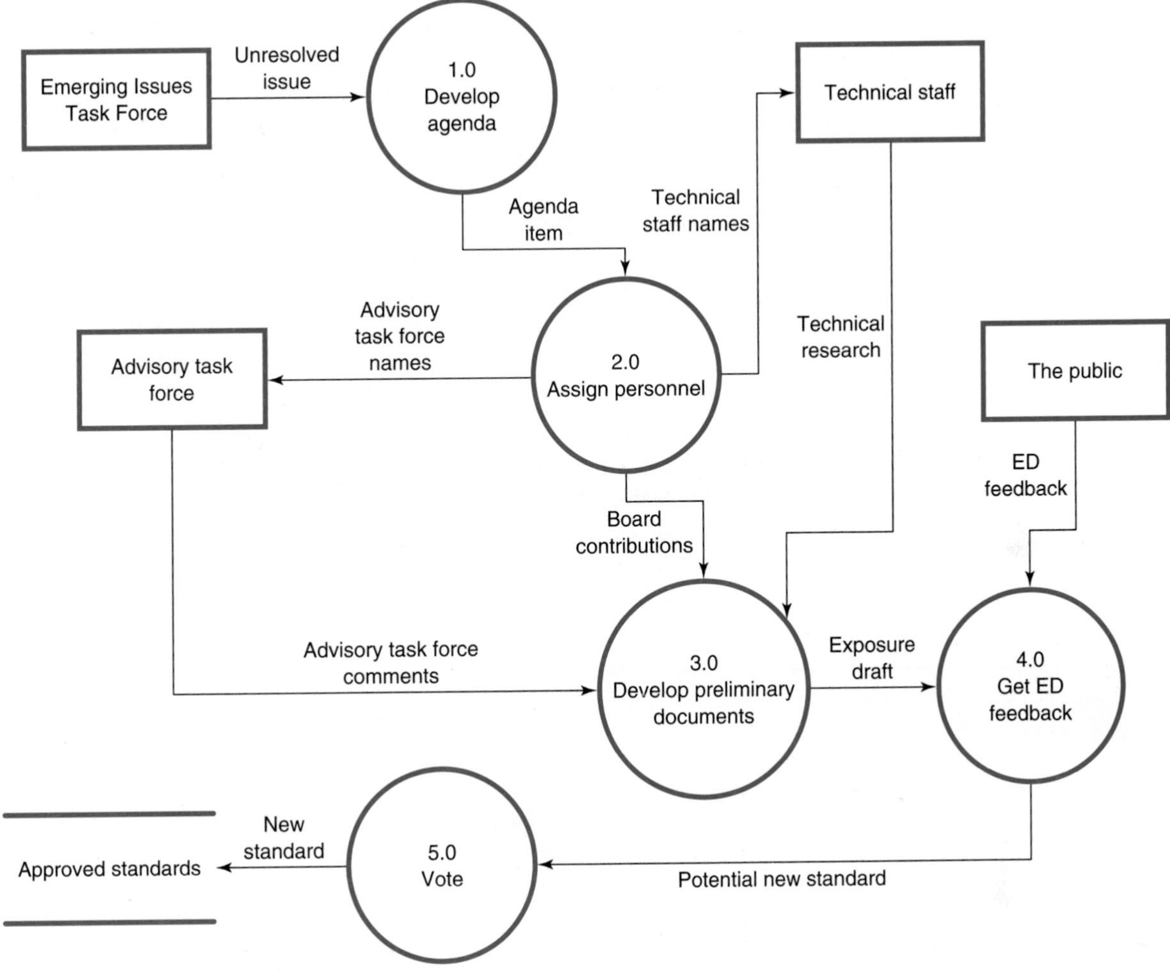

Summary

Data flow diagrams and relational databases are powerful tools in the design, implementation, use, and evaluation of accounting information systems. Here is the chapter summary:

1. *Explain the symbols and design considerations associated with DFDs.* Data flow diagrams incorporate four symbols. Processes are represented with circle, data flows are depicted by arrows, parallel horizontal lines denote data stores, and rectangles represent external entities. DFDs are prepared in leveled sets, with each set revealing more detail than the one before it.
2. *Compare and contrast flowcharts and DFDs with regard to purpose, content, structure, and use in accounting information systems.* Both flowcharts and DFDs are methods of conceptualizing an information system. Flowcharts incorporate more symbols than DFDs, but both are read from top to bottom and left to right (generally). DFDs can be used more easily to design relational databases.
3. *Discuss ways DFDs are used in AIS work.* DFDs can be used in at least four ways in accounting information systems design, development, and implementation. They can

(*a*) ensure an adequate understanding of an accounting information system, (*b*) help accountants make process improvements to the system, (*c*) help others understand the flows of data and information, and (*d*) assist in designing relational database tables that capture data and report information.

4. *Construct a leveled set of DFDs.* As with flowcharting, DFDs are designed iteratively and cooperatively. Two different systems professionals can create two different DFDs based on the same situation; as usual, there is no deterministic solution for most DFD problems.
5. *Design normalized database tables from a DFD.* Many elements of a DFD require database tables in an accounting information system. Tables should be normalized; each must include a primary key that uniquely identifies each record within the table. Foreign keys can link tables together in a database. Junction tables are used when items in two separate tables have a many-to-many relationship, such as the relationship between customers and inventory or purchasing agents and vendors.

As noted in the conclusion for the flowcharting chapter, you will likely be challenged as you develop familiarity and skill in using DFDs. Keep in mind that, like flowcharting, data flow diagramming and database design are at least as much "art" as "science." The point isn't to get to the "one right answer"; it probably doesn't exist anyway. The point here is to produce DFDs and database tables that are both effective and efficient from multiple points of view.

Key Terms

balanced, *113*
context diagram, *111*
data flow, *107*
data store, *107*
database tables, *114*
external entity, *107*
foreign keys, *115*
Level Zero diagram, *111*
leveled sets, *110*
primary key, *114*
primitive, *113*
process, *106*
queries, *115*
rules/conventions, *107*
systems development life cycle, *114*

Chapter References

Bradford, M., S. Richtermeyer, and D. Roberts. 2007. "System Diagramming Techniques: An Analysis of Methods Used in Accounting Education and Practice." *Journal of Information Systems,* Spring, pp. 173–212.

DeMarco, T. 1979. *Structured Analysis and Systems Specifications.* Englewood Cliffs, NJ: Prentice Hall.

Hoffner, J., J. George, and J. Valacich. 1996. *Modern Systems Analysis and Design.* Reading, MA: Benjamin/Cummings.

Ricciardi, S. 1994. "Database Design: Redundancy and Normalization." *PC Magazine,* January 25, pp. 285–89.

End-of-Chapter Activities

1. *Reading review questions.*
   a. What is a data flow diagram? How are data flow diagrams used in accounting information systems?
   b. List and discuss the four symbols used in the development of data flow diagrams. Give an example of each symbol in an AIS context.
   c. What rules/conventions should accountants follow when creating DFDs?
   d. Define the following terms as they relate to the material presented in this chapter: relational database, table, primary key, foreign key, field, record, and query.
   e. Respond to the questions for this chapter's "AIS in the Business World."

2. *Reading review problem.* Home Depot (www.homedepot.com) is one of the nation's largest retailers of home improvement products. But, according to Flick and Subu, "manual processes, high transaction volumes and a lack of information technology resources have plagued the Home Depot treasury for years." Managers and treasury analysts were unable to make accurate, timely predictions of the company's cash position; the company's old system was "inefficient, time-consuming and [had] no integrated system to support it."

   Subu assembled an interdisciplinary team from expense payables, receivables, and the treasury department. Together, with the aid of a well-constructed data flow diagram and primary research with system users, the group built a new cash management system that satisfied eight basic needs:

   - Input and approve wire requests.
   - Track the status of wire requests at any time.
   - Access reports and files of wire payments.
   - Manage the company's wire policy automatically.
   - Interpret bank files to provide meaningful information.
   - Automate the process of entering wire transfers.
   - Calculate the company's net cash position.
   - Manage cash and identify money available for investment.

   The system produced over $34 million in cost savings and increased efficiencies—enough to construct two new Home Depot stores.

   a. List the symbols included in data flow diagrams. Explain the meaning of each symbol.
   b. For each symbol, suggest two examples you would expect to find in Home Depot's data flow diagram.
   c. Explain the concepts of "leveling" and "balancing" as they relate to data flow diagrams.

Source: R. Flick and M. Subu, "Home Improvement Requires Creative Thinking and a New Toolbox," *AFP Exchange*, May/June 2004.

3. *Making choices and exercising judgment.* Bumble Beasley is a recently enrolled accounting major at your university. In a conversation about accounting information systems, he said: "I don't know why we have to learn about flowcharts *and* data flow diagrams. One documentation technique should be enough; besides, both techniques give basically the same information if you know how to read them." Do you agree or disagree with Bumble? Why?

4. *Field exercises.*

   a. Contact an information systems professional such as a professor or systems analyst. Ask him or her about how flowcharts and data flow diagrams could be used in the design and evaluation of an accounting information system.
   b. Point your Web browser to www.download.com and search for flowcharting and/or data flow diagramming software there. Identify and describe two pieces of software that are capable of creating *both* flowcharts and data flow diagrams.
   c. Look up the Bradford article listed in the chapter references. Summarize its main points.

5. *Data flow diagram creation.*

   a. The Geek Squad (www.geeksquad.com) offers a variety of telephone, in-office, and in-home computer services. When a call for assistance comes into their 800 number, the Geek Squad determines its geographical origin and routes the call to an agent in the area. The agent confers with the customer by phone, determining the nature of the problem and the type of service desired. The agent also will find out if the customer has previously done business with Geek Squad. The agent will respond to the customer's request and report the problem's resolution to the corporate office. The corporate office bills the customer and collects payment; a fixed fee is remitted to the local agent based on the type and nature of the service call. Point your Web browser to the Geek Squad Web site to get more information about their operations. Then, prepare a context diagram, Level Zero diagram, and one Level One diagram for Geek Squad.

b. Every year, the Institute of Management Accountants sponsors a student case competition to help students build their technical, analytical, and communication skills. In the student case competition, the IMA solicits cases from accounting faculty; an IMA committee chooses the best case and publishes it in an issue of *Strategic Finance.* Teams of students prepare videotaped responses to the case and submit them to the IMA. The videotaped presentations are evaluated and the team with the best presentation in each geographic region presents their case "in person" to a panel of judges at the IMA annual meeting. The team with the best presentation receives an award; all teams presenting at the annual meeting receive an engraved plaque with the members' names on it. The IMA maintains a database of case topics and authors; it also keeps a record of the name and university affiliation of all teams submitting videotapes as well as the status of those submissions. (For more information about the IMA student case competition, point your Web browser to www.imanet.org.) Consider the preceding narrative, and prepare a leveled set of data flow diagrams (context, Level Zero, and Level One).

c. Consider the narratives presented in Chapter 5 for Cori's Catering Services and University Bookstore. Use those narratives to prepare a leveled set of data flow diagrams.

6. *Critiquing database tables.* Bumble Beasley attempted to design a database to capture data about inventory purchases. He thought it would be easier to create one table with all the data rather than separate tables for different data items. The table he created contained the following fields:

Vendor phone	Inventory description
Purchasing agent ID	Cost per item
Vendor ID	Vendor code
Purchasing agent home address	Invoice total (number of items × cost per item)
Vendor state	Payment terms (e.g., 2/10, n/30)
Vendor address	Inventory ID
Vendor city	Purchasing agent first name
Purchasing agent last name	Transaction number
Transaction date	Quantity purchased
Vendor ZIP	

a. Is Bumble's database table in normal form? Discuss.

b. How many normalized database tables would be required for the data?

c. Group the data into the required number of normalized database tables. Specify a primary key for each table.

7. *Creating database tables.* (Your instructor may want you to use Access or some other relational database software to complete this problem.)

a. Create at least two database tables for each Level One data flow diagram you created in Problem 5 (data flow diagram creation).

b. In most states, the Department of Motor Vehicles keeps records of individual driver's licenses and vehicle license plates. Create two database tables that capture relevant information for the DMV; information in the driver's license table would include, but not be limited to, an individual's name, license number, and birth date. Information in the vehicle license plate table would include, but not be limited to, the license plate number and information about the vehicle itself. What foreign key(s) would you use to link the two tables together?

c. Robert Half International (www.roberthalf.net) pairs up potential employees with companies seeking accountants and other financial information professionals. Their Web site states: "With 325 offices and 55 years of experience, Robert Half is the world's first and largest specialized financial recruiting firm, placing quality candidates at all levels." Point your Web browser to the company's Web site and click the link for Robert Half United States. What information does Robert Half collect on new job seekers? Organize that information into a database table.

8. *Crossword puzzle.* Please complete the puzzle below using terminology from the chapter.

Across

3. The number of symbols in data flow diagrams.
5. Type of phrase associated with a process.
7. In a ______ diagram, the entire information system is represented by a single process.
9. A general ledger account can be thought of as one of these.
10. Type of phrase associated with a data flow.

Down

1. A process that cannot be decomposed.
2. For example, "pay vendors."
4. A properly constructed set of DFDs.
6. Data stores do not specify this.
8. Descriptor for entities outside the system.

9. *Terminology.* Please match each item on the left with the most appropriate item on the right.

1. Data flow	a. A compilation of fields in a database.
2. Data store	b. A primary key posted to another table.
3. External entity	c. Accounts receivable file.
4. Field	d. Customer last name.
5. Foreign key	e. First detailed look at an information system.
6. Level Zero	f. First National Bank.
7. Primary key	g. Paid invoices.
8. Process	h. Prepare financial statements.
9. Query	i. Uniquely identifies records in a database.
10. Record	j. Which customers have balances over $500?

10. *Multiple choice questions.*

1. Which of the following statements about data flow diagrams is not true?
   a. Processes should always be numbered and named.
   b. A context diagram cannot include any data stores.
   c. Data flows should be labeled with noun phrases.
   d. Data flow diagrams incorporate four symbols.
2. In creating a data flow diagram for a course registration process, which of the following is most likely to be an external entity?
   a. Parents
   b. Student
   c. Registration system
   d. Bank
3. Which of the following best describes a context diagram?
   a. A flowchart that shows the relationship of an accounting information system to its environment.
   b. A data flow diagram that does not include any processes.
   c. A data flow diagram that cannot be decomposed further.
   d. A data flow diagram that shows the highest level view of an information system.
4. John is designing a database table to keep track of his customers. Which of the following would most likely be the primary key in the table?
   a. Customer number generated automatically by the information system
   b. Customer last name
   c. Customer address
   d. Customer telephone number
5. A foreign key
   a. Is another name for a table's primary key.
   b. Is a primary key in another database table.
   c. Is a primary key written in a foreign language.
   d. Cannot be incorporated in a normalized database table.
6. Database tables in first normal form eliminate
   a. Repeating groups.
   b. Redundant data.
   c. Columns not dependent on the primary key.
   d. All of the above.

7. A database junction table
   a. Is needed when an item in one table can be associated with many items in a second table.
   b. Is needed when many items in one table can be associated with one item in a second table.
   c. Is needed when many items in one table can be associated with many items in a second table.
   d. Violates the rules of data normalization.
8. Which of the following is not a symbol associated with data flow diagrams?
   a. Triangle
   b. Circle
   c. Line
   d. Rectangle
9. If data about a customer reside in a junction table, the table is not in
   a. First normal form.
   b. Second normal form.
   c. Third normal form.
   d. Compliance with rules about derivable data.
10. Which of the following is derivable?
   a. A customer's Zip code
   b. A student's age
   c. Cost per unit of inventory
   d. All of the above are derivable.

11. *Statement evaluation.* Specify whether each statement below is (i) always true, (ii) sometimes true, or (iii) never true. For those that are (ii) sometimes true, explain when the statement is true.
   a. A context diagram does not include data stores.
   b. A database table in 2NF is in 3NF as well.
   c. A salesperson is an external entity in a data flow diagram.
   d. Data flow diagrams are better than flowcharts for documenting accounting information systems.
   e. Database forms can be used to look up information in a table.
   f. Database queries store instructions, not data.
   g. Database tables are needed for processes, external entities, and data stores in a DFD.
   h. Database tables in 3NF are, by definition, also in 1NF and 2NF.
   i. Decomposing a process numbered 2.0 would lead to numbers like 2.1, 2.2, and so on.
   j. Lines in a data flow diagram should be labeled with verb phrases to show the movement of data.

Chapter Seven

REAL Modeling

AIS in the Business World

Beta Alpha Psi

Beta Alpha Psi (www.bap.org) is the international honor society for students and professionals in accounting, finance, and information systems. According to its Web site:

> The primary objective of Beta Alpha Psi is to encourage and give recognition to scholastic and professional excellence in the business information field. This includes promoting the study and practice of accounting, finance and information systems; providing opportunities for self-development, service and association among members and practicing professionals, and encouraging a sense of ethical, social, and public responsibility.

Each BAY chapter is required to complete certain activities each year; they also may earn extra recognition and rewards by going beyond the minimums specified by the national office. Events include things like meet the firms, professional speaker meetings, community service projects, and national and regional meetings. Each BAY chapter tracks its members' participation in the various events, reporting periodically to the national office via BAY's reporting intranet.

As you can tell, the information needs of a typical BAY chapter go far beyond general purpose financial statements. To facilitate information gathering and decision making, a BAY chapter might choose to develop a REAL model as the basis for an event-driven accounting information system.

Discussion Questions

1. What is a REAL model?
2. What is an event-driven accounting information system?

So far, we've looked at two documentation techniques for accounting information systems: flowcharting and data flow diagramming. In this chapter, we'll examine a third technique: REAL modeling. A relative newcomer to accounting information systems, REAL modeling is an important part of designing event-driven accounting information systems.

McCarthy (1982) is considered by many to be a pioneer in the development of event-driven accounting systems. Event-driven systems capture a broader range of data than view-driven systems; relational database technology underlies most event-driven systems. Enterprise resource planning (ERP) systems are a sophisticated version of event-driven AIS. In this chapter, we'll take a closer look at event-driven accounting information systems and REAL modeling, the documentation technique often used in their development.

When you finish studying this material, you should be able to:

1. Compare and contrast view-driven and event-driven accounting information systems.
2. Use REAL modeling to represent an event-driven AIS.
3. Use a REAL model to design a relational database for an event-driven AIS.

In some accounting curricula, professors devote entire courses to the topic of event-driven AIS. Although REAL modeling is used less frequently in accounting practice than systems flowcharts, it represents an important way of thinking about the AIS. As with flowcharting and data flow diagramming, two people may come up with slightly different REAL models for the same event-driven AIS. And, as with the other two systems documentation techniques, skill in REAL modeling is developed with practice over time.

TYPES OF ACCOUNTING INFORMATION SYSTEMS

At a very basic level, accounting information systems can be divided into two broad groups: view-driven and event-driven. Think of view-driven systems as traditional accounting systems—they may incorporate some forms of information technology, but their defining characteristic is their focus on the general purpose financial statements. If a manager or other decision maker is interested in producing an income statement, a balance sheet, a statement of changes in equity, or (in a few cases) a statement of cash flows, the task can be accomplished with a few simple, well-defined steps (i.e., completing the accounting cycle).

Stove piping refers to separating organizational functions and their information systems; for example, treating accounting as though it is unrelated to marketing, operations, or human resource management.

However, managers and other organizational stakeholders frequently need different and/or additional information for effective decision making. As business processes have become more integrated, the need for information has grown exponentially. Business professionals no longer have the luxury of "stove piping" the disciplines. And, unfortunately, view-driven accounting systems foster the idea that departments can remain separate and unrelated.

Walker and Denna (1997) summarized five key problems with view-driven accounting information systems:

1. They focus on a very small, well-defined group of important business events—those that are recordable in the accounting information system with debits and credits.
2. They often process data in batches, frequently at the end of the month. Thus, the data in a view-driven accounting system are often outdated.
3. Even for those transactions described in (1), the system captures a very limited set of data—dates, accounts, and amounts. Other transaction details, such as product characteristics, are omitted.

4. Data in a view-driven system are highly aggregated and stored in multiple places. Important data from source documents such as purchase orders and customer invoices are summarized and rearranged to conform to generally accepted accounting principles. Those changes may facilitate the production of financial statements, but they limit the information available for making decisions.
5. In view-driven systems, the internal control process is often protective and expensive. Controls such as separation of duties are focused on preventing collusion in an effort to safeguard assets.

Consider, for example, a simple, common transaction in most businesses: the sale of inventory on account. If the cost of inventory was $100 and the selling price was $150, a view-driven accounting information system would record the sale as follows:

Accounts receivable	$150	
Cost of goods sold	100	
Sales		$150
Inventory		100

And, while that information is vital for the production of financial statements, consider the following questions related to the transaction: Was the merchandise delivered on time? Was its quality acceptable to the customer? Has this customer ordered similar merchandise before? How close is the customer to reaching/exceeding its established credit limit? Those questions are virtually impossible to answer with a view-driven accounting information system.

In contrast to view-driven systems that capture, organize, and summarize data by business function, event-driven accounting systems focus on business processes. Processes may cut across disciplinary lines, so the data captured about business processes must be more comprehensive than in a view-driven system.

Walker and Denna (1997, p. 24) offer the following comments about event-driven accounting information systems:

> The event-driven approach assumes that the purpose of accounting (and other) information systems is to provide information about economic events that is useful in a variety of decision contexts. Events proponents say, "Let's collect raw business data that can be used by a variety of information customers, each with its own set of values and weights to assign to the data." It is the events view that provides an avenue to the next generation of business information systems.

So, in contrast to view-driven systems, event-driven systems

1. Capture more data about individual transactions.
2. Organize the data so that they can be accessed and understood by people from a variety of organizational functions.
3. Are equipped to answer questions like those posed above regarding the inventory transaction.

By their nature, event-driven systems are more complex than view-driven systems. They must be designed to meet the information needs of many groups of users—not just accountants interested in preparing general purpose financial statements. Because of that complexity and the importance of following good design principles, systems professionals needed a new modeling tool. In the next section, we'll look at REAL modeling—a documentation technique that facilitates the design and implementation of event-driven accounting information systems.

REAL MODELING

REAL is an acronym referring to the *r*esources, *e*vents, *a*gents, and *l*ocations in an event-driven accounting information system. Most AIS designers and auditors find it best to start a REAL model by identifying its relevant events. In general, "events" come in three broad categories:

- *Operating events* focus on activities involved with providing goods and services to customers. Examples include purchasing and selling inventory, paying employees, and converting raw material into finished goods.
- *Information events* deal with recording and maintaining data, as well as reporting information. Think of information events as preparing financial statements or updating accounting records.
- *Decision/management events* are concerned with human decision making. They can range from simple things, such as which software and hardware to buy, to more complex decisions such as changing compensation packages.

REAL models capture data on strategically significant operating events; they do not incorporate information events or decision/management events. Once strategically significant operating events have been identified, the rest of the details (resources, agents, and, when necessary, locations) can be filled in around them.

Agents are the people involved in the information system. Internal agents include employees in all departments; external agents refer to customers, vendors, and other stakeholders "outside" the business. Resources are the things agents need to complete the events: cash, inventory, equipment, supplies, and other assets. Locations are not strictly required in every REAL model. However, if an event occurs at a particular geographic location, it should be noted in the REAL model. For example, if a company maintains an operating bank account in one bank and a payroll account in a different bank, the event "disburse cash" would need to include a location.

REAL models are organized in columns, with the **events** appearing in the middle, **resources** to the left, and **agents** to the right. **Locations** can be included wherever they fit most logically. The REAL model presented in Figure 7.1 has one event: rent car for cash. It includes one resource—automobile—and it incorporates two agents: client (an external agent) and a rental agent (an internal agent). That REAL model describes the process of renting a car to a client.

FIGURE 7.1
REAL Model Illustration

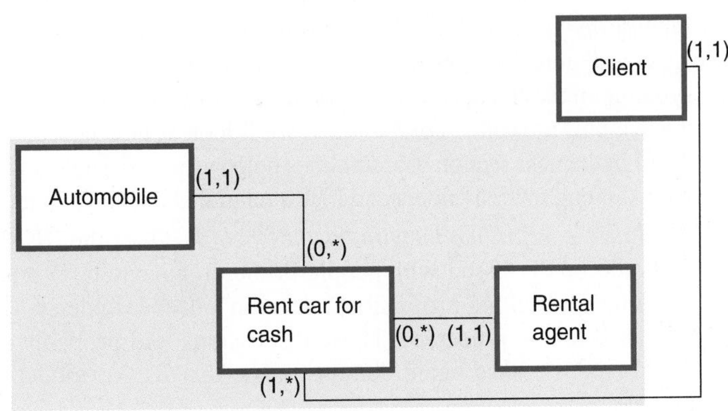

So how do you develop a REAL model? Hollander, Denna, and Cherrington (2000) recommend a **six-step process:**

1. *Understand the organization's environment and objectives.* To become trusted business advisors, accounting professionals need to have a thorough grasp of what the organization does. In 1995, I was privileged to work in Swaziland, a small country next to South Africa. Part of my job there was to consult with local organizations about the development and implementation of activity-based costing systems. One such organization was Mhlume Sugar Company. But, before I could help the organization as a consultant, I had to understand how sugar is manufactured—everything that happens from the time the sugar cane is planted until the sugar is in its final form. The same logic applies to REAL modeling. You'll have to observe the operations, read manuals and articles from the literature, and talk with managers and workers before developing a REAL model.
2. *Review the business process and identify the strategically significant operating events.* REAL modeling focuses on business processes—the everyday activities employees undertake to create value for their customers and other stakeholders. Every business process is made up of events; the focus in REAL modeling is on the strategically significant operating event. As I write this chapter, I'm sitting in the airport in Las Vegas, waiting for a flight back home. The strategically significant operating events associated with the flight process would include checking baggage, checking in passengers, and boarding the airplane. Identifying the strategically significant operating events for a REAL model is both subjective and iterative. The process is subjective because two different designers might come up with two slightly different sets of events and/or give them different names. The process is iterative because you'll normally need several "tries" to capture all the events.
3. *Analyze each strategically significant operating event to identify the event resources, agents, and locations.* For example, checking in passengers would include two agents (a passenger and an airline employee) and two resources (a computer and a boarding pass). The location would be optional in this case, but could be the city name.
4. *Identify the relevant behaviors, characteristics, and attributes of the REAL model elements.* This step helps you create database tables. For example, what data would you want/need to capture about an airline employee in your database? Fields in the "employee" table might include last name, first name, Social Security number, phone number, address, job position, and emergency contact. The relevant data for a boarding pass would include the passenger's name, seat assignment, departure and destination cities, gate assignment, and boarding and departure times.
5. *Identify and document the direct relationships among elements of the REAL model.* Look again at Figure 7.1; notice the lines between the various REAL model elements and the symbols on the end of each line. The lines show which elements are related to one another; the symbols are called *cardinalities.* We'll look at how to establish cardinalities in more detail in the next section. Cardinalities help systems designers, auditors, and fraud examiners (among others) understand how a relational database should be constructed.
6. *Validate the REAL model with businesspeople.* Once the REAL model is constructed, it should be discussed with people in the organization. Discussing the REAL model helps the accounting professional develop a deeper understanding of the organization and its business processes. Those discussions will probably result in changes to the REAL model, once again demonstrating that REAL modeling is a highly iterative process.

You won't be able to complete this step in homework problems, but it is vital in practice.

You'll need to practice developing REAL models to become comfortable and proficient at the process. Try not to become discouraged or frustrated—REAL modeling is a new way of thinking for most accounting students. Remember, for example, when you first started making journal entries in introductory accounting? You may have thought you'd never remember that debits are on the left and credits are on the right; now, though, you probably don't give that whole process a lot of conscious thought—it's second nature to you. REAL modeling will likely be the same: some initial confusion and discomfort leading to success in the long term.

Reflection and Self-Assessment 7.1

If you're like most accounting students, you love pizza. Think about the process of ordering and making a pizza. Identify the strategically significant operating events associated with those two processes; then identify the relevant resources and agents. What information would you want to capture in a relational database about each item you identify?

Now, let's take a closer look at establishing relationships between the elements of a REAL model by creating cardinalities.

CARDINALITIES

As you read earlier, **cardinalities** tell an accounting professional about the relationships between elements of a REAL model. A well-constructed set of cardinalities is a huge help in using a REAL model to create a relational database. Ask yourself four questions when establishing cardinalities for a REAL model:

1. *For each* x, *what is the minimum number of* y *involved?* Consider, for example, the relationship between "rent car for cash" and "rental agent" in Figure 7.1. If "rent car for cash" is *x* and "rental agent" is *y,* you're asking: for each "rent car for cash" transaction, what is the minimum number of rental agents involved? In this case, the answer is one. Could the minimum number of rental agents ever be zero? Sure—if the process was entirely automated; for example, a client might access a Web site to make a reservation for a car. Situations such as that illustrate why it's important to understand an organization's environment when you develop a REAL model.
2. *For each* x, *what is the maximum number of* y *involved?* Extending that illustration, this question becomes: for each "rent car for cash" transaction, what is the maximum number of rental agents involved? Assuming that each transaction is handled by only one agent, the answer here is also one. Setting the maximum number of agents to "one" promotes strong internal control; if two or more agents were involved in a transaction, collusion between them could lead to errors and/or fraud.

Once you've answered the first two questions, record the cardinalities on the *y* side of the relationship. So, the (1,1) notation next to the "rental agent" box in Figure 7.1 explains how many rental agents are involved in each "rent car for cash" transaction.

3. *For each* y, *what is the minimum number of* x *involved?* In our example, this question is asking about the minimum number of rental transactions each rental agent could

complete. To answer this question, envision a rental agent who just stands around behind the counter or sits behind the desk, reading magazines and surfing the Internet instead of helping customers. If you had an employee like that, who never completed a rental transaction, you'd want to know it! So, the minimum number of rental transactions for a given rental agent is zero.

4. *For each* y, *what is the maximum number of* x *involved?* On the other hand, envision an employee who works tirelessly—who handles each rental transaction effectively and efficiently. Would you limit the number of transactions that agent could complete? Probably not. When there's no upper limit on a relationship between two elements of a REAL model, we refer to the maximum as *many,* and symbolize it with an asterisk (*).

After answering questions 3 and 4, note the cardinalities on the *x* side of the relationship. So, the (0,*) notation next to "rent car for cash" tells us that each rental agent can complete from zero to many car rental transactions.

If you're like most students who read this material for the first time, you're saying to yourself, "Hmmm, maybe I don't want to be an accounting major after all." But don't give up! Remember: cardinalities are a very new way of thinking for most accounting students. You've probably never encountered anything like this notation in your other accounting classes. You'll need to practice and think very deliberately about establishing cardinalities for a while—after that, it'll become as second nature to you as creating a balance sheet.

Reflection and Self-Assessment 7.2

Examine the remaining relationships in Figure 7.1. Write out, in plain English, what each relationship means. Use the four questions as a guide.

The final element of our discussion of REAL modeling involves how to translate the REAL model into a **relational database.** We'll take up that topic in the next section.

DATABASE CREATION FROM A REAL MODEL

In general, you're going to need at least one table for each "box" in the REAL model. So, in our ongoing rental car example, you'd need the tables listed below. Possible fields in each table are indicated, with the primary key signified by an underline. The rules for data normalization, explored earlier in the text, also apply to creating databases for event-driven accounting information systems based on REAL models. When finished, database tables should be in third normal form; they should contain neither repeating groups (1NF) nor redundant data (2NF). In addition, every field in the table should provide additional information about its primary key (3NF). As you may recall from your study of data flow diagramming in Chapter 6, the rules of **normalization** are

1. Focus each database table on a single "thing," such as customer data or inventory data. Each table must have a primary key that uniquely identifies each record.
2. Eliminate redundant data in each table. If a table has a compound primary key, each data element in the table must depend on both parts of the primary key. If a data element depends on only one part of the key, it should go in a separate table.

3. Ensure that all fields in a database table contain data that describe the table's primary key. If a field is not dependent on the primary key, it should be removed to a separate table.

- Automobile table
  - <u>Identification number</u>
  - Make
  - Model
  - Year
- Client table
  - <u>Client last name</u>
  - <u>Client first name</u>
  - Client date of birth
  - Street address
  - City
  - State
  - ZIP
  - Phone
- Rental agent table
  - <u>Employee ID</u>
  - Address
  - Date of birth
  - Emergency contact information
  - First name
  - Job classification
  - Last name
  - Phone
- Rental transaction table
  - <u>Transaction number</u>
  - [Automobile identification number]
  - [Client first name]
  - [Client last name]
  - [Employee ID]
  - Transaction date

In the rental transaction table, notice the presence of primary keys from the other three tables. Referring to the REAL model in Figure 7.1, notice the cardinalities between the automobile table and rental transaction table (as well as the others). The maximum cardinalities between the automobile and rental transaction are one and many, bringing us to the first "rule" of creating database tables from a REAL model:

> When the maximum cardinalities between two elements of a REAL model are one and many, include the primary key from the "one side" in the table on the "many side."

In our example, that rule tells us to put the primary key from the automobile table (the "one side") into the rental transaction table (the "many side").

In some REAL models, relationship cardinalities include maximums of many on both sides. Consider, for example, a database that tracks the academic progress of students in your AIS class. Each student can take many classes; each class includes many students. The REAL model relationship between student and class would look like this:

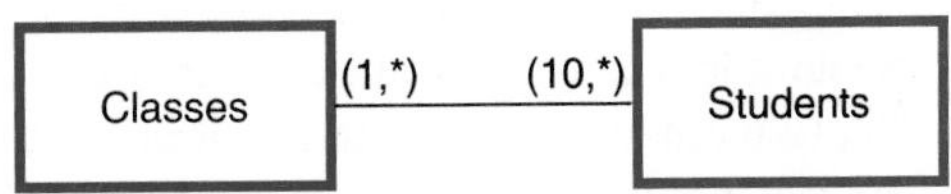

The cardinalities there indicate that every class can have from 10 to many students; every student can take between one and many classes. Situations like that one bring us to the second important rule of creating database tables from a REAL model:

> When the maximum cardinalities between two elements of a REAL model are many and many, create a separate junction table to reflect the combined relationship.

So, in creating a database to reflect the relationship above, you would need three tables: a student table, a classes table, and a student/classes table. The student/classes table is referred to as a **junction table.** Junction tables don't normally contain more than a few fields; many of them will simply comprise the primary keys from the other two tables. So, if the primary key of the student table is the student identification number and the primary key from the classes table is the class identification number, the student/classes table would look like this:

- Student/classes table
  - [Student identification number]
  - [Class identification number]

In creating a relational database table, you would enforce referential integrity between the tables (i.e., between the student and student/classes table and between the classes and student/classes table). Enforcing referential integrity tells the database to update the junction table whenever the separate tables are updated. Junction tables are necessary to make databases more efficient. Consider the alternative: creating separate fields in the student table for each class a student takes. The problem is not knowing the maximum number of fields to create. If you created 10, for example, where would you record information about an 11th class? On the other hand, creating too many fields (i.e., enough so that you never "run out") makes the database too large to store and search.

Reflection and Self-Assessment 7.3

Suppose one of the strategically significant operating events for a pizza restaurant is "sell pizza." Assume the agents involved are "customer" and "employee," and the one resource is "pizza." Create a REAL model, including cardinalities, for those four items. Then, create specifications for the "sell pizza" database table.

Remember: it takes patience and practice to get comfortable with creating REAL models and databases for event-driven accounting systems. The idea is to create a workable REAL model that reflects an organization's **strategically significant operating activities**—not to search for the "one right answer" in any particular situation.

CRITICAL THINKING

So now, let's take a look at a different example of REAL model and database creation. Netflix (www.netflix.com) is an online service that supplies DVDs to its clients. We'll use the six-step process outlined above to create a REAL model for Netflix.

1. *Understand the organization's environment and objectives.* In the company's sales/ collection process, clients subscribe to Netflix and create a "rental queue" of DVDs they want. The client pays a fixed monthly fee, and Netflix ships the DVDs one at a time. When a client returns one DVD to Netflix, Netflix ships the next DVD on the list.
2. *Review the business process and identify the strategically significant operating events.* From Netflix's point of view, the strategically significant operating events in the sales/ collection process are

a. Subscribe new clients.

b. Ship DVDs.

c. Collect payment.

d. Receive returned DVDs.

So, at this point, the REAL model would look like the diagram shown in Figure 7.2.

FIGURE 7.2
Strategically Significant Operating Events—Netflix

Subscribe new clients.

Ship DVDs.

Collect payment.

Receive returned DVDs.

3. *Analyze each strategically significant operating event to identify the event resources, agents, and locations.*

   a. Subscribe new clients.

      i. Agent: client

      ii. Resource: DVDs

   b. Ship DVDs.

      i. Agents: client, Netflix employee

      ii. Resource: DVDs

   c. Collect payment.

      i. Agents: client, Netflix employee

      ii. Resource: cash

   d. Receive returned DVDs.

      i. Agents: client, Netflix employee

      ii. Resource: DVDs

   In this case, locations aren't especially important; they are therefore omitted from the model. And I've chosen to put all Netflix employees into a single table; as a result, the table must include information about the employee's position. Another option would be to create separate tables for different kinds of employees (mailroom, cash receipts, receiving, and so on). So, we can add the resources and agents to the REAL model, as shown in Figure 7.3.

4. *Identify the relevant behaviors, characteristics, and attributes of the REAL model elements.* (In anticipation of creating the database, primary keys are underlined; foreign keys are in brackets.)

   a. Resources

      i. DVDs: <u>DVD ID, Title,</u> year, genre, director, synopsis

      ii. Cash: <u>Account number,</u> bank, beginning balance date, beginning balance

   b. Events

      i. Subscribe new clients: <u>Subscription date,</u> [<u>client ID</u>], number of DVDs per month

      ii. Ship DVDs: <u>Shipping transaction number,</u> shipment date, [client ID], [Netflix employee ID], [DVD ID]

      iii. Receive returned DVDs: <u>Receipt transaction number,</u> receipt date, [client ID], [Netflix employee ID], [DVD ID]

   c. Agents

      i. Client: <u>Client ID,</u> last name, first name, address, city, state, ZIP, area code, phone, e-mail address, credit card number, credit card expiration date

      ii. Netflix employee: <u>Employee ID,</u> last name, first name, address, city, state, ZIP, area code, phone, emergency contact, department, date employed, pay rate, date terminated, reason for termination

5. *Identify and document the direct relationships among elements of the REAL model.* In this step, we'll create cardinalities using the four questions noted above. Note that

FIGURE 7.3
REAL Model without Cardinalities—Netflix

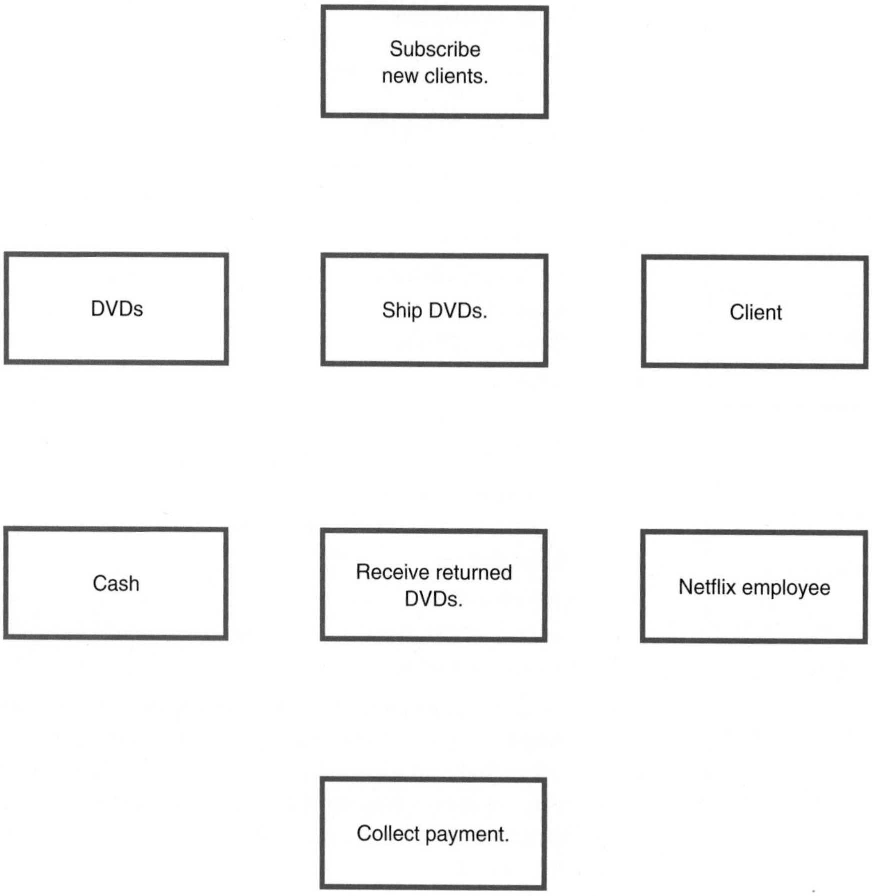

"client" has a relationship with "DVDs" outside of any event because the client establishes a rental queue as part of the subscription event. The REAL model with cardinalities is shown in Figure 7.4.

6. *Validate the REAL model with businesspeople.* In practice, you would review the REAL model with Netflix employees and others to ensure that it portrays the business rules clearly and accurately.

After creating the REAL model, you'd be ready to construct a relational database. Notice how step four above helps you create the database—if you've completed it diligently, you have the field names for most of the database tables. In this case, let's assume that DVD ID refers to a specific title—not a specific copy. Netflix could create as many copies as it needs to distribute to clients; tracking each copy separately would involve extensive recordkeeping. If you didn't want to create a separate DVD ID, you could use a compound primary key of title *and* year for the DVD table—the title alone wouldn't be enough because of the common practice of "remaking" films in different years—consider, for example, the two versions of *The Man in the Iron Mask, Cheaper by the Dozen,* or *When a Stranger Calls.*

The REAL model in Figure 7.4 would require one junction table to document the relationship between client and DVDs. Again, recall that those two have a relationship

FIGURE 7.4 REAL Model with Cardinalities—Netflix

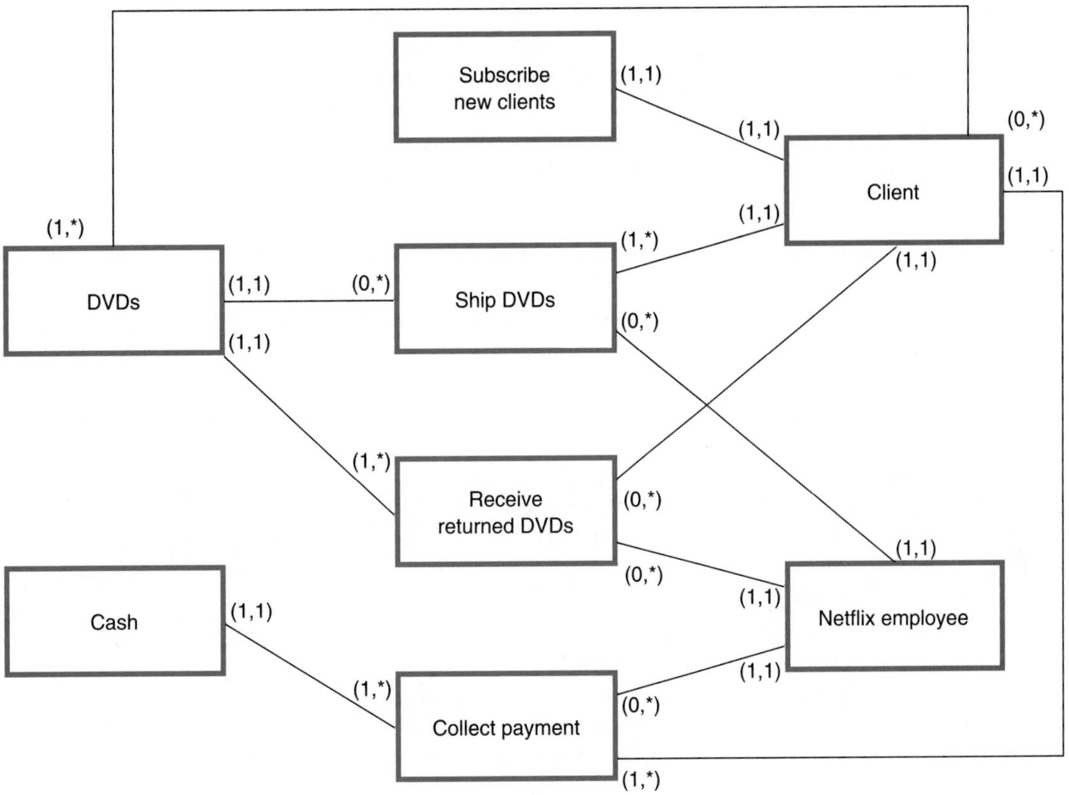

independent of any event because the client establishes a rental queue during the subscription process. The client/DVD junction table would have just a few fields: client ID, DVD ID, position in queue, date added. It would have a compound primary key (client ID and DVD ID); in the Access table, you'd have to specify "duplicates OK" for both the client and DVD ID fields, as each client can have many DVDs in the queue *and* each DVD can be associated with multiple clients.

Summary

In this chapter, then, we've examined event-driven accounting information systems and REAL modeling. Here's a summary of the chapter's important points, seen through the lens of its learning objectives:

1. *Compare and contrast view-driven and event-driven accounting information systems.* Both types of systems are designed to collect data and process it into information; both typically involve various forms of information technology. View-driven systems are designed to present that information in one principal way: the general purpose financial statements. Event-driven systems are built on relational database technology; they capture more data and offer greater flexibility in terms of reporting via queries and reports.
2. *Use REAL modeling to represent an event-driven AIS.* REAL modeling begins by understanding an organization's environment and business processes. Then, for each process, it identifies the resources, events, agents, and (optionally) locations needed to capture

the essential nature of transactions. System designers use cardinalities to explain the relationships between the elements of a REAL model.

3. *Use a REAL model to design a relational database for an event-driven AIS.* Once the REAL model has been established and validated, it can be translated into a series of relational database tables. In most cases, each element of a REAL model requires at least one table in a relational database. Where the maximum cardinalities between elements of the model are many to many, system designers create a junction table to denote the relationship.

The relational database technology that forms the basis for REAL modeling is also the basis for enterprise resource planning systems. So, a solid understanding of this area of AIS will give you an appreciation for that important technology, as well as help you "speak the same language" as the IT professionals with whom you'll be working.

Key Terms

agents, *129*
cardinalities, *131*
events, *129*
junction table, *134*
locations, *129*
McCarthy, *127*
normalization, *132*
relational database, *132*
resources, *129*
six-step process, *130*
strategically significant operating activities, *134*

Chapter References

Hollander, A. S., E. L. Denna, and J. O. Cherrington. 2000. *Accounting, Information Technology, and Business Solutions.* 2nd ed. New York: Irwin/McGraw-Hill.

McCarthy, W. E. 1982. "The REAL Accounting Model: A Generalized Framework for Accounting Systems in a Shared Data Environment." *Accounting Review,* July, pp. 554–77.

Walker, K. B., and E. Denna. 1997. "Arriveder ci, Pacioli? A New Accounting System Is Emerging." *Management Accounting,* July, pp. 22–30.

End-of-Chapter Activities

1. *Reading review questions.*

a. What are the similarities and differences between view-driven and event-driven accounting information systems?

b. What does the acronym REAL stand for? Give examples of each element.

c. List the six steps for creating a REAL model.

d. Explain how to establish a set of cardinalities between two elements of a REAL model.

e. How would you use a REAL model to design a relational database?

f. Prepare a response to the questions for this chapter's "AIS in the Business World."

2. *Reading review problem.* Coral's See-the-Reef, located on the Gulf of Mexico, is famous for its fast service. Coral's business is renting scuba and snorkeling gear. Coral needs someone to analyze her business and help her use that analysis to plan and design a new information system. Coral employs four fitting clerks, three rental clerks, and four cashiers. The fitting clerks enter equipment items, sizes, and experience codes into the computer. The computer searches the rental inventory, by experience code, for the requested equipment. For example, a beginner is code one, which tells the computer to locate the oldest equipment available in the requested size. Once the requested equipment is located, a duplicate rental invoice is printed. The rental clerk uses the second copy to retrieve the equipment. While this clerk gets the equipment, the customer pays the rental fee to a cashier. A deposit is added to the rental fee, and a code indicating the condition of the equipment is noted.

Source: A. S. Hollander, E. L. Denna, and J. O. Cherrington, *Accounting, Information Technology, and Business Solutions,* 2nd ed. (New York: Irwin/McGraw-Hill, 2000).

a. What are Coral's basic choices with respect to developing a new information system? What are the advantages and disadvantages associated with each choice?

b. If Coral wants to develop an event-driven information system, what steps will she (or the analyst) need to take?

c. Prepare a REAL model for an event-driven information system for Coral.

3. *Making choices and exercising judgment.* Consider the REAL model you created in the reading review problem for this chapter.

a. Create database tables for one resource, one event, and one agent.

b. Suggest two queries Coral should incorporate in her database; justify your suggestions. Which tables and fields would she need to create the queries you suggest?

c. Design a form a fitting clerk could use for entering equipment items, sizes, and experience codes.

4. *Field work.*

a. Enterprise resource planning (ERP) systems are an advanced form of the event-driven concepts discussed in this chapter. Examples of ERP systems include PeopleSoft, SAP, and Oracle. Use your school's library resources to find case examples of ERP systems in action. Prepare a brief PowerPoint presentation of your findings.

b. Relational database software can be used very effectively in detecting fraud in the accounting information system. Use your school's library resources to find and read R. Marden and R. Edwards, "Internal Controls for the Small Business: Skimming and the Fraud Triangle," *Internal Auditing* (January/February 2005). If Pinewoods of the Blue Ridge Mountains (the company discussed in the article) captured transactions in a relational database based on a REAL model, what queries and reports would you construct in an attempt to discover the fraud?

5. *Constructing REAL models.* (Case situations *a* through *d* come from Hollander, Denna, and Cherrington, 2000.) In each independent case situation below, construct a REAL model and a database structure.

a. *Tom's Trailers.* Tom owns a small recreational trailer business in a suburban community located close to the mountains. The community is relatively small but growing at a fast rate. Tom's business is growing, not because of his effective sales style and personality, but by growth of the community. Currently, Tom's competition has been nearly nonexistent but, as the area grows, he expects to encounter increasing competition.

Tom sells mostly trailers for vacationing and camping. When customers arrive on Tom's lot, they are greeted by a salesperson. The salesperson may show the customers the trailers on the lot, but the salesperson need not be present during the entire showing. Depending on customer preference, either the salesperson will take the customer on a tour or the customer may roam the lot freely, inspecting trailers at his or her leisure.

Since recreational trailers are fairly large-ticket items, customers often will leave the lot without making a purchase, only to return another day after making the decision to purchase a trailer. When a customer decides to make a purchase, the salesperson initiates a series of procedures to properly document the order and sale transaction. First, the salesperson determines the model of the selected trailer and offers the customer a list of options that correspond to the particular model. The customer may (1) purchase a trailer off the lot with no added features, (2) purchase a trailer off the lot with additional features, or (3) special order a trailer not currently on the lot.

In most cases, customers do not pay cash for their trailers. If, however, the customer pays cash, a simple sales contract is prepared and the customer drives off with his or her trailer. The majority of customers use an installment method of purchase. Before an installment purchase is authorized, the customer's credit must be verified to determine creditworthiness.

With an installment purchase, an installment agreement is prepared in addition to the sales contract. Tom has arranged financing through a local bank for all installment sales. When an installment sale is made, the bank sends Tom a lump-sum payment equal to the price of the trailer. Instead of making a payment to Tom, customers pay the bank plus interest. In either case, Tom receives a lump-sum payment for each trailer sold, whether that lump sum comes from the customer or the bank.

Once the customer's credit is approved, the customer can take delivery of the trailer. This involves a delivery person who checks the trailer before delivering it to the customer. The customer may pick up the trailer or have it delivered by Tom.

b. *Maple Bluff Pharmacy.* Maple Bluff Pharmacy sells prescription drugs and over-the-counter medications and supplies. All prescriptions and over-the-counter items are sold using a cash register. Each cash register retains on the cash register's journal tape a record of the transactions and who performed them. This information is subsequently entered into a computer.

Prescriptions received over the phone are taken by the pharmacist and recorded on a prescription slip. Also, prescriptions received over the phone are entered into a computer that matches the prescription with guideline dosage levels and instruction information and prints the necessary information for the prescription. After entering the prescription information into the computer, the prescription is filled and a hard copy of the prescription slip is filed numerically for future reference.

All sales items are paid for with cash, check, or credit card. On occasion, credit is extended to a customer, but he or she must be approved through the chief pharmacist. If credit is extended, a separate billing account is established. If a customer does not pay the bill within 120 days of the initial billing date, the account is turned over to a collection agency.

At the end of the day, cash in the register till is counted and compared with the total amount of credit card receipts and accounts receivable slips. This check is performed by two employees in the safe room and is always monitored on camera. In addition, total cash receipts recorded in the computer are compared with the deposit totals each day before Deposits Express picks up the money for deposit.

c. *Western Steel Company.* Western Steel Company produces steel for a variety of customers. When customers order steel, an order clerk enters information into a computer that prepares a purchase order to track the order from production to collection of payment. If the customer's credit has been approved, production of the order begins immediately. If the customer is new, a credit check is performed.

After the order is filled, a tally count is made of the produced steel and the steel is shipped to the customer. If the steel is to be shipped by railroad, rail cars are checked for weight before shipping the order. The weight of the load is then compared to the order to ensure an accurate delivery. Accompanying the shipment is a computer-generated bill of lading and a copy of the purchase order.

Shortly after shipping an order, Western invoices the customer using prices on an approved price list. The invoice total is obtained by multiplying the quantity ordered and shipped by the standard price. Steel prices are set by the Sales Department, which determines competitive prices based on market conditions and cost information.

Customers send payments directly to a lockbox account in selected cities across the United States. The bank where a particular customer sends payment is located in the city closest to the customer's location. Western receives no payment, but Western receives a record of customer deposits from the bank maintaining the lockbox account. Accounting personnel maintain the billing and collection accounts, while the Credit Department issues credit to customers and follows up on past due accounts.

d. *Payroll process for a CPA firm.* The payroll and personnel function represents a large expense for many companies—especially the audit divisions of accounting firms. Clients are frequently billed based on staff, manager, and partner involvement in the audit. Firms bill clients based on a predetermined rate for each person involved. For example, a company bills a partner's hours at a substantially higher rate than it bills the staff's hours. Partners also trade employees to work on different projects for different clients. Careful tracking and planning go into each audit to maintain both audit quality and the lowest possible cost to the client.

For each client engagement, an audit plan is developed to identify the type and quantity of hours necessary to complete each audit step. For example, the audit plan might specify 30 hours to count warehouse inventory. Each week, auditors record their time on a time-and-expense report and submit it to the audit supervisor. The supervisor compares the actual time to the budgeted time in the audit plan. The time-and-expense reports are then submitted to the Payroll Department, which prepares paychecks for the auditors. Each week, the Payroll Department calculates pay based on a yearly salary and overtime for each employee. In addition, the Payroll Department must track deductions for taxes, insurance, and benefits. Once the deductions are withheld, the net pay is deposited into the employee's checking account, or a check is issued in the name of the employee.

e. *Textbook ordering and purchasing process.* Six weeks before the start of each academic term, accounting instructors at AIS University of America inform the department secretary of the books they're planning to use for each class. Instructors may use one or more books for an individual class; different instructors may use different textbooks for various sections of the same course. The department secretary compiles the instructor-provided data and transmits them via e-mail to the bookstore's purchasing agent. The purchasing agent prepares a purchase order and sends it to the textbook publisher; a single purchase order may combine textbooks for several different courses, so long as all the textbooks come from the same publisher. When the publisher ships the books, the bookstore's receiving department records the shipment; stock clerks put the books on the shelves. The textbook publisher invoices the bookstore, which then writes a check in payment; unused textbooks are returned to the publisher roughly one month after the term begins.

6. *Interpreting a REAL model.* Consider the REAL model presented below. Write a narrative description of the business process it depicts.

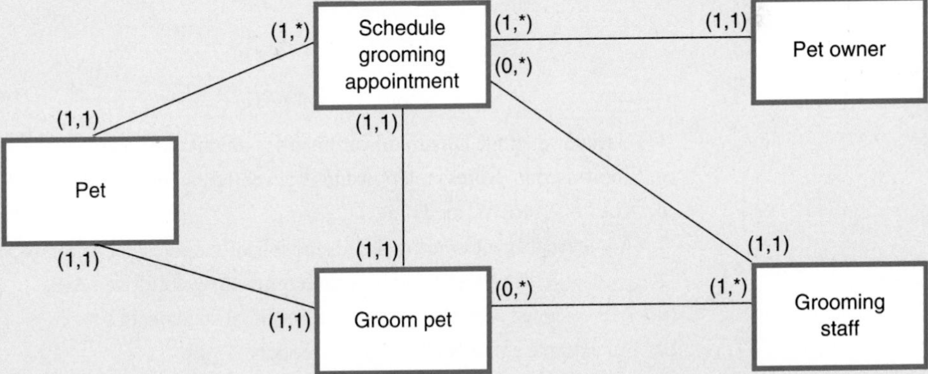

7. *Crossword puzzle.* Please fill in the crossword puzzle below using appropriate terminology from the chapter.

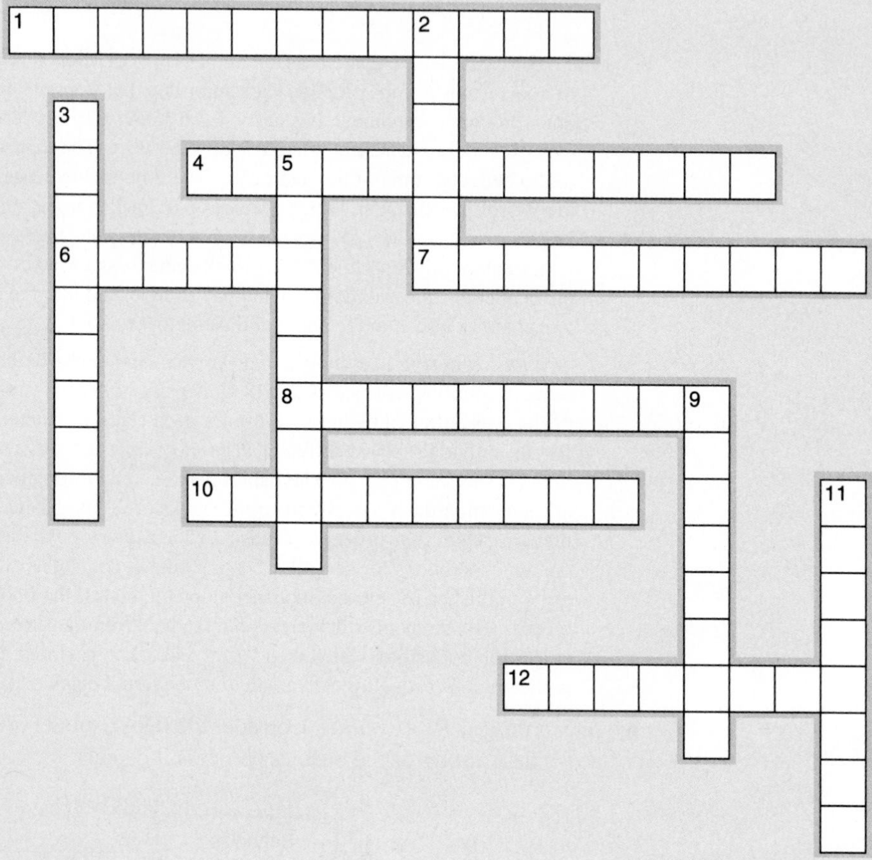

Across

1. Needed when the maximum cardinalities are many to many.
4. Tools used to express relationships between elements of a REAL model.
6. The "E" in REAL modeling.
7. An internal agent in many REAL models of the sales/collection process.
8. ________ database technology undergirds an event-driven AIS.
10. AIS designed primarily to produce financial statements.
12. An external agent in many REAL models.

Down

2. The "A" in REAL modeling.
3. Referential ________ refers to the ability to update junction tables.
5. The "R" in REAL modeling.
9. The "L" in REAL modeling.
11. The inventor of REAL modeling.

8. *Terminology.* Match each item on the left with the most appropriate item on the right.

1. Cardinality	a. Unique record identifier in a database table
2. Decision/management event	b. Supports the preparation of financial statements
3. Enterprise resource planning	c. Purchasing supplies
4. Information event	d. Preparing journal entries
5. Junction table	e. Opening an office in a new city
6. Primary key	f. Internal agent
7. Purchasing agent	g. External agent
8. Strategically significant operating event	h. Combines the primary keys of two tables
9. Vendor	i. A sophisticated form of event-driven AIS
10. View-driven AIS	j. (1,*)—(1,1)

9. *Multiple choice questions.*

1. Which of the following is least likely to be classified as a strategically significant operating event in a REAL model?
   a. Selling inventory to customers
   b. Updating a client database
   c. Purchasing supplies from a vendor
   d. Paying employees
2. In a REAL model, the maximum cardinalities between an agent and an event are many and many. How many tables would you need to create?
   a. Two
   b. Three
   c. One
   d. More than three
3. A REAL model contains the following cardinality: customer (1,1)—rent equipment (1,*). Which of the following is the best interpretation?
   a. Every piece of equipment can only be rented one time.
   b. A single equipment rental can involve many different customers.
   c. An individual customer can only rent equipment one time.
   d. Every rental transaction involves exactly one customer.
4. Which of the following statements is most true regarding the cardinalities in the previous question?
   a. The customer table will have a compound primary key.
   b. A junction table is required.
   c. The primary key from the customer table will be posted to the rent equipment table.
   d. The cardinality is invalid.
5. Identifying the relevant behaviors and characteristics of the elements of a REAL model helps the designer
   a. Create cardinalities.
   b. Create database tables.
   c. Both of the above.
   d. None of the above.

6. Consider the Netflix example presented in the chapter. "Record cash receipts in the accounting information system" would be considered a(n)
   a. Operating event.
   b. Information event.
   c. Decision/management event.
   d. Value-added event.
7. A junction table is required in a relational database when
   a. One item A is associated with many item Bs.
   b. One item B is associated with many item As.
   c. Both of the above.
   d. None of the above.
8. Consider the Netflix REAL model presented in Figure 7.4. Which of the following relationships indicates strong internal control through separation of duties?
   a. DVDs and ship DVDs
   b. Collect payment and cash
   c. Client and collect payment
   d. Netflix employee and receive returned DVDs
9. REAL models can include
   a. Internal agents and external agents.
   b. Internal agents and strategic agents.
   c. External agents and strategic agents.
   d. Internal agents, external agents, and strategic agents.
10. Which of the following is most likely to require locations in a REAL model?
    a. A company uses both UPS and FedEx to ship products.
    b. A company maintains multiple manufacturing facilities around the United States.
    c. Both A and B.
    d. Neither A nor B.

10. *Statement evaluation.* Please indicate whether each of the following statements is (i) always true, (ii) sometimes true, or (iii) never true. For those that are (ii) sometimes true, explain when the statement is true.

a. "Choose AIS software" would be included as an event in a REAL model.
b. Events can be related to one another in a REAL model.
c. Events in a REAL model are shown in the second column.
d. If an accountant can construct a REAL model, data flow diagrams and flowcharts are unnecessary.
e. Most REAL models will include both internal and external agents.
f. REAL models include locations.
g. Resources and agents are unrelated in a REAL model.
h. Strong internal controls are evident in a REAL model.
i. Understanding an organization's environment is important in designing a REAL model.
j. View-driven accounting systems do not provide information for decisions.

Part Three

Systems Analysis and Information Technology

Now that we've looked at some of the fundamental topics in AIS (Part One) and systems documentation techniques (Part Two), let's turn our attention to information technology. You may have expected this material much earlier in the text—after all, when most people think about "information systems," they think almost immediately about information technology. But keep in mind what you read in Chapter 1: Accounting was an information system long before the advent of computers and information technology.

This section contains three chapters; here's a short overview of each one:

- Chapter 8: Information Systems Concepts. We'll look at three main topics in this chapter: the systems development life cycle, the capability maturity model, and factors to consider when selecting information technology. All three topics can be applied to virtually any information system, including the AIS.
- Chapter 9: XBRL. XBRL stands for the eXtensible Business Reporting Language. It's a way of tagging financial data so that it can be interpreted across software and hardware platforms. Starting in April 2009, the SEC required companies to use XBRL in their filings with the commission.
- Chapter 10: E-business and Enterprise Resource Planning Systems. E-business is no longer an "up-and-coming" trend—it's firmly planted all across the world economy. In this chapter, we'll look at various forms of e-business, along with costs and benefits. We'll also talk about enterprise resource planning systems—sophisticated database applications that can help organizations run more smoothly.

WHY DO WE CARE ABOUT SYSTEMS ANALYSIS AND INFORMATION TECHNOLOGY

The chapters in this section effectively describe tools that accountants use to help collect, store, process, and communicate information to the right people, in the right form, at the right time. These essentially help to provide more transparency, pertaining to a company's financial situation, to potentially avoid a fiscal calamity.

Quality information is critical to an organization's success. The information environment in organizations is an extremely complex system of interrelated subsystems that connect users across organizations. These chapters provide an excellent foundation for understanding how information is communicated between various applications, the end user, suppliers, vendors, and customers.

The key to this section of the text is to promote electronic data exchanges to enhance efficiency of the information that accountants spend so much time aggregating, copying, and pasting. The fact is poor information management adds costs, exposes security gaps, and even leads to erroneous movements of information. Over time all of this contributes to increased costs and organizational inefficacy.

For example, take the case of a customer address database that is manually updated. Imagine in this database some addresses have not been updated or were incorrectly updated. As a result, the organization wouldn't be able to reach some of its customers; the organization will incur unnecessary costs due to returned mail and a potential customer loss. Direct costs are easy to track such as the unnecessary costs of returned mail. On the other hand, indirect costs are more difficult to track and even more difficult to value. In many cases, these costs can be a lost costumer, lost efficiency of work, or lost money based on bad decisions that were based on bad data.

Chapter Eight

Information Systems Concepts

AIS in the Business World

Diverse Systems Development Projects

As organizations grow and change, their information systems must change as well. Consider these examples:

- Gazing more at the rowers on the [Schuylkill River] below than on the automobiles ahead, a [Center City Philadelphia] driver slams into the car in front of him, causing an accident that increases the ride home for many commuters—and sets in motion a series of legal and insurance steps. Such a traffic incident is only one of more than 70,000 automobile accidents reported each year in Philadelphia, and the city's police department prepares a report for each one. Accident reports are necessary for insurance companies to process claims and ultimately pay settlements to their customers. Until recently, processing an accident report was a costly, time-consuming process, taking up to six weeks for a paper copy to become available. Thanks to the efforts of a unique public/private partnership and the power of Internet technology, Philadelphia accident reports are now available to insurance companies in less than one week. [Coghlan and vonMechow, 2004]
- When Wacoal [Corporation] analyzed their information technology systems, what they found wasn't very encouraging. Their technology had been growing as the company grew—systems were added on an as-needed basis, which resulted in a patchwork quilt of 32 independent legacy systems. Many of these legacy systems were more than 10 years old. To improve the quality of business-decision information, Wacoal sought a solution that would connect its disparate systems together in a seamless data flow. These system changes would allow the company to achieve operational efficiency and concentrate on its core competence. The question was how to accomplish a seemingly complex task of system and platform integration in a very short time frame with a limited project budget. The answer came from Wacoal's technology partner—Hitachi—and the freely available eXtensible Business Reporting Language for General Ledger (XBRL-GL), the Journal Taxonomy. [Hasegawa et al., 2004]

Discussion Questions

1. What steps do organizations use to develop or change information systems?
2. How can systems professionals evaluate the sophistication of an organization's business processes?
3. What factors should managers consider when choosing information technology?

Sources: T. Coghlan and T. vonMechow, "Driving Auto Accident Costs Down," *Strategic Finance,* January 2004; M. Hasegawa, T. Sakata, N. Sambuichi, and N. Hannon, "Breathing New Life into Old Systems with XBRL-GL: The Wacoal Story," *Strategic Finance,* March 2004.

Early in your study of accounting information systems, you learned that most AIS have five parts: inputs, processes, outputs, storage, and internal controls. But did you ever wonder how those elements of the AIS come into existence in the first place? After all, they don't "spring full blown" like Minerva from the brow of Jupiter! (That's your multicultural, interdisciplinary lesson for this chapter. Hope you liked it.) And once the elements are in place, how can we judge, in a macro sense, the extent to which an organization's processes need improvement? Finally, what factors should professionals take into account when choosing which information technology to implement?

In this chapter, we're going to explore three topics that help answer those questions: the systems development life cycle (SDLC), the capability maturity model (CMM), and software selection.

When you've finished studying this chapter, you should be able to:

1. List and discuss, in order, the steps in the systems development life cycle.
2. Explain the advantages and disadvantages of using the SDLC.
3. Apply the SDLC in accounting contexts.
4. List and discuss the levels of the capability maturity model.
5. Classify organizations' processes according to the CMM.
6. Explain factors managers should consider when choosing IT for an AIS.

SYSTEMS DEVELOPMENT LIFE CYCLE

As the name implies, the **systems development life cycle** (SDLC) is a methodology for designing, implementing, and maintaining virtually any kind of information system. It's certainly not the only such methodology; it may not even be the best methodology. But many organizations use the SDLC in their systems projects, so you're highly likely to run across it in your career.

The SDLC comprises seven parts (see Figure 8.1):

1. Initiation/planning
2. Requirements analysis
3. Design
4. Build
5. Test
6. Implementation
7. Operations and maintenance

FIGURE 8.1
Systems Development Life Cycle

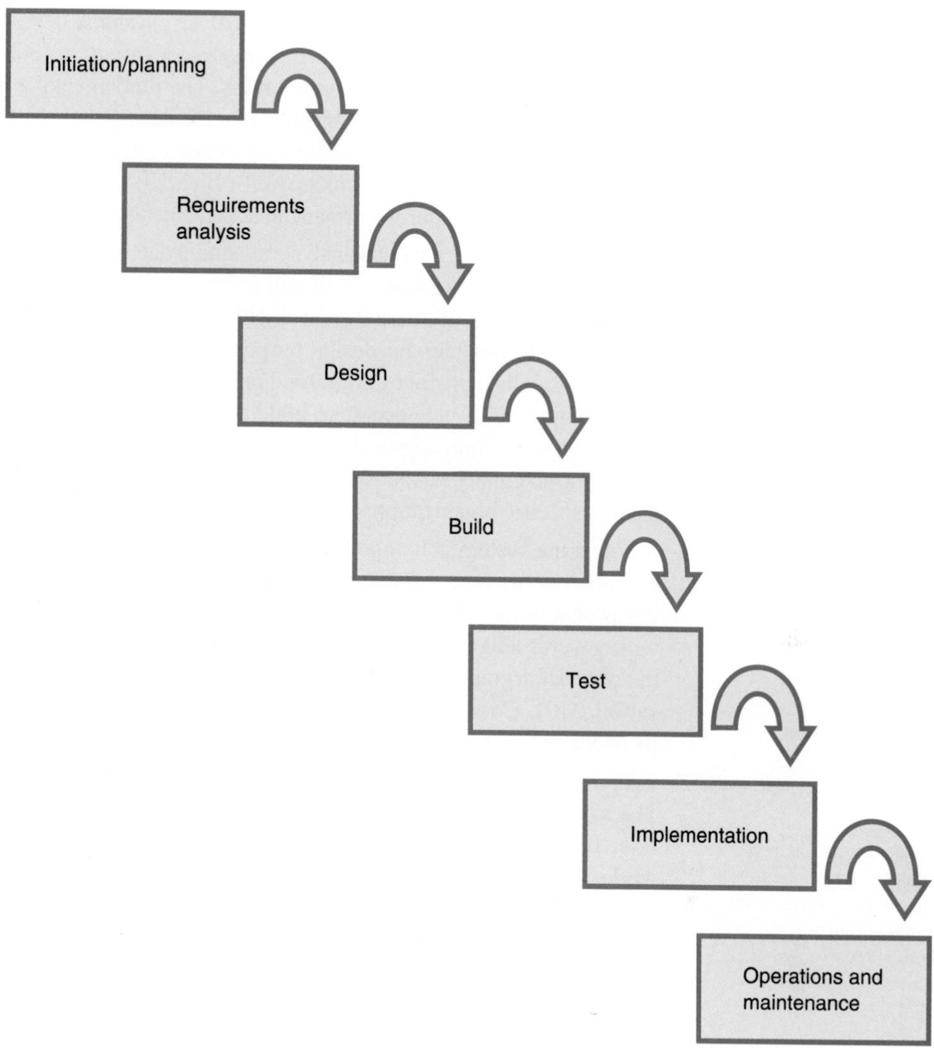

Although the seven steps appear very linear in nature, the SDLC is actually highly **iterative** in practice—similar to systems documentation. In other words, information systems professionals don't move from one step to another in a rigid way. Rather, they move back and forth between the steps as needed in a specific project. So, for example, an organization might be engaged in testing, only to find that it must change the way a system is built; or, a team might be partially done designing a system when it discovers that the requirements analysis needs additional work.

Let's look at each of the seven steps in more detail, along with how you might apply them in an accounting information system:

1. *Initiation/planning.* Most systems development projects start because someone in an organization recognizes an unfilled need. For example, a small organization might have been using a checkbook as its only accounting information system. But if the organization is growing, its needs for accounting information will quickly outpace the capabilities of a simple checkbook. This first phase of the SDLC often includes a feasibility study to determine if the project is possible from economic, operational, and technical perspectives. The feasibility study results may be used to try to get the project funded.

2. *Requirements analysis.* In requirements analysis, systems designers figure out what the new system needs to accomplish. They may use a variety of tools at this stage, including flowcharts and interviews with system users. The fundamental goal of requirements analysis is to develop a clear set of objectives for the new system—in much the same way that every chapter in this book starts with a set of objectives. The requirements analysis for our fictional small organization, which we'll call MCL Company, could include objectives like "produce general purpose financial statements" or "prepare end-of-year tax returns."

Enterprise resource planning systems come in different versions based on generic organizational types. For example, PeopleSoft has one version designed for the needs of colleges and universities.

3. *Design.* With the requirements analysis in hand, systems designers can begin to think about how the system should look—how will screen layouts look, what kinds of documents are needed, what forms of internal control will be involved. Very often, the overall AIS is broken down into modules for design purposes; modules could be based on business processes (sales/collection, for example) and/or stakeholders (such as customers and employees). At this point, MCL may decide to build a system "from scratch" or to evaluate "off-the-shelf" software. Both approaches have costs and benefits. Building a system from scratch takes time and may be expensive; off-the-shelf software may not be completely customizable to a specific organization.
4. *Build.* If the system is being built "from scratch," this phase involves writing the actual computer code. If an organization is using off-the-shelf software, like Peachtree, building probably includes customizing it to the particular organization. If you've worked with general ledger software in your AIS course, you probably customized things like the chart of accounts, inventory records, and personnel information. As a small organization, MCL Company may be more likely to use off-the-shelf software, particularly if its needs are as generic as those mentioned in (2) above.

This step may help you understand the iterative nature of systems development more clearly, as it may involve revisiting earlier phases of the SDLC.

5. *Test.* You probably wouldn't want to buy a new car without test driving it first, right? The same holds true for information systems! During the testing phase, users can critique the system and make suggestions for its improvement. One of my former students works for the U.S. Navy; when the Navy was preparing to implement new software for procurement/purchasing, the software was installed on a few machines. Users had the opportunity to work with the new software and make suggestions about it. If MCL's management decided to build a system from scratch using relational database software, testing would involve setting up the database so users could "check it out" before starting to use it. It's much easier to make design changes at this stage than it would be after the system has been implemented. If the information system has been designed in modules, testing also helps ensure that the modules work well together.
6. *Implementation.* After any revisions based on testing, the system is at last ready for implementation—for actual use by the organization to achieve the purposes set out in requirements analysis. Managers have many choices when it comes to systems implementation. They may, for example, run the old system and the new system simultaneously for a time (parallel implementation). They may completely take down the old system and put the new system in its place (direct cutover or "big bang"). They may implement the system in modules, as well. MCL's management could continue using its simple checkbook system alongside its newly developed/purchased system for a time. Even with such a parallel approach, MCL could use modular implementation for the new system. Every implementation approach has costs and benefits; there's no "one right way" or even "one best way" to approach this important task.
7. *Operations and maintenance.* Information systems, particularly accounting information systems, are dynamic. As people, processes, products, and services of the organization change, the AIS should change along with them. For example, MCL's management might decide to incorporate at some point; at a minimum, incorporation would require

a change in the chart of accounts. Other issues to consider over the life of a new system include internal control, accessibility for the disabled, and hardware and software requirements.

Some descriptions of the SDLC break it down into more than seven phases. The U.S. Department of Justice lists 10 steps in its SDLC (www.usdoj.gov/imd/irm/lifecycle/ch1.htm#para1.2); regardless of the level of detail, the same basic tasks are involved.

Reflection and Self-Assessment 8.1

The SDLC has both strengths and weaknesses. Some of its strengths include strong control and opportunity for user input; weaknesses include rigidity and difficulty estimating costs. What other strengths and weaknesses can you identify for the SDLC?

Now, we'll turn our attention to the capability maturity model.

CAPABILITY MATURITY MODEL

Humphrey first wrote about the CMM in Managing the Software Process.

The **capability maturity model** (CMM) was first suggested by **Watts Humphrey** in the late 1980s. Humphrey was a software engineer, and he developed the CMM as a framework to assess business processes in an objective way—with particular reference to government contractors and software projects. In the intervening years, the CMM has been applied in many other organizational contexts: project management, software maintenance, risk management, and business school accreditation. Whatever the context, the CMM has five levels: chaotic, repeatable, defined, managed, and optimized (see Figure 8.2). Let's look at each level's characteristics and apply them to accounting information systems.

- *Level one: chaotic.* These processes are unstable and noncohesive; think of this level as an "every person for him/herself" mentality, or like a bunch of Lone Rangers in an organization. Individuals may be highly motivated and put forth extraordinary effort in making a process "work," but the organization's processes as a whole are jumbled and confused. As a graduate student, I did some consulting with small businesses that often had chaotic accounting information systems. I recall one client, a marine supply business, in which the AIS consisted of a shoebox full of receipts, check stubs, and other documents. And, as a reviewed them, I discovered that the collection was incomplete. Hopefully, in your professional career, you won't run across an organization with such a chaotic AIS.
- *Level two: repeatable.* This level involves some planning; it may result in consistent results over time. One way to recognize this maturity level is the development of "major milestones" for projects and/or processes, with specific deliverables at each milestone. If the marine supply business wanted to move from its chaotic AIS to this level, managers might focus on producing monthly financial statements. They could establish a process for collecting source documents, making journal entries, and keeping accounting records up-to-date to achieve that goal.

FIGURE 8.2
Capability Maturity Model

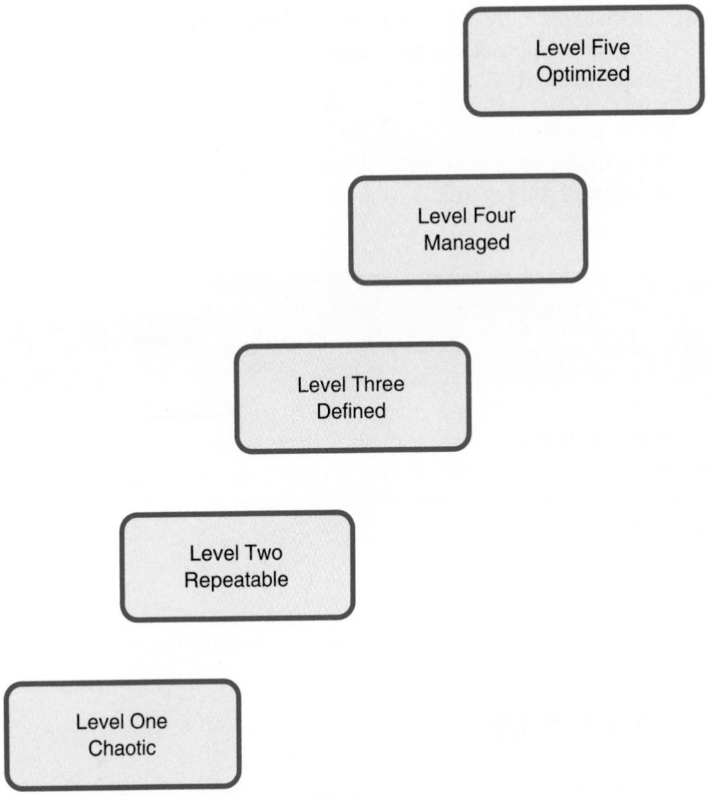

- *Level three: defined.* In describing this level, Hurst (2007, p. 4) noted:

  > At maturity level 3, the standards and procedures for an individual project are derived from organizational standards to suit that particular project. This is a key distinction between levels 2 and 3. Both levels require project standards, procedures, and process descriptions. In level 2, they might be unique to a project. In level 3, they are tailored from broader organizational standards. It is expected in level 3 that processes will be described in more detail and with more rigor. Management is expected to understand relationships between processes and to collect detailed metrics of performance.

  So, in the marine supply business, the accounting information system moves from being a "necessary evil" to something that supports the organization in other ways. The business would likely develop a procedures manual to standardize the way the AIS is maintained; such a manual would be particularly useful during times of transition and expansion.

- *Level four: managed.* In level three, processes are defined but not measured. When an organization moves to level four, its management develops metrics to establish goals and control processes. When a process doesn't achieve those goals, management can look for ways to improve the process. The management of the marine supply business might, for example, set a goal of producing quarterly financial statements within one week of the end of each quarter. If the quarterly financials took longer than a week, management would look for ways to improve the process to achieve that goal.

The idea of continuous improvement is called-*kaizen* in Japan. You may have encountered this idea in a cost accounting or operations management course.

- *Level five: optimized.* This level is characterized by a "continuous improvement" mentality in the organization. At this level, organizations look at the "big picture" of process improvement. Hurst (2007, p. 4) offered these comments: "A key distinction between level 4 and level 5 is the types of process variation that are addressed. At level 4, the concern is with individual projects experiencing delays and variations. Level 5 organizations develop processes to address the common causes of process delay and variation, and to change processes to improve performance." If our marine supply business moved to this level, managers would think beyond the accounting information system, considering ways to improve other business processes. Level five is really about an attitude of improvement—one that permeates the organization and affects nearly everything it does.

Reflection and Self-Assessment 8.2

You've started the process of entering the accounting profession by going to college. Based on the CMM levels, how would you describe that process? Why?

We'll look more closely at business processes in Part Four of the text.

Ideally, an organization will move all of its business processes sequentially through the levels. Since each level builds on those that precede it, skipping levels can be frustrating and counterproductive. At the same time, processes at different levels within the same organization can create problems; for example, a sales/collection process at level four would be problematic if the acquisition/payment process was at level two.

INFORMATION TECHNOLOGY SELECTION

The eight issues here are but a small subset of many considerations managers must weigh in IT decisions. Later, you'll have a chance to research and/or brainstorm additions.

Managers need to consider two kinds of issues when they think about selecting an appropriate form of information technology for their AIS: **macro-level issues** and **micro-level issues.** Figure 8.3 provides a list of all the factors we'll consider in this section.

Managers must first specify the *need* they are trying to meet with a new form of information technology. Often, company personnel want the "latest and greatest" form of information technology just because it looks cool or is fun to play with. But IT resources represent a major investment of time and money for most firms, so establishing a clear need is critical. Johnston (2003) offered the following insights in this area:

Notice how Johnston's comments tie into the phases of the SDLC.

> Assign the managers . . . to prepare a [needs analysis] for their sections. It should include all the things they do—from invoice preparation to inventory operations. Using the data, ask them to prepare flowcharts to diagram how they perform those tasks . . . or even how they get bottled up. During this analysis have the managers gather samples of every form . . . and every report the current software produces. From this analysis you will be able to develop a requirements definition—a detailed document that defines what your business needs.

Strategic fit is also important when investing in new information technology. As you may know, a strategy indicates how an organization competes in its markets. Most good strategic plans begin with a strong, yet concise, mission statement. For example, the mission of the McGraw-Hill Companies (www.mcgraw-hill.com) is to provide essential information and insight that help individuals, markets, and societies perform to their potential. A mission statement, as part of a strategic plan, explains why an organization exists; it outlines how the organization plans to differentiate itself from its competitors. Information

FIGURE 8.3
Factors to Consider in IT Selection

Macro-Level Factors	Micro-Level Factors
Need	Cost
Strategic fit	Adaptability
Personnel involvement	Training
Financing	Vendor reliability

technology investments should align with (support) the organization's strategic plan; that is, managers and employees should be able to state clearly how a given information technology fulfills the organizational mission.

Personnel involvement is another key factor in new IT investments. Johnston (2003) recommended two items in this area: a technology advisory committee and independent consultants. While he considers a technology advisory committee essential, he states that hiring an independent consultant may or may not be a good idea. A technology advisory committee should, according to Johnston, comprise five to seven members from various departments/functions/offices of the organization. Subcommittees also may be in order to manage more focused tasks and involve more personnel. Employees on the committee need not necessarily be technology experts, but they should be able to think globally for the good of the company, rather than representing the (perhaps) parochial interest of their own area.

Reflection and Self-Assessment 8.3

Under what circumstances would you want to hire an independent consultant for an IT investment project? Suggest three questions you would ask during a selection interview for an independent consultant; also, identify and discuss three adjectives that would describe the ideal consultant.

Finally, on the macro side of the equation, managers need to consider *financing*—how do they plan to pay for the IT? Key questions here include

- Will external funding be required for the investment?
- If so, how will the company raise it: debt or equity?
- Is leasing an option? If so, what are its advantages and disadvantages?
- Are any tax credits available based on the investment?

Well-developed, detailed operational and capital budgets will help address those issues.

Now, let's look at some of the *micro-level issues* involved in IT investments. Most managers will immediately consider *cost* when they think about micro-level issues. Cost, however, is much broader than just the money spent for the investment. Managers need to consider the total cost of information technology: its upfront cost, training, maintenance, and customization to name a few.

We'll look at business process management later in be text.

Adaptability is another micro-level issue managers need to consider. In other words, can the proposed information technology be adapted effectively to the organization? Or will its adoption involve major business process redesign? Investments in new IT are challenging under most circumstances. But, if they disrupt or create change in the way a company does business, they become even more so.

Employees need to learn to use a new information technology, so *training* becomes another issue. How easy will it be to learn to use new hardware and/or software? Will the training be provided by the vendor as part of the contract, or will the company have to pay extra for it? Can the training be made available online, or does it require classroom attendance to be effective? While a hardware or software vendor will certainly have answers to most of those questions, many organizations seek answers from companies that have already implemented the same or similar systems.

Finally, what about *vendor reliability?* Is the supplier of the technology a well-established, reputable company? You don't want to make a significant investment with a company only to find them bankrupt or out of business within a few months or years. Naturally, no-one can predict those kinds of events with perfect certainty, so managers have to rely on their judgment and independent data collection as assessment tools.

Sylla and Wen (2002) proposed a **three-stage process** for evaluating information technology investments; their ideas are depicted in Figure 8.4.

So how can you make sense of all those factors in an IT investment situation? I've often used a **weighted-rating technique** as a guide. Here's how it works:

1. Develop a list of factors that are important in your decision. I generally stick with around five factors, but you could use fewer or more depending on the circumstance.
2. Weight each factor on a scale from 1 to 10 based on its importance, with higher numbers assigned to factors that are more important.
3. Evaluate each piece of hardware and/or software on each factor. Assign each item a score (again from 1 to 10) based on how well it fulfills the factor.
4. Multiply the weightings by the ratings and add everything up to determine an overall "score" for an individual item.
5. Use the weighted ratings as one input to your investment decision.

FIGURE 8.4
Sylla and Wen Framework

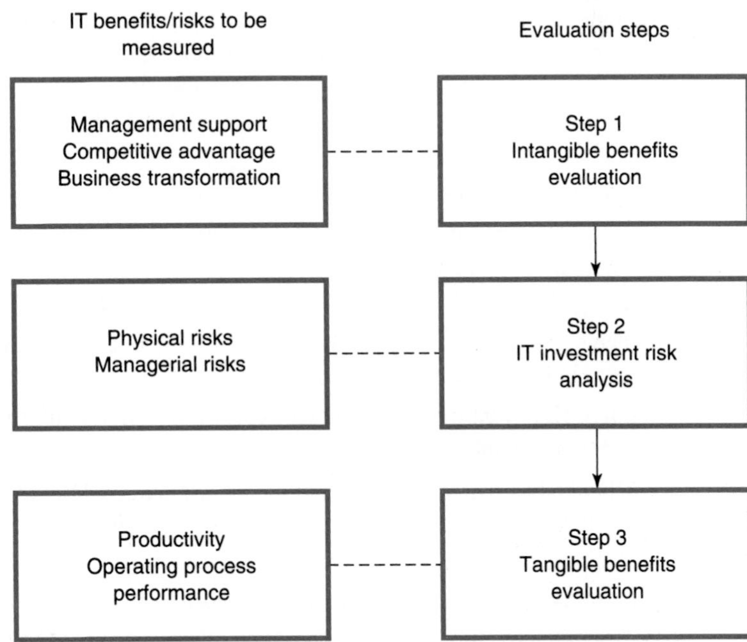

Here's an example:

Factor	Factor Weighting
Adaptability	7
Cost	8
Strategic fit	9
Training	9

	Ratings				
Software package	**Adaptability**	**Cost**	**Strategic Fit**	**Training**	**Weighted Score**
1	6	10	8	5	239
2	10	10	9	7	294
3	8	7	10	9	283

So, in the preceding analysis, the numeric results argue in favor of software package 2. Notice, though, that its "score" is very close to that of package 3. In cases such as this, where the scores are so close, managers need to use judgment in making the final choice—rather than slavishly following the numeric results.

CRITICAL THINKING

As I'm working on this section, 2008 is about to turn into 2009. And lots of people are making resolutions for the New Year—like losing weight. I've been seeing a lot of television ads along those lines, including one that offers an online program. Let's take a look at how the SDLC could be applied to develop an information system for that purpose.

- *Initiation/planning.* Weight loss programs have been around a long time—even longer than the Internet. And just like many businesses took advantage of information technology to expand, weight loss programs did the same. Someone recognized a need/opportunity—the first step in the systems development life cycle.
- *Requirements analysis.* So the question became: What does an information system for an online weight loss program need to accomplish? Objectives for such a system might include
  - Allow users to create personalized accounts.
  - Develop a mechanism for billing members and collecting payment.
  - Track food, exercise, and weight loss.

  Systems designers would use at least one documentation tool at this point, as well: a systems flowchart, data flow diagram, or REAL model. Figure 8.5 shows a sample flowchart; Figure 8.6 shows a REAL model.
- *Design.* How would database tables be structured in the information system? Here are some suggestions:
  - Client table: <u>E-mail address,</u> first name, last name, address, city, state, ZIP code, payment type, credit card number, starting date, starting weight
  - Recipes table: <u>Recipe name,</u> total calories, total fat, total carbohydrates
  - Exercise table: <u>Exercise name,</u> calories burned per hour
  - Program activities table: <u>Transaction number,</u> [e-mail address], date

FIGURE 8.5
Weight Loss Systems Flowchart

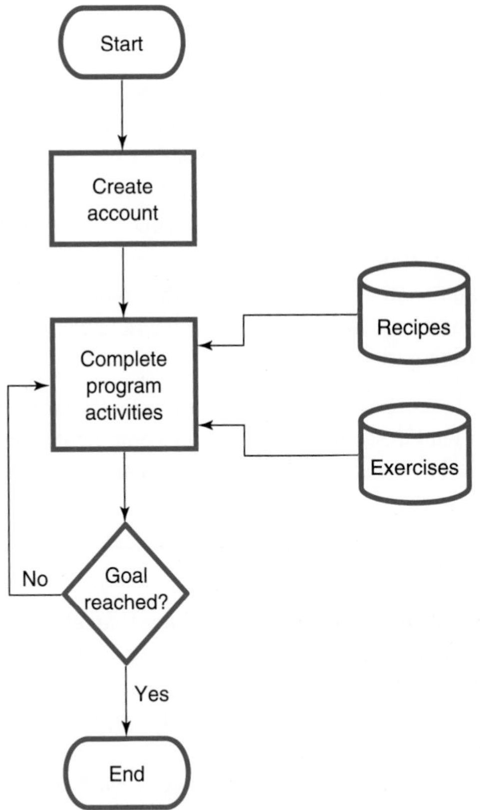

FIGURE 8.6
Weight Loss System REAL Model

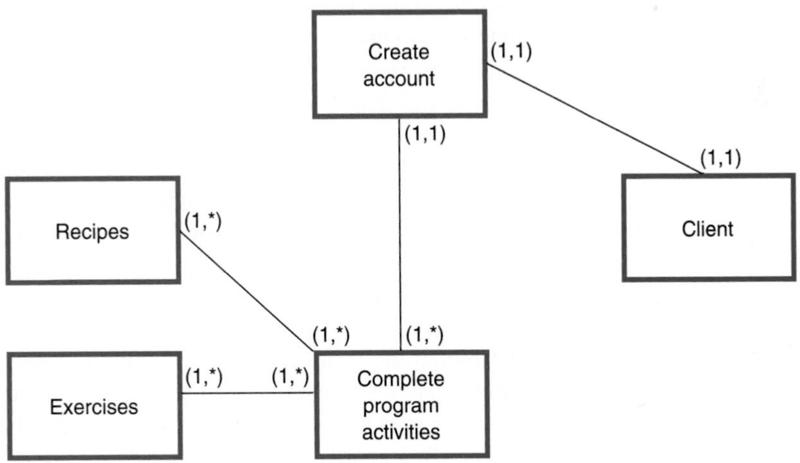

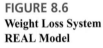

- Program activities/recipes table: [Transaction number], [recipe name]
- Program activities/exercise table: [Transaction number], [exercise name]

In addition to the tables themselves, systems designers would probably create forms for easy information input. Queries would allow users to look up recipes or exercises easily. And users should be able to generate reports to track their progress.

- *Build.* In the build phase, systems designers would use the specifications for tables, forms, queries, and reports to create a database file.
- *Test.* The company could create a "dummy transaction" database; they also could pilot test the system with actual users. Keeping in mind the iterative nature of systems development, testing might require going back to earlier phases of the cycle.
- *Implementation.* After testing, the system could "go live." Marketing staff would likely get involved at this stage to help promote the new system; customer service personnel should be available to address questions from users.
- *Operations and maintenance.* At a minimum, the company should create a help desk to address ongoing questions. In addition, the recipes and exercise tables would be updated with new information periodically.

For me, the most challenging aspects of a project like this are the requirements analysis and systems design. That's not to say that the other steps aren't challenging—but, if the requirements analysis and design are sound, the other steps can be accomplished relatively easier.

Summary

Here's a look back at what we've covered in this chapter:

1. *List and discuss, in order, the steps in the systems development life cycle.* The SDLC is a methodology many organizations use to develop and implement information systems. It comprises seven steps, which are highly iterative in nature: initiation/planning, requirements analysis, design, build, test, implementation, and operations and maintenance.
2. *Explain the advantages and disadvantages of using the SDLC.* The SDLC is very structured and offers organizations a lot of control over information systems projects; in addition, it is widely recognized and used in business. On the other hand, the steps in the SDLC can take a lot of time to complete, thereby resulting in high costs relative to other systems development strategies.
3. *Apply the SDLC in accounting contexts.* Since accounting is fundamentally an information system, the SDLC steps can be applied to it. In the *initiation/planning* stage, an organization would recognize the need for changes in its AIS—for example, the need to generate a variance analysis or consolidate results from subsidiary companies. *Requirements analysis* focuses on what the system needs to accomplish; staying with the variance analysis example, the system would probably need to generate quantity and cost variances for product costs. *Designing* such a system gets still more specific: What would a user see on the screen? Which source documents, paper or electronic, would be required to collect the data? How would the data be input? Systems professionals would move next to *building* the system—actually putting together the screens, documents, and programming code for computing variances. Users would have the opportunity to *test* the system prior to it being *implemented* with a parallel approach, direct cutover approach, or some other approach. Finally, in *operations and maintenance,* the system would be changed as the organization and its information needs change.
4. *List and discuss the levels of the capability maturity model.* The capability maturity model consists of five levels, each more sophisticated than the previous level: chaotic, repeatable, defined, managed, and optimized.
5. *Classify organizations' processes according to the CMM.* When an organization's processes are *chaotic,* they lack cohesion; each individual in the organization does what seems best to him/her. *Repeatable* processes involve some standards and procedures,

but they are probably applied to a single project. When processes are *defined,* they are connected to broader organizational standards; standards are developed and data are collected about the process. Processes move to the *managed* stage when the collected data are used to improve and control the process. When the idea of managing and improving business processes is ingrained in the organization, becoming part of its culture, it moves to the last level of the CMM: *optimized.*

6. *Explain factors managers should consider when choosing IT for an AIS.* The chapter considers both macro- and micro-level factors. Macro-level factors include need, strategic fit, personnel involvement, and financing. Micro-level factors are cost, adaptability, training, and vendor reliability. The weighted-rating technique can be used to balance the factors.

When accounting information systems courses started becoming a part of undergraduate accounting programs, they often focused on ideas common to all information systems like the SDLC. Although the content of AIS courses has become more specific over time, those ideas can still be an integral part of AIS study.

Key Terms

capability maturity model, *151*
iterative, *149*
macro-level issues, *153*
micro-level issues, *153*
systems development life cycle, *148*
three-stage process, *155*
Watts Humphrey, *151*
weighted-rating technique, *155*

Chapter References

Hurst, J. 2007. *The Capability Maturity Model and Its Applications.* www.giac.org/resources/whitepaper/application/242.php (last visited September 15, 2008).

Johnston, R. 2003. "A Strategy for Finding the Right Accounting Software." *Journal of Accountancy,* September, pp. 39–46.

Sylla, C., and H. J. Wen. 2002. "A Conceptual Framework for Evaluation of Information Technology Investments." *International Journal of Technology Management,* pp. 236–61.

End-of-Chapter Activities

1. *Reading review questions.*

a. What are the steps in the systems development life cycle? What activities does each step involve?

b. What are the costs and benefits of using the SDLC?

c. How can the SDLC be useful in accounting information systems?

d. What are the levels in the capability maturity model? What characteristics distinguish each level?

e. What factors should managers consider when choosing information technology resources?

f. Respond to the questions for this chapter's "AIS in the Business World."

2. *Making choices and exercising judgment.*

a. Business professionals have debated whether or not an organization should strive to ensure that all its processes are "optimized" according to the CMM. What do you think? Regardless of your response, what benefits might an organization realize at the earlier levels?

b. Common forms of information technology in AIS include spreadsheets, databases, general ledger software, and ERP systems. List and discuss three AIS-related tasks you could accomplish with each type of software; for example, you could develop a budget with spreadsheet software.

c. FTP (file transfer protocol) software is used to transfer files between a computer and the Internet. In considering an FTP package, managers might consider factors such as cost, popularity, documentation, and ease of use. Point your Web browser to www.download.com and identify three FTP software packages available there. Evaluate them using the weighted-rating technique described in the chapter.

3. *Field exercises.*

a. The SDLC is only one methodology for designing and implementing information systems. Others include rapid application development, open source development, joint applications design, and prototyping. Investigate one or more of those alternatives. Describe it, then compare and contrast it to the systems development life cycle.

b. Arrange an interview with an accounting or information systems professional in an environment where you'd like to work after earning your degree. Ask your interviewee to describe a business process in his/her organization. On your own, based on that description, classify the process according to the capability maturity model. Explain your classification.

c. Read "Commercializing the Back Office at Lloyds of London: Outsourcing and Strategic Partnerships Revisited" in *European Management Journal* (April 2004, pp. 127–40). Summarize the article's contents in no more than one single-spaced page. Did Lloyds use IT strategically? Justify your response.

4. *Capability maturity model classification.* Several business processes are described below. Which CMM level best characterizes each one?

a. Alastor owns a lawn care business. Each time he mows a client's lawn, he sets a goal for how long it should take.

b. Big State University was engaged in three building projects simultaneously: an addition to the library, a new parking structure, and upgrades to the student center. Although each project was over budget for both time and money, the university president focused on analyzing the situation for the parking structure only.

c. CHL Corporation's management team meets monthly to address issues of process improvement and product quality.

d. Christina is a sales representative with clients all over eastern Michigan. At the beginning of each day, she decides which clients she will contact that day and whether she will contact them in person, over the phone, or via e-mail.

e. Hong and Meihua build wooden doghouses based on requests from clients. They frequently disagree about the best way to build each one.

f. Magdy is the vice president of finance at TCH Corporation. At the end of each year, he consults with the president and other vice presidents to determine the corporation's optimal capital structure. He then compares the optimal structure to the actual one, making recommendations for needed changes.

g. Rodrigo, Miguel, and Ana own a mobile pet grooming service with eight employees. Every quarter, as part of their overall quality improvement plan, they send two employees to a continuing education seminar.

h. Sebastian is a manager at PPK Corporation. The last time he hired a new employee, he asked his favorite current employee if any of her relatives were looking for a job; he then hired one based on that conversation.

i. The payroll manager at BHN Corporation has proposed outsourcing part of the payroll function. In accordance with BHN policy, the manager prepared a flowchart of how the new process would work.

j. When the production manager at STK Corporation suggested converting from a process-costing system to a job-costing system, the vice president of operations asked how the change would affect the amount of inventory available for sale.

5. *Systems development life cycle.* Which phase of the SDLC is described by each independent case below?

a. Dolores used design specifications to create database tables for employee records.

b. Eric works at a "help desk" answering questions about patching issues in World of Warcraft.

c. Esther must decide how many "action buttons" to put on an Access form for entering purchase requisitions.

d. Liliane completed several simulations of a new inventory control system, then made recommendations for changes in how the system was designed and built.

e. Marcel prepared a leveled set of data flow diagrams for a new sales/collection process, then used the set as a basis for discussion with the sales staff.

f. Tony wants to move from incremental budgeting to zero-based budgeting.

g. When the accounting staff of CHF Corporation arrived at work on Monday morning, their old manual accounting system had been replaced.

6. *Requirements analysis.*

a. Jeff is the warehouse manager for Alta Pasa Unified School District; he wants an online inventory tracking system for computers and other technology resources in the warehouse. List and discuss at least five questions you would ask Jeff and his staff as part of the requirements analysis for the project.

b. Amanda is a hypnotherapist in Dallas, Texas. She currently maintains her appointment schedule in a paper-based calendar but wants to start using information technology for that purpose. List and discuss at least five questions you would ask Amanda as part of the requirements analysis for the project.

7. *Designing, building, and testing an information system.* Working on your own or with a group of students, consider one of the following cases from the indicated chapters on business processes. Design and build at least one database table with an associated form for the case you select. Test your application by letting another student/group from your AIS class use it.

a. Sales/collection process: Dreambox Creations, Dr. Sanjay Doshi, Richards Furniture Company.

b. Acquisition/payment process: Dreambox Creations, Big State University library.

c. Other business processes: Mhlume Sugar Company, Damian Information Inc., Dreambox Creations.

8. *AICPA Top Technology Initiatives.* Point your Web browser to www.infotech.aicpa.org. Investigate the 2008 list of AICPA Top Technology Initiatives; describe the process used to develop the list. Work with a group of students to investigate one or more of the technologies, summarizing your work in a form specified by your instructor.

9. *Crossword puzzle.*

Across

1. What users do during testing.
7. Often analyzed through interviews.
9. Philosophy associated with optimized processes.
10. CMM level at which processes are based on organizational standards.

Down

2. First step in the SDLC.
3. Associated with the design phase of the SDLC.
4. First suggested the CMM.
5. Direct ________: another way to implement a new system.
6. Must be developed for CMM level two.
8. Implementation style that runs old and new systems at the same time.

10. *Terminology.* Match each item on the left with the most appropriate item on the right.

1. "Ad hoc" processes
2. Business rules
3. Consistent project standards
4. Cost overrun
5. Discrete project standards
6. Feasibility study
7. Improvement part of organizational culture
8. Modular programming code
9. Simulations
10. Statistical project control

a. Test (SDLC)
b. Risk of SDLC
c. Repeatable (CMM)
d. Optimized (CMM)
e. Managed (CMM)
f. Initiation/planning (SDLC)
g. Design (SDLC)
h. Defined (CMM)
i. Chaotic (CMM)
j. Build (SDLC)

11. *Multiple choice questions.*

1. As a future accounting professional, which phase of the SDLC are you least likely to be involved in?
   a. Build
   b. Requirements analysis
   c. Operations/maintenance
   d. Test
2. If a system does poorly during the testing phase of the SDLC, it may be due to issues in
   I. Requirements analysis.
   II. Design.
   III. Build.
   a. I and II only
   b. II and III only
   c. I and III only
   d. I, II, and III
3. Data flow diagrams are most likely to be used first in which step of the SDLC?
   a. Initiation/planning
   b. Requirements analysis
   c. Design
   d. Data flow diagrams are not used in the SDLC.
4. Which of the following is the best example of the "initiation/planning" stage of the SDLC?
   a. "We need to use XBRL to produce financial statements."
   b. "We should adopt Peachtree as our general ledger software."
   c. "Let's compare PeopleSoft with SAP."
   d. "Our inventory controls are weak."
5. Which of the following statements is most true?
   a. Failure of a new system is a bigger risk in direct cutover implementations than in parallel implementations.
   b. Failure of a new system is a bigger risk in parallel implementations than in direct cutover implementations.
   c. Smaller organizations should use parallel implementation more often than direct cutover.
   d. Larger organizations should use direct cutover implementation more often than parallel.

6. John plans to use the SDLC to develop a balanced scorecard for his department. Which stage of the capability maturity model is John's organization in?
   a. Chaotic
   b. Repeatable
   c. Managed
   d. Cannot be determined from the information given
7. The vice president of TRT Corporation doesn't care how managers develop budgets, as long as they do it on time. Which stage of the capability maturity model best describes TRT?
   a. Chaotic
   b. Repeatable
   c. Defined
   d. Managed
8. Which of the following statements is most true?
   a. An organization with optimized business processes is more efficient than an organization with managed business processes.
   b. All organizations should strive to optimize all their business processes as quickly as possible.
   c. Information technology can be used at any stage of the CMM.
   d. Organizations with optimized business processes are in compliance with SOX.
9. The CMM has been applied in
   a. Project management.
   b. Risk management.
   c. Business school accreditation.
   d. All of the above.
10. The CMM was first developed as a way to assess
   a. Government contractors working on military equipment.
   b. Private sector software developers.
   c. Organizations developing software for the government.
   d. Risk.

12. *Statement evaluation.* Indicate whether each of the following statements is (i) always true, (ii) sometimes true, or (iii) never true. For those that are (ii) sometimes true, explain when the statement is true.

a. The systems development life cycle is the best way to develop new information systems.
b. The SDLC can never be used as a tool for managing business processes.
c. Interviews with system users can be an important element of requirements analysis.
d. Results in the build stage of the SDLC may require an organization to revisit its requirements analysis.
e. Cost growth and schedule delays are risks associated with using the SDLC.
f. If the business processes in Department X are optimized, the business processes in Department Y are also optimized.
g. An organization can move from repeatable processes to managed processes without having defined processes.
h. An organization should move through the stages of the CMM sequentially.
i. An organization using activity-based management is at the managed stage of the CMM.
j. Publicly traded corporations are required to optimize their business processes for SOX and the Foreign Corrupt Practices Act.

Chapter Nine

XBRL

AIS in the Business World

XBRL at the Federal Deposit Insurance Corporation

According to its Web site (www.fdic.gov), "The Federal Deposit Insurance Corporation (FDIC) is an independent agency created by the Congress that maintains the stability and public confidence in the nation's financial system by insuring deposits, examining and supervising financial institutions, and managing receiverships."

On a quarterly basis, banks submit a Report of Condition and Income, otherwise known as a "Call Report," to the FDIC. The Web site provides the following information about the Call Report:

> FDIC collects, corrects, updates and stores Reports of Condition and Income data submitted to us by all insured national and state nonmember commercial banks and state-chartered savings banks on a quarterly basis. Reports of Condition and Income data are a widely used source of timely and accurate financial data regarding a bank's condition and the results of its operations. The Reports of Condition and Income data are the only publicly available source of information regarding the status of U.S. banking system; therefore, the FDIC's actions in this regard are of paramount importance, and every precautionary measure is taken to preserve data integrity and accuracy.

In 2004, the FDIC began requiring member banks to use the eXtensible Business Reporting Language in filing Call Reports. XBRL has been particularly useful in Call Report formulas, which check for logical consistency in the reports.

Discussion Questions

1. What is XBRL? How does it facilitate the exchange of financial information?
2. How are accountants likely to be involved with XBRL?

One of the really interesting things about accounting information systems is its dynamic nature. Because AIS involves information technology, there are always new ideas, new tools, and new topics to explore. We'll look at one of those topics in this chapter: XBRL. XBRL is an acronym for the eXtensible Business Reporting Language; it's an example of business exchange technology, which has appeared on many AICPA Top Technologies lists over the years. The basic purpose of XBRL is to facilitate information exchange, particularly financial information, between all different kinds of organizations, regardless of the hardware and software platforms they use individually.

XBRL is a "standard" in the broadest sense of the term. It is not, however, a new accounting standard in the FASB sense. XBRL is simply a way to code information for easier interpretation.

You may have heard of HyperText Markup Language (HTML), the language used to develop Web pages on the Internet. **XBRL** is to financial information what HTML is to Web page development. XBRL is a subset of a much broader language, XML (eXtensible Markup Language). As an accountant, you will likely be called upon to convert standardized financial statements into XBRL format; you also may have to interact with information technology professionals in organizations about this important new standard.

When you've finished studying this chapter, you should be able to:

1. Define the following terms as they relate to XBRL: *extensible, specification, taxonomy, namespace,* and *instance document.*
2. Explain the history and structure of XBRL.
3. Discuss ways XBRL can benefit organizations.
4. Identify software tools for creating XBRL-tagged documents.
5. Discuss internal control issues for XBRL.

According to the Web site of XBRL International (www.xbrl.org):

> XBRL is a language for the electronic communication of business and financial data which is set to revolutionize business reporting around the world. It provides major benefits in the preparation, analysis and communication of business information. It offers cost savings, greater efficiency and improved accuracy and reliability to all those involved in supplying or using financial data. XBRL is being developed by an international non-profit consortium of approximately 250 major companies, organizations and government agencies. It is an open standard, free of license fees. It is already being put to practical use in a number of countries and implementations of XBRL are growing rapidly around the world.

Except where specifically stated otherwise, the material in this chapter is based on material found on that Web site as well as materials provided at the first American Accounting Association workshop on XBRL Teaching.

TERMINOLOGY

I often tell my students that accountants (and other professionals) invent new words for things people already understand, and new meanings for words they already know.

As you may have learned in your very first accounting course, accounting is often referred to as the "language of business." And, like most languages, accounting has some specialized terminology/idiomatic expressions that should be mastered. Consider, for example, the term *depreciation.* If you ask a friend who is a nonaccounting major what depreciation is, he or she likely will talk about a loss in value—as in "when you drive a new car off a lot, it depreciates 50 percent." But, in accounting, *depreciation* takes on a completely different meaning: the periodic allocation of an asset's cost to the periods that benefit from its use. In accounting, we say that depreciation is a process of allocation, not valuation.

In the same way that accounting (and most "regular" languages) involves specialized terminology, so does XBRL. You should understand at least five terms before you begin reading about XBRL in the rest of this chapter.

- *Extensible.* The "X" in XBRL stands for *extensible.* In other words, the XBRL language is "able" to be "extended." The same is true for English. Think about words and expressions we use in the 21st century that hadn't even been invented a decade ago: WiFi, iPod, and the like. In the same way that English grows and changes, users can add new ideas and phrases to the basic XBRL without changing its fundamental purpose, structure, or existing terminology. This idea is critically important in any discussion of XBRL. The original creators of the language could not possibly have anticipated every term needed by every organization over the course of even a few years—let alone a longer time period.
- *Specification.* Think of a specification as a particular (specific) example of a larger group. For example, "California" is a specification of "United States." Or "goodwill" is a specification of "assets." XBRL is part of a larger group of languages referred to as XML (eXtensible Markup Language). One common feature of all XML specifications is their "extensible" nature; another is their use as "markup" languages. So, XML consists of a series of descriptors added to various kinds of information that help users make sense of the information. As a specification of XML, XBRL is focused on descriptors of business reporting information—most often, accounting information.
- *Taxonomy.* Broadly speaking, a taxonomy is a way to organize knowledge. The table of contents of a book is a taxonomy. If someone asked you about the information contained in a balance sheet, you would likely describe it as "assets, liabilities, and equity." Those three elements of financial statements are a taxonomy—they are a way of grouping items together for ease of presentation and discussion. XBRL is made up of several taxonomies, which, for the most part, are focused on specific industry groups. For example, the terminology that describes financial information in a manufacturing firm (such as material, labor, overhead, work in process) has some significant differences from financial terminology in a government entity (fund, encumbrance).
- *Namespace.* If you were reading and ran across a word you didn't know, where would you look to find its meaning? Probably a dictionary—online or in book form. A namespace is like an XBRL dictionary. Remember what the "X" stands for: *extensible.* So, if someone invents a new XBRL term (i.e., extends XBRL), he or she has to let others know what it means. The meaning (definition) of the new term would reside in a namespace. Namespaces have Internet addresses (URLs) just like Web pages.
- *Instance document.* An instance document is a specific example of properly tagged XBRL information. For example, a publicly traded company like Microsoft might mark up its balance sheet with XBRL tags. The balance sheet, then, would be an instance document.

Those five terms will come up again as you read the chapter. You might find it helpful to mark these pages in some way in case you need to refer back to them later.

HISTORY AND STRUCTURE

Take a look at this number:

59.77.85.91

What do you suppose it means? If you're like most students, you're thinking "it could mean anything!" The problem is you don't have any *context* for interpreting the number. On the other hand, if I provide you the following facts, the number might make more sense:

- I was born in 1959.
- I graduated from high school in 1977.

- I earned my master's degree in 1985.
- I defended my doctoral dissertation in 1991.

I'm grateful to Dr. Roger Debreceny (University of Hawaii, Manoa) for providing a similar illustration at the AAA XBRL Teaching workshop (Debreceny and White, 2005).

Now, extrapolate the difficulty of interpreting a relatively simple number in a relatively easy-to-understand language to the complexity of an accounting information system.

- Organizations can have significantly different structures and titles in their chart of accounts.
- Every account in the system has its own balance.
- The balances can be measured in hundreds of world currencies.
- Some of the numbers in the system reflect results for a period of time (e.g., revenues), while others reflect position at a point in time (e.g., assets).
- The numbers in an accounting system can be produced with or without information technology. When information technology is used, the specific hardware and software variations are practically limitless.

Reflection and Self-Assessment 9.1

Consider the list of complexities inherent in accounting information presented above. Suggest one or two more items that make it difficult to interpret accounting information without some context.

Suppose, for example, ASR Corporation has two divisions: RBE Division in the United States and CLG Division in Mexico. RBE collects and processes accounting information using an enterprise resource planning system; CLG is a much smaller division and keeps its accounting records in Peachtree. At the end of a recent accounting period, RBE sent the following accounting information to corporate headquarters:

Account Number	Account Title	Balance
101	Cash	$80,000
105	Accounts receivable	15,000
108	Inventory	7,000

At the same time, CLG sent this information:

Account Number	Account Title	Balance (pesos)
102	Seguro	10,000
107	Seguridades comerciales	9,000
109	Fuentes	5,000

How could ASR's corporate controller combine the information from RBE and CLG to produce corporate financial statements? One solution might be to reenter all the information into Excel or some other piece of software—but that would be time-consuming and inefficient. In addition, reentering the information creates the risk of making an error that could impact the corporate financial statements.

Enter XBRL—the eXtensible Business Reporting Language. XBRL is one application of XML, the eXtensible Markup Language. According to the XBRL Web site (www.xbrl.org), XML "is a standard for the electronic exchange of data between businesses and on the Internet. Under XML, identifying tags are applied to items of data so that they can be processed efficiently by computer software." Let's dissect the pieces of the name *XBRL* to understand it more clearly.

1. XBRL is *extensible.* In other words, users can "extend" the language beyond its original parameters based on their own needs. Certain terms are commonly used in accounting: assets, liabilities, revenue, gross profit, and the like. But suppose a company has its own unique labels for its financial information: revenue from the southern division, gross profit on products, gross profit on services, and similar terms. If XBRL wasn't extensible, users would be "stuck with" whatever labels its creators built into the language. As it stands, users can create their own unique tags for financial data as the need arises.
2. XBRL is for *business reporting.* It is specifically designed to tag and transmit financial information—the kind produced by an accounting information system. Other languages in the XML family include the Resource Description Framework (RDF), Rich Site Summary (RSS), Mathematical Markup Language (MathML), and Scalable Vector Graphics (SVG).
3. XBRL is a *language.* Just like English, French, or Visual Basic, XBRL has its own rules regarding things like syntax and punctuation. The XBRL Web site provides this example of how the language looks:

```
<ifrs-gp:AssetsHeldSale contextRef="Current_AsOf" unitRef="U-Euros"
  decimals="0">100000</ifrs-gp:AssetsHeldSale>
<ifrs-gp:ConstructionProgressCurrent contextRef="Current_AsOf"
  unitRef="U-Euros" decimals="0">100000</ifrs-
  gp:ConstructionProgressCurrent>
<ifrs-gp:Inventories contextRef="Current_AsOf" unitRef="U-Euros"
  decimals="0">100000</ifrs-gp:Inventories>
<ifrs-gp:OtherFinancialAssetsCurrent contextRef="Current_AsOf"
  unitRef="U-Euros" decimals="0">100000</ifrs-
  gp:OtherFinancialAssetsCurrent>
<ifrs-gp:HedgingInstrumentsCurrentAsset contextRef="Current_AsOf"
  unitRef="U-Euros" decimals="0">100000</ifrs-
  gp:HedgingInstrumentsCurrentAsset>
<ifrs-gp:CurrentTaxReceivables contextRef="Current_AsOf" unitRef="U-
  Euros" decimals="0">100000</ifrs-gp:CurrentTaxReceivables>
<ifrs-gp:TradeOtherReceivablesNetCurrent contextRef="Current_AsOf"
  unitRef="U-Euros" decimals="0">100000</ifrs-
  gp:TradeOtherReceivablesNetCurrent>
<ifrs-gp:PrepaymentsCurrent contextRef="Current_AsOf" unitRef="U-Euros"
  decimals="0">100000</ifrs-gp:PrepaymentsCurrent>
<ifrs-gp:CashCashEquivalents contextRef="Current_AsOf" unitRef="U-
  Euros" decimals="0">100000</ifrs-gp:CashCashEquivalents>
<ifrs-gp:OtherAssetsCurrent contextRef="Current_AsOf" unitRef="U-Euros"
  decimals="0">100000</ifrs-gp:OtherAssetsCurrent>
<ifrs-gp:AssetsCurrentTotal contextRef="Current_AsOf" unitRef="U-Euros"
  decimals="0">1000000</ifrs-gp:AssetsCurrentTotal>
```

Keep in mind that the preceding example of XBRL is designed to be read by computers, not people. In fact, the XBRL Web site says: "Ordinary users of XBRL may be largely or totally unaware of the technical infrastructure which underpins the language. However, software companies, such as accountancy software providers, need to take account of XBRL and its features when producing their products." We won't get further into the technical details of XBRL as a language in this text; we'll focus the rest of our discussion on XBRL at a conceptual level.

XBRL, then, is a **specification** of XML. XBRL itself is comprised of several **taxonomies;** taxonomies are developed by professional organizations and industry groups based on their unique accounting standards and needs. The XBRL Web site defines taxonomies as

> The dictionaries used by XBRL. They define the specific tags for individual items of data (such as "net profit"). Different taxonomies will be required for different financial reporting purposes. National jurisdictions may need their own financial reporting taxonomies to reflect their local accounting regulations. Many different organizations, including regulators, specific industries or even companies, may require taxonomies to cover their own business reporting needs.

As of December 2008, XBRL International had approved 12 XBRL taxonomies in the United States:

- Accountants' Report Taxonomy 1.0
- Country Taxonomy 1.0
- Currency Taxonomy 1.0
- Document and Entity Information Taxonomy 1.0
- Exchange Taxonomy 1.0
- GAAP Taxonomy 1.0
- Management's Discussion and Analysis Taxonomy 1.0
- Management Report Taxonomy 1.0
- North American Industrial Classification System (NAICS) Taxonomy 1.0
- SEC Certification Taxonomy 1.0
- Standardized Industrial Classification (SIC) Taxonomy 1.0
- State-Province Taxonomy 1.0

Most current software, such as Microsoft Excel and Great Plains Dynamics, can interpret XBRL tags. Namespaces must be "declared" at the beginning of an XBRL document so the software knows where to look on the Internet for its interpretive rules.

Figure 9.1 shows the relationship between XML, XBRL, and the XBRL taxonomies. The rules and terminology associated with a specific taxonomy reside in a **namespace** on the Internet; that way, XBRL-enabled software can reference the taxonomy simply by locating its namespace.

Reflection and Self-Assessment 9.2

Choose one of the approved U.S. taxonomies listed above. Point your Web browser to www.xbrl.org/FRTApproved/. Click the link for the taxonomy you selected and prepare a summary of what you find.

FIGURE 9.1
Basic XBRL Concepts

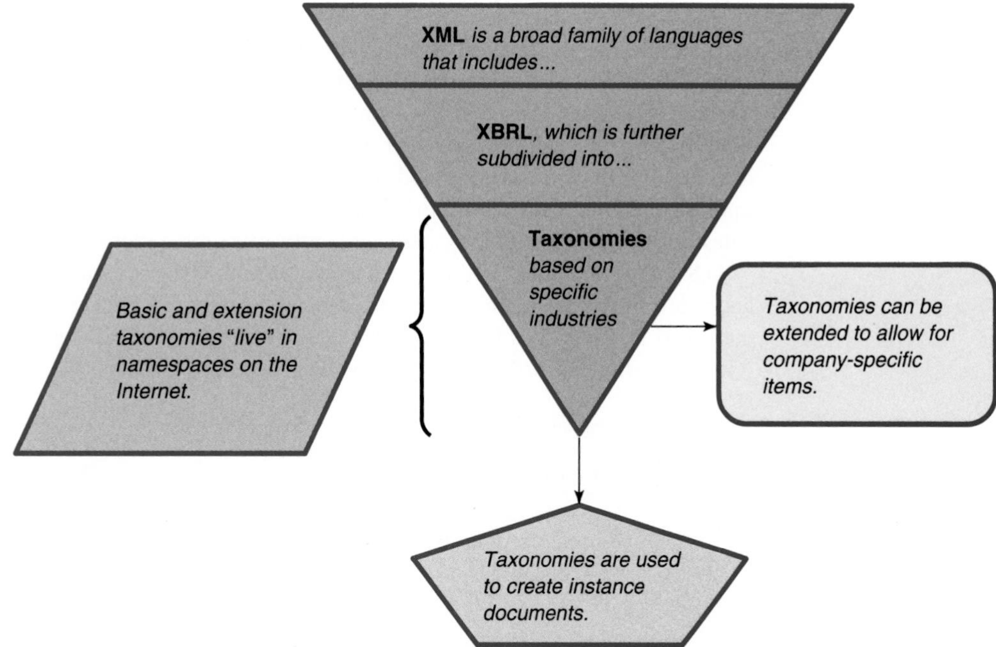

Here's one more piece of terminology associated with XBRL: **instance document.** One of the Big Four CPA firms, KPMG International, provides the following definition of an instance document (www.kpmg.com/xbrl/jargon.asp):

> A business report in XBRL form that provides information in context, complying with the definitions set down in a taxonomy and one or more extension taxonomies. For example, a company's financial statements might be published as an instance document in compliance with the U.S. GAAP commercial and industrial taxonomy. Quarterly, half yearly, weekly or hourly business reports also take the form of an instance document.

So, for example, the illustration provided in item 3 on page 169 ("XBRL is a language") is part of an XBRL instance document.

GLOBAL TAXONOMIES AND TAGGING TOOLS

Many XBRL taxonomies are country-based; that is, approved taxonomies in the United States are different from approved taxonomies in, for example, China or Ireland. But two taxonomies cut across national borders: the International Financial Reporting Standards (IFRS) taxonomy and the Global Ledger (GL) taxonomy.

As of December 2008, the IFRS taxonomy was acknowledged by XBRL. An acknowledged taxonomy has to conform to a specific version of XBRL. Acknowledged taxonomies are differentiated from approved taxonomies; the latter must conform to a specific version of XBRL and XBRL guidelines for the specific taxonomy type (e.g., financial reporting). The official name of the IFRS taxonomy is "International Financial Reporting Standards General Purpose Financial Reporting for Profit-Oriented Entities, Incorporating Additional Requirements for Banks and Similar Financial Institutions (IFRS-GP) 2006," but people commonly refer to it as IFRS-GP. (I'm sure you can tell why!) The purpose of IFRS-GP is to allow for-profit organizations to prepare XBRL-tagged financial statements based on International Financial Reporting Standards.

The Global Ledger taxonomy, commonly known as XBRL-GL, helps organizations manage internal information. According to the XBRL Web site discussion of XBRL-GL, "the XBRL Global Ledger taxonomy allows the representation of anything that is found in a chart of accounts, journal entries or historical transactions, financial and non-financial. It does not require a standardised chart of accounts to gather information, but it can be used to tie legacy charts of accounts and accounting detail to a standardised chart of accounts to improve communications within a business." Like other XBRL taxonomies, XBRL-GL cuts across organization types, hardware/software combinations, and languages.

U.S.-based taxonomies, along with IFRS-GP and XBRL-GL, are going to become more and more important as time goes on. The Securities and Exchange Commission (SEC) published its final rules for XBRL in December 2008. The SEC will phase in mandatory XBRL reporting according to the following schedule:

Type of Filer	XBRL Reporting Deadline
Large, accelerated filers using U.S. GAAP	2009
All other accelerated filers using U.S. GAAP	2010
All remaining filers using U.S. GAAP	2011

As you can tell, XBRL is massive. And if organizations had to tag every piece of data manually, they would probably need an entire staff devoted to that one task! Thankfully, there are many automated tools available for that purpose. Here are some examples:

Tool Name	Web Site
Dragon Tag	www.rivetsoftware.com
EDGAR Online I-Metrix	i-metrix.edgar-online.com/
CoreFiling Ltd.	www.corefiling.com/
Fujitsu Interstage XWand	www.fujitsu.com/global/services/software/interstage/xbrltools/
TagEzee	www.simplexdtech.com/tagezee.html

You can check out www.xbrl.org/Tools/ for more examples of tagging software. The use of tagging software doesn't eliminate the need to understand the purpose, nature, and structure of XBRL, any more than the use of general ledger software eliminates the need to understand principles of debit and credit, the accounting cycle, and the purpose and structure of financial statements. Rather, tagging software is a tool that helps organizations tag their documents more efficiently than they could with manual coding.

ORGANIZATIONAL BENEFITS

Fundamentally, XBRL helps organizations in two major ways. First, it allows for more efficient data collection and reporting. Consider, for example, a corporate controller in an international organization. The controller would be receiving reports from all over the world that are prepared using a multitude of software packages. If all the information came into the controller's office with appropriate XBRL tags, it could be collected and summarized quickly and easily, then reported to both internal and external stakeholders in a relatively short time.

Second, XBRL facilitates data consumption and analysis. Using XBRL, our corporate controller can collect data and report information much more quickly and easily—leaving more time for analysis and interpretation. Additionally, XBRL-tagged documents can be searched for specific kinds of information, such as sales revenue by geographic region.

The XBRL Web site lists 10 specific **benefits** organizations can derive from implementing this important new technology:

- Save costs by preparing data in one form and automatically generating many outputs. Companies will avoid re-keying of data and other manual tasks.
- Consolidate results across divisions and subsidiaries with much greater speed and reliability.
- Improve accuracy and reliability of financial data.
- Focus effort on analysis, forecasting, and decision making, rather than on laborious tasks in gathering, compiling, and preparing data.
- Achieve quicker and more efficient decisions.
- Make more effective use of the internet in communicating with investors. Companies will benefit from the growing importance of web sites as a means of communication.
- Improve investor relations through provision of more transparent and user-friendly information.
- Simplify the process and reduce the costs involved in regulatory reporting to tax and other authorities.
- Obtain quicker responses from counterparties, including banks and regulators.
- Free themselves from proprietary systems and software which are difficult and costly to replace.

As accountants, we can benefit from XBRL as well. Again, XBRL International cites the following advantages for accountants using XBRL:

- Obtain more rapid and reliable data on company financial performance.
- Greatly reduce effort and costs in gathering and analyzing data.
- Simplify and automate tasks.
- Focus effort on analysis and value-added work.
- Make better use of software to improve efficiency and speed.

The XBRL Web site also identifies specific advantages for other kinds of organizations and groups of financial information professionals.

Reflection and Self-Assessment 9.3

Point your Web browser to www.xbrl.org. Click the "XBRL and Business" link on the left side of the page. Choose one of the groups listed there (e.g., regulators and government, stock exchanges, and investment analysts) and prepare a summary of XBRL's specific advantages.

INTERNAL CONTROL

First, a bit of review. In general, internal control has four main purposes: safeguard assets, ensure reliable financial statements, encourage adherence to management directives, and promote operating efficiency. And, with respect to information technology, recall the C-I-A triad; we want to ensure that data are *c*onfidential, have *i*ntegrity, and are *a*vailable when needed.

What risks, then, do organizations face when they use XBRL? Consider the list below:

- XBRL moves data between and within information systems electronically. Therefore, the data are subject to theft, loss, and manipulation in the same ways all electronic data are.

- XBRL tagging, while not complex, is detail oriented. So, the coding process is subject to the risk that humans will make errors in coding.
- Since XBRL is so technology dependent, we also must consider the risks of hardware and software failure in an XBRL environment.

Trites (2002), working under the auspices of the Canadian Institute of Chartered Accountants (www.cica.ca), suggested two additional risks associated with XBRL: inappropriate/missing authorizations for document changes and selection of an inappropriate taxonomy. Given those five risks, then, what internal controls should organizations consider when adopting XBRL? Here are some suggestions:

Risk	Suggested Control(s)
Compromised data	Daily data backups Firewalls Mandatory password changes "Strong" password requirements Password-protected access Virus protection software
Tagging errors	Electronic tagging (as opposed to manual) Independent review after tagging (e.g., by internal auditors) Periodic user training
Hardware and software failure	Disaster recovery plan Physical security (e.g., locked doors, alarms) Uninterruptible/backup power supplies
Inappropriate/missing authorizations	Internal audit review of selected transactions Periodic user training Up-to-date procedures manuals
Selection of an inappropriate taxonomy	Periodic review and approval of taxonomies used Centralized approval process for taxonomy additions

Does XBRL create new risks for organizations that adopt it? Yes. But, with strong internal controls (such as those listed above), the benefits of adopting XBRL far outweigh its associated costs and risks.

CRITICAL THINKING

Consider the following data about current assets, drawn from the XBRL International Web site (www.xbrl.org).

Assets Held for Sale	100,000
Construction in Progress, Current	100,000
Inventories	100,000
Other Financial Assets, Current	100,000
Hedging Instruments, Current [Asset]	100,000
Current Tax Receivables	100,000
Trade and Other Receivables, Net, Current	100,000
Prepayments, Current	100,000
Cash and Cash Equivalents	100,000
Other Assets, Current	100,000
Current Assets, Total	1,000,000

Here's the XBRL coding that would produce it:

```
<ifrs-gp:AssetsHeldSale contextRef="Current_AsOf" unitRef="U-Euros"
  decimals="0">100000</ifrs-gp:AssetsHeldSale>
<ifrs-gp:ConstructionProgressCurrent contextRef="Current_AsOf"
  unitRef="U-Euros" decimals="0">100000</ifrs-
  gp:ConstructionProgressCurrent>
<ifrs-gp:Inventories contextRef="Current_AsOf" unitRef="U-Euros"
  decimals="0">100000</ifrs-gp:Inventories>
<ifrs-gp:OtherFinancialAssetsCurrent contextRef="Current_AsOf"
  unitRef="U-Euros" decimals="0">100000</ifrs-
  gp:OtherFinancialAssetsCurrent>
<ifrs-gp:HedgingInstrumentsCurrentAsset contextRef="Current_AsOf"
  unitRef="U-Euros" decimals="0">100000</ifrs-
  gp:HedgingInstrumentsCurrentAsset>
<ifrs-gp:CurrentTaxReceivables contextRef="Current_AsOf" unitRef="U-
  Euros" decimals="0">100000</ifrs-gp:CurrentTaxReceivables>
<ifrs-gp:TradeOtherReceivablesNetCurrent contextRef="Current_AsOf"
  unitRef="U-Euros" decimals="0">100000</ifrs-
  gp:TradeOtherReceivablesNetCurrent>
<ifrs-gp:PrepaymentsCurrent contextRef="Current_AsOf" unitRef="U-Euros"
  decimals="0">100000</ifrs-gp:PrepaymentsCurrent>
<ifrs-gp:CashCashEquivalents contextRef="Current_AsOf" unitRef="U-
  Euros" decimals="0">100000</ifrs-gp:CashCashEquivalents>
<ifrs-gp:OtherAssetsCurrent contextRef="Current_AsOf" unitRef="U-Euros"
  decimals="0">100000</ifrs-gp:OtherAssetsCurrent>
<ifrs-gp:AssetsCurrentTotal contextRef="Current_AsOf" unitRef="U-Euros"
  decimals="0">1000000</ifrs-gp:AssetsCurrentTotal>
```

Notice a few things about the XBRL coding:

1. XBRL tags are enclosed in brackets.
2. Every tag has both a beginning, such as <ifrs-gp:AssetsHeldSale contextref="Current_AsOf" unitRef="U-Euros"decimals="0">, and an ending, such as </ifrs-gp:AssetsHeldSale>.
3. Elements of an XBRL tag include capital letters within a label, such as "AssetsHeld-Sale." We refer to that style as *camelCase.*
4. Each tag includes the following information:
   a. The taxonomy used. In this example, "ifrs-gp" stands for General Purpose International Financial Reporting Standards. You can find more information about that taxonomy at http://xbrl.iasb.org/int/fr/ifrs/gp/2005-05-15/summary page.htm.
   b. The element name from the taxonomy. In this example, those element names include AssetsHeldSale and ConstructionProgressCurrent.
   c. Time data. Since we're looking at a schedule of current assets, we're dealing with data at a point in time—not data for a period of time.
   d. Currency data. Each item in the schedule is measured in euros.
   e. Number of decimals to display. In this example, we're displaying zero decimals.

Keep in mind that you're looking at a *partial* instance document. The full document would "declare" a namespace—that means telling a computer where to look on the Internet to find the "translation" of the IFRS-GP taxonomy. The taxonomy is quite extensive—over 700,000 bytes of data. And the PDF file that lists the taxonomy elements is 189 pages long! Nevertheless, if an organization needed to extend the IFRS-GP taxonomy, it could definitely do so. The organization would then have to create a namespace for the extension and identify ("declare") it within the XBRL instance document.

Summary

Here is a summary of the chapter's main points for your review:

1. *Define the following terms as they relate to XBRL:* extensible, specification, taxonomy, namespace, *and* instance document.
   a. *Extensible:* The characteristic of XBRL that allows users to create new tags as the need arises.
   b. *Specification:* Describes the relationship between XBRL and its parent language (XML). XBRL is a specification (example) of the eXtensible Markup Language.
   c. *Taxonomy:* The organizational unit of XBRL. Taxonomies typically are linked to industry groups, such as commercial and industrial or investment management.
   d. *Namespace:* An XBRL dictionary. This is an Internet location that defines some of the tags used in a taxonomy.
   e. *Instance document:* A specific example of properly tagged XBRL information.
2. *Explain the history and structure of XBRL.* The eXtensible Business Reporting Language grew out of a need for increased efficiency in collecting, analyzing, and reporting financial information. XBRL is one specification of XML, the eXtensible Markup Language. XBRL comprises several approved taxonomies that are used to create individual instance documents.
3. *Discuss ways XBRL can benefit organizations.* XBRL allows organizations to collect data from disparate accounting systems, combining it quickly and easily. It smoothes the data collection process and automates many tasks previously completed by hand. Just as general ledger software allowed accountants to automate many repetitive tasks, XBRL helps managers accomplish the same goal. Automating tedious tasks such as consolidating financial statements provides more time for analysis and decision making.
4. *Identify software tools for creating XBRL-tagged documents.* Accountants can avail themselves of a plethora of software tools for creating XBRL-tagged documents. Tagging software such as Rivet's Dragon Tag does not replace human judgment on preparing instance documents. Rather, it is a tool that makes such preparation more efficient and less tedious.
5. *Discuss internal control issues for XBRL.* XBRL exposes an organization to many risks commonly associated with any information technology. Internal controls to combat those risks include proper authorizations and approvals, periodic user training, virus protection software, password procedures, and up-to-date procedures manuals.

XBRL is the future of financial reporting. It provides a language for understanding financial information that transcends national borders, differences in GAAP, languages, currencies, and software packages.

Key Terms

benefits, *173*
instance document, *171*
namespace, *170*
specification, *170*
taxonomies, *170*
XBRL, *166*

Chapter References

XBRL International, www.xbrl.org.
Debreceny, R., and S. White. 2005, June. *XBRL Working Paper.*
Trites, G. D. 2002. *Audit and Control Implications of XBRL.* Toronto, Ontario: Canadian Institute of Chartered Accountants.

End-of-Chapter Activities

1. *Reading review questions.*
   a. What is XBRL? How is it related to XML?
   b. Define the following terms related to XBRL: *specification, taxonomy, instance document.*
   c. How can XBRL benefit organizations?
   d. Will most accountants need to learn to write "code" in XBRL? If not, how can they create XBRL-tagged documents?
   e. Respond to the questions for this chapter's "AIS in the Business World."
2. *Reading review problem.* Willis and Saegesser offered the following comments about using XBRL as a tool for credit risk management:

   XBRL enables disparate reporting systems and software to communicate with each other directly. By providing universal codes for the information which existing software already has and uses, XBRL makes the credit assessment process more automated. The bottom line is that XBRL enables creditors to better manage credit risk from several directions at once. XBRL is helpful because it eliminates distortion and loss of information and artificial delay in the process of getting data from borrower to creditor.

   Source: M. Willis and B. Saegessert, "XBRL: Streamlining Credit Risk Management," *Credit & Financial Management Review,* 2nd quarter 2003.

   a. Explain how XBRL accomplishes the tasks described in the Willis and Saegessert quote.
   b. How are XBRL-tagged documents prepared?
   c. What internal control issues does the use of XBRL raise in accounting information systems?
3. *Making choices and exercising judgment.* The chapter discussed several benefits of implementing XBRL. What are the costs associated with an adoption? Think in terms of financial, organizational, and behavioral costs.
4. *Field work.*
   a. Interview a practicing accountant, in either a CPA firm or a corporate environment. Find out what your interviewee knows about XBRL and its advantages for accounting firms and their clients.
   b. Refer to the list of XBRL tagging software referenced in the chapter. Choose two or three of the software packages on the list; apply the software evaluation methodology discussed earlier in the text. As your evaluation criteria, use cost (weight = 5), ease of use (weight = 3), and support services (weight = 2).
   c. Complete the XBRL tutorial developed by KPMG, which you'll find at www.us.kpmg.com/microsite/xbrl/train/86/86.htm. Prepare a summary of what you learned to discuss in class.

5. *Contextual categories of XBRL.* The purpose of XBRL is to provide a context for understanding financial information. Several contextual categories associated with financial information are listed below; for each category listed, give at least two examples of how it might vary across organizations and financial reporting systems. The first item is done as an example.
   a. Type of balance: debit, credit
   b. Time period
   c. Currency
   d. Account type
   e. Accounting rules (i.e., GAAP)
   f. Reporting language
   g. Preparation tools
6. *XBRL tags.* Consider the sample of XBRL tags shown in the chapter. Use your critical-thinking skills and accounting background to suggest what each of the following pieces of information might denote. The first item is done as an example.
   a. IFRS: International Financial Reporting Standards
   b. ContextRef
   b. UnitRef
   c. Decimals
7. *XBRL tagging.* Read "Six Steps to XBRL" by Phillips, Bahmanziari, and Colvard in the February 2008 issue of *Journal of Accountancy.*
   a. Is XBRL relevant to companies that don't file with the SEC? Justify your response.
   b. List the six steps the authors recommend for creating XBRL-tagged documents.
   c. How many XBRL-tagged filings did the SEC receive as part of its voluntary program?
   d. With respect to Dragon Tag software:
      i. What are the elements of an entity profile?
      ii. What is a "hopper"?
      iii. What is "validation"? Why is it important?
8. *Benefits of XBRL.* Fill in the blanks below with terminology that describes the benefits of XBRL for organizations and accountants.
   a. Consolidate results across _______ with much greater speed and reliability.
   b. Focus effort on _______, rather than on laborious tasks in _______ data.
   c. Free themselves from _______ and software that are difficult and costly to replace.
   d. Greatly reduce _______ in _______.
   e. Improve _______ through provision of more _______ information.
   f. Make better use of _______ to improve _______.
   g. Make more effective use of the _______ in _______.
   h. Obtain _______ data on company financial performance.
   i. Save costs by _______ and automatically generating many _______.
   j. Simplify the process and reduce the costs involved in _______ to tax and other authorities.

9. *Internal control issues for XBRL.* Point your browser to the Web site of the Canadian Institute of Chartered Accountants (www.cica.ca). Find and download Trites' paper on audit and internal control issues. In consultation with your instructor, and working with a group of students, write a paper or prepare a presentation that summarizes at least one of the following sections of the Trites report: control issues, assurance issues, emerging issues.
10. *Crossword puzzle.* Complete the puzzle below with appropriate terminology from the chapter.

Across

3. XBRL's relationship to XML.
5. Items like currency and time period.
7. The "B" in XBRL.
9. The parent language of XBRL.
10. The type of document created using XBRL.

Down

1. The "R" in XBRL.
2. The "L" in XBRL.
4. The "X" in XBRL.
6. What XBRL adds to information.
8. The type of profile created with Dragon Tag.

11. *Terminology.* Please match each item on the left with the most appropriate item on the right.

1. Acknowedged and approved	a. "Levels" of XBRL taxonomies
2. Business exchange technology	b. AICPA Top Ten Technology that describes XBRL
3. Context	c. Dragon Tag item that specifies "as of" or "duration"
4. Dragon Tag	d. An Excel add-on that facilitates tagging
5. Focus effort on analysis	e. An XBRL taonomy
6. NAICS 1.0	f. Marking up data with XBRL codes
7. Namespace	g. Relationship between XBRL and XML
8. Open source	h. What XBRL provides for information
9. Specification	i. Why no-one "owns" XBRL
10. Tagging	j. XBRL "dictionary"

12. *Multiple choice questions.*

1. XBRL is based on
   a. XBRL-GL.
   b. U.S. GAAP.
   c. XML.
   d. Visual Basic.
2. XBRL is an open standard, meaning
   a. Only public organizations can implement it.
   b. It is related to open-book management.
   c. It does not cost anything to implement.
   d. It does not involve license fees.
3. The notation <ifrs-gp> is referred to as a(n)
   a. Tag.
   b. Instance document.
   c. Specification.
   d. Taxonomy.
4. The Web site for XBRL International is
   a. www.xbrl_international.org.
   b. www.xbrl.com.
   c. www.xbrl.org.
   d. www.xbrl_taxonomies.org.
5. XBRL is independent of
   a. Software and GAAP.
   b. Hardware and GAAP.
   c. Software and hardware.
   d. Software, hardware, and GAAP.
6. Where would you look to find the meaning of an XBRL tag created by an organization?
   a. Textbook
   b. Namespace
   c. Instance document
   d. XBRL Web site

7. Which of the following statements is most true?
   a. Internal controls that work for many forms of information technology are inappropriate for XBRL.
   b. The risks associated with implementing XBRL are too great given the cost of addressing them.
   c. Internal controls for other forms of IT can be adopted for XBRL.
   d. XBRL eliminates the need for internal control.
8. As a language, XBRL has rules associated with
   a. Syntax.
   b. Punctuation.
   c. Both of the above.
   d. None of the above.
9. Which of the following is not a benefit associated with XBRL?
   a. Eliminates the need for financial statement audits
   b. Consolidates results across divisions and subsidiaries with much greater speed and reliability
   c. Obtains quicker responses from counterparties, including banks and regulators
   d. All of the above are benefits associated with XBRL.
10. Dragon Tag is
   a. An XBRL taxonomy.
   b. A namespace.
   c. Software used to generate XBRL tags.
   d. The only software that translates documents into XBRL.

13. *Statement evaluation.* Indicate whether each of the following statements is (i) always true, (ii) sometimes true, or (iii) never true. For those that are (ii) sometimes true; explain when the statement is true.

a. All necessary XBRL tags were developed by the XBRL Consortium.
b. Companies should use Dragon Tag to create XBRL documents.
c. Companies that do business in a single country do not need XBRL.
d. Diversified organizations should use XBRL.
e. General ledger software can create XBRL tags.
f. Organizations that adopt XBRL must create their own namespace.
g. Publicly traded companies can use XBRL for SEC reporting.
h. XBRL adopters must create specific internal controls for XBRL.
i. XBRL is a nonproprietary system.
j. XBRL is an example of business exchange technology.

Chapter Ten

E-business and Enterprise Resource Planning Systems

AIS in the Business World

The Business of Managing People

Information technology and computer networks have changed nearly every aspect of business in the last decade. Consider the following comments about human resource (HR) management:

> Large US employers continue to take a selective approach to outsourcing their benefits administration, recruiting, payroll and other HR functions rather than relying exclusively on a single provider, according to research by consultancy Watson Wyatt. Selective outsourcing is popular because it can be tailored to meet an organization's exact needs. The key to successful outsourcing is finding the solutions that fit the organization's needs and culture, Hubbard notes. Watson Wyatt's Changing Strategies in HR Technology and Outsourcing survey of 182 US companies found that many expect to do more outsourcing in areas such as health and welfare programs. However, few companies, 21%, direct their HR function to outsource programs automatically. The majority, 63%, look to use their internal or enterprise resource planning systems whenever possible to deliver HR services.

In this chapter, we'll consider three important topics that tie in with that case: e-business, enterprise resource planning systems, and application service providers.

Discussion Questions

1. What is *selective outsourcing?*
2. What is an enterprise resource planning system? How do such systems benefit organizations?

Source: Stephen Miller, "Companies Continue to Selectively Outsource HR Programs," *HRMagazine: SHRM's 2009 HR Trend Book,* January 2009, pp. 76–78, from ABI/INFORM Global database (Document ID: 1607406711; accessed January 4, 2009).

E-business systems have become a fact of life in most sectors of the economy; we truly live in a networked world. Think of all the ways information technology impacts your life today, from the hundreds of television and radio stations available via satellite, to the process of registering for classes and ordering textbooks at your university, to the ways you've done research and completed assignments for your AIS class.

When you've finished studying this chapter, you should be able to:

1. Explain the nature of e-business, comparing and contrasting it with traditional "brick-and-mortar" organizations.
2. Discuss major forms of e-business, including business-to-business, consumer-to-consumer, business-to-consumer, government-to-business, and government-to-consumer.
3. Describe the basic nature, purpose, and structure of enterprise resource planning systems.
4. Give examples and analyze the causes of ERP system failures.
5. List and discuss steps associated with successful ERP implementations.
6. Discuss the role of application service providers in e-business.

While this chapter won't make you an expert on these topics, it will give you sufficient background to ask the right questions and engage in intelligent professional conversation about them.

E-BUSINESS

We'll use the terms e-business and e-commerce interchangeably throughout this chapter.

Encarta (www.encarta.msn.com) offers the following definition of e-business:

> **E-commerce** is the exchange of goods and services by means of the Internet or other computer networks. E-commerce follows the same basic principles as traditional commerce—that is, buyers and sellers come together to exchange goods for money. But rather than conducting business in the traditional way—in stores and other "brick and mortar" buildings or through mail order catalogs and telephone operators—in e-commerce buyers and sellers transact business over networked computers.

The central feature of e-business is business is transacted over computer networks. Completing business transactions over **computer networks** offers many costs and benefits, including those summarized in the following table.

Benefits of E-business	Costs of E-business
• Marketing: geographic market expansion, hard-to-reach markets, more targeted marketing • Reduced operating costs: marketing, telecommunications, transaction processing • Streamlined operations • Quicker, easier product and service delivery	• Financial costs associated with setting up networks • Need to develop different, better internal control systems • Potential for customer distrust • Severe consequences for technology breakdowns

From a *marketing* point of view, e-business allows companies to reach customers they might never be able to contact in a traditional brick-and-mortar operation. Late in 2005, I visited Budapest, Hungary, for a week of consulting and teaching with MBA students at the Budapest University of Technology and Economics (www.bme.hu/en/). Part of my travels included a flight on Malev, the Hungarian national airline (www.malev.hu/bp/eng/index.asp). Without the benefit of e-business, I might never have known about or considered flying with Malev; their routes are restricted to a few geographic areas.

E-business also can help organizations *reduce their operating costs*. Consider, for example, services such as Moviefone.com or Fandango.com, which allow moviegoers to purchase their tickets before arriving at the theater. Moving a significant portion of ticket sales to the Internet would help theaters reduce personnel costs in the box office; such systems also would reduce the costs of transaction processing, since online ticket sales could be fed directly into the company's accounting information system or enterprise resource planning system, lessening the need for employees to make manual journal entries and updates to the accounting records.

Companies also can *streamline their operations* using e-business. For example, tourists in southern California can purchase tickets to Disneyland and other attractions online. They can print them out on their own computers, thus eliminating the need to stop at a ticket booth once they arrive at the park. The same is true for airlines; most carriers now offer the option of printing boarding passes before arriving at the airport.

Finally, e-business can promote *quicker, easier product and service delivery*. I'm reminded of this advantage every year during the holiday season. Most of my family and friends live in the Midwest, not in southern California. Prior to the advent of e-business, holiday shopping was extremely stressful: Pick out gifts, fight traffic to shop for them, package them securely, and ship them well in advance to ensure they would arrive on time. With e-business, the process is much simpler; I can complete virtually all of my holiday shopping in just an hour or two at home.

Of course, almost everything in business that has a benefit also involves a cost. Organizations that are just starting their venture into e-business may experience *significant financial costs* associated with developing, purchasing, and configuring software and hardware to support the e-business operation. In addition, e-business systems necessarily require different kinds of *internal controls* than brick-and-mortar operations. Such controls would probably include customer identity authentication via usernames and passwords. Many e-business operations also require customers to input the "control number" from the back of a credit card. A control number is typically a three-digit number printed next to the card number itself, above the signature panel on the back of the card. Billing addresses must match the credit card company's records as a preventive internal control as well. Most companies engaged in e-business operations also process their transactions using a secure server dedicated to that purpose. You may have seen the VeriSign logo on Web pages, indicating an added layer of security for online transactions.

The AICPA's WebTrust and SysTrust projects also provide extra security. The AICPA Web site (http://infotech.aicpa.org) offers the following comments about trust services, WebTrust, and SysTrust:

> Trust Services (including WebTrust® and SysTrust®) are defined as a set of professional assurance and advisory services based on a common framework (that is, a core set of principles and criteria) to address the risks and opportunities of IT. Trust Services principles and criteria are issued by the Assurance Services Executive Committee of the AICPA.
>
> WebTrust is the accounting profession's answer to concerns relating to electronic commerce. WebTrust is based on Trust Services Principles and Criteria, which constitute professional guidance and serve as best practices for electronic commerce. Using these Principles and Criteria either separately or in combination, CPAs can offer a range of advisory and assurance services to help either clients or employers address security, online privacy, availability, and confidentiality needs.
>
> SysTrust is the accounting profession's answer to concerns relating to system reliability. SysTrust is based on the Trust Services Principles and Criteria, which constitute professional guidance as well as serving as best practices for system reliability. Using these Principles and Criteria either separately or in combination, CPAs can offer a range of advisory and assurance services to help either clients or employers address their security, availability, processing integrity, and confidentiality needs.

You can get more information about both services at www.cpawebtrust.org.

Data encryption is another common internal control found in e-business systems. With data encryption, the party that receives data over the Internet must have a decryption key to make it understandable; without encryption, computer criminals can use high-tech techniques to intercept data as they are transmitted electronically. Finally, e-business systems also can incorporate their own form of segregation of duties. You may recall reading about segregation of duties earlier in the text; for any asset, three important responsibilities should be vested in three different people: physical custody, authorization for use, and recordkeeping. In e-business operations, designers can restrict access to various parts of the system based on organizational level and/or job function. For example, faculty members can access certain student information that is unavailable to others at a university.

Beyond the development and internal control costs of e-business, doing business online can create significant amounts of *customer distrust*—particularly for customers who are accustomed to doing business in a traditional brick-and-mortar context. Perhaps you know someone who simply refuses to buy things on the Internet because of concerns over data security and related issues. Finally, the effects of *technology breakdowns* can be severe in an e-business environment: Loss of customer confidence, lost sales, overloaded customer service phone lines, and generalized damage to a company's reputation are just a few.

Reflection and Self-Assessment 10.1

Which of the above benefits and costs have you experienced in doing business on the Internet? What other items could you add to the list based on your experience and/or previous study?

Business professionals and researchers have developed many taxonomies, or **e-business categories,** to describe e-business. I've generally found it helpful to classify e-businesses by the parties they connect, leading to a five-part classification system:

Type	Abbreviation	Example
Business-to-consumer	B2C	Travelocity
Business-to-business	B2B	Dell Computers
Government-to-consumer	G2C	Internal Revenue Service
Government-to-business	G2B	EDGAR (SEC)
Consumer-to-consumer	C2C	eBay

You may have experienced examples of one or more categories of e-business as a consumer. For example, if you've ever purchased anything online, you've been a part of a B2C transaction. C2C transactions are associated with organizations like eBay (www.ebay.com), where people deal with each other directly in selling goods and services. B2B transactions take place when two organizations do business over a computer network; for example, your university bookstore may use e-business techniques to order textbooks from publishers each semester.

Government at all levels is moving head on into the networked economy as well. For example, the Internal Revenue Service (www.irs.gov) provides a lot of information to taxpayers on its Web site; taxpayers also can file their taxes electronically there. And the U.S. Securities and Exchange Commission's EDGAR database (www.sec.gov/edgar.shtml)

Reflection and Self-Assessment 10.2

Suggest one other specific example for each of the five categories presented in the table above. You might find www.cio.com helpful in completing this exercise.

allows publicly traded companies to file their required SEC reports. Investors, researchers, and potential investors also can access companies' documents via EDGAR.

How would e-business impact the accounting information system? Let's go back to the basic model of AIS discussed earlier in the text: inputs, processing tools, storage media, outputs, and internal controls.

We've already discussed a few of the internal controls associated with an e-business environment (data encryption, segregation of duties, access restrictions). From an input perspective, e-business can cut down on the number of paper documents in an accounting information system; it also can shift data entry responsibilities from accounting clerks to customers, since transaction data can be captured directly from a Web site. Consider the process of buying a book from a retail bookstore such as Barnes and Noble. In a brick-and-mortar environment, the steps might include

1. Customer locates book and brings it to a cash register.
2. Register clerk rings up the sale and provides the customer with a paper receipt.
3. At the end of the day, the register clerk retrieves data on the day's sales from the cash register and transmits them to a corporate office or an accounting department.
4. Clerks in the accounting department make journal entries to record the day's transactions.

Contrast those steps with purchasing a book online:

1. Customer identifies books and adds them to an electronic "shopping cart."
2. Customer provides billing and shipping information electronically.
3. E-business system creates and posts journal entries and related inventory information in the accounting information system.

The flowchart in Figure 10.1 depicts the brick-and-mortar process. Figure 10.2 shows what the process would look like in an e-business environment.

Purchasing airplane tickets is another business process that has been profoundly streamlined via e-business. In a brick-and-mortar environment, most people who wanted to purchase airline tickets would consult a travel agent. The travel agent would communicate with the airline, then present options to the client. The client would make a choice; the agent would buy the tickets from the airline, sometimes charging an additional fee for the service. The process could often take several days, and paper tickets were required in the overwhelming majority of transactions.

Consider the process you probably follow now if you want to fly. You log on to an airline or travel-related Web site (for example, www.jetblue.com or www.travelocity.com). You put in the parameters of your travel; the computer searches for tickets and can even compare nearby airports. You submit your payment information on a secure server, and an e-mail arrives in your mailbox confirming the transaction. When you get to the airport, you don't need a paper ticket in most cases.

While e-business probably cannot remove the need for human intervention in an accounting information system, it can significantly reduce that need—and all the attendant problems that accompany it (e.g., data entry mistakes, billing problems, incorrect journal entries).

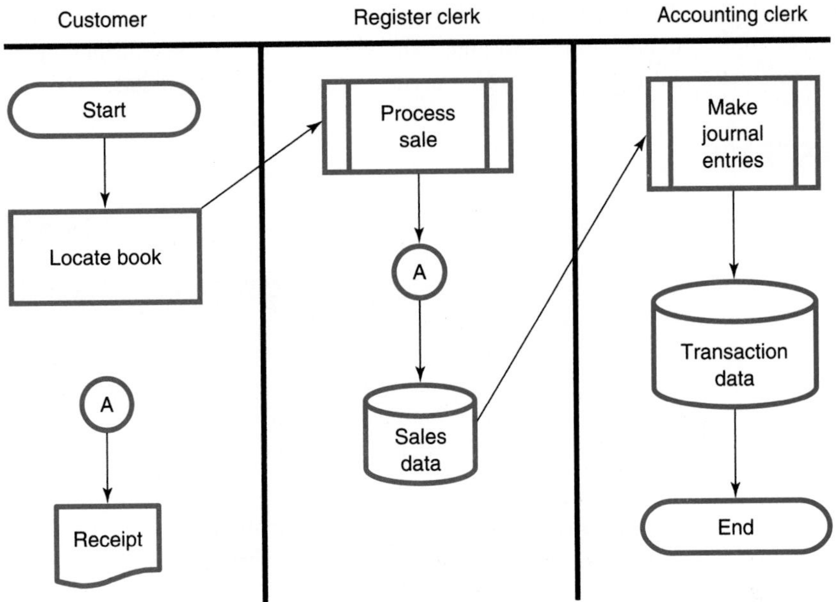

FIGURE 10.1
Brick-and-Mortar Sales Process

From an output perspective, e-business systems facilitate the preparation of general purpose financial statements and other reports. In an early job in my accounting career, I worked for a heavy-equipment manufacturer with consistently large amounts of outstanding accounts receivable. At the end of each business day, I manually prepared an accounts receivable aging, showing each customer's name, balance owed, and length of time the balance had been outstanding. In an e-business system, generating an accounts receivable aging is normally a matter of "pushing a button." The computer does the analysis and prints out the results with little or no human effort.

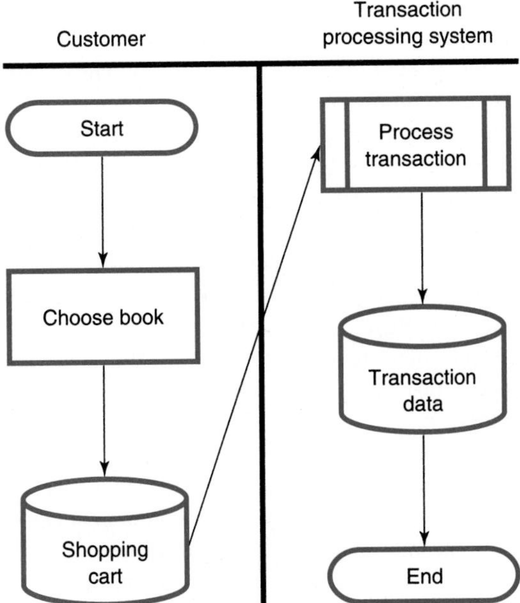

FIGURE 10.2
E-business Sales Process

So, with that very brief overview of e-commerce as background, let's turn our attention to one of the most important, yet most controversial, technologies associated with the networked economy: enterprise resource planning systems.

ERP SYSTEMS

An **enterprise resource planning system** is a modular, relational database designed to provide internal organizational stakeholders with more timely, comprehensive information for decisions. Arguably, the two best-known ERP systems today are PeopleSoft (www.peoplesoft.com) and SAP (www.sap.com). Because most ERP systems are modular, they can be implemented one piece at a time according to an organization's needs and budget. Because they are relational in nature, they organize information in database tables, much like those you learned about earlier in this text.

Typical modules in an ERP system include

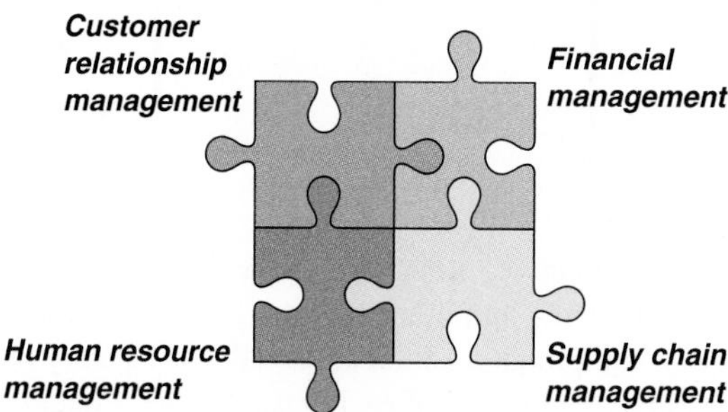

The modules depicted above are not unique to any particular ERP vendor; rather, they provide a broad organizational structure for most ERP systems.

Think back to your study of database development earlier in the text. Since ERP systems are built on relational databases, the principles we discussed there apply here as well. Customer relationship management, as the name implies, helps organizations manage customer data. Beyond basic data such as customer name, address, and phone number, organizations also can capture data on credit limits, transaction histories, contacts, and appointments and referrals. For example, when I log on to Amazon.com to buy books, the system has recommendations for me based on my past purchases; the same is true for NetFlix.

Human resource management concerns itself with employee data. Again, an organization can track "mundane" data such as name and address. However, an HRM module also might include details on work goals, disciplinary problems, and training and development plans. For example, the university where I work maintains a database of faculty experts for the media and other purposes. So, if a newspaper reporter wants a quote on the impact of recycling on the environment, public affairs personnel can consult the database and give them some recommendations.

Supply chain management focuses on vendors—the usual data, plus transaction histories, comments about product quality, and personnel interactions, among other items. Financial management would incorporate the accounting information system, but also would go far beyond the basic general purpose financial statements. For example, organizations can input their budget data into a financial management module, then generate variance reports quickly and easily at any point in time. In universities, a financial management module also might track scholarship records. Financial forecasting is another important function of most financial management ERP modules.

Notice that the four parts of most ERP systems provide information associated with four key stakeholder groups: customers (customer relationship management), employees (human resource management), vendors (supply chain management), and stockholders (financial management). Managing an organization in terms of its relationships with key stakeholder groups has been referred to as the "resource dependency model of the firm" (RDM). The RDM assumes that organizations enter into relationships with stakeholders to get the resources they need to operate (Barnard, 1968). So, most ERP systems help managers stay aware of the importance of those relationships; they also allow an individual manager to concentrate on the relationship(s) that are most important to him or her, while simultaneously providing access to comprehensive information throughout the organization.

Reflection and Self-Assessment 10.3

Suggest at least five pieces of information an ERP system should capture in each module shown above.

Many organizations experience significant difficulty in implementing ERP systems; consider the example below:

> [A major soft drink bottler], which implemented a major ERP system, completed the implementation, but not without losing significant personnel and system functionality. After committing millions of dollars to purchase ERP software, the soft drink maker tried cutting corners during implementation. Relying too heavily on its own people instead of consultants, the bottler expected too much from its already-taxed employees. Trying to minimize setup costs and reduce expenses, the company overlooked many of the planning team's recommendations regarding the project. This ERP implementation created high turnover and communication problems, which led to the termination of key people and animosity among employees. All of these factors, in turn, led to a system that was grossly underused, and in the beginning, a hindrance to the overall business. (Barker and Frolick, 2003)

Umble and Umble (2002) identified 10 major **causes of ERP implementation failures**:

1. *Poor leadership from top management.* Selecting and installing an ERP system is an enormous undertaking in terms of time, money, and energy. Clear, strong leadership and support from top management are essential for a successful implementation—without them, employees are likely to view the ERP system as just another "initiative du jour."
2. *Automating existing redundant or non-value-added processes in the new system.* An ERP implementation project is a terrific time to reconsider the company's business processes. In other words, do policies, procedures, document flows, and internal controls make sense from a business point of view? Do the processes add value to organizational stakeholders? In most organizations, at least a few policies and processes will need to be changed to make the most of the ERP system. Otherwise, managers will be doing the same, ineffective things—only faster.
3. *Unrealistic expectations.* An ERP system is designed to collect, process, and report data and information for making management decisions more effectively. Systems are not a panacea for problems with organizational culture, poorly designed business

processes, or inadequate internal controls. Expecting an ERP system to fix those kinds of problems is a forlorn hope and will seriously jeopardize the project's success.

4. *Poor project management.* ERP system selection, testing, and implementation are time-intensive, long-term projects. To be successful, managers have to apply solid project management techniques for selecting the right people, completing tasks in the right order, and staying on schedule. You may have had coursework in operations management that taught you about project management. Gray and Larson's *Project Management: The Managerial Process* (McGraw-Hill, 2006) would be a good reference if you need a review.
5. *Inadequate education and training.* This failure cause is linked to many of the others in this list. Without good training and education, employees may have unrealistic expectations of what the ERP system can do; they also may see the ERP implementation as solely an information technology project, rather than as an opportunity to analyze business processes and make them better.
6. *Trying to maintain the status quo.* Since an ERP system is such a major undertaking, implementation will almost always create fear and uncertainty throughout an organization. When people are fearful about their job security and future in the firm, they will likely act in very dysfunctional ways, either intentionally or unintentionally. To avoid this problem, be upfront and honest from the start about the purpose and possible results of implementing the ERP system.
7. *A bad match between ERP software and organizational processes.* Every organization has its own ways of doing business. And, while ERP systems can be customized to a degree based on specific organizational contexts, such modifications are time-consuming and expensive. Managers would be well advised to consult with colleagues in the field about which ERP software has worked well, and which has worked poorly, in a specific industry.
8. *Inaccurate data in the system.* As the old saying goes: "garbage in, garbage out." The reports and information generated by an ERP system are only as valid and useful as the data that undergird them. Faulty or inaccurate data in the ERP system can be even worse than the same condition in less-integrated systems, since they will be used throughout the organization for decision making. Once inaccurate data have been discovered in a system, every other prior and future output are called into question until the situation has been resolved.
9. *ERP implementation viewed as an IT project.* As discussed above, implementing an ERP system goes far beyond the information technology requirements. Fundamentally, an ERP project needs to be viewed as holistic, touching not only information technology, but also business processes and organizational behavior issues.
10. *Significant technical difficulties.* Of course, even though an ERP project is not solely concerned with IT issues, some technical problems may arise. Bugs in the software, problems interfacing with existing information systems, and hardware difficulties are just three identified by Umble and Umble.

Similarly, Umble and Umble (2002) discussed six necessary **conditions for a successful ERP implementation**:

1. *Obtain organizational commitment.* This condition speaks most clearly to poor leadership from management and trying to maintain the status quo. The ERP project team needs to get a clear, strong commitment to the project throughout the organization, but especially from top management. Without a psychological and financial commitment to see the project through to its completion, the project may "lose steam" when encountering difficult problems.

2. *Communicate strategic goals clearly.* This idea also relates to two of the common causes of ERP implementation failure: unrealistic expectations and inadequate education and training. Employees in all functions at all levels of the organization need to understand the goals of the ERP project—typically, providing better information more quickly for decision making.
3. *View ERP as an enterprisewide venture.* An ERP system will eventually touch every aspect of operations; therefore, it must be viewed as a companywide project. If the project is viewed as "just another information technology initiative," managers will lose the opportunity to examine business processes thoughtfully and critically—possibly leading to automating redundant or non-value-added processes.
4. *Select a compatible ERP system.* Here, we're talking about items 7 and 10 from the list of common causes of failure: a bad match between ERP software and organizational processes and significant technical difficulties. The bottom line: Don't believe everything the software vendor or implementation consultants tell you! Do your own research; ask for other companies that have had successful (and unsuccessful) implementations.
5. *Resolve multisite issues.* ERP implementations are inherently complicated. But they become more complicated when an organization is geographically dispersed. The project management plan (see item 4 in the preceding list) must deal specifically with multisite issues.
6. *Ensure data accuracy.* The final key to success in ERP implementation is directly related to item 8 on previous page. The project team needs to do significant employee education about the importance of accurate data entry; test runs with fictitious data before the system "goes live" also can help achieve this goal.

Many of those conditions were found at Marathon Oil, leading to a successful implementation of SAP ERP software (Stapleton and Rezak, 2004). Marathon used a change-management approach in implementing its ERP system, recognizing that the goal was "the transfer of ownership from the project team that designed and configured the new system and processes to the end users, the internal clients who would employ these tools and processes in their day-to-day operations." Other keys to Marathon's successful experience included constant communication via newsletters, workshops, and hands-on interaction to increase employees' comfort level with the software.

APPLICATION SERVICE PROVIDERS

Organizations that want to move into an e-business environment have two basic choices for doing so: create applications "from scratch" or hire an **application service provider** (ASP). ASPNews.com (2002) offers the following comments about application service providers:

> An ASP is a third party entity that deploys, hosts and manages access to a packaged application and delivers software-based services and solutions to customers across a wide area network from a central data center. Applications are delivered over networks on a subscription or rental basis. In essence, ASPs are a way for companies to outsource some or almost all aspects of their information technology needs.
>
> ASPnews.com breaks the industry into five subcategories:
>
> - Enterprise ASPs—deliver high-end business applications.
> - Local/Regional ASPs—supply wide variety of application services for smaller businesses in a local area.
> - Specialist ASPs—provide applications for a specific need, such as Web site services or human resources.

- Vertical Market ASPs—provide support to a specific industry such as healthcare.
- Volume Business ASPs—supply general small/medium-sized businesses with prepackaged application services in volume.

COSO's *Enterprise Risk Management: Integrated Framework* discusses ASPs as a form of risk sharing, one way of responding to risks in an organization's environment. (Refer back to Chapter 4 for a complete discussion of the COSO ERM framework.)

In addition to the human resources example discussed in this chapter's "AIS in the Business World," organizations and individuals have used ASPs to

- Process insurance claims (www.processclaims.com).
- Complete the steps in the accounting cycle (www.epeachtree.com).
- Manage stock market transactions electronically (www.tradingtechnologies.com).
- Provide personal financial planning (www.naviplan.com).
- Prepare income tax returns (www.taxslayer.com).

Just as with e-business in general, ASPs offer both benefits and risks to organizations. The table below summarizes a few:

ASP Benefits	ASP Risks
Less costly than purchasing software outright	Psychological and behavioral factors
Increased flexibility	Service interruptions
Potentially improved customer service	Compromised data
Role in disaster recovery plans	Inability to pay monthly fees

Internal controls like those listed below can help address some of those risks:

- Establishing a budget for the ASP project.
- Backing up data on a daily basis.
- Providing ongoing training for employees using the ASP.
- Creating firewalls and encryption protocols.

Application service providers are one type of service organization addressed by Statement of Auditing Standards 70, developed by the AICPA in 1992. Here's part of what SAS70.com has to say about the standard:

> Statement on Auditing Standards (SAS) No. 70, *Service Organizations,* is a widely recognized auditing standard developed by the American Institute of Certified Public Accountants (AICPA). A service auditor's examination performed in accordance with SAS No. 70 ("SAS 70 Audit") is widely recognized, because it represents that a service organization has been through an in-depth audit of their control objectives and control activities, which often include controls over information technology and related processes. In today's global economy, service organizations or service providers must demonstrate that they have adequate controls and safeguards when they host or process data belonging to their customers. In addition, the requirements of Section 404 of the Sarbanes-Oxley Act of 2002 make SAS 70 audit reports even more important to the process of reporting on the effectiveness of internal control over financial reporting.

So, if an ASP has had a service audit, its clients can have more confidence that their data are safe, secure, and accessible when they need them.

CRITICAL THINKING

I've been in a quandary as to the focus of this chapter's critical thinking application. In previous chapters, this section has focused on some example of a topic previously covered in the chapter, but that general idea seemed less than relevant and interesting for this chapter. So, for this one, I'm going to show you how to apply two of the concepts we've discussed in other chapters in an e-business environment: systems documentation and database design.

Check out www.youbars.com, the Web site for You Bars and You Shakes; the company makes custom-designed nutrition bars and shakes. Here are the steps that might go into receiving an order of You Bars:

1. Customer accesses Web site.
2. Customer completes 10-step process for designing a nutrition bar.
3. Customer submits billing, shipping, and other information.
4. You Bars verifies information submitted.
5. You Bars prepares product.
6. You Bars ships the product.

The "other information" in step three includes options for overnight shipping, gift wrapping, and personalized greeting cards. A systems flowchart of those steps could look like Figure 10.3.

I've used a predefined process symbol for "design bar" and "make bar" to indicate that there are predefined steps associated with each process; additional systems flowcharts would spell out those details. The details could be included in Figure 10.3, but the flowchart would rapidly become crowded and difficult to read.

FIGURE 10.3
You Bars Ordering Process

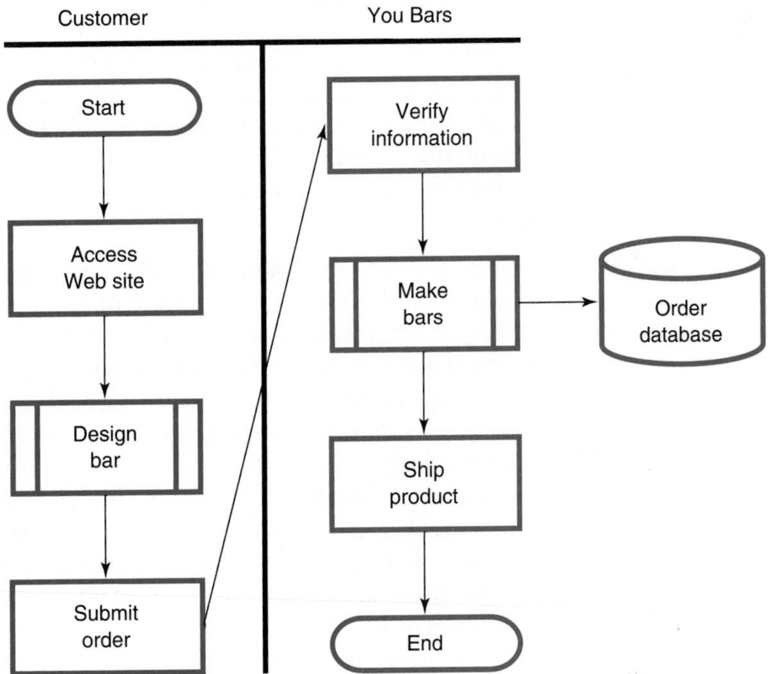

If you wanted to do a leveled set of data flow diagrams, it would definitely include one context diagram and one Level Zero diagram. At Level One, you could decompose "design bar" and "make bars" into their separate steps. The table below suggests elements for a REAL model of the same process:

REAL Model Element	Examples
Events	Design bar, place order, make bar, ship order
Resources	Bar ingredients
Agents	Customer, production employee, shipping employee

You Bars' accounting information system would need several database tables: customer, order history, product, employee. It also might include a raw materials table for the various ingredients in the finished product. Customer and employee tables are fairly common; their design doesn't change much from one company to another.

The product table, though, would be unique. As you can see on the Web site, the last step in creating a bar is to give it a name. But the name alone won't uniquely identify each bar; two customers might independently come up with the same bar name. So, the product table would need a compound primary key composed of the customer ID and the bar name. Customer ID would be a foreign key in the product table; it would be the primary key in the customer table. The product table would need fields for the various ingredients: Base 1, Base 2, Protein 1, Protein 2, Protein 3, and such.

The order history table would include data like order number (as the primary key), order date, and customer ID. Since each order can comprise many products, and since each product can be ordered many times, the database would need an order/product junction table as well.

I hope this example has reinforced some of the ideas we've examined in previous chapters. As always, I encourage you to e-mail me with suggestions for improvement.

Summary

After reading the chapter, I'm confident you can see that e-business and ERP systems, like most other aspects of AIS, are full of judgments—they are almost certainly a blend of "art" and "science," at the very least. Here's a summary of the chapter's main points in terms of its learning objectives:

1. *Explain the nature of e-business, comparing and contrasting it with traditional "brick-and-mortar" organizations.* The essential feature of e-business is the computer network. It is otherwise very similar to traditional businesses in terms of its stakeholder groups, information needs, and organizational structures.
2. *Discuss major forms of e-business, including business-to-business, consumer-to-consumer, business-to-consumer, government-to-business, and government-to-consumer.* E-businesses often are classified by the types of entities connected via computer networks. B2B arrangements partner organizations, such as when a company purchases inventory from a supplier. B2C transactions are characterized by operations such as Travelocity or Amazon. G2B partners government agencies with businesses, as with EDGAR. G2C operations allow consumers to obtain information from the government; consider the Web site of the Internal Revenue Service (www.irs.gov) in this category. C2C sites, like eBay, facilitate business between individuals.

3. *Describe the basic nature, purpose, and structure of enterprise resource planning systems.* An ERP system is a relational database designed to capture data and provide for reports and analyses via queries. Common modules include financial, human resources, vendors, and customer relationships.
4. *Give examples and analyze the causes of ERP system failures.* ERP implementations fail for one or more of a few common reasons, including poor leadership from top management, failure to analyze business processes thoroughly, unrealistic expectations, poor project management, inadequate education and training, bad match between software and organization, technical problems, and inaccurate data.
5. *List and discuss steps associated with successful ERP implementations.* Successful ERP implementations commonly follow a six-step implementation process: (1) Obtain organizational commitment. (2) Communicate strategic goals clearly. (3) View ERP as an enterprisewide venture. (4) Select a compatible ERP system. (5) Resolve multisite issues. (6) Ensure data accuracy.
6. *Discuss the role of application service providers in e-business.* Application service providers can facilitate an organization's entry into the networked economy. ASPs deliver a wide range of applications on a subscription or rental basis: managing elements of the human resource function, preparing tax returns, and completing the steps in the accounting cycle. Organizations using ASPs must modify their internal control systems to address the risks they present. SAS 70 audits help promote the integrity of an ASP's accounting information system.

Now, please proceed to the end-of-chapter activities assigned by your instructor to get some practical applications of the concepts discussed in this chapter.

Key Terms

application service provider 191
causes of ERP implementation failure, *189*
computer networks, *183*
conditions for a successful ERP implementation, *190*
e-business categories, *185*
e-commerce, *183*
enterprise resource planning system, *188*

Chapter References

ASPNews.com. 2002. "ASPNews Glossary." www.aspnews.com/strategies/asp_basics/article.php/759691 (January 11).

Barker, T., and M. Frolick. 2003. "ERP Implementation Failure: A Case Study." *Information Systems Management,* Fall, pp. 43–49.

Barnard, C. I. 1968. *The Functions of the Executive.* 30th anniversary ed. Cambridge, MA: Harvard University Press.

Stapleton, G., and C. Rezak. 2004. "Change Management Underpins a Successful ERP Implementation at Marathon Oil." *Journal of Organizational Excellence,* Autumn, pp. 15–22.

Umble, E., and M. Umble. 2002. "Avoiding ERP Implementation Failure." *Industrial Management,* January/February, pp. 25–34. Reprinted with the permission of the Institute of Industrial Engineers. 3577 Parkway Lane, Suite 200, Norcross, GA 30092, 770-449-0461. Copyright © 2002.

End-of-Chapter Activities

1. *Reading review questions.*

a. What is the distinguishing characteristic of e-business that makes it different from traditional brick-and-mortar businesses?

b. The chapter discusses five basic types of e-business arrangements. Identify and describe each one; give an example of each type other than the example in the chapter.

c. What is an enterprise resource planning system?

d. What common problems cause ERP implementations to fail? What can managers do to promote successful ERP implementations?

e. Prepare a response to the questions for this chapter's "AIS in the Business World."

2. *Reading review problem.* Point your Web browser to www.baselinemag.com. Locate and read "Hershey's Sweet Victory" by David F. Carr. Read the article, then respond to the following questions:

a. Visit Hershey's Web site. Discuss the corporation's involvement in e-business.

b. Explain the purpose and nature of enterprise resource planning software, referred to in the article as "enterprise client/server software."

c. What factors may have contributed to Hershey's problems with Enterprise 21?

d. In 2002, Hershey announced an upgrade to its ERP system using SAP; the upgrade was both ahead of schedule and under budget. Visit www.SAP.com. Is SAP an application service provider? Explain your response.

3. *Making choices and exercising judgment.*

a. Consider Question 2. In the blinding light of hindsight, which of the common causes of ERP failure did Hershey experience? What could management have done to avoid those problems?

b. The e-business model can be applied very effectively in some industries, but not as effectively in others. You may remember early attempts to establish online grocery shopping with companies such as Web Grocer and Net Grocer. Think of another industry where the value of e-business might be considered questionable. Explain your reasoning.

c. Chapter 8 discussed a weighted rating model for software evaluation. If you were using such a model to evaluate ERP systems, what factors would you want to consider? What relative weights would you assign each of them? Explain your choices.

4. *Field work.*

a. Use your university's library resources to investigate ERP implementation failures other than those discussed in the chapter. Analyze the failures in terms of the common causes discussed in the chapter; explain how a manager could have used Steps for Better Thinking to avoid ERP implementation problems.

b. Conduct research into WebTrust and/or SysTrust. Prepare an oral or written report summarizing at least the following items: historical development, nature and purpose of the system, financial and nonfinancial benefits, and costs and examples of companies using the technology. You can start your research at www.webtrust.org.

c. Visit a company in your geographic area that uses an ERP system. Ask for a demonstration of the system (or at least one part of it) and prepare a brief oral or written presentation to the class on your findings.

5. *Internal controls in e-business.* The chapter mentioned three potential internal controls for an e-business environment: encryption, segregation of duties, and access restrictions. Consider your study of internal controls throughout this text; suggest five additional internal controls for e-business environments. Explain specifically how you would apply them.

6. *Types of computer networks.* As you read in the chapter, the presence of a computer network is the defining characteristic of e-business. Research the topic and define each of the following terms related to networks and networking.

a. Local area network

b. Network architecture

c. Network protocol

d. Network topology
e. Node
f. Server
g. Wide area network

7. *Forms of e-business.* Which category of e-business (B2B, B2C, G2B, or G2C) best describes each of the following items?

a. Buying materials for professional practice from www.aicpa.org
b. Electronic reporting of state unemployment taxes
c. Filing personal income taxes with TaxSlayer.com
d. Getting medical advice from www.webmd.com
e. Making appointments with the Department of Motor Vehicles
f. Online banking
g. Paying traffic citations online
h. Purchases from Amazon.com
i. Receiving the online newsletter from the Institute of Management Accountants
j. Registration for seminars sponsored by the Association of Certified Fraud Examiners

8. *Causes of ERP failure.* Fill in the blanks below with appropriate terms related to the causes of ERP failure.

a. _____ expectations
b. A bad _____ between ERP software and _____ _____
c. Automating existing _____ or _____ processes in the new system
d. ERP implementation is viewed as an _____ _____
e. Inaccurate _____ in the system
f. Inadequate _____ and _____
g. Poor _____ _____
h. Poor _____ from _____ management
i. Significant _____ _____
j. Trying to _____ the _____ _____

9. *Promoting ERP success.* Choose one or more of the organizations listed below (or another specified by your instructor); investigate it on the Internet and through your university's library. Work with a group of students to prepare a PowerPoint presentation to fulfill the first three of Umble and Umble's six conditions for promoting ERP success (obtain organizational commitment, communicate strategic goals, and view ERP as an enterprisewide venture).

a. Kitchen Stuff Plus (www.kitchenstuffplus.com)
b. Woodbury University (www.woodbury.edu)
c. DreamBox Creations (www.dreamboxcreations.com)
d. Atomic Dog (www.atomicdogpublishing.com/home.asp)
e. Yankee Candle Company (www.yankeecandle.com)

10. *Application service providers.*

a. Companies considering utilizing an ASP might start the process by identifying a need to lower costs and increase flexibility. What other steps would a manager likely take in selecting an ASP? Who should be involved in such a decision?

b. Refer to www.sas70.com to determine which of the following statements are true about service audits conducted under that standard.
   i. The audit provides positive proof that an ASP is not vulnerable to fraud.
   ii. An SAS 70 audit is sometimes called a "service auditor's examination."
   iii. An SAS 70 audit can be an important component of an internal control examination and assessment.
   iv. The audit consists of going through a checklist of required controls and activities.
   v. As defined in the standard, a "service organization" can be an ASP.
   vi. Service auditors can issue a Type I report or a Type II report.
   vii. A Type I report means that the service organization has good internal control; a Type II report indicates internal control problems.
   viii. Without an SAS 70 examination, an ASP may need to be audited by its clients' independent auditors.
   ix. SAS 70 audits are generally performed by professionals with a background in accounting, auditing, and information security.
   x. Section 404 of the Sarbanes-Oxley Act of 2002 has increased the importance and relevance of SAS 70 examinations.

c. All professional accounting certifications and licenses (such as the CPA and CFE) require continuing professional education (CPE) on an annual basis. Suppose you and a group of friends started an ASP designed to track CPE requirements for accounting professionals. Design a database that would capture the required information about your clients. What internal controls would you implement to promote the integrity of those data?

11. *Crossword puzzle.* Please complete the crossword puzzle below using appropriate terminology from the chapter.

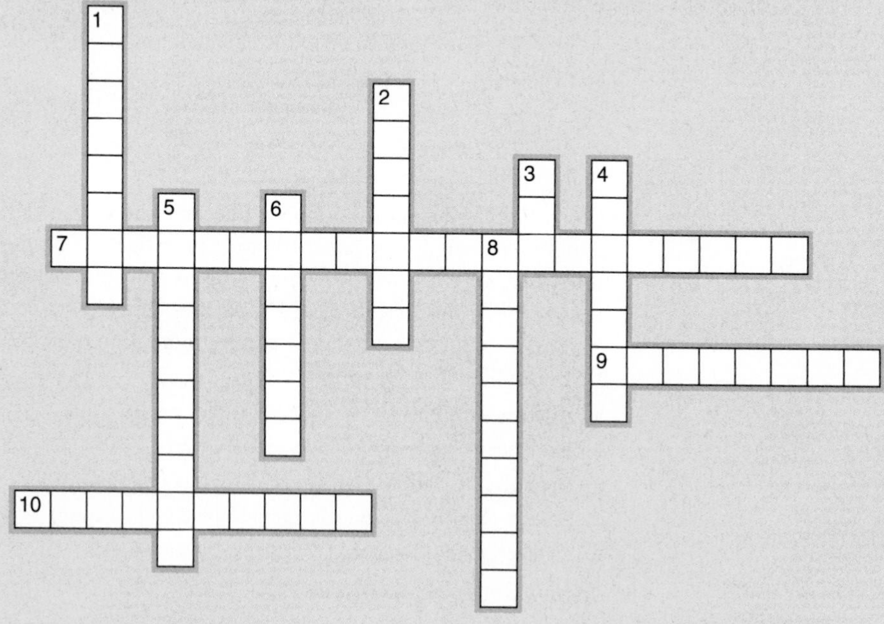

Across

7. ERP implementations should not be seen as mere ______ projects.
9. The "R" in ERP.
10. Resource ______ model of the firm.

Down

1. The "P" in ERP.
2. The distinguishing feature of e-business.
3. Making hotel reservations on the Internet.
4. The stakeholder group associated with supply chain management.
5. Obtaining organizational ______ to an ERP project is critical.
6. ______ in, ______ out: a phrase associated with ERP failures.
8. The "E" in ERP.

12. *Terminology.* Please match each item on the left with the best item on the right.

1. Brick and mortar	a. A well-known ERP system
2. Computer network	b. Another name for "old economy" organizations
3. Financial management	c. Associated with G2C and G2B e-commerce
4. Hershey	d. B2C e-commerce example
5. Human resource management	e. ERP module associated with employees
6. Internal Revenue Service	f. Had a "not so sweet" experience with ERP
7. Multisite issues	g. Module in an ERP system associated with stockholders
8. Online banking	h. Need to be resolved for a successful ERP project
9. PeopleSoft	i. Technology underlying ERP
10. Relational database	j. The salient feature of e-business

13. *Multiple choice questions.*

1. The common element in all forms of e-business is
   a. A computer.
   b. The involvement of a government agency.
   c. Doing business on the Internet.
   d. A network of computers.
2. Which of the following costs would you expect to incur in an e-business but not in a traditional brick-and-mortar business?
   a. Transaction processing costs
   b. Information technology costs
   c. Human resource costs
   d. All of the above would be found in both e-businesses and traditional businesses.
3. An enterprise resource planning system is most similar to which of the following?
   a. PowerPoint
   b. Access
   c. QuickBooks
   d. FrontPage
4. Which of the following is not a common cause of ERP failure?
   a. Assembling a committee or task force for the project
   b. Expecting too much from the system
   c. Lack of information seminars for employees
   d. All of the above are common causes of ERP failure.
5. An ERP system should be viewed as
   a. An information technology project.
   b. An accounting project.
   c. A human resources project.
   d. An organizational project.

6. Netflix is an example of which form of e-business?
   a. B2C
   b. C2C
   c. G2C
   d. None of the above
7. Which of the following internal controls would be applicable in an e-business environment but not in a traditional environment?
   a. Segregation of duties
   b. Adequate documentation
   c. Data encryption
   d. Appropriate supervision
8. Benefits of e-business can include reduced operating costs in
   a. Marketing.
   b. Telecommunications.
   c. Transaction processing.
   d. All of the above.
9. Trust Services principles and criteria are issued by the
   a. Securities and Exchange Commission.
   b. International Accounting Standards Board.
   c. Committee of Sponsoring Organizations.
   d. Assurance Services Executive Committee of the AICPA.
10. WebTrust relates to ______; SysTrust focuses on ______.
    a. Electronic commerce, enterprise systems
    b. System reliability, enterprise systems
    c. Electronic commerce, system reliability
    d. Internal control, risk management

14. *Statement evaluation.* Indicate whether each of the following statements is (i) always true, (ii) sometimes true, or (iii) never true. For those that are (ii) sometimes true, explain when the statement is true.

a. Companies involved in e-business report higher profit margins than traditional companies.
b. Computer networks are the defining feature of e-business.
c. E-business expands an organization's geographic markets.
d. E-business removes the need for human intervention in accounting information systems.
e. Every aspect of Porter's value chain can be impacted by e-business.
f. Implementing an ERP system ensures that data will be accurate and accessible.
g. Many enterprise resource planning systems are modular in nature.
h. Organizations enter into relationships with stakeholders to get the resources they need to operate.
i. Successful ERP implementations often require business process redesign.
j. WebTrust and SysTrust can strengthen internal controls in e-business.

Part **Four**

Business Processes

11. Sales/Collection Process

12. Acquisition/Payment Process

13. Other Business Processes

14. Business Process Management

Many accounting information systems courses focus on business processes. In this section, we'll apply the material from previous chapters (internal control, systems documentation, transaction processing, ethics, and information technology) to a comprehensive set of business processes. The first two chapters in this section are devoted to processes that generalize easily across organizations; the third chapter discusses processes that often vary in detail (conversion, financing, human resources). The last chapter in this section explores ways to manage business processes to make them more efficient and effective.

WHY DO WE CARE ABOUT BUSINESS PROCESSES

In your principles of financial accounting course, and in Chapter 2 of this book, you learned how to record basic transactions—but you may not have learned much about how these transactions are "born," that is, what happens in the organization that lets an accountant know it's time to record a transaction. The business processes chapters discuss, from start to finish, inputs and outputs, documents to journal entries, where these financial transactions are derived.

Take a recent experience with Quad-City General Hospital, a small rural hospital. Quad-City was losing around $25,000 per month in revenue by not properly obtaining "pre-approvals" for necessary procedures. Should a physician fail to obtain the pre-approval properly, the hospital would not get paid for a procedure it had already performed. Part of the responsibility of the Accounting Department was to understand why the hospital was losing this revenue from billing for some key procedures being denied by the payers (third-party insurance companies, HMOs, and PPOs).

To fix the problem, the Accounting Department reviewed existing business processes and developed a set of procedures to resolve the problems. (You can probably make a connection back to systems documentation as well.) Additionally, the new processes required assigning responsibilities to hospital staff. In the end, they eliminated the denials by verifying certifications and obtaining certifications where none could be verified.

To engage in the problem-solving process of this particular situation required an understanding of business processes (in this case, hospital business processes) and financial implications. What may seem to be small or insignificant, or the responsibility of another party, can have a significant impact upon operations and operating and financial results. Being an accountant requires caring about the business and financial processes to identify solutions to business problems.

Chapter Eleven

Sales/Collection Process

AIS in the Business World

AIM Mail Center

Dean is the owner and manager of the AIM Mail Center in Rancho Cucamonga, California; the store is a franchise of AIM Mail Centers. The corporate Web site (http://www.aimmailcenters.com/index.html) provides this list of the company's services:

- Authorized UPS shipping outlet
- FedEx authorized ShipCenter
- Packing needs
- Money orders
- Photocopies
- Fax
- Mail service
- Metered mail
- Keys
- Office gifts
- Banners
- Notary public
- Money transfer
- Mailbox rentals
- Gift wrapping
- Business cards
- Greeting cards
- Frequent faxer service
- Signs
- Rubber stamps
- Engraving
- Shipping
- Office supplies
- Letterhead and envelopes

Often, a customer brings in material to be mailed without proper packaging. In that situation, Dean selects appropriate packaging from the store's inventory. He prepares the package for shipment and tells the customer how much shipping will cost based on the carrier and expected delivery date. The customer makes a choice; Dean prepares the shipping documents and collects payment. The store accepts cash and major credit cards, but not checks. Dean then puts the package with others to be shipped via the same carrier; major common carriers make daily visits to the store to pick up the packages.

Discussion Questions

1. How does the sales/collection process at Dean's store compare to a generic sales/collection process?
2. What risk exposures does Dean face? What risk exposures does the customer face?
3. What internal controls can help address those risk exposures?
4. What forms of systems documentation and information technology would be useful for Dean?

This chapter, and the two that follow it, put together much of what you've already learned within the context of specific business processes. So what is a "business process"? At its most simplistic, a **business process** is a set of procedures and policies designed to create value for some organizational stakeholder. Those stakeholders might include customers, stockholders, employees, or vendors.

Consider, for example, the value created by your university. If you were extraordinarily hardworking and diligent, you might be able to get the knowledge afforded by your degree on your own—but very few students have that kind of determination. So, instead, it's much more effective and efficient for you to gain that knowledge through an organization (your university) and its business processes.

In AIS study, we combine sales and collection activities because of their logical relationship to one another. But, as you're probably aware, a "collection" does not necessarily constitute a "sale" according to GAAP. The rules of accrual-basis accounting still apply—we just organize the knowledge a little differently in AIS.

While the details of processes can vary significantly from one organization to another, most of them share some common features. Those common features will be our focus in the next three chapters, starting here with the sales/collection process.

When you finish studying this chapter, you should be able to:

1. Explain the elements of Porter's value chain.
2. Explain the role and purpose of the sales/collection process.
3. List and discuss, in order, the steps in the process.
4. Identify and describe documents commonly used in the process.
5. Suggest and evaluate internal controls associated with sales/collection activities.
6. Explain how information technology can make the sales/collection process more effective and efficient.
7. Create and interpret systems documents related to sales and collections.

Keep in mind the overarching theme of your AIS study this term: single, correct, deterministic responses to problems seldom exist. Your goal should not be, therefore, to memorize the content of this chapter. Rather, focus on learning the underlying concepts and applying them to specific situations. In practice, you'll be asked to evaluate costs and benefits of various sales/collection scenarios, not to look up formulaic solutions in a textbook somewhere.

PORTER'S VALUE CHAIN

Porter (1998) developed the "value chain" as a way to think about the processes organizations use to create value for their stakeholders. The value chain (shown in Figure 11.1) is organized into two parts: primary activities are directly involved in value creation, while support activities provide essential services to the organization.

NetMBA (www.netmba.com) describes the value chain activities like this:

- *Inbound logistics:* the receiving and warehousing of raw materials, and their distribution to manufacturing as they are required.
- *Operations:* the processes of transforming inputs into finished products and services.
- *Outbound logistics:* the warehousing and distribution of finished goods.
- *Marketing & sales:* the identification of customer needs and the generation of sales.
- *Service:* the support of customers after the products and services are sold to them.
- *Procurement:* purchasing inputs such as materials, supplies, and equipment.
- *Infrastructure:* organizational structure, control systems and company culture
- *Human resource management:* employee recruiting, hiring, training, development, and compensation.
- *Information technology:* technologies to support value-creating activities.

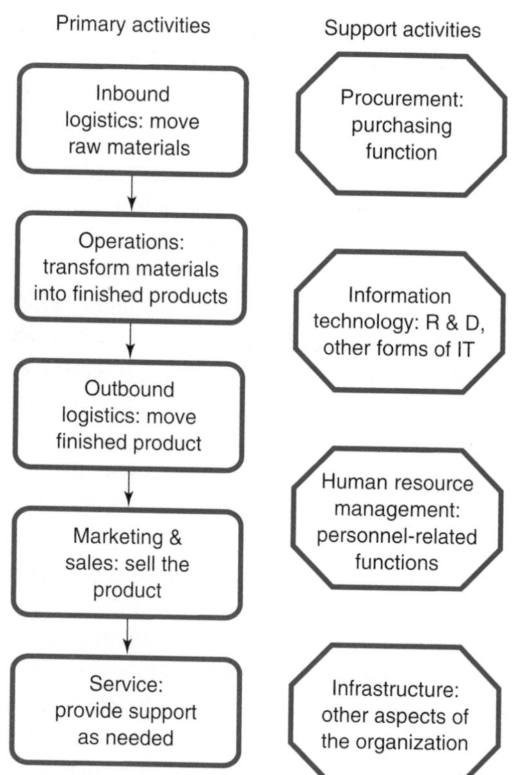

FIGURE 11.1
Porter's Value Chain

In studying accounting information systems, we collapse and reorganize the value chain activities to facilitate discussion and learning. The sales/collection process discussed in this chapter comprises marketing and sales and, to some extent, service from the value chain; the acquisition payment process (in the next chapter) focuses on procurement, inbound logistics, and outbound logistics. We'll explore other business processes such as conversion (operations), human resources (human resource management), and financing (related to infrastructure) in the third chapter in this section.

PROCESS DESCRIPTION

The fundamental purpose of the sales/collection process is to provide goods and services to clients and to collect payment from them. Without an effective sales/collection process, an organization will soon cease to exist. Ineffective processes may arise from lack of demand for a company's product or service, inadequate exposure in the marketplace, and/or poor credit policies (with the attendant difficulty in cash collections).

Reflection and Self-Assessment 11.1

Via brief library research and/or your own thinking, suggest an example company that suffered from an ineffective sales/collection process. What made the process ineffective? (Don't limit yourself to the reasons discussed above!)

So, what exactly are the **steps** involved in an effective sales/collection process? Consider the list below (Hollander, Denna, and Cherrington, 2000):

1. *Take a customer's order.* Sales staff can take a customer's order in a variety of ways: face-to-face, via the Internet, through the mail, over the phone, and others.
2. *Approve the customer's credit.* Once the customer's order is in hand, the organization often must approve his/her credit. When you shop in a store, credit approval comes from scanning your credit card. Organizations doing business with one another, though, often extend credit directly—without the use of a credit card.
3. *Fill the order based on approved credit.* If the customer's credit is approved, the warehouse staff can fill the order and prepare it for shipment.
4. *Ship the product (if necessary).* In the best-case scenario, a separate shipping department actually sends the product to the customer (we'll talk more about this idea when we consider internal controls later in the chapter). If a customer is paying cash, she might take the product on a cash-and-carry basis, rather than having it shipped. In some cases, a customer may be forced to pay cash for goods and services if his credit is insufficient or he has a poor payment history.
5. *Bill the customer.* When goods and services are sold on credit, the billing department will typically send an invoice or statement on a monthly basis. Your credit card company, for example, follows that process. They are a third-party intermediary between you and the company that sold the goods and services, but the process is basically the same.
6. *Collect payment.* In a perfect world, the client timely remits payment. The client may take advantage of cash discounts for early payment. Customers that fail to pay timely may undergo more extensive collection processes and/or be denied further credit. Systems for recording cash collections fall into two broad groups: open invoice and balance forward. In an open invoice system, a customer's remittance is tied to a specific invoice or set of invoices. While more complex to maintain, open invoice systems do provide more detail for decision making. In a balance forward system, remittances are not applied to a particular invoice; rather, they are simply applied to a customer's total outstanding balance.
7. *Process uncollectible receivables as necessary.* In a worst-case scenario, when all attempts to collect cash have failed, the organization may be forced to write off its bad debts using a method approved under GAAP.

Figure 11.2 presents a data flow diagram that captures the seven steps at a high level (we'll look at a more detailed flowchart later in the chapter).

Keep in mind that the seven steps are very generic in nature. In your accounting career, you may be called upon to design an effective sales/collection process and/or to evaluate one as part of an audit. In either case, use the seven steps as a guide, but make allowances for individual company practices.

Next, let's consider some of the documents that are commonly involved in the sales/collection process.

Reflection and Self-Assessment 11.2

Consider a recent purchase you made as an individual. How were the generic steps in the sales/collection process operationalized in that transaction?

FIGURE 11.2 Sales/Collection DFD

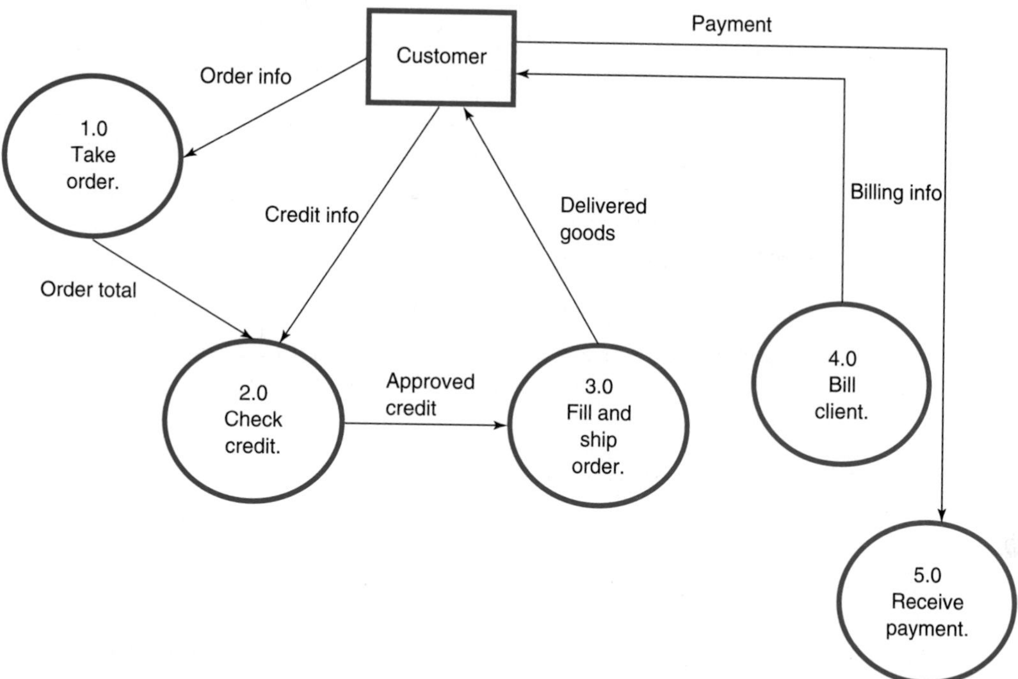

DOCUMENTS AND MODELING

Most of the time, people think of "documents" as pieces of paper. But they also can be developed and transmitted entirely electronically these days. So, our definition of a document includes both types: paper and electronic.

As we discuss **documents** associated with the sales/collection process, keep in mind that we're examining them from the point of view of the *selling* organization. The customer will have its own names and formats for the same documents; we'll explore those in the next chapter. Table 11.1 gives you a broad overview of the documents we'll be discussing in the next few pages.

In the first step of the sales/collection process (take customer order), a sales clerk (or someone with a similar title) notes the type and quantity of merchandise the customer is requesting. The customer's order, then, might be filled out by the sales staff or the customer him- or herself. In many cases, the customer may simply bring the needed merchandise to a cash register; in that situation, a formal "order" does not exist. See Figure 11.3 for an illustration of a customer order form.

The picking list comes into play when an order is filled based on approved credit. A picking list typically tells warehouse or stockroom staff what products to take (pick) off the shelves to fill the customer's order. In some cases, the picking list doubles as the packing list as well. If you've ever ordered any merchandise from the Internet or a catalog, you've probably seen a packing list. It serves as a final check of what is actually loaded into the box before the goods are shipped to the customer.

A bill of lading is used when the goods are shipped to the customer. A bill of lading is a contract between the seller (such as Amazon.com) and a common carrier (such as Federal Express or United Parcel Service). The bill of lading tells the common carrier where to

TABLE 11.1 Documents Associated with the Sales/Collection Process

Document Name	Basic Purpose	Originator	Recipient
Customer order	To summarize items ordered and prices	Sales department	Warehouse
Picking list	To guide selection of items from warehouse	Warehouse	Shipping department
Packing list	To specify contents of shipment	Shipping department	Customer
Bill of lading	To specify freight terms	Shipping department	Common carrier
Customer invoice	To bill client	Billing department	Customer
Customer check	To remit payment	Customer	Cash receipts department
Remittance advice	To provide a source document for AIS	Customer	Accounting department
Deposit slip	To transmit cash receipts to bank	Cash receipts department	Bank

deliver the goods. It also explains the freight terms associated with the shipment. **Freight terms** identify two important items: who is responsible for the goods while they're in transit and who ends up paying the freight bill. For each question, there are two possible answers:

1. Who is responsible for the goods while they're in transit?
   a. FOB destination: The buyer takes responsibility for the goods when they arrive at the destination. The seller is therefore responsible for them en route.
   b. FOB shipping point: The buyer takes responsibility for the goods when they are loaded on the truck. The buyer is therefore responsible for them en route.
2. Who pays the freight bill?
   a. Prepaid: The seller pays the freight company up front.
   b. Collect: The buyer is responsible for paying the freight company.

So, with two questions and two possible answers each, a bill of lading can show four different freight terms:

- *FOB destination, freight prepaid.* In this case, the seller pays the freight company up front, and the buyer takes responsibility for the goods when they arrive at the destination. So, the seller is responsible for dealing with the common carrier throughout the transaction. The seller will pay the freight company and charge the cost to "delivery expense" or some similar account.
- *FOB destination, freight collect.* Here, the buyer takes responsibility for the goods when they arrive and pays the freight bill at the same time. This alternative is seldom seen in practice—if the seller is responsible for the goods en route, it doesn't make much sense for the buyer to be paying the freight bill.
- *FOB shipping point, freight prepaid.* The buyer takes responsibility for the goods as soon as they are loaded on the truck/train/plane. But the seller pays the freight company up front. The seller will therefore include the freight bill on the buyer's invoice; the buyer effectively reimburses the seller for the freight cost when the invoice is paid. If a cash discount is available on the merchandise shipped, the discount does not apply to the freight bill.

FIGURE 11.3 Customer Order

Your Name: ______________________________

Shipping Address: ______________________________
(No PO box, please)

City: ____________________ State: ________ ZIP code: ________

Phone (days): ______________________________

Phone (eves): ______________________________

Credit Card #: ____________________ Exp. Date: ________
(MasterCard, Visa, or Discover only, please)

Signature: ______________________________
Your Distributor's ID #: **Name:**
(Check on the e-rep's page for this name & number.)

Please send a free Fuller Brush Master Catalog.____Yes ____ No

Item Number	Qty:	Description:	Price each	Total

Handling Charge Chart:

$0 to	$24.99	$3.95
$25 to	$49.99	$4.95
$50.00	and up	$5.95

Sales Tax Policy: Since we have a business presence in all states, we are required by law to collect sales tax for every state. Need help finding your area's sales tax? Just call us at: 1-800-522-0499.

Merchandise total	
Handling from chart	
Merchandise subtotal	
Sales tax on subtotal	
Total amount due	

Make checks payable to: The Fuller Brush Company
PO Box 420130
Great Bend, KS 67530-1247

- *FOB shipping point, freight collect.* The buyer takes responsibility for the goods at the shipping point and pays the freight company when the goods arrive. The freight cost is a reasonable and necessary cost of obtaining the goods, so it is capitalized to an asset account rather than being charged to an expense.

Failing to take a cash discount with terms of 2/10, n/30 is the same as borrowing money at an interest rate of around 37 percent (2/98 × 365/20). In that formula, 2 refers to the 2 percent discount; 98 is the difference between 100 percent and 2 percent; 365, the number of days in a year, is a constant; and 20 is the difference between 30 and 10—the number of "extra days" a customer has to pay the invoice without the discount.

Customer invoices vary as much as the companies that issue them. Typically, though, they will contain some key information: the customer's name and address, the mailing address for the company, the total amount due, and the due date. To foster good internal control (discussed later in the chapter), invoices should be prepared by a billing department once the goods have been received by the customer.

To motivate customers to pay as quickly as possible, a company may offer a cash discount. Cash discounts commonly look like this: 2/10, n/30. Read that notation as "two-ten, net thirty." In plain English, it says that the customer may take a 2 percent discount off the merchandise cost if the bill is paid within 10 days. Otherwise, the full (net) amount of the invoice is payable within 30 days. The discount will not apply to any freight charges included on the invoice.

Suppose, for example, CLM Corporation sends an invoice dated February 2, 2009, to a customer that includes $6,200 for merchandise and $100 for freight. If the cash discount is 2/10, n/30, the customer may pay the bill on or before February 12. The total remitted will be 6,200 × 98% + $100 for freight = $6,176. Otherwise, the full invoice amount ($6,300) is due within 30 days of February 2.

Collecting payment from a customer on open account involves two documents: the customer check and the remittance advice. While I'm sure you know what a check is, you may not be familiar with the term *remittance advice.* Basically, the purpose of a remittance advice is to *advise* the company that you are *remitting* payment on an invoice. Consider, for example, your monthly credit card bill. When you receive it, you tear off a portion to send back with your check. The portion you tear off is the remittance advice. It becomes the source document for journal entries related to cash receipts. The check itself goes to the bank; the remittance advice goes to the accounting department for recordkeeping. You can see a generic remittance advice in Figure 11.4.

Ideally, all cash received by a company is deposited daily in the bank. A deposit slip typically lists each item to be deposited with some identifying information (such as an ABA or routing number for checks), the account holder's name and account number, and the date. The bank issues a receipt as evidence that the deposit has been accepted.

So, a typical sales/collection process that incorporates the seven steps and eight documents discussed so far might look like the process shown in Figure 11.5.

As we discussed in Chapter 5 (flowcharting), you should be able to look at a flowchart and generate a narrative *and* use a narrative to generate a flowchart. The same applies to data flow diagrams and REAL models.

FIGURE 11.4
Remittance advice

REMITTANCE ADVICE FOR CPD INC.
CHECK # 3225 - CHECK DATE 04/14/09

INVOICE #	INV DATE	ORIG AMT	PAYMENT	REFERENCE
145216	03/12/09	$ 40.00	$ 40.00	WARRANTY REPLACEMENT
144540	03/04/09	158.00	158.00	SSI STOCK
146035	03/25/09	1,890.00	1,700.00	CIVIC PLAZA
TOTALS		$ 2,088.00	$ 1,898.00	

FIGURE 11.5 **Generic Sales/Collection Process**

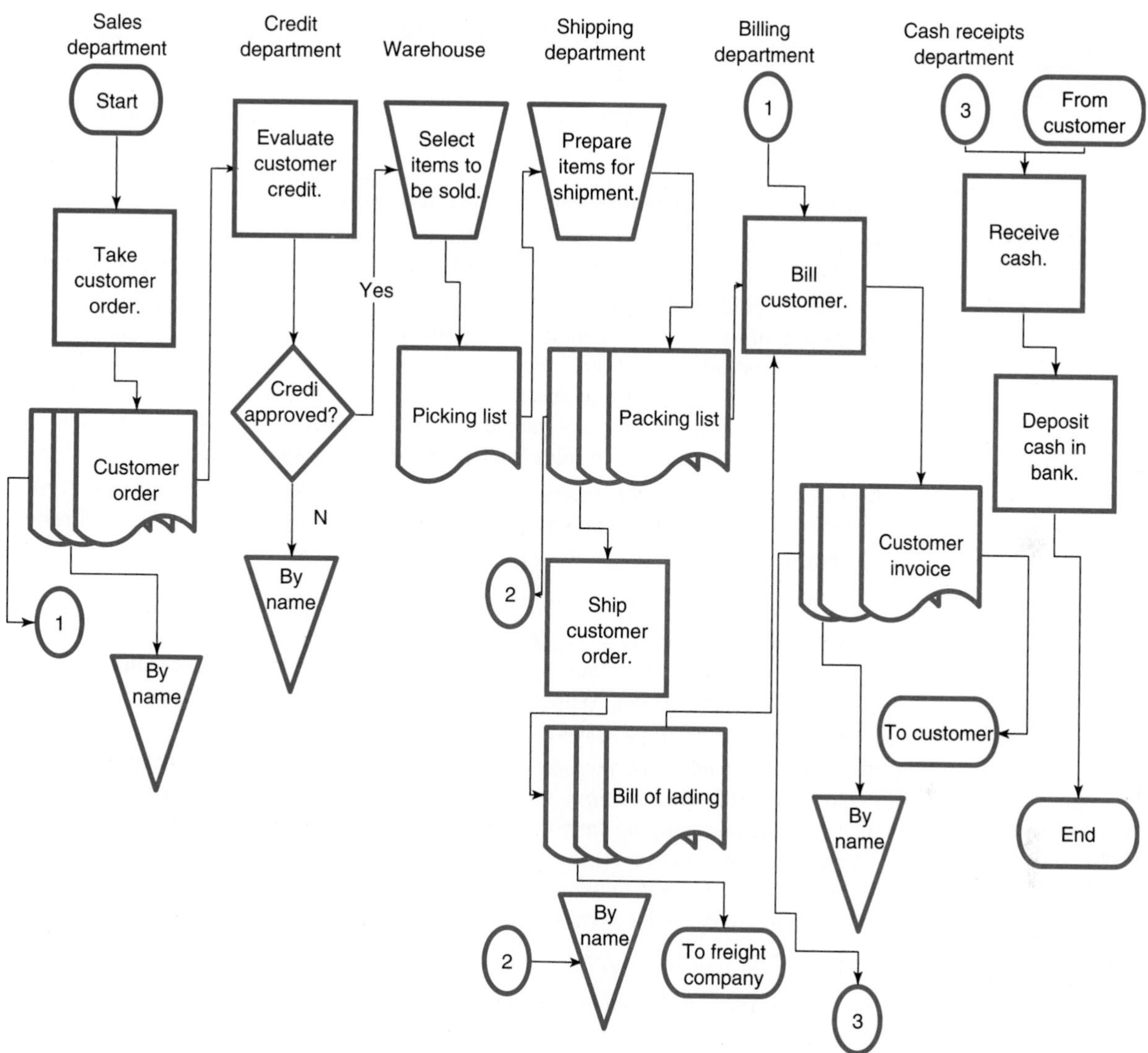

INTERNAL CONTROLS

You may want to review the purposes of internal control presented in Chapter 4. Also, keep in mind that internal controls are subject to a cost–benefit constraint—the idea isn't to design controls that will eliminate risk, but to incorporate those that will mitigate it.

Organizations commonly encounter various kinds of risks in the sales/collection process. Accountants, therefore, must design internal controls to ameliorate those risks as efficiently and effectively as possible.

The numbered items below are common risks faced in the sales/collection process. The associated lettered items represent **internal controls** that might lessen those risks. Keep in mind that the list is illustrative, not definitive; that is, each organization's risks and controls must be assessed and developed individually, based on time, money, and human constraints.

Reflection and Self-Assessment 11.3

A list of common risks in the sales/collection process follows. Before you read it, look over the process steps presented earlier in the chapter. See if you can identify at least three risks suggested by those steps before you read the list.

1. Granting credit to customers who are not creditworthy.
   a. *Relying on third-party vendors to grant credit.* A company may choose not to extend credit itself. Rather, it may rely on third parties such as Visa, Discover, or American Express to approve customers' credit.
   b. *Establishing a formal credit-approval process, independent of the sales function.* In the best possible situations, salespeople will not have the authority to grant credit directly. If you've ever purchased a new car, for example, you may have observed that the salesperson does not handle the financing part of the transaction. Granting credit independently from sales is an example of separation of duties.
   c. *Conducting a cash-only business.* Smaller organizations may opt not to grant credit or accept third-party credit cards at all. While they may lose some sales as a result, they do not run the risk of inappropriately granting credit.
2. "Selling" products that are not available.
   a. *Checking stock-on-hand before completing a customer's order.* While salespeople should not grant credit, they should be able to check inventory levels directly or via an information system. Without that ability, customers may be frustrated and the organization may lose business.
   b. *Maintaining adequate inventory.* An organization must constantly balance the need to have sufficient inventory on hand with the costs of maintaining that inventory. Costs include tying up cash in inventory, insurance, maintenance (such as keeping perishable products cool), and supervision/security costs. Although beyond the scope of this text, you may be familiar with terms like just-in-time, economic order quantity, and reorder point as methods for maintaining adequate inventory.

Bergan Mercy Medical Center (www.alegent.com/bergan) in Omaha, Nebraska, uses the Homerus system in their pharmacy to fill daily prescriptions for in-patients. With Homerus, pharmacy technicians create individual packaging and stock the machine with required pharmaceuticals. A registered pharmacist inputs drug orders to the hospital's information system based on physician orders; Homerus fills the next day's orders, putting medications in individual packets labeled with patient names. A pharmacist verifies a sample for accuracy, and the drugs are delivered manually to the patient the next day.

3. Filling the customer's order incorrectly.
   a. *Incorporating independent order checking.* Warehouse personnel may misread the picking slip, select the wrong inventory from the shelves, or put incorrect quantities in the customer's order. Ideally, the organization should find and correct those errors before turning the merchandise over to the customer. An independent check by another member of the warehouse staff, or a member of the shipping staff, can reduce the chances that the wrong goods are shipped to the customer.
   b. *Using information technology to fill orders.* Computerized order-filling is becoming more and more common in some sectors of the economy. Many hospital pharmacies, for example, use computers to fill prescriptions. While the orders should still be checked by a pharmacist for accuracy, using IT first can be much more efficient.
4. Damaging goods in the delivery process.
   a. *Packing merchandise adequately prior to shipment.* Whether handled by a common carrier or the organization's own shipping department, goods should be properly packaged prior to shipment. Omaha Steaks (www.omahasteaks.com), for example, ships its products in Styrofoam containers with dry ice. The food therefore arrives at the customer's location fresh.

b. *Insuring goods in transit.* If you have ever shipped anything valuable, you may have purchased insurance for it. While insurance cannot prevent damage to the goods, it can mitigate financial risk by providing the customer reimbursement for the insured value if the goods are damaged in transit.

5. Billing the customer incorrectly.

   a. *Matching documents prior to billing.* The customer should only be billed for what has been ordered and shipped. So, the billing department should receive a copy of both the customer's order and the bill of lading. Once those documents are received, billing clerks can generate customer invoices from the accounting information system.

   b. *Using information technology to ensure numerical accuracy.* In most accounting information systems, computers generate invoices. Mathematical errors are thus avoided.

6. Mishandling cash receipts.

The three basic duties to be separated include custody of an asset, its recordkeeping, and authorization for its use.

   a. *Separating duties.* As you learned in Chapter 4, separation of duties is a basic internal control in most accounting information systems. When it comes to the sales/collection process, cash should be deposited daily in the bank (custody). Accountants should use remittance advices as the source documents for journal entries (recordkeeping). And signatories on the checking account should not be allowed to handle cash received from customers (authorization).

   b. *Restrictively endorsing checks when they are received.* When you deposit checks in your bank account, you have to sign the back first—that's an endorsement. A restrictive endorsement includes the phrase "for deposit only" before the signature. Many banks encourage or require customers also to include their account number as part of the endorsement. Although managers should take great care not to lose or misplace checks once they have been endorsed, a restrictive endorsement can ensure that misplaced or lost checks are not cashed.

   c. *Reconciling the bank statement at least monthly.* At the very least, an independent accountant or someone who does not handle cash receipts or payments should reconcile the bank statement when it is received. The Association of Certified Fraud Examiners (www.cfenet.com) recommends that checking accounts be reconciled at least weekly—a process that is now entirely achievable with online banking records. As you may know, reconciling the bank statement involves accounting for timing differences in what the bank knows versus what the depositor knows; it also helps correct errors made by either the depositor or the bank. A typical bank reconciliation is presented in Figure 11.6.

FIGURE 11.6
Bank Reconciliation

HLN Corporation
Bank reconciliation
For the month ended January 31, 2009

Bank statement balance		$ 1,500	Checkbook balance	$ 1,575
Deposits in transit			Interest earned	15
28 Jan	$ 300			
30 Jan	275	575	Bank service charges	85
Outstanding checks				
#1801	$ 150			
#1803	450	600		
Adjusted balance		$ 1,475	Adjusted balance	$ 1,475

Those six risks, and the suggested internal controls that accompany them, are by no means exhaustive. In designing and evaluating internal controls for the sales/collection process, you must develop an intimate knowledge of an organization's processes and personnel. Use your own creativity and critical-thinking abilities, coupled with your sense of cost–benefit issues, when confronted with the important task of internal control assessment in practice.

INFORMATION TECHNOLOGY IN THE SALES/COLLECTION PROCESS

Although the sales/collection process can be completed in many organizations without the benefit of information technology, the use of IT can make the process more efficient. IT also can promote strong internal controls. Consider the examples below:

- *Maintain customer lists.* Organizations often use relational database software to maintain contact and other relevant information about customers. In a larger company, enterprise resource planning systems might be used for this task.
- *Generate sequentially numbered forms.* Whether a form is designed using relational database technology or generated automatically by general ledger or ERP systems, sequential numbering promotes good internal control. Sales orders and customer invoices can be accounted for quickly and accurately; their sequential numbers also can be used as easy references for queries. If a number is out of sequence or missing, internal auditors (or other designated staff) can determine whether it was simple oversight or a red flag for possible fraud.
- *Look up inventory status.* ERP systems can maintain up-to-date inventory records very easily; with a little effort, relational databases can do the same. Some general ledger software offers real-time inventory tracking as well. Not only would electronic access to inventory help prevent stockouts and shortages; it also would provide a reference for physical inventory counts.
- *Identify unpaid and past-due invoices.* A relational database query allows a user to extract information from one or more database tables based on specified conditions; queries are also a feature of enterprise resource planning systems. In Access, users can create a "find unmatched" query to identify invoices that have not been paid; that is, invoices that are "unmatched" with a corresponding cash receipt. Most general ledger software can accomplish this same task fairly easily, in addition to creating an aged schedule of accounts receivable to focus collection efforts.
- *Record transactions in the general ledger.* Of course, general ledger software and/or ERP packages can be used to make journal entries and complete related steps in the accounting cycle.
- *Report financial information.* Whether publicly traded or not, an organization could prepare XBRL-tagged documents for information sharing and reporting purposes. As we discussed in Chapter 9, such documents could include financial statements and tax returns (for both external and internal users), as well as cost analyses, profit projections, and budgets (for internal users only).

CRITICAL THINKING

Consider the following description of a sales/collection process:

> Smoothies-R-Us prepares fresh, healthy fruit smoothies; at present, their menu includes six choices, each of which can be ordered in two sizes (small and large). Management expects to update and expand the menu as time goes on. When a customer enters the store, a staff member takes his/her order and inputs the details, including the customer's first name, into the cash register. The cash register is connected to a visual display in the smoothie-making area. The customer pays (cash, credit card, or gift card) and receives his/her order a few minutes afterward. All Smoothies-R-Us employees are cross-trained, so any one of them can perform any of the preceding tasks.

Let's look at how some of the concepts from this chapter would be applied to Smoothies-R-Us' sales/collection process.

We've considered three ways to document an information system: flowcharts, data flow diagrams, and REAL models. The figures below (11.7, 11.8 and 11.9) use each technique to document the process:

FIGURE 11.7
Smoothies-R-Us sales / collection process

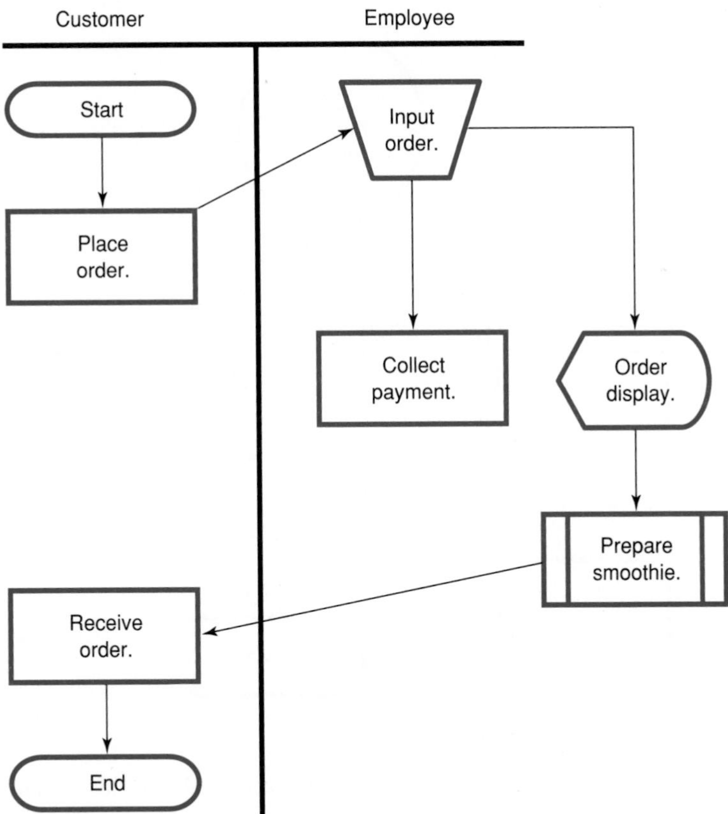

FIGURE 11.8
Smoothies-R-Us sales / collection process Level Zero DFD

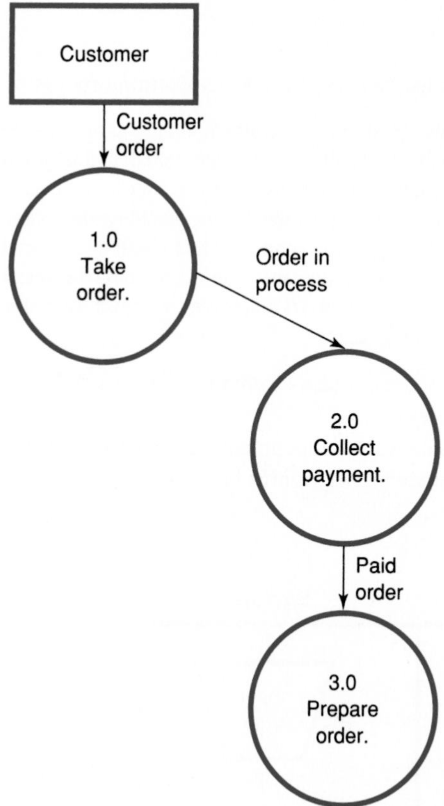

FIGURE 11.9
REAL model of Smoothies-R-Us sales / collection process

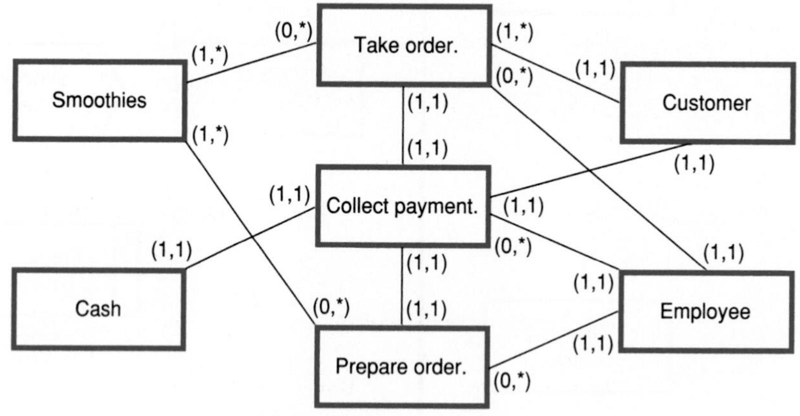

Although it might be done most easily from the REAL model, any one of the figures could be used to create database specifications for the system. Here are some examples:

1. Take order table
   a. <u>Order number</u>
   b. Date
   c. [Customer name]

2. Smoothies table
   a. Smoothie name
   b. Small smoothie price
   c. Large smoothie price
3. Take order / smoothies table
   a. [Order number]
   b. [Smoothie name]
   c. Smoothie size
   d. Number ordered

Smoothies-R-Us would use queries to calculate the total cost of each order; periodically, the store could run a report to determine the popularity of each smoothie.

The table below identifies some risks associated with the sales/collection process; it also shows internal controls to address each risk:

Risk	**Control**
Order taken incorrectly	• Repeating order back to customer • Visual display of order
Incorrect prices charged	• Prices programmed in cash register • Prices displayed on menu
Poor quality smoothies	• Employee training • Standardized recipes

Finally, let's consider what forms of information technology would be useful at Smoothies-R-Us. If the store is a "stand-alone" operation (as opposed to being part of a larger corporation), it might incorporate relational database software to track orders and store recipes. A wireless network, with appropriate network security, could transmit orders to the video display in the production area. Of course, a cash register is also a form of information technology—albeit one so common we seldom give it a second thought.

Summary

This chapter is the first of four discussing issues in various business processes. Here is the chapter summary, structured according to its learning objectives:

1. *Explain the elements of Porter's value chain.* The value chain comprises the following primary activities: inbound logistics, operations, outbound logistics, marketing and sales, and service. It also includes four support activities: infrastructure, procurement, human resource management, and information technology. Collectively, the activities represent the ways an organization creates value for its stakeholders (vendors, customers, employees, stockholders, and others).
2. *Explain the role and purpose of the sales/collection process.* The sales/collection process is concerned with providing goods and services to clients, then collecting the related payment.
3. *List and discuss, in order, the steps in the process.* The sales/collection process comprises seven steps:
   a. Take a customer's order.
   b. Approve the customer's credit.

c. Fill the order based on approved credit.
d. Ship the product (if necessary).
e. Bill the customer.
f. Collect payment.
g. Process uncollectible receivables as necessary.

4. *Identify and describe documents commonly used in the process.* Documents associated with the sales/collection process include
   a. Bill of lading
   b. Customer check
   c. Customer invoice
   d. Customer order
   e. Deposit slip
   f. Packing list
   g. Picking list
   h. Remittance advice
5. *Suggest and evaluate internal controls associated with sales/collection activities.* Internal controls in the sales/collection process should be based on a comprehensive risk analysis. Depending upon its risk exposures, an organization can implement internal controls such as document matching, separation of duties, bank reconciliations, and formalized policies for granting credit to customers.
6. *Explain how information technology can make the sales/collection process more effective and efficient.* Information technology can promote strong internal control via prenumbered documents and segregation of duties. In addition, IT such as relational databases can prepare reports for decision making regarding A/R collections and other processes.
7. *Create and interpret systems documents related to sales and collections.* The conventions and rules discussed in previous chapters apply here. Flowcharts and data flow diagrams should be uncluttered and easy to read; their preparation should involve consultation with personnel involved in the sales/collection process. Flowcharts should be organized in columns depicting levels of responsibility, while data flow diagrams must be balanced between levels.

Keep in mind that what you've just read is necessarily generic in nature. While most organizations will use documents, processes, and internal controls similar to those discussed here, each situation must be evaluated individually in the art of designing and implementing accounting information systems.

Key Terms

business process, *204*
documents, *207*
freight terms, *208*
internal controls, *211*
steps, *206*

Chapter References

Hollander, A. S., E. L. Denna, and J. O. Cherrington. 2000. *Accounting, Information Technology and Business Solutions.* 2nd ed. New York: Irwin/McGraw-Hill.

Porter, M. 1998. *Competitive Advantage: Creating and Sustaining Superior Performance.* New York: Free Press.

End-of-Chapter Activities

1. *Reading review questions.*
   a. What activities are involved in Porter's value chain?
   b. What is the basic purpose of the sales/collection process?
   c. What steps do companies commonly complete as part of the sales/collection process?
   d. What documents are important in the sales/collection process?
   e. What risks do managers face as part of the sales/collection process? What internal controls help reduce exposure to those risks?
   f. Respond to the questions for this chapter's "AIS in the Business World."

2. *Reading review problem.* Dreambox Creations (www.dreamboxcreations.com) was incorporated as an S Corporation in November 1999 by six founding members, two of whom are still involved in the business along with several other employees. The firm's operations focus on Web development and hosting, design and implementation of corporate intranets, systems integration, and back-office management systems.

   Dreambox's sales/collection proess typically begins with an initial contact from a client, via either phone or e-mail. Dan, one of the two founders, consults with the client and develops an initial requirements assessment; the firm then submits a written cost estimate for the client's consideration. In a few cases, Dreambox is part of a formal bidding process. If the client accepts the cost estimate, Dan writes up a formal contract and then collects half the proposed fee in advance. The firm issues invoices periodically throughout the work; those invoices are generally payable on receipt.

   Once the initial work is completed, the client may stay with Dreambox for subsequent maintenance. Maintenance is handled via monthly billing; no client signs up for a contract for a certain maintenance time period, although Dreambox does offer financial incentives for bulk purchases. Dreambox accepts payment via check only; Dan deposits all cash receipts weekly in the bank and reconciles the bank statement daily. At year-end, the company provides its tax preparer with a summary of revenues and expenses compiled by hand. Dreambox utilizes Quicken for printing its checks.

   a. Using one or more techniques specified by your instructor, document Dreambox's sales/collection process.
   b. Consider the list of common documents in Table 11.1. How do the items in the list correlate with Dreambox's operations?
   c. What are Dreambox's risk exposures? What internal controls would you recommend to address them?
   d. Design the following tables for Dreambox's accounting information system: client, provide services, client/provide services.
   e. What forms of information technology would be useful to Dreambox?

3. *Making choices and exercising judgment.* Rob, Teri, Kirk, and Peggy are students in the accounting program at Big State University. They have worked together on several projects throughout their classes and are considering starting a business together when they graduate. Their preliminary idea is a firm called Reliable Reminder Services (RRS). RRS would assist its clients in remembering important dates, purchasing and sending greeting cards, and providing specialized shopping services for important dates (birthdays, anniversaries, and the like). Using the seven generic sales/collection steps presented in the chapter, list and discuss the activities the students would likely incorporate in RRS's sales/collection process. Using one or more techniques specified by your instructor, create a document depicting the steps you develop.

4. *Field exercises.*
   a. Find examples of the documents discussed in the chapter. You may want to visit a local office supply store such as Office Depot or Staples or do an Internet search using the document names for your research.
   b. Contact a practicing accountant involved in auditing (either external or internal). Discuss the risks involved in the sales/collection process and internal controls he or she has observed in various organizations that address those risks.
5. *Modeling sales/collection processes.* In each of the following independent cases, use a systems documentation technique specified by your instructor to model the process.
   a. Dave's Pool Service is based in Upland, California; the firm offers a variety of pool- and spa-related services, including acid washing, routine maintenance, solar panel installation, and repair services. For regular customers, Dave prepares and mails paper invoices on a monthly basis; for one-time services, Dave leaves the invoice at the client's home. Dave accepts payment via check only; if a client fails to pay amounts billed within 30 days, Dave turns the case over to a collections firm. Dave deposits cash receipts in his personal checking account on a weekly basis; he does not maintain a separate business checking account.
   b. Steve and Mike Nauertz own an insurance agency with offices in Upland, Arcadia, and Pasadena, California; they offer several types of insurance, including automobile, motorcycle, homeowners, and whole life. When a client comes into one of the offices, one of the owners does a "needs assessment," which they record both on a paper form and in a relational database file. The client is then assigned to an office employee who presents the available options based on the needs assessment. Options include type of insurance, insurance providers, costs, and policy features. The client makes a choice; the employee writes the policy and collects the initial payment in cash or check. Thereafter, the insurance company bills the client directly; Nauertz Insurance collects a commission from the insurance company. Steve or Mike deposits client receipts in a business bank account daily; commissions are transmitted to the same account electronically.
   c. Chapter 10's critical thinking application focused on "You Bars" (www.youbars.com); the company also sells "You Shakes." Visit the company's Web site and document the sales/collection process for You Shakes.
   d. Choose any organization where you do business regularly, such as a gas station, bookstore, or restaurant. Write a description of the sales/collection process, then document the process you described.
6. *Document design.* Consider the list of documents presented in the chapter; choose three from the list. Using whatever forms of information technology your instructor specifies, design a generic example of the form. Keep in mind that forms should have a title, be logically arranged for easy data input, and have plenty of white space. Be prepared to present and discuss your documents in class.
7. *Sales/collection transactions.* ABL Corporation sells on credit terms of 2/10, n/30; all merchandise is shipped FOB shipping point, freight collect. During the month of February 2009, ABL completed the following transactions:

Date	Transaction
2	Collected cash on account from HLN Corporation. Invoice dated January 28, $1,100.
3	Sold merchandise on account to VRA Corporation, $3,000. Inventory cost, $1,400.
5	Sold merchandise for cash to RKH Corporation, $2,200. Inventory cost, $1,025.
11	Collected cash on account from PNB Corporation. Invoice dated January 27, $3,000.

13	Collected cash on account from VRA Corporation for two invoices. The first, dated January 31, totaled $4,200. The second, dated February 3, totaled $3,000.
17	Wrote off bad debts totaling $1,800.
20	Sold merchandise on account to CHR Corporation, $7,000. Inventory cost, $3,300.
21	Sold merchandise on account to HLN Corporation, $3,400. Inventory cost, $1,500.
28	Completed monthly adjustment for bad debts, 1% of February credit sales.

a. Record the preceding transactions in general journal format.

b. Beyond the journal entries, what information would you want to capture in a relational database about the transactions?

8. *Document information.* The sales/collection process documents discussed in the chapter are listed below on the right. Various information items that might appear in them are listed on the left. For each information item listed on the left, indicate the document(s) in which it would most likely appear with the appropriate letter(s).

— 1. Amount paid	a. Bill of lading
— 2. Common carrier name	b. Customer check
— 3. Cost per unit	c. Customer invoice
— 4. Credit rating	d. Customer order
— 5. Customer name	e. Deposit slip
— 6. Freight terms	f. Packing list
— 7. Inventory quantities	g. Picking list
— 8. Items shipped	h. Remittance advice
— 9. Total due	
— 10. Unit prices	

9. *Risk and internal control classification.* Consider the six risks and related internal controls presented in the chapter. Use the taxonomies presented in Chapter 4 to classify the risks as financial, operational, strategic, or hazard and the controls as preventive, detective, or corrective in nature. Be prepared to discuss your classifications.

10. *Porter's value chain.* Which value chain element is most closely associated with each item below? Use each element of the value chain only once.

a. A Glaxo-Smith-Kline (www.gsk.com) representative visits a doctor's office.

b. Dell Computer ships a Latitude notebook to a customer.

c. Dreambox Creations purchases the latest version of McAfee Security Suite.

d. General Motors uses trucks and trains to move steel from Pennsylvania to Michigan.

e. Hewlett-Packard is organized on functional lines (marketing, accounting, and so on).

f. Pei Wei Asian Diner (www.peiwei.com) prepares Blazing Noodles with Tofu and Vegetables.

g. Robert Half Inc. screens candidates for temporary accounting positions.

h. Toyota changes the oil in a recently purchased automobile.

i. University Bookstore buys textbooks in preparation for a new academic term.

11. *Database creation.* Consider the Level Zero data flow diagram presented in Figure 11.2. Create database specifications for at least three tables indicated by the diagram.

12. *Data flow diagram completion.* Consider the Level Zero data flow diagram, depicting the generic sales/collection process, presented below. Fill in any missing information based on the generic process described in the chapter.

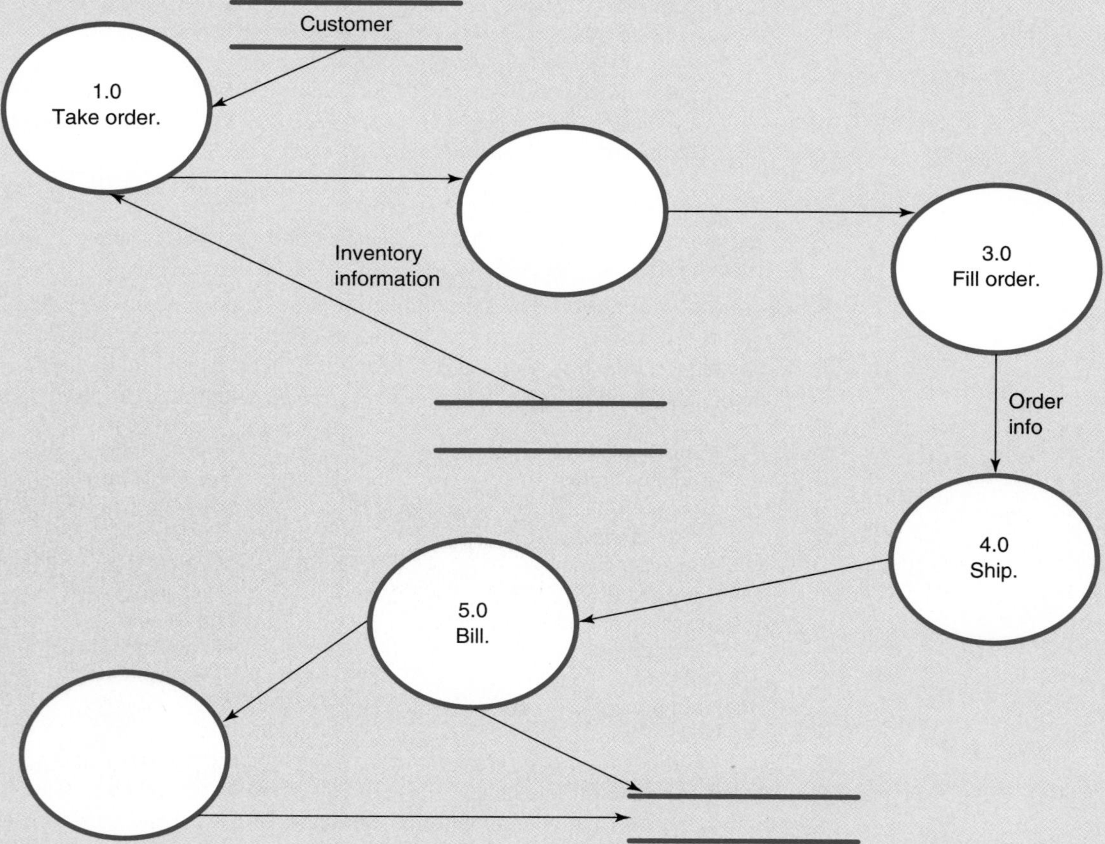

13. *Internal controls.* (CMA adapted, December 1993) Abid and Company manufactures a variety of pumps and valves that it distributes through several thousand plumbing supply houses as well as 100 manufacturer's representatives. As a result of the less-than-favorable business conditions that have existed over the last several years, Abid's cash flow situation has deteriorated. Accounts receivable have continually grown due to creeping extensions of time that Abid's customers have been taking in remitting payments for supplies. In addition, as Abid has been easing credit to its customers, bad debts have grown to 3 percent of sales.

Abid's president has hired Joe Jackler, an experienced cash manager, to improve Abid's liquidity position. Jackler met with Dora Mooney, Abid's controller, and ascertained that Abid's (1) product sales prices have a 20 percent margin over the sum of direct operating costs and all delivery and selling costs; (2) production is currently slightly less than full capacity; (3) current credit terms are 2/12, n/45, which is in line with industry practices; and (4) dunning notices are sent monthly on all past due accounts with telephone follow-ups for delinquent accounts in excess of $8,000. On average, customers currently pay 35 days after the sale. Delinquent accounts are sent to collection agencies when they reach a past due status of 12 months.

From a review of credit records, Jackler was able to group Abid's customers into risk classes according to the probability of loss associated with sales to a customer, as follows:

Risk Class	Probable Loss (%)
1	None
2	0% to 0.5%
3	0.6% to 1%
4	2% to 3%
5	4% to 6%
6	7% to 12%
7	13% to 20%
8	Over 20%

After considering the available alternatives, Jackler has implemented the following changes to Abid's credit policies in order to improve cash flow:

- The credit terms extended to customers will change to 2/10, n/30. Jackler believes the current customers will accept this change as a sound business decision and, consequently, there will be minimal effect on sales. The overall effects of this change will be to improve accounts receivable turnover, reduce the opportunity costs of carrying receivables, and identify potentially troubled accounts sooner to minimize write-offs.
- Customers in risk groups 1 through 5 will continue to have the customary credit extended to them; selling to groups 6 and 7 will be under more stringent credit terms, such as cash on delivery; and sales to group 8 will require advance payments. Jackler believes this change will cause a reduction in sales; however, this reduction will come from the high-risk customer profile.
- Collection efforts will be increased to ensure better compliance with the new credit terms. Dunning notices will continue to be sent monthly; however, telephone follow-ups will be initiated for all delinquent accounts in excess of $2,000. Accounts outstanding nine months or more will be turned over to a collection agency. Jackler believes this action, coupled with the other changes in policy, will reduce bad debts to a level of 1 to 1.5 percent of sales.

Mooney is responsible for extending credit to customers who deal directly with the company and for establishing the guidelines under which manufacturer's representatives operate. Mooney has tailored credit to various customers to meet their needs and over time has developed a close relationship with a number of the larger customers. In view of the indicated impact the new policies will have on company sales and production, as well as on some of the larger customers, Mooney performed her own risk study. She concluded that some of Jackler's "risk classifications" were inappropriate and believes that some of the larger customers are better business risks than indicated in Jackler's analysis.

Mooney did not share her findings with Abid's president or with Jackler. She decided that to follow the policies in their entirety would reduce sales more than Jackler estimates and result in idle manufacturing capacity. Consequently, Mooney does not intend to totally comply with the new policies, particularly as they affect her larger customers.

What internal control strengths and weaknesses are indicated by the narrative? What additional internal controls would you recommend in this situation? Evaluate Mooney's actions using the IMA code of ethics.

14. *Flowchart interpretation and internal controls analysis.* (CMA adapted, June 1994) The flowchart below depicts the sales/collection process for Richards Furniture Company, a mid-sized retailer of living room and bedroom furniture. Use the flowchart to generate a narrative description of Richards' sales/collection process. Comment on the company's strengths and weaknesses with regard to internal controls; suggest ways to address the weaknesses you identify.

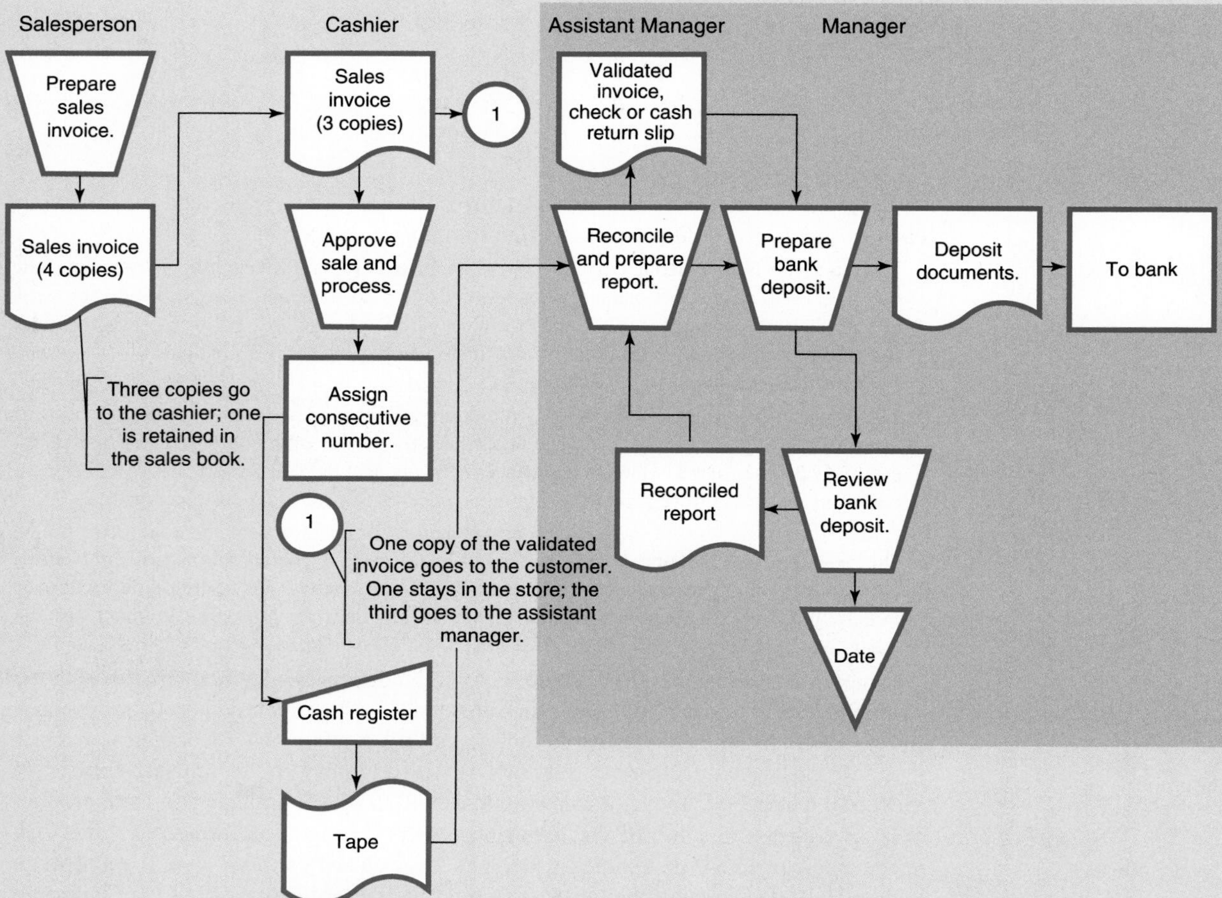

15. *Crossword puzzle.* Please complete the puzzle below using terminology from the chapter.

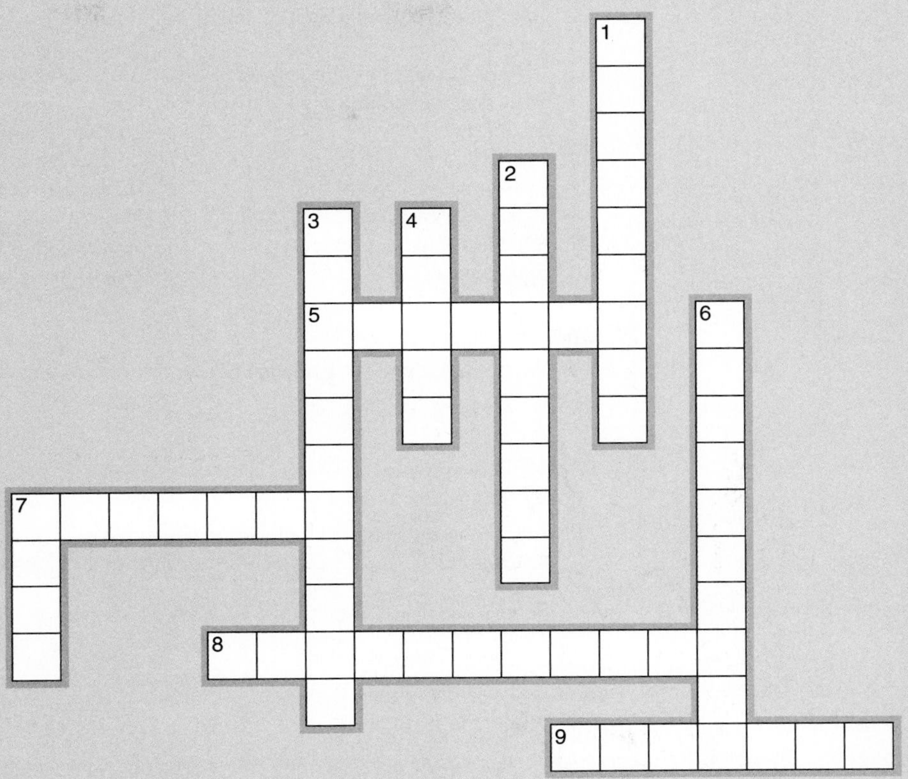

Across

5. Freight ______: buyer is responsible for freight costs.
7. Originates customer invoice.
8. FOB ______: client takes responsibility for merchandise when it arrives.
9. Order-filling technology example.

Down

1. Internal control relationship between custody, recordkeeping, and authorization.
2. Recipient of customer order.
3. Guides inventory selection in the warehouse.
4. Business processes create this.
6. A ______ advice typically accompanies a client's check.
7. Recipient of deposit slip.

16. *Terminology.* Please match each item on the left with the most appropriate item on the right.

1. Associated with separation of duties	a. Business processes create value for them.
2. Deposit slip	b. Buyer capitalizes freight costs to inventory.
3. FOB destination, freight prepaid	c. Can reduce the risk of damaged goods.
4. FOB shipping point, freight collect	d. Custody, recordkeeping, authorization.
5. Insurance	e. For deposit only.
6. Internet	f. Internal control for granting customer credit.
7. Outsource	g. Method for taking customer orders.
8. Restrictive endorsement	h. Packing list.
9. Specifies shipment contents	i. Seller charges freight cost to delivery expense.
10. Stakeholders	j. Transmits cash receipts to bank.

17. *Multiple choice questions.*

1. What interest rate is a company paying if it fails to take a discount of 3/15, n/60?
   a. 3%
   b. 25%
   c. 15%
   d. Some other amount
2. An accounting clerk debited cash and credited accounts receivable for $500. Which of the following is the most likely source document for that transaction?
   a. Deposit slip
   b. Sales invoice
   c. Remittance advice
   d. Customer order
3. Which of the following duties should be separated in the sales/collection process?
   a. Purchasing inventory and reconciling the bank statement
   b. Reconciling the bank statement and signing checks
   c. Signing checks and purchasing inventory
   d. Signing checks, purchasing inventory, and reconciling the bank statement
4. When goods are shipped FOB shipping point, freight prepaid,
   a. The buyer pays the freight cost to the seller.
   b. The selling company cannot use a common carrier.
   c. The buyer pays the freight company directly.
   d. The freight cost is absorbed by the common carrier.
5. Which of the following steps in the sales/collection process typically happens first?
   a. Checking customer credit
   b. Verifying that inventory is on hand
   c. Taking the customer's order
   d. Generating a picking list
6. Primary activities in Porter's value chain include all of the following except
   a. Infrastructure.
   b. Inbound logistics.
   c. Marketing and sales.
   d. Operations.

7. Which of the following is a support activity in Porter's value chain?
   a. Service
   b. Human resource management
   c. Outbound logistics
   d. Operations
8. Which of the following would be represented by a line in a DFD of the sales/collection process?
   a. Check customer credit
   b. Ship merchandise
   c. Customer information
   d. All of the above
9. Bumble Beasley created a relational database table for the "check customer credit" activity in the sales/collection process. Which of the following would be the most likely primary key in the table?
   a. Credit decision
   b. Customer ID
   c. Credit employee ID
   d. Customer ID and credit employee ID
10. A data flow diagram of the sales/collection process includes "common carrier" as an external entity. The external entity would most likely be connected to
    a. Customer (external entity).
    b. Ship merchandise (process).
    c. Inventory (data store).
    d. Collect payment (process).

18. *Statement evaluation.* Indicate whether each of the following statements is (i) always true, (ii) sometimes true, or (iii) never true. For those that are (ii) sometimes true, explain when the statement is true.

a. A junction table would be required in a relational database for the sales/collection process.
b. Cash receipts clerks should reconcile a company's bank statement at least monthly.
c. Companies complete all activities in the value chain to serve their stakeholders.
d. Customers should borrow money to take advantage of cash discounts in paying their bills.
e. Documents in the sales/collection process can be paper or electronic.
f. In the sales/collection process, separation of duties can be applied to credit decisions.
g. Restrictive check endorsements eliminate the need for other internal controls over cash.
h. Separation of duties helps safeguard inventory in the sales/collection process.
i. Transactions in the sales/collection process require a bill of lading.
j. Web sites assist companies in the sales/collection process.

Chapter Twelve

Acquisition/Payment Process

AIS in the Business World

Wal-Mart

Wal-Mart is the largest retail organization in the world; in fiscal year 2008, its net sales were $374.5 billion, resulting in operating income of $22.0 billion. Earnings per share increased for the fifth consecutive year, and free cash flow increased by 25 percent from fiscal year 2007 to fiscal year 2008 (www.walmartstores.com).

While there are many important factors leading to Wal-Mart's impressive results, one of the firm's critical success factors is its ability to manage its inventory, which totaled over $35 billion at the end of fiscal 2008. According to Powanga and Powanga (2008), Wal-Mart uses RFID technology to help manage its inventory. They explain RFID like this (p. 1):

> RFID technology encompasses any electronic system employing radio or electromagnetic waves to collect, store and retrieve digital data that uniquely identifies an item, usually a serial number called an electronic product code (EPC) [which is] similar to a Universal Product Code (UPC). The EPC matching the identifying information about a product stored in a single or networked database is programmed into a tag equipped with a miniature chip to store the data. The tag contains an antenna to receive and respond to radio-frequency queries from the reader. The reader interrogates the tag for information by generating a magnetic field bubble. The tag, once it enters this bubble, is activated and transmits the EPC to the reader. Through a network interface, the EPC is passed on to the database where information related to the tag is identified and retrieved.

During its pilot test phase, stores using RFID had 16 percent fewer stock-outs than stores not using RFID.

Discussion Questions

1. Which element(s) of Porter's value chain are enhanced through the use of RFID?
2. What are the steps in the acquisition/payment cycle? Which steps benefit most directly from RFID?
3. What are the risks associated with RFID? What internal controls would help address those risks?

Source: M. Powanga and L. Powanga, "Deploying RFID in Logistics: Criteria and Best Practices and Issues," *The Business Review, Cambridge,* Summer 2008.

The acquisition/payment process is the flip side of the sales/collection process. Like the sales/collection process, it follows a fairly common set of steps and uses some consistent documents and internal controls across a wide range of companies and industries.

The chapter follows the same structure as Chapter 11. By carefully studying it and completing the activities your instructor assigns, you should be able to:

1. Explain the role and purpose of the acquisition/payment process.
2. List and discuss, in order, the steps in the process.
3. Identify and describe documents commonly used in the acquisition/payment process.
4. Suggest and evaluate internal controls associated with it.
5. Explain the role of information technology in the acquisition/payment process.
6. Create and interpret systems documents related to acquisitions and payments.

Although it can be applied to virtually anything an organization needs to acquire, our discussion of the acquisition/payment process will focus on inventory. We'll leave the discussion of payroll to the next chapter; although it can be considered part of the acquisition/payment process, its details are more complex than "ordinary" acquisition/payment activities; they also can vary significantly across companies and industries. In addition, the acquisition/payment process also incorporates noninventory purchases such as fixed assets (equipment, furniture, and similar items) and other current assets (such as supplies).

PROCESS DESCRIPTION

The primary purpose of the acquisition/payment process is to obtain the resources the organization needs and to pay for them. Fundamentally, organizations exist to create value for their stakeholders; the acquisition/payment process is one element of that basic purpose. In the last chapter, we looked at Porter's value chain as a way to think about business processes; the acquisition/payment process is principally related to procurement and inbound logistics. Procurement is a synonym for purchasing; inbound logistics refers to the process of getting resources from "where they are" to "where they are needed." For example, McGraw-Hill might use air and ground transportation to ship books to university bookstores.

For more information on value creation and its importance, consult the writings of Chester Barnard, Peter Drucker, or Michael Porter.

Reflection and Self-Assessment 12.1

What resources does your university gather to help you achieve your educational goals?

Although an acquisition/payment process can have slight differences across organizations and industries, its basic **steps** include (Hollander, Denna, and Cherrington, 2000)

1. *Request goods and services based on monitored need.* Organizations use all sorts of tools and techniques to establish the need for a good or service. Inventory levels, for example, might be monitored with a reorder point; orders could be based on an economic order quantity formula. Other resources may be time-sensitive; for example, your car insurance bill may be paid monthly or semiannually. A special project, such as the design and implementation of an accounting information system, may lead to a request for goods or services on a more episodic basis. In many organizations, requests for inventory, supplies, and services are coordinated through a central purchasing department, thus creating economies of scale and discounted purchase prices.

Consult a cost accounting or operations management text for details about EOQ and reorder point.

2. *Authorize a purchase.* This step promotes good internal control (discussed in greater depth later in the chapter). For example, your AIS instructor may be authorized to select her own textbook for the course. Or the decision may be a collaborative one, with a department chair or course coordinator having the final authorization for placing a textbook order with your university bookstore. Even in the bookstore, not every employee is authorized to deal with publishers and other suppliers; rather, that right is probably vested in one employee or a small group of employees.

At Cal Poly Pomona, employees in the Facilities Planning and Management Department can use a departmental credit card to purchase small supplies such as light bulbs if none are available in the warehouse.

3. *Purchase goods/services.* Once a purchase has been authorized, the appropriate documentation must be submitted to the vendor/supplier. We'll look at purchase documentation requirements in more detail later in the chapter.
4. *Receive goods and services.* Major purchases of goods, particularly inventory, are received through a dedicated receiving department for stronger internal control. Individual employees, however, may be authorized to make small purchases using company credit or debit cards.

An audit trail consists of source documents, journal entries, and ledger postings; it also may involve electronic data in a computer-based accounting information system.

5. *Disburse cash.* Once the goods have been properly purchased and received, accounting personnel generate payment to the vendor. Keeping a solid audit trail is very important here, as it is in the other steps and in the sales/collection process.
6. *When necessary, process purchase returns.* If received goods are defective, do not meet quality standards, or are otherwise unacceptable to the buyer, they may need to be returned to the vendor.

As with our discussion of the sales/collection process, keep in mind that those six steps are very generic. Each organization will have its own modifications to the basic steps; the fundamental idea is purchasing the goods and services you need, when you need them, and paying for them timely. Figure 12.1 shows a Level Zero data flow diagram depicting the basic steps in the acquisition/payment process.

FIGURE 12.1
Generic Acquisition/ Payment Process

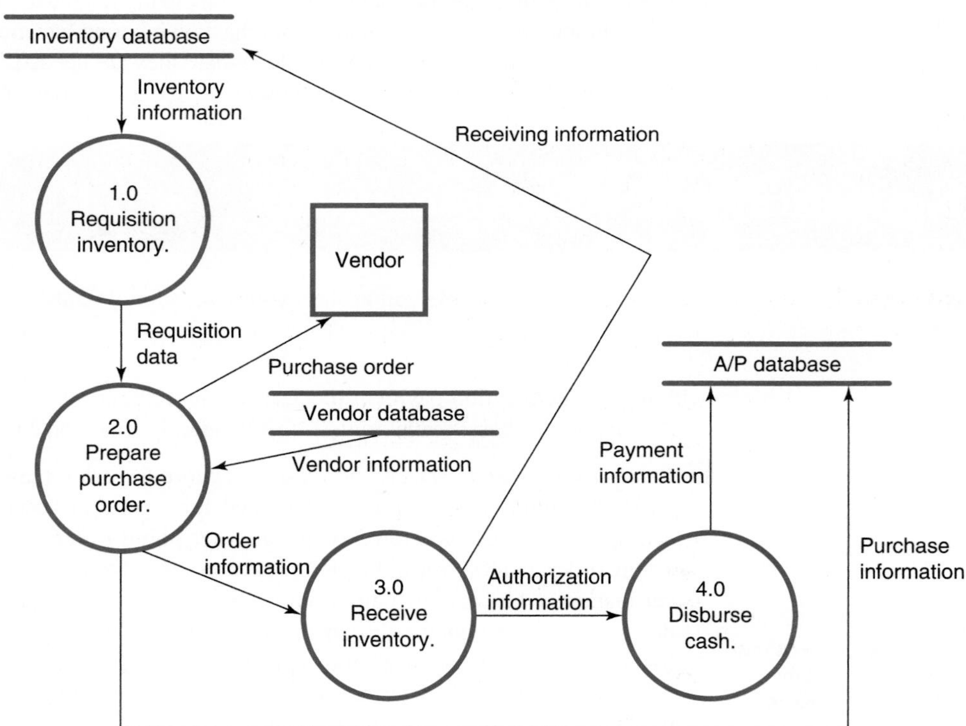

The steps in the sales/collection process are related to those in the acquisition/payment process as shown in the table below:

Sales/Collection	Acquisition/Payment
Take customer order	Purchase goods and services
Ship the product	Receive goods and services
Collect payment	Disburse cash

Next, let's turn our attention to some of the documents commonly found in the acquisition/payment process.

DOCUMENTS AND MODELING

You can find a lot of information about EDI, XBRL, and other technologies at www.itpapers.com.

As in the sales/collection process, a document can be either paper or electronic. Documents in both processes can be transmitted electronically using **electronic data interchange** (EDI) or the **eXtensible Business Reporting Language** (XBRL).

Common **documents** in the acquisition/payment process include those listed in Table 12.1.

Reflection and Self-Assessment 12.2

How do the documents listed in Table 12.1 relate to those discussed for the sales/collection process? Which documents would generate journal entries in the accounting information system? What would those entries be?

Once an operating department establishes the need for a good or service, its personnel generate a purchase requisition. The purchase requisition, like all forms, should have a clear title and plenty of white space for easy reading. Information should be complete and logically laid out. In most cases, the operating department keeps a copy of the purchase requisition for its own files and sends a copy to the purchasing department. Figure 12.2 shows an example of a purchase requisition.

TABLE 12.1
Documents Used in the Acquisition/Payment Process

Document Name	Basic Purpose	Originator	Recipient
Purchase requisition	To request that the purchasing department order goods or services from a vendor	Operating department	Purchasing department
Purchase order	To specify the items to be ordered, freight terms, shipping address, and other information for the vendor	Purchasing department	Vendor
Receiving report	To ensure that goods have been ordered and received in good condition	Receiving department	Various departments
Vendor invoice	To request payment from a customer	Vendor	Accounting department
Check	To pay the vendor	Accounting department	Vendor

FIGURE 12.2 **Purchase Requisition**

George Mason University

PURCHASE REQUISITION **835457**

Sample Sample

SUGGESTED VENDOR	DELIVERY INSTRUCTIONS	DEPARTMENTAL APPROVAL
	DELIVER TO:	DATE NEEDED:
	DEPARTMENT:	FUND CODE:
	TELEPHONE:	APPROVAL SIGNATURE:
	BUILDING:	
	ROOM NUMBER:	TITLE:
		DATE APPROVED:

ITEM NUMBER	DESCRIPTION OF ITEM/SERVICE DESIRED		QUANTITY	UNIT	UNIT PRICE	EXTENSION
			TOTAL AMOUNT OF REQUISITION:			

+++ FOR BUYER'S USE ONLY +++

VENDOR ADDRESS:	CONTRACT NO:
	FOB:
	DELIVERY:
CONTACT:	BUYER:
PHONE:	REMARKS
EIN/SSN:	

The purchasing department, then, will consolidate various purchase requisitions into a single purchase order. Consolidating purchase requisitions may allow the company to take advantage of quantity discounts. Creating a separate purchasing department also facilitates strong internal control through separation of duties. Purchasing agents may be in charge of dealing with a specific set of vendors, a certain group of parts or supplies, or the purchase requisitions from one or more operating departments. While the purchase requisition generated by the operating department is an informal, internal document, the signed purchase order functions as a "contract" between the company and the vendor. The purchase requisition will normally include the goods and quantities requested; the purchase order will specify the vendor, the expected price, the freight terms, and other important data for the transaction. In most cases, the purchasing department keeps a copy on file; it also sends copies to the receiving department and the accounting department. Figure 12.3 shows an example of a purchase order.

FIGURE 12.3
Purchase Order

Purchase Order

Purchase Order No.:________________________
Requisition No.:________________________
Vendor Code:________________________
Vendor Name:________________________
Vendor Address:________________________

Vendor Contact: Vendor Phone: (____) _____-______

Order Description

Product Item No.	Product Description	Quantity	Estimated Cost	Tax	Total

When the goods arrive from the vendor, the receiving department prepares a receiving report. The goods should be matched and verified against an existing purchase order so that the company does not receive goods that were not properly ordered. The receiving personnel also may verify the quality and condition of the goods before accepting delivery. Commonly, the receiving department copies the accounting department and purchasing department as well.

Point your Web browser to www.ita.doc.gov/ofm/forms/receiving_insp_text.htm for a summary of information commonly included in a receiving report.

Notice that the accounting department receives both a copy of the purchase order and a copy of the receiving report. When the vendor mails an invoice for payment, then, accounting personnel use those documents to ensure that the invoice reflects goods that were properly ordered and received before generating payment. The department then issues a check in payment of the invoice, taking advantage of any discounts offered.

Reflection and Self-Assessment 12.3

Use the narrative description above to prepare a flowchart of a generic acquisition/payment process.

Now, let's turn our attention to internal controls in the acquisition/payment process.

INTERNAL CONTROLS

As with the sales/collection process, our discussion is centered on the various risks managers confront in the acquisition/payment process. Many of the controls discussed in the last chapter also apply here, so don't consider the list that follows comprehensive or exhaustive. Remember: The idea is to implement internal controls that provide *reasonable* assurance—not *absolute* assurance. Even if the latter were possible, it almost certainly would not be cost-effective in most organizations.

As in the previous chapter, the numbered items below suggest risks to be addressed; the lettered items beneath them discuss possible **internal controls**.

1. Ordering unneeded goods.
   a. *Institute a system for monitoring inventory levels.* In addition to traditional systems like EOQ, many organizations use information technology to monitor inventory levels. Jonietz (2001) reported on the use of wireless systems in a Tulsa-based retail warehouse for inventory control.
   b. *Require justification for unusual orders or orders over a specified dollar amount.* If an employee is ordering goods unnecessarily, or is attempting to defraud the organization by ordering goods for personal benefit, an additional authorizing signature or approval process can be effective in detecting the problem.
   c. *Specify the business purpose for ordered goods.* This control is connected to the previous one. Consider, for example, a company with unusually high travel expenses; employees should be required to justify the business purpose of a trip before taking it.
2. Purchasing goods from inappropriate vendors.
   a. *Develop and enforce a conflict-of-interest policy.* Such policies make clear the actions that constitute a conflict of interest, as well as the consequences for engaging in those actions. The World Wide Web Consortium (www.w3.org) established a

detailed policy in 2003; you may view it at their Web site: www.w3.org/2000/09/06-conflictpolicy.html.

b. *Establish criteria for supplier reliability and quality of goods.* Managers may establish standards for delivery time, product quality, and availability for their suppliers. Home Depot (www.homedepot.com), for example, requires its vendors to maintain adequate inventory levels in their own operations so that they can fill Home Depot's inventory needs. Many organizations use a "preferred vendor list" for that purpose.

The value chain consists of four support activities (infrastructure, human resource management, technology development, and procurement) and five primary activities (inbound logistics, operations, outbound logistics, marketing and sales, and service).

c. *Create strategic alliances with preferred vendors.* Porter (1985, p. 33) conceptualized the value chain as a way of "examining all the activities a firm performs and how they interact. . . . The value chain disaggregates a firm into its strategically relevant activities in order to understand the behavior of costs and the existing and potential sources of differentiation." When an organization is particularly expert at one or more value chain activities, it may form a strategic alliance with organizations that are more adept at other value chain components. For example, an outstanding manufacturer may establish a strategic alliance with a particular common carrier, thus creating value for both organizations.

3. Receiving unordered or defective goods.
   a. *Match receiving reports with approved purchase orders.* Document matching is a fundamental internal control found in many organizations. In the acquisition/payment process, the receiving clerk should verify that goods have been ordered by an authorized company representative before accepting them. Goods received without a purchase order are suspicious; such receipts should either be refused outright or investigated more carefully to ensure that no fraud is involved.
   b. *Inspect goods before accepting a shipment.* This control is especially applicable when dealing with very specialized goods. Receiving clerks should have a clear grasp of acceptable quality standards and verify that (at least) a sampling of products meets those standards.
   c. *Insure products en route.* Purchasing transit insurance cannot necessarily prevent damage, but it can help organizations recover financially if goods are damaged in transit.
4. Experiencing theft of inventory and/or cash.
   a. *Establish an internal audit function.* The Sarbanes-Oxley Act of 2002 has done a lot to establish the importance of internal audits in organizations. Your university may have a separate class on internal auditing; you also can get more information about the field from the Institute of Internal Auditors (www.theiia.org/).
   b. *Reconcile bank statements promptly.* Consider the case of Wholelife Counseling Center (Hurt, 1994). In that organization, failure to reconcile bank statements promptly led to a major loss of cash due to embezzlement.
   c. *Separate authorization, custody, and usage functions for both inventory and cash.* Separation of duties is another common, and essential, internal control procedure. Three important duties should always be separated to foster good internal control: physical custody of an asset, authorization for its use, and recordkeeping associated with it.
   d. *Install employee monitoring systems.* Systems like these are controversial and may involve ethical and legal issues. Consider, for example, one company that put detection sensors in its employees' identification badges. The sensors allowed management to track employee movements inside the corporate headquarters.
   e. *Bond employees who handle high-value goods.* Fidelity bonding is a form of insurance focused on employee behavior. According to Kishel and Kishel (1993), three

types of fidelity bonds are common. "Individual bonds cover theft by a specific named individual. Schedule bonds list every name or position to be covered. Blanket bonds, the most encompassing of the three, cover all employees without reference to individual names or positions."

5. Making errors in paying invoices.
   a. *Require document matching (purchase order, receiving report, invoice) before issuing a check.* This control technique is especially effective when incorporated with good separation of duties. When the accountant/cash payments clerk has all three documents in hand, he or she will know that goods were properly ordered and received. The invoice will show the amount due, and the accountant/cash payments clerk will cut a check for the vendor.
   b. *Employ information technology to take advantage of available discounts.* Most general ledger software packages, such as QuickBooks or Great Plains Dynamics, can prompt users to pay invoices before cash discounts expire.
   c. *Stamp documents "paid" to avoid duplicate payments.* This control seems simple (and it is!), but it is very effective in avoiding duplicate payments. Whether documents are stamped electronically or physically, they should be somehow marked so they are not paid more than once.

Forensic accounting and fraud detection are concerned with uncovering internal control breaches. For more information about this growing area of accounting practice, point your Web browser to www.cfenet.com, the Web site for the Association of Certified Fraud Examiners.

Those risks, and the suggested internal controls that accompany them, are by no means exhaustive. In designing and evaluating internal controls for the acquisition/payment process, you must develop an intimate knowledge of an organization's processes and personnel. Use your own creativity and critical thinking abilities, coupled with your sense of cost–benefit issues, when confronted with the important task of internal control assessment in practice.

INFORMATION TECHNOLOGY IN THE ACQUISITION/ PAYMENT PROCESS

Information technology can make the acquisition/payment process more effective and more efficient, just as you learned for the sales/collection process in the last chapter. In addition to the general internal controls described there (prenumbered documents, segregation of duties, and the like), IT can assist immeasurably in completing the steps in the acquisition/payment process. Consider the following examples:

- *Paying vendors online.* You may have participated in electronic banking activities on your own; those same sorts of processes can easily apply to organizations. Most online banking systems have strong internal controls built in: passwords, lockouts, and transaction numbers. In addition, online payments make the process much more efficient.
- *Utilizing bar codes for inventory.* Bar codes can be used to monitor inventory levels and to make pricing changes easily.
- *Instituting radio frequency identification for inventory.* Often referred to as RFID technology, this technology "is a method of storing and remotely retrieving data using devices called RFID tags or transponders" (www.wikipedia.org). RFID technology can be used to track goods from the receiving function to the warehouse. In addition, the technology can be used for remote data transfer in virtually any business process.

Wal-Mart now requires its vendors to equip products with RFID technology to facilitate acquisition/payment activities.

In addition, most forms of IT discussed previously are easily applied to the acquisition/payment process.

CRITICAL THINKING

As you read at the start of this chapter, the acquisition/payment process can involve virtually anything an organization needs to buy. Since our previous examples have involved inventory, I thought you might like to see something a bit different for this chapter's critical thinking exercise. This example focuses on an internal service; specifically, building and grounds maintenance.

The Facilities Management Department of ETR Corporation is in charge of all building and grounds maintenance; some tasks are completed routinely (e.g., weekly or monthly), while others are done based on service call requests from other ETR departments. Consider the systems flowchart of the process shown in Figure 12.4.

A narrative description of the process would look like this: When an ETR department needs a service call, the manager prepares a service request; the request becomes part of a master "service request database" in the Facilities Management Department. Each day, facilities employees consult a video display to determine which tasks will be addressed; those tasks include both routine maintenance and service requests. The facilities employee completes the required tasks. For each service request, the facilities employee prepares a "completed job report," which is sent back to the requesting manager; for both service requests and routine maintenance, the service request database is updated. The department manager who requested the service call files a copy of the original service request and a copy of the completed job report.

FIGURE 12.4
ETR maintenance

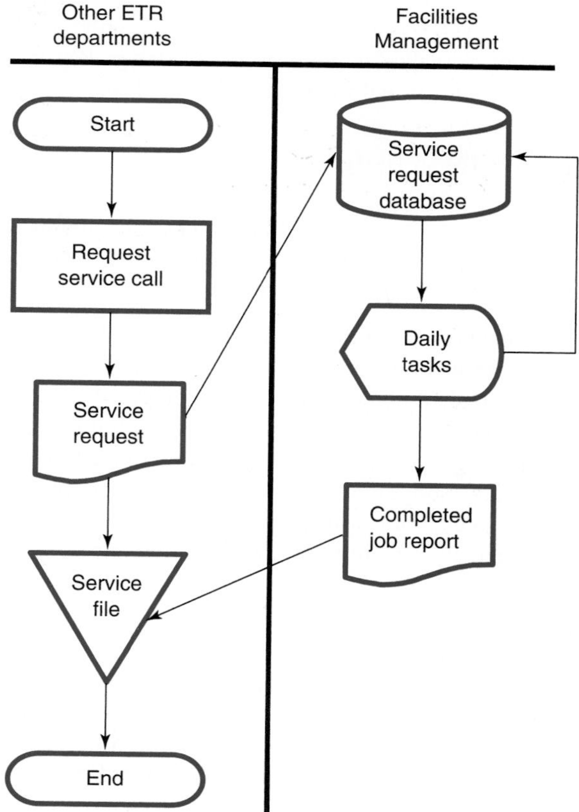

Here are some risks and associated internal controls for the process:

Risk	Control
Too many service call requests	Expand staffing. Hire temporary employees. Create a transfer pricing system.
Poor quality work	Periodic employee training Customer satisfaction reports Post-audits of completed jobs
Damage to database/files	Backup copies (electronic and hard copy)

Here are some sample specifications for the service request database:

Request number

Date requested

[Requesting manager]

Description

Date completed

[Facilities employee]

The primary key (request number) could be an auto-numbered field, thus promoting stronger internal control through sequential numbering. Since one manager can initiate many service requests, but each service request comes from only one manager, the primary key from the "requesting manager" table becomes a foreign key in the service request database; the same logic holds true for the "facilities employee."

BUSINESS PROCESS RELATIONSHIPS

So now we've looked at both the sales/collection process and the acquisition/payment process. Keeping in mind that the two complement one another in two different organizations, here's a comprehensive view of both processes:

1. An operating department in the buying organization requests goods and services. For example, the production department might need additional raw materials. Or the accounting department might need new computers. A purchase requisition is the relevant document in this step. The purchase requisition serves as an important internal control by allowing the organization to respond to legitimate needs, take advantage of quantity discounts, and establish relationships with suppliers based on objective criteria. A purchase requisition would indicate the items needed and their quantities; one copy would typically remain with the requisitioning department, while another copy would go to purchasing.
2. The purchasing department in the buying organization authorizes the purchase. Having a central location that handles all purchasing for an organization is an important element of internal control. It promotes adequate supervision, helping ensure that the organization is only buying things that are legitimately needed; in addition, it promotes operating efficiency through coordination. A purchasing agent would complete a serially numbered purchase order based on one or more requisitions; the purchase order would be transmitted to the supplier electronically and/or in paper form. One copy of the purchase order, without the quantities of items ordered, would be sent to the receiving department; a second copy would go to the accounting department.

3. The sales department in the selling organization takes the customer's order. Taking a customer order can refer to receiving a purchase order; on the other hand, the selling organization can receive orders over the phone, electronically (such as through a Web site), or via electronic data interchange. The sales staff member would fill out an order form based on the data in the purchase order.
4. The credit department in the selling organization approves the customer's credit. Having a credit department promotes good separation of duties. If the sales staff is allowed to grant credit, internal control is weakened; customers might be allowed to purchase items on credit when they are not creditworthy, which can lead to collection problems later.
5. The warehouse in the selling organization fills the order based on approved credit. Again, we see good separation of duties here—physical custody of inventory is separated from its recordkeeping (handled in the accounting department) and from authorization for its use (which comes from the sales and credit departments). The warehouse employee would complete a picking slip to show what merchandise he or she took off the shelves.
6. The selling organization's shipping department ships the product. The shipping department would verify the customer's name and address; shipping also would fill out a packing slip to enclose with the goods, showing what was shipped. If the seller uses a common carrier such as UPS to ship the goods, a bill of lading also would be required. Insurance could be an important internal control here as well. The shipping department would send a copy of the shipping documents to the accounting department, as the shipment would trigger a journal entry recording the sale.
7. The buying organization's receiving department receives the goods. The receiving department would have a "blind copy" of the related purchase order(s). A blind copy contains all the usual information but not the quantities ordered. Thus, the receiving department can verify that the goods really were ordered (an important element of internal control) but would have to count the merchandise received physically, rather than simply verifying quantities against the purchase order. Receiving would send a copy of the receiving report to accounting and the merchandise itself to the warehouse or the location where it is needed.
8. The billing department in the selling organization bills the client. Document matching is an important internal control in this step and the ones that follow. Before issuing a bill, the selling organization needs to ensure that the client has indeed ordered the goods *and* that the goods have actually been shipped. Separation of duties also comes into play here, as the authorization to bill is separated from the physical custody of the inventory. The invoice (bill) could be mailed, faxed, and/or transmitted electronically; it would normally include the payment terms (e.g., 2/10, n/30) and the seller's address.
9. The cash disbursements department in the buying organization disburses cash. The cash disbursements department needs to ensure that the goods really were ordered (purchase order), that they were received (receiving report), and that the company is being billed for the correct amount (invoice). If all three documents match, the company could issue a check and/or an electronic funds transfer in payment of the invoice. The cash disbursements clerk would typically not be a signatory on the company's checking account; rather, the clerk would prepare the check and send it to an authorized signer—once again promoting good internal control through separation of duties. Checks would be sequentially numbered; they should ideally be kept in a locked filing cabinet until needed.
10. The cash receipts department in the selling organization collects payment. If the payment is mailed, it would be received in the selling organization's mailroom. Adequate supervision in the mailroom is an important internal control, as it is throughout most business processes. Most companies will not accept currency and coin through the

mail, as it weakens internal control. The mail clerk would separate the check from the remittance advice; the check would be endorsed restrictively and prepared for deposit. The remittance advice would go to the accounting department to serve as a source document for the related journal entry.

So, that's a comprehensive picture of both the acquisition/payment and sales/collection business processes. I've described an "ideal" situation here; as an accounting professional, you might be called upon to audit or recommend improvements to similar systems in practice.

Summary

This chapter is the second of four discussing issues in various business processes. The chapter objectives are listed below, each with a brief summary of important points.

1. *Explain the role and purpose of the acquisition/payment process.* The activities in the acquisition/payment process are concerned with two main tasks: how an organization acquires the resources it needs and how it pays for them. Those resources include inventory, supplies, insurance, and plant assets.
2. *List and discuss, in order, the steps in the process.* The acquisition/payment process involves six steps:
   a. Request goods and services based on monitored need.
   b. Authorize a purchase.
   c. Purchase goods/services.
   d. Receive goods and services.
   e. Disburse cash.
   f. When necessary, process purchase returns.
3. *Identify and describe documents commonly used in the acquisition/payment process.* The documents involved in the acquisition/payment process can be paper-based or electronic. They include purchase requisition, purchase order, receiving report, vendor invoice, and check.
4. *Suggest and evaluate internal controls associated with it.* As in the sales/collection process, internal controls should be based on risk exposures. Additionally, they should be designed to reduce, not eliminate, risk. Specific controls in the acquisition/payment process include separation of duties, adequate documentation, conflict-of-interest policies, strategic alliances, and employee monitoring systems.
5. *Explain the role of information technology in the acquisition/payment process.* In addition to the forms of IT discussed in previous chapters, this chapter introduced applications of online banking, bar coding, and radio frequency identification and their applications in the process.
6. *Create and interpret systems documents related to acquisitions and payments.* Flowcharts, data flow diagrams, and REAL models can help accountants interact intelligently and efficiently with personnel in an organization. They are developed iteratively and interactively; they are also subject to the same general criteria and conventions as those in the sales/collection process. Remember: a single, correct, deterministic solution does not exist for most systems documentation cases.

Keep in mind that what you've just read is necessarily generic in nature. While most organizations will use documents, processes, and internal controls similar to those discussed here, each situation must be evaluated individually in the art of designing and implementing accounting information systems.

Key Terms

documents, *231*
electronic data interchange, *231*
eXtensible Business Reporting Language, *231*
internal controls, *234*
steps, *229*

Chapter References

Hollander, A. S., E. L. Denna, and J. O. Cherrington. 2000. *Accounting, Information Technology, and Business Solutions.* 2nd ed. New York: Irwin/McGraw-Hill.
Hurt, R. 1994. "Wholelife Counseling Center." *Journal of Accounting Case Research,* pp. 97–98.
Jonietz, E. 2001. "Wireless Stockroom." *Technology Review,* July/August, p. 32.
Kishel, G., and P. Kishel. 1993. "Safeguarding Your Business." *Black Enterprise,* July, pp. 98–104.
Porter, M. 1985. *Competitive Advantage: Creating and Sustaining Superior Performance.* New York: Free Press.

End-of-Chapter Activities

1. *Reading review questions.*

a. What is the basic purpose of the acquisition/payment process?
b. What steps do companies commonly complete as part of the acquisition/payment process?
c. What documents are important in the acquisition/payment process?
d. What risks do managers face as part of the acquisition/payment process? What internal controls help reduce exposure to those risks?
e. Prepare a response to the questions for this chapter's "AIS in the Business World."

2. *Reading review problem.* You were introduced to Dreambox Creations in the reading review problem for Chapter 11. Dreambox follows a fairly simple process in its acquisition/payment activities. Its monthly payments to vendors include rent, telephone, Internet access, and insurance. Regular, nonmonthly expenditures include office supplies, advertising, and equipment purchases. Regardless of the type of payment, Dreambox simply receives a bill or invoice in the mail and uses Quicken to write a check. Checks are typically mailed to the vendor within 10 days of receiving the bill. The co-owners, Danielle and Dan, are both authorized to sign checks for Dreambox; Dan reconciles the bank statement daily.

a. What risks is Dreambox exposed to based on the preceding narrative?
b. What internal controls would you recommend to address those risks?
c. What documents would Dreambox use to complete the transactions mentioned above?

3. *Making choices and exercising judgment.* Use your school's library to locate the Kishel and Kishel article in this chapter's references. Read the article and discuss the costs and benefits associated with each type of insurance coverage discussed. Considering the risks of the acquisition/payment process in the chapter, which risk management approaches would you consider most appropriate for each one? Why?

4. *Field exercises.*

a. Point your Web browser to www.admin.rpi.edu/purchasing/ie40_index.asp, the Web site for Rensselaer Polytechnic Institute's purchasing process. Explore the site and prepare a written or oral presentation comparing and contrasting its contents with the generic information discussed in the chapter.
b. Contact a practicing accountant involved in auditing (either external or internal). Discuss the risks involved in the acquisition/payment process and internal controls he or she has observed in various organizations that address those risks.
c. Contact a practicing accountant in a corporate environment. Ask about forms of information technology the company employs in its acquisition/payment process. Also find out how various functional managers use the AIS data from the process for making decisions.

5. *Modeling acquisition/payment processes.*

   a. Figure 12.1 presents a Level Zero data flow diagram of the acquisition/payment process. Based on directions from your instructor, complete at least one of the following three tasks: (i) decompose Process 1.0 in a Level One DFD; (ii) prepare a systems flowchart of the acquisition/payment process; (iii) prepare a REAL model, with cardinalities, of the process.

   b. The library at Big State University routes all purchase requests through its requisitions department. Faculty, staff, and students can suggest titles for books, periodicals, electronic media, and other items via e-mail or by using a paper form sent to the requisitions librarian. The requisitions librarian tracks the various requests in a database; once at least 10 requests for the same item have come in, the requisitions librarian orders it from an appropriate vendor using a standard purchase order. The requisitions librarian e-mails the requestors to tell them the item has been ordered and files a copy of the purchase order by title. When the item is received, the receiving clerk matches it against the purchase order supplied by the requisitions librarian; if it matches, the item moves out of the receiving department into the library, where it is filed. A copy of the receiving report goes to the requisitions librarian and to the financial services department; financial services clerks match the invoice against the receiving report and purchase order. They also reconcile any differences between them with the vendor. Invoices are paid on a monthly basis according to the company name of the vendor; for example, vendors starting with A through C are paid the first five days of the month. The financial services clerk creates a payment packet of all relevant documents, stamps "Paid" on the top, and files it alphabetically by vendor name, and by date within vendor name. Create a flowchart or data flow diagram that depicts the preceding process.

   c. The four articles listed below summarize acquisition/payment processes in various organizational contexts. Working with a group of students, select one of the four articles. Prepare a one-page summary of the acquisition/payment process described in the article you select, then create a flowchart or data flow diagram that depicts your summary. You'll have to use some creative and critical-thinking skills to fill in some of the details in each case.

      - David Hannon, "Easing into E-Procurement with Indirect Spend," *Purchasing,* February 19, 2004, pp. 35–36.
      - "P-card Makes Purchasing Easier," *CA Magazine,* www.camagazine.com/pcard.
      - Susan Avery, "Building a Print Spend Supply Chain," *Purchasing,* November 18, 2004, pp. 51–52.
      - "Ordering Books from APHA Now Easier Than Ever Before," *Nation's Health,* October 2004, p. 5.

6. *Document design.* The chapter presented examples of a purchase order and a purchase requisition; it also pointed you to a Web site with information about a receiving report. Consider Dreambox Creations, which you read about in this chapter's reading review problem; use the examples and your imagination to design at least one of the three forms for its acquisition/payment process. Use whatever form of information technology your instructor specifies.

7. *Acquisition/payment transactions.* As of January 31, 2005, the accounts payable subsidiary ledger of ABL Corporation revealed the following information:

Vendor Name	Invoice Number	Invoice Date	Invoice Amount	Terms
FNA Corp.	5525	1/6/2005	$1,700	2/15, n/30
FRS Corp.	6217	1/15/2005	1,840	3/15, n/60
CNF Corp.	1457	1/18/2005	1,350	2/10, n/30
APR Corp.	8071	1/22/2005	550	2/10, n/30
CRL Corp.	4687	1/29/2005	360	2/10, n/30

ABL uses a perpetual inventory system; purchases are debited to Inventory and credited to Accounts Payable. The terms shown in the table on the previous page apply to all purchases from a given vendor. During the month of February 2005, ABL completed the following transactions related to its acquisition/payment cycle:

Date	Transaction
1	Purchased equipment for use in the business from FRP Corporation. List price, $10,000. 30% cash down payment, with the remainder on a 3-month, 12% note.
2	Purchased inventory on account from CNF Corporation, $1,500.
3	Paid amount due to CRL Corporation.
11	Purchased supplies on account from FNA Corporation, $700.
13	Paid amount due to CNF Corporation.
17	Purchased supplies on account from FNA Corporation, $500.
20	Paid total amount due to FNA Corporation.
21	Paid half the amount due to FRS Corporation.
24	Returned unused materials to APR Corporation, $100. The materials were part of Invoice 8071.
28	Accrued one month's interest on note payable to FRP Corporation.

a. Record the preceding transactions in general journal format.

b. In addition to that provided by the journal entries, what information would you want to capture in a database about the transactions?

8. *Document information.* The documents discussed in this chapter are listed below on the right. Various information items that might appear in them are listed on the left. For each information item listed on the left, indicate the document(s) in which it would most likely appear with the appropriate letter(s).

__ 1. Vendor name	a. Purchase requisition
__ 2. Items needed	b. Purchase order
__ 3. Vendor address	c. Receiving report
__ 4. Purchasing agent's name	d. Vendor invoice
__ 5. Operating manager's name	e. Check
__ 6. Transaction date	
__ 7. Cost per unit	
__ 8. Total cost of all items	
__ 9. P.O. number	
__10. ABA routing number	

9. *Risk and internal control classification.* Consider the five risks and related internal controls presented in the chapter. Use the taxonomies presented in Chapter 4 to classify the risks as financial, operational, strategic, or hazard and the controls as preventive, detective, or corrective in nature. Be prepared to discuss your classifications.

10. *Internal controls.* (CMA adapted, June 1991) Brock Company is a manufacturer of children's toys and games. The company has been experiencing declining profit margins and is looking for ways to increase operating income. Because of the competitive nature of the industry, Brock is unable to raise its selling prices and must either cut costs or increase productivity.

As the company purchases a variety of raw materials, the volume of paperwork in the Accounts Payable Department is very large, and there are several accounting clerks involved in processing and paying the invoices. The repetitive nature of this work leads to errors because of inattention to details such as part numbers and unit prices. These errors have led to double payments, payments for goods not yet received, and delays in the receipt of raw materials because suppliers that should have been paid have not been paid. These situations often require a great deal of supervisory time to resolve.

The department manager has recommended that increased emphasis be placed on quality control. This would be achieved by increased monitoring of daily output, curtailing talking among staff members, and strict adherence to work hours. All errors would be discussed with the employee, and the staff would be informed that performance evaluations will be negative if errors are not reduced.

Comment on the costs and benefits of Brock's proposed new internal control system in Accounts Payable. Suggest an alternative system that would achieve the same results.

11. *Internal control analysis.* (CMA adapted, December 1992) LCK Corporation manufactures small tools such as hammers and screwdrivers. Many of LCK's employees pocket some of the firm's manufactured tools for their personal use. Since the quantities taken by any one employee were typically immaterial, the individual employees did not consider their actions detrimental to LCK. As the company grew larger, management instituted an internal audit department. The internal auditor charted gross profit percentages for particular tools and discovered higher gross profit rates for tools related to industrial use than for personal use. Subsequent investigation uncovered the fraudulent acts.

As an internal auditor, what steps would you take to uncover the fraud? What additional internal controls should LCK Corporation institute to prevent this problem from occurring in the future?

12. *Crossword puzzle.* Please complete the puzzle below using terminology from the chapter.

Across

2. Purchase ______ : received by vendor from purchasing department.
4. One method for monitoring inventory needs.
6. A ______ -of-interest policy is a recommended internal control.
7. Important in tracking cash disbursements.
8. Organizations exist to create this.
9. The acquisition/payment cycle is concerned with obtaining these.

Down

1. Issues an invoice for customer payment.
3. Purchase ______ : request for purchasing department to order goods.
5. Document ______ can enhance internal control.
7. Companies can create strategic ______ with vendors.

13. *Terminology.* Please match each item on the left with the most appropriate item on the right.

1. Authorize a purchase
2. Bank reconciliation
3. Purchase order
4. Purchase requisition
5. Quantity discounts
6. Receiving report
7. Reorder point
8. Source documents, journal entries, ledger postings
9. Strategic alliance
10. Vendor invoice

a. A way to monitor inventory needs.
b. Audit trail components.
c. Internal control to manage the risk of embezzlement.
d. One reason for consolidating purchase requisitions.
e. Possible internal control for purchasing from inappropriate vendors.
f. Prepared by purchasing department.
g. Promotes separation of duties.
h. Requests customer payment.
i. Several can be combined on one purchase order.
j. Step in the acquisition/payment process.

14. *Multiple choice questions.*

1. PLP Corporation maintains an electronic database file for all its vendors and purchases. Which of the following amounts would you be least likely to find in the "vendor" table?
   a. Total amount owed
   b. Vendor name
   c. Part numbers commonly purchased
   d. All of the above would be included in the vendor table.
2. An accounting clerk debited inventory and credited accounts payable for $500. Which of the following is the most likely source document for that transaction?
   a. Purchase order
   b. Receiving report
   c. Vendor invoice
   d. Purchase requisition
3. In the context of an acquisition/payment process, the three-way match concept applies to which of the following sets of documents?
   a. Purchase requisition, vendor invoice, and remittance advice
   b. Vendor invoice, receiving report, and purchase requisition
   c. Receiving report, purchase order, and vendor invoice
   d. Remittance advice, purchase order, and receiving report

4. Although the ideas associated with the acquisition/payment process are most commonly associated with ______, they also can be applied to ______.
   a. Sales, purchases
   b. Purchases, sales
   c. Inventory, other assets
   d. Supplies, intangibles
5. Which of the following steps in the acquisition/payment process typically happens first?
   a. Purchase goods/services.
   b. Authorize a purchase.
   c. Check vendor credit.
   d. Disburse cash.
6. The difference between a purchase requisition and a purchase order is
   a. Purchase orders are paper, while requisitions are electronic.
   b. Purchase requisitions are electronic, while purchase orders are paper.
   c. Purchase requisitions are purely internal documents; purchase orders leave the company.
   d. Purchase requisitions often have different prices than purchase orders.
7. Which of the following is the best example of a conflict of interest?
   a. RKH Corporation established a list of preferred vendors.
   b. RKH's conflict-of-interest policy was developed by their auditors.
   c. RKH purchases 80 percent of its inventory from a firm where its purchasing agent is a stockholder.
   d. All of the above constitute conflicts of interest.
8. Which documents must be matched before paying a vendor's invoice?
   a. Purchase order, invoice, remittance advice
   b. Purchase requisition, invoice, packing list
   c. Purchase order, invoice, receiving report
   d. Purchase requisition, purchase order, invoice
9. Which of the following would be represented in a data flow diagram with a line?
   a. Prepare purchase order
   b. Inventory file
   c. Vendor
   d. Purchase requisition
10. Which of the following is a form of insurance for employee behavior?
   a. Bonding
   b. Workers' compensation insurance
   c. Property insurance
   d. Life insurance

15. *Statement evaluation.* Indicate whether each statement below is (i) always true, (ii) sometimes true, or (iii) never true. For any statements that are (ii) sometimes true, explain when the statement is true.

a. A bill of lading is required in the acquisition/payment process.
b. A data flow diagram of the acquisition/payment process has six numbered circles.
c. A vendor invoice triggers a cash disbursement event in a well-organized acquisition/payment process.
d. Companies without a conflict-of-interest policy have weak internal control over the acquisition/payment process.

e. Daily bank reconciliations eliminate the need for other forms of internal control over cash.
f. Most of the documents in the acquisition/payment process are paper-based, rather than electronic.
g. Purchase orders are binding contracts between a customer and a vendor.
h. The passage of time triggers events in the acquisition/payment process.
i. The receiving department should have a blind copy of the purchase order.
j. When two signatures are required, blank checks should be signed by one person to promote operating efficiency.

16. *Process relationships.* The steps in the sales/collection and acquisition/payment processes are listed below, but they are out of order. Put the statements in the proper order based on how they occur in organizations.

a. An operating department in the buying organization requests goods and services.
b. The billing department in the selling organization bills the client.
c. The buying organization's receiving department receives the goods.
d. The cash disbursements department in the buying organization disburses cash.
e. The cash receipts department in the selling organization collects payment.
f. The credit department in the selling organization approves the customer's credit.
g. The purchasing department in the buying organization authorizes the purchase.
h. The sales department in the selling organization takes the customer's order.
i. The selling organization's shipping department ships the product.
j. The warehouse in the selling organization fills the order based on approved credit.

Chapter Thirteen

Other Business Processes

AIS in the Business World

Dr. Mohamed Ali

Dr. Mohamed Ali is an internal medicine physician in Upland, California; his office employs two nurses and a physician's assistant. Dr. Ali offers a variety of services, including smoking cessation and weight loss programs, in addition to his regular medical practice. In response to a trend that started as early as 2004, Dr. Ali maintains his patients' medical records electronically using software from Cerner Corporation (www.cerner.com).

Consider the following comments about electronic medical records (EMR) technology:

> [A study discussed in the *Journal of the American College of Surgeons*] reported that in just 16 months the University of Rochester (N.Y.) Medical Center recouped its initial $485,000 cost for an EMR system serving five outpatient offices and 28 doctors. The study compared actual before- and after-EMR costs of activities such as pulling and filing charts, creating new charts and transcription. The savings with electronic medical records added up to $394,000 a year, meaning annual savings of $280,000 after operating costs, the study said.

Advantages of EMR include labor cost savings, improved records accessibility, and the ability to query databases of patient information. Although security and privacy issues create some concern, information security techniques like encryption can help address them.

Discussion Questions

1. What steps would a doctor take to investigate EMR software?
2. How might an accounting professional be involved with EMR software?

Source: R. Roberts, "Electronic Records Provide Good Return on Investment," *Kansas City Business Journal,* June 8–14, 2007, www.cerner.com/public/Cerner_2.asp?id=26328 (January 22, 2009).

The last two chapters have examined, respectively, the sales/collection and acquisition/payment processes. While those two share many commonalities across a variety of contexts, they are not the only important business processes in organizations. In this chapter, we'll look at three additional business processes: conversion, financing, and human resources. These three processes are summarized in a single chapter, not because they are less important or interesting than the others, but because they vary significantly depending upon the size and type of organization in question.

When you finish studying this chapter, you should be able to:

1. Explain the purpose and nature of the conversion, financing, and human resource business processes.
2. Compare and contrast job order and process production systems; explain how they are reflected in the accounting information system.
3. Identify and describe common transactions associated with the financing business process.
4. Identify and describe the forms used in payroll processing.
5. Identify and discuss risks associated with each business process; design and critique internal controls for each risk.
6. Prepare and critique systems documentation for each process.

Our discussion here will be far more conceptual than in the last two chapters; we'll also touch on a few areas that you'll learn about in more depth in other accounting courses.

CONVERSION PROCESS

Your study of cost accounting elsewhere in your accounting curriculum will discuss the conversion process in much greater depth.

Organizations can be classified in several ways in today's economy; one such way is by the basic nature of their operations: service, merchandising/retail, and manufacturing. The **conversion process** is typically associated with manufacturing enterprises; its basic purpose is to convert direct material, direct labor, and manufacturing overhead into a finished product. Collectively, direct material, direct labor, and manufacturing overhead are often referred to as "factors of production." Direct material refers to the major kinds of materials in a product—those you can easily "see" when you look at it. Direct labor refers to the salaries, wages, and benefits of assembly-line workers—people who are directly involved in the manufacture of the product. Manufacturing overhead, sometimes referred to as factory overhead, comprises everything else in the production operation. Items such as factory equipment depreciation, salaries of factory supervisors, factory utilities, and custodial costs are typically included in manufacturing overhead.

Reflection and Self-Assessment 13.1

Pizza, for better or worse, is a staple in the diet of many college students. List at least three specific examples of direct material, direct labor, and overhead associated with making pizza.

Conversion processes can be organized in many different ways, but the three most common are job costing, process costing, and hybrid costing. In **job costing**, goods are produced "to order." Units of product are differentiated; that is, you can tell the difference between them by looking at them. **Process costing**, on the other hand, is most closely associated with undifferentiated, mass-produced goods. While some systems are purely job costing or purely process costing, many combine the two into a hybrid system. In a hybrid system, a "basic unit" might be mass produced, but then customized based on a client's order. You also may have studied standard costing systems, which are often used to track differences (variances) between actual and budgeted performance.

Reflection and Self-Assessment 13.2

Which basic production process (job or process) would be most applicable in each of the following manufacturing settings? Justify your response.

- Automobiles
- Homes
- Office buildings
- Pizza
- Swimming pools
- Textbooks

In a job costing system, costs are accumulated in the accounting information system according to the "job." Generic journal entries associated with job costing are shown below:

Raw materials inventory
  Accounts payable
To record the purchase of raw materials
Job 123A
  Raw materials inventory
  Direct labor
  Manufacturing overhead
To assign costs to Job 123A
Cost of goods sold
  Job 123A
To record the sale of Job 123A

In a process costing system, on the other hand, costs are accumulated according to production processes. Units are undifferentiated, so they cannot be tracked in separate jobs. Generic journal entries associated with process costing are shown below:

Raw materials inventory
  Accounts payable
To record the purchase of raw materials
Work in Process—Department A
  Raw materials inventory
  Direct labor
  Manufacturing overhead
To assign costs to Department A
Work in Process—Department B
  Work in Process—Department A
To transfer costs from Dept. A to Dept. B
Work in Process—Department B
  Direct labor
  Manufacturing overhead
To add labor & overhead costs incurred in Dept. B
Finished Goods
  Work in Process—Department B
To move units from Dept. B to Finished Goods
Cost of Goods Sold
  Finished Goods
To record the sale of finished units

TABLE 13.1 Forms Used in Manufacturing

Form Name	Purpose	Originator	Recipient
Materials requisition	Requests raw material from the warehouse for production	Production	Warehouse
Job cost sheet	Summarizes the material, labor, and overhead costs in a job costing system	Production	Accounting
Labor time ticket	Accumulates labor data (time, pay rate, total labor cost)	Production	Accounting
Production cost report	Summarizes cost and quantity information in a process costing system	Production	Accounting
Materials move ticket	Documents the movement of materials from the warehouse into production	Warehouse	Production

As with the other business processes we've examined, you'd expect to find some common forms in a manufacturing environment. Table 13.1 discusses some of them.

Many of the internal control processes we've discussed already can be applied to conversion cycle activities as well. For example, raw materials must be safeguarded; in many cases, raw materials require special storage conditions to remain usable. Internal controls such as adequate documentation (as with the forms listed above), physical safeguards (such as locked doors and cameras), and backup power supplies for air conditioners and other environmental regulators can help an organization achieve its objectives with respect to raw materials. Separation of duties applies here as well—in many organizations, physical custody of raw materials is in the warehouse. Authorization for their use comes from production in the form of material requisitions; the accounting department takes care of journal entries. To the extent that a conversion process involves equipment, that equipment must be kept safe and properly maintained to ensure efficient operations. Periodic training on issues such as equipment operations and safety are important internal controls for the human element of conversion systems.

Consider the process of writing a textbook like this one. Authors and publishers typically go through a set of steps such as those listed below:

1. *Author:* Develop a textbook proposal. The proposal includes a general overview of the book and a sample first chapter. The author sends the materials to the publisher for review.
2. *Publisher:* Accept or reject the proposal. If accepted, prepare standard contracts governing the development and publication process.
3. *Author:* Write chapter drafts based on the proposal. Submit the drafts to the publisher in batches.
4. *Publisher:* Solicit professors in the field to review the chapters as they are submitted. Reviews consist of responses to a common set of questions.
5. *Publisher:* Summarize and analyze the reviewers' responses. Send them to the author.
6. *Author:* Revise chapters as necessary based on reviewer feedback. Submit revised chapters to publisher.
7. *Publisher:* Publish and print the text.

Figure 13.1 shows a flowchart depicting those steps.

Misek (2004) discussed the conversion process for Purcell Productions, "a full-service digital video production studio located in Alta Loma, California." Purcell follows a job costing system, as each job is unique. The steps in the company's conversion process include

FIGURE 13.1 Conversion Process Flowchart

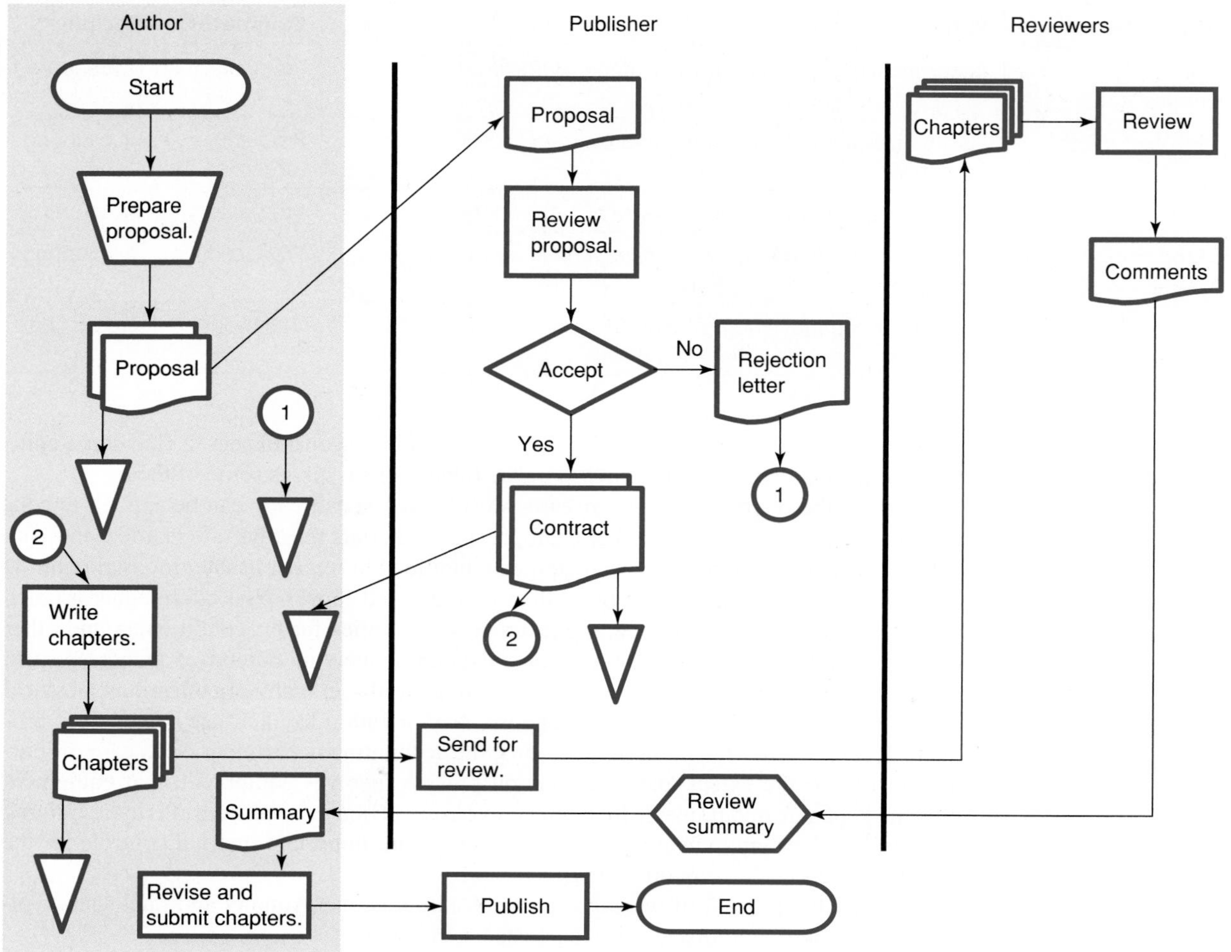

1. Assemble a video crew for the job.
2. Two days before the event, clean, label, and pack all the cameras and tapes for transport to the job site. The company typically employs at least half a dozen cameras for a single job, thus increasing the chance of getting important parts of the event on film.
3. One day before the event, put all the cameras in place.
4. Shoot the event.
5. Use computer software to synchronize the views from the various cameras.
6. Edit the synchronized views according to client length specifications (e.g., roughly an hour for an automobile race or other motor sports event).
7. Output the edited film to a master camera and make copies according to the client's formatting needs (e.g., DVD, VHS, MPG).

Purcell would likely use a database to maintain names and contact information for video crew candidates. Naturally, the steps in this company's conversion process are significantly different than what you'd expect to find in, for example, an agricultural company or heavy-equipment manufacturer. The key in understanding the conversion process is to understand

Reflection and Self-Assessment 13.3

Draw a flowchart to depict the conversion process at Purcell Productions. What information would you want to capture in the "video crew" database? What other databases are indicated by the narrative? (You may find it helpful to read the Misek article.)

the company's operations. AIS designers and auditors can gather data via direct observation, interview, and/or survey, then prepare a flowchart to ensure that they understand the process thoroughly.

The risks managers confront in the conversion cycle are as unique as the steps in the cycle itself. In the Purcell Productions case, risks and controls that may help address them include

Risk	Control
Stolen equipment	Engraved identification Recorded serial numbers
Unreliable staff	Fidelity bonding Regular performance evaluations
Malfunctioning equipment	Backup equipment Regular periodic testing
Bad weather contributing to poor output	Production insurance Extra lighting for cloudy days
Software malfunction	Backup software

As you learned in Chapter 4, the idea in risk assessment and internal control design is to understand the overall operation. Then, you can think of the most likely problems and create controls to mitigate those problems.

FINANCING PROCESS

Courses in intermediate accounting cover the technical aspects of these transactions, while finance courses explore them from a conceptual perspective with discussions of optimal capital structure and weighted average cost of capital.

The **financing process** deals with transactions between an organization and its stockholders, as well as between an organization and its long-term creditors. Financial statement users see the results of the financing process in the long-term debt and equity sections of a balance sheet; those same sections are associated with cash flows from financing activities on the statement of cash flows.

From an accounting information systems point of view, we need to track data associated with the following **financing process transactions**:

1. Issuance of capital stock:
   a. Number of shares
   b. Par value per share
   c. Market value per share
   d. Shareholder identification data (such as name and address)
2. Purchase of treasury shares:
   a. Number of shares
   b. Price per share
   c. Shareholder identification data

Treasury shares can be accounted for at par, but most organizations use the cost method.

3. Long-term debt transactions (issuance and repayment):
   a. Principal
   b. Coupon interest rate
   c. Market interest rate at time of issuance
   d. Time to repayment
   e. Number of annual interest payments
   f. Lender identification data
4. Dividend distributions:
   a. Type of dividend (cash, stock, property)
   b. Shareholder identification data
   c. Amount of dividend
   d. Dates
      i. Declaration
      ii. Record
      iii. Distribution

An initial public offering (IPO), as the name implies, marks the first time a company offers its securities for sale on a recognized stock exchange. The recordkeeping is more involved in an IPO than in subsequent securities transactions; for more information, point your Web browser to www.entrepreneur.com or do a Google search.

While those four transactions are by no means exhaustive, they are the most common types you're likely to encounter in an accounting information system.

Reflection and Self-Assessment 13.4

Select one of the four common transactions listed above. Using a software tool specified by your instructor, create a database that contains the necessary information for the transaction you select. Keep in mind the principles of database normalization as you complete this task.

In August 2005, Federated Department Stores (www.fds.com) completed an acquisition of the May Department Stores Company. Federated's Web site described the financial arrangements for stockholders associated with the merger: "Under terms of the merger agreement, May Company shareholders as of the time of merger on Aug. 30, 2005, will receive $17.75 in cash and 0.3115 shares of Federated common stock for each share of May Company common stock." Consider the data flow diagram in Figure 13.2 illustrating the steps involved in fulfilling that agreement.

Clearly, the biggest risk associated with the financing business process is the misappropriation of cash, either through skimming or larceny. The internal controls over cash discussed in the previous chapters are at least as applicable to the financing business process: separation of duties, bank reconciliations, and adequate documentation, to name a few. Other risks here include missing payment deadlines and insufficient cash to repay principal. Missing payment deadlines can be addressed via automatic electronic funds transfers or simple scheduling software installed on accounting department computers. A sinking fund can be used to mitigate the risk of insufficient cash to repay principal. As you may know, a sinking fund is a pool of money restricted to just one purpose: debt repayment. Because of the time value of money, a borrower can put small amounts of cash into a sinking fund throughout the life of the debt; when it matures, then, the sinking fund has sufficient cash to handle the transaction. Finally, a lender also may institute a debt covenant as

FIGURE 13.2 Stock Conversion Data Flow Diagram

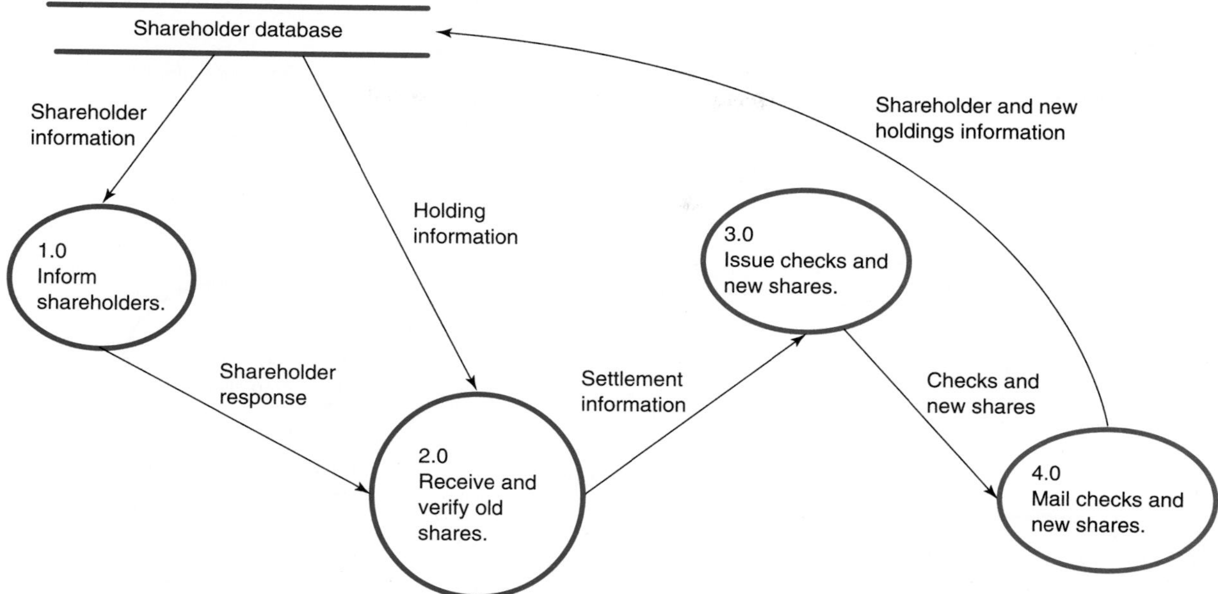

an internal control. Debt covenants may restrict the borrower's ability to pay dividends to shareholders, specify a minimum current ratio level throughout the life of the debt, or hold the borrowing organization accountable for its overall financial leverage.

HUMAN RESOURCE PROCESS

The **human resource process** may be the most complex of all business processes today. Whole textbooks, courses, and fields of study have been devoted to its objectives, which include

- Hiring employees.
- Paying them.
- Coordinating employee benefits (insurance, pensions, and the like).
- Evaluating their performance.
- Managing their departures from the firm via termination, quitting, or retirement.

Consider the data flow diagram in Figure 13.3, which illustrates the preceding steps in the human resource process.

The Web site of the Professionals in Human Resources Association (www.pihra.org) lists many similar organizations involved in virtually all facets of the human resource process.

Because of its complexity and legal implications, many organizations outsource their human resource functions to organizations such as ADP.

In accounting information systems, the main concern is capturing the data necessary to make informed decisions in each of the preceding areas, as well as providing sufficient cost-effective internal controls to mitigate human resource risks. Capturing necessary data is most often accomplished via paper-based or electronic **payroll forms,** such as those listed in Table 13.2.

The risks associated with the human resource process fall into two major groups: financial and human. Financially, managers must ensure that they have sufficient cash on hand

FIGURE 13.3 Human Resource Process Data Flow Diagram

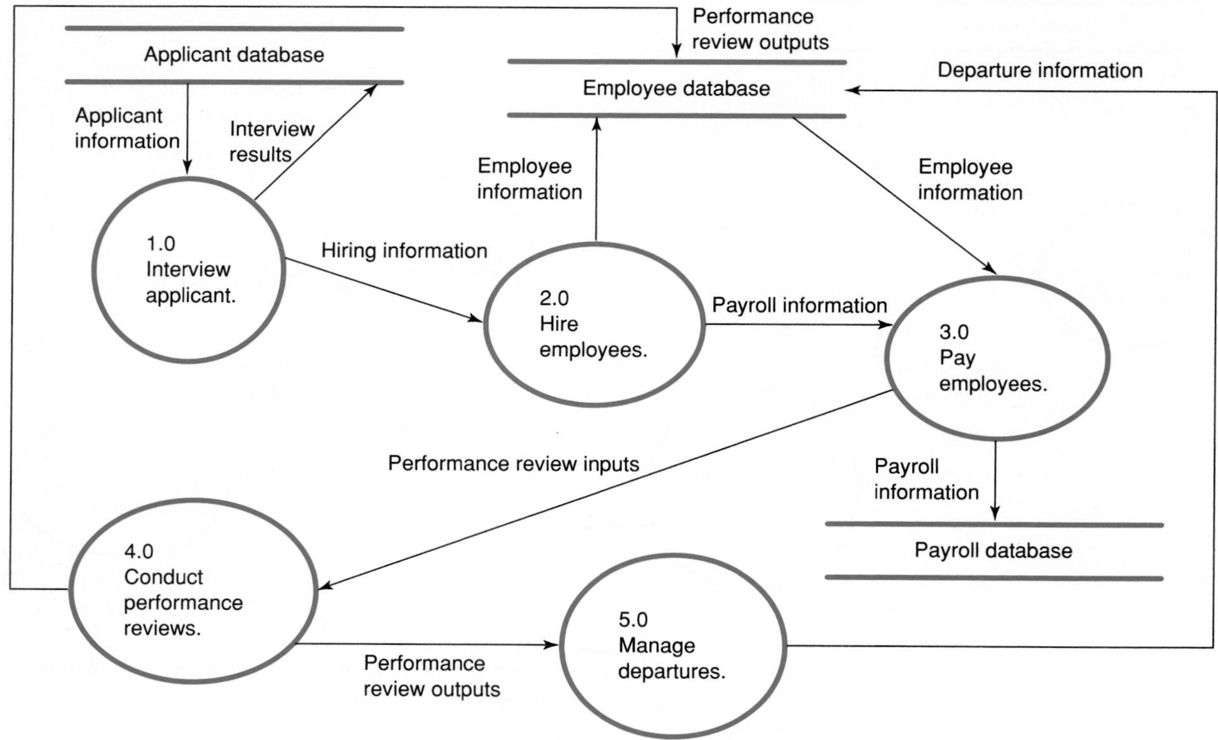

to meet payroll obligations; for that reason, companies often maintain a payroll checking account separate from their regular operating accounts. In addition, companies that pay employees by the hour typically need a way of tracking hours worked; Internet time-tracking systems or even simple time clocks mitigate the risk that hours will be recorded and reported inaccurately. When employees depart the company, whether through quitting, termination, or retirement, their access to organizational information systems (e.g., intranet accounts, passwords) should be eliminated to mitigate the risks of hacking, sabotage, and other forms of fraud.

Human risks in this business process are equally significant; some might say the human risks are weightier than the financial risks because of their long-term nature and potential for costly litigation. Human risks associated with the HR business process include hiring unqualified workers, failing to follow applicable laws (such as the Americans with Disabilities Act), engaging in acts of sexual harassment, and illegal or inappropriate employee terminations. Perhaps the best internal control for all those risks is a well-informed, educated human resources staff. Seeking the advice of legal counsel also may be appropriate in some cases; adequate documentation of human resource processes is essential, regardless of the type of organization under consideration.

Fraud is also a significant risk associated with employees. Internal controls that can help prevent and detect fraud include

- *Thorough background checks.* Several years ago, one of my students applied for a job with the federal government. The agency sent a representative to my home to ask me about the student, who had listed me as a reference.

TABLE 13.2 Payroll Forms

Form Name	Purpose	Data Included
Form W-4	Establishes payroll withholding status	Employee identification data Withholding status Number of withholding allowances
Form W-2	Reports year-end information for tax purposes	Employee identification data Employer identification data Gross pay and tax withholdings 401(k) contributions
Payroll register	Computes payroll data for all employees for a given pay period	Employee identification data Hours worked Pay rate Total gross pay Tax and benefit withholdings Net pay
Employee earnings record	Summarizes payroll data for a single employee for multiple pay periods	Virtually the same as the payroll register
Form 1099	Reports amounts paid to an independent contractor (I.C.)	I.C. identification data Payer's identification data Total amount paid
Form 940	Reports employer's federal unemployment taxes	Company name Amount paid
Form 941	Reports amounts withheld by employer to IRS	Company name Employee identification data Amounts withheld

Reflection and Self-Assessment 13.5

Visit the Web site of the Internal Revenue Service (www.irs.gov) and find examples of all the preceding forms except the payroll register and employee earnings record. (The design of those two forms can vary significantly from organization to organization.)

- *Forced vacations.* You may be thinking, "Why would anyone need to be forced to take a vacation?" Consider the case of accounts receivable lapping. A/R lapping occurs when a clerk steals money sent by one client, then uses money from another client to cover up the theft. For example, a clerk might steal money from Smith; then, when Jones pays her bill, the clerk would credit Jones's cash to Smith's account. Maintaining a lapping system requires an ongoing fraud; so, if an employee is forced to take a vacation, there's a greater chance of detecting the fraud than if vacations are not mandatory.
- *Adequate training and supervision.* We've looked at this control in connection with other business processes, but it's worth repeating here. Training can help promote effective and efficient operations, while adequate supervision can help safeguard assets.

While those controls will not prevent problems completely, they will be very effective in limiting opportunities to commit fraud.

CRITICAL THINKING

On January 1 of every year, the Tournament of Roses Parade winds its way down Colorado Boulevard in Pasadena, California. And, later that day, two football teams square off for the Rose Bowl. Check out www.tournamentofroses.com for information about both events.

As part of the Rose Parade, organizations from all over the world prepare floats; in 2009, the list included the City of Anaheim, Jack in the Box, and the National Association of Realtors. The two polytechnic universities in the California State University system (Cal Poly Pomona and Cal Poly San Luis Obispo) have a unique way of creating a float for the parade. The schools solicit design ideas from their students; after selecting a winner, each university builds half of the float. The two halves are joined in Pasadena, where the float is finished.

The tournament's Web site, referenced above, describes the float-building process like this:

> Float construction begins shortly after the previous year's Parade is over. The process starts with a specially built chassis, upon which is built a framework of steel and chicken wire. In a process called "cocooning," the frame is sprayed with a polyvinyl material, which is then painted in the colors of the flowers to be applied later. Every inch of the float must be covered with flowers or other natural materials, such as leaves, seeds, or bark. Volunteer workers swarm over the floats in the days after Christmas, their hands and clothes covered with glue and petals. The most delicate flowers are placed in individual vials of water, which are set into the float one by one.

Creating a Rose Parade float is an application of the conversion process because the factors of production (material, labor, and overhead) are combined into a finished product. Figure 13.4 presents a flowchart of how the float creation process works for the Cal Poly universities. The processes depicted in the flowchart (solicit ideas, submit proposals,

FIGURE 13.4
Systems Flowchart of Rose Parade Float Conversion Process

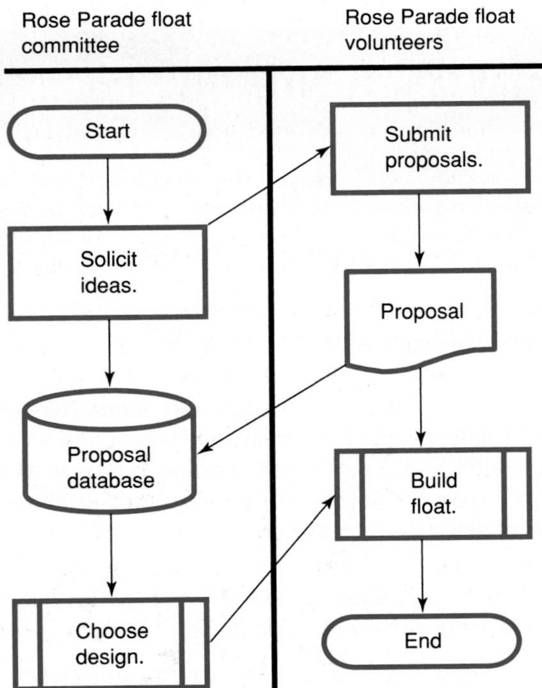

choose design, and build float) would be represented with numbered circles in a leveled set of data flow diagrams. The "build float" process would probably be decomposed at least one level based on the steps described above.

At Cal Poly Pomona, many student organizations, such as Beta Alpha Psi, work on the Rose Parade float as part of their community service efforts. Thus, the system would need a database for tracking volunteer participation. One good way to organize that database would be with three tables. A "task table" would list the various tasks available to volunteers (build chassis, cocoon float, place materials), while a "volunteer table" would provide details for each volunteer (volunteer ID, last name, first name, organizational affiliation, e-mail, phone number). Because each volunteer can complete many tasks and each task can be completed by many volunteers, a "task/volunteer" junction table also would be required. Each record in the junction table would need fields for the date, number of hours worked (or starting and finishing times), task name, and volunteer ID.

PROCESS RELATIONSHIPS

This chapter concludes our examination of business processes. In total, we've looked at five: sales/collection, acquisition/payment, conversion, financing, and human resources. We studied the business processes separately to focus attention on the issues for each one, but, in real organizations, the processes are interrelated and highly dependent on one another.

Organizations typically need three kinds of resources to function effectively: people, money, and other assets (such as supplies, inventory, and equipment). The *human resource* process is concerned with people—how do organizations find them, train them, compensate them, and manage their separation from the company (e.g., through retirement or termination)? The *financing* process is associated with money—in particular, funds obtained from outside the company. Those funds typically come in the form of debt and equity financing. The *acquisition/payment* process is concerned with other kinds of assets: inventory, office equipment, factory machinery, supplies, and furniture, for example. The *conversion* process is particularly applicable to manufacturers, but also has implications for other types of organizations. In the conversion process, manufacturing companies combine raw material, direct labor, and manufacturing overhead to create a finished product. Finally, then, the company sells its product (or service) through the *sales/collection* process.

Summary

This chapter has provided an overview of the conversion, financing, and human resource business processes. Here is a summary of the chapter's main points:

1. *Explain the purpose and nature of the conversion, financing, and human resource business processes.* The conversion process covers the ways in which organizations manufacture products from raw materials; its concepts and ideas also can be applied in limited ways to service and retail organizations. The financing process deals with the right side of a balance sheet—long-term debt and equity transactions. It deals with ways in which an organization acquires external financing. The human resource business process is extremely comprehensive, covering the activities from hiring to termination.
2. *Compare and contrast job order and process production systems; explain how they are reflected in the accounting information system.* Job order costing systems are most applicable when goods are differentiated from one another; that is, when you can tell them apart just by looking at them. In the AIS, ledger accounts are organized based on specific jobs. Process costing systems are best used with undifferentiated goods; costs are tracked by processes, rather than jobs.

3. *Identify and describe common transactions associated with the financing business process.* Common transactions associated with the financing process include
   a. Issuing capital stock.
   b. Purchasing treasury shares.
   c. Distributing dividends.
   d. Borrowing money via long-term debt.
   e. Re1paying borrowed funds.
4. *Identify and describe the forms used in payroll processing.* Payroll processing forms include
   a. Form W-4.
   b. Form W-2.
   c. Payroll register.
   d. Employee earnings record.
   e. Form 1099.
   f. Form 940.
   g. Form 941.
5. *Identify and discuss risks associated with each business process; design and critique internal controls for each risk.* Risks in the conversion, financing, and human resources processes can be somewhat unique; understanding an organization's overall operation is important. Specific risks common to many organizations include (but are not limited to) damaged inventory in the conversion process, embezzlement in the financing process, and failure to follow applicable laws in the human resource process. The risk of damaged inventory can be mitigated by carefully designed production systems; embezzlement opportunities can be reduced by such common controls as bank reconciliations and separation of duties. Failure to follow applicable human resource laws can be controlled by good training and documentation.
6. *Prepare and critique systems documentation for each process.* The chapter provides examples of systems documentation for each of the processes discussed in it. Those generic documents may require significant modification in specific organizational contexts due to the specialized nature of the conversion, human resource, and financing business processes.

As with the sales/collection and acquisition/payment processes, however, the key is developing a broad and deep understanding of the organization for which you're working. That understanding will facilitate your analysis of the accounting information systems issues associated with all three processes.

Key Terms

conversion process, *249*
financing process, *253*
financing process transactions, *253*
human resource process, *255*
job costing, *249*
payroll forms, *255*
process costing, *250*

Chapter Reference

Misek, M. 2004. "Home Is Where the Art Is." *Emedia,* August, pp. 36–38.

End-of-Chapter Activities

1. *Reading review questions.*
   a. What is the basic purpose of each business process discussed in this chapter (conversion, financing, human resources)?
   b. What are the similarities and differences between job costing and process costing systems? How is each system reflected in the organization of the accounting information system?
   c. What are the four common transactions associated with the financing business process? What information must be tracked for each transaction?
   d. What forms are commonly used in processing payroll transactions?
   e. How are the purposes of internal control fulfilled in each business process discussed in the chapter?
   f. Respond to the questions for this chapter's "AIS in the Business World."
2. *Reading review problem.* Mhlume Sugar Company Ltd. (MSC) is a sugar refinery in the kingdom of Swaziland, a small nation bordering South Africa. Here's a description of MSC's conversion process for changing sugarcane into raw sugar.

   MSC's harvesting cycle begins roughly around May 1 each year and ends roughly in November or December. Harvesting the cane involves two basic steps. First, the standing fields of sugarcane are burned; burning removes the leaves from the standing cane and facilitates the harvesting process. For harvesting, migrant workers are engaged each year to cut down the cane by hand. Workers are paid a fixed daily salary with the possibility of earning incentive pay for cutting more than their daily quota. Harvesting the cane is a very labor-intensive process, making it well-suited to the Swazi economy, where labor resources are plentiful but machinery is not. The cut cane is transported to Mhlume's mill. On arrival at the mill, the cut cane is crushed to extract the liquid from its core. The liquid is heated, causing the sucrose to fall to the bottom, where it can be collected for further processing. At this point, the sucrose itself is dark and thick, resembling molasses. Chemicals are added to the sucrose to cause crystallization into the brown sugar that is the mill's principal product.

   Source: R. Hurt, "Mhlume Sugar Company Limited: A Case Study in Costing and Pricing," *Journal of Interdisciplinary Studies,* Fall 1996.

   a. What kind of costing system is Mhlume using? Explain your response.
   b. Why is it important for accounting professionals to understand the operational aspects of an organization in designing and evaluating its AIS?
   c. How are the other business processes you've studied related to Mhlume's conversion process?
3. *Making choices and exercising judgment.*
   a. In the last three chapters, you've learned about five different business processes: sales/collection, acquisition/payment, conversion, financing, and human resources. Draw a diagram or write a paper that explains the connections between the five.
   b. Phil and Lil are the owners of Planters for All, a company that makes small decorative planters for homes and offices. Their planters come in various shapes, including a well with a bucket, a telephone, a wheelbarrow, and others. Each shape can be made in two sizes: large and small. If you were advising Phil and Lil about setting up their production process, would you recommend a job costing system or a process costing system? Why?
   c. PKT Corporation has annual sales of $1,600,000 and a profit margin averaging 8 percent. The corporation employs 40 people and currently does its payroll processing internally. Typically, the two accounting staff spend one day every two weeks calculating and processing payroll; each accounting staff member's annual salary is $48,000. The president of PKT has asked your advice regarding outsourcing payroll processing. List and discuss at least three factors you would tell the president to consider in making this decision. Based on the data provided, should PKT outsource its payroll or keep doing it internally?

4. *Field exercises.*
   a. Look online or in your local Yellow Pages for a company that manufactures a product. Arrange an interview with a member of the company's accounting staff and a tour of its production facilities. Prepare a brief presentation or paper discussing the results of your research.
   b. Contact a local human resources professional or an attorney that specializes in labor law. Ask about legislation that impacts the human resource function in organizations, such as the Americans with Disabilities Act, the Family and Medical Leave Act, the Occupational Safety and Health Act, or the Immigration Reform and Control Act, or about the company's policies with regard to sexual harassment, substance abuse testing, or use of information technology. Prepare a brief presentation or paper discussing the results of your research.
5. *Costing systems.* Indicate whether each of the following types of businesses would be more likely to use a job or process costing system. Justify your choices.
   a. Architect
   b. Attorney
   c. Dentist
   d. Heavy-equipment manufacturer
   e. House painter
   f. Landscaper
   g. Magazine publisher
   h. Management consultant
   i. Pet groomer
   j. Tax preparer
6. *Transaction and business processes.* Which business process (conversion, financing, or human resources) is most closely associated with each transaction listed below?

a. Payroll taxes expense
   Cash
	f. Retained earnings
	   Capital stock

b. Manufacturing overhead
   Accumulated depreciation
	g. Work in process
	   Manufacturing overhead

c. Treasury stock
   Cash
	h. Interest expense
	Premium on bonds payable
	   Interest payable

d. Cash
   Capital stock
   Additional paid-in capital
	i. Cash
	Discount on bonds payable
	   Bonds payable

e. Payroll expense
   Wages payable
   Withholding taxes payable
	j. Cost of goods sold
	   Finished goods

7. *Transaction explanations.* Explain what is happening in each transaction presented in the previous exercise. For example, in transaction (*a*), the company is paying its share of payroll taxes.
8. *Payroll computations and analysis.* Eric is the president and chief executive officer of his own management consulting firm. He has five employees: Jon Jones, Lupe Bana, Austin Pei, Diane Driscoll, and Yu Chung Wright. Selected information for each employee is listed in the table below:

	Marital Status	Withholding Allowances	Hourly Wage	Hours Worked
Jon	Single	0	$50	80
Lupe	Single	1	65	85
Austin	Married	3	60	81
Diane	Married	3	55	90
Yu Chung	Married	4	40	75

Employees have three kinds of taxes withheld from their wages: federal income, state income, and Social Security. Social Security is withheld from all employees at 9.75 percent of their gross pay. Single employees have federal income tax withheld at a base rate of $200 plus $50 for each withholding allowance; married employees' federal tax withholding is $150 plus $25 for each withholding allowance. State income tax is withheld at 30 percent of the federal amount for each employee. Employees are paid every two weeks and receive 1.5 times their regular hourly wage for any hours in excess of 80. In addition, Jon and Austin contribute $50 each pay period to an employee pension fund; Lupe and Diane contribute $75 each pay period for group health insurance.

Using Access or Excel, prepare a payroll register based on the preceding data. Then, prepare a report for Eric that shows the average gross pay and the average hourly wage for all five employees. Finally, prepare a pie-chart graph for each employee showing the breakdown of gross pay into each amount withheld and net pay. (An example for Jon is shown below.)

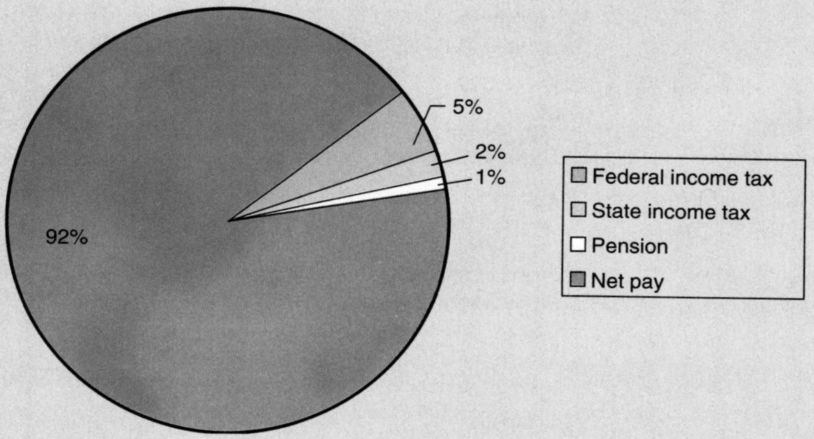

9. *Payroll forms data.* Several data items that might be included on a payroll form are listed below on the left. The standard payroll forms discussed in the chapter are listed below on the right. For each data item, indicate the form(s) on which you'd find it.

a. Address of employee	1. Form 940
b. Employee name	2. Form 941
c. Employer identification number	3. Form 1099
d. Federal income tax withheld	4. Form W-2
e. Location of employer	5. Form W-4
f. Marital status	
g. Number of withholding allowances	
h. Social Security number	
i. State income tax withheld	
j. Unemployment tax paid—federal	

10. *Forms design.*

a. Use Access (or another software tool specified by your instructor) to design a form that captures basic data for the human resource process. At a minimum, it should include the employee's name, address, and phone; department or job classification; and e-mail address. Populate the form with data from yourself and three of your friends.

b. Design a materials requisition form for the conversion process. The materials requisition form should include the requestor's name and department, the date of the request, and the type and amount of material issued. It also may include a place to indicate the type and amount of any material returned to the warehouse.

c. Design a labor time ticket for a job costing environment. The document should include the employee's name and identification number, as well as the hours worked on each job. It also should incorporate the date(s) worked.

11. *Risk analysis and internal controls.* In each independent situation below, identify and describe at least three risks. For each risk, suggest two internal controls to address it.

a. (CMA adapted, June 1992) Midwest Electronics Corp. manufactures computers. Recently, its products have met stiff competition from lower-priced imports, and the firm is seeking ways to improve its workers' productivity in order to maintain its market share. Over lunch in the company cafeteria, Alice Kumar (manager of the Accounting Department) and Greg Mossman (manager of the Sales Department) recently discussed a presentation made to the management of Midwest by a consultant on employee motivation. In the course of the conversation, Kumar recalled what happened at Spokane Computer Associates, her former employer. A national labor union had sought repeatedly to unionize the workers at the plant but had never succeeded. There was very little turnover among the workers, and the plant was considered a safe and pleasant place to work. Salaries were relatively high, and workers earned not only a base salary but incentive bonuses based on their individual output and company profits.

b. (CMA adapted, June 1992) Alaire Corporation manufactures several different types of printed circuit boards; however, two of the boards account for the majority of the company's sales. The first of these boards, a television circuit board, has been a standard in the industry for several years. The market for this type of board is competitive and, therefore, price sensitive. Alaire plans to sell 65,000 television circuit boards next year at a price of $150 each. The second high-volume product, a personal computer circuit board, is a recent addition to the company's product line. Because it incorporates the latest technology, it can be sold at a premium price; next year's budget calls for the sale of 40,000 personal computer boards at a price of $300 each.

c. (CMA adapted, December 1991) Microtronics Inc. is a private company involved in genetic engineering. The company was started several years ago by Joseph Graham, a scientist, and is financed by a group of venture capitalists. Microtronics has had some successful research, and one of its products recently received approval from the Federal Drug Administration (FDA). Two other products have been submitted to the FDA and are awaiting approval. Because of these successes, the investors believe the time is right for preparing the company for a public stock offering.

d. (CMA adapted, December 1991) Princess Corporation grows, processes, packages, and sells three apple products: sliced apples used in frozen pies, applesauce, and apple juice. The outside skin of the apple, which is removed in the Cutting Department and processed as animal feed, is treated as a by-product. In the company's conversion process, the Cutting Department washes the apples and removes the outside skin. The apples are then cored and trimmed for slicing; the three main products and the by-product are recognizable after processing in the Cutting Department. Each product is then transferred to a separate department for final processing. The trimmed apples are forwarded to the Slicing Department, where they are sliced and frozen. Any juice generated during the slicing operation is frozen with the slices. The pieces of apple trimmed from the fruit are processed into applesauce in the Crushing Department. Again, the juice generated during this operation is used in the applesauce. The core and any surplus apple generated from the Cutting Department are pulverized into a liquid in the Juicing Department. The outside skin is chopped into animal feed and packaged in the Feed Department.

e. (CMA adapted, June 1994) Damian Information Inc. is a four-year-old information processing and software development company serving a number of small clients in the midwestern

United States. As its customer base has grown, DAI has increased its staff to 30 employees. The company has been considering an arrangement whereby they would lease employees. Currently, there are in excess of 400 employee leasing companies in the United States representing nearly one million workers. The major users of this service are companies that need fewer than 100 workers. If DAI were to enter into an employee-leasing arrangement, all of DAI's current employees would become employees of the leasing company and then leased back to DAI.

f. (CMA adapted, June 1994) Richmond Inc. operates a chain of department stores located in the northwest. The first store began operations in 1965 and the company has steadily grown to its present size of 44 stores. Two years ago, the board of directors of Richmond approved a large-scale remodeling of its stores to attract a more upscale clientele. Before finalizing these plans, two stores were remodeled as a test. Linda Perlman, assistant controller, was asked to oversee the financial reporting for these test stores, and she and other management personnel were offered bonuses based on the sales growth and profitability of these stores. Based on the apparent success of the test (sales growth for the two stores was reported at 11 percent and profitability showed a 14 percent increase), the board is now considering two alternatives for financing the balance of the remodeling effort. Alternative one involves pure debt financing. The company would make a public offering of bonds with a face value of $30 million and a stated interest rate of 11 percent. Alternative two is a combination alternative. It would involve $12 million in 9 percent bonds, common stock of $14.5 million, and retained earnings of $4.5 million. The current market value of Richmond's common stock is $30 per share; the dividends per share have held steady at $3.00 per share for the last year, but investors are expecting growth of 6 percent in the dividend.

12. *Systems documentation.* In each of the following independent cases, document the system using whatever technique(s) your instructor specifies.

a. The two previous chapters introduced you do Dreambox Creations, Dreambox partners with Automatic Data Processing Inc. (ADP) for its payroll processing. Dreambox employs Internet-based time tracking. Employees log in and out based on the client for whom they're working; in that way, the company can track billable hours, which feed into the sales/collection process. (The concept of billable hours is also important in other professional organizations such as law firms and CPA firms.) Dan, in charge of operations and information technology, summarizes each employee's hours on a biweekly basis. He transmits them to ADP electronically or via telephone; ADP then processes the payroll, including all tax withholdings and deposits. ADP also handles Dreambox's year-end reporting via W-2 forms. Dreambox maintains a payroll account separate from its regular operating cash account for internal control purposes. ADP sends paper checks drawn on the payroll account back to Dan, who distributes them to the employees. The checks lag the pay period by one week; for example, checks for the pay period January 10 to January 21 are distributed on January 28.

b. Point your Web browser to www.sba.gov, the Web site for the Small Business Administration. The SBA is a federal organization that helps entrepreneurs start and manage businesses. Click the link for "Financing Your Business." Browse the topics under "Financing Eligibility Topics" as the basis for documenting the system.

c. Hiring new faculty is one of the most important human resource processes for universities. The department chair requests funding for a new full-time position and sends it to the dean, who approves or rejects the request. If approved, the department selects a faculty hiring committee. Their first task is to prepare a position description, which must be approved by the university's human resource office. The position description is submitted by the search committee to various Web sites, professional organizations, and periodicals; candidates submit required documentation for consideration. The committee reviews the required documentation and selects a small number of candidates for phone interviews. Based on the phone interviews, a few candidates (perhaps three to five) are invited to an on-campus interview. Based on feedback from references and on-campus interviews, the hiring committee forwards names to the dean, who makes the final selection. The dean's office sends out offer letters, which are either accepted or rejected by the applicant.

d. Geoff is a Registered Tax Preparer in the State of California. Each year, he renews his registration on the Web site of the California Tax Education Council (www.ctec.org/). Geoff then makes his advertising plans for the year, which usually include direct mail flyers and classified ads in local newspapers. He also sends out appointment cards to his clients from the previous year; about 80 percent of them hire Geoff again. Clients call Geoff to make an appointment; Geoff maintains his appointment schedule in his personal digital assistant (PDA). He uses commercial software to prepare and e-file each client's return.

e. Corporations that want to prepare for an initial public offering (IPO) generally follow a seven-step process for doing so. (1) Hire an investment bank. (2) Work with the investment bank to prepare an underwriting agreement—a contract that governs the IPO. (3) File a registration statement with the Securities and Exchange Commission. (4) Wait for SEC staff to verify the information in the registration statement—this step is often referred to as a "cooling off period." (5) Issue a preliminary prospectus. (6) Conduct one or more due diligence meetings with accountants, lawyers, and company management. (7) Issue the final prospectus.

13. *Database design.*

a. Consider the May Company/Federated Department Stores data flow diagram presented in Figure 13.2. What information would you want to capture in the shareholder database to facilitate the conversion transaction?

b. Consider the generic human resource process data flow diagram presented in Figure 13.3. What information would you want to capture in the employee database and/or payroll database to facilitate the indicated processes?

c. Consider one or more of the diagrams you prepared in Activity 12 above. Create the specifications for any database tables, included in those diagrams.

14. *Crossword puzzle.* Please complete the puzzle below using terminology from the chapter.

Across

1. Factory equipment depreciation classification.
6. Risk associated with financing process.
8. One of three business processes discussed in the chapter.
9. One type of dividend.

Down

2. One of three business processes discussed in the chapter.
3. Costing system for undifferentiated goods.
4. What many companies do with payroll processing.
5. One of three business processes discussed in the chapter.
7. Stated interest rate on long-term debt.
8. Method used for most treasury stock transactions.

15. *Terminology.* Please match each item on the left with the most appropriate item on the right.

1. Custom-made bicycles
2. Date of record
3. Direct material
4. Electronic funds transfer
5. Factory supplies
6. Number of interest payments
7. Observation
8. Par value of a share
9. Pencils
10. Time clock

a. Associated with dividend payments
b. Human resource process internal control
c. Internal control for missed payments
d. Job costing product
e. Method for gathering data
f. Needed for stock issuance transaction
g. Overhead
h. Process costing product
i. Required data for long-term debt transactions
j. Steel, for an automobile

16. *Multiple choice questions.*

1. The after-tax cost of debt would be most closely associated with the ______ process.
   a. Conversion
   b. Human resource
   c. Financing
   d. Bookkeeping
2. A company that reproduces fine works of art, such as the Mona Lisa, would most likely use what kind of production process?
   a. Hybrid
   b. Conversion
   c. Job
   d. Process
3. A journal entry in a company's accounting information system debited retained earnings. The purpose of the journal entry is most likely
   a. To record the declaration of a cash dividend.
   b. To account for the sale of finished goods inventory.
   c. To apply manufacturing overhead.
   d. To account for an employee leasing arrangement.
4. TRN Corporation produces a product that is highly perishable. Which of the following internal controls is the best alternative for controlling the risk of product spoilage?
   a. Separation of duties
   b. Adequate documentation
   c. Employee training
   d. Specialized storage containers

5. Whadda Ya Know University recently discovered that one of its professors had falsified his educational transcripts and does not actually hold any college degree. Which of the following constitutes an appropriate corrective control in this situation?
   a. Background checks
   b. Well-established performance evaluation procedures
   c. Termination
   d. All of the above
6. Forced vacations
   a. Are irrelevant in most companies, as employees are eager to take vacations.
   b. Can reveal fraudulent activities.
   c. Violate federal employment laws.
   d. Save a company money.
7. A production cost report
   a. Is most applicable to process costing systems.
   b. Is most applicable to job costing systems.
   c. Is one of the general purpose financial statements for manufacturers.
   d. Originates in the warehouse.
8. An independent contractor is most closely associated with which of the following forms?
   a. 940
   b. 941
   c. W-2
   d. 1099
9. In a DFD of the human resources business process, "evaluate employees" would be represented with a
   a. Line.
   b. Circle.
   c. Rectangle.
   d. Triangle.
10. RKH Corporation maintains its job costing system using a relational database. Which of the following pieces of information would not be stored in a table in their system?
    a. Total cost of Job A244
    b. Manufacturing employee names
    c. Department affiliations of each employee
    d. Location of manufacturing equipment

17. *Statement evaluation.* Indicate whether each statement below is (i) always true, (ii) sometimes true, or (iii) never true. For statements that are (ii) sometimes true, explain when the statement is true.

a. All five business processes discussed in the text are required to create value for stakeholders.
b. Companies with long-term debt establish sinking funds.
c. Conversion process forms are paper-based.
d. Individual units of product in a process costing system are homogeneous.
e. Information technology eliminates the problem of accounts receivable lapping.
f. Separation of duties can be applied to fixed assets used in the conversion process.
g. The "date of record" determines who receives dividends on capital stock.
h. The par value of a share of capital stock is determined by the stock market.
i. The total cost of a batch of units should be calculated and stored in a relational database table.
j. With respect to long-term debt, the "coupon interest rate" and the "market interest rate" are two ways of referring to the same thing.

Chapter Fourteen

Business Process Management

AIS in the Business World

Employee Expense and Vendor Invoice Processing at America Online

America Online (AOL) describes itself as "a leading global advertising-supported Web company, with the most comprehensive display advertising network in the U.S., a substantial worldwide audience, and a suite of popular Web brands and products. The company's strategy focuses on increasing the scale and sophistication of its advertising platform and growing the size and engagement of its global online audience through leading products and programming" (http://corp.aol.com/about-aol/company-overview).

Given the size of its staff and operations, you can probably imagine the transaction volume AOL's accounting information system handles on a daily basis. In 2004, AOL used the principles and processes of business process management to develop an electronic funds transfer system (EFTS) for processing employee expense reimbursements and vendor invoices. Prior to the EFTS, such requests were processed manually, consuming a lot of time and resources while offering very little flexibility for customers.

AOL's management used two pieces of software from Interfacing (www.interfacing.com) in its BPM project: Charter (an add-on for Visio) and Designer (process simulation software). As a result of the EFTS implementation, AOL experienced improvements in time, cost, customer satisfaction, and management control.

Discussion Questions

1. What is business process management?
2. Does business process management always involve information technology?
3. Why should accounting students learn about business process management?

Source: America Online, Inc. Financial Services white paper, http://interfacing.com/uploads/File/aol.pdf (September 9, 2008).

In prior chapters, we've looked at generic business processes: sales/collection, acquisition/payment, and others. But organizations are dynamic; they must adapt to changes in their environment. So what happens when managers need to change business processes? Changes can be as simple as redesigning a form to make it more useful or as complex as introducing some new form of information technology to streamline a business process. **Business process management** (BPM) gives managers some guidelines to help them with that sometimes daunting task. As an accounting professional, you may be called upon to help organizations manage their business processes so that they can create value for their stakeholders more efficiently and effectively.

Like so many things in AIS, business process management is at least as much "art" as "science." This chapter will provide some basic principles and ideas about BPM that you'll be able to apply in various organizational contexts. When you complete your study of this chapter, you should be able to:

1. Explain what business process management is and how it is related to your study of accounting information systems.
2. List and discuss some basic principles of business process management.
3. Identify and describe tools and techniques commonly used in managing business processes.
4. Apply the basic principles, tools, and techniques in diverse organizational contexts.

In addition to presenting brand new material in this chapter, I'll also draw on some of the things you've learned already about AIS: business processes, information technology, and systems documentation techniques.

NATURE OF BUSINESS PROCESS MANAGEMENT

Business process management has been defined in many different ways, including

- A business improvement strategy based on documenting, analyzing, and redesigning processes for greater performance (SmartDraw.com, 2008).
- A method of efficiently aligning an organization with the wants and needs of clients (Wikipedia.com, 2008).
- A systematic approach to analyzing, redesigning, improving and managing a specific process (Harmon and Wolf, 2008, p. 12).

Notice the important ideas in each definition of BPM: improving performance, promoting efficiency, responding to the needs of clients, and analyzing processes systematically and strategically.

Reflection and Self-Assessment 14.1

Consult at least two other sources that provide definitions of business process management. Based on those sources and what you've just read, develop your own definition of BPM.

Although every BPM project is unique in some way, certain generic activities are common to most of them. Seppanen, Kumar, and Chandra (2005) suggested the following sequence as a **generalized model of BPM**.

1. Select the process and define its boundaries.
2. Observe, document, and map the process steps and flow.
3. Collect process-related data.
4. Analyze the collected data.
5. Identify and prioritize potential process improvements.
6. Optimize the process.
7. Implement and monitor process improvements.

How is BPM related to your study of accounting information systems? Good question! Consider the following points to help understand why AIS students should know something about business process management:

1. BPM can assist managers in providing accounting information that conforms to elements of the FASB Conceptual Framework. Refer back to Figure 1.1, which illustrates the conceptual framework. Managing business processes can ensure that relevant, reliable information is furnished in a cost-effective way.
2. BPM can help managers promote strong internal control. You probably recall from Chapter 4 that internal control has four main purposes, one of which is enhancing operating efficiency. Periodically examining business processes to see how they can be improved helps achieve that goal.
3. BPM frequently involves strategic uses of information technology, such as those discussed in Chapter 8: relational databases, enterprise resource planning systems, and general ledger software. In addition, the 2008 list of AICPA Top Ten Technologies includes business process improvement.
4. BPM is a natural outgrowth of accountants' intimate involvement with business processes. As a future accounting professional, your work will frequently focus on business processes: documenting them (flowcharts, data flow diagrams, REAL models), designing inputs and outputs for them (sales invoices, purchase requisitions, production cost reports), and auditing them (financial, operational, compliance).

Next, let's turn our attention to some fundamental ideas associated with business process management.

BASIC PRINCIPLES

You can learn more about Robert's company on its Web site: www.erpsolutions.net.

You learned about Porter's value chain in Chapter 11. His book, *Competitive Strategy: Techniques for Analyzing Industries and Competitors,* is considered a classic work on strategy.

As part of my background research for this chapter, I interviewed my friend and former student, Robert J. Eppele II. Robert is the chief information officer (CIO) for ERP Solutions LLC. He shared these important ideas about business process management:

1. *Understand how business processes interact with/support organizational strategy.* As you may have learned in a management class, "strategy" refers to the ways an organization gains a competitive advantage in its markets. In today's on-demand, knowledge-driven economy, organizations' business processes can be key to creating and sustaining a competitive advantage in the marketplace.
2. *Move away from the "we've always done it this way" mentality. Be open to alternatives.* Business processes often originate based on some organizational need. For example, in the

Accounting Department at Cal Poly Pomona, we monitor students' progress through upper-division accounting courses independently of the university's recordkeeping system. Until recently, that process required faculty to report students' grades to the department office in addition to reporting them to the university. That process had a clearly defined reason when it was developed over 20 years ago; within the last year, however, through the innovative thinking and expertise of the department administrative support coordinator (Ms. Nan Miller), we streamlined the process while still achieving the same goal.

3. *Enlist top management support; ensure that top management can describe current business processes before trying to reengineer/maintain/modify the processes.* In Chapter 4, you learned about the COSO frameworks for internal control and enterprise risk management; in both frameworks, the "tone at the top" is an important factor. The same is true for BPM: Without top management support, most efforts will be doomed to failure. In addition, to support and lead BPM efforts effectively, top management needs to understand the way things currently work in the organization.

Hamel and Prahalad's 1989 article in *Harvard Business Review,* "Strategic Intent," has a lot to say about this point.

4. *Managing business processes is fundamentally about people, not technology/documents. It's important to hire people who can think beyond their little piece of the world and see how what they do fits into the "bigger picture."* In the next section of this chapter, we'll look at some of the tools managers can use to improve business processes; however, all the tools in the world won't help without a good team of people to use them! BPM requires a holistic view of the organization—one that moves beyond thinking about what's best for your department to thinking about how the organization as a whole can create value for its stakeholders.
5. *Don't rely on external consultants to the exclusion of internal employees, Value the experience of people in the organization who are close to the process.* This point might strike you as a bit odd, since both Robert and I have worked as external consultants in many organizations. But it is 100 percent true! Far too many managers, when confronted with a complex problem, advocate hiring an external consultant as a first step. While doing so has many advantages, external consultants rarely have the intimate familiarity of internal employees when it comes to BPM. I've often found that a team approach, combining both employees and consultants, produces very positive results.
6. *When using consultants, make sure the task is well defined, with specific deliverables defined by the company.* This idea reminds me of something Lewis Carroll wrote in *Alice's Adventures in Wonderland:* "If you don't know where you are going, any road will take you there." In other words, outcomes for a BPM project should be defined in advance; otherwise, the project may grow out of control, costing both time and money without achieving solid results.
7. *Communicate early; communicate often. Deal immediately with objections/issues as they arise.* BPM, like most important organizational initiatives, needs to be an open, transparent process. The best plans are developed by a team of people through a process of dialogue and feedback, not by one or two people sitting in an office for several hours.

As we look at specific tools and techniques for BPM in the next section of this chapter, please keep those **basic principles** in mind.

BPM TOOLS AND TECHNIQUES

Keeping in mind that the overall goal of BPM is to enable an organization to create more value for its stakeholders, managers have many options when it comes to improving organizational processes. In this section, we'll look at information technology, activity-based management, and flowcharting and their applications in BPM.

FIGURE 14.1
Integrify BPM Software Screen Shot

Source: www.integrify.com.

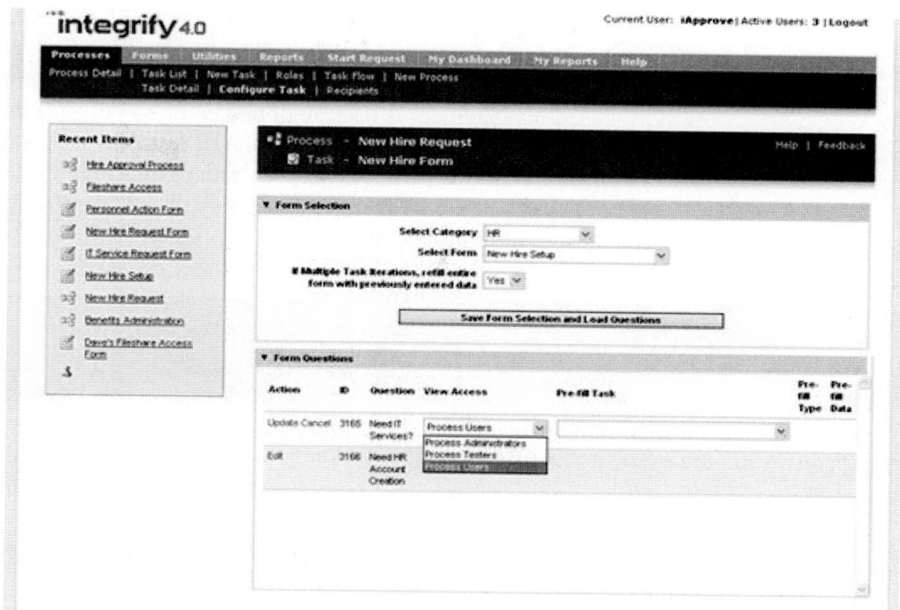

Information Technology

If you do a Web search on BPM, you'll most likely come up with several Web sites that talk about **software;** Harmon and Wolf (2008, p. 31) found that 74 percent of their survey respondents use at least a graphics modeling tool (like Visio) for BPM. Companies also use information technology specifically designed for business process modeling (such as Casewise, ProVision, or Integrify).

Figure 14.1 shows a screen shot from Integrify.

Reflection and Self-Assessment 14.2

Do a Web or literature search for process modeling tools like those mentioned above (or others). What features do they offer that differentiate them from simpler graphics modeling tools like Visio or SmartDraw?

Refer back to Chapter 2 for a discussion of people- versus IT-related tasks in transaction processing.

Although IT can be useful for BPM, keep in mind the fourth principle above: managing business processes is fundamentally about *people,* not technology/documents. Just as general ledger software can assist in maintaining an organization's accounting records but cannot replace human thinking and judgment, IT for business process management is only a tool—not an end in itself.

Activity-Based Management

If you've had an introductory course in management or cost accounting, you're probably familiar with activity-based costing (ABC). ABC is a method of assigning overhead costs to products and services that is more rational and accurate than traditional labor-based allocation methods. But using ABC to compute product costs is only the beginning!

Brewer, Garrison, and Noreen (2008, p. 132) offered the following comments about **activity-based management.** "Basically, activity-based management involves focusing on activities to eliminate waste, decrease processing time, and reduce defects. Activity-based management is used in organizations as diverse as manufacturing companies, hospitals and the U.S. Marine Corps." ABM projects focus on differentiating value-added from non-value-added activities—a process that involves significant amounts of judgment. Once non-value-added activities have been identified, managers can look for ways to redesign or eliminate them using the principles of business process management.

Reflection and Self-Assessment 14.3

How would you decide the extent to which a process is "value added"?

Cost Management: Strategies for Business Decisions (4th ed.) by Hilton, Maher, and Selto (Irwin/McGraw-Hill, 2008) discusses this topic in much greater depth.

Consider the following example: CHR Corporation's activity-based costing system includes a pool called "order taking," which CHR's managers further subdivided into several activities. Managers ranked each activity on a three-point scale, where "3" stood for an activity with very high value and "1" stood for an activity with very low value. Note: Three-point scales are just one good option for the ranking. While a two-point classification (value-added or non-value-added) may be too restrictive, scales might include four or more points. The activities, their costs, and rankings are shown below:

Activity Name	Total Cost for a Typical Order	Ranking
Take phone order	$30	3
Input phone order to computer system	10	1
Correct errors	15	1
Transmit order information to warehouse	5	2
Transmit order information to accounting	5	1
	$65	

Notice that "level one" activities (those that add the least value) constitute nearly half of the total cost for a typical order!

Ranking	Cost	Percent of Total Cost
3	$30	46%
2	5	8
1	30	46

If CHR used business process management to reduce, or even eliminate, the three lowest-ranked activities, its product cost would decline significantly, enabling it to compete more effectively in its markets.

For example, CHR could eliminate "input phone order to computer system" as a separate activity if the people taking the orders completed that task as part of the order-taking process. Various IT controls, such as echo checks and limit checks, would be useful in reducing the number of input errors; thus, the need to correct errors would be reduced/eliminated. And, if the organization kept its records in a relational database or enterprise resource planning system, managers could assign access privileges that would eliminate the need to transmit orders. "Access privileges" means limiting systems users' ability to look at various parts of a system. For example, as a faculty advisor, there are things I can see in my school's ERP system that students cannot see; likewise, there are things my department chair can see that I cannot see.

Flowcharting

You might find it helpful to review "Flowcharting and Accounting Information Systems" in Chapter 5.

A well-designed **flowchart** also can help with managing business processes. Flowcharts, as you're aware, require attention to detail and precision; they typically involve dialogue about business processes and several drafts before they are complete. The dialogue alone can help managers focus on ways to improve business processes, particularly for those that have "been around" in organizations for extended periods of time.

In the list of basic principles above, I mentioned a process redesign for grade reporting in the Accounting Department at Cal Poly Pomona. Figure 14.2 shows a systems flowchart of the old process.

FIGURE 14.2 Original Grade Update Process

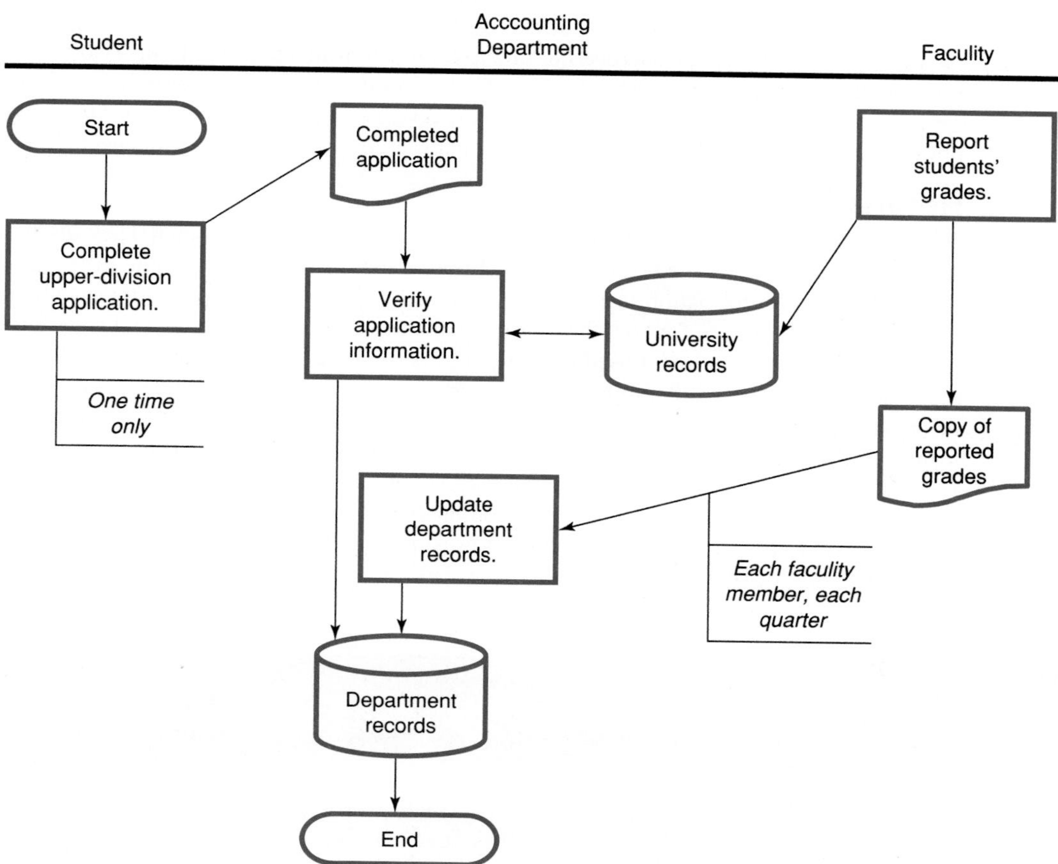

Can you spot the redundancy in the original process? Faculty were submitting grades twice: once to the university's database and separately to the Accounting Department. Frequently, the Accounting Department staff had to make multiple requests for copies of reported grades—an especially difficult task at the start of long breaks (like the summer). When our new department secretary, Ms. Nan Miller, came on board, she figured out a way to extract the grades directly from university records, thus removing the redundancy.

Next, let's look at some additional examples of actual BPM projects.

CASE STUDIES

We'll look at three specific **examples of BPM** in this section: governmental activities in Tyler, Texas; enterprise design team project at a large midwestern hospital; and special order processing in a Swiss bank.

Tyler, Texas

You can see some of the results of the city's efforts at www.tylertexas.com

Fagan (2006, p. 104) described how the City of Tyler implemented "e-government initiatives that involve city, county and state government entities along with a number of local citizens and community organizations." One initiative focused on providing information via the Web; the project involved BPM in the sense that the city was changing the way people accessed information about economic issues, tourism, and business in the area. In addition to information gathering, people using the Web site can download commonly used forms (such as building permits), query the local library database, and pay traffic tickets online.

After describing the Web portal and two other BPM projects in Tyler, Fagan concluded (p. 107): "Future efforts to improve the online offerings available through the Tyler Texas portal will require new approaches to identify the specific services that citizens need. An approach based upon a BPM mindset can help the diverse participants work toward breaking down organizational and departmental barriers in order to focus on their client's needs."

Hospital

Since the Tyler example focused on information technology, this case will describe the top-down BPM effort.

Huq and Martin (2006) studied BPM efforts in a large midwestern hospital They discuss two different projects at the hospital; the first used a top-down approach while the second focused more on information technology as a tool for BPM. The hospital's management surveyed its customers to find out the extent to which customers were pleased with the hospital's products and services. Based on those results (p. 580), "the hospital noted that their major weaknesses were inflexibility, poor service delivery performance, bureaucracy, lack of cross training and high cost of services." Management established a cross-functional team (the "Enterprise Design Team") to address customers' concerns. The team then identified eight processes split into two categories: (a) core and (b) management and support. After working with that structure for six months, the hospital completed a major merger; the new executive team dismantled the Enterprise Design Team and started a technology-based approach for BPM.

Reflection and Self-Assessment 14.4

The hospital's top-down BPM effort was largely viewed as a failure, leading to the change in approach. What factors might have contributed to the failure, and how could they have been addressed successfully?

Swiss Bank

Kung and Hagen (2007) looked at four BPM efforts in a Swiss bank, one of which was a "special orders" process. Many banking transactions can be accomplished in a fairly routine way: opening accounts, cashing checks, receiving deposits, and such. But customers often request products and services that fall outside those routine transactions. Prior to its BPM effort, the Swiss bank's special order processing presented several challenges (Kung and Hagen, pp. 483–84):

- Involvement of many different functions and roles throughout the bank.
- Unique steps, often requiring different tools and methods of communication.
- Long cycle times.

To address those challenges and provide better customer service, the bank designed a loosely structured, generic process for handling special orders. Customers' special orders are managed via a database that tracks both progress and the people involved. According to Kung and Hagen (p. 485), "This setup makes it possible that responsibility of each special order is determined and for each case the current state as well as the currently involved agent can be identified." The BPM effort resulted in reduced cycle times, faster task completion, and improved productivity; employees were therefore able to focus more on providing excellent customer service.

CRITICAL THINKING

So far in this chapter, we've looked at some basic principles and tools for business process management, along with a few case examples. But, like nearly everything in organizations, business process management isn't a simple matter of deciding to do something. Especially in tight economic times (such as we're experiencing as I write this in January 2009), every new idea needs to pass a cost-benefit test. So, let's take a look in this section at how you might conduct such an analysis for a BPM project.

At least three important principles govern most cost–benefit analyses:

- Only incremental costs and benefits are financially relevant in decision making.
- Not all costs and benefits can be expressed financially, so every analysis involves some subjectivity and judgment.
- For projects that will span more than one year, cash flows should be discounted to their present value.

By this time in your accounting education, you've probably had at least one introductory management accounting course; the first two principles should seem familiar from there. You probably applied those principles in short-term decision contexts, such as make or buy, special orders, and product discontinuance. Because I'm fairly certain you've studied that material, I'm not going to talk more about it here; if you need a review, check out a management or cost accounting text.

If you've had a finance and/or intermediate accounting class, you've probably run across the idea of the "time value of money" and how to discount future cash flows. In case you haven't, here's a *very* brief overview of the basic concepts:

- Money has a time value, meaning that a fixed amount of cash received today is worth more than the same amount of cash received in the future. Why? Because the cash today can be invested so that it will be greater in the future.
- The time value of money is unrelated to the idea of inflation. Even in an inflation-free economy, money would still have a time value.

- *Present value* refers to money exchanged today, while *future value* refers to money exchanged at some point in the future. A *discount rate* is the assumed interest rate at which money will be invested.

If you received \$100 today and invested it at 10 percent, how much money would you have in a year? \$110, calculated as \$100 + \$100 × 10%, or \$100 × 1.1. If you left the \$110 for another year, how much would you have? \$121, calculated as \$110 + \$110 × 10%, or \$110 × 1.1, or \$100 × 1.1 ^ 2. Here's how it would look in equation form:

$$\$121 = \$100 \times 1.1^2$$

In that equation:

- \$100 is the present value
- \$121 is the future value
- 10% is the discount rate
- 2 is the number of periods

So, in a more generalized format, the equation would look like this:

$$\text{Future value} = \text{Present value} \times (1 + \text{Interest rate})^{\text{Number of periods}}$$

or

$$FV = PV \times (1 + i)^n$$

or

$$FV / (1 + i)^n = PV$$

I'm sure your head is spinning right about now—that's some pretty technical information in a really summarized format. So, you might want to take a minute to reread it before we look at an example.

Now, consider the following example: The management at TBL Corporation wants to make changes to its product shipment process; they're considering closing their internal shipping department and outsourcing shipping to a firm specializing in that element of the value chain. If TBL keeps the shipping department as it is, the annual cost to operate it is \$12,000. If TBL follows through with the idea of outsourcing, management plans to phase out the shipping department, gradually decreasing its costs over the next few years; at the same time, the cost of outsourcing will increase. Here are some numbers:

	Cost of:		
Year	**Shipping Department**	**Outsourcing**	**Total**
0	\$12,000	\$3,000	\$15,000
1	9,000	4,000	13,000
2	6,000	5,000	11,000
3	3,000	6,000	9,000
4	3,000	6,000	9,000

Year 0 is the current year. The cost of the shipping department might decrease as a result of employee layoffs or retirements; the cost of outsourcing might increase as more packages are shipped in that way. So, if the annual cost of keeping things the same is \$12,000, the incremental benefit/(cost) of outsourcing would be

Year	Incremental Benefit/ (Cost) of Outsourcing
0	$(3,000)
1	(1,000)
2	1,000
3	3,000
4	3,000

If TBL's discount rate is 8 percent, the present value of those future cash flows would be

Year	Present Value of Incremental Benefit/(Cost)
0	$(3,000)
1	(926)
2	857
3	2,381
4	2,205

The sum of the present value of the cash flows is $1,518. From a strictly financial perspective, TBL would be better off from outsourcing. After conducting the quantitative analysis, though, TBL management should consider qualitative issues such as service quality and the impact on shipping department employees. They also must consider how accurate the estimates of future cash flows are, as well as whether 8 percent is the appropriate discount rate.

Summary

Here's a summary of the chapter's main points, as usual, structured according to its objectives:

1. *Explain what business process management is and how it is related to your study of accounting information systems.* Companies create value for their stakeholders via their business processes. And, as stakeholders' needs change, managers should update their business processes, too. BPM, therefore, refers to the tools and techniques managers use to adapt and change their business processes.

   In the most generic sense, BPM comprises seven basic steps: (a) Select the process and define its boundaries. (b) Observe, document, and map the process steps and flow. (c) Collect process-related data. (d) Analyze the collected data. (e) Identify and prioritize potential process improvements. (f) Optimize the process. (g) Implement and monitor process improvements.

   BPM is an important part of accounting information systems for many reasons: (a) Business processes are at the heart of AIS study; (b) business professionals, including accounting professionals, must think critically to manage processes appropriately; and (c) BPM frequently, though not always, involves information technology.
2. *List and discuss some basic principles of business process management.* The chapter discussed seven principles managers should keep in mind when engaged in BPM activities: (a) Understand how business processes interact with/support organizational strategy. (b) Move away from the "we've always done it this way" mentality. Be open to alternatives. (c) Enlist top management support; ensure that top management can

describe current business processes before trying to reengineer/maintain/modify the processes. (d) Managing business processes is fundamentally about people, not technology/documents. It's important to hire people who can think beyond their little piece of the world and see how what they do fits into the "bigger picture." (e) Don't rely on external consultants to the exclusion of internal employees. Value the experience of people in the organization who are close to the process. (f) When using consultants, make sure the task is well defined, with specific deliverables defined by the company. (g) Communicate early; communicate often. Deal immediately with objections/issues as they arise.

3. *Identify and describe tools and techniques commonly used in managing business processes.* Although every BPM project has some unique characteristics, certain tools are common across a variety of them. Managers may use various forms of information technology for BPM; whether something as simple as flowcharting software, or something more complex like an enterprise resource planning system, IT can be an asset for business process management. Activity-based management, an extension of activity-based costing, also can help realign business processes, particularly with a view toward cost savings versus value added. Finally, systems documentation techniques, whether using information technology or not, can help see both opportunities for improvement and possible new process configurations.
4. *Apply the basic principles, tools, and techniques in diverse organizational contexts.* The chapter looked at three specific cases of BPM projects: the city of Tyler, Texas; a midwestern hospital; and a Swiss bank.

In completing the activities that follow, I hope you'll draw upon your prior study of systems documentation, information technology, and business processes.

Key Terms

activity-based management, *274*
basic principles, *272*
software, *273*
business process management, *270*
examples of BPM, *276*
flowchart, *275*
generalized model of BPM, *271*

Chapter References

Brewer, P. R. Garrison, and E. Noreen. 2008. *Introduction to Managerial Accounting.* 4th ed. New York: Irwin/McGraw-Hill.

Fagan, M. 2006. "Exploring City, County and State E-government Initiatives: An East Texas Perspective." *Business Process Management Journal* 12, no. 1, pp. 101–12.

Harmon, P., and C. Wolf. 2008. *The State of Business Process Management.* San Francisco: Business Process Trends.

Huq, Z., and T. Martin. 2006. "The Recovery of BPR Implementation through an ERP Approach: A Hospital Case Study." *Business Process Management Journal* 12, no. 5, pp. 576–87.

Kung, P., and C. Hagen. 2007. "The Fruits of Business Process Management: An Experience Report from a Swiss Bank." *Business Process Management Journal* 13, no. 4, pp. 477–87.

Seppanen, M., S. Kumar, and C. Chandra. 2005. *Process Analysis and Improvement: Tools and Techniques.* 1st ed. New York: Irwin/McGraw-Hill.

SmartDraw.com. 2008. "Standards and Methodologies." www.smartdraw.com/tutorials/bpm/methodologies.htm (August 27).

Wikipedia.com. 2008. "Business Process Management." http://en.wikipedia.org/wiki/Business_process_management (August 27).

End-of-Chapter Activities

1. *Reading review questions.*
   a. Define *business process management* in your own words. Explain why BPM can be considered part of accounting information systems.
   b. List seven generic steps involved in many BPM projects.
   c. List and discuss seven fundamental principles to keep in mind when undertaking a BPM initiative.
   d. How can information technology, flowcharting, and activity-based management come into play in BPM?
   e. Summarize the three BPM cases discussed in the chapter.
   f. In a format specified by your instructor, respond to the questions for this chapter's "AIS in the Business World."
2. *Making choices and exercising judgment.* The chapter mentions three specific pieces of software organizations often use for BPM: Casewise, ProVision, and Integrify. Use the weighted rating methodology described in Chapter 8 to compare two of them *and* one other BPM software you find on your own. Use the following factors with the weights indicated: features (5), availability of successful case studies (3), and flexibility (4).
3. *Field exercises.*
   a. Search the internet and/or your school's library to find an example of a successful BPM project. Summarize the project. To what extent does the case follow the seven basic steps suggested by Seppanen, Kumar, and Chandra?
   b. Interview an accounting or other business professional who has participated in a BPM project. Ask your interviewee to describe the project and to comment on the basic BPM principles discussed in the chapter.
4. *BPM cases.* Read and summarize one of the following articles from the *Business Process Management Journal.* Be prepared to present and discuss your results in whatever form your instructor specifies.
   a. Sentonin et al., "Business Process Management in a Brazilian Public Research Centre," *Business Process Management Journal* 14, no. 4.
   b. Romero-Hernandez et al., "Business Process Modeling for a Central Securities Depository," *Business Process Management Journal* 14, no. 3.
   c. Suhaimi et al., "Information Systems Outsourcing: Motivations and the Implementation Strategy in a Malaysian Bank," *Business Process Management Journal* 13, no. 5.
5. *Risk analysis.* Consider one of the cases described in the chapter and/or one that you summarized in Activity 3(b) above. Use Brown's risk taxonomy (Chapter 4) to identify and describe at least three risks associated with the case(s) you choose. How would you suggest managers address the risks?
6. *BPM applications.* Reexamine at least one of the following cases presented previously in the text. Make at least two suggestions for improvements in the business process described, then draw a flowchart depicting the new business process.
   a. Chapter 5, Case 1: Cori's Catering Services.
   b. Chapter 5, Case 2: University Bookstore.
   c. Chapter 11, Activity 2, reading review problem: Dreambox Creations Inc.
   d. Chapter 12, Activity 10, internal controls: Brock Company
7. *BPM information technology.* Point your Web browser to www.download.com and search for free software related to business process management. Could any of the forms of IT discussed previously in the text (spreadsheets, relational databases, general ledger, Web development, ERP) accomplish the same tasks? If so, how? If not, why not?

8. *Activity-based management.* BLZ Corporation designs and produces massively multi-player online role-playing games (MMORPG). Designing a completely new game can take up to two years, while expanding an existing game usually takes 8 to 10 months. Some of BLZ's activities, with approximate costs, are shown below:

   - Beta testing new games, $2,400
   - Developing content for expansions, $7,680
   - Fixing software bugs, $16,470
   - Manufacturing game software CDs, $50,625
   - Marketing and advertising, $7,000
   - Processing returned CDs, $3,800
   - Responding to player questions, $1,900
   - Shipping CDs to retail stores, $8,100
   - Writing instructional manuals, $4,200
   - Recording transactions in the accounting information system, $9,430

   a. Use a four-point scale to categorize the value added by each process, where "1" stands for an activity with little or no value and "4" stands for an activity with very high value.
   b. Prepare a pie chart that shows the percentage of cost in each category.
   c. Consider at least two activities you classify as having the lowest value. For each activity, suggest at least two ways it could be improved. Explain your reasoning.

9. *Crossword puzzle.*

Across

2. Software that can be used in BPM.
4. Should be used cautiously in BPM, and always with well-defined outcomes.
7. _____-based management is one tool for BPM.
9. Must be defined at the start of a BPM project.
10. The "B" in BPM.

Down

1. The "M" in BPM.
3. BPM is fundamentally about _____.
5. BPM minimizes or eliminates processes that don't do this (two words).
6. Purpose of internal control closely related to BPM.
8. The "P" in BPM.

10. *Terminology.* Please match each item on the left with the most appropriate item on the right.

1. Best motivation for starting BPM	a. Activity-based management
2. Essential element of all BPM projects	b. Boundaries
3. Focuses on eliminating waste	c. Communication
4. How an organization competes in its markets	d. Consultants
5. Internal control purpose associated with BPM	e. Efficiency
6. Must be defined before starting a BPM project	f. Information technology
7. Often used in, but not essential to, BPM	g. Non-value-added activities
8. Should be frequent in BPM	h. People
9. Should be reduced or eliminated	i. Stakeholders' needs
10. Should be used cautiously in BPM	j. Strategy

11. *Multiple choice questions.*

1. Business process management can be defined as
   a. A business improvement strategy based on documenting, analyzing, and redesigning processes for greater performance.
   b. A method of efficiently aligning an organization with the wants and needs of clients.
   c. Both A and B.
   d. Neither A nor B.
2. The first step in many BPM projects is selecting a process and defining its boundaries. Which of the following is the best example of a well-defined process?
   a. Keeping clients happy
   b. Motivating employees
   c. Producing goods
   d. Issuing capital stock
3. The fourth step in many BPM projects is analyzing data, which could be accomplished with
   a. A flowchart.
   b. A value-added study.
   c. An analysis of the organization's strategy.
   d. The FASB Conceptual Framework.

4. Which of the following is the best example of a BPM project that promotes strong internal control?
   a. Developing an online order-taking process
   b. Drawing a flowchart of a company's new production process
   c. Hiring an external consultant to make recommendations about internal control
   d. Increasing supervision over employees
5. Accountants can be involved in business process management through
   I. Documenting processes.
   II. Designing process inputs and outputs.
   III. Auditing.
   a. I and II only
   b. II and III only
   c. I and III only
   d. I, II, and III
6. Business processes should support
   a. Organizational strategy.
   b. Top management.
   c. Information technology.
   d. Employees.
7. All of the following are elements of a value-added activity except
   a. A customer is willing to pay for it.
   b. It involves a transformation of a process or activity.
   c. It is performed correctly the first time.
   d. It involves information technology.
8. Which of the following statements is most true?
   a. Organizations that use activity-based costing must use activity-based management.
   b. An organization must implement activity-based management before it can implement activity-based costing.
   c. Organizations that use activity-based management are likely to use activity-based costing as well.
   d. Activity-based management is the best way to manage business processes.
9. Examples of value-added activities include
   I. Ordering raw materials.
   II. Testing product quality.
   III. Fueling delivery trucks.
   a. I and II only
   b. I and III only
   c. II and III only
   d. I, II, and III
10. Which of the following generic BPM steps occurs first?
    a. Analyze process-related data.
    b. Collect process-related data.
    c. Identify potential improvements.
    d. Optimize the process.

12. *Statement evaluation.* Indicate whether each statement below is (i) always true, (ii) sometimes true, or (iii) never true. For those that are (ii) sometimes true, explain when the statement is true.

   a. Information technology is an important part of business process management projects.
   b. "Value added" is defined by external customers.
   c. External consultants are always necessary for successful BPM projects.
   d. A process can be value added if it helps employees work more efficiently.
   e. Fixing product defects is not a value-added activity.
   f. Many forms of information technology can be used in managing business processes.
   g. Business processes are only value added if external customers are willing to pay for them.
   h. A service-based business has more opportunities for BPM projects than a manufacturing business.
   i. Managing business processes requires critical thinking and judgment.
   j. Data flow diagrams are less useful than flowcharts in managing business processes.

Other Topics in Accounting Information Systems

15. Computer Crime and Information Technology Security

16. Decision-Making Models and Knowledge Management

17. Professional Certifications and Career Planning

18. Auditing and Evaluating the AIS

The final section of the text is designed to give AIS instructors some flexibility and the opportunity to innovate. I considered three types of topics for inclusion in this section: topics of current interest in accounting information systems (computer crime and IT security), topics that link accounting information systems with other areas of accounting and other areas of business (decision-making models and knowledge management and auditing), and topics that have consistently interested my own students (professional certifications).

WHY DO WE CARE ABOUT THESE SPECIAL TOPICS

This final section of the text exposes you to a variety of topics that are relevant to an accountant in today's business environment. Technology is more infused in the business environment than ever before; becoming proficient with information technology is no longer an option for any business professional—particularly for accountants. Criminals understand technology weaknesses and setup; as an accountant, you must be one step ahead to maintain the quality of the accounting system.

In addition to worrying about the security of your IT system, as an accountant you must understand how to evaluate your firm's accounting information system. If your firm's system has a material weakness, and you are unable to detect it, your firm is susceptible to anything and everything that could go wrong. This would make any accountant's job impossible, no matter in what area he or she is involved.

The interesting aspect of AIS is the tremendous career paths you may take. Unlike the traditional areas of accounting, AIS provides you with exposure that cuts across many disciplines—think about how the topics we've examined so far have involved not only accounting, but also information technology, human resource management, legal issues, and operations management. Just like a city planner designs a city from scratch to work in perfect harmony, an AIS accountant has the ability to develop an ideal system that fits the ideology and personality of himself or herself and the firm. The opportunities are endless.

Chapter Fifteen

Computer Crime and Information Technology Security

AIS in the Business World

Identity Theft

The growth of information technology has been a positive force in business; but, as with all innovations, it has a downside risk as well. Consider the following case of identity theft:

> Federal prosecutors charged 11 men in five countries with orchestrating a high-tech operation that stole more than 40 million credit-card numbers from U.S. retailers. The case is the biggest identity-fraud heist ever prosecuted in the U.S. The government said the defendants engaged in a sophisticated scheme involving wireless interception of retailers' data transmissions, "sniffer" programs that stole card numbers as they were being swiped at cash registers, bulk fencing of stolen cards at less than $1 apiece on the Internet, and encrypted computer servers that stored the thieves' digital plunder in Latvia and Ukraine. [One retailer] says it has set aside $202 million to cover costs including settlements with consumers and card-issuing banks. In a statement, the company said that the number of retailers attacked "demonstrates the much broader challenges in protecting sensitive consumer data from this increasing threat."

As a future accounting professional, you may be called upon to help prevent, detect, or correct situations like that one in your career.

Discussion Questions

1. What broad categories can be used to describe computer crime?
2. How can accountants help safeguard organizations against computer crime?

Source: J. Pereira, J. Levitz, and J. Singer-Vine, "U.S. Indicts 11 in Global Credit-Card Scheme," *The Wall Street Journal* (Eastern Edition), August 6, 2008, p. A1.

With individuals becoming more than simply computer literate and the emergence of the Internet as a tool for global information exchange, accounting information systems and the information they store and process will increasingly fall victim to computer crime and fraud. Computers also have become facilitators for criminals, providing them with new methods of perpetrating classic forms of crimes and creating many new "business opportunities" for these criminals. This chapter examines many facets of computer crime and fraud: associated risks and threats, the use of accounting information systems, and investigation of computer crime.

When you've finished studying this chapter, you should be able to:

1. Explain Carter's taxonomy of computer crime.
2. Identify and describe business risks and threats to information systems.
3. Name and describe common types of computer criminals.
4. Discuss ways to prevent and detect computer crime.
5. Explain CoBIT's information criteria and accountability framework.
6. Explain how CoBIT can be used to strengthen internal controls against computer crime.

Understanding the various types of computer crime will allow you to understand more clearly how the AIS can be affected by common malicious acts. Carter (1995) suggested a four-part **taxonomy for computer crime:**

- *Target.* This category is comprised of computer crimes where the criminal targets the system or its data. The objective of these crimes is to impact the confidentiality, availability, and/or integrity of data stored on the computer.
- *Instrumentality.* Computer as the instrumentality of the crime uses the computer to further a criminal end. In crimes *targeting* the computer, the data are the object of the crime; in this case, the computer is used to commit a crime.
- *Incidental.* This type of computer crime encompasses crimes where the computer is not required for the crime but is related to the criminal act. The use of the computer simplifies the criminal actions and may make the crime more difficult to trace.
- *Associated.* The simple presence of computers, and notably the growth of the Internet, has generated new versions of fairly traditional crimes. In these cases, technological growth essentially creates new crime targets and new ways of reaching victims.

I am deeply indebted to Mr. Jean-Francois Legault for contributing most of the text for this chapter.

The lines between each type of crime can be blurry at times and some criminal transactions may overlap the different types of crimes.

BUSINESS RISKS AND THREATS TO INFORMATION SYSTEMS

Organizations, both large and small, have come to rely heavily on information systems to provide timely information used in making critical business decisions. As such reliance on information systems grows, so do the risks the organization faces. So, anyone involved in decision making should understand those risks and how they can impact the organization.

We'll discuss the following business **risks and threats:**

- Fraud
- Error
- Service interruption and delays

- Disclosure of confidential information
- Intrusions
- Information theft
- Information manipulation
- Malicious software
- Denial-of-service attacks
- Web site defacements
- Extortion

Fraud

In 1989, the U.S. Department of Justice defined computer fraud as being any illegal act for which knowledge of computer technology is used to commit the offense. Fundamentally, computer fraud is people fraud; no computer system can perpetrate fraud without at least some human intervention.

Computer skills required will vary greatly depending on the type of fraud being perpetrated. Frauds such as data diddling—the intentional modification of information—require only basic skills; on the other hand, theft of information in a secure database will require more advanced computer skills from the fraudster.

Following a series of scandals and lapses in corporate governance, the Sarbanes-Oxley Act was introduced to restore customer confidence in the stock markets. It was introduced with the firm resolve to increase corporate responsibility and requires that companies establish extensive governance policies to prevent and respond to fraudulent activities. The act and the accompanying SEC regulations require that organizations produce a report of the internal controls it has in place to ensure compliance with the act itself.

We looked at SOX in more detail in Chapter 4 on internal controls.

Error

Losses associated with errors can vary widely depending on where the error originated and the time it may take to identify and correct it. A single error when entering a product code will lead to the wrong item being shipped; a programming error in a financial institution's transaction system could lead to many millions lost and some very angry customers. Implementing preventive controls that will detect and correct errors before they occur can prevent financial losses and negative impacts to the organization's image.

Service Interruption and Delays

A delay in processing information or a service interruption can bring an organization to a standstill; such delays can lead to missed deadlines for payables and receivables. Service interruptions can be due to many factors, but they all fall into three main categories: accidental, willful neglect, and malicious behavior. Accidental service interruption can be caused by someone shutting down the wrong machine. Willful neglect could be due to outdated antivirus software; a malicious service interruption could be caused by a hacker launching a denial of service attack against an organization's Web site.

Disclosure of Confidential Information

The disclosure of sensitive information can have major impacts on an organization's financial health. No organization wishes to imagine its customer or employee data being made available to all on the Internet, but such disclosure has become an important risk for most organizations. Privacy laws have made managers and other stakeholders aware of the critical need to protect information assets.

Intrusions

The main objective of an intrusion is to gain access to a network or a system by bypassing security controls or exploiting a lack of adequate controls. An intruder's motivations will vary widely: Some hack for profit while others hack for fun. Hackers for profit will often target specific organizations or specific information before beginning their attack; hackers looking for entertainment will often choose "low-hanging fruit": data and/or systems that are relatively unprotected and easy to access.

Information Theft

This form of computer crime targets the organization's most precious asset: information. Trade secrets, marketing plans, advertising campaigns, research and development data for new products, and customer lists are just a few examples of data in this category. These assets, which are represented in a numeric format, often have a higher value than other traditionally targeted assets, resulting in potentially higher losses for the organizations.

Information Manipulation

Information manipulation can occur at virtually any stage of information processing, from input to output. Input manipulation in computer systems is probably the most common form of fraud since it is easy to perform, requiring only basic computer skills. Furthermore, it is hard to detect, since the fraudulent input may look valid until an in-depth examination is performed. Such a situation could occur when an employee creates fake refunds in the payables system to benefit a family member.

Program manipulation is a complex task and is extremely difficult to detect as both the modification and detection require advanced computer programming knowledge. Manipulating computer programs involves the modification or insertion of specific functions in the computer information system.

Other forms of manipulation involve taking advantage of the automatic repetitions of a computer program. Such manipulation is characteristic of the "salami technique," where unnoticeable slices of a financial transaction are removed and transferred to another account. Under such a scenario, a computer programmer employed in a bank could redirect interest smaller then a penny to his own account. Over time, those fractional amounts can add up to a large sum.

Malicious Software

We'll look at the C-I-A triad in the next section of this chapter.

Malicious software, or malware, can take many different forms. All of them have a direct impact on the C-I-A triad, whether it be a virus infecting a system and modifying its data, a worm replicating over the network causing a bottleneck, or a Trojan horse allowing an unauthorized backdoor into a system that directly impacts the confidentiality of the files residing on the system.

Logic bombs are another example of malicious software. In a payroll system, for example, software validates whether a specific employee's number is present or not when paychecks are issued. If the employee was ever dismissed, his employee number would no longer be present and, upon execution of the payroll application, the logic bomb would detect the missing employee number and trigger the deletion of all employee records.

Denial-of-Service Attacks

Denial-of-service (DOS) attacks prevent computer systems and networks from functioning in accordance with their intended purpose. These attacks cause loss of service to the users by consuming scarce resources such as bandwidth, memory, or processor cycles; they also can disrupt configuration information or physical components.

In a distributed denial-of-service attack, many compromised systems under the control of one or many attackers are used to multiply the impact by launching concurrent attacks against a determined target. These attacks can be devastating to an organization as they will bring computer operations to a complete standstill; in many cases, distributed DOS attacks are virtually impossible to block as they come from so many sources.

Web Site Defacements

Web site defacements are a form of digital graffiti where intruders modify pages on the site in order to leave their mark, send a message, or mock the organization. Politically motivated defacement, often called hacktivism, attempts to send a message to the organization or some part of the online community.

Extortion

Online extortion is often the result of the computer being the object of a crime; the extortionist contacts an organization after successfully stealing information or launching a DOS attack. The criminal then threatens either to reveal the information to the public or to launch a prolonged denial of service if demands are not met.

PERPETRATORS OF COMPUTER CRIME

A wide variety of individuals have been known to commit computer crimes: students, amateurs, terrorists, and members of organized crime groups. What distinguishes them is the intent of their crime: a youth attempting to break into a system without any further intent is much different than an employee embezzling funds. Any person of any age with computer skills, motivated by the technical challenge; by the potential for gain, notoriety, or revenge; or by the promotion of ideological beliefs is a potential computer criminal.

The following paragraphs discuss seven common types of computer criminals, or **perpetrators**:

- Script kiddies
- Hackers
- Cyber-criminals
- Organized crime
- Corporate spies
- Terrorists
- Insiders

A *script kiddie* describes a young, inexperienced hacker who uses tools and scripts written by others for the purpose of attacking systems. Most of them do not possess enough programming and system knowledge to write or understand such scripts and tools. The growth of the script kiddie has been exponential since the rise of the Internet, as it made available detailed information on breaking into systems and networks. Script kiddies will most often scan thousands of computers looking for those presenting vulnerabilities that they know how to exploit. They often act out of boredom, curiosity, or a desire to "play war" on the Internet.

Today, a *hacker* refers to someone who invades an information system for malicious purposes; for example, a hacker might steal clients' Social Security numbers or change student information. Originally, a hacker simply referred to a person who wanted to further his or her knowledge of computers and attempted to push the system to the limit.

Cyber-criminals are hackers driven by financial gain. These individuals possess advanced skills and have turned to hacking—not for the challenge, but for the money. Many of these cyber-criminals are members of or contractors for criminal organizations who have turned to the Internet to continue their rackets.

With computer crime being so profitable, it is no surprise that *organized crime* has expanded part of its operations into this new area. These criminal organizations have been getting into spamming, phishing, extortion, and all other profitable branches of computer crime. To assist them in their foray into computer crime, criminal organizations have begun recruiting talented hackers to handle the technical aspects of the crime, turning them into cyber-criminals.

As organizations have moved into the digital age, so have *corporate spies*. Information is now stored on network systems with physical access no longer required to access it. Corporate spies have begun taking advantage of this by turning to computer intrusion techniques to gather the information they desire.

As critical infrastructures become reliant on computers and networks for their operations, *terrorists* could seriously disrupt power grids, telecommunications, transportation, and others if they were to exploit vulnerabilities to disrupt or shut down critical functions. This new form of terrorism, known as cyber-terrorism, targets the underlying computers and networks of a nation's critical infrastructure with the intent of provoking public disturbances and threatening life and health.

According to many studies, *insiders* represent the largest threat to a company's information systems and underlying computer infrastructure, but, as the network perimeter gradually disappears, the threat from external sources is likely to increase. The insider threat is generally due to employees finding themselves in positions of extraordinary privilege in relation to the key functions and assets of their organization.

Less stringent supervisory controls over information systems personnel are often due to the highly technical and specialized nature of the work, which is difficult to understand and control. In addition, IS personnel often enjoy a degree of freedom quite different from that considered normal in a more traditional employment area.

Whether the threat is from malicious or subversive activities or from honest errors on the part of staff members, the human aspect is perhaps the most vulnerable aspect of information systems. In light of this, adequate controls should be implemented to ensure that employee wrongdoing is deterred and can be detected.

Reflection and Self-Assessment 15.1

Consult your university's library resources to find examples of one or more of the preceding types of computer criminals.

So, now that you know something about computer crime and computer criminals, let's examine ways to reduce the risk of computer crime in organizations.

INFORMATION SECURITY

The three principles are often referred to as the C-I-A triad.

Information security is defined as the protection of data in a system against unauthorized disclosure, modification, or destruction, and protection of the computer system itself against unauthorized use, modification, or denial of service. It is based on three fundamental principles: confidentiality, availability, and integrity. While the level of security varies from one organization to the next, controls are implemented to achieve one or more of these three **basic principles** (see Figure 15.1):

- *Confidentiality:* Condition that exists when data are held in confidence and are protected from unauthorized disclosure.
- *Data integrity:* State that exists when data stored in an information system are the same as those in the source documents or have been correctly processed from source data and have not been exposed to accidental or malicious alteration or destruction.
- *Availability:* Achieved when the required data can be obtained within the required time frame.

These three principles must be maintained throughout the information life cycle from creation to destruction.

Failure to protect the organization's information adequately could lead to financial losses, legal action, and loss of trust. Controls are thus implemented to protect the information. Much like the preventive/detective/corrective taxonomy we explored in Chapter 4, IT controls can be classified as physical, technical, or administrative (see Figure 15.2).

Physical security controls are required to protect computers, related equipment, and their contents from espionage, theft, and destruction or damage by accident, fire, or natural disasters (e.g., floods, earthquakes, and hurricanes). They involve the use of locks, security guards, badges, alarms, and similar measures to control access to computers, network equipment, and the processing facility. Other forms of controls such as smoke and fire detectors and generators are implemented to protect against threats such as fire and power outages.

Sometimes referred to as logical controls, **technical security controls** involve the use of safeguards incorporated in computer and telecommunication hardware and software. Firewalls, encryption, access control software, antivirus software, and intrusion detection systems fall into the category of technical security controls.

Firewalls are the first line of defense in protecting the corporate network from network-based threats. An access control policy determines which packets can flow between the network segments protected by firewalls; common techniques include examining packet information (such as source and destination address) and/or determining a message's transmission protocol. A firewall will only be as secure as the policy that it implements, the most effective being designed to restrict all traffic except that which is expressly permitted. You may be familiar with Windows Firewall or McAfee Security Suite, which incorporates firewall technology.

FIGURE 15.1
C-I-A Triad

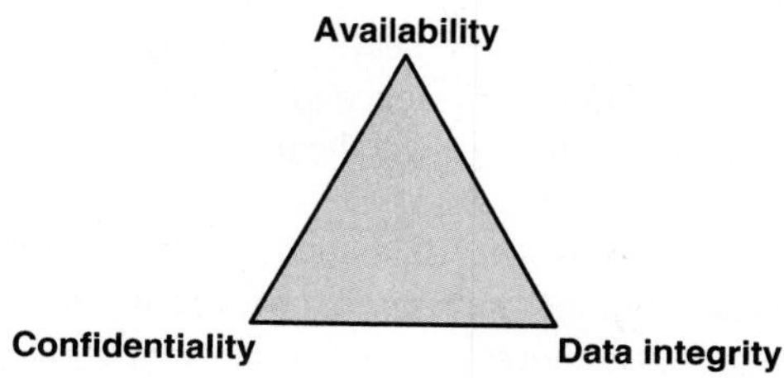

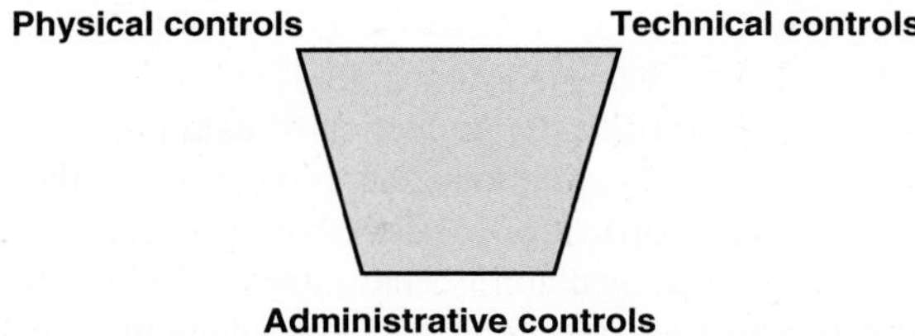

FIGURE 15.2
Control Taxonomy

Intrusion detection systems and intrusion prevention systems detect potentially malicious data and access patterns. Both system types operate at both network and individual computer levels. Network-based systems examine network traffic; they look for specific patterns of anomalous behavior or deviations from the standard behavior of the network. Individual systems detect malicious activity by examining system calls, event logs, critical system files, and other valuable system information.

Access controls protect the confidentiality, integrity, and availability of information resources. Access control can usually be seen as a three-step process: identification (the user provides information in order for the system to recognize him or her), authentication (once identified, the user must prove his or her identity), and authorization (the user is granted the privileges associated with his or her profile). Fundamentally, access controls ensure that only the "right" people have access to specific types of information. For example, as a faculty advisor at my university, I can access the records of any student, but an individual student has access only to his or her own academic records.

Cryptography transforms data to (*a*) hide them, (*b*) prevent them from being modified, and/or (*c*) prevent unauthorized access to them. Most cryptography uses mathematical functions (algorithms) to turn ordinary data into an incomprehensible format.

Management constraints, as well as operational and accountability procedures, are known as **administrative security controls**. Examples include security policies and procedures, security awareness and training, adequate supervision of employees, and security reviews and audits.

A security policy is a clear and concise set of guiding statements supported by management; it provides a framework that ensures that information assets are secured. It is the key component to an organization's information security management system; without it, internal stakeholders have no specific guidance with respect to information system security issues.

Security awareness training is an often-overlooked part of a security management program. Communicating the roles and responsibilities of employees as they are defined in the security policy is the first line of defense in protecting critical computing infrastructures.

Organizations should conduct security reviews in which they monitor the program to ensure compliance, fine-tune the security policy and controls in accordance with the organization's goals, and ensure that any deficiencies are corrected. Security audits will examine whether the information systems operate in accordance with the security policy and ensure that the controls are effective in protecting these systems. The information system auditing process collects and examines evidence to determine whether the information system possesses controls that adequately protect the organization's informational assets in an effective way.

Administrative security controls are established for three main reasons: (1) to provide supplemental controls, (2) to protect information processing resources, and (3) to ensure that all employees have proper authorization to access computing resources.

You might recall reading about these classifications in Chapter 4.

Physical, technical, and administrative controls can further be classified as preventive, detective, or corrective controls. Preventive controls are implemented to keep unwanted events from occurring, detective controls attempt to identify anomalous and unwanted events once they have occurred, whereas corrective controls remedy problems discovered by detective controls.

Reflection and Self-Assessment 15.2

Under what circumstances could each of the preceding information systems controls be classified as preventive, detective, and/or corrective?

Let's conclude our discussion of computer crime with a look at an important set of internal control ideas: ISACA's Control Objectives for Information and Related Technology (CoBIT).

COBIT

You may recall the reference to ISACA (Information Systems Audit and Control Association) in Chapter 4 (internal control); in Chapter 17 (professional certification and career planning), we'll look at the CISA certification sponsored by ISACA. ISACA's well-respected Control Objectives for Information and Related Technology framework gives accountants and other information systems professionals clear guidance in establishing strong internal controls, thereby deterring fraud. Earlier, we talked about COSO's (www.coso.org) contributions: *Internal Control: Integrated Framework* and *Enterprise Risk Management: Integrated Framework.* Singleton (2006, p. 12) explained the relationship between CoBIT and COSO as follows: "COSO does not directly provide guidance on assessing controls, especially IT controls, but CoBIT is well-suited to assess IT controls. Thus, a map from CoBIT to COSO is useful to IT auditors and managers alike in complying with Sarbanes-Oxley adequately and efficiently."

You'll find ISACA's Web site at www.isaca.org.

Now in Version 4.1, the **CoBIT framework** looks at the issue of internal control from three points of view: business objectives, information technology resources, and information technology processes. Further, CoBIT is organized in four "domains" of knowledge: plan and organize, acquire and implement, deliver and support, and monitor and evaluate. Poole (2006, p. 24) provides a context for the CoBIT framework by discussing CoBIT's seven **information criteria**:

- *Effectiveness.* The information is relevant and pertinent to the business process and is delivered in a timely, correct, consistent and usable manner.
- *Efficiency.* The information is provided through the optimal (most productive and economical) use of resources.
- *Confidentiality.* Sensitive information is protected from unauthorized (sic) disclosure.
- *Integrity.* The information is accurate and complete and is in accordance with business values and expectations.
- *Availability.* The information is available when required by the business process, now and in the future. It also concerns the safeguarding of necessary resources and associated capabilities.

- *Compliance.* The information complies with those laws, regulations and contractual arrangements to which the business process is subject, i.e., externally imposed business criteria.
- *Reliability of information.* Appropriate information is provided for management to operate the entity and exercise its financial and compliance reporting responsibilities.

Notice the way many of the information criteria relate to preventing and detecting computer crime. Computer crime often involves the disclosure of sensitive information—customer lists, employee records, and the like. By putting controls into place with sufficient confidentiality, managers can reduce the risk of computer crime. Such controls might include authorizing employees to access certain parts of the information system based on their position; for example, human resource employees would be able to access employee records, while purchasing department employees would not. The availability criterion talks about the importance of keeping resources safe; those resources would include hardware, software, and the information they contain. Internal controls in this area might include surveillance systems, locked and alarmed doors, and password protection with mandatory password rotation. As an accountant, you may be called upon to design or audit an information system for compliance with Sarbanes-Oxley. A strong internal audit function can be very helpful in achieving CoBIT's compliance criterion. Finally, information that has been compromised by computer crime, such as through Web site defacement, malicious software, or some form of information theft or manipulation, would violate the reliability of information criterion. Applicable internal controls here would include clear policy statements on installing software and various kinds of internal checks on data and information, such as validation rules in a relational database.

Refer to Chapter 4 and/or www.soxlaw.com for a review of that legislation.

Poole also discussed the issue of accountability as it relates to information governance. Business professionals and other stakeholders need to understand the role and responsibilities of at least six parties in keeping information safe and combating computer crime. Those six parties are shown in the **CoBIT accountability framework** in Figure 15.3 (Poole, 2006, p. 24).

Notice how accountability flows downward from stakeholders, through the board of directors, to IT and information security management. In this context, *stakeholders* refers to anyone with an interest in the business; it therefore could refer to customers, employees, investors, and a host of other parties. How does the issue of accountability relate to the topic of computer crime? Stakeholders put their trust in the board of directors, who in turn rely on the expertise of IT and information security management, to guard the organization against the kinds of computer crime discussed in this chapter. When either or both parties fail to meet their responsibilities, stakeholders (including the public) can lose confidence in an organization; some of the officers might even be held legally accountable.

The three parties on the right (audit committee, internal audit, and external audit) work with one another and with IT and information security management to assess and attest to the scope and adequacy of internal controls over information technology. Your accounting degree probably includes at least one required course in auditing, so we won't go into a lot of depth with it in this text. But Figure 15.3 might be the first time you've run across the term *audit committee.* Whittington and Pany (2004, p. 74) offer the following comments about audit committees:

Chapter 18 includes a brief overview of some important concepts in auditing to give you a feel for the discipline and its relationship to AIS.

> The New York Stock Exchange, the American Stock Exchange and NASDAQ have established requirements for independent audit committees by all listed companies. According to these requirements, audit committees must consist of at least three independent and financially literate individuals, and the chairman must have accounting or financial management expertise. In addition, the Sarbanes-Oxley Act of 2002 makes the audit committee directly responsible for the appointing, compensating and overseeing [of] the public accounting firm. The SEC regulations require public companies to file a copy of the audit committee's charter every three years and disclose whether its members are independent of management.

FIGURE 15.3 CoBIT Accountability Framework

Source: Poole, 2006, p. 24.

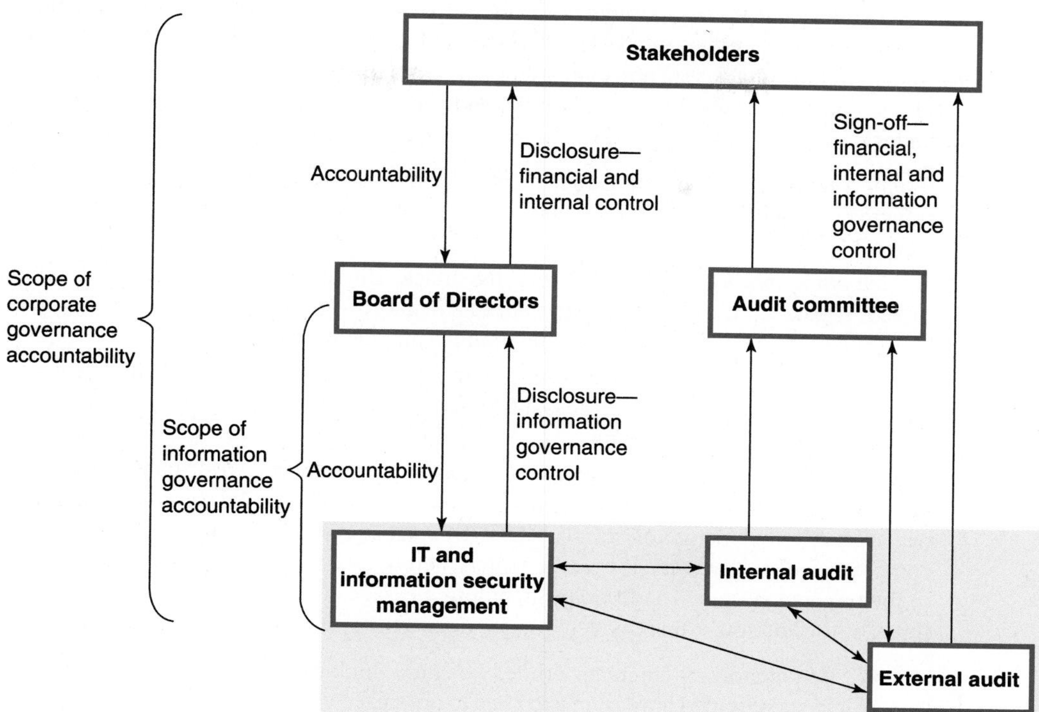

As you can see in Figure 15.3, the audit committee takes some responsibility for internal controls—including those that will prevent, detect, and correct computer crime. With most large accounting information systems employing some form of information technology, a clear understanding of computer crime and CoBIT will be helpful to you as an AIS professional.

CRITICAL THINKING

We've looked at several topics related to computer crime and IT security in this chapter: Carter's taxonomy, risks and threats, perpetrators of computer crime, internal controls, and CoBIT. In this section, I want to tie all of those together with an example.

Consider the following true account of a situation at Blue Security, an anti-spam firm that is now out of business (Lemos, 2006):

> Blue Security had created a small program called Blue Frog to turn a spam flood back on the advertiser, thus raising the cost of sending spam. The program would send a single opt-out request to the advertisers' Web sites for every registered user who received a spam message. Blue Security had about 500,000 subscribers to its service, so if a spam flood hit 20 percent of those users, then 100,000 opt-out requests would hit the advertisers who requested that the spam be sent. In revenge, one of the spammers—reportedly the one called PharmaMaster—attacked Blue Security and all Internet services associated with it for more than two weeks. The attack was so crippling that Blue Security was forced to close its doors.

How would the attack on Blue Security be classified using Carter's taxonomy of computer crime? As with many cases, it would fit in more than one category. We could think of it in

Carter's *target* classification; the attack targeted Blue Security's information system and its data to stop it from using Blue Frog. Since a computer was used to launch the attack, it also could be considered in the *instrumentality* classification. The incident wouldn't be appropriately classified as either incidental or associated; the computer was an integral part of the attack, but the attack was not simply a new version of an old crime.

The chapter discussed 11 business risks and threats associated with computer crime. The attack on Blue Security could be considered an example of any of the following:

- *Fraud.* According to the U.S. Department of Justice definition, the Blue Security case constitutes fraud. Knowledge of computer technology was critical in launching the attack.
- *Service interruption and delays.* During the attack, Blue Security's services were interrupted. If your campus has ever experienced a denial-of-service attack, as mine has, you know the kind of frustration those interruptions and delays can create.
- *Malicious software.* Attackers also sent incredible amounts of spam to Blue Security's customers. They were able to access customers' e-mail addresses by comparing e-mail lists based on responses to spam.
- *Denial-of-service attack.* The attack is a classic example of a distributed denial-of-service attack (DDOS). SearchSecurity.com describes DDOS like this: "On the Internet, a distributed denial-of-service (DDOS) attack is one in which a multitude of compromised systems attack a single target, thereby causing denial of service for users of the targeted system. The flood of incoming messages to the target system essentially forces it to shut down, thereby denying service to the system to legitimate users."

In terms of perpetrators of computer crime, we could think of Blue Security's attackers as hackers; some sources also have suggested ties to organized crime in the Blue Security case.

Most experts agree that there is no 100 percent foolproof way to prevent situations like the one at Blue Security. But managers can still implement some internal controls to reduce their likelihood and lessen their effects on an information system. Here are some ideas:

- Develop a business continuity plan that lays out how the organization will respond to cyber-attacks.
- Ensure that the information system isn't stretched to its capacity limits. If a system has excess capacity, denial-of-service attacks may not be as severe.
- Purchase insurance to cover the costs associated with system attacks.
- Store data and Web pages on multiple servers so that attackers don't have a single focal point.
- Track activity on the system so that you can detect denial-of-service attacks and other forms of intrusion. By knowing what a system's traffic usually looks like, it's easier to determine when an attack has occurred.

While I was researching material for this section, I came across a good, comprehensive paper talking about DDOS attacks: "Managing the Threat of Denial of Service Attacks" by Householder et al., October 2001. You can find the paper on the Internet; I encourage you to read it if you'd like to know more about this important topic. You can also check out http://staff.washington.edu/dittrich/misc/ddos/ for a comprehensive set of references about DDOS attacks.

How does the Blue Security case relate to the CoBIT framework? The case really touches all four domains of knowledge from CoBIT. Organizations need to plan for such attacks and organize themselves to respond. They need to acquire and implement tools and policies, like those just suggested, to ensure that their response is efficient and effective. With regard to the third CoBIT domain (deliver and support), information systems professionals need to make sure that the tools are available to users. And someone in the organization (whether the IT staff, internal auditors, or some other group) must take responsibility for monitoring the protection plan and evaluating it periodically.

Developing a strong information security response plan helps fulfill CoBIT's information criteria as well. It also promotes the kind of accountability relationships illustrated in Figure 15.3. Finally, organizations can move through the stages of the CoBIT maturity model as their security plans become more sophisticated.

Summary

Here is a summary of the chapter's important points based on its learning objectives:

1. *Explain Carter's taxonomy of computer crime.* Carter identified four basic types of computer crime: target (where the object is to attack the computer itself, often with the intent of compromising its data), instrumentality (where the computer is used to commit the crime), incidental (where the computer is not necessarily required for the crime but is used to make it easier to complete and/or harder to detect), and associated (where the computer is used to commit old crimes in a new way).
2. *Identify and describe business risks and threats to information systems.* Computers expose businesses to at least four specific risks, some of which are also present in noncomputerized information systems. First is the risk of fraud; while not unique to a computerized environment, the risk of fraud is increased because of the unique ways computers can be used to commit crime (refer to Carter's taxonomy for specific examples). Error is also an information systems risk; people can make data entry errors or create inaccurate processing instructions, just as they can in noncomputerized systems. Service interruptions and delays are unique to information technology environments; for example, without adequate internal controls, power failures can cause service interruptions. Finally, companies must consider the risk of disclosing confidential information; while not unique to a computerized environment, that risk is enhanced when data are stored electronically.

   The chapter discussed seven specific threats associated with computerized information systems. Intrusions allow a computer criminal to bypass information security and internal controls. Information theft is self-evident; it involves stealing sensitive or proprietary information from the system. Information manipulation doesn't necessarily mean that the information is stolen outright; however, it changes information, often resulting in inaccurate reports or less-than-optimal decision making. Malicious software, for example, a logic bomb, can exist in an information system benignly until a date, event, or condition activates it. At that point, it may change or delete data or cut off access to the information system. In a denial-of-service attack, a computer criminal bombards the information system with requests for information, thus preventing it from fulfilling its legitimate purpose. Think of Web site defacement as digital "tagging" or graffiti. Finally, extortion involves threats from a computer criminal (such as disclosing confidential information) unless the organization meets the criminal's conditions (such as paying cash).
3. *Name and describe common types of computer criminals.* A script kiddie is a relatively inexperienced computer criminal who uses techniques and code written by others. Hacker is a more generalized term referring to anyone who accesses an information system for any criminal/illicit purpose. Cyber-criminals are a subset of hackers; typically, cyber-criminals are motivated by financial gain. Organized crime groups have

taken advantage of information systems as well, often getting involved in phishing, extortion, and other profit-oriented types of computer crime. Corporate spies use computers and technology to gain access to confidential information, trade secrets, and the like. Terrorists may threaten life and public health by their actions, while insiders are employees of an organization who compromise the information system.

4. *Discuss ways to prevent and detect computer crime.* Internal control is at least as important in a computerized information system as it is in manual systems. Physical controls are perhaps the simplest type: locking doors, installing alarms, and requiring identification badges are some examples. Technical controls are part of the computer hardware and software themselves; think of firewalls, virus detection software, and access controls in this group. Finally, administrative controls refer to management policies and procedures designed to promote information security. For example, organizations may develop a clear information security policy and/or require periodic security training for employees.
5. *Explain CoBIT's information criteria and accountability framework.* The Information Systems Audit and Control Association (ISACA) developed and published a well-respected internal control framework specifically focused on IT security: Control Objectives for Information and Related Technology (CoBIT). The framework considers internal control from three perspectives: business objectives, information technology resources, and information technology processes. It identifies seven information characteristics essential to strong IT control: effectiveness, efficiency, confidentiality, integrity, availability, compliance, and reliability. CoBIT's accountability framework discusses the roles and responsibilities of six groups with respect to IT security: stakeholders, the board of directors, the audit committee, IT and information security management, internal audits, and external auditors.
6. *Explain how CoBIT can be used to strengthen internal controls against computer crime.* CoBIT's information criteria, accountability framework, and other components can help information systems professionals identify and assess risk. They also can help assign responsibility and designate authority for various tasks related to information systems security.

Key Terms

administrative security controls, *296*
basic principles of information security, *295*
CoBIT accountability framework, *298*
CoBIT framework, *297*
CoBIT information criteria, *297*
perpetrators, *293*
physical security controls, *295*
risks and threats, *290*
taxonomy for computer crime, *290*
technical security controls, *295*

Chapter References

Carter, D. 1995. "Computer Crime Categories." *FBI Law Enforcement Bulletin,* pp. 21–28.

Lemos, R. (2006, August). "Gangland Web Attacks; How Not to Get Whacked by the Botnet Mafia. *PC Magazine* 25(13), 116. ABI/INFORM Trade & Industry database (Document ID: 11070446111; February 1, 2009).

Poole, V. 2006. "Why Information Security Governance Is Critical to Wider Corporate Governance Demands—A European Perspective." *Information Systems Control Journal* 1, pp. 23–25.

Singleton, T. 2006. "CoBIT—A Key to Success as an IT Auditor." *Information Systems Control Journal* 1, pp. 11–13.

Whittington, R., and K. Pany. 2004. *Principles of Auditing and Other Assurance Services.* 14th ed. New York: McGraw-Hill/Irwin.

End-of-Chapter Activities

1. *Reading review questions.*
   a. What four common classifications are often associated with computer crime?
   b. What computer crime–related risks and threats are associated with information systems?
   c. What categories are commonly associated with computer criminals? Describe each category.
   d. How can organizations safeguard against computer crime? How can they detect it and recover from it if it happens? What role does CoBIT play in those tasks?
   e. What is CoBIT? What are the seven information criteria discussed in the CoBIT framework?
   f. Respond to the questions for this chapter's "AIS in the Business World."

2. *Reading review problem.* Consider the following examples of computer crime:
   - In June of 2005, news broke that breach at a third-party payment processor had affected 40 million credit cards. The intruders were able to export names, card numbers, and card security codes from approximately 20,000 of the affected cards. (CNN.com)
   - Beginning early Saturday, January 25, 2003, a worm known as Sapphire (aka SQL Slammer) began propagating through the Internet. It was the fastest-spreading worm ever released on the Internet, the number of infected hosts doubling every 8.5 seconds during the first minutes of propagation. Sapphire exploited vulnerability in MS-SQL, for which Microsoft had released a patch in July 2002. It is estimated that the worm infected at least 75,000 hosts, causing major network slowdowns and outages that led to canceled flights, ATM failures, and many other impacts to both large and small organizations. (CAIDA.org)
   - In recent years, online gambling sites have become the targets of cyber-extortionists threatening to bring down sites unless the companies behind these sites pay "protection" money. Online gambling sites are particularly vulnerable to online extortion as transactions are high volume and high impulse, customers turning to another site if the one they are attempting to access is unavailable. The perpetrators of these schemes have started taking advantage of information technology to launch large-scale denial-of-service attacks against the sites. (TheRegister.co.uk)
   - On June 8, 2005, the former IT manager of a software maker pleaded guilty to computer crime charges. Within two weeks of his termination, he gained unauthorized access to the computer system of his former employer and deleted an e-mail server domain, accessed the e-mail account belonging to the president, and made configuration changes to the mail servers that caused e-mails to be rejected. (Cybercrime.gov)

   a. Use Carter's taxonomy for computer crime to classify each of the preceding examples.
   b. What business risk(s)/threat(s) are exemplified by each situation?
   c. Which element(s) of the C-I-A triad was/were compromised in each example?
   d. What internal controls would you recommend to address each example?
   e. Discuss elements of the CoBIT framework that are relevant to each example.

3. *Making choices and exercising judgment.*
   a. What would motivate someone to engage in computer crime?
   b. Choose one of the AICPA Top Ten Technologies and explain how it might be used to engage in computer crime.
   c. Suggest at least three specific internal controls you'd employ to prevent, detect, or correct the computer crime you identified above.
   d. Brad Willman contributed to the arrest of several pedophiles in Canada and the United States. But he collected evidence for his investigation by hacking into others' computers. Read about this case in Cori Howard, "Internet Vigilante," *Maclean's* (June 6, 2005). What model of ethics, discussed in Chapter 3, best describes Willman's actions? Were Willman's actions ethical? What legal action, if any, should be taken against Willman?

4. *Field work.*
   a. Use your university library or www.findarticles.com to locate and read T. McCollum, "Computer Crime Surveys Yield Mixed Results," *Internal Auditor* (August 2004). Prepare a brief oral or written report on the article, relating it to the material presented in this chapter.
   b. Use a literature search to investigate one or more of the following computer criminals. Describe each one's crime; also compare and contrast them in terms of personal characteristics and motivations.
      i. Christopher Phillips (University of Texas)
      ii. Gary McKinnon (aka "Solo")
      iii. Julian Lush (Manchester, Connecticut)
5. *Applying Carter's taxonomy.* Which element(s) of Carter's taxonomy apply to each of the following situations? If more than one category applies, explain why.
   a. A bookkeeper steals cash as it comes into the company. The bookkeeper later falsifies accounting entries using general ledger software to cover the trail.
   b. A bored teenager initiates a denial-of-service attack on his Internet service provider's information system.
   c. A disgruntled employee uses a previously installed "back door" into an information system to lock out other users by changing their passwords.
   d. A gang of criminals breaks into a local retail store. They steal all the store's computers and then later hack into them for the purpose of identity theft.
   e. A pair of computer criminals uses e-mail to contact victims for an illegal pyramid scheme. They use money from new investors, rather than profits, to pay off old investors, keeping most of the money themselves.
   f. A recently fired employee laid the groundwork for corporate espionage by installing spyware on the company's network.
   g. A student discovers the password to his university's information system. He then hacks the system to change grades for himself and his friends.
   h. A woman impersonates her wealthy employer, stealing personal information about the employer from her bank's information system.
6. *Identifying business risks and threats.* Which type(s) of business risks/threats described in the chapter best applies to each situation below? If more than one applies, explain why.
   a. Blackmail based on stolen information.
   b. Concurrent attacks against a determined target.
   c. Digital graffiti.
   d. Discovery of customer Social Security numbers by external parties.
   e. Hacking.
   f. Intentional modification of information.
   g. Mistakes in data entry.
   h. Power failure.
   i. Salami technique.
   j. Stealing research and development data for new products.
   k. Trojan horse.
7. *Classification of computer criminals.* Fill in the blanks below with appropriate terms related to the types of computer criminals discussed in the chapter.
   a. ______ represent the largest threat to a company's information systems and underlying computer infrastructure.

b. ______ has been getting into spamming, phishing, extortion, and all other profitable branches of computer crime.

c. ______ could seriously disrupt power grids, ______, transportation, and others if they were to exploit vulnerabilities to disrupt or shut down critical functions.

d. A ______ describes a young inexperienced hacker who uses tools and scripts written by others for the purpose of attacking systems.

e. Corporate ______ have begun turning to ______ techniques to gather the information they desire.

f. Cyber-criminals possess ______ and have turned to hacking, not for the ______ but for the ______.

g. The term *hacker* originally described someone who wanted to ______ of computers and attempted to ______ to the limit.

8. *Classification of controls.* Classify each of the following controls as physical, technical, or administrative. Then, describe each control in your own words.

a. Access control software
b. Adequate supervision of employees
c. Badges
d. Encryption
e. Firewalls
f. Internal audits
g. Intrusion detection systems
h. Locks
i. Ongoing training regarding security issues
j. Security guards
k. Security policy
l. Smoke detectors
m. Universal power supplies

9. *CoBIT information criteria.* Indicate which of the CoBIT information criteria are violated in each of the following independent scenarios. Justify your choices.

a. Financial statements for the year ended December 31, 2008, are completed and published in June 2009.

b. A company with $1 million in annual revenues maintains an accounting information system with paper journals and ledgers.

c. Employee names, identification numbers, job classifications, and addresses are posted on a company Web site.

d. A careless employee spilled a soft drink on a file server. The server was damaged and could not be used for three days.

e. The CEO and CFO fail to provide the documents required by the Sarbanes-Oxley Act.

10. *Internal controls.* For each situation presented in the preceding problem, suggest one or more internal controls. Classify the controls as preventive, detective, or corrective. You may find it helpful to refer back to Chapter 4 to complete this problem.

11. *CoBIT.* Point your Web browser to www.isaca.org. Create a free account that will give you access to the CoBIT documents; then, work with a group of students to address one or more of the following questions:

a. What are the five IT Governance Focus Areas identified in the framework? Describe at least one of them.

b. How is CoBIT related to the COSO frameworks on internal control and enterprise risk management?

c. What are the components of CoBIT? How do they relate to one another?

d. How would managers apply the systems development life cycle to develop strong controls using CoBIT?

e. Compare and contrast the CoBIT maturity model with the capability maturity model discussed earlier in the text.

12. *C-I-A triad.* The C-I-A triad contains three elements: confidentiality, integrity, and availability. Refer back to one or more of the professional codes of ethics discussed in the first part of the text. How are the elements of the ethical code(s) you selected related to the triad? For example, confidentiality and integrity are explicitly mentioned in the IMA code of ethics.

13. *Crossword puzzle.* Please complete the puzzle below using terminology from the chapter.

Across

7. Developed a four-part taxonomy for computer crime.
8. Another name for technical security controls.
10. Type of computer crime that exploits weak internal controls.

Down

1. Element of the C-I-A triad that refers to timely access to necessary information.
2. The most precious asset of most organizations.
3. Type of behavior associated with service interruptions and delays.
4. For many hackers, fraud is this type of crime.
5. Key component of an organization's information security management system.
6. Control type concerned with identifying unwanted events.
9. A type of malicious software that reproduces over a network.

14. *Terminology.* Please match each item on the right to the most appropriate item on the left.

1. Confidentiality
2. Creating fake refunds to benefit a friend
3. Data diddling
4. Human element
5. Incidental
6. Instrumentality
7. Logic bomb
8. Salami technique
9. Sarbanes-Oxley Act
10. Willful neglect

a. Computers used to carry out a crime.
b. Crime classification that does not necessarily require a computer.
c. Data are protected from unauthorized disclosure.
d. Designed to help restore consumer confidence.
e. Information manipulation.
f. Intentionally changing information in a system.
g. Interest of less than one cent diverted to computer criminal's account.
h. Most vulnerable part of an information system.
i. One type of service interruption/delay.
j. Shuts down a payroll system if a specific employee number is deleted.

15. *Multiple choice questions.*

1. The name most closely associated with a taxonomy of computer crime is
   a. Sarbanes.
   b. Oxley.
   c. Legault.
   d. Carter.
2. Computer crime has been defined as any illegal act for which knowledge of ______ is used to commit the offense.
   a. Database software
   b. Hacking techniques
   c. Computer technology
   d. Spamming
3. Which of the following is most closely associated with a computer worm?
   a. Sapphire
   b. Online gambling
   c. Organized crime
   d. All of the above are associated with computer worms.
4. Which of the following is not a type of computer criminal?
   a. Script kiddie
   b. Hacker
   c. Salami criminal
   d. Terrorist

5. Administrative security controls include
   a. Management constraints.
   b. Operational procedures.
   c. Accountability procedures.
   d. All of the above.
6. The CoBIT framework includes ______ information criteria.
   a. Three
   b. Four
   c. Seven
   d. Some other number
7. Which of the following is not a domain in CoBIT?
   a. Prevent and correct
   b. Plan and organize
   c. Acquire and implement
   d. Monitor and evaluate
8. In CoBIT, accountability flows downward from
   a. External auditors to internal auditors.
   b. The audit committee to internal auditors.
   c. Stockholders to the audit committee.
   d. Stakeholders to the board of directors.
9. Which of the following uses an algorithm to secure information transmitted between computers?
   a. Password rotation
   b. Firewalls
   c. Encryption
   d. Security audit
10. In CoBIT, which of the following flows upward from the board of directors to stakeholders?
    a. Financial and internal control disclosures
    b. Accountability
    c. Disclosures regarding information governance control
    d. All of the above

16. *Statement evaluation.* Indicate whether each of the following statements is (i) always true, (ii) sometimes true, or (iii) never true. For those that are (ii) sometimes true, explain when the statement is true.

a. A specific instance of computer crime can involve multiple categories from Carter's taxonomy.
b. Computer crime involves using a computer to commit a crime.
c. Computer crime is perpetrated by organized crime groups.
d. Confidentiality, availability, and data integrity comprise the C-I-A triad.
e. Each element of the C-I-A triad is also mentioned in CoBIT's information criteria.
f. Hackers may be motivated by profit or by entertainment.
g. Information technology controls can be physical, technical, or administrative.
h. Organizations that implement CoBIT are immune to computer crime.
i. Perpetrators of computer crime come from outside the organization.
j. The "salami technique" is an example of information manipulation.

Chapter Sixteen

Decision-Making Models and Knowledge Management

AIS in the Business World

Knowledge Sharing in CPA Firms

To build an effective knowledge management system, people in organizations must first be willing to share knowledge. Vera-Muñoz, Ho, and Chow (2006) studied the idea of knowledge sharing in CPA firms. They point out that CPA firms should improve knowledge sharing due to increased regulation of the accounting profession, pressures to improve the audit process, and the need to leverage knowledge across an entire firm. They offer three recommendations (pp. 134–35) for increasing knowledge sharing:

- Recommendation 1: While the emergence and proliferation of new information technologies increase the ability of CPA firms to share knowledge, effective knowledge sharing requires more than a technological solution. Successful knowledge sharing further demands an organizational solution that includes the firm's employees, their practices, and their know-how.
- Recommendation 2: To encourage knowledge sharing, CPA firms need to develop and nurture a culture that simultaneously rewards knowledge sharing and discourages knowledge hoarding as a source of power or job security.
- Recommendation 3: To enhance the prospects of knowledge sharing in team-based settings, CPA firms should seek synergistic ways of combining extrinsic motivation with intrinsic motivation.

Although their study focused on public accounting firms, the recommendations apply to virtually any accounting context.

Discussion Questions

1. What is knowledge management?
2. What steps should firms follow to implement the recommendations listed above?

Source: S. C. Vera-Muñoz, J. L. Ho, and C. W. Chow, "Enhancing Knowledge Sharing in Public Accounting Firms," *Accounting Horizons,* June 2006, pp. 133–55.

Accounting is all about decision making—whether you're making decisions about the design and implementation of an accounting information system or using accounting information as the basis for decision making or in some other context. But, at the same time, the information available to business professionals for those decisions is increasing exponentially. So, how do accounting professionals manage all that information? And how do they make decisions based on it? We'll explore those two questions in this chapter.

When you've finished studying it, you should be able to:

1. Discuss and give examples of the concept of information overload, including causes, symptoms, and countermeasures.
2. Explain the nature of decision models and knowledge management.
3. Explain why those two topics are important in the study of accounting information systems.
4. Describe and apply decision-making models, including Wolcott and Lynch's Steps for Better Thinking.
5. Develop a personal strategy for making decisions and managing knowledge, including available information technology and other resources.

The principles and ideas we'll discuss in this chapter have broad application across a wide range of business and nonbusiness disciplines. We'll keep our focus, though, on their application and meaning in the context of accounting information systems.

INFORMATION OVERLOAD AND OTHER BARRIERS TO GOOD DECISIONS

Even Albert Einstein is often credited with acknowledging that he couldn't deal with more than seven variables simultaneously—surely a sign that even he was susceptible to information overload!

The idea that managers can be receiving "too much information" goes back to at least the 1960s, according to Eppler and Mengis (2004). They provide several definitions of **information overload,** including (p. 328):

> The decision maker is considered to have experienced information overload at the point where the amount of information actually integrated into the decision begins to decline. Beyond this point, the individual's decisions reflect a lesser utilization of the available information.
>
> Information overload occurs when the volume of the information supply exceeds the limited human information processing capacity. Dysfunctional effects such as stress and confusion are the result.
>
> Information overload occurs when the information-processing requirements (information needed to complete a task) exceed the information-processing capacity (the quantity of information one can integrate into the decision-making process).
>
> Information overload occurs when the decision maker estimates he or she has to handle more information than he or she can efficiently use.

Notice what all those definitions have in common: our brains have a limited capacity for processing information. When too much information starts coming in, or information comes in faster than we can process it, information overload is the result.

So what are the **causes of information overload?** Eppler and Mengis distilled the writing of more than a dozen authors spanning over 30 years of research in this area. They suggest five fundamental causes of information overload (2004, p. 332), as shown in Figure 16.1.

Personal factors refer to everyone's individual limitations to process information. For example, I process information much better in the afternoon and evening than I do in the morning—something my own students can easily verify! If you've ever stayed up all night finishing a school project, you may have noticed your own ability to process information erodes. But, on the positive side, you can probably process more information today than

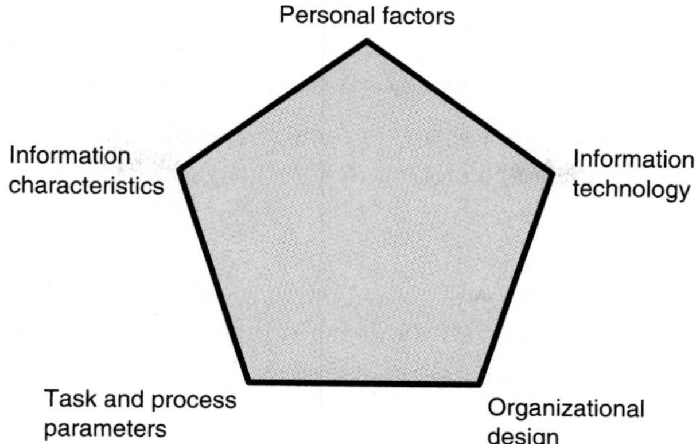

FIGURE 16.1
Causes of Information Overload

Source: Eppler and Mengis, 2004, p. 332.

you could 10 years ago, simply because you have more life experience and skills to help you manage information.

Readability indexes, such as the Gunning Fog index, can give an objective measure of a text's difficulty. A Web search on readability indexes or the Gunning Fog index will return a lot of information, including how to calculate a readability level.

Information characteristics also play an important part in triggering information overload. Information can be uncertain, ambiguous, complex, and intense—all of which create a greater opportunity for decision makers to become overloaded. Consider, for example, the complexity of information you read in an accounting text compared to the information complexity in a newspaper or novel. Newspapers and novels are likely to be much easier to "digest" than an accounting book, simply because of the nature of the information they contain.

Task and process parameters are the third cause of information overload identified by Eppler and Mengis. Have you ever had to make a decision under significant time pressure? If you're like most accounting students, the answer is a resounding "Yes!" Time pressure is one process parameter than can contribute to information overload. If you've taken any intermediate accounting courses, or perhaps a course or two in taxation, you may have found the rules and standards in one or both areas both numerous and incredibly detailed. Other causes of information overload in this area include nonroutine tasks, task complexity and interdependencies, and interruptions.

Fourth, Eppler and Mengis discuss *organizational design.* You've probably experienced this cause of information overload if you've ever worked on a group project in school or in practice. People in groups have differing ideas and approaches for problem solving and decision making; integrating all those different points of view can easily lead to information overload.

The final cause of information overload, according to Eppler and Mengis, is *information technology.* Think of all the ways IT provides you with information: e-mail, instant messaging, cell phones, the Internet, increased numbers of television channels. Every day, people are bombarded with information—much more so than in the past. Having all that information coming at you virtually all the time is bound to create some information overload.

Reflection and Self-Assessment 16.1

Think of a recent experience you had with information overload. What caused it? Can you classify the causes according to the five items in Figure 16.1? For example, as I started to write this chapter, I did a quick online library search for articles dealing with information overload—the search returned over 500 separate sources! My information overload came from three of the five sources: information characteristics, task and process parameters, and information technology.

Since you've probably experienced information overload at one time or another, you probably have at least some idea of its symptoms and effects. Eppler and Mengis grouped the symptoms and effects into four categories and provided several examples of each (2004, p. 333):

- Limited information search and retrieval strategies (information overload causes people to be less effective when looking for information).
  - Less systematic searching.
  - Increased problems differentiating relevant and irrelevant information.
- Arbitrary information analysis and organization (too much information coming in too fast impairs a person's ability to organize and classify information).
  - Overlapping and inconsistent categories.
  - Difficulty seeing "the big picture."
- Suboptimal decisions (decision making is weakened, producing poor results).
  - Inefficient work.
  - Reduced quality and accuracy of decisions.
- Strenuous personal situations (information overload takes its toll on people physically, psychologically, mentally, and spiritually).
  - Stress, confusion, and cognitive strain.
  - Overconfidence.

Are you experiencing information overload right now? Can you describe how it is impacting you?

Of course, the examples given above are but a few of many ways people respond to information overload.

So, since information overload is such a widespread problem, and since its impacts can be diverse and severe, how can managers deal with it? Returning to the five-part framework suggested in Figure 16.1, Eppler and Mengis examined the literature and noted the following **countermeasures** for information overload (2004, pp. 335–36):

- Allow more time to complete important tasks.
- Compress, aggregate, categorize, and structure information.
- Create small, self-contained tasks rather than trying to do everything at once.
- Define decision models and rules for common decision contexts.
- Focus on creating value-added information.
- Formalize the language used to describe information.
- Handle information as it comes to you—don't put it off!
- Improve personal information management.
- Improve personal time management skills and techniques.
- Use graphs and other visual aids.

The list could go on for another page or two, but I don't want you to experience information overload from reading it!

Reflection and Self-Assessment 16.2

Classify the countermeasures noted above using the five categories in Figure 16.1. For each category, suggest at least one other strategy you could use to combat information overload.

Simon (1997) talked about two additional reasons people don't always make the "best" decisions: **satisficing** and **bounded rationality**. *Satisficing* refers to people's tendency to stop looking for solutions to a problem when they find a solution that works—whether that decision is the "best" or not. For example, an accountant trying to choose a piece of general ledger software might "settle" for the first package that came along, rather than continuing to search for software that might meet his or her needs even better.

Bounded rationality is a separate, but related, idea; it means that people will inherently avoid uncertainty and rely on proven "rules" for problem solving whenever they can. Suppose your friend rides with you to school one day and later tells you that there's a better route to take than the way you usually go. The concept of bounded rationality would predict that you'll keep going the same way as always, avoiding the uncertain (and perhaps better) alternative. In our example above, bounded rationality might cause a decision maker to reject hiring a consultant if he or she has had poor experience with consultants in the past.

Betsch et al. (2004) talked about the idea of **relapse errors** in decision making. Their research revealed that people will follow a familiar routine, even if the routine is ineffective and even if they have a positive intention to change. Perhaps you know a student who spends most weekends partying instead of studying. That student may say to him/herself: "I really need to stop partying so much on the weekends. It's starting to impact my grades, and I don't like that." The idea of relapse errors indicates that, even with the positive intention to change, the student is likely to continue repeating the same behavior over and over again. And, in the AIS example, relapse errors might cause a decision maker just to adopt a newer version of an old piece of software, without considering a broad range of choices.

Do the ideas of satisficing, bounded rationality, and relapse errors mean that people are doomed to make bad decisions? Of course not! But it takes tremendous effort to change ineffective decision-making processes, and being aware of those three important ideas may help.

Reflection and Self-Assessment 16.3

Kathy has just started her own business after graduating from college. She is a management consultant, specializing in the development of business plans. She comes to you, a recent accounting graduate, for help in setting up her accounting information system. How would the ideas of satisficing and bounded rationality affect your advice to Kathy?

If you'd like to know more about the ideas in this section of the chapter, use your school's library to locate and read the Eppler and Mengis article. They do an excellent job of distilling and synthesizing the work of many other authors on this important topic.

DECISION MODELS AND KNOWLEDGE MANAGEMENT

One of the ways to combat information overload is to apply effective models for making decisions and managing knowledge. A "model" in this context refers to a generalized set of processes employed to accomplish a specific task. For example, you may have a model for how you get ready to go to school; it is probably significantly different from the model you use when you get ready to go out with friends.

Within the context of an organization, the generalized set of processes people use to gather, organize, and retain information has become known as *knowledge management,* defined as "the organization of intellectual resources and information systems within a business environment" (MSN Encarta dictionary). Santosus and Surmacz (2005) defined **knowledge management** as "the process through which organizations generate value from their intellectual and knowledge-based assets. Most often, generating value from such assets involves sharing them among employees, departments and even with other companies in an effort to devise best practices. It's important to note that the definition says nothing about technology; while [knowledge management] is often facilitated by IT, technology by itself is not [knowledge management]." In today's world, knowledge is power. Organizations no longer derive most of their wealth from physical assets such as cash in the bank or property, plant, and equipment. Information drives the 21st-century economy, and business professionals need strategies for capturing and organizing information, as well as for using that information for making decisions.

Rowley (1999) identified four objectives of knowledge management:

1. *To create knowledge repositories.* Think of this objective as developing a "library" for your organization. Knowledge here can refer to information on the competitive landscape, results of internal research, and the experiences of others in the organization.
2. *To improve knowledge access.* Here, we're talking about making knowledge more available throughout an organization. The most competitive organizations today share knowledge among individuals and responsibility centers. In fact, Drucker (1993) pointed out that knowledge may be the only genuinely sustainable economic resource in the modern economy.
3. *To enhance the knowledge environment.* This objective means stakeholders have a responsibility to create conditions that facilitate knowledge creation and sharing. Techniques that fall into this category include participative management, 360-degree performance evaluation, and decentralized management structures. Fundamentally, creating an environment of knowledge sharing is an issue of organizational culture.
4. *To manage knowledge as an asset.* The strict accounting definition of an asset is a probable future economic benefit obtained or controlled by a particular entity as a result of past transactions or events. While "knowledge" probably falls within that definition, we simply don't know how to measure its economic value for financial-reporting purposes. But, even though you won't see "knowledge" listed as an asset on organizational balance sheets, it must be managed for organizational benefit.

Call (2005) pointed out that "effective knowledge management changes the way organizations and individuals function." Building on the ideas of Nesbitt (2002), Call advocated seven **steps to create a knowledge management system**. Those steps are listed below; the text that follows each step provides an example of how it might "work" in practice.

For more information on organizational culture and its importance, consult the writings of Edgar Schein and/or Vijay Sathe.

1. *Create an organizational culture that supports the ideas of knowledge sharing and development.* You may recall reading about Dreambox Creations (www.dreambox creations.com/) in Part Four of this book. Dreambox provides Web site creation and other information systems services to its clients. As an information systems service company, Dreambox has a culture that relies on knowledge sharing and development. "Culture" in this case refers to the set of behaviors, values, and assumptions present in an organization. Establishing a strong organizational culture is no easy task—it depends principally on the people involved.

2. *Define the business goals the knowledge management system will address.* At Dreambox, the goal of a knowledge management system might be to compete more effectively by providing better client service through information sharing in the office. In other words, although each project at Dreambox is somewhat unique, certain lessons carry from one project to the next. As an information-based organization, developing a knowledge management system will enable Dreambox to compete more effectively in its markets.
3. *Perform a knowledge audit to identify any duplication, gaps, and overlaps in an organization's knowledge base.* A knowledge audit could be as simple as a series of staff meetings or as complex as a formal research project. Although every organization will have its own approach to a knowledge audit, one good approach would involve Dreambox staff asking questions such as: What do we need to know to compete? What lessons has each staff member learned from various client engagements? Do any of those lessons contradict one another? How do they interact? Who are the experts in each knowledge area? How can everyone learn from their expertise to provide better services to clients?
4. *Create a visual map that describes units of knowledge and the relationships between them.* If critical areas of knowledge at Dreambox include technical, communications, financial, and marketing, a visual map might look like Figure 16.2.
5. *Develop a knowledge management strategy based on the content management, integration, search mechanisms, information delivery, and collaboration.* A strategy refers to a consistent

FIGURE 16.2
Sample Knowledge Map

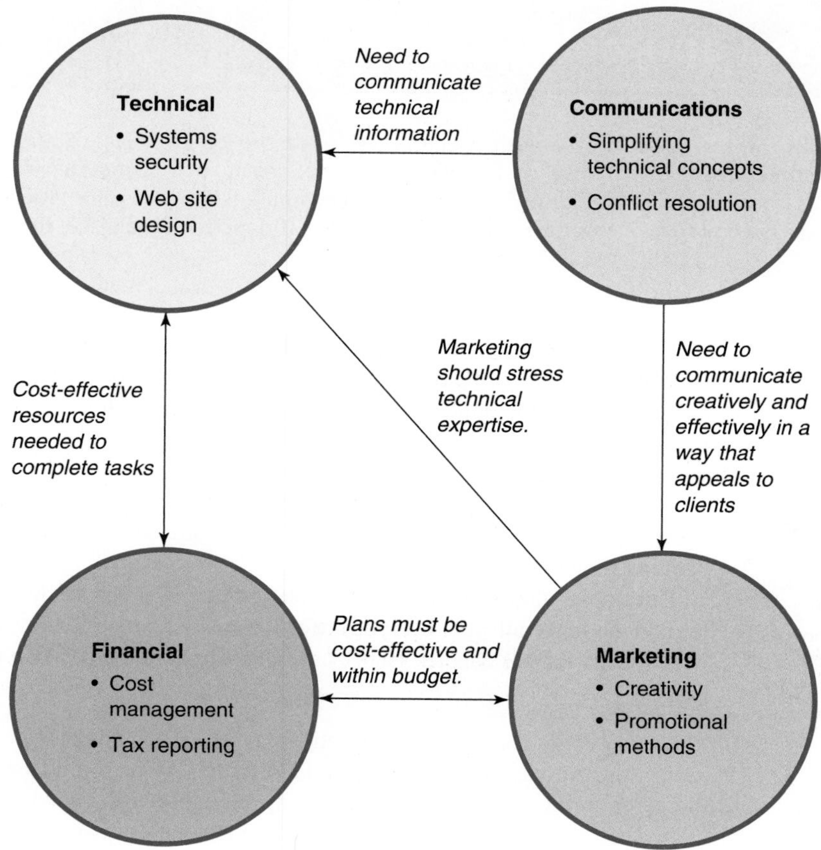

set of processes, policies, and procedures designed to achieve a specific purpose. Dreambox's knowledge management strategy might include project debriefing reports, periodic staff meetings, and client surveys to determine staff strengths and weaknesses.

6. *Purchase or build appropriate tools for capturing, analyzing, categorizing, and distributing knowledge.* As an information services firm, Dreambox might employ an Access database for this purpose. Tables could be organized around the four themes in the visual map; each table might contain fields for comment number (auto-generated), contributor (staff member name), client name, and "lesson learned" (perhaps a "memo" field). Queries and reports could be based on any of those fields; for example, what lessons were learned from our engagement with ABC Corporation.
7. *Periodically reassess the value of the knowledge management system and make necessary adjustments.* Knowledge is not static; therefore, knowledge management systems cannot be static either. The staff at Dreambox could review the system annually to determine any needed changes in organizational culture, visual map categories, database layout, and other aspects of the system.

Of those seven tasks, the first one is probably the most daunting. A detailed analysis of how to change organizational culture is far beyond the scope of this text, but you probably have run across the idea of organizational culture in management and/or organizational behavior courses.

Reflection and Self-Assessment 16.4

You might think of the FASB pronouncements that govern financial reporting as a form of knowledge management—although some would say those pronouncements are becoming too extensive and complex to do the job effectively. Suggest at least one other way we organize information in accounting; draw your example from your prior study of any area of accounting (financial, managerial, taxation, etc.).

The idea that accounting involves complex, open-ended problems may come as a surprise to you. In many accouning texts, the focus is on presenting problems with single correct responses. They form the foundation of the Steps for Better Thinking process but are not completely representative of the kinds of problems you'll have to solve in practice.

Business problems today require creative, critical thinking—bringing us to a discussion of Wolcott and Lynch's Steps for Better Thinking (2005). **Steps for Better Thinking** (SBT) is a developmental problem-solving and decision-making process. It is especially relevant to the kinds of problems we face in business today—complex and open-ended, without single, "correct," deterministic responses.

SBT starts with a foundation level, and proceeds through four problem-solving processes. Each process is more complex than the one before it. Wolcott (2005) presented the steps as shown in Figure 16.3.

Developing the skills in SBT is a lifelong process. It takes deliberate, intensive practice to ingrain the steps into your everyday decision-making process. Consider the "AIS in the Business World" for this chapter. Here's how an analysis of the decision might look using SBT.

1. *Identifying.*
   a. Problem: The problem investigated by Vera-Muñoz, Ho, and Chow was how to improve knowledge sharing in CPA firms. We're going to look at this problem from the point of view of a CPA trying to improve knowledge sharing in his/her own firm—an issue you're highly likely to encounter in your own professional career.

FIGURE 16.3
Steps for Better Thinking

Source: Adapted with permission; Copyright 2005 by Susan K. Wolcott. Steps for Better Thinking and related materials can be accessed at www.wolcottLynch.com.

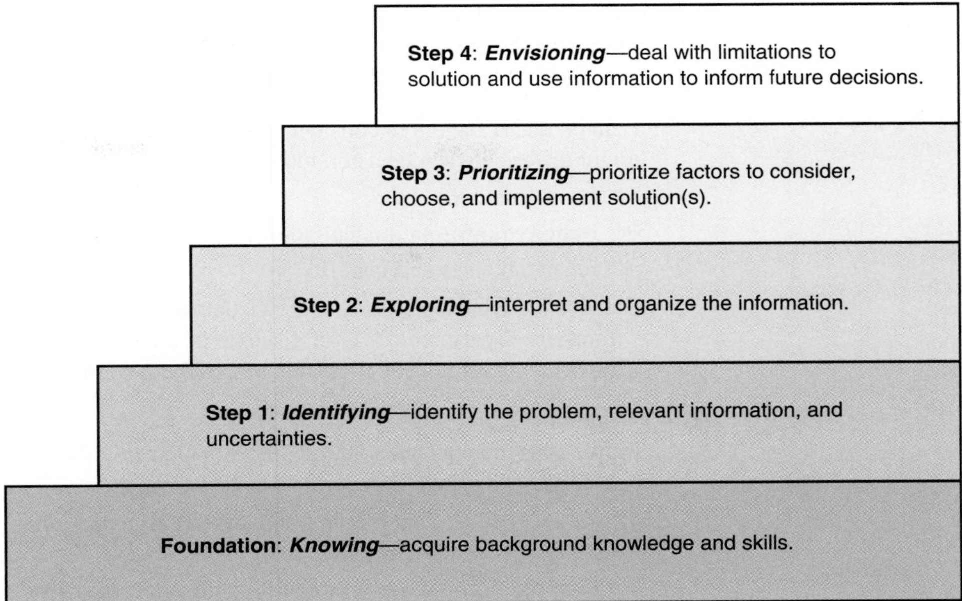
Step 4: Envisioning—deal with limitations to solution and use information to inform future decisions.
Step 3: Prioritizing—prioritize factors to consider, choose, and implement solution(s).
Step 2: Exploring—interpret and organize the information.
Step 1: Identifying—identify the problem, relevant information, and uncertainties.
Foundation: Knowing—acquire background knowledge and skills.

b. Relevant information: As background, a decision maker would have to acknowledge the legal and regulatory requirements, such as SOX and the PCAOB, that increase the need for knowledge sharing. In addition, particularly in the current economy, organizations are trying to control costs as much as they can; knowledge sharing may help reduce costs since people won't have to "reinvent the wheel" every time an issue arises.

c. Uncertainties: As with most decisions, there are plenty of uncertainties here! Are people in the organization willing to share knowledge? Do they know how to do so efficiently and effectively? What information technology tools, if any, will be needed to promote knowledge sharing?

The steps are presented in a very linear way in this example. In "real life," decision makers might move back and forth between the steps as new information comes to light.

2. *Exploring.*

a. Biases: While some people are very open to sharing knowledge, others are likely to be resistant (biased against it). The second of the researchers' three recommendations acknowledges this idea.

b. Assumptions: Knowledge sharing is a good idea. The recommendations offered are practical and legitimate.

c. Qualitative interpretation from various points of view:

i. Inexperienced CPAs may feel they don't have much knowledge to share, so they may be less willing to express an opinion or offer suggestions.

ii. Experienced CPAs may believe they don't have much to learn from others.

iii. Some clients may be in favor of knowledge sharing as a way to reduce the cost of an audit; on the other hand, clients that have something to hide may not want CPAs to share knowledge.

d. Information organization: A professional trying to decide whether (and how) to implement knowledge sharing could develop a simple list of costs and benefits, based on reading, self-reflection, and conversation with others. To the extent that those costs and benefits can be quantified reliably, a projected overall cost–benefit of knowledge sharing could be estimated.

3. *Prioritizing.*
   a. Ranked list of factors to consider (note that this ranking is still highly subjective and might differ between decision makers):
      i. Human factors.
      ii. Required information technology knowledge and tools.
      iii. Financial costs and benefits.
   b. Conclusion: Develop a limited knowledge-sharing program on a pilot basis—perhaps within one department or with a subset of clients. The pilot project would help the CPA firm work out some problems before the system was more widely disseminated.
4. *Envisioning.*
   a. Limitations of endorsed solution (decision makers would monitor and report on these over time, using them to inform later decisions):
      i. Knowledge sharing requires a change in organizational culture—seldom an easy thing to accomplish.
      ii. Pilot testing in a subset of the organization may lead to rumors and later bias against knowledge sharing.
   b. Skills integration: Once the pilot test was done, decision makers could use the information to spread the knowledge-sharing project throughout the firm. The program should be monitored and assessed periodically; that is, people should ask whether the program is working. In that way, any needed changes can be implemented.

Reflection and Self-Assessment 16.5

Consider the case of Kathy presented in Reflection and Self-Assessment 16.3. Use the Steps for Better Thinking model to prepare your advice to Kathy.

As you can see, using the Steps for Better Thinking to reach a decision is a detailed process. As noted above, the ability to use the steps must be deliberately, consistently, and continually developed over time; a decision maker's comfort level with the steps will increase with practice, though, and careful application of SBT will typically result in high-quality decisions.

CRITICAL THINKING

In this chapter, we've looked at three important topics: information overload, knowledge management systems, and Steps for Better Thinking. Let's look at a comprehensive example that connects all three topics.

Consider the following situation:

> Ricardo, Erika, Stephen, Travis, and Qian all work in the Accounting Department of CHL Corporation; they all have undergraduate degrees in accounting and professional licenses/

certifications (CPA, CMA, and the like). Erika is the vice president and corporate controller; the other four are associate vice presidents for specific functions. CHL was getting ready to expand its operations into Brazil, and the five accountants were on a team charged with finding out more about Brazil in anticipation of the expansion. They were supposed to prepare a report with the following sections: country background (history, language, geography), environmental factors (national culture, legal and political systems, business environment), financial matters (currency, exchange rates, taxation), accounting standards (local GAAP, International Financial Reporting Standards), and conclusions/ recommendations. Their boss had given them two weeks to complete the task; during that time, they would be relieved of some (but not all) of their usual responsibilities.

What sources of information overload is the team likely to experience? And how should they deal with them? Here are some thoughts on those two questions:

Information Overload Source	Strategy for Managing
Personal factors	Set aside specific times for working on the project and for team meetings to discuss progress.
Information characteristics	Develop a detailed outline of the topics to include in each section of the report.
Task and process parameters	Create a schedule that will allow them to complete the project on time. Ask for additional time if necessary.
Organizational design	Estimate the amount of time each section of the report will take; divide up the responsibility as evenly as possible.

With so much information to synthesize, the team might decide to create a knowledge management system (KMS) as an organizational aid. The report will have five sections, so the KMS could be organized in that way. Each section will have multiple pieces of information; suppose (for the sake of simplicity) that each piece of information applies to only one section. The team could create a database table with the following fields: record number, report section, date, contributor, information source, summary. "Record number" would be the primary key, and could be set up as an "auto-number" field. The team could develop a data input form that would incorporate drop-down lists (i.e., combo boxes) for the "report section" and "contributor" fields. "Information source" should provide a complete reference for accessing the information after its initial input; the field could include (for example) Web addresses, book and article citations, and interview details. The team could set up queries based on report sections and/or other criteria; reports based on those queries would be useful in preparing the report.

The team's task would fit into the Steps for Better Thinking model like this:

1. *Knowing:* The team members would have acquired the skills they need to complete the research as part of their educational experience; the research itself would give them the background knowledge they need about Brazil.
2. *Identifying:* The problem and relevant information are defined by the nature of the task. The team might be uncertain about where to find the information they need and how long the task will take.
3. *Exploring:* Designing the knowledge management system would be part of this step. A properly designed database (or some other way of managing the information they collect) would assist in organizing the information. Team discussions would be useful in interpreting it.

4. *Prioritizing:* The team's basic task is to develop a report that will inform the expansion decision. Once the research is complete, they will have to prioritize the information they've collected, choose what to include in the report, and write the report.
5. *Envisioning:* With such a short time to prepare such a comprehensive and important report, it is almost certain to have some limitations. After the project is complete, the team should meet to discuss those limitations and identify ways to overcome them in similar future situations.

I hope this example has improved your understanding of this chapter's main topics, and that you'll be able to apply them in your own professional career.

Summary

As usual, here's a brief synopsis of this chapter's main points:

1. *Discuss and give examples of the concept of information overload, including causes, symptoms, and countermeasures.* Information overload occurs when people have information coming in faster than they can process that information. Information technology has definitely contributed to information overload in modern organizations; other factors include human, task, process, and information characteristics. Symptoms and responses include suboptimal decisions and arbitrary analysis. Managers can effectively combat information overload with good time management, personal discipline, and knowledge management systems.
2. *Explain the nature of decision models and knowledge management.* A model is a generalized framework for completing a task. Knowledge management systems achieve four important objectives: create knowledge repositories, improve knowledge access, enhance the knowledge environment, and manage knowledge as an asset.
3. *Explain why those two topics are important in the study of accounting information systems.* The essence of accounting is decision making. As accountants, we need to collect information that is relevant and helpful in specific decision contexts.
4. *Describe and apply decision-making models, including Wolcott and Lynch's Steps for Better Thinking.* The Steps for Better Thinking is an example of a decision-making model; it involves four levels of increasing complexity: identifying, exploring, prioritizing, and envisioning.
5. *Develop a personal strategy for making decisions and managing knowledge, including available information technology and other resources.* Practice using the models and strategies presented in this chapter will help you become a more effective decision maker. The ideas discussed here can be molded and adapted to a decision style that suits you as an individual—once again reinforcing the idea of "art" over "science."

You make personal and professional decisions every day. Some of them are more mundane (what to wear to school, what to eat for lunch), while others are of vital long-term importance (how to allocate your time, which job offer to accept at graduation). The information presented in this chapter will assist you in developing your own decision-making style and process.

Key Terms

bounded rationality, *313*
causes of information overload, *310*
countermeasures, *312*
information overload, *310*
knowledge management, *314*
relapse errors, *313*
satisficing, *313*
Steps for Better Thinking, *316*
steps to create a knowledge management system, *314*

Chapter References

Betsch, T., S. Haberstroh, B. Molter, and A. Glockner. 2004. "Oops, I Did It Again—Relapse Errors in Routinized Decision Making." *Organizational Behavior and Human Decision Processes* 93, no. 1, pp. 62–74.

Call, D. 2005. "Knowledge Management—Not Rocket Science." *Journal of Knowledge Management* 9, no. 2, pp. 19–30.

Drucker, P. 1993. *Post-Capitalist Society.* New York: Harper Row Publishing.

Eppler, M., and J. Mengis. 2004. "The Concept of Information Overload: A Review of Literature from Organization Science, Accounting, Marketing, MIS and Related Disciplines." *Information Society,* pp. 325–44.

Nesbitt, K. 2002, February 8. "Designing a Knowledge Management System." http://academic.edu.2081/products/faulknerlibrary/00018382.htm (May 2, 2005).

Rowley, J. 1999. "What Is Knowledge Management?" *Library Management,* pp. 416–19.

Santosus, M., and J. Surmacz. 2005. "The ABCs of Knowledge Management." www.cio.com (April 28).

Simon, H. 1997. *Administrative Behavior.* 4th ed. New York: Free Press.

Wolcott, S., and C. Lynch. 2005. "Steps for Better Thinking." www.wolcottlynch.com (April 29).

End-of-Chapter Activities

1. *Reading review questions.*
   a. What is information overload? What causes it? What are its effects? How can decision makers deal with information overload in their professional lives?
   b. Explain the idea of knowledge management. Why is it important? What are some techniques you can use to manage knowledge now and in the future?
   c. Summarize the ideas and steps associated with Wolcott and Lynch's Steps for Better Thinking.
   d. Prepare a response to the questions for this chapter's "AIS in the Business World."
2. *Reading review problem* Suppose an organization is considering three ways to provide improved information technology to its sales staff:
   - *Alternative 1:* Invest in a large mainframe computer and software that will provide a variety of services to various divisions, including sales. The system will allow the salespeople to send the order by phone at the end of each day, have it filled in by the order entry clerk at the corporate head office, edit the order for errors, and input the order into the system. The software will analyze the order, configure the product price, and prepare the order that night on the mainframe computer. The next day, the order (with the expected date of shipment and value) is sent to the customer/salesperson. The approximate total cost of this option is $9 million.
   - *Alternative 2:* Invest in a large software package that will do product configuration and ordering for the sales personnel. This software is put on a minicomputer and is networked via leased lines/modems to various sales offices, so that salespeople can access it. The total cost of the investment is $3.5 million. The organizational intent remains the same: Provide access to expert advice for product configuration and process orders online so a salesperson can order the product correctly and provide the customer the needed service.
   - *Alternative 3:* Invest in 400 notebook computers and software for sales personnel so they can use them to configure products for customers and prepare business orders at the customer site. This investment, totaling about $3 million, is intended to improve the productivity of sales professionals, that is, enable them to correctly order the product and service the customer effectively.

   a. What sources of information overload are likely to impact decision makers in evaluating the three alternatives?
   b. What strategies would you recommend for dealing with those sources?
   c. What information would you capture about the three alternatives in a knowledge management system?
   d. Use the first three steps of the Steps for Better Thinking to choose one of the alternatives. You may omit the fourth step (envisioning).

3. *Making choices and exercising judgment.* Betsy and Mark are bookkeepers for CTC Corporation; both have been employed by CTC for over 20 years. They currently use a paper-based accounting information system to complete the steps in the accounting cycle, but the company president (Raj) wants to move to a more automated environment. Use Steps for Better Thinking to analyze the choice of staying with the current paper-based system or moving to an automated system. (*Note:* This problem is not asking you to evaluate technology alternatives for the AIS. Rather, you are to compare the idea of staying with a paper-based system with the concept of using information technology to complete the steps in the accounting cycle.)
4. *Field work.*
   a. Use your university's library to locate and read "Knowledge Management in Three Financial Organisations: A Case Study" by Martie M. Squier and Retha Snyman. What conclusions do they reach regarding knowledge management?
   b. Talk with other students at your university about their decision-making processes. Compare and contrast the decision-making processes based on at least two of the following factors: age, year in school, major, GPA.
   c. Interview a practicing accountant in an area of the profession that interests you. Ask about a recent major decision your interviewee has made and the process he or she used to make it. Write a short paper that summarizes the accountant's decision process. Analyze the decision process through the lens of Steps for Better Thinking as well.
5. *Analyzing current issues in accounting.* Consider the list of current and classic issues in accounting presented below (or others specified by your instructor). With your instructor's help and guidance, form a team of students to investigate one of the issues. Use the Steps for Better Thinking to analyze the issue and prepare a short oral report for the class.
   a. What are the obstacles associated with adopting International Financial Reporting Standards?
   b. Should the provisions of the Sarbanes-Oxley Act be extended to nonpublic corporations?
   c. Will principles-based accounting become the norm for U.S. GAAP?
   d. Has the 150-hour requirement for becoming a CPA been a success?
   e. What systems documentation techniques should be taught in AIS courses?
   f. Has the conceptual framework of accounting fulfilled its purpose?
   g. What issues should managers consider with regard to corporate governance?
   h. Should social and environmental reporting be mandatory?
   i. How, if at all, should fair-value accounting be implemented?
6. *Software acquisition decision using SBT.*
   a. Critter Sitters (www.stlouiscrittersitters.com/) is an in-home pet care company based in St. Louis, Missouri. Their Web site lists several services available to pet owners, including mid-day dog walking, puppy care, and in-home dog training. Suppose Critter Sitters is considering three general ledger packages for its accounting information system: ePeachtree, Quickbooks, and Great Plains Dynamics. Use the Steps for Better Thinking to help the company's president make a choice.
   b. According to its Web site (www.40debts.org/counseling/default.asp), Harbour Credit Management "provides credit management services to families and individuals experiencing financial stress." Suppose the firm is searching for software that will help manage spam on

its information system. Point your Web browser to www.download.com, and investigate three different software packages that fulfill that purpose. Make a recommendation to Harbour's management using the Steps for Better Thinking to inform your decision.

c. Katy is the owner of Active Bodyworks and Wellness in Ontario, California. She has been taking appointments, maintaining her accounting information system, and managing client information using a paper-based system for the last several years but now wants to move to a more computerized environment. She's heard about voice recognition systems and comes to you for a recommendation between three specific packages: Dragon Naturally Speaking, Realize Voice Lite, and e-Speaking. Point your Web browser to www.download.com, and investigate each package. Use the Steps for Better Thinking to make a recommendation to Katy.

7. *Knowledge management tools.* Point your Web browser once again to www.download.com. Search for knowledge management software; choose one example and prepare a short oral report for the class on its capabilities and cost.

8. *Creating knowledge management systems.*

a. Viola completed her accounting degree in 2000; she has had three professional positions since that time. She summarized information about each position as indicated below. Organize the information into a knowledge management system.

Dewey, Cheatam and Howe, CPAs (2000 to 2001)

Responsibilities: Small-business auditing

Salary: $40,000 annually

Comments: I like working with small-business clients, but it's tough getting to know them.

ENZ Corporation (2001 to 2003)

Responsibilities: AIS design, accounts receivable management

Salary: $45,000 annually

Comments: More stable hours, interesting work—but not really diverse.

FNN Corporation (2003 to present)

Responsibilities: Divisional controller

Salary: $50,000 annually

Comments: Plenty of responsibility; interesting corporate culture

b. Most university accounting curricula cover a fairly standard range of topics: financial accounting, cost accounting, taxation, systems, and auditing. Think about the classes you've taken so far within your accounting program; develop a list of at least five topics for each class. Also, develop a list of other abilities (like writing, speaking, and use of information technology) that cut across the accounting classes you've had. Using a software tool of your choice (or one specified by your instructor), develop a system to organize and manage the items in the lists.

c. Sebastian is a self-employed AIS consultant. He has several books on the subject in his library, as shown in Table 16.1, covering a variety of topics. Develop a knowledge management system based on the information provided. (Your instructor may ask you to use a relational database such as Microsoft Access to complete this task.)

9. *Personal decision making and knowledge management system.* Based on what you've learned in this chapter, prepare a brief written report that summarizes your personal plan for making better decisions and managing knowledge. Use a specific example of a recent past or upcoming decision to illustrate your decision-making model.

TABLE 16.1 Table of Books for Activity 7(c)

	Books					
Title	*Accounting Information Systems*	*Adventures in AIS*	*Basic AIS Concepts*	*Auditing AIS*	*The Role of AIS in Organizations*	*Safeguarding the AIS*
Author	Brady	Legault	Ogan	Barbagallo	James	Burkett
Publisher	Prentice Hall	Thomson	McGraw-Hill	Thomson	McGraw-Hill	McGraw-Hill
Copyright	2000	2003	2003	2005	2004	2005
Strengths	Easy to read; lots of illustrations	Real-world examples	Real-world examples; Sarbanes-Oxley	Topic breadth; checklists	End-of-chapter materials; independent organization	Small-business focus; easy to read
Weaknesses	Cost	Difficult to read	End-of-chapter materials	Sarbanes-Oxley	Difficult to read	Web materials
Number of Pages	300	150	275	300	185	210
Topics	• Information technology • Internal controls • Data modeling	• Accounting cycle • Fraud detection • Information technology • Data modeling	• Accounting cycle • Internal controls • Data modeling • Information technology	• Fraud detection • Internal controls • Accounting cycle • Data modeling • Information technology	• Information technology • Internal controls	• Internal controls • Fraud detection • Information technology

10. *Crossword puzzle.* Please complete this puzzle using appropriate terminology from the chapter.

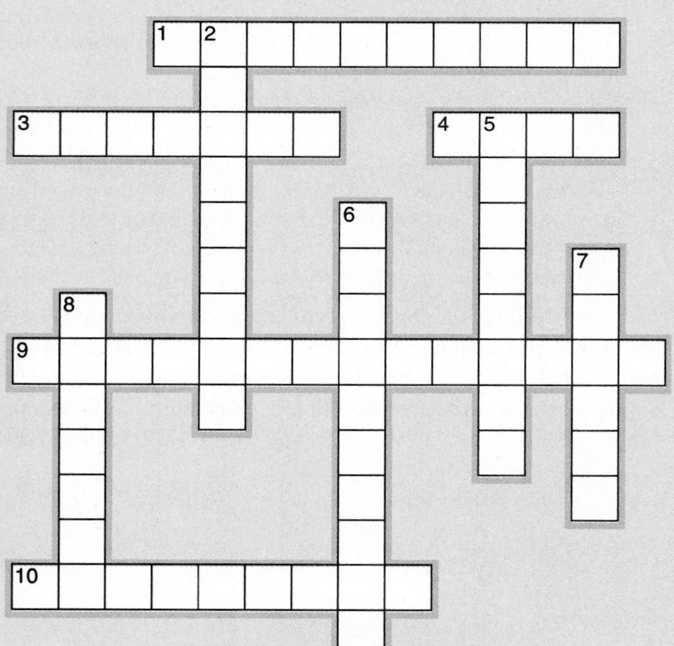

Across

1. Creating a knowledge ______ is one purpose of knowledge management systems.
3. Error type that describes repeating past ineffective behaviors.
4. Number of SBT levels after the foundation.
9. ______ design: one cause of information overload.
10. Type of information analysis that may result from information overload.

Down

2. SBT level focused on interpreting and organizing information.
5. Occurs when too much information comes in too quickly.
6. Task and process ______: a cause of information overload.
7. Along with visual aids, can help combat information overload.
8. Author who believed that knowledge may be the only economically sustainable resource.

11. *Terminology.* Please match each item on the left with the most appropriate item on the right.

1. Wolcott and Lynch	a. A system for creating value from intellectual assets
2. Satisficing	b. Software that can be used to implement a KMS
3. Relapse errors	c. Human tendency to rely on rules for making decisions
4. Prioritizing	d. Looking at information from multiple points of view
5. Knowledge management	e. SBT step that involves identifying personal bias
6. Identifying	f. Simon's notion that people will accept the first reasonable solution for a problem
7. Exploring	g. Starting place for Steps for Better Thinking
8. Envisioning	h. Tendency to make the same mistakes repeatedly
9. Bounded rationality	i. The creator(s) of Steps for Better Thinking
10. Database	j. The last step in SBT

12. *Multiple choice questions.*

1. Which of the following types of information is most likely to create information overload for an experienced accountant?
   a. Elements of financial statements
   b. Tax pronouncements
   c. The Sarbanes-Oxley Act
   d. Rules of debit and credit
2. The Gunning Fog Index is most closely related to
   a. Task and process parameters.
   b. Information characteristics.
   c. Organizational design.
   d. Personal factors.
3. Which of the following statements about Steps for Better Thinking is most true?
   a. Using the steps effectively requires a college degree as a precursor.
   b. SBT is the best model for decision making available to accountants today.
   c. Each step requires more complex tasks than the steps that precede it.
   d. SBT is most applicable to ethical decision-making situations.
4. A group of accounting students told their accounting professor to "give them the right answer to a problem so they could memorize it for the exam." The students were exhibiting
   a. Satisficing.
   b. Bounded rationality.
   c. Relapse errors.
   d. Good knowledge management skills.

5. Knowledge should be managed as a(n)
   a. Asset.
   b. Element of shareholders' equity.
   c. Liability.
   d. Source of revenue.
6. Which of the following is not a cause of information overload?
   a. Personal factors
   b. Relapse errors
   c. Information technology
   d. Task and process parameters
7. Which element of Steps for Better Thinking focuses on dealing with limitations of problem solutions?
   a. Identifying
   b. Exploring
   c. Prioritizing
   d. Envisioning
8. The concepts discussed in this chapter can be applied to
   a. Evaluating software for an accounting information system.
   b. The job search process.
   c. Studying for professional exams.
   d. All of the above.
9. Which of the following is not an effective way to deal with information overload?
   a. Leave important decisions to others.
   b. Define decision models and rules for common decision contexts.
   c. Focus on creating value-added information.
   d. Formalize the language used to describe information.
10. Who first suggested the ideas of satisficing and bounded rationality?
    a. Drucker
    b. Wolcott
    c. Simon
    d. Pacioli

13. *Statement evaluation.* Indicate whether each of the following statements is (i) always true, (ii) sometimes true, or (iii) never true. For those that are (ii) sometimes true, explain when the statement is true.

a. A supportive organizational culture is an important step in knowledge management.
b. Bounded rationality prevents people from making good decisions.
c. Breaking up a complex job into smaller tasks can help combat information overload.
d. Even the smartest human beings have a limited capacity for processing information.
e. Information characteristics can contribute to information overload.
f. Information technology is a cause of information overload.
g. Information technology is a solution for information overload.
h. Knowledge management systems involve relational database software.
i. The levels of Steps for Better Thinking involve increasingly complex tasks.
j. Visual maps resemble data flow diagrams.

Chapter Seventeen

Professional Certifications and Career Planning

AIS in the Business World

Career Paths for Accountants

Accounting is a great field of study for many people, as it opens up a variety of career paths. Understanding the financial aspects of organizations is a highly sought skill, and the employment market is very competitive.

Consider the following comments from practicing accountants in diverse working environments:

> I would say my career progressed in a way that is quite typical . . . where you start as a graduate, you do your qualification, you become a senior accountant after a couple of years, then you become a manager. You continue to work in an audit practice. You continue to do client facing work, but start to take on some internal responsibilities.
>
> I don't have an end point where I've got to be a Vice President or I've got to be anything in particular.
>
> Should I be poor but seek happiness. Or should I make us comfortable before I break off. Where I am now is 75% there, but in order to get the other 25% I might have to go back to zero. Am I able to . . . get a better work life balance . . . or will I have to reassess?

You'll have to confront similar issues in your own professional career, so it's a good idea to start planning that career now—not to lock yourself into a path, but to have some concept of where you're headed professionally.

Discussion Questions

1. What is the relationship between earning an accounting degree and becoming professionally certified?
2. What professional certifications are available in the accounting profession? How are they related to your study of AIS?
3. What are the costs and benefits associated with professional certification?

Source: T. Smith-Ruig, "Making Sense of Careers through the Lens of a Path Metaphor," *Career Development International* 13, no. 1 (2008).

At my university, AIS is the first upper-division accounting course in a student's curriculum, so it's a good time for talking about career planning issues—that's why I'm including this chapter in an AIS text.

Earning your undergraduate accounting degree is the first step in a lifetime of your professional development as an accounting professional. A good second step is earning one or more professional licenses or certifications, many of which we'll discuss in this chapter. Earning a professional certification or license demonstrates your mastery of a common body of knowledge, shows you are self-disciplined and eager to learn, and opens up many more professional doors than your degree alone.

You're probably already familiar with the Certified Public Accountant (CPA) license. But did you know that many other accounting certifications exist beyond being a CPA? Each one is rigorous in its own way; each one has a distinct purpose and benefit for a practicing accountant. My advice to my own students is to decide where you see your career headed, and then choose a certification or license that matches your professional goals. Earning a professional certificate or license doesn't necessarily lock you into a given career direction—plenty of CPAs, for example, move out of public practice into the corporate world after earning their license. The important thing at this stage in your career is to get a clear picture of your interests and abilities, then pursue a certification/licensure option that aligns with them. In this chapter, we'll examine the following professional certifications related to accounting information systems: Certified Management Accountant, Certified Fraud Examiner, Certified Internal Auditor, and Certified Information Systems Auditor.

By the time you've finished studying this chapter and completing its related learning activities, you should be able to:

1. Describe the process for obtaining each certification.
2. Explain career options associated with each certification.
3. Discuss your personal career plans and certifications that align with it.

The four certifications we'll discuss in this chapter are by no means the only ones available to you, nor are they intended to downplay the value of licensure as a Certified Public Accountant. I've chosen them for three main reasons: (*a*) they are closely connected to many of the topics discussed in this text, (*b*) they are nationally and internationally recognized, and (*c*) they have been subjects of keen interest from my own accounting students.

You're probably wondering why this chapter doesn't discuss the CPA license. After all, it is the oldest and best-recognized professional certification for accountants. First, the CPA credential is a license, not a certificate; like a driver's license or a marriage license, the CPA credential gives its holder permission to do a specific task. CPAs have permission to sign audit opinions; the four credentials discussed in this chapter are certificates. They demonstrate mastery of a body of knowledge but do not confer any special privileges on their holders. CPAs have a fiduciary responsibility to their clients and the public—although the recent ethics scandals in the accounting profession suggest that not all CPAs take that responsibility as seriously as they should. That fiduciary responsibility is granted by a particular "jurisdiction," which most often refers to a state. So, the process of becoming a Certified Public Accountant varies from state to state. For example, in California currently, there are at least four paths that can lead to becoming a CPA; although each path allows you to put the letters "CPA" after your name, the meaning of those letters varies across the paths. You'll find a problem at the end of this chapter that asks you to investigate the licensure requirements for your state; the Web site of the National Association of State Boards of Accountancy (www.nasba.org) is a good place to start.

CERTIFIED MANAGEMENT ACCOUNTANT

The **CMA** certificate is sponsored by and promoted through the **Institute of Management Accountants** (www.imanet.org). Like most certification processes, becoming a CMA is a three-part process: education, examination, and experience.

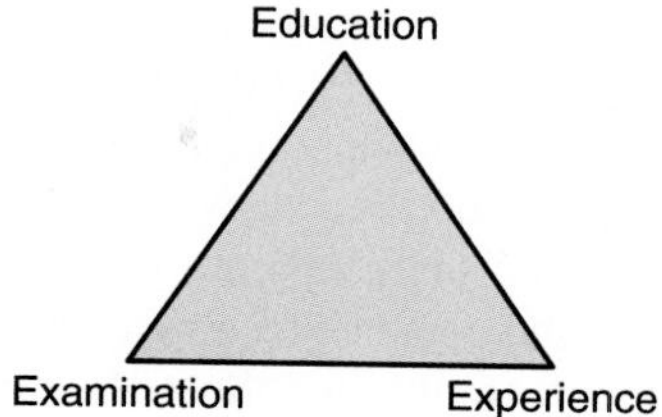

Education generally refers to earning an undergraduate degree. Although the discipline (major) for the degree is completely open, some background in accounting and other facets of business are highly advisable. Some practicing accountants, in fact, have undergraduate degrees in a field completely unrelated to accounting; they pursue accounting in their graduate work for a variety of reasons.

The CMA examination is in four parts: business analysis, management accounting and reporting, strategic management, and business applications. The IMA provides suggested reading lists and content specification outlines to guide candidates' study. The exam is given in an entirely online format; the first three parts contain objective, multiple-choice questions, while the fourth part (business applications) focuses on case analyses and essay questions.

To earn the CMA designation, candidates also must complete two years of relevant experience. The experience must be full time (with some exceptions) and professional in nature; it must require the candidate to make "judgments . . . employing the principles of management accounting and financial management." The two years of experience can be completed before or after passing the exam, but must be completed within seven years of doing so.

Several topics on the CMA exam are closely associated with accounting information systems, including

- Ethical issues.
- Internal controls.
- Decision-making models.
- Enterprise resource planning systems.
- Development of accounting information systems.
- Behavioral issues.

In-depth knowledge of information technology, such as spreadsheets and databases, also would be an enormous asset in taking the CMA exam. Conceptual and application questions about the uses of information technology are common. For example, the exam might contain a short case dealing with AIS design. Associated questions might call on you to explain differences between file-oriented and database-oriented accounting systems, to discuss the advantages and disadvantages of each type, and/or to explain the duties and responsibilities of a database administrator.

Reflection and Self-Assessment 17.1

Explore the content of the CMA exam in greater depth on the IMA Web site (www.imanet.org). In addition to your accounting studies, what other university courses have you had that would help you prepare for the exam?

As a certified management accountant, you might be called upon to recommend information technologies, set up or evaluate internal controls, or resolve behavioral issues associated with the design and implementation of a new accounting information system. Many CMAs are also CPAs; they earned their CPA license first, and then the CMA certificate after entering the corporate world. The combination of credentials is very powerful and may give the person's resume added appeal for prospective employers; the same could be said about combining the CPA license with any of the credentials discussed in this chapter.

CERTIFIED FRAUD EXAMINER

The **CFE** designation is promulgated by the **Association of Certified Fraud Examiners,** "a global, 33,000-member professional association whose members are dedicated to fighting fraud" (www.cfenet.com). The importance of fraud examination has been underscored recently by many of the high-profile cases discussed previously in this text.

CFEs come from diverse educational and professional backgrounds, including accounting, sociology, the law, and criminology. The certification process involves the same three elements as the CMA: education, experience, and examination. Prospective CFEs earn "points" based on their educational and professional background; for example, a bachelor's degree is worth 40 points toward the required total of 50. Regardless of the number of points earned based on education, CFEs must have two years of fraud-related experience to qualify for certification.

The CFE exam tests knowledge in four main areas:

- *Criminology and ethics.* This section examines the ACFE Code of Ethics (discussed earlier in the text). It also looks at various theories of fraud causation; that is, what pressures and circumstances combine to motivate people to commit fraud.
- *Financial transactions.* This section deals most closely with accounting and auditing. For example, questions might ask you to explain the purpose of a trial balance or identify the advantages and disadvantages of sample selection methods in auditing.
- *Fraud investigation.* Although every fraud investigation is different, fraud examiners often follow a series of basic steps and conventions; those items are discussed in this section. For example, most fraud examinations begin with careful analysis of documents; interviewing suspects occurs much later in the process.
- *Legal elements of fraud.* In the final section of the exam, you have to know about the laws that govern fraud examination; most of the emphasis here is on federal law since it is consistent across the United States. For example, a question might ask you about the importance of the fourth and fifth Amendments to the U.S. Constitution.

The test itself contains 125 questions in each of the four areas; it is administered entirely online and is available only from the ACFE. Many candidates (myself included!) prepare for the exam using the ACFE's study materials. Not only does the CFE Exam Prep Course allow candidates to proceed at their own pace, but it also provides a pass guarantee if the candidate meets specific conditions.

Internal controls are a key component of the financial transactions section of the CFE exam. Candidates should have a solid understanding of how to design and evaluate controls; they also should be intimately familiar with the provisions of the Sarbanes-Oxley Act of 2002 and principles of auditing. The first section of the CFE exam also tests candidates' knowledge of the ACFE Code of Ethics.

Reflection and Self-Assessment 17.2

Point your Web browser to the ACFE home page. Click the "CFE Quiz" link and take the 20-question practice test. How would you gain the knowledge needed to pass the exam and establish a career as a fraud examiner?

Check out JPL's ethics office on its Web site (http://eis.jpl.nasa.gov/ethics/).

Fraud examiners can be effective participants in the design and implementation of accounting information systems. In organizations that suspect fraudulent activity, they also may be called upon to use their skills to ferret it out. The Jet Propulsion Laboratory in Pasadena, California, has an entire staff devoted to fraud detection and ethics.

CERTIFIED INTERNAL AUDITOR

The Sarbanes-Oxley Act of 2002 has strengthened the need for internal auditors, particularly in publicly held corporations. The **Institute of Internal Auditors** (www.theiia.org) publishes "Tone at the Top" on a monthly basis; the March 2005 issue provides an excellent, succinct comparison of internal and external auditing in 12 main areas:

- Focus
- Management
- Audit committee
- Standards
- Approach
- Independence
- Results
- Control
- Risk
- Fraud
- Recommendations
- Follow-up

To demonstrate competence in internal auditing, professionals can become a **CIA** (Certified Internal Auditor) through the IIA. The usual requirements apply (bachelor's degree, two years of experience in internal auditing, and passing the CIA exam). Like the CFE exam, the CIA exam is structured in four parts of 125 multiple-choice questions each. The four parts are

- The internal audit activity's role in governance, risk, and control.
- Conducting the internal audit engagement.
- Business analysis and information technology.
- Business management skills.

The CIA exam is available on a computer-based format like the CFE and CMA exams.

Reflection and Self-Assessment 17.3

Point your Web browser to the IIA home page (www.theiia.org). Check out the exam content. Which topics from accounting information systems are relevant in preparing for the CIA exam?

Professionals with the CFE or CMA certificates, or a CPA license, can waive the fourth part of the CIA exam.

CERTIFIED INFORMATION SYSTEMS AUDITOR

You may recall one of ISACA's important contributions to our understanding of internal control: CoBIT. Refer back to Chapter 4 or Chapter 15 for more information on CoBIT.

The **Information Systems Audit and Control Association** (www.isaca.org) offers this certificate for professionals with backgrounds in both accounting and information systems.

The **CISA** exam is given twice a year; according to ISACA's Web site:

> CISA, the Certified Information Systems Auditor is ISACA's cornerstone certification. Since 1978, the CISA exam has measured excellence in the area of IS auditing, control and security. CISA has grown to be globally recognized and adopted worldwide as a symbol of achievement. The CISA certification has been earned by more than 38,000 professionals since inception.

ISACA provides the following content breakdown for the CISA exam:

- IS audit process (10 percent).
- IT governance (15 percent).
- Systems and infrastructure life cycle (16 percent).
- IT service delivery and support (14 percent).
- Protection of information assets (31 percent).
- Business continuity and disaster recovery (14 percent).

Information systems auditing is a relatively new field in business. In addition to passing the exam, candidates also must have five years of related professional experience to become certified. However, an undergraduate degree can be substituted for two years of the required experience.

Reflection and Self-Assessment 17.4

Point your Web browser to ISACA's home page (www.isaca.org). How often is the exam content revised? What process is used to determine the appropriate areas to test on the CISA exam?

Information systems auditors can be involved in both internal and external audits. They can help managers identify issues and solve problems related to, and at the intersection of, accounting, auditing, and information systems.

CAREER PLANNING

How do professional certifications interact with your career in accounting? While you may be able to have a career without one, earning a certification will enhance your resume and credibility with potential employers. While your **career plan** will almost certainly change as your career progresses, consider the steps listed below as you develop your initial ideas:

1. *Determine your strengths, aptitudes, and abilities.* You can complete this important step in many ways, one of which is with assessment tools likely available in your campus career center. The Discover Inventory (http://webapps01.act.org/eDISCOVER/) will give you a three-letter code that denotes the kinds of working environments in which you're most comfortable. The code is based on Holland's Hexagon (www.learning4liferesources.com/holland_codes.html), which classifies working environments into six broad categories: enterprising, conventional, realistic, social, artistic, and investigative. Another good instrument for completing this step is the Gallup Organization's StrengthsFinder (www.strengthsquest.com/). StrengthsFinder identifies your five top "themes" based on your responses to a series of objective questions. The themes were developed from extensive research and statistical analyses of hundreds of individuals and can be used to help you find a career that builds on those innate abilities.

For example, my career mission is to help others become the best professionals they can be and make informed choices about their education.

2. *Create a career mission statement.* You may have run across the idea of organizational mission statements in your management coursework. Basically, an organizational mission statement explains its reason for being—the way(s) it expects to achieve a competitive advantage in its markets. Your career mission statement can work the same way. It gives you a goal to work toward—one that will not absolutely dictate your educational and professional choices, but one that will provide some direction as you enter the accounting profession.
3. *Research employment opportunities related to the first two items.* This research might involve conducting informational interviews with practicing accountants, attending student organization events related to career opportunities on your campus, or finding an internship in an environment where you think you might eventually like to work. The earlier you can start that research, the better off you'll be; that way, if you discover you don't have the interest, aptitude, or ability to sustain a particular career, you can change your career plan accordingly. In a very fundamental sense, your career planning process started the day you started college; too many students wait until the year they expect to graduate to think about their career. I encourage you to start the process early, so you can make more informed choices when you graduate.
4. *Build your resume.* Your campus career center can give you clear, specific guidance about how to create a strong resume. Too many students wait until they're ready to graduate to visit the career center. I encourage you to visit it early in your academic career. You'll find your job search process goes a lot more smoothly if you take advantage of the career center's services regularly.
5. *Practice your interviewing skills.* Most career centers offer practice (mock) interviews; if your school has an accounting society, an IMA student chapter, and/or a chapter of Beta Alpha Psi, they also may host mock interview events throughout the year. Practicing your interviewing skills in those settings will make you a lot more comfortable when you're ready for the "real thing." While you'll always be somewhat nervous during an interview situation, practicing in advance can significantly reduce those feelings, allowing you to put your best foot forward with potential employers.

Those five steps certainly aren't the sum total of career planning efforts, but they are a good beginning. The earlier you begin developing a plan, the more time you'll have to explore it.

CRITICAL THINKING

One of the reasons I love working in accounting information systems is its interdisciplinary nature. I really believe that, in modern organizations, there is virtually no such thing as an "accounting problem"; that is, there are very few situations in which knowing accounting alone is enough to address an issue. Rather, organizations have problems that may be informed by accounting—but are probably informed by other business (and nonbusiness!) disciplines, too. Think about all the topics we've examined throughout the text: internal control, systems documentation, business processes, information technology, and ethics. While it's true that we've discussed all of them in an accounting context, those same topics are important in other areas of business, too.

Let's take a look at one of those broad topics (internal control) and think about how it might come into play in the various certification exams discussed in this chapter.

At a minimum, you'd expect to find questions on internal control in Part 1 of the CMA exam (business analysis), Part 2 of the CFE exam (financial transactions), Part 3 of the CIA exam (business analysis and information technology), and Parts 1 and 5 of the CISA exam (information systems audit process and protection of information assets). Such questions might be relatively simple multiple-choice items, computational problems, or short-answer questions.

A multiple-choice question might look like this:

1. Approvals, verifications, and reconciliations are most closely associated with which part of the COSO internal control framework?

   a. Control environment

   b. Risk assessment

   c. Control activities

   d. Information and communication

A problem-based question on internal control could ask you to reconcile a bank statement based on the following data:

Statement balance	$3,000
Outstanding checks	95
Interest earned	160
Deposits in transit	450
Book balance	3,200
Bank service charge	5

A short-answer question on the same topic could be

> You are an information systems auditor. While conducting a review of an organization's business processes, you discover that a key preventive control has been removed. Explain what you should do with respect to your discovery.

Now, don't panic if you can't respond to all of those questions without doing some research—after all, your accounting education isn't complete yet, nor is the purpose of your AIS course to enable you to pass a certification exam. My goal here is to show you more specifically how your AIS course can tie into your professional accounting career, regardless of the direction it takes.

Summary

This chapter has discussed four professional accounting certifications: Certified Management Accountant, Certified Fraud Examiner, Certified Internal Auditor, and Certified Information Systems Auditor. The chapter did not discuss the Certified Public Accountant license, as its requirements vary from one state to another. We also looked at the steps involved in developing your first career plan. Here's a summary of the chapter in terms of its learning objectives:

1. *Describe the process for obtaining each certification.* In general, accounting certifications require a three-step process. First, finish your undergraduate education; while an accounting degree isn't necessarily a prerequisite for becoming certified, it certainly provides a solid foundation. Second, pass an exam. Each exam has its own content specifications, which can be obtained through the various sponsoring organizations. Finally, accumulate relevant professional experience; the type and length also vary with the certification.
2. *Explain career options associated with each certification.* Earning a particular certification does not lock you into a specific career; rather, it broadens your options. Earning a professional certification shows that you are organized and determined; it also demonstrates an attitude of lifelong learning.
3. *Discuss your personal career plans and certifications that align with it.* As with most questions in accounting, there is no "one right way" to develop your career plan. But a good start involves three steps: assessing your personal characteristics relative to career environments, establishing a career mission statement, and researching opportunities related to the statement. Building your professional resume and practicing your interviewing skills are also important as you plan your career.

The four professional credentials discussed in this chapter are globally recognized. Earning one or more of them, or some other certification or license, will distinguish you from accounting professionals with a degree alone, giving you a "leg up" in starting your professional career.

Key Terms

Association of Certified Fraud Examiners, *330*
career plan, *333*
CFE, *330*
CIA, *331*
CISA, *332*
CMA, *329*
Information Systems Audit and Control Association, *332*
Institute of Internal Auditors, *331*
Institute of Management Accountants, *329*

End-of-Chapter Activities

1. *Reading review questions.*
   a. What are the benefits of obtaining professional certification?
   b. What three common components are associated with most professional certifications in accounting?
   c. Describe the content and process associated with taking one or more of the professional exams discussed in the chapter.
   d. Respond to the questions for this chapter's "AIS in the Business World."
2. *Reading review problem.* As an undergraduate, I had a friend named Gary. Although he started off as an accounting major (like me), he changed to a computer-related field after one semester. When I asked him why, he said, "By the time we graduate, all accountants will have been replaced by computers." I don't know what happened to Gary after we left college, but, clearly, his prediction didn't come true. Use the concepts discussed in the chapter to explain why it's unlikely all accountants will ever be replaced by computers.
3. *Making choices and exercising judgment.* Visit your campus career center; talk with a career counselor about your future career plans. Take an aptitude or interest assessment, such as the Discover Inventory or StrengthsQuest; what does the assessment tell you about yourself? Map out a tentative plan for your accounting career, starting with earning your accounting degree.
4. *Field work.* Choose one of the professional associations discussed in the chapter. Attend a meeting of a local chapter; talk with professionals in the field about their job responsibilities and the costs and benefits of certification. Prepare to share your findings with your classmates as directed by your instructor.
5. *Certification and curriculum alignment.* Choose one of the four certifications discussed in the chapter. Consider its exam requirements in light of your accounting curriculum; which accounting courses are particularly relevant in preparing for the exam? (Don't limit yourself to accounting courses alone here—consider the totality of your degree, including general education.)
6. *Job responsibilities.* Choose one of the four certifications discussed in the chapter. Then, look online or in your local newspaper for job listings that seem related to the certification. Make a list of the companies, job titles, responsibilities, and (if available) salaries for each position you locate. (Consider using a relational database to complete this problem.)
7. *Ethics.*
   a. Summarize the ethical code of one of the four professional organizations discussed in the chapter. Prepare a short oral presentation of your summary for the class.
   b. Through research or your own imagination, identify a situation in which an accountant would have to consult the ethical code you summarized in (*a*). Write a one-page case study of the situation and explain how it should be resolved under the appropriate set of ethical principles.
8. *CPA licensure.* Research the requirements to become a Certified Public Accountant in your state. Prepare a brief oral or written report discussing your findings. Start your research at www.nasba.org; also visit www.cpa-exam.org for details of the CPA exam.

9. *Crossword puzzle.* Please complete the crossword puzzle below using appropriate terminology from the chapter.

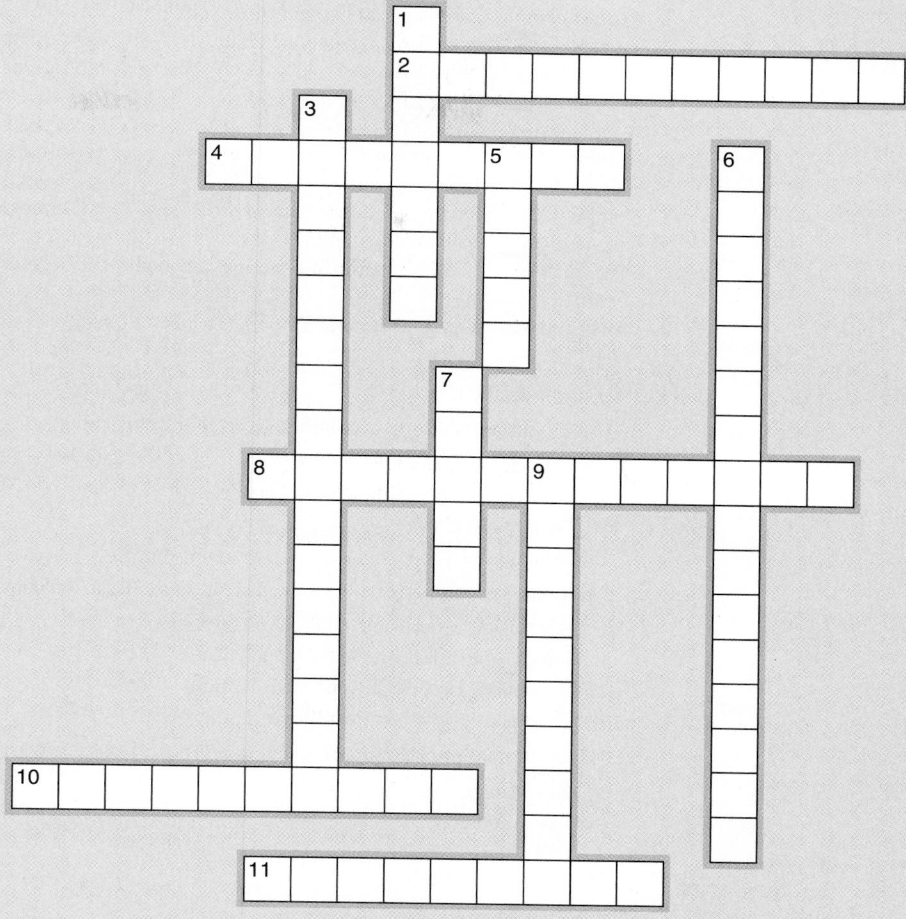

Across

2. One of three parts of a generalized certification process.
4. One of three parts of a generalized certification process.
8. An important piece of legislation tested on many certification exams.
10. One way to research employment opportunities.
11. Try to achieve this when it comes to certification and your career interests.

Down

1. Holland's __________: a tool that classifies employment environments in six categories.
3. One of the four parts of the CMA exam.
5. The sponsoring organization for CISAs.
6. An exam topic common to many accounting certification exams.
7. Legal elements of __________: one of the areas tested on the CFE exam.
9. One of three parts of a generalized certification process.

10. *Terminology.* Match each item in the left column with the best item in the right column.

1. A certification exam given online
2. A short, simple statement that explains how you expect to create value for a prospective employer
3. A topic tested on the CFE exam
4. A topic tested on the CISA exam
5. A topic tested on the CMA exam
6. Number of career options available with most accounting certifications
7. Number of elements in most certification processes
8. One element of Holland's hexagon
9. Other than exams and education, a common element of certification
10. Professional exam given "in person"

a. Career mission statement
b. Certified Fraud Examiner
c. Certified Information Systems Auditor
d. Experience
e. Financial transactions
f. Investigative
g. Protection of information assets
h. Strategic management
i. Three
j. Unlimited

11. *Multiple choice questions.*

1. Which of the following is common to all four certifications discussed in the chapter?
   a. They are globally recognized.
   b. They require professional experience.
   c. Both of the above.
   d. None of the above.
2. The common components associated with professional accounting certification are
   a. Education, experience, and oral examination.
   b. Ethics, education, and experience.
   c. Education, experience, and examination.
   d. Graduate-level education, ethics, and experience.
3. Which professional exams are given in an entirely online environment?
   a. CMA and CISA
   b. CISA and CFE
   c. CMA and CFE
   d. CISA and CIA
4. Which of the following statements is most true?
   a. All accountants should become CPAs.
   b. Professional certification really isn't necessary if you have a master's degree.
   c. Most accounting certifications require at least some knowledge of accounting information systems.
   d. Earning a given certification, such as the CMA, locks a professional into a very specific career.
5. Which of the certifications discussed in the chapter covers the broadest range of topics?
   a. CFE
   b. CMA
   c. CISA
   d. CIA
6. The difference between a "license" and a "certificate" is
   a. A certificate is issued by a state; a license is issued by a federal agency.
   b. A license is issued by a state; a certificate is issued by a federal agency.
   c. A license confers permission; a certificate demonstrates knowledge.
   d. A certificate confers permission; a license demonstrates knowledge.

7. CPA licenses are issued by
   a. The American Institute of CPAs.
   b. Universities.
   c. The federal government.
   d. States.
8. Which of the following gives you a three-letter code based on Holland's Hexagon?
   a. Discover
   b. StrengthsQuest
   c. Myers-Briggs Type Indicator
   d. Minnesota Multiphasic Personality Inventory
9. Holland's Hexagon contains all of the following except
   a. Enterprising.
   b. Conventional.
   c. Realistic.
   d. Numeric.
10. "People with math and science abilities, who like working alone and solving complex problems" most clearly describes which element of Holland's Hexagon?
    a. Artistic
    b. Investigative
    c. Social
    d. Conventional

12. *Statement evaluation.* Please indicate whether each of the following statements is (i) always true, (ii) sometimes true, or (iii) never true. For those that are (ii) sometimes true, explain when the statement is true.

a. A professional resume should be limited to a single page.
b. Accounting information systems topics are important in most certification exams.
c. Certification leads to higher salaries.
d. Certifications in accounting require two years of working experience.
e. Fraud investigators have earned the Certified Fraud Examiner credential.
f. Professional certification exams are given online.
g. Professional resumes should use action verbs like "coordinated" and "implemented."
h. Successful accountants have a Holland code of CSI.
i. The purpose of earning an accounting degree is to become a CPA.
j. The Sarbanes-Oxley Act of 2002 can be tested on any accounting professional exam.

Chapter Eighteen

Auditing and Evaluating the AIS

AIS in the Business World

Internal Auditing

We conclude our discussion of accounting information systems by looking at one of the most important elements of professional practice: auditing. As you'll read in the following pages, accountants perform many different types of audits. One of the most interesting, fastest-growing fields in accounting is internal auditing; you probably recall reading about the Certified Internal Auditor designation in the chapter on professional certification and career planning.

In the article referenced below, Nolan pointed out that internal auditing is at a crossroads. Many large corporations pumped significant money into internal auditing departments when the Sarbanes-Oxley Act of 2002 passed; in today's stressed economy, those same corporations are trying to trim those budgets back. At the same time, organizations face many significant business issues and risks, such as fraud, systems, corporate social responsibility, corporate governance, privacy, and liquidity. Internal auditors need a broad skill set to address those risks and create value for organizations. Nolan's article advocates outsourcing parts of the internal auditing function to promote good cost control.

Discussion Questions

1. How are the topics we've examined in accounting information systems related to the audit process?
2. What are the costs and benefits of outsourcing internal auditing?

Source: M. Nolan, "Internal Audit at the Crossroads," *Risk Management,* November 2008.

Auditing is the area of accounting associated with AIS evaluation. The corporate scandals of the late 20th and early 21st centuries such as Parmalat, Global Crossing, and Enron point to the need for regular, thorough AIS evaluation as part of accountants' professional responsibility and fiduciary duties to shareholders and the public.

When you finish studying this chapter, you should be able to:

1. Describe the various kinds of audits you might encounter in your accounting career.
2. Explain the AICPA's 10 generally accepted auditing standards (GAAS).
3. Discuss the basic steps associated with a financial statement audit.
4. Explain the connection between auditing and accounting information systems.

I am deeply indebted to Steve Flores and Ahmed Abo-Hebeish for their assistance in developing this chapter.

Your accounting curriculum probably includes at least one course in auditing, so this chapter certainly will not make you an expert in the field, but it will give you an introduction to this important area of professional practice.

TYPES OF AUDITS

Ahmed is a lecturer in the accounting program at Cal Poly Pomona, focusing on auditing. He is a CPA and formerly worked for Northrop-Grumman. He has practiced accounting all over the world.

Dictionary.com lists several definitions for *audit,* but the one that seems most appropriate here is "a methodical examination or review of a condition or situation." My friend and colleague Ahmed Abo-Hebeish identified seven types of audits in our discussion about this chapter:

1. *Financial audit.* A financial audit involves the examination of a company's accounting information system and financial statements. Auditors express one of four types of opinions on the company's financial statements. An *unqualified* opinion (also known as a *clean* opinion) says that the company's statements are prepared in accordance with generally accepted accounting principles (GAAP). Auditors issue a *qualified* opinion when one or more items don't conform to GAAP—but not so many items as to compromise the overall fairness of the statements. An *adverse* opinion means the statements are not prepared in accordance with GAAP, while a *disclaimer* of opinion denotes that the auditors could not tell if they were. Adverse and disclaimers of opinion are hard to find—most companies would change auditors (or the auditors would resign) before such an opinion was issued.
2. *Operational audit.* In an operational audit, auditors examine a company's rules and procedures for conducting business. They're asking if a company's rules make sense, and if they're followed. Systems documentation techniques such as flowcharting are particularly important in operational audits; for example, a flowchart of the purchasing process would give the operational auditor a standard for comparison against a company's actual practice in the same area. Internal auditors often are involved in operational auditing.
3. *Systems audit.* As we've discussed before, information technology is an integral part of most accounting information systems today. A systems audit determines whether the various forms of information technology in an AIS are producing expected results. It also examines the issue of systems security very closely, making sure the data are safe within the system. Basically, a systems audit looks "inside the box," rather than treating the computer as an unknown quantity in an audit. In the chapter on professional certification, you read about Certified Information Systems Auditors—professionals who have a clear, deep command of both accounting and information technology issues. CISAs are well qualified to conduct systems audits. Another issue in systems auditing is the *service organization* audit discussed in Statement of Auditing Standards 70. Many organizations outsource certain duties and responsibilities to external parties; for

example, a corporation might hire ADP to do its payroll processing. Auditors need to know that those service organizations are maintaining adequate internal controls for their client; SAS 70 speaks to that knowledge. According to www.sas70.com, "SAS No. 70 is the authoritative guidance that allows service organizations to disclose their control activities and processes to their customers and their customers' auditors in a uniform reporting format. A SAS 70 examination signifies that a service organization has had its control objectives and control activities examined by an independent accounting and auditing firm. A formal report including the auditor's opinion ('Service Auditor's Report') is issued to the service organization at the conclusion of a SAS 70 examination."

4. *Compliance audit.* Governmental and not-for-profit organizations (GNFPs) are subject to compliance audits. Although almost every audit involves some sort of judgment on the part of the auditor, compliance audits are virtually devoid of judgment. GNFPs are subject to very strict government rules and regulations, many of which are contained in the **Yellow Book** published by the Government Accountability Office (GAO). You can learn a lot more about the Yellow Book and compliance auditing on the GAO's Web site: www.gao.gov. A compliance audit determines whether or not a GNFP is following the rules and regulations in the Yellow Book.
5. *Management audit.* Of all the kinds of auditing discussed here, the management audit may involve the greatest degree of judgment. A management audit determines the degree to which the assumptions underlying decisions are valid; it also examines the ways in which management decisions are supported. In the chapter on decision-making models, you read about the Steps for Better Thinking; a management audit would be looking for that type of support for major decisions.
6. *Investigative audit.* Also known as a *fraud audit,* it is associated with the broader field of forensic accounting. The recent ethics scandals at Enron, WorldCom, Global Crossing, and other firms have raised awareness of the costs of occupational fraud and abuse in organizations. An investigative audit, which may be conducted by a Certified Fraud Examiner, may be triggered by observation of unusual behavior or discrepancies in the accounting information system. Figure 18.1 lays out a common order for gathering evidence in an investigative audit (www.cfenet.com).

FIGURE 18.1
Investigative Audit Tools

Source: Wells, 2004.

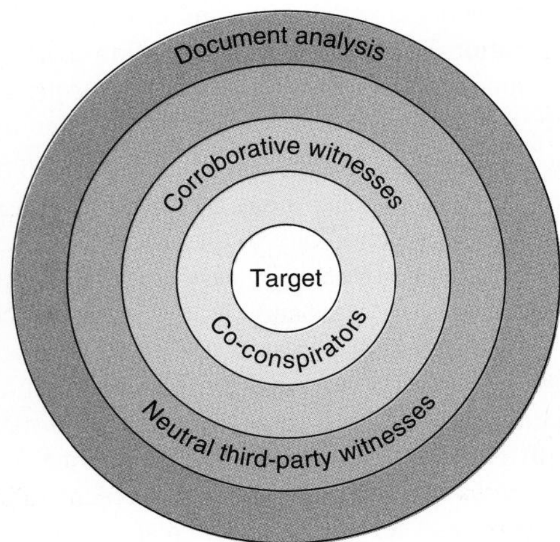

Most investigative audits start with reviewing pertinent *documents;* for example, the auditor might examine physical or electronic copies of checks in cases where embezzlement is suspected. Interviews of *neutral third-party witnesses* often come next. For example, an employee might have observed a co-worker taking computer equipment out of the office; the employee might have assumed a perfectly innocent, legitimate reason/motivation, even if fraud was involved. *Corroborative witnesses* can lend additional information to the investigation by (for example) confirming information collected in the first two stages—or even in subsequent stages. *Co-conspirators* are involved in the fraud, but often not as deeply or as seriously as the target of the investigation. For example, a purchasing agent might collude with a receiving department employee to steal merchandise; the receiving department employee would be considered a co-conspirator. Finally, the investigative auditor interviews the *target.* By that time, the auditor has a clear idea of how the fraud occurred—an idea supported by evidence from the other steps.

7. *International audit.* This type of audit is really a "basket" of the other types. It can be conducted in a U.S.-based firm with international operations or a non-U.S.-based firm. International auditing is exceptionally challenging. It requires the auditor to understand the accounting rules in another country, but it also necessitates an intimate understanding of national culture, laws, religion, and other nonaccounting issues.

While the degree, role, and type of **professional judgment** vary among the seven types of audits discussed here, all of them incorporate judgment to some degree. Other commonalities between the seven types of audits include

- Checking existing conditions against some predetermined standard.
- Questioning, firmly but professionally, managers and employees of the organization being audited.
- Maintaining an independent attitude and appropriate professional "distance" from the client.

Reflection and Self-Assessment 18.1

What type of audit is indicated by each of the following descriptions? Justify your choices, particularly if more than one type of audit seems applicable.

1. Ray and Gary, partners in a psychotherapy practice, hire Rob to determine if their secretary has been embezzling cash.
2. An internal auditor works with managers in the purchasing department to determine a more efficient way to handle inventory transactions.
3. An audit client uses Peachtree for transaction processing. An auditor examines the system to ensure that the software is processing the transactions correctly.
4. A German-based organization hires a U.S. firm to check out its accounting information system. The overall objective is enabling the German firm to list its securities on the NYSE.
5. A CPA firm conducts its annual evaluation of CHC Corporation's accounting information system. After the evaluation, the CPA firm issues an unqualified opinion.

Financial audits are further guided by 10 generally accepted auditing standards (GAAS), discussed in the next section.

GENERALLY ACCEPTED AUDITING STANDARDS

The Auditing Standards Board (ASB) of the American Institute of Certified Public Accountants (AICPA) identified 10 **auditing standards** that govern external audits by CPAs (Whittington and Pany, 2004, pp. 31–56). See Figure 18.2. Of course, the 10 standards aren't the only guidelines for conducting an audit. We're discussing them here because they represent the foundation of the rest; you'll explore the standards and related issues in significantly greater depth in your auditing course.

The three *general standards* focus on the auditor's background and approach to the audit. First and foremost, an auditor must be well-trained in auditing before an engagement commences. Generalized knowledge of accounting principles and information systems is important, but specific *training* related to auditing is essential. Auditing is an important element of professional practice in accounting; without good auditing, decision makers cannot rely on the financial statements to be fair. *Independence* speaks to the auditor's mental attitude; that is, the auditor must always remain independent from the client. While some have questioned how independent an auditor can be from the organization signing his or her paychecks, maintaining a professional distance and appropriate professional skepticism are key to the conduct of a successful audit. Finally (in this group), the auditor must exercise due *professional care* in preparing for and completing the audit. The engagement must be properly planned in terms of personnel on the audit team and specific audit procedures. The duty of professional care also extends to preparing the audit report.

The second group of standards focuses on *field work;* in other words, they set out important ideas for conducting the audit itself. The audit is to be properly planned, and all staff members must be adequately *supervised.* Most audit teams comprise professionals at various stages of their careers, with varying levels of experience in auditing. As a team member's

FIGURE 18.2
Generally Accepted Auditing Standards

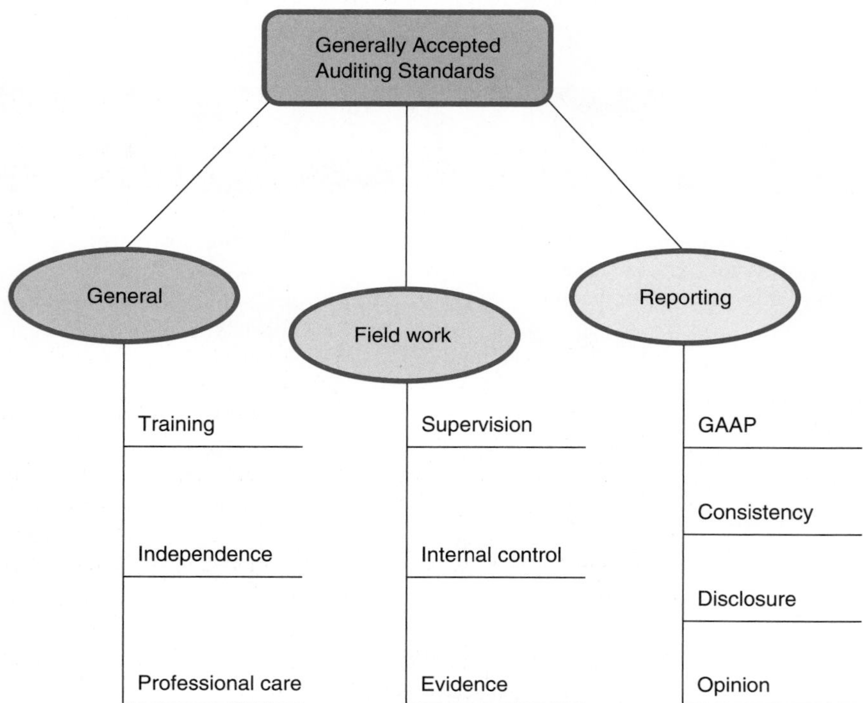

experience increases, the need for supervision may decrease. A thorough assessment of *internal controls* is a critical step early in the audit process. While such an assessment has always been critical, the Sarbanes-Oxley Act of 2002 has placed even greater emphasis on internal control issues. Auditors must assess an organization's risk exposures and determine the degree to which the organization's internal controls ameliorate those risks. The *evidence* standard speaks to the importance of having an objective, reasonable basis for expressing an opinion on the company's financial statements. Evidence can be obtained in many different ways, including observing organizational processes, inspecting documents, and obtaining external confirmations of account balances.

You may find it helpful to revisit Chapter 4, where we discussed these topics in greater detail.

GAAS also contains four *reporting standards,* which speak to the ultimate opinion the auditors express on the financial statements. First, the opinion must state whether or not the statements are presented in accordance with *generally accepted accounting principles* (GAAP). The language of an audit opinion is very specific; unqualified opinions always include such a statement. You may recall that *consistency* is one of the qualitative characteristics of accounting information in the conceptual framework; it is also one of the reporting standards. The audit report must explain any inconsistencies between the current period's application of GAAP and the prior period's application. Full *disclosure* is another commonality between GAAS and the conceptual framework. Financial statement users can assume the disclosures in the financial statements are appropriate unless the audit opinion specifically states they are not. Finally, the audit report must clearly state the auditor's *opinion* on the financial statements (unqualified, qualified, disclaimer, or adverse). The auditor also must explain the reason(s) for the opinion.

Whittington and Pany (2004, p. 32) offer these summary comments on the 10 standards:

> The 10 standards set forth by the American Institute of Certified Public Accountants include such subjective terms of measurement as "*adequate* planning," "*sufficient* understanding of internal control," and "*adequate* disclosure." To decide under the circumstances of each audit engagement what is adequate, sufficient and competent requires the exercise of *professional judgment.* Auditing cannot be reduced to rote; the exercise of judgment by the auditor is vital at numerous points in every engagement. However, the formulation and publication of carefully worded auditing standards are of immense aid in raising the quality of audit work, even though these standards require professional judgment in their application.

That professional judgment must be developed deliberately and consistently over time, starting with your formal undergraduate education as an accountant. Critical thinking and interpersonal communication skills are important keys in developing and honing them.

GENERIC AUDIT STEPS

Steve is an emeritus lecturer in accounting at Cal Poly Pomona. He maintains his own CPA practice in Orange County, California.

Although professional judgment is an important aspect of auditing, auditors commonly follow a generalized set of steps when conducting an audit. My friend and colleague Steve Flores suggested the generic steps for an audit that are shown in Figure 18.3 and discussed in the following paragraphs.

Ultimately, and particularly since Sarbanes-Oxley, management is responsible for the content of the organization's financial statements. So, assessing management's integrity is a necessary first step in the audit process. Dictionary.com defines "integrity" as "steadfast adherence to a strict moral or ethical code." Managers have a **fiduciary duty** to their employees and stockholders to act in the best interests of the organization—even when those interests may conflict with their own. COSO's *Internal Control: Integrated Framework* (Committee of Sponsoring Organizations, 2002) alludes to this step in its discussion of an organization's control environment:

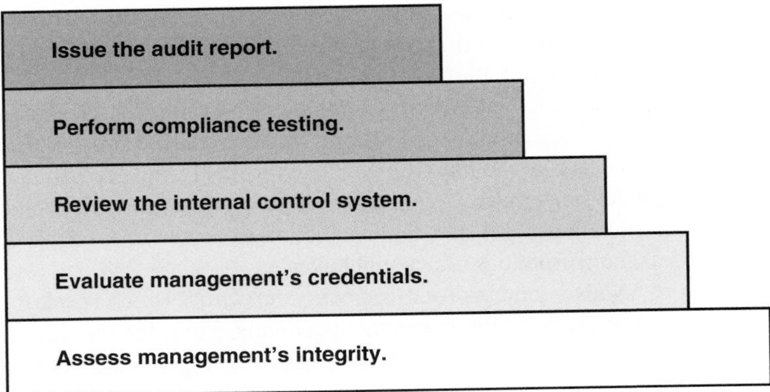

FIGURE 18.3
Audit Steps

> The control environment sets the tone of an organization, influencing the control consciousness of its people. It is the foundation for all other components of internal control, providing discipline and structure. Control environment factors include the integrity, ethical values and competence of the entity's people; management's philosophy and operating style; the way management assigns authority and responsibility, and organizes and develops its people; and the attention and direction provided by the board of directors.

Management must set the example by demonstrating integrity and ethical behavior; otherwise, employees throughout the organization are likely to feel justified in engaging in unethical actions.

Reflection and Self-Assessment 18.2

What tools and techniques would you use to assess management's integrity?

After evaluating management's integrity, the auditor should consider management's credentials. This evaluation focuses on two questions: (*a*) Is management technically competent? (*b*) Is management financially competent? Notice that the evaluation of management's competence comes *after* the evaluation of integrity. Managers can understand the organization at a deep and fundamental level; they can even comprehend clearly the role, purpose, and importance of accounting as a reporting mechanism. But those credentials mean very little without a generalized disposition toward ethical behavior. Managers can develop technical and financial competence via formal education and/or experience.

The next step is evaluating the organization's internal control system. The auditor must assess the organization's risk exposures and then determine whether the controls are in place to address those risks successfully. Remember: the goal is not to eliminate risk—that's impossible anyway. Rather, the goal is to address, manage, and/or reduce risk. Common controls you'd expect to find include

- Adequate documentation of business processes.
- Background checks for prospective employees.
- Comprehensive employee training.

- Document matching.
- Multiple signatures for checks over a specified threshold.
- Physical safeguards for assets.
- Regular bank reconciliations.
- Separation of duties.

Computerized AIS environments often require unique internal controls. Louwers et al. (2005, p. 732) listed the following examples:

Administrative Controls	Physical Controls	Technical Controls
Security checks on personnel	Controlled access	Data encryption
Segregation of duties	Computer room entry log record	Access control software and passwords
Program testing after modification	Data backup storage	Transaction logging reports
Rotation of computer duties	Preprinted limits on documents (e.g., checks)	Range and reasonableness checks on transaction amounts
Transaction limit amounts	Inconspicuous location	Control totals

Control Objectives for Information and Related Technology (CoBIT) were discussed in the chapter on computer crime. Those standards also examine internal control issues within the context of computerized information systems.

The auditor's confidence in an organization's internal control system dictates the extent and character of compliance testing conducted in the next phase. Compliance testing involves examining a sample of transactions and verifying that they have been recorded in accordance with GAAP, thus leading to fair account balances on the financial statements. For example, an auditor might conduct a physical count of the inventory. Independent verification of major accounts receivable and accounts payable balances are also common compliance tests at this stage of an audit.

A company's financial statements implicitly involve several assertions by management that must be evaluated as part of auditing. Those assertions are commonly organized into five groups (Louwers et al., 2005, p. 9):

- *Existence or occurrence.* Did the recorded sales transactions really occur? Do the assets listed on the balance sheet really exist?
- *Rights and obligations.* Does the company really own the assets? Are related legal responsibilities identified?
- *Valuation and allocation.* Are the accounts valued correctly? Are expenses allocated to the period(s) benefited?
- *Completeness.* Are the financial statements (including footnotes) complete? Were all the transactions recorded in the right period?
- *Presentation and disclosure.* Were all the transactions recorded in the correct accounts? Are the disclosures understandable to users?

You may recall that a risk-control matrix can include an area for these assertions.

Note that the questions listed above are illustrative, not comprehensive. A well-designed accounting information system that incorporates strong internal controls and appropriate forms of information technology can assist auditors in verifying the five assertions related to financial statements.

The audit culminates with the issuance of the audit report, or opinion. As stated earlier, audit opinions fall into four broad categories: unqualified, qualified, disclaimer, or adverse. Each opinion has very specific language; the audit opinion expressed by KPMG on the financial statements of Home Depot Inc. appears in Figure 18.4.

The Sarbanes-Oxley Act has increased the role of judgment and the responsibility of management for financial statements. In addition, SOX requires its own compliance audit,

FIGURE 18.4 KPMG's Audit Opinion on Home Depot's Financial Statements

We have audited management's assessment, included in the accompanying Management's Report on Internal Control over Financial Reporting, that The Home Depot, Inc. and subsidiaries maintained effective internal control over financial reporting as of January 30, 2005, based on criteria established in *Internal Control-Integrated Framework* issued by the Committee of Sponsoring Organizations of the Treadway Commission (COSO). The Company's management is responsible for maintaining effective internal control over financial reporting and for its assessment of the effectiveness of internal control over financial reporting. Our responsibility is to express an opinion on management's assessment and an opinion on the effectiveness of the Company's internal control over financial reporting based on our audit.

We conducted our audit in accordance with the standards of the Public Company Accounting Oversight Board (United States). Those standards require that we plan and perform the audit to obtain reasonable assurance about whether effective internal control over financial reporting was maintained in all material respects. Our audit included obtaining an understanding of internal control over financial reporting, evaluating management's assessment, testing and evaluating the design and operating effectiveness of internal control and performing such other procedures as we considered necessary in the circumstances. We believe that our audit provides a reasonable basis for our opinion.

A company's internal control over financial reporting is a process designed to provide reasonable assurance regarding the reliability of financial reporting and the preparation of financial statements for external purposes in accordance with generally accepted accounting principles. A company's internal control over financial reporting includes those policies and procedures that (1) pertain to the maintenance of records that, in reasonable detail, accurately and fairly reflect the transactions and dispositions of the assets of the company; (2) provide reasonable assurance that transactions are recorded as necessary to permit preparation of financial statements in accordance with generally accepted accounting principles, and that receipts and expenditures of the company are being made only in accordance with authorizations of management and directors of the company; and (3) provide reasonable assurance regarding prevention or timely detection of unauthorized acquisition, use, or disposition of the company's assets that could have a material effect on the financial statements.

Because of its inherent limitations, internal control over financial reporting may not prevent or detect misstatements. Also, projections of any evaluation of effectiveness to future periods are subject to the risk that controls may become inadequate because of changes in conditions, or that the degree of compliance with the policies or procedures may deteriorate.

In our opinion, management's assessment that The Home Depot, Inc. and subsidiaries maintained effective internal control over financial reporting as of January 30, 2005, is fairly stated, in all material respects, based on criteria established in *Internal Control-Integrated Framework* issued by the Committee of Sponsoring Organizations of the Treadway Commission (COSO). Also, in our opinion, The Home Depot, Inc. and subsidiaries maintained, in all material respects, effective internal control over financial reporting as of January 30, 2005, based on criteria established in *Internal Control-Integrated Framework* issued by the Committee of Sponsoring Organizations of the Treadway Commission (COSO).

We also have audited, in accordance with the standards of the Public Company Accounting Oversight Board (United States), the Consolidated Balance Sheets of The Home Depot, Inc. and subsidiaries as of January 30, 2005 and February 1, 2004, and the related Consolidated Statements of Earnings, Stockholders' Equity and Comprehensive Income, and Cash Flows for each of the fiscal years in the three-year period ended January 30, 2005, and our report dated March 11, 2005 expressed an unqualified opinion on those consolidated financial statements.

conducted by a different firm, in addition to the financial audit. SOX is divided into 11 titles (similar to chapters in a book), which are further subdivided into sections. Some of the most important sections that relate to auditing and the accounting information system include

- *Section 302.* This section relates to the evaluation of internal controls in an audit. Specifically, it obligates the chief executive officer and chief financial officer to attest that they have personally reviewed internal controls within the preceding 90 days. The CEO and CFO also acknowledge that they are responsible for the financial statements and the internal controls that promote their reliability and integrity. The responsibilities outlined in this section of SOX cannot be delegated, even via power of attorney.

- *Section 401.* This section is titled "Disclosures in Periodic Reports." The financial statements must be "accurate and presented in a manner that does not contain incorrect statements or admit to state material information. These financial statements shall also include all material off-balance-sheet liabilities, obligations or transactions" (www.soxlaw.com). If you've made any study of the Enron debacle in this or another course, you may recall that off-balance-sheet transactions were one of the corporation's primary problems. Enron accountants structured transactions to conform to the "letter" of accounting rules and regulations while disregarding the "spirit" of those regulations.
- *Section 404.* Entitled "Management Assessment of Internal Controls," this section reemphasizes the importance of a sound internal control system as part of maintaining AIS integrity and reliability. As part of their annual reports, SOX-compliant organizations must discuss the scope and adequacy of internal controls. Independent auditors also must comment on the opinion expressed by the organization's management. In practice, you may hear this practice referred to as a "404 audit."
- *Section 409.* Real-time reporting is the primary issue in this section. If an organization experiences a material change in its financial condition or operations, it is required to disclose that change "on an urgent basis." In other words, the company cannot wait until its quarterly or annual SEC filings to communicate the change; it must be disclosed as quickly as possible. Additionally, section 409 requires that the disclosure be made in nontechnical, easy-to-understand terms. The disclosures should be supported by qualitative information as well.
- *Section 802.* This section spells out the penalties for noncompliance with the Sarbanes-Oxley Act. According to www.soxlaw.com, "This section imposes penalties of fines and/or up to 20 years imprisonment for altering, destroying, mutilating, concealing, falsifying records, documents or tangible objects with the intent to obstruct, impede or influence a legal investigation. This section also imposes penalties of fines and/or imprisonment up to 10 years on any accountant who knowingly and willfully violates the requirements of maintenance of all audit or review papers for a period of 5 years."

With my own students, I've often referred to SOX as the "full employment act for accountants." So long as SOX remains in effect, accountants will have jobs because of the responsibilities the act imposes on organizations.

ACCOUNTING INFORMATION SYSTEMS AND AUDITING

So how does this discussion of auditing relate to your study of accounting information systems? Many of the topics we've discussed in this text, as well as many of the skills you have developed in your study of AIS, have direct relevance when it comes to auditing.

First, this text has emphasized the importance of critical thinking in the design and implementation of accounting information systems. Developing and exercising your professional judgment have been consistent themes in this book—whether they relate to selecting information technology tools, evaluating internal controls, documenting accounting information systems with flowcharts, or making recommendations for improving business processes. Decision-making models such as Wolcott and Lynch's Steps for Better Thinking (www.wolcottlynch.com) provide a rational, systematic approach for making complex decisions. Professional judgment is critically important in the auditing process. It is an integral component of the general standards of independence and professional care; critical thinking also comes into play in maintaining appropriate levels of professional skepticism in the audit process.

Second, the discussion of internal controls throughout the text has an important relationship to auditing. Understanding the four broad purposes of internal control, the risk exposures for a specific organization, and the types of controls that can reduce those risk exposures are key elements of the third step in an audit: reviewing internal controls. Because no two organizations are likely to have identical sets of risk exposures and internal controls, accounting professionals must consistently return to the bedrock principles and ideas of this important area in their examination and evaluation of accounting information systems.

Third, in our examination of business processes, we talked about the importance of understanding an organization's environment as part of understanding its accounting information system. Understanding the organization's internal and external environment is also an important skill for the auditor. Specialization in specific industries is therefore a somewhat common practice among auditing firms. For example, Vicenti, Lloyd and Stutzman (www.vlsllp.com) in southern California maintains a strong practice in the government and not-for-profit sector.

Finally, information technology skills link accounting information systems and auditing in very important ways. Familiarity and skill with common forms of IT, such as spreadsheets and databases, can enable an auditor to examine the accounting information system much more effectively and efficiently. Auditors with backgrounds in both accounting and information systems may conduct information technology audits. As more and more large organizations move to enterprise systems and the utilization of enterprise resource planning software, this connection will only become more important.

CRITICAL THINKING

I'm using the fraud audit as an example in this section because most of my students find discussions of fraud and forensic accounting really interesting. Also, as a certified fraud examiner, I like to use any opportunity I can to educate people about fraud detection and prevention.

Like accounting information systems, auditing is a multidisciplinary field. Of course, it requires an in-depth knowledge of accounting; but auditors also need to master various aspects of information technology, business law, and human behavior. Let's look at how each of those topics might impact one of the seven types of audits listed at the beginning of this chapter: the fraud audit.

Information technology can certainly be used to commit fraud; just this weekend, a friend of mine had his bank account hacked for the third time in three years. The good news is, information technology also can be used to detect fraud. IT allows auditors to examine transaction databases quickly and efficiently; here are some tasks auditors can complete more easily using information technology when conducting a fraud audit:

- *Graphical trend analysis.* Consider the data below, which shows total cash disbursements by week for two years:

Week	20x2	20x1
1	$2,245	$2,720
2	1,557	1,886
3	3,710	4,494
4	4,792	2,441
5	1,657	2,008

If you were looking for anomalies between the two years, a graphical representation of the data would be a lot easier to evaluate than a table of numbers. Here's that same data in graphic form:

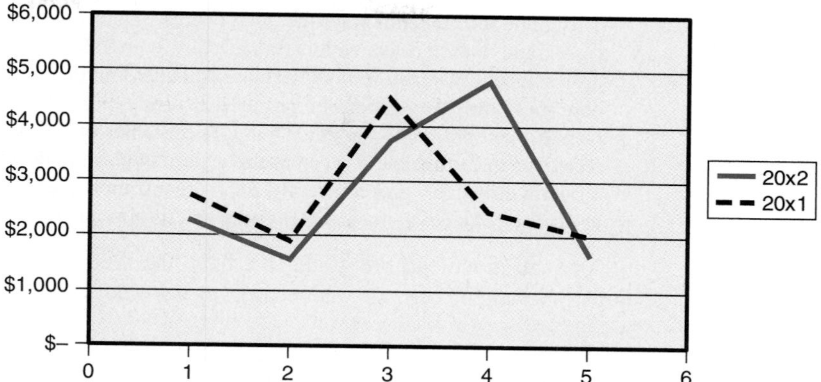

- *Statistical tests.* You've probably completed at least one statistics course by this time in your education. You may recall some of the tests that can be used to analyze differences between two samples, such as a *t*-test. While *t*-tests can be performed without the use of information technology, they are much easier and quicker when IT is used—whether the IT is a simple spreadsheet or some more complex statistics software like SPSS.
- *Database queries.* A "find unmatched" query could be used to generate a list of unpaid purchase invoices or uncollected receivables. If a fraud auditor finds significant numbers of those transactions associated with a particular manager, department, or location, additional investigation is probably a good idea. A "just under limit" query can be used to locate suspicious amounts. For example, if an organization requires two signatures on purchase orders over $10,000, a "just under limit" query could identify purchase orders that are more than $9,000 but less than the $10,000 limit. Too many of those transactions may indicate that someone is trying to circumvent internal controls.

We've talked a lot about the Sarbanes-Oxley Act and its impact on accounting and auditing, but forensic auditors need to be aware of many other laws and legal issues, too. The Bank Secrecy Act, for example, requires banks to file a Currency Transaction Report for cash transactions that exceed $10,000 in a single day—whether from a single transaction or a series of transactions. The Act also requires banks to keep a Monetary Instrument Log that records cash purchases between $3,000 and $10,000 of money orders, cashier's checks, traveler's checks, and other monetary instruments; finally, banks must file a Suspicious Activity Report for any transaction where it seems the customer is trying to avoid other reporting requirements, launder money, or engage in other potentially illegal activity.

While no single behavior provides conclusive evidence of fraud, there are some behavioral indications that a person may be lying or otherwise distorting the truth during a fraud audit. Some of them include nervous gestures (like tapping a pencil on the table), answering a question with a question ("What possible motivation would I have for stealing money?"), trying to cast suspicion on someone else in the organization, or an employee obviously living beyond his/her means (e.g., an employee who makes $20,000 a year driving an expensive new sports car to work).

If you'd like to know more about fraud auditing, check out *Managing the Business Risk of Fraud: A Practical Guide,* recently published by the Institute of Internal Auditors, the American Institute of CPAs, and the Association of Certified Fraud Examiners. According to its introduction (pp. 5–6):

> This guide recommends ways in which boards, senior management, and internal auditors can fight fraud in their organization. Specifically, it provides credible guidance from leading professional organizations that defines principles and theories for fraud risk management and describes how organizations of various sizes and types can establish their own fraud risk management program. The guide includes examples of key program components and resources that organizations can use as a starting place to develop a fraud risk management program effectively and efficiently. Each organization needs to assess the degree of emphasis to place on fraud risk management based on its size and circumstances.

You can download the guide free from the Web site of any one of the three organizations: www.theiia.org, www.aicpa.org, or www.acfe.com.

Summary

In this chapter, then, you've had the briefest introduction to auditing—the evaluation of an accounting information system. Here is a summary of the chapter in terms of its learning objectives:

1. *Describe the various kinds of audits you might encounter in your accounting career.*
   a. Financial
   b. Operational
   c. Systems
   d. Compliance
   e. Management
   f. Investigative
   g. International
2. *Explain the AICPA's 10 generally accepted auditing standards (GAAS).*
   a. General standards: training, independence, and professional care.
   b. Field work standards: supervision, internal control, and evidence.
   c. Reporting standards: GAAP, consistency, disclosure, and opinion.
3. *Discuss the basic steps associated with a financial statement audit.*
   a. Assess management's integrity.
   b. Evaluate management's credentials.
   c. Review the internal control system.
   d. Perform compliance testing.
   e. Issue the audit report.
4. *Explain the connection between auditing and accounting information systems.* Auditing and AIS are linked via at least four important skill areas: critical thinking, internal controls analysis, understanding of business processes, and effective use of information technology.

Recent financial scandals have shaken public confidence in financial reporting and the accounting profession in general. Therefore, conducting audits with diligence and integrity is even more important today than in the past.

Key Terms

auditing, *341*
auditing standards, *344*
fiduciary duty, *345*
professional judgment, *343*
Yellow Book, *342*

Chapter References

Committee of Sponsoring Organizations of the Treadway Commission. 2002. *Internal Control: Integrated Framework.* New York: AICPA.

Louwers, T., R. Ramsay, D. Sinason, and J. Strawser. 2005. *Auditing and Assurance Services.* 1st ed. New York: McGraw-Hill/Irwin.

Wells, J. 2004. *Principles of Fraud Examination.* 1st ed. New York: John Wiley & Sons.

Whittington, R., and K. Pany. 2004. *Principles of Auditing and Other Assurance Services.* 14th ed. New York: McGraw-Hill/Irwin.

End-of-Chapter Activities

1. *Reading review questions.*

a. List and discuss the seven types of audits described in the chapter.

b. Explain the 10 generally accepted auditing standards that guide financial audits.

c. Describe the common steps associated with an audit.

d. Prepare a response to the questions for this chapter's "AIS in the Business World."

2. *Reading review problem.* The National Aeronautics and Space Administration (NASA) conjures up images of rockets and voyages to the stars. And all its research and operations require a fairly sophisticated, detailed accounting information system. When NASA's 2003 financial statements and accounting information system were audited by PricewaterhouseCoopers (PwC), the CPA firm issued a disclaimed audit opinion. According to Frieswick, "PwC complained that NASA couldn't adequately document more than $565 billion in year-end adjustments to the financial-statement accounts, which NASA delivered to the auditors two months late." NASA's chief financial officer, Gwen Brown, testified before a congressional committee in May 2004 about $2 billion it could not trace through the AIS. "In her testimony, Brown assured subcommittee members that the missing $2 billion was not the result of 'fraud, waste or abuse.' But when pressed on what did cause the money to go missing, she admitted the agency wasn't sure." NASA's inspector general, Robert Cobb, talked about problems with the implementation of the agency's new AIS. He believed NASA wouldn't get a clean audit opinion until at least 2007.

Source: K. Frieswick, "NASA, We Have a Problem," *CFO: The Magazine for Senior Financial Executives,* May 2004, and K. Frieswick, "System Failure," *CFO: The Magazine for Senior Financial Executives,* July 2004.

a. What elements of an accounting information system are evaluated in an audit?

b. What are the processes and attitudes associated with an audit?

c. What types of audits are involved in professional accounting?

d. List and describe the four types of opinions associated with financial statement audits.

3. *Making choices and exercising judgment.* Barb is an auditor for Vicenti, Lloyd and Stutzman (VLS), a regional CPA firm; she earned her CPA license three years ago and is supervising the audit team for CDR Corporation, a company that manufactures blank CDs. Last year's audit resulted in a qualified opinion, and both Barb and CDR's management are highly motivated to achieve a clean opinion this year. The audit team comprises four individuals (including Barb):

- Richard has been with VLS a little over two years. He has passed three parts of the CPA exam and is currently working on the fourth part. He graduated with a 3.8 GPA from a prestigious local university and is working on CDR's audit for the first time. In previous audits, Richard has been in charge of inventory observation and bank reconciliations.

- Laura joined VLS at the same time as Barb. She was licensed as a CPA one year ago. Laura has a Master's degree in accounting from a local university and is an experienced auditor. In previous audits, she has taken the lead in evaluating internal controls and discussing audit matters with company management. This audit is her first for CDR Corporation.
- Albert came to work for VLS from one of the Big Four CPA firms about six months before the CDR audit started. He is an experienced CPA and made the move to get better working hours and a better chance at becoming a partner. The CDR audit will be Albert's first for VLS.

What responsibilities should Barb assign to each member of the audit team for the CDR audit? Explain your choices.

4. *Field work.*

a. Contact an experienced auditor in your area for an interview about common audit procedures. Compare the process with the generic one presented in Figure 18.3. Prepare a short report or presentation comparing and contrasting the two.

b. Reviewing internal controls is an important part of any AIS evaluation. Visit a local business such as a restaurant, movie theater, bank, or amusement park; observe one or more common transactions and assess the strength of internal control over those transactions. Classify the internal controls as preventive, detective, or corrective. If you wanted to circumvent the internal control system, how would you do it?

c. Using your work in (*b*) above as a basis, create a flowchart/data flow diagram/REAL model of the transaction process.

d. Point your Web browser to www.soxtoolkit.com. Review and summarize the tools available for accountants and managers seeking to comply with the Sarbanes-Oxley Act of 2002.

e. Use your school's library to find Greg Rogers, "Environmental Transparency: Five Areas for Concern," *Financial Executive,* June 2004. Summarize the article and suggest at least three ways an auditor would discover undisclosed environmental liabilities.

5. *Internal controls.* Consider the list of internal controls discussed in this chapter (e.g., security checks on personnel, controlled access, and data encryption). Choose one control from each category (administrative, physical, and technical). Prepare an oral and/or written report that describes its nature and importance in the accounting information system.

6. *Audit types.* What type of audit is indicated in each of the following situations?

a. Checking internal controls over the sales/collection process.

b. Determining how an employee embezzled cash.

c. Establishing whether an audit conformed to all provisions of Sarbanes-Oxley.

d. Evaluating the accounting policy choices management made for conformity with GAAP.

e. Expressing an opinion on the fairness of a company's financial statements.

f. Inputting sample transactions and verifying the output from Peachtree.

g. Observing internal controls over inventory to improve process effectiveness.

h. Performing a comprehensive analysis of an Italian firm's accounting information system.

i. Using test data to determine how QuickBooks processes transactions.

j. Validating the assumptions made for a major capital investment.

7. *Generally accepted auditing standards.* Figure 18.2 presents a diagram of the 10 standards that govern financial audits. Prepare a similar, but original, diagram that illustrates the same concepts.

8. *Violations of GAAS.* Which of the 10 standards is violated in each of the following independent situations? Some situations may violate more than one.
   a. A team of auditors, each with varying levels of experience, divided up the audit tasks and completed them independently before expressing an opinion on the statements.
   b. An audit client changed its inventory cost flow assumption from LIFO to FIFO in the last year. The audit opinion makes no mention of the change.
   c. Auditors relied solely on the client's assertions in evaluating account balances.
   d. Austin supervised the audit team for a company in which he has an investment.
   e. Chip relied solely on the client's assessment of its AIS integrity in determining compliance tests for an audit.
   f. Sebastian conducted his first audit during his last semester of college. He audited the accounting information system of a nonprofit organization where he volunteers.
9. *Generic audit steps.* Fill in the blanks in each statement below with appropriate terminology to describe the generic steps in a financial statement audit. Then, put the steps in the correct order.
   a. Assess _____ integrity.
   b. Evaluate management's _____ .
   c. Issue the _____ .
   d. Perform _____ testing.
   e. Review the _____ system.
10. *Investigative audit.* For each independent case presented below, use Figure 18.1 as a guide in explaining the steps you would take to uncover fraud. Also suggest at least two internal controls that could have prevented the fraud described.
    a. KC Group is basically a high-integrity company with sound approaches to financial reporting. Associates involved in financial reporting are of high competence and ethical values. KC Group has grown in recent years. There are new systems, sometimes administered by those who do not fully understand them. KC Group is performance driven, and managers are under tremendous pressure to make their goals. KC Group has acquired several new companies. Some of the associates in the acquired companies do not share certain values inherent in the KG culture. Consequently, reporting and integrity in some of these subsidiaries have proven to be a problem. At an acquired subsidiary, certain executives who never traveled had traditionally been allowed $2,000 to $25,000 in travel advances. These permanent travel advances were essentially noninterest-bearing loans. The subsidiary had been told to stop the practice. Instead, the subsidiary's controller obtained repayment checks from the executives and credited the travel advance account. Rather than actually depositing the checks at the bank before year-end, he held them until after the end of the year. He then issued company checks to the executives to replace the travel advances purportedly repaid. The executives thus could cover their own checks by depositing company checks before their checks cleared. The controller back-dated the deposit slip reflecting the repayments from the executives and a fictitious deposit in transit. Although the amount was minor, the controller was knowingly and intentionally making false entries in the company records. (Source: C. Thompson, "The Reporting Challenge,"*Internal Auditor,* December 2002.)
    b. During a routine audit of your client, you discover the price the company pays for widgets has doubled in the past year. Moreover, you notice all of the business is going to a new vendor. You check further and find the price of widgets on the open market is half what your client is currently paying. Maybe there is a legitimate reason for this anomaly. Or maybe it's a fraud. (Source: J. Wells, "Sherlock Holmes, CPA—Part 1,"*Journal of Accountancy,* August 2003.)

11. *Crossword puzzle.* Use appropriate terminology from the chapter to complete the puzzle below.

Across

3. A common aspect of all types of audits.
4. The group of GAAS with the most individual elements.
5. One of the three groups of auditing standards.
7. Certification most closely associated with a systems audit.
8. Audit type that examines business processes for reasonableness.
9. An audit opinion that indicates statements are not presented in accordance with GAAP.
10. Audit type that results in an opinion on statements.

Down

1. Starting point for a fraud audit.
2. One of the groups of GAAS.
6. Audit type that relies on the Yellow Book.

12. *Terminology.* Please match each item on the left with the most appropriate item on the right.

1. Bank reconciliation
2. Compliance
3. Disclosure
4. Flowcharting
5. GAAP
6. Independence
7. Internal control
8. Laws and religion
9. Target
10. Unqualified

a. A "clean" opinion
b. Field work standard
c. General standard
d. Important in international audits
e. Internal control example
f. Reporting standard
g. Standard associated with financial statement audits
h. Systems documentation technique often used in operational audits
i. Type of audit most closely associated with governmental entities
j. Ultimate subject of an investigative audit

13. *Multiple choice.* Please select the best answer for each of the following questions.

1. Which type of audit requires the broadest knowledge of nonfinancial issues?
   a. Financial
   b. Investigative
   c. Compliance
   d. International
2. Which of the following information sources would you consult first in an investigative audit?
   a. Target
   b. Co-conspirators
   c. Documents
   d. Neutral third-party witnesses
3. Which of the following is not a classification associated with generally accepted auditing standards?
   a. Information technology
   b. Field work
   c. Reporting
   d. General
4. An ERP system could be associated with _____ audits.
   a. Systems
   b. Financial
   c. Investigative
   d. All of the above
5. In a financial audit, which of the following can someone assume is adequate unless specifically told otherwise?
   a. Consistency
   b. Disclosure
   c. Internal controls
   d. All of the above
6. In an investigative audit, co-conspirators are interviewed before the target
   a. Because the information they can provide is more important.
   b. So the investigative auditor will be certain to get a confession from the target.
   c. Because they can be offered a "deal" that will help prove the fraud.
   d. Because they are younger.

7. Which of the following is not associated with field work standards?
   a. Supervision
   b. Internal control
   c. Evidence
   d. Risk management
8. Which type of audit opinion ensures that financial statements are true and correct?
   a. Unqualified
   b. Qualified
   c. Both of the above
   d. None of the above
9. The standard for government audits is
   a. The Yellow Book.
   b. SAS 70.
   c. COSO's internal control framework.
   d. SOX.
10. As part of their annual reports, SOX-compliant organizations must discuss the scope and adequacy of internal controls. That requirement comes from section
    a. 302.
    b. 401.
    c. 404.
    d. 802.

14. *Statement evaluation.* Determine whether each of the following statements is (i) always true, (ii) sometimes true, or (iii) never true. For those that are (ii) sometimes true, explain when the statement is true.

a. A disclaimed audit opinion means the financial statements contain errors.
b. Audits focus on a company's financial statements.
c. Field work standards contain guidelines for conducting an audit.
d. Financial statement audits result in an unqualified opinion.
e. Following the provisions of Sarbanes-Oxley, CEOs can delegate their responsibility to examine internal controls.
f. In an investigative audit, the target should be interviewed first.
g. Independent auditors in the United States help determine whether financial statements are true.
h. Investigative audits examine five main assertions about financial statements.
i. U.S. companies need to undergo annual financial statement audits.
j. Weak internal controls lead to qualified audit opinions.

Glossary

A

accounting Accounting is the process of identifying, measuring, and communicating economic information to permit informed judgments and decisions by users of the information. (Ch. 2)

accounting cycle The set of repetitive activities used to prepare general purpose financial statements. Although many parts of the accounting cycle can be completed more easily with information technology, some parts require significant human judgment and decision making. (Ch. 2)

accounting information system A collection of interrelated processes, technologies, and documents designed to capture primarily financial data and process them into information for making decisions. (Ch. 1)

accounting information system (AIS) structure Most accounting information systems comprise five parts: inputs (such as source documents), processing tools (such as general ledger software), outputs (such as the general purpose financial statements), storage (such as computer disks), and internal controls (such as separation of duties). (Ch. 1)

activity-based management A system that extends the principles of activity-based costing, helping managers see how they can function more effectively by focusing on activities. (Ch. 14)

Adelphia Communications Corporation Well-known fraud case involving a cable company. Key figure was John Rigas. (Ch. 3)

adjusting entries Journal entries made at the end of an accounting period to account for timing differences between cash flow and accrual basis revenues and expenses. Types include accrued revenue, accrued expense, deferred revenue, prepaid assets, uncollectible receivables, and depreciation. (Ch. 2)

administrative security controls One of three internal control types necessary to protect data integrity in a computerized information system. (Ch. 15)

agents One element of a REAL model. Agents can be internal (such as a sales clerk) or external (such as a customer). In laying out a REAL model, agents should be in the third column from the left. (Ch. 7)

AICPA Code of Professional Conduct One of three ethics codes discussed in the text. Seven parts: Principles of Professional Conduct; Rules: Applicability and Definitions; Independence, Integrity, and Objectivity; General Standards; Accounting Principles; Responsibilities to Clients; Responsibilities to Colleagues; and Other Responsibilities and Practices. (Ch. 3)

Association of Certified Fraud Examiners The premiere professional organization for people with an interest in forensic accounting and fraud examination. The association's Web site is www.cfenet.com. (Ch. 17)

auditing A systematic review of an organization's accounting information system, often for the purpose of expressing an opinion on the financial statements. (Ch. 18)

auditing standards The rules auditors use to promote integrity and consistency in the audit process. Often referred to collectively as GAAS (generally accepted auditing standards). (Ch. 18)

B

balanced Characteristic of a set of data flow diagrams. Balanced diagrams do not allow symbols to disappear between levels. (Ch. 6)

basic principles of business process management The text discusses seven principles suggested by Eppele. The seven principles focus on the relationship between BPM and strategy, attitude toward change, top management support, focusing on people, external consultants, task definition, and communication. (Ch. 14)

basic principles of information security Confidentiality, availability, and data integrity are the three basic principles of information security. They are often referred to as the C-I-A triad. (Ch. 15)

benefits of XBRL XBRL facilitates information exchange regardless of hardware or software platform. In addition, XBRL is flexible, allowing users to create their own tags when the need arises. (Ch. 9)

bookkeeping The process of recording transactions in a journal, posting them to ledger accounts, and preparing basic financial statements. Though often confused with accounting, bookkeeping is distinct; it focuses on the mechanical aspects and rules of accounting and often can be completed more easily with the aid of information technology. (Ch. 2)

bounded rationality The idea that most decision makers will avoid uncertainty; rather, they will depend on a set of rules for making decisions. (Ch. 16)

BPM software Information technology tools that can assist organizations in business process management. (Ch. 14)

Brown's taxonomy of risk A way of looking at and categorizing risk. Four broad categories include financial, operational, strategic, and hazard. (Ch. 4)

business process The set of steps associated with an activity; one way an organization creates value. The processes discussed in the text include sales/collection, acquisition/payment, conversion, financing, and human resources. (Ch. 11)

business process management Analyzing business processes with a view toward making them more efficient and/or effective. (Ch. 14)

C

capability maturity model A five-stage model developed by Humphrey, used to categorize and improve business processes. (Ch. 8)

cardinalities Relationships between elements of a REAL model. Cardinalities are set up in pairs, with each element of the pair having a minimum value and a maximum value. Proper design of cardinalities facilitates the development of a relational database. (Ch. 7)

career plan The plans an accountant makes for his/her career in the profession. (Ch. 17)

causes of ERP implementation failure ERP systems most often fail because of poor planning and lack of strategic vision. The chapter discusses other causes of ERP failure. (Ch. 10)

causes of information overload As discussed in the chapter, at least five things can cause information overload: personal factors, information technology, information characteristics, organizational design, and task and process parameters. (Ch. 16)

Certified Fraud Examiner Abbreviated CFE. A professional certification demonstrating knowledge and competence in fraud examination. (Ch. 17)

Certified Fraud Examiner Code of Professional Ethics One of three ethics codes discussed in the text. Contains eight statements covering personal behavior and demeanor, conduct of fraud examinations, and other areas. (Ch. 3)

Certified Information Systems Auditor Abbreviated CISA. A professional certification demonstrating knowledge and competence in information systems auditing. (Ch. 17)

Certified Internal Auditor Abbreviated CIA. A professional certification demonstrating knowledge and competence in internal auditing. (Ch. 17)

Certified Management Accountant Abbreviated CMA. A professional certification demonstrating knowledge and competence in management accounting. (Ch. 17)

characteristics of a professional Bell's list includes seven components: communicates effectively; thinks rationally, logically, and coherently; appropriately uses technical knowledge; integrates knowledge from many disciplines; exhibits ethical professional behavior; recognizes the influence of political, social, economic, legal, and regulatory forces; and actively seeks additional knowledge. (Ch. 3)

Charles Ponzi Originator of the fraud, now labeled a "Ponzi scheme," that involves paying off old investors with money from new investors, rather than money generated by an investment itself. (Ch. 3)

CoBIT accountability framework The accountability framework shows the relationships between six groups of people as part of that process: stakeholders, board of directors, audit committee, IT and information security management, internal audit, and external audit. (Ch. 15)

CoBIT framework The CoBIT framework (Control Objectives for Information and Related Technology) was developed by the Information Systems Audit and Control Association (ISACA) to provide guidance for information systems internal controls. (Ch. 15)

CoBIT information criteria The ideal characteristics for information. They include effectiveness, efficiency, confidentiality, integrity, availability, compliance, and reliability. (Ch. 15)

computer networks The defining feature of e-commerce. Computers can be networked via hardware or software, in the same physical location or different physical locations. (Ch. 10)

conceptual framework of accounting A document produced by the Financial Accounting Standards Board in 1977, intended to guide the development of future accounting principles. Parts include objective of financial reporting, elements of financial statements, qualitative characteristics of accounting information, assumptions, principles, and constraints. (Ch. 1)

conditions for a successful ERP implementation Conditions include organizational commitment, clearly communicated strategic goals for the project, and involvement of the entire organization. (Ch. 10)

context diagram Highest-level data flow diagram. Contains the least detail. Depicts a business process in a single circle, showing its interaction with external entities. (Ch. 6)

conversion process The process of combining raw material, labor, and overhead in the production of finished goods. (Ch. 13)

COSO Committee of Sponsoring Organizations of the Treadway Commission. Includes five organizations: the Institute of Management Accountants, the American Institute of Certified Public Accountants, the American Accounting Association, the Institute of Internal Auditors, and the Financial Executives Institute. Created two important documents (integrated frameworks) related to internal control and risk management. (Ch. 4)

countermeasures Actions people can take to avoid, or reduce the effects of, information overload. Examples include allowing additional time to complete important tasks and using graphs or other visual aids. (Ch. 16)

D

data flow One of four elements of a data flow diagram. Depicted with an arrow. Always contains a noun phrase as a label, such as "purchase order information." (Ch. 6)

data store One of four elements of a data flow diagram. Depicted with two parallel lines containing a noun phrase label, such as "employee database." (Ch. 6)

database tables Primary organizational element of a relational database. Composed of fields and records. Each record must contain a primary key that uniquely identifies it. (Ch. 6)

definitions of ethics Rules or standards governing the conduct of a person or the members of a profession (www.dictionary.com). Others are presented in the chapter as well. (Ch. 3)

document flowcharts One of four flowchart types discussed in the chapter. Follows the flow of one or more documents through an information system. (Ch. 5)

documents Hard copy or electronic forms, often used as the basis for data entry in an accounting information system. For the sales/collection process, they may include remittance advices and customer invoices; in the acquisition/payment process, they may include purchase orders and receiving reports. (Chs. 11, 12)

E

e-business categories Most taxonomies in this area identify five categories: business-to-business, business-to-consumer, government-to-consumer, government-to-business, and consumer-to-consumer. (Ch. 10)

e-commerce The process of conducting business using computer networks. (Ch. 10)

eight-step model Generic process for responding to ethical problems developed by Langenderfer and Rockness. (Ch. 3)

electronic data interchange A protocol used to transmit data electronically between a vendor and a customer. (Ch. 12)

Enron/Arthur Andersen At the time, the largest bankruptcy in U.S. history. Issues of organizational culture and reward systems contributed to financial statement fraud through the use of special-purpose entities and non-GAAP revenue recognition policies. Andersen served as Enron's independent auditor; the scandal led to the demise of both firms. (Ch. 3)

enterprise resource planning system A very large relational database, designed to capture data for use in decision making. Most ERP systems are organized into modules such as human resource management and supply chain management. (Ch. 10)

Enterprise Risk Management: Integrated Framework One of two COSO documents. Contains eight elements to help professionals think about managing risk: internal environment, objective setting, event identification, risk assessment, risk response, control activities, information and communication, and monitoring. (Ch. 4)

events One element of a REAL model. Events typically fall into one of three categories: operating, information, and decision/management. Only strategically significant operating events appear in a REAL model; examples include selling services to a client or paying employees. Information events, such as updating ledger account balances, focus on recording and maintaining data, as well as reporting information. Decision/management events involve human decision making, such as changing compensation packages. (Ch. 7)

examples of BPM The chapter discusses e-government in Tyler, Texas, customer-related issues in a hospital, and special orders in a Swiss bank.

eXtensible Business Reporting Language Also known as XBRL. A markup language that allows users to tag data so that they can be read by virtually any computer program on any hardware platform. (Chs. 9, 12)

external entity One of four elements of a data flow diagram. Depicted with a rectangle. Represents an entity outside the boundary of an information system, such as a vendor. (Ch. 6)

external transactions Transactions that involve parties external to the organization. Typically do not require adjusting entries at the end of a period. Examples include selling inventory, purchasing plant assets, and paying vendors. (Ch. 2)

F

fiduciary duty The responsibility of an accountant to act in the best interests of others, such as stockholders. (Ch. 18)

financing process The process of acquiring external funding, most commonly through debt or equity. (Ch. 13)

financing process transactions Issuance of capital stock, purchase of treasury shares, issuance and repayment of long-term debt, and dividend distributions. (Ch. 13)

Flow chart Flowcharts can be an important tool in business process management.

Foreign Corrupt Practices Act One of the earliest laws focused on business ethics. Passed in 1977. Prohibits conduct that would be considered illegal in the United States, even if that conduct is acceptable in foreign countries. (Ch. 4)

foreign keys A field in a database table that is a primary key in another table. For example, a customer identification number would be a primary key in the customer table and a foreign key in a sales transaction table. (Ch. 6)

freight terms Terms that govern when title to merchandise passes from the seller to the buyer (destination or shipping point) and who is responsible for the cost of freight (collect or prepaid). (Ch. 11)

G

general purpose financial statements Collective term referring to the balance sheet, income statement, statement of changes in equity, and statement of cash flows. Must be prepared in accordance with generally accepted accounting principles. (Ch. 2)

generalized model of BPM Seven generic steps associated with many business process management initiatives. (Ch. 14)

H

hardware flowcharts One of four flowchart types discussed in the chapter. Depicts the hardware layout of an information system. (Ch. 5)

human judgment A critical element of accounting and accounting information systems. For example, accountants exercise judgment in deciding which transactions are recordable in the AIS and in making decisions based on financial information. (Ch. 2)

human resource process Associated with personnel activities in an organization, from the time of hiring to the time of discharge via retirement, termination, or quitting. (Ch. 13)

I

information competence The ability to formulate research questions, locate the information to answer the questions, evaluate information quality, and use it for decision making. (Ch. 1)

information overload One factor that negatively impacts decision making. Symptoms and effects include limited information retrieval strategies, increased stress, arbitrary analysis, and suboptimal decisions. (Ch. 16)

Information Systems Audit and Control Association Abbreviated ISACA. Professional organization that sponsors the CISA credential. The association's Web site is www.isaca.org/. (Ch. 17)

information technology Computer hardware and software, often employed in accounting information systems to make routine tasks more efficient. Examples include general ledger packages and enterprise resource planning software. (Ch. 2)

instance document As applied in XBRL, an instance document refers to properly tagged information. For example, a balance sheet with XBRL tags would be an instance document. (Ch. 9)

Institute of Internal Auditors Abbreviated IIA. Professional organization that sponsors the CIA credential. Their Web site is www.theiia.org. (Ch. 17)

Institute of Management Accountants Abbreviated IMA. Professional organization that sponsors the CMA credential. Their Web site is www.imanet.org. (Ch. 17)

Institute of Management Accountants ethics code One of three ethics codes discussed in the chapter. Divided into two large sections (principles and standards). Principles include honesty, fairness, objectivity, and responsibility. Standards include competence, confidentiality, integrity, and credibility. (Ch. 3)

internal control One element of an accounting information system. Policies and procedures designed to achieve four objectives: safeguarding assets, ensuring financial statement reliability, promoting operational efficiency, and encouraging compliance with management's directives. (Chs. 4, 11, 12)

Internal Control: Integrated Framework One of two COSO documents. Contains five elements to help professionals think about internal control: control environment, risk assessment, control activities, information and communications, and monitoring. (Ch. 4)

internal transactions Transactions that do not involve parties external to the organization. Typically require adjusting entries at the end of an accounting period. Examples include depreciation of fixed assets and the use of prepaid assets such as supplies. (Ch. 2)

iterative In the context of accounting information systems, iterative refers to the idea that steps don't always proceed in a linear fashion and/or that the development of systems documentation, internal controls, and other AIS elements is rarely accomplished in a single attempt. (Ch. 8)

J

job costing A production operation typically associated with unique, customized, or made-to-order goods. Examples include consulting assignments and custom-built homes. (Ch. 13)

junction table Type of relational database table used to capture cardinalities where the maximum is many on both ends. For example, consider this cardinality: Sales (0,*)—(1,*) Inventory. That cardinality indicates that each sale involves one to many items of inventory; each item of inventory can be included in zero to many sales transactions. A junction table would be required in this situation. It would capture data such as the sales transaction number and inventory item numbers for each transaction. (Ch. 7)

justice model One of four schools of ethical thought discussed in the chapter. Relies on the idea that people should get what they deserve. (Ch. 3)

K

knowledge management The way(s) managers and other decision makers organize knowledge to facilitate decision making. (Ch. 16)

L

Level Zero diagram One element of a leveled set of data flow diagrams. The next level down from a context diagram. Shows the processes, data flows, data stores, and external entities of an information system at a high level, but with more detail than a context diagram. (Ch. 6)

leveled sets Applied to data flow diagrams. Refers to the idea that business processes are decomposed into greater levels of detail until they cannot be decomposed any more. Leveled sets of data flow diagrams must be balanced. (Ch. 6)

locations One element of a REAL model. Used when differentiating locations is important, such as with geographic divisions or bank accounts. Locations are not always included in a REAL model, and should be placed wherever they fit most logically. (Ch. 7)

M

macro-level issues The "big picture" issues to be considered in adopting a specific form of information technology. The chapter discusses need, strategic fit, personnel involvement, and financing. (Ch. 8)

McCarthy Professor credited with the development of REAL modeling techniques and their application to accounting information systems. (Ch. 7)

micro-level issues The more focused issues to be considered in adopting a specific form of information technology. The chapter discusses cost, adaptability, training, and vendor reliability. (Ch. 8)

Microsoft Visio Software that can be used to create flowcharts and other forms of systems documentation. (Ch. 5)

N

namespace Related to XBRL. A place on the Internet that defines tags used for coding. Users can use an existing namespace and/or create one of their own. (Ch. 9)

normalization The rules for creating an efficient, effective relational database. Although six normal forms exist, most organizations use only the first three as a practical matter. The rules are summarized at www.datamodel.org/NormalizationRules.html. (Ch. 7)

normative ethics Statements about what is right and what is wrong. For example, "people shouldn't cheat" or "lying is wrong." (Ch. 3)

P

payroll forms The forms commonly used to process payroll transactions. Examples include Form W-4, Form W-2, payroll register, employee earnings record, Form 1099, Form 940, and Form 941. (Ch. 13)

perpetrators People who commit crimes, specifically involving information systems. (Ch. 15)

physical security controls One of three internal control types necessary to protect data integrity in a computerized information system. (Ch. 15)

popular/practitioner information One of three information types used in accounting information systems. This type of information has often been through some review and editing process but may not rely on strict research protocols. Examples include *Strategic Finance, Fraud Magazine,* and the *Journal of Accountancy.* (Ch. 1)

primary key The field in a database table that uniquely identifies each record in the table. For example, a product identification code in an inventory table. (Ch. 6)

primitive The lowest level of decomposition for processes in a data flow diagram. Systems analysts and designers use judgment in selecting/establishing primitive processes. (Ch. 6)

principles of debit and credit The rules used to record transactions in a journal. Assets and expenses increase with debits and decrease with credits; liabilities, equity, and revenue follow the opposite rules. (Ch. 2)

process Any set of procedures an organization uses to gather data, change the data into information, or report the information to system users. Depicted in data flow diagrams with circles, each of which has both a number and a name. (Ch. 6)

process costing A production operation typically associated with mass-produced, undifferentiated goods such as computer disks or blank video tape. (Ch. 13)

professional judgment A key element of the audit process and accounting information systems design and implementation. (Ch. 18)

program flowcharts One of four flowchart types discussed in the chapter. Illustrates the logic of a computer program and the steps required to complete it. (Ch. 5)

Q

queries One object in relational databases. Allow the user to ask questions of the database based on specific conditions. For example, what are the names of all customers with credit limits exceeding $10,000? (Ch. 6)

R

relapse errors The human tendency to make the same mistakes repeatedly, even when determined not to. (Ch. 16)

relational database A type of software that allows users to enter data, ask questions about the data, and create reports in response to those questions. Microsoft Access is an example of relational database software, which forms the basis for event-driven accounting systems. Enterprise resource planning systems are a sophisticated form of relational databases. (Ch. 7)

resources One element of a REAL model. Resources refer to items such as inventory, cash, and supplies, which are required to carry out the events in a REAL model. In a properly constructed REAL model, all resources appear in the leftmost column. (Ch. 7)

rights and duties One of four schools of ethical thought discussed in the chapter. Relies on the idea that people have specific rights that should not be compromised by others. (Ch. 3)

risks and threats Potential hazards for information systems. The development of internal controls often begins by identifying risks and threats. (Ch. 15)

rules/conventions The rules associated with creating data flow diagrams. (Ch. 6)

S

Sarbanes-Oxley Act of 2002 Federal legislative response to the corporate scandals of the late 20th century. Imposes specific duties on managers and auditors for the review of internal controls, disclosures, and related issues. Specifies fines and penalties for noncompliance. (Ch. 4)

satisficing The idea that decision makers will not necessarily look for the best solution to a problem—just a solution that solves the problem. (Ch. 16)

scholarly information One of three information types used in accounting information systems. This type of information is intended primarily for an academic audience and has been through a rigorous review process before publication. Typically follows strict research protocols. Examples include *Accounting, Behavior and Organizations* and the *Journal of Accounting Research.* (Ch. 1)

six-step process The steps AIS designers take to develop a REAL model. (Ch. 7)

SmartDraw Software that can be used to create flowcharts and other forms of systems documentation. www.smartdraw.com. (Ch. 5)

source documents Paper-based or electronic documents often used as the basis for journal entries in an accounting information system. Examples include remittance advices, purchase orders, and check stubs. (Ch. 2)

specification A specific example of a larger group. For example, "California" is a specification of "U.S. states." XBRL is a specification of a larger family of languages called XML (eXtensible Markup Language). (Ch. 9)

sponsored/commercial information One of three information types used in accounting information systems. This type of information may be less objective than the other two forms but can be useful in researching specific products or gaining a company's point of view on an issue. Examples include www.peoplesoft.com and www.findaccountingsoftware.com. (Ch. 1)

steps The common activities associated with a business process. Although the steps may vary slightly for some processes between organizations, certain common elements are nearly always present. (Chs. 11, 12)

Steps for Better Thinking A decision-making model developed by Wolcott and Lynch. The model is organized in five levels: knowing, identifying, exploring, prioritizing, and envisioning. (Ch. 16)

steps to create a knowledge management system The seven-step process for creating a knowledge management system (recommended by Call) begins with developing an organizational culture that supports knowledge sharing and concludes with periodically reevaluating the system's value and making needed adjustments. (Ch. 16)

strategically significant operating activities The subset of operating activities depicted in a REAL model. AIS designers use judgment to identify strategically significant operating activities, which may include things such as purchasing inventory and paying vendors. (Ch. 7)

symbols Elements of a flowchart and other forms of systems documentation. (Ch. 5)

systems development life cycle Generic set of steps used to develop, implement, and maintain information systems. Four iterative phases include analysis, logical design, physical design, and implementation and maintenance. (Chs. 6, 8)

systems flowcharts One of four flowchart types discussed in the chapter. Shows the components of an information system. Of the four types, this one is used most often in accounting information systems work. (Ch. 5)

T

taxonomies In general, a taxonomy is a way of organizing knowledge. In XBRL, a taxonomy refers to a specific set of tags, most often associated with an industry group. For example, XBRL contains government accounting taxonomies and manufacturing industry taxonomies. (Ch. 9)

taxonomy for computer crime A classification system for computer crime. Carter's taxonomy has four parts: target, instrumentality, incidental, and associated. (Ch. 15)

technical security controls One of three internal control types necessary to protect data integrity in a computerized information system. (Ch. 15)

three-stage process Framework proposed by Sylla and Wen regarding the adoption of information technology.

Stages include intangible benefits evaluation, IT investment risk analysis, and tangible benefits evaluation. (Ch. 8)

U

unstructured problems Frequently encountered in the study of accounting information systems and the practice of accounting. Refers to problems without single, correct responses/solutions that require creativity and judgment. Unstructured problems may have more than one acceptable answer, although some responses to them may clearly be incorrect or inappropriate. (Ch. 1)

utilitarian model of ethics One of four schools of ethical thought discussed in the chapter. Relies on the idea that the "end justifies the means." (Ch. 3)

V

virtues model One of four schools of ethical thought discussed in the chapter. Relies on the idea that people should do what is right/moral/virtuous. (Ch. 3)

W

Watts Humphrey First suggested the capability maturity model. (Ch. 8)

weighted-rating technique System for comparing specific software packages. The user selects a list of criteria, such as cost and ease of use, and assigns each criterion a weight. Then, each software package is rated on each criterion. The rating is multiplied by the weighting to arrive at an overall weighted score, which informs (but does not dictate) the choice. (Ch. 8)

X

XBRL The eXtensible Business Reporting Language. A software- and hardware-independent way of coding financial data. According to www.xbrl.org, it is "a language for the electronic communication of business and financial data which is set to revolutionize business reporting around the world." (Ch. 9)

Y

Yellow Book A document published by the Government Accountability Office (GAO) that explains the rules for conducting a compliance audit. (Ch. 18)

Comprehensive Chapter References

ASPNews.com. 2002. "ASPNews Glossary." www.aspnews.com/strategies/asp_basics/article.php/759691 (January 11).

Association of Certified Fraud Examiners. 2004. *Code of Professional Ethics.* www.cfenet.com/about/codeethics.asp (October 11).

Barker, T., and M. Frolick. 2003. "ERP Implementation Failure: A Case Study." *Information Systems Management,* Fall, pp. 43–49.

Barnard, C. I. 1968. *The Functions of the Executive.* 30th anniversary ed. Cambridge, MA: Harvard University Press.

Bell, N. 2004. "Characteristics of a Risk Management and Insurance Professional." www.wsu.edu/~belln/ (October 4, 2004).

Betsch, T.. S. Haberstroh, B. Molter, and A. Glockner. 2004. "Oops, I Did It Again—Relapse Errors in Routinized Decision Making." *Organizational Behavior and Human Decision Processes* 93, no. 1, pp. 62–74.

Bradford, M., S. Richtermeyer, and D. Roberts. 2007. "System Diagramming Techniques: An Analysis of Methods Used in Accounting Education and Practice." *Journal of Information Systems,* Spring, pp. 173–212.

Brewer, P., R. Garrison, and E. Noreen. 2008. *Introduction to Managerial Accounting.* 4th ed. New York: Irwin/McGraw-Hill.

Brown, B. 2001. "Step-by-Step Enterprise Risk Management." *Risk Management,* September, pp. 43–49.

Call, D. 2005. "Knowledge Management—Not Rocket Science." *Journal of Knowledge Management* 9, no. 2, pp. 19–30.

Carter, D. 1995. "Computer Crime Categories." *FBI Law Enforcement Bulletin,* pp. 21–28.

Committee of Sponsoring Organizations of the Treadway Commission. 1985. *Internal Control: Integrated Framework.* New York: Committee of Sponsoring Organizations of the Treadway Commission.

Committee of Sponsoring Organizations of the Treadway Commission. 2002. *Internal Control: Integrated Framework.* New York: AICPA.

Committee of Sponsoring Organizations of the Treadway Commission. 2006. *Internal Control over Financial Reporting—Guidance for Smaller Public Companies.* New York: Committee of Sponsoring Organizations of the Treadway Commission.

Committee of Sponsoring Organizations of the Treadway Commission. 2004. *Enterprise Risk Management: Integrated Framework.* New York: Committee of Sponsoring Organizations of the Treadway Commission.

Curzon, S. 1995. *Information Competence in the CSU.* www.calstate.edu/LS/Archive/info_comp_report.shtml (May 25, 2005).

Debreceny, R., and S. White. 2005, June. *XBRL Working Paper.*

DeMarco, T. 1979. *Structured Analysis and Systems Specifications.* Englewood Cliffs, NJ: Prentice Hall.

Dictionary.com. 2004. "Ethics." http://dictionary.reference.com/search?q=ethics (October 4).

Drucker, P. 1993. *Post-Capitalist Society.* New York: Harper Row Publishing.

Egerdahl, R. 1995. "A Risk Matrix Approach to Data Processing Facility Audits." *Internal Auditor,* June, pp. 34–40.

Eppler, M., and J. Mengis. 2004. "The Concept of Information Overload: A Review of Literature from Organization Science, Accounting, Marketing, MIS and Related Disciplines." *Information Society,* pp. 325–44.

Fagan, M. 2006. "Exploring City, County and State E-government Initiatives: An East Texas Perspective." *Business Process Management Journal* 12, no. 1, pp. 101–12.

Halbert, J. 2003. "Mining Back Office Operations May Bolster the Bottom Line." *Los Angeles Business Journal,* April 14. www.findarticles.com (last visited November 4, 2004).

Harmon, P., and C. Wolf. 2008. *The State of Business Process Management.* San Francisco: Business Process Trends.

Hoffner, J., J. George, and J. Valacich. 1996. *Modern Systems Analysis and Design.* Reading, MA: Benjamin/Cummings.

Hollander, A. S., E. L. Denna, and J. O. Cherrington. 2000. *Accounting, Information Technology, and Business Solutions.* 2nd ed. New York: Irwin/McGraw-Hill.

Houle, C. 1980. *Continuing Learning in the Professions.* San Francisco: Jossey-Bass.

Huggett, K. 2000. "Professional Development in an Uncertain Profession: Finding a Place for Academic and Career Advisors." *NACADA Journal,* Fall, pp. 46–51.

Huq, Z., and T. Martin. 2006. "The Recovery of BPR Implementation through an ERP Approach: A hospital Case Study." *Business Process Management Journal* 12, no. 5, pp. 576–87.

Hurst, J. 2007. *The Capability Maturity Model and Its Applications.* www.giac.org/resources/whitepaper/application/242.php (September 15, 2008).

Hurt, R. 1994. "Wholelife Counseling Center." *Journal of Accounting Case Research,* pp. 97–98.

Internet Encyclopedia of Philosophy. 2004. "Ethics." www.utm.edu/research/iep/e/ethics.htm (October 4).

Johnston, R. 2003. "A Strategy for Finding the Right Accounting Software." *Journal of Accountancy,* September, pp. 39–46.

Jonietz, E. 2001. "Wireless Stockroom." *Technology Review,* July/August, p. 32.

Kishel, G., and P. Kishel. 1993. "Safeguarding Your Business." *Black Enterprise,* July, pp. 98–104.

Kung, P., and C. Hagen. 2007. "The Fruits of Business Process Management: An Experience Report from a Swiss Bank." *Business Process Management Journal* 13, no. 4, pp. 477–87.

Lander, G. 2004. *What Is Sarbanes-Oxley?* New York: McGraw-Hill.

Langenderfer, H., and J. Rockness. 1989. "Integrating Ethics into the Accounting Curriculum: Issues, Problems, and Solutions." *Journal of Accounting Education,* Spring, pp. 58–69.

Lemos, Robert 2006. "Gangland Web Attacks; How Not to Get Whacked by the Botnet Mafia." *PC Magazine* 25, no. 13 (August), p. 116. ABI/INFORM Trade & Industry database (Document ID: 1107044611, February 1, 2009).

Louwers, T., R. Ramsay, D. Sinason, and J. Strawser. 2005. *Auditing and Assurance Services.* 1st ed. New York: McGraw-Hill/Irwin.

McCarthy, W. E. 1982. "The REAL Accounting Model: A Generalized Framework for Accounting Systems in a Shared Data Environment." *Accounting Review,* July, pp. 554–77.

McDonald, C. 2001. "A Review of Continuing Professional Education." *Journal of Continuing Higher Education,* Winter, pp. 29–40.

Merchant, K., and W. Van der Stede. 2003. *Management Control Systems.* Upper Saddle River, NJ: Prentice Hall.

Misek, M. 2004. "Home Is Where the Art Is." *Emedia,* August, pp. 36–38.

Nesbitt, K. 2002, February 8. "Designing a Knowledge Management System." http://academic.edu.2081/products/faulknerlibrary/00018382.htm (May 2, 2005).

New York State Office of the State Comptroller. 2004. *Standards for Internal Control in New York State Government.* www.osc.state.ny.us/audits/audits/controls/standards.htm (October 18, 2004).

Poole, V. 2006. "Why Information Security Governance Is Critical to Wider Corporate Governance Demands—A European Perspective." *Information Systems Control Journal* 1, pp. 23–25.

Porter, M. 1985. *Competitive Advantage: Creating and Sustaining Superior Performance.* New York: Free Press.

Porter, M. 1998. *Competitive Advantage: Creating and Sustaining Superior Performance.* New York: Free Press.

Roth, J., and D. Espersen. 2004. "The Matrix Revisited." *Internal Auditor,* August, pp. 87–88.

Rowley, J. 1999. "What Is Knowledge Management?" *Library Management,* pp. 416–19.

Santosus, M., and J. Surmacz. 2005. "The ABCs of Knowledge Management." www.cio.com (April 28).

Seppanen, M., S. Kumar, and C. Chandra. 2005. *Process Analysis and Improvement: Tools and Techniques* 1st ed. New York: Irwin/McGraw-Hill.

Simon, H. 1997. *Administrative Behavior.* 4th ed. New York: Free Press.

Singleton, T. 2006. "COBIT—A Key to Success as an IT Auditor." *Information Systems Control Journal* 1, pp. 11–13.

SmartDraw.com. 2008. "Standard and Methodologies." www.smartdraw.com/tutorials/bpm/methodologies.htm (August 27).

Spiceland, J. D., J. Sepe, M. W. Nelson, and L. A. Tomassini 2009. *Intermediate Accounting.* 5th ed. New York: Irwin/McGraw-Hill.

Stapleton, G., and C. Rezak. 2004. "Change Management Underpins a Successful ERP Implementation at Marathon Oil." *Journal of Organizational Excellence,* Autumn, pp. 15–21.

Stoica, R. 2000. *Development of a Procedural Manual for Newly Hired Treasury Analysts at Company X.* California State Polytechnic University Pomona.

Sylla, C., and H. J. Wen. 2002. "A Conceptual Framework for Evaluation of Information Technology Investments." *International Journal of Technology Management,* pp. 236–61.

Thorp, J. A. 1991. "European Uniform Chart of Accounts." *Management Accounting,* July/August, pp. 20–23.

Trites, G. D. 2002. *Audit and Control Implications of XBRL.* Toronto, Ontario: Canadian Institute of Chartered Accountants.

Umble, E., and M. Umble. 2002. "Avoiding ERP Implementation Failure." *Industrial Management,* January/February, pp. 25–34.

Verschoor, C. 2005. "Do the Right Thing: IMA Issues New Ethics Guidance." *Strategic Finance,* November, pp. 42–46.

Walker, K. B., and E. Denna. 1997. "Arrivederci, Pacioli? A New Accounting System Is Emerging." *Management Accounting,* July, pp. 22–30.

Wells, J. 2004. *Principles of Fraud Examination.* 1st ed. New York: John Wiley & Sons.

Whittington, R., and K. Pany. 2004. *Principles of Auditing and Other Assurance Services.* 14th ed. New York: McGraw-Hill/Irwin.

Wikipedia.com. 2008. "Business Process Management." http://an.wikipedia.org/wiki/Business_process_management (August 27).

Williamson, D. 2006. "Coding Systems for Accountants: An Introduction." www.duncanwil.co.ukcu.de.htm (June 10, 2006).

Wolcott, S., and C. Lynch. 2005. "Steps for Better Thinking." www.wolcottlynch.com (April 29).

XBRL International. www.xbrl.org.

Index

Page numbers followed by "n" indicate footnotes and sourcenotes. **Bold** page numbers indicate glossary definitions.

C

D